Andreas Lochbihler

AF238998

A Machine-Checked, Type-Safe Model of Java Concurrency

Language, Virtual Machine, Memory Model, and Verified Compiler

A Machine-Checked, Type-Safe Model of Java Concurrency

Language, Virtual Machine, Memory Model, and Verified Compiler

by
Andreas Lochbihler

Dissertation, Karlsruher Institut für Technologie (KIT)
Fakultät für Informatik, 2012

Impressum

Karlsruher Institut für Technologie (KIT)
KIT Scientific Publishing
Straße am Forum 2
D-76131 Karlsruhe
www.ksp.kit.edu

KIT – Universität des Landes Baden-Württemberg und
nationales Forschungszentrum in der Helmholtz-Gemeinschaft

KIT Scientific Publishing 2012
Print on Demand

ISBN 978-3-86644-885-8

A Machine-Checked, Type-Safe Model of Java Concurrency
Language, Virtual Machine, Memory Model, and Verified Compiler

zur Erlangung des akademischen Grads eines

Doktors der Naturwissenschaften

der Fakultät für Informatik
des Karlsruher Instituts für Technologie (KIT)

genehmigte
Dissertation

von

Andreas Lochbihler

aus Memmingen

Tag der mündlichen Prüfung: 12. Juli 2012

Erster Gutachter: Prof. Dr.-Ing. Gregor Snelting

Zweiter Gutachter: Prof. Tobias Nipkow, PhD

Contents

Abstract

Klein and Nipkow's formalisation Jinja [83] of a Java-like programming language was the first that unifies source code, bytecode, and a compiler, is executable, and has been shown type safe – with Isabelle/HOL [128] having mechanically checked all definitions and proofs. In this thesis, I extend Jinja to JinjaThreads with concurrency in the form of Java threads and the Java memory model (JMM). Moreover, I transfer the existing theorems of type safety and compiler correctness, and prove the important JMM guarantee that data-race free programs behave like under interleaving semantics. Furthermore, I present the first formally-verified compiler for multithreaded Java.

JinjaThreads splits in two dimensions. On the one hand, like in Jinja, the compiler connects source code with bytecode on the level of languages. On the other hand, the semantics spans across different layers ranging from the implementation of the shared memory via the formalisation of the languages to the interleaving of threads and the axiomatic JMM. JinjaThreads is more than the sum of its parts, because it is their integration in a unified model that permits to correctly capture their interaction and to make reliable statements about the theory of the Java programming language.

Jinja has simplified Java in many places for clarity. In contrast, JinjaThreads investigates concurrency as described in the Java language specification in detail. On the language level, JinjaThreads covers dynamic thread creation, synchronisation via locks and monitors, wait and notify, interruption, and joining on threads. To obtain a tractable model, I have structured JinjaThreads in modules which encapsulate language-independent parts and which source code and bytecode share. For example, the interleaving semantics is parametrised over the single-threaded semantics and responsible for managing the thread pool, locks, interrupts, wait sets and notifications. By instantiating the parameters, I directly obtain the semantics for source code and bytecode. This modularity allows to formally define deadlock caused by synchronisation, which the type safety proof has to account for.

The second aspect of concurrency is the JMM. In this thesis, I connect its axiomatic specification with an operational semantics of Java for the first time. The intuitive memory model sequential consistency interleaves the individual steps of the threads and makes changes to memory immediately visible for all threads. In comparison, the JMM allows more executions such that compilers and the virtual machine itself may optimise more aggressively. Here, I prove – across all layers of the semantics – that for the important class of data-race free programs, the JMM allows only those intuitive executions that sequential consistency also allows. It is this link to an operation semantics that allows to formally apply this guarantee to concrete programs. Conversely, I also prove that the JMM is consistent by showing that it allows all (interleaved) executions that sequential consistency allows – even for programs with data races. Regarding type safety of Java with the JMM, I show that it depends on how type information is managed at runtime.

The JinjaThreads compiler connects source code with bytecode; its verification shows that both fit together. In particular, the compiler addresses the interaction between synchronisation and exceptions. Non-termination, intermediate output, and non-determinism constitute the challenges for the verification. Here, modularity of the model directly translates into manageable proofs. For example, I completely resolve the non-determinism at the level of interleaving semantics – independent of the language. Unlike for the semantics and type safety, I was not able to adapt the verification proofs of Jinja, because they were conducted against the big-step semantics of Jinja source code, which cannot express interleaving adequately.

Since JinjaThreads is a definitional artefact, one must argue that it faithfully models Java. In this case, formal verification is not possible, because Java is not specified formally. Instead, using Isabelle's code generator, I have automatically extracted from the formalisation an interpreter, compiler, and virtual machine in Standard ML. Using them, I have validated the semantics of source code and bytecode by running and compiling a test suite of Java programs, which a conversion tool translated to JinjaThreads abstract syntax. To achieve reasonable execution times, the interpreter and the virtual machine use verified efficient data structures and formalised schedulers to resolve the non-determinism. This way, they perform as good as other formalised virtual machines for Java.

This work demonstrates that today, it is possible to build tractable models of sizeable programming languages in a theorem prover. Jinja-Threads now provides the basis for verifying the program analyses for information flow control that our group is developing. Machine support has been crucial, because it reliably detects the impact of changes and extensions on other parts of the model.

Zusammenfassung

Jinja von Klein und Nipkow [83] ist die erste Formalisierung einer Java-ähnlichen Programmiersprache, die Quellcode, Bytecode und einen Übersetzer vereinigt, ausführbar ist und mittels Isabelle/HOL [128] maschinengeprüft als typsicher nachgewiesen wurde. Diese Dissertation erweitert Jinja zu JinjaThreads um Nebenläufigkeit durch Java-Threads und das Java-Speichermodell (JMM). Sie überträgt die bisherigen Theoreme zu Typsicherheit sowie Übersetzer-Korrektheit und beweist die für Programmierer wichtige Garantie des JMMs, dass wettlauffreie Programme sich wie bei verschränkter Ausführung verhalten. Dabei entstand der auch erste formal verifizierte Übersetzer für nebenläufiges Java.

JinjaThreads fächert sich in zwei Dimensionen in seine Komponenten auf. Einerseits verbindet es – wie schon Jinja – auf der Ebene der Sprachen Quellcode mit Bytecode durch den Übersetzer. Andererseits erstreckt sich die Semantik über die verschiedenen Schichten von einer Implementierung des gemeinsamen Speichers über die Beschreibung der Sprachen bis hin zur verschränkten Ausführung und zum axiomatischen JMM. Erst die Integration aller Einzelteile in einem einzigen Modell erlaubt es, deren Interaktion korrekt zu erfassen und belastbare Aussagen zur Theorie der Programmiersprache Java zu machen.

Während Jinja an vielen Stellen aus Gründen der Verständlichkeit Java vereinfacht, untersucht JinjaThreads den Aspekt der Nebenläufigkeit gemäß der Java Sprachspezifikation [56] im Detail. Auf Sprachebene umfasst JinjaThreads dynamische Thread-Erzeugung, Synchronisation über Monitore, Warten auf Benachrichtigung sowie Unterbrechung und Beitreten von Threads. Wesentlich für die Handhabbarkeit der Formalisierung ist die modulare Struktur, die sprachunabhängige Teile herausfaktorisiert, so dass Quell- und Bytecode diese wiederverwenden können. Beispielsweise definiert diese Arbeit für die verschränkte Ausführung aller Threads eines Programms eine parametrisierte Semantik, welche die Threads, Sperren, Unterbrechungen, Wartemengen und Benachrichtigungen verwaltet; durch Instanziierung der Parameter erhält man jeweils direkt die Semantiken von Quell- und Bytecode. Erst diese Modularität erlaubt es, sprachunabhängig durch Synchronisation erzeugte Verklemmungen zu definieren und im Typsicherheitsbeweis zu berücksichtigen.

Zur Nebenläufigkeit gehört auch das JMM [115], dessen axiomatische Spezifikation diese Arbeit erstmals mit einer operationalen Semantik von Java verbindet. Verglichen mit dem intuitiven Modell für sequenzielle Konsistenz, bei der die Thread-Einzelschritte verschränkt ausgeführt werden und Speicherveränderungen sofort für alle Threads sichtbar werden, erlaubt das JMM mehr Ausführungen, um aggressive Optimierungen bei der Übersetzung nach Bytecode und in der virtuellen Maschine selbst zu ermöglichen. Diese Arbeit beweist über alle Schichten der Semantik hinweg, dass für die wichtige Klasse der wettlauffreien Programme alle vom JMM erlaubten Ausführungen nicht von sequenzieller Konsistenz zu unterscheiden sind. Erst durch die Verbindung mit einer operationalen Semantik wird diese Garantie für konkrete Programme formal nutzbar. Umgekehrt weist diese Arbeit auch die Konsistenz des JMMs nach, indem gezeigt wird, dass es alle verschränkten Ausführungen gemäß sequenzieller Konsistenz erlaubt – auch für Programme mit Wettläufen. Hinsichtlich der Typsicherheit von Java mit dem JMM wird gezeigt, dass diese davon abhängt, wie Typinformationen zur Laufzeit verwaltet werden.

Der in dieser Arbeit entwickelte Übersetzer verbindet Quell- und Bytecode; seine Verifikation zeigt, dass beide Sprachen zusammenpassen. Bei der Kompilation ist die Herausforderung das Zusammenspiel der Synchronisationsprimitive mit Ausnahmen, bei der Verifikation sind es nicht terminierende Programme, Ausgaben und Nichtdeterminismus. Hier zeigt sich, wie wesentlich die Modularität der Semantik für die Handhabbarkeit der Beweise ist; beispielsweise lässt sich Nichtdeterminismus auf der Ebene der verschränkten Ausführung vollkommen sprachunabhängig auflösen. Anders als bei Semantik und Typsicherheit ließen sich dabei die alten Jinja-Beweise nicht anpassen, da diese in Bezug auf die Gesamtschrittsemantik der Quellsprache geführt wurden, die Nebenläufigkeit nicht adäquat ausdrücken kann.

Da JinjaThreads ein definitorisches Artefakt des Modellierungsprozesses ist, muss begründet werden, dass JinjaThreads Java adäquat abbildet. Eine formale Verifikation ist hier nicht möglich, weil die Spezifikation von Java nicht formal ist. Stattdessen wurde mit Isabelles Codegenerator vollautomatisch aus der Formalisierung ein Interpreter, ein Übersetzer und eine virtuelle Maschine für JinjaThreads-Programme in Standard ML extrahiert. Damit wurde die Semantik von Quell- und Bytecode durch eine Testsuite von Java-Programmen validiert, nachdem diese ein Konvertierungswerkzeug in die abstrakte Syntax von Jinja-

Threads übersetzt hatte. Um akzeptable Ausführungszeiten zu erzielen, verwenden der Interpreter und die virtuelle Maschine verifizierte effiziente Datenstrukturen und eigens formalisierte Abwickler zur Auflösung des Nichtdeterminismus. Damit sind sie ähnlich schnell wie andere formalisierte virtuelle Maschinen für Java.

Diese Arbeit zeigt, dass heutzutage umfangreiche Programmiersprachen in handhabbarer Form in Theorembeweisern abgebildet werden können. So stellt JinjaThreads jetzt die semantische Grundlage für die Verifikation der am Lehrstuhl entwickelten Programmanalysen zur Informationsflusskontrolle. Umgekehrt wäre diese Arbeit wegen der Komplexität des Modells ohne Maschinenunterstützung unmöglich gewesen, da nur so Auswirkungen von Änderungen und Erweiterungen auf andere Teile des Modells zuverlässig festgestellt werden konnten.

Acknowledgements

First, I would like to thank my advisor Prof. Gregor Snelting for his support, advice and the opportunity to pursue my own ideas without pressure. I also thank Prof. Tobias Nipkow for reviewing this thesis.

I would also like to thank my former and current colleagues in the Isabelle group at Passau and Karlsruhe, Daniel Wasserrab and Denis Lohner, for the numerous discussions ranging from technical issues with Isabelle to possible directions to pursue. Whenever I ran into a problem or had a sketchy idea, they never denied me to scribble inintelligible symbols and formulae on *their* whiteboards, but always helped to arrange my ideas and sort things out. Further, I thank Martin Hecker for sharing with me his understanding of the Java memory model. Neither must I forget to mention the discussions with all the other members of the group, which helped to set my views in perspective. In particular, they are Matthias Braun, Sebastian Buchwald, Andreas Zwinkau, and Manuel Mohr from the compiler group, and Christian Hammer, Dennis Giffhorn, Jürgen Graf, and Martin Mohr, who develop VALSOFT/Joana.

I am also indebted to the Isabelle developers in Munich, for answering my questions on the Isabelle mailing list and on the phone. In particular, I thank Stephan Berghofer and Florian Haftmann for introducing me to Isabelle's code generator at TPHOLs 2008 in Montreal. They and Lukas Bulwahn set me on track for code generation and always helped to fix or circumvent its limitations. Jasmin Blanchette and his tool Nitpick have saved me from trying to prove wrong lemmata. The cooperation with Peter Lammich set the ground for extracting efficient code from JinjaThreads.

Furthermore, I thank the students Jonas Thedering and Antonio Zea, who developed the converter Java2Jinja and solved all the annoyances of Eclipse by themselves.

Finally, I thank Wolfgang Pausch, Denis Lohner, Martin Hecker, and Claudia Reinert for reading preliminary drafts of this thesis. Their comments helped to make the presentation more intelligible and focused.

The work in Chapters 2, 3, and 6 has been partially funded by the Deutsche Forschungsgemeinschaft grants Sn11/10-1 and Sn11/10-2.

Threads cannot be implemented as a library.
Hans-J. Boehm

1

Introduction

The Java programming language provides safety and security guarantees for all programs, which distinguish it from other mainstream programming languages like C and C++. Two are particularly important: type safety and Java's security architecture. Type safety expresses that "nothing bad", e.g., a segmentation fault, will happen during execution. The security architecture permits to execute untrusted code safely in a sandbox, i.e., without access to critical system resources [54].

Another distinctive feature of Java is its built-in support for multi-threading and its semantics for executing threads in parallel [56, §17]. Yet, while it is well-known that multithreading non-trivially interacts with type safety and Java's security guarantees [56, 145], their combination has never been considered formally.

In this thesis, I build a machine-checked model of Java concurrency called JinjaThreads for both Java source code and bytecode, and investigate the effects of multithreading on type safety and Java's security guarantees. Moreover, I formalise a compiler from source code to bytecode and prove it correct. As the starting point of this work, I have used Jinja, a sequential Java-like language with compiler and type-safety proofs by Klein and Nipkow [83].

This work originates in the Quis custodiet (QC) project [147]. Using the proof assistant Isabelle/HOL [128], QC aims at mechanically verifying program analyses for information flow control (IFC) [53, 64, 65] that are developed in the VALSOFT/Joana project [173]. In QC, JinjaThreads defines the programming language and semantics against which program analyses like Wasserrab's formalisation of program slicing [175–177] are verified. In the long term, QC aims to build a verified, trusted prototype for analysing and executing security-critical Java programs.

1.1 Java concurrency

For this thesis to be self-contained, this section gives a quick tour of the concurrency features of Java 6. Since Java itself is widely used today, I do not explicitly introduce sequential Java, but refer unfamiliar readers to the Java language specification (JLS) [56].

Java concurrency revolves around threads, i.e., parallel strands of execution with shared memory. A program controls a thread through its associated object of (a subclass of) class *Thread*. To spawn a new thread, one allocates a new object of class *Thread* (or any subclass thereof) and invokes its *start* method. The new thread will then execute the *run* method of the object, in parallel with all other threads. Each thread must be spawned at most once, every further call to *start* raises an *IllegalThreadState* exception. The thread terminates when *run* terminates, either normally or abruptly due to an exception. The static method *currentThread* in class *Thread* returns the object associated with the executing thread.

Java offers four kinds of synchronisation between threads: locks, wait sets, joining and interrupts. The package `java.util.concurrent` in the Java API [76] builds sophisticated forms of synchronisation from these primitives and atomic compare-and-set operations.

Every object (and array) has an associated monitor with a lock and a wait set. Locks are mutually-exclusive, i.e., at most one thread can hold a lock at a time, but re-entrant, i.e., a thread can acquire a lock multiple times [56, §17.1]. For locking, Java uses `synchronized` blocks that take a reference to an object or array. A thread must acquire the object's lock before it executes the block's body, and releases the lock afterwards. If another thread already holds the lock, the executing thread must wait until the other thread has released it. Thus, `synchronized` blocks on the *same* object never execute in parallel. The method modifier `synchronized` is equivalent to wrapping the method's body in a `synchronized` block on the *this* reference [56, §8.4.3.6]. Java bytecode has explicit instructions for locking (`monitorenter`) and unlocking (`monitorexit`) of monitors. The major difference to `synchronized` blocks is that they can be used in unstructured ways; if the executing thread does not hold the lock, `monitorexit` fails with an *IllegalMonitorState* exception.

To avoid busy waiting, a thread can suspend itself to the wait set of an object by calling the object's method *wait*, which class *Object* declares [56, §17.8]. To enter the wait set, the thread must have locked the object's monitor and must not be interrupted; otherwise, an *IllegalMonitorState* exception or *InterruptedException*, respectively, is thrown. If successful, the call also releases the monitor's lock completely. The thread remains in the wait set until (i) another thread interrupts or notifies it, or (ii) if *wait* is called with a time limit, the specified amount of time has elapsed, or (iii) it wakes up spuriously. After having been removed, the thread reacquires the lock on the monitor before its execution proceeds normally or, in case of interruption, by raising an *InterruptedException*. The methods *notify* and *notifyAll* remove one unspecified or all threads from the wait set of the call's receiver object. Like for *wait*, the calling thread must hold the lock on the monitor. Thus, the notified thread continues its execution only after the notifying thread has released the lock.

When a thread calls *join* on another thread, it blocks until (i) the thread that the receiver object identifies has terminated, or (ii) another thread interrupts the joining thread, or (iii) an optionally-specified amount of time has elapsed. In the second case, the call raises an *InterruptedException*; otherwise, it returns normally.

Interruption [56, §17.8.3] provides asynchronous communication between threads. Calling the *interrupt* method of a thread sets its interrupt status. If the interrupted thread is waiting or joining, it aborts that, raises an *InterruptedException*, and clears its interrupt status. Otherwise, interruption has no immediate effect on the interrupted thread. Instead, class *Thread* implements two methods to observe the interrupt status. First, the static method *interrupt* returns and resets the interrupt status of the *executing* thread. Second, the method *interrupted* returns the interrupt status of the receiver object's thread without changing it.

Apart from that, class *Thread* also declares the methods `yield` and `sleep` [56, §17.9]. They instruct the scheduler to prefer other threads and cease execution for the specified time, respectively. Since these are only recommendations to the scheduler, they cannot be used for synchronisation.

Figure 1.1 shows some examples of synchronisation in a program with three threads that are run in parallel. However, it is prone to various forms of deadlock caused by locking, waiting and joining. Note that interruption alone cannot lead to deadlocks, because it is asynchronous.

For a start, suppose that threads `t1` and `t2` first acquire the locks on the shared objects p and q, respectively. Then, all threads are in deadlock for the following reasons: `t1` must acquire the lock on q, which `t2` is

thread t1	thread t2	thread t3

`synchronized (p) {`
`  synchronized (q) {`
`    synchronized (q) {`
`      q.wait();`
`}}}`
	`synchronized (q) {`
	`  synchronized (p) {`
	`    q.notify();`
	`}}`
		`t2.join();`
		`if (...)`
		`  t1.interrupt();`

Figure 1.1: Three Java threads with different deadlock possibilities

holding, but t2 itself must acquire the lock on p that t1 is holding, i.e., they are waiting for each other cyclically. Moreover, t3 is waiting for either t2 terminating or itself being interrupted, but t2 cannot terminate and there is no other thread which could interrupt t3.

A slightly different situation arises when t1 executes first until it suspends itself to q's wait set. In terms of locks, it has first acquired p's, then q's twice, and finally released both on q, but it is still holding the lock on p. Hence, when t2 starts to execute, it can acquire q's lock, but not p's. Consequently, all threads are again in deadlock: t1 waits to be removed from the wait set, but none of the other threads could do so, because t2 waits for t1 releasing p's lock and t3 waits for t2 to terminate or some other thread interrupting itself. Note that spurious wake-ups do not matter in this case. If t1 wakes up spuriously, then it must reacquire its locks on q first, i.e., t1 and t2 again end up waiting for each other.

Now suppose that t2 starts and is the first to acquire both locks q and p. Then, the call to *notify* has no effect since q's wait set is empty. Thus, it releases p and q (in that order) and terminates. Hence, t3's call to *join* terminates normally. Suppose further that t3's **if** condition evaluates to false, i.e., t1 is not interrupted and t3 terminates. When t1 subsequently enters q's wait set, it is immediately deadlocked, because there is no thread to remove it from the wait set. Note that in this case, there is only a single thread in deadlock, which is not possible if deadlock is due to locks and joins only. In case of a spurious wakeup, t1 terminates normally.

Finally, consider the same scenario again, but let t3 interrupt t1. Under this schedule, no deadlock occurs. If t3 calls *interrupt* before t1 calls *wait*, the latter call does not suspend t1 to q's wait set, but raises the *InterruptedException* immediately. Otherwise, the interrupt removes t1 from q's wait set. Then, t1 first reacquires the locks on q before it raises

```
class C { static int x = 0, y = 0; }
```

thread t1	thread t2
1: C.y = 1;	3: C.x = 2;
2: int i = C.x;	4: int j = C.y;

(a)

1 2 → 3 4	1 2 → 3 4	3 4 → 1 2
i == 2	i == 0	i == 2
j == 1	j == 1	j == 0

(b)

Figure 1.2: Program with two threads (a) and three of its sequentially consistent schedules (b), adapted from [2, Fig. 1 & 2]

the exception. In either case, t1's synchronized blocks correctly release all locks despite the exception.

Beyond threads and synchronisation, Java also specifies how shared memory behaves under concurrent accesses, which is known as the Java memory model (JMM) [56, §17.4]. Let me sketch the main ideas behind the JMM with Figure 1.2. The program on the left has two threads, each of which sets one of C's static fields x and y and subsequently reads the other into a local variable. Figure 1.2b shows three schedules for the program and for each schedule, the final values stored in the threads' local variables. There are three further schedules, but they result in the same assignments to i and j. All these schedules assume sequential consistency (SC) [93], which is the most intuitive memory model: There is a global notion of time, one thread executes at a time, and every write to a memory location immediately becomes visible to all threads. In particular, the result i == j == 0 is impossible under SC as the following argument shows. If it was possible, then l. 1 must execute after l. 4 and l. 3 after l. 2. Since l. 1 and l. 3 literally precede l. 2 and l. 4, respectively, one obtains the contradiction that l. 1 executes after l. 4 after l. 3 after l. 2 after l. 1.

For efficiency reasons, modern hardware implements memory models that are weaker than SC to allow for local caches and optimisations [3,165]. For example, if threads t1 and t2 execute on different processors, the writes in ll. 1 and 3 might still be queued in the processors' write buffers, when the reads in ll. 2 and 4 execute. Thus, the reads retrieve the initial values for C.x and C.y, i.e., 0, from main memory, which results in i == j == 0. Similarly, compiler optimisations might reorder the independent statements in each thread. Then, i == j == 0 is possible

5

```
static Object data;
volatile static boolean done = false;
```

thread t1	thread t2
1: data = ...;	3: **while** (!done) {}
2: done = **true**;	4: ... = data;

Figure 1.3: Synchronisation and publication of data through a **volatile** field

for the transformed program even under SC. Therefore, a correct implementation of SC must take extra precautions and conservatively disable such optimisations in *all* code, because the code does not provide any clues when it should do so. To avoid the ensuing slow-down, the JMM relaxes SC and allows the outcome i == j == 0 in the example.

Nevertheless, the JMM provides the intuitive SC semantics under additional assumptions – known as the data-race freedom (DRF) guarantee [4]. Two accesses to the same location conflict if (i) they originate from different threads, (ii) at least one is a write, and (iii) the location is not explicitly declared as **volatile**. A data race occurs if two conflicting accesses may happen concurrently, i.e., without synchronisation in between. If the program contains no data races, the JMM promises that it behaves like under SC. In other words: If a programmer protects all accesses to shared data via locks or declares the fields as **volatile**, she can forget about the JMM and assume interleaving semantics, i.e., SC.

In the above example, there are two data races: the write of C.y in l. 1 races with the read in l. 4 and similarly l. 2 and l. 3 for C.x, i.e., the DRF guarantee does not apply. To eliminate these data races, one can use the synchronisation mechanisms from above, e.g., wrapping every line in its own **synchronized** block on C's class object.

Alternatively, one can declare C's static fields x and y as **volatile**, because accesses to such fields never conflict.[1] Since these fields are marked, Java implementations know when to take appropriate measures. Thus, programmers can use volatile fields to implement their own

---

[1]When a thread reads from a volatile field, it synchronises with all other threads that have written previously to that field. Hence, the reading thread can be sure that everything that should have happened in the other threads prior to their writes in fact has happened prior to its read. For the formal semantics, see §4.3.2.

synchronisation mechanisms like in the example in Figure 1.3. After thread t1 has finished the construction of the data object to be passed, it releases thread t2 from spinning in l. 3 by setting the volatile flag done. Volatile semantics of the JMM guarantees that thread t2 sees the correct data, even though data itself is not volatile, i.e., no precautions slow down accesses to data.

Java also gives semantics to programs with data races, which is the main cause for the technical complexity of the JMM. This is essential, since malicious code could otherwise exploit data races to break type safety and Java's security architecture. This semantics, however, is weaker than SC in that it allows more behaviours. Still, it is too strong, because it does not allow as many compiler optimisations as desired [38, 115, 162]. Conversely, it is unclear whether it is strong enough to ensure type safety and the Java security guarantees.

1.2 Historical overview

In the mid-1990s, Nipkow's group started their work on the Bali project [11, 84] which lead to a comprehensive model (called Java^{light}) of the JavaCard language, a sequential subset of Java. They formalised the type system and a big-step semantics with a proof of type safety, and an axiomatic Hoare-style semantics that is shown sound and relatively complete with respect to the big-step semantics [129, 135–138, 156, 157]. At the same time, they studied the interaction between Java source code and bytecode for a smaller subset that was named μJava [85]. This line of work [24, 79–81, 86, 87, 126, 130, 146, 167, 168] lead to formal models of the virtual machine (VM), of the bytecode verifier, and to a compiler from source code to bytecode. These are complemented by proofs of type safety for source code and bytecode, and preservation of type correctness and semantics for the compiler.

Both Bali and μJava only consider sequential Java, although multithreading has been envisioned as future work from the start [129]. An important step towards this goal was Jinja by Klein and Nipkow [83], because they developed a small-step semantics for Jinja source code that they proved equivalent to the big-step semantics. Additionally, they redesigned the type safety proof to use the small-step semantics, and they considerably slimmed down Bali and μJava.

Thus, when I started to work on a formal semantics for *concurrent* Java in 2007, the choice for the sequential semantics was obvious: Jinja. Isabelle/HOL as the proof assistent was set, because the Quis custodiet project used it already and the semantics should become part of it – and Jinja was the most complete semantics of Java in Isabelle/HOL that featured a small-step semantics. A small-step semantics is crucial, because big-step semantics cannot express interleaving semantics adequately.

Of course, there have already been other formalisations of concurrent Java source code or bytecode [104, 20] in other provers (see §3.4.1 for an in-depth discussion), which could have been ported to Isabelle. However, none of them had been used in large proofs about the semantics. Hence, it was unclear whether they would be easy to use in verifying the program analyses of the QC project. In contrast, Jinja had evolved over ten years and the type safety proof and compiler verification demonstrate its usability. Thus, it seemed reasonable to extend Jinja with concurrency.

In retrospect, I have not regretted this choice. For validating the semantics, it would have been better if Jinja had included all the Java features that Bali and μJava had already covered. Hence, I have reintroduced arrays and the full set of binary operators – see §2.3 for a detailed comparison.

Adding multithreading to a sequential language is pervasive, because almost every definition and every proof needs to be adapted. Although I have tried to reuse in JinjaThreads as much as possible from Jinja, it is more the general ideas and concepts that have survived than their literal formulation in Isabelle/HOL. Hence, JinjaThreads is incompatible with Jinja, but every Jinja program can be trivially transformed into a JinjaThreads program.

1.3 Contributions

The technical contributions of this thesis are the following:

- a model of Java threads for source code and bytecode (Chapter 3);
- proofs of type safety with deadlocks (§3.3);
- modular single-threaded semantics shared between SC and the JMM (Chapter 4);
- a proof of the DRF guarantee (§4.3.3), consistency (§4.3.4), and type safety (§4.3.5) of the JMM;

- an example that the JMM corrupts Java security in theory (§4.3.5);
- a verified compiler from source code to bytecode (Chapter 5);
- an efficient, executable interpreter, virtual machine, type checker, and compiler that are extracted automatically from the formal model (Chapter 6); and
- validating the model by compiling and running Java programs in a test harness (§6.5).

The complete model and all proofs are formalised in the proof assistant Isabelle/HOL and available online [106] in the Archive of Formal Proofs.[2]

My model JinjaThreads covers all concurrency features from the Java language specification [56] except

- the methods `stop`, `destroy`, `suspend`, and `resume` in class *Thread*, as they are deprecated;
- timing-related features like timed `wait` and `Thread.sleep`, because JinjaThreads does not model time;
- the compare-and-swap operations for the `java.util.concurrent` package, since these are vendor-specific extensions of Java; and
- spurious wake-ups, because the JLS discourages VMs to perform those and they would obscure deadlocks. Standard Java coding practice circumvents this; see §4.3.6 for details.

The concurrency features that JinjaThreads covers are embedded in (an extension of) Jinja [83] by Klein and Nipkow, which I introduce in Chapter 2. The sequential features include classes with objects, fields, and methods, inheritance with method overriding and dynamic dispatch, arrays, exception handling, assignments, local variables, and standard control structures. Like its predecessor, JinjaThreads omits some sequential features from Java to remain tractable, e.g., static and final fields and methods, visibility modifiers, interfaces, class initialisation, and garbage collection. §7.4 contains the complete list, and in §6.5.1, I discuss how some of them can be emulated.

Thus, JinjaThreads is the first machine-checked model that unifies multithreaded Java source code, bytecode, and a compiler. In particular, JinjaThreads subsumes all of Jinja except for the big-step semantics and the proof of equivalence to the small-step semantics.

---

[2]In this thesis, I describe version e7d44e610544 in the archive. It works with Isabelle development version 915af80f74b3.

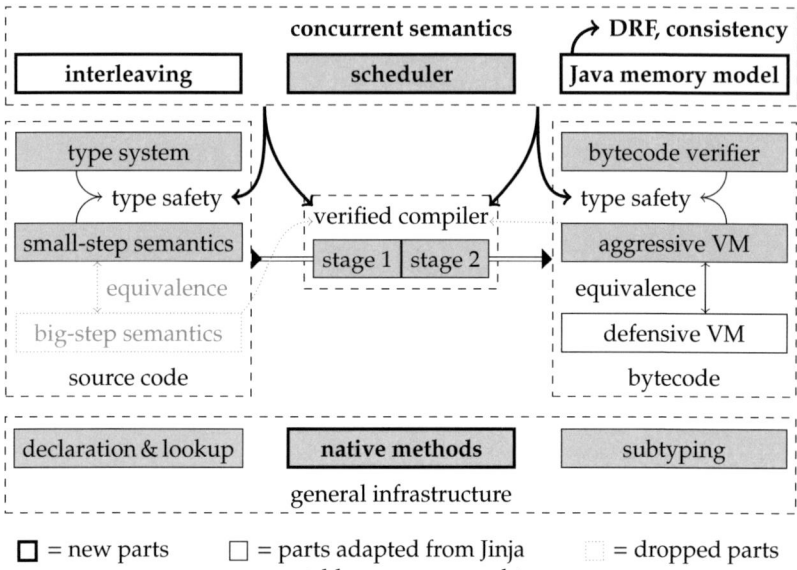

$\square$ = new parts $\square$ = parts adapted from Jinja $\square$ = dropped parts
$\blacksquare$ = executable $\rightarrow$ = used to prove

Figure 1.4: Structure of JinjaThreads in comparison with Jinja's

Figure 1.4 shows the resulting structure of JinjaThreads. New parts are set in bold, adapted ones normally, and dropped ones in grey with dotted lines. The source code part defines the syntax, the type system, and a small-step semantics. The bytecode part formalises bytecode instructions, a virtual machine for individual threads in two equivalent flavours (aggressive and defensive), and a bytecode verifier. Both parts share some general infrastructure, the interleaving semantics and the JMM formalisation. The compiler translates source code into bytecode in two stages.

I prove type safety using the standard approach by Wright and Felleisen [180]. Subject reduction, i.e., preservation of well-typedness, easily carries over from Jinja. However, potential deadlocks severely complicate the progress theorem, which shows that execution does not get stuck. In fact, formalisations of type soundness for concurrent programming languages typically leave out the progress theorem or their notion of deadlock is implicit in the theorem's assumptions, e.g., [57, 73, 94, 166, 169]. This way, one cannot be sure that the theorem's

layer	source code		bytecode	
7	Java memory model			concurrent semantics
6	complete interleavings			
5	interleaved small-step			
4	thread start & finish events			single-threaded semantics
3	statements & expressions	call stacks		
		exception handling		
		single instruction		
2	native methods			
1	heap operations			

Figure 1.5: JinjaThreads stack of semantics

notion coincides with the intuitive understanding of deadlock, especially because deadlock can arise in many different ways (§1.1). In contrast, I formalise deadlock semantically (§3.3) and then prove type safety with respect to this notion.

Furthermore, JinjaThreads advances the state of the art in modelling concurrency. Previous formal semantics for multithreaded Java source code or bytecode [9, 14, 15, 20, 48, 70, 104, 166] stopped at interleaving semantics, i.e., sequential consistency. On the contrary, I formally connect the Java programming language with the Java memory model for the first time. Nevertheless, JinjaThreads models sequential consistency, too.

Here, separation of concerns and sharing of definitions and proofs are crucial to obtain a tractable model – not only between source code and bytecode, but also between the different memory models. To disentangle sequential aspects, the concurrency features, and the memory model from one another, I have built the semantics as a stack of seven layers (Figure 1.5). For example, to switch from source code to bytecode, one only needs to exchange layer 3, which defines the semantics of the language primitives. Analogously, the type safety proof at level 3 holds for both memory models, because they differ only in layers 1, 4, 6, and 7.

Furthermore, I have identified several previously unknown corner cases that the JMM misses and show how to deal with them. Moreover, I prove that the JMM indeed provides the DRF guarantee. Previous proofs [8,69] made assumptions about the sequential semantics, this work shows that these assumptions were justified. Regarding the other two promises of the JMM, namely type safety and Java's security guarantees, the answers are less positive. Only a weak form of type safety holds, which excludes allocation of objects, i.e., the JMM allows Java programs to access unallocated objects (albeit in a type-correct fashion); and the JMM compromises Java's security guarantees.

JinjaThreads also extends Jinja's non-optimising compiler to handle the synchronisation primitives, and proves that it preserves semantics, well-typedness, and data race freedom of programs. Preservation of well-typedness is a straightforward extension of Jinja's proofs, but semantic preservation requires a completely different approach, because Jinja used the big-step semantics, which no longer exists. In particular, verification must deal with the non-determinism of concurrency and different granularity of atomic operations. Using a bisimulation approach, I obtain a stronger correctness statement than Klein and Nipkow for Jinja, which also covers non-terminating executions. Again, JinjaThreads's modular structure ensures that the result holds for both SC and the JMM. Thus, this is the first verified compiler for Java threads.

The various proofs about the semantics and the compiler demonstrate that JinjaThreads is indeed a tractable model, albeit large, and that today's prover technology can handle such large models. Nevertheless, one must also make sure that it *faithfully* abstracts reality, i.e., Java. However, JinjaThreads' size is beyond the point up to which good common sense suffices to convince oneself. Therefore, I have undertaken the effort to validate the model by executing smallish Java programs in both the source code and bytecode semantics. To that end, I have used Isabelle's code generator to generate code for all definitions in grey boxes in Figure 1.4. Chapter 6 discusses the necessary steps and what the pitfalls were. This way, I have automatically extracted an executable well-formedness checker, interpreter, virtual machine and compiler for JinjaThreads programs from the Isabelle formalisation.

To make the vast supply of Java programs available for experimenting and testing with the semantics, I have developed together with the students Jonas Thedering and Antonio Zea the (unverified) conversion tool Java2Jinja[3] as a plugin to the Eclipse IDE. It converts Java class

---

[3]Java2Jinja is availabe for download at
http://pp.info.uni-karlsruhe.de/projects/quis-custodiet/Java2Jinja/

declarations into JinjaThreads abstract syntax and provides a front-end to the well-formedness checker, interpreter and VM. Validation was not in vain, it discovered a bug in JinjaThreads' implementation of the division and modulus operators (§6.5.2).

The size of the formalisation also poses a challenge for presentation. To keep the presentation intelligible, Chapter 2 starts with the sequential subset of JinjaThreads and omits everything that is related to multithreading. Then, I extend this subset with Java concurrency (Chapter 3) and the memory models (Chapter 4). This also demonstrates how Jinja evolved to JinjaThreads and what adaptations to the sequential semantics were necessary. Since I show most definitions only in excerpts or informally and change some of them multiple times, I have included the complete formal definition of the languages and semantics for source code and bytecode in Appendix B. Most of the proofs are only sketched or omitted completely, but they can be found in [106] with all the gory details of a machine-checked formalisation.

1.4 Isabelle/HOL

I have used the theorem prover Isabelle with higher-order logic (HOL) [128] as meta-language to formalise this work. Isabelle is able to check formalised definitions for being type-correct in the meta-language and formalised proofs for correctness. Although Isabelle offers sophisticated tools for proof automation, users must still decompose proofs into many small steps and guide the proof search. Yet, being an interactive proof assistant, Isabelle also supports the user in devising a formalised proof. For example, it correctly generates all non-trivial inductive cases for her and solves the trivial ones automatically. Conversely, Isabelle does not accept proofs of the form "analogous to . . . " or "without loss of generality, . . . " In such a case, the user must either repeat the proof or generalise it such that it works for all relevant cases. Thus, constructing elegant formal proofs still remains a business for experts. I have omitted most proofs in the presentation and only sketched the line of argument. Since I have written most proofs in the human-readable language Isar [25,179], the interested reader may consult the formalisation sources [106] for full details.

Despite Isabelle having formally checked all lemmas and theorems of this thesis, typing errors may have slipped in during typesetting.

13

Although Isabelle can in principle typeset definitions and theorems automatically to rule out such mistakes, I have transcribed all formulae in this thesis from the formalisation manually for two reasons. First, complex locale hierarchies (locales are Isabelle's module system, §1.4.2) confuse Isabelle's pretty-printer such that it loses track of pretty-printing syntax and outputs all fixed parameters, i.e., its output becomes unintelligible. Second, the presentation simplifies the formalisation in a few places for the sake of readability. For example, it glosses over some technical details such as trivial type coercions (see Footnotes 29 and 30). Chapters 2 and 3 present the definitions without the generalisations that later chapters add, although there is only one set of formal definitions with all extensions and generalisations. Consequently, I show how to adapt the simplified presentations in the later chapters. Appendix B contains the unsimplified definitions with all extensions.

1.4.1 Notation

The meta-language HOL mostly uses standard mathematical notation. This section introduces further notation and in particular some basic data types and operations on them.

Implication in Isabelle/HOL is written $\longrightarrow$ or $\Longrightarrow$ and associates to the right. Since the latter form stems from Isabelle's environment for natural deduction, it separates the assumptions in proof rules, but cannot occur inside other HOL formulae. I abbreviate multiple assumptions by enclosing them in $[\![$ and $]\!]$ with the separator ";". Displayed implications are often printed as inference rules. For example, modus ponens is written $P \longrightarrow Q \Longrightarrow P \Longrightarrow Q$ or $[\![P \longrightarrow Q;\ P]\!] \Longrightarrow Q$ or

$$\frac{P \longrightarrow Q \qquad P}{Q}$$

Biimplication $P \longleftrightarrow Q$ is shorthand for $P \longrightarrow Q$ and $Q \longrightarrow P$.

The set of *HOL types* includes the basic types of truth values, natural numbers, integers and 32 bit machine words, which are called *bool, nat, int,* and *word32,* respectively. The space of total functions is denoted by $\Rightarrow$. Type variables are written $'a, 'b$, etc. $t :: \tau$ means that the HOL term t has HOL type τ. To distinguish variables from defined constants, I typeset variables in italics (e.g., x, y, f) and defined names slantedly (e.g., x, y, f).

Pairs come with two projection functions *fst* :: $'a \times 'b \Rightarrow 'a$ and *snd* :: $'a \times 'b \Rightarrow 'b$. Tuples are identified with pairs nested to the right, i.e., (a, b, c) is identical to $(a, (b, c))$ and $'a \times 'b \times 'c$ to $'a \times ('b \times 'c)$. Dually, $'a + 'b$ denotes the *disjoint sum* of $'a$ and $'b$; the injections are *Inl* :: $'a \Rightarrow 'a + 'b$ and *Inr* :: $'b \Rightarrow 'a + 'b$. *Records* are tuples with labelled components, e.g., $(\!| x = 1, y = 2 |\!)$.

Sets (type $'a\ set$) are isomorphic to predicates (type $'a \Rightarrow bool$) with bijections $\_ \in \_$ and $\{x \mid x. \_ x\}$, where $\mid x$ denotes the bound variable and can be omitted if equal to the preceding term, e.g., $y \in \{x. P\ x\} \longleftrightarrow P\ y$. *UNIV* :: $'a\ set$ is the set of all elements of type $'a$, $\emptyset$ denotes the empty set. The image operator $f\ '\ A$ applies f to all elements of A, i.e., $f\ '\ A = \{f\ a \mid a.\ a \in A\}$. For example, $f\ '\ UNIV$ (written *range* f) denotes f's range. The predicate *finite* on sets characterises all finite sets. The operator $\uplus$ :: $'a\ set \Rightarrow 'b\ set \Rightarrow ('a + 'b)\ set$ denotes disjoint union on sets.

The definite description operator $\iota x.\ P\ x$ is known as Russell's ι-operator. It denotes the unique x such that $P\ x$ holds, provided exactly one exists. Hilbert's ε-operator (indefinite description operator), written $\varepsilon x.\ P\ x$, denotes one (fixed, but underspecified) x such that $P\ x$ holds, provided P is satisfiable at all. Otherwise, both operators are unspecified.

Lists (type $'a\ list$) come with the empty list $[]$ and the infix constructor $\cdot$ for consing. Variable names ending in "s" usually stand for lists. The function *append*, written @ as infix operator, concatenates two lists, $|xs|$ denotes the length of xs, and *set* converts lists into sets. If $i < |xs|$, $xs_{[i]}$ denotes the i-th element of xs, and $xs[i := x]$ replaces the i-th element of xs with x. Further standard operations on lists are available: *hd xs* returns (*tl xs* removes) the first element of (from) xs, and *take n xs* returns (*drop n xs* removes) the first n elements of (from) xs; *replicate n x* constructs the list $[x, x, \ldots, x]$ of length n; *rev xs* reverses xs *map f xs* applies the function f to all elements of the list xs; *filter P xs* with syntax $[x \leftarrow xs.\ P\ x]$ retains only elements from xs that fulfill P; *zip xs ys* combines xs and ys elementwise into a list of pairs; *foldl f a xs* and *foldr f xs a* reduce the list xs with the binary operator f and start value a, associating to the left and right, respectively; *concat* = *foldl append* $[]$ concatenates a list of lists; *distinct xs* checks whether the elements in xs occur only once.

datatype $'a\ option = None \mid Some\ 'a$

adjoins a new element *None* to $'a$, all existing elements in type $'a$ are also in $'a\ option$, but prefixed by *Some*. For succinctness, I write $\lfloor a \rfloor$

15

for *Some a*. For example, *bool option* consists of the three values *None*, $\lfloor True \rfloor$, and $\lfloor False \rfloor$. The underspecified inverse *the* of *Some* satisfies *the* $\lfloor x \rfloor = x$. Variables whose name ends in "o" usually have *option* type. *Option.map f* maps *None* to *None* and $\lfloor x \rfloor$ to $\lfloor f\, x \rfloor$.

Case distinctions on datatypes use guard-like syntax. For example, *case xo of None* $\Rightarrow a \mid \lfloor x \rfloor \Rightarrow f$ pattern-matches on *xo*. If *xo* is *None*, it returns *a*; if *xo* is $\lfloor x \rfloor$, the result is *f* where *f* may refer to *x*.

Function update is defined as follows: Let $f :: {}'a \Rightarrow {}'b$, $a :: {}'a$, and $b :: {}'b$. Then, $f(a := b) = \lambda x.\ \textit{if } x = a \textit{ then } b \textit{ else } f\, x$.

As all functions in HOL are total, *partial functions* are modelled as functions of type $'a \Rightarrow {}'b$ *option* where *None* represents undefinedness and $f\, x = \lfloor y \rfloor$ means that *f* maps *x* to *y*. I abbreviate $'a \Rightarrow {}'b$ *option* by $'a \rightharpoonup {}'b$ and call such functions *maps*. The notation $f(x \mapsto y)$ is shorthand for $f(x := \lfloor y \rfloor)$, and it extends to lists: $f\ (xs\ [\mapsto]\ ys)$ means $f\big(x_{[0]} \mapsto y_{[0]}\big) \ldots \big(x_{[i]} \mapsto y_{[i]}\big)$ where *i* is the minimum of $|xs| - 1$ and $|ys| - 1$. Multiple updates like $f(x \mapsto y)\ (xs\ [\mapsto]\ ys)$ can be written as $f(x \mapsto y, xs\ [\mapsto]\ ys)$. The everywhere undefined map $\lambda\_.\ None$ is written *empty*. Updates of *empty* are written $[x \mapsto y]$, $[xs\ [\mapsto]\ ys]$, etc. The domain of *f* (written *dom f*) is the set of points at which *f* is defined, *ran f* denotes the range of *f*. Function *map-of* turns an association list, i.e., a list of pairs, into a map:

$$map\text{-}of\ [] = empty$$
$$map\text{-}of\ ((x, y) \cdot xs) = (map\text{-}of\ xs)(x \mapsto y)$$

The order $m_1 \subseteq_m m_2$ on maps denotes that m_2's domain contains m_1's and m_1 and m_2 are equal on *dom* m_1. I say that m_1 is a *restriction* of m_2 and m_2 an *extension* of m_1.

FinFuns [109] (type $'a \Rightarrow_f {}'b$) are functions that are almost everywhere constant, which Isabelle's code generator implements as associative lists (§6.1.3). For this thesis, one may treat them just like ordinary functions except for some notation. Function application and update are written $f_f\, x$ and $f(x :=_f y)$, respectively; $K^f\, y$ denotes the FinFun that maps everything to *y*. The decoration with subscripts f extends to other update notation for maps, e.g., $f\ (x \mapsto_f y)$ denotes $f(x :=_f \lfloor y \rfloor)$ and $[x \mapsto_f y]$ abbreviates $(K^f\, None)(x :=_f \lfloor y \rfloor)$.

1.4.2 Locales

Locales [12] are Isabelle's approach to modularisation. A locale declaration defines the signature of a context, which consists of the locale parameters with fixed types (fixes) and the assumptions about the parameters (assumes). It also defines a predicate with the locale's name that collects all assumptions.

For example, the following locale *monoid* declares a module monoid whose parameters, i.e., abstract operations, are the binary operator $\odot$ and the neutral element e. It has three assumptions: *assoc* states associativity and *neutral* states that e is left and right neutral – free variables in the assumptions (such as a, b, and c) are implicitly universally quantified. Note that the type of the elements of the monoid is the type variable $'a$ rather than an opaque type. This way, module implementations can instantiate $'a$ as needed.

> **locale** *monoid* = fixes $\odot :: 'a \Rightarrow 'a \Rightarrow 'a$ and $e :: 'a$
> assumes *assoc*: $(a \odot b) \odot c = a \odot (b \odot c)$
> and *neutral*: $a \odot e = a \qquad e \odot a = a$

A locale context collects declarations such as theorems and definitions, which may depend on the parameters and assumptions. If a definition or proof uses the module, but does not need to look at one concrete implementation, it goes in such a locale context. For example:

> **fun** (in *monoid*) *pow* $:: 'a \Rightarrow nat \Rightarrow 'a$ where
> $pow\ x\ 0 = e$
> $\mid pow\ x\ (n+1) = x \odot pow\ x\ n$

> **lemma** (in *monoid*) *pow-plus*: $pow\ x\ (n+m) = pow\ x\ n \odot pow\ x\ m$

Locale interpretations correspond to module implementations – they instantiate the parameters of a locale and discharge the assumptions. This specialises all collected declarations to the given parameters, optionally adding a name prefix. For example,

> **interpretation** *list*: *monoid* @ $[\,]$ ⟨proof⟩

interprets the monoid for lists. This yields the function *list.pow* and the lemma *list.pow-plus*, in which the type $'b\ list$ instantiates the type variable

$'a$ for the monoid elements and @ and $[]$ replace $\odot$ and e, respectively, i.e.,

$$list.pow\ x\ 0 = []\qquad list.pow\ x\ (n+1) = x\ @\ list.pow\ x\ n$$
$$list.pow\ x\ (n+m) = list.pow\ x\ n\ @\ list.pow\ x\ m$$

To use or extend a module, locales can inherit from other locales where parameters may be renamed, specialised and names prefixed as necessary. From the module point of view, the inherited locale exports all the declarations it has collected. Here is an example for monoid homomorphisms:

locale $monoid\text{-}hom = m_1 : monoid \odot_1\ e_1 + m_2 : monoid \odot_2\ e_2$
  for $\odot_1 :: 'a \Rightarrow 'a \Rightarrow 'a$ and $e_1 :: 'a$ and $\odot_2 :: 'b \Rightarrow 'b \Rightarrow 'b$ and $e_2 :: 'b +$
  fixes $h :: 'a \Rightarrow 'b$
  assumes $h\ e_1 = e_2$ and $h\ (a \odot_1 b) = (h\ a) \odot_2 (h\ b)$

lemma (in $monoid\text{-}hom$) $hom\text{-}pow$: $h\ (m_1.pow\ x\ n) = m_2.pow\ (h\ x)\ n$

The locale $monoid\text{-}hom$ imports the locale $monoid$ twice and redeclares the inherited parameters in the for clause. To avoid ambiguities, references to the first (second) are prefixed with m_1 (m_2) and the parameters renamed to $\odot_1$ and e_1 ($\odot_2$ and e_2), respectively. Additionally, it fixes another parameter h and assumes that it is a monoid homomorphism. The lemma demonstrates how imported declarations are referenced.

JinjaThreads heavily uses locales to define interfaces between the different layers in the stack of semantics such that the development on higher levels can be reused by different implementations of the lower levels. For example (Chapter 3), the locale for interleaving semantics fixes a parameter for the single-threaded semantics. Then, source code and bytecode reuse the definitions and theorems for the interleaving semantics by interpretation. From the module point of view, source code and bytecode implement the module for single-threaded semantics on which the interleaving semantics builds.

To overcome incompatibilities between the code generator and the locale infrastructure, which I explain in §6.1.4, I have separated the declaration of parameters from the assumptions by splitting the locales whenever executability is a concern. Locales with names ending in -base only fix the parameters, the others inherit from them and add the assumptions.

1.4.3 Induction and coinduction

JinjaThreads heavily uses inductive and coinductive definitions, e.g., for the type system, small-step semantics, and complete interleavings. Since coinductive definitions and coinduction are less known than inductive ones, I contrast the former with the latter. Moreover, I briefly show how Isabelle's automation supports such definitions and proofs.

Consider, for example, the following introduction rules of the reflexive and transitive closure (RTC) r^{**} of a binary relation r.

$$\frac{}{r^{**}\, a\, a} \qquad \frac{r^{**}\, a\, b \qquad r\, b\, c}{r^{**}\, a\, c} \tag{1.1}$$

When one interprets them as an inductive definition, the binary prediate r^{**} is defined as follows:

1. $r^{**}\, a\, a$ holds for any a, and
2. $r^{**}\, a\, c$ holds if $r^{**}\, a\, b$ already holds for some b such that $r\, b\, c$, and
3. r^{**} holds for nothing else – or, equivalently, r^{**} is the *strongest* predicate satisfying 1 and 2.

The last clause is characteristic for inductive definitions. In particular, r^{**} holds for concrete x and y only if one can prove $r^{**}\, x\, y$ in finitely many steps using the rules of (1.1).

Now, consider the coinductive definition of r_{**} with the same introduction rules as for r^{**}:[4]

$$\text{REFL}: \frac{}{r_{**}\, a\, a} \qquad \text{STEP}: \frac{r_{**}\, a\, b \qquad r\, b\, c}{r_{**}\, a\, c} \tag{1.2}$$

This definition characterises r_{**} as follows:

1. $r_{**}\, a\, a$ holds for any a, and
2. $r_{**}\, a\, c$ holds if $r_{**}\, a\, b$ holds for some b such that $r\, b\, c$, and
3. $r_{**}\, a\, b$ is the *weakest* predicate with the property that whenever it holds, this can be justified by 1 or 2.[5]

---

[4]I use double horizontal bars for coinductive definitions to distinguish them from inductive ones.

[5]Pierce calls this property "'self-justifying': every assertion in it [the predicate considered as a set] is justified by other assertions that are also in it" [143, §21.1].

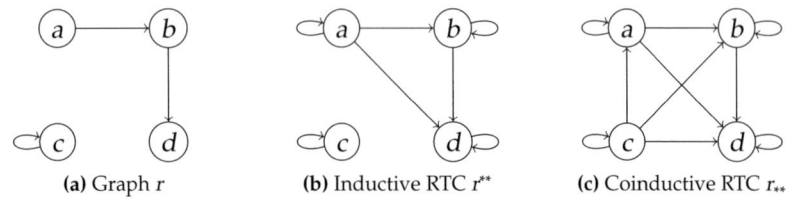

(a) Graph r (b) Inductive RTC r^{**} (c) Coinductive RTC r_{**}

Figure 1.6: Example to illustrate the difference between inductive and coinductive definitions

Again, the last clause is characteristic for coinductive definitions. In particular, r_{**} does *not* hold for concrete x and y only if one can prove $\neg\, r_{**}\, x\, y$ in finitely many steps.

To appreciate the difference between inductive and coinductive definitions, consider Figure 1.6. Let r be the binary predicate on a type with four elements a, b, c, and d as shown as a graph in Figure 1.6a, i.e., only $r\, a\, b$, $r\, b\, d$, and $r\, c\, c$ hold. The inductive RTC r^{**} adds the missing loops at a, b, and d, and the transitive edge from a to d (Figure 1.6b). Figure 1.6c shows the coinductive RTC. It includes everything from the inductive RTC, but adds edges from c to every other element, too – even though c is disconnected from the rest of the graph. These edges are justified, because the loop at c permits to apply STEP infinitely often. Hence, one cannot prove that these edges do not belong to r_{**}. When defining predicates coinductively, one must be careful to avoid such infinite recursion when it is not intended.

Isabelle/HOL provides a package to automate inductive and coinductive definitions [142] of predicates and sets. Given the introduction rules for a (co)inductive predicate, it computes the corresponding functional F over predicates and defines the predicate as the least (greatest) fixed point *lfp F* (*gfp F*) of F. Next, the package proves monotonicity of F to ensure that the fixed point exists. Unless the premises involve user-defined operators that take as a parameter the predicate to be defined, this is completely automatic. Then, the package derives from the definition the specified introduction rules, a rule for case analysis, and a (co)induction rule.

The functional F for the introduction rules in (1.1) and (1.2) is the same, namely

$$\lambda P\, x_1\, x_2.\, (\exists a.\, x_1 = a \wedge x_2 = a) \vee (\exists a\, b\, c.\, x_1 = a \wedge x_2 = c \wedge P\, a\, b \wedge r\, b\, c)$$

where the parameter P abstracts the predicates r^{**} and r_{**} to be defined. Since F is automatically proven monotone, r^{**} is defined as $lfp\,F$ and r_{**} as $gfp\,F$.

The induction rule (1.3) stems from the fact that $lfp\,F$ is the intersection of all F-closed binary predicates, where P is F-closed iff $F(P)\,x\,y$ implies $P\,x\,y$. Hence, to prove that some property P holds for all points x and y with $r^{**}\,x\,y$, it suffices to prove that P is F-closed.

$$\frac{r^{**}\,x\,y \qquad \forall a.\,P\,a\,a \qquad \forall a\,b\,c.\,r^{**}\,a\,b \longrightarrow P\,a\,b \longrightarrow r\,b\,c \longrightarrow P\,a\,c}{P\,x\,y} \tag{1.3}$$

Dually to (1.3), the package derives the coinduction rule (1.4) for r_{**} from the fact that $gfp\,F$ is the union of all F-consistent binary predicates, where P is F-consistent iff $P\,x\,y$ implies $F(P)\,x\,y$.

$$\frac{P\,x\,y \qquad \begin{array}{c}\forall x_1\,x_2.\,P\,x_1\,x_2 \longrightarrow \\ (\exists a.\,x_1 = a \wedge x_2 = a)\,\vee \\ (\exists a\,b\,c.\,x_1 = a \wedge x_2 = c \wedge (P\,a\,b \vee r_{**}\,a\,b) \wedge r\,b\,c)\end{array}}{r_{**}\,x\,y} \tag{1.4}$$

Duality of (1.3) and (1.4) extends to how they are used in proofs: Induction (1.3) serves to prove properties P of all elements of r^{**}; it eliminates the premise $r^{**}\,x\,y$ towards the goal $P\,x\,y$. Conversely, the coinduction rule (1.4) has the coinductive predicate r_{**} in the conclusion. Hence, it can only establish that r_{**} contains all elements that satisfy the (F-consistent) property P, but it is useless in deriving properties of *all* elements of r_{**}.

Sometimes, it is convenient to strengthen the coinduction rule such that one may delay to show the consistency requirement for P. To that end, P is replaced by a family $Q\,k$ of predicates indexed over a well-founded relation R (written $wf\,R$), where k measures how often one may delay to show the consistency requirement. For r_{**}, the strengthened coinduction rule is

$$\frac{wf\,R \qquad Q\,k\,x\,y \qquad \begin{array}{c}\forall k\,x_1\,x_2.\,Q\,k\,x_1\,x_2 \longrightarrow \\ (\exists k'.\,(k',k) \in R \wedge Q\,k'\,x_1\,x_2)\,\vee \\ (\exists a.\,x_1 = a \wedge x_2 = a)\,\vee \\ (\exists a\,b\,c.\,x_1 = a \wedge x_2 = c \wedge ((\exists k'.\,Q\,k'\,a\,b) \vee r_{**}\,a\,b) \wedge r\,b\,c)\end{array}}{r_{**}\,x\,y}$$

21

The additional case $\exists k'.\ (k',k) \in R \wedge Q\,k'\,x_1\,x_2$ in the last premise permits to defer showing consistency if one can descend in R from k to k' without changing the elements. After one step in the consistency proof, one may freely choose the new index k' in the last case. For examples of such strengthened coinduction rules, see Lemmata 4.16 and 5.2.

Proof. Isabelle does not automatically prove the strengthened coinduction rule, i.e., the user has to prove it manually for every coinductive definition for which she needs it. From the last premise, one proves by well-founded induction that the last premise of (1.4) holds for P instantiated with $\lambda x\,y.\ \exists k.\ Q\,k\,x\,y$. The claim $r_{**}\,x\,y$ then follows directly with (1.4). $\qquad\square$

(Co-)Induction is the main proof principle for (co-)datatypes, too. Isabelle's datatype package [26] defines algebraic datatypes. The package automatically derives the induction rule and a combinator for primitive recursion, which *de*structs the term towards a result. For example, the type of finite lists $'a\ list$ is defined by

$$\textbf{datatype}\ 'a\ list = [\,]\ |\ 'a \cdot 'a\ list$$

Again, coalgebraic datatypes (codatatypes) are dual: Users must construct them manually, e.g., [110, 142], and the corecursion operator *con*structs them. Possibly infinite lists (HOL type $'a\ llist$), e.g., have the corecursion operator

$$llist\text{-}corec\ a\ f = (case\ f\ a\ of\ None \Rightarrow [\,]\ |\ \lfloor(x,a')\rfloor] \Rightarrow x \cdot llist\text{-}corec\ a'\ f)$$

It can be used, e.g., to define the iteration of a function f:

$$[b, f\ b, f\ (f\ b), f\ (f\ (f\ b)), \ldots] = llist\text{-}corec\ b\ (\lambda a.\ \lfloor(a, f\ a)\rfloor])$$

For a good introduction to corecursive definitions in Isabelle, see [142] by Paulson. The coinduction rule is used to prove such terms equal.

Bernard of Chartres used to say that we are like dwarfs on the shoulders of giants, so that we can see more than they, and things at a greater distance, not by virtue of any sharpness of sight on our part, or any physical distinction, but because we are carried high and raised up by their giant size.

John of Salisbury, Metalogicon

2

Sequential JinjaThreads

In this chapter, I present the abstract syntax, type system, and semantics of sequential JinjaThreads including a proof of type safety, for both source code (§2.1) and bytecode (§2.2). In Chapters 3 and 4, I extend the sequential parts to Java concurrency. JinjaThreads also comes with a compiler and bytecode verifier, whose presentation I defer to Chapters 5 and 6, respectively, since this chapter focusses on the languages, type systems, and semantics.

As JinjaThreads builds on Jinja, I have taken the vast bulk of sequential features from Jinja, but made some adaptations and extensions. Klein and Nipkow have presented most of these features in detail [83], so I do not treat the sequential constructs in depth, here. Rather, this chapter introduces the main ideas and notation relevant for the rest of this thesis. Consequently, I present most definitions only in excerpts or informally. Appendix B contains the complete formal definitions, which include all generalisations of the later chapters. In §2.3, I compare sequential JinjaThreads to its predecessors Jinja, Bali, and μJava, and discuss the relevant changes.

2.1 Source code

This section describes the sequential part of JinjaThreads source code called J. First, I define the abstract syntax, covering values and types, expressions and statements, and program declarations with lookup operations on them (§2.1.1). The static semantics of the language is completed by the type system (§2.1.2) and well-formedness constraints (§2.1.4). In §2.1.5, I sketch the small-step semantics, focussing on native methods. Finally, the type safety proof (§2.1.6) shows that static and dynamic semantics fit together.

2.1.1 Abstract syntax

In this section, I present the abstract syntax for JinjaThreads source code, bottom up. I start off with values and types, continue with expressions and statements, and conclude with program declarations and lookup functions on them. Abstract syntax falls into a generic part and one specific to source code. This way, bytecode can reuse the generic parts (see §2.2.1). JinjaThreads only defines an abstract syntax, but no concrete input syntax. In §6.5, I discuss how to translate the concrete syntax of Java into JinjaThreads abstract syntax.

There are HOL types *cname* for class names, *mname* for method names, and *vname* for variable names and field names. To make the semantics executable (Chapter 6), all of them are isomorphic to strings – as opposed to leaving them unspecified. For example, the special reference *this* to the current object is modelled as a local variable with name "this". In the sequel, I use the following variable conventions: C, D for class names, M for method names, V for variable names, and F for field names. v stands for values, T for JinjaThreads types, a for addresses and e for expressions.

Values and types

There are five kinds of JinjaThreads values (of HOL type *val*, see Figure 2.1): a dummy value *Unit*, booleans *Bool b* where $b :: bool$, 32-bit integers *Intg i* where $i :: word32$, the null reference *Null*, and references *Addr a* where $a :: addr$. For the moment, I treat the type of addresses *addr* as an opaque type, the memory models in Chapter 4 add more structure.

JinjaThreads types (of HOL type *ty*, see Figure 2.1) are the type *Void* for *Unit*, primitive types *Boolean* and *Integer*, and three kinds of reference types, namely *NT* for the null reference, *Class C* for classes, and *Array T* for arrays with element type T. $T[]$ is shorthand for *Array T*. The predicate *is-refT* on types *ty* tests for reference types.

The map *typeof* statically assigns types to values, see Figure 2.1 for the definition. References (*Addr a*) are statically not typable, because

datatype $val = Unit \mid Bool\ bool \mid Intg\ word32 \mid Null \mid Addr\ addr$
datatype $ty\ = Void \mid Boolean \mid Integer \mid NT \mid Class\ cname \mid Array\ ty$

$$typeof\ Unit\ = \lfloor Void \rfloor$$
$$typeof\ (Bool\ b) = \lfloor Boolean \rfloor \qquad typeof\ Null\ = \lfloor NT \rfloor$$
$$typeof\ (Intg\ i)\ = \lfloor Integer \rfloor \qquad typeof\ (Addr\ a) = None$$

Figure 2.1: JinjaThreads values and types

their type may depend on the object or array that gets allocated at a at run time.

Expressions

JinjaThreads source code J is an imperative language where everything is an expression (HOL type $expr$) with a return value: statements are modelled as expressions that return $Unit$. Table 2.1 shows the sequential subset of expressions that JinjaThreads supports. It extends Jinja's source code language by the following expressions (marked with *): (i) test on run time types with $instanceof$ and (ii) array creation, array cell access and update, and reading the length of an array. Expressions whose syntax has been generalised are marked with ‡: casts are now possible between arbitrary types, not only classes; and local variable blocks carry an optional explicit initialisation $vo :: val\ option$. Figure 2.2 introduces abbreviations for frequent expressions.

The binary operator bop ranges over the binary operators (HOL type bop) known from Java: $==, !=, <, <=, >, >=, +, -, *, /, \%, \&, |, \hat{\ }$, $<<, >>$, and $>>>$. The two other binary operators in Java, short-circuit conjunction && and disjunction ‖, are represented by the conditional operator:

$$e_1\ «\&\&»\ e_2 = if\ (e_1)\ e_2\ else\ false$$
$$e_1\ «\|»\ e_2\ = if\ (e_1)\ true\ else\ e_2$$

To implement static binding of fields, field access and assignment are annotated with the class D that declares the field. Jinja provides a preprocessor [83, §2.6] that computes these annotations and converts unqualified field accesses into $Var\ this.F\{D\}$, where D is the class being processed. JinjaThreads extends this preprocessor (see Appendix B.9.4

expression		description
$new\ C$		allocation of an object of class C
$new\ T[e]$	*	allocation of an array with element type T
$Cast\ T\ e$	‡	checked cast of e to type T
$e\ instanceof\ T$	*	check if $e \neq Null$ is assignment-compatible to T
$Val\ v$		literal value
$e_1\ \ll bop \gg e_2$		binary operator
$Var\ V$		local variable access
$V := e$		assignment to local variable
$e_1[e_2]$	*	array cell access
$e_1[e_2] := e_3$	*	array cell assignment
$e.length$	*	array length
$e.F\{D\}$		field access
$e_1.F\{D\} := e_2$		field assignment
$e.M(es)$		method call
$\{V : T = vo; e\}$	‡	local variable declaration with opt. initial value
$e_1;;\ e_2$		sequential composition
$if\ (e_1)\ e_2\ else\ e_3$		conditional
$while\ (e_1)\ e_2$		while loop
$throw\ e$		exception throwing
$try\ e_1\ catch(C\ V)\ e_2$		exception handling

Table 2.1: Sequential JinjaThreads expressions

$$
\begin{aligned}
null &= Val\ Null & unit &= Val\ Unit \\
true &= Val\ (Bool\ True) & false &= Val\ (Bool\ False) \\
addr\ a &= Val\ (Addr\ a) & Throw\ a &= throw\ (addr\ a) \\
\{V : T; e\} &= \{V : T = None; e\}
\end{aligned}
$$

Figure 2.2: Abbreviations for common expressions

for the definition) to handle (i) the super qualifier for fields and (ii) array lengths like fields. Regarding the latter, the JLS specifies [56, §6.4.5] that array lengths be stored in a final field length. However, JinjaThreads provides the special syntax $e.length$ for accessing array lengths, because Java bytecode and the Java memory model (JMM) treat array lengths specially anyway. Therefore, the preprocessor replaces the unannotated

datatype	$'m\ prog = Program\ 'm\ cdecl\ list$
type_synonym	$'m\ cdecl = cname \times 'm\ class$
type_synonym	$'m\ class = cname \times fdecl\ list \times 'm\ option\ mdecl\ list$
type_synonym	$fdecl = vname \times ty \times fmod$
record	$fmod = volatile :: bool$
type_synonym	$'m\ mdecl = mname \times ty\ list \times ty \times 'm$
type_synonym	$J\text{-}mb = vname\ list \times expr$
type_synonym	$J\text{-}prog = J\text{-}mb\ prog$

Figure 2.3: Type definitions for program declarations

access $e.length\{\}$ by $e.length$ if e's type is an array. This correctly implements that array length hides the field *length* of class *Object* if it declares such.

Program declaration

Figure 2.3 shows the type definitions for program declarations. A program declaration (of type $'m\ prog$, variable convention P)[6] is a list of class declarations (type $'m\ cdecl$), each of which consists of the class name and the class itself. The class (type $'m\ class$) declares its direct superclass, its fields and methods. A field declaration (type $fdecl$) is a tuple of field name, type and field modifiers. For field modifiers, JinjaThreads features only *volatile*. A method declaration (type $'m\ mdecl$) consists of the method name, a list of the parameters' types, the return type, and the method body. Class declarations specialize $'m$ to $'m\ option$ to allow for optional method bodies. If the method body is *None* (written *Native*), only the signature of a native method is declared.

The method body is left as a type parameter $'m$ such that all JinjaThreads languages reuse this generic format for declarations. For the source code language, a method body consists of the list of formal parameter names and the expression itself (type $J\text{-}mb$). Then, a source code program has type $J\text{-}prog$, which plugs in $J\text{-}mb$ for $'m$ in $'m\ prog$.

---

[6]In JinjaThreads, $'m\ prog$ is a type of its own (with injection *Program*) rather than an abbreviation like the other types for declarations and $'m\ prog$ in Jinja, because this permits data refinement of programs in Isabelle's code generator (see §6.3.3). This is only of technical interest since $'m\ prog$ and $'m\ cdecl\ list$ are isomorphic.

Although JinjaThreads requires certain system classes to work properly, it does not distinguish between them and user-defined classes. System classes are like ordinary classes except that JinjaThreads specifies their class names and every proper program declaration must define them. For the sequential part, the following system classes are needed: *Object*, *Throwable*, and the system exceptions

$sys\text{-}xcpts =$

$[NullPointer, ClassCast, ArithmeticException, OutOfMemory,$

$\quad ArrayIndexOutOfBounds, ArrayStore, NegativeArraySize]. \quad (2.1)$

The class *Object* is the root of the class hierarchy and *Throwable* the root of all exception and error classes that can be thrown. The names for the system exceptions are self-explanatory, their Java counterparts reside in the `java.lang` package.

Lookup functions

For most parts of JinjaThreads, the exact representation of programs is irrelevant. Instead, they access declaration information via the following lookup functions:

- *class* $P\ C$ extracts the class with name C from P.

- *is-class* $P\ C$ predicates that P declares a class with name C,

- $P \vdash C <^1 D$ denotes that C is a direct subclass of D in P.

- $P \vdash C\ sees\ M{:}Ts{\to}T = meth\ in\ D$ means that class C sees a method named M implemented in class D, taking method overriding into account. Ts is the list of parameter types, T the return type, and *meth* :: '*m option* the optional method body. For JinjaThreads source code, *meth* is either *Native* or of the form $\lfloor (pns, body) \rfloor$, i.e. the formal parameter names *pns* and the expression *body*.

- $P \vdash C\ has\ F{:}T\ (fm)\ in\ D$ denotes that in P, the superclass D of C declares the field F with type T and field modifiers fm.

- $P \vdash C\ sees\ F{:}T\ (fm)\ in\ D$ is like $P \vdash C\ has\ F{:}T\ (fm)\ in\ D$ except that F must also be visible in C, i.e. there is no intervening declaration of F in the subclass hierarchy between C and D that hides the field F in D.

The following example (in an imaginary concrete syntax) from [83] illustrates method overriding and field hiding:

```
class B extends A {field F:TB
                   method M:TBs->T1 = mB}
class C extends B {field F:TC
                   method M:TCs->T2 = mC}
```

We have both $P \vdash C$ has F:TC (fm) in C and $P \vdash C$ has F:TB (fm) in B, where fm is $(volatile = False)$. In constrast, we have $P \vdash C$ sees F:TC (fm) in C, but not $P \vdash C$ sees F:TB (fm) in B, because the declaration of F in C hides the one in B.

Method overriding only considers names, not the declared types. Consequently, JinjaThreads does not allow method overloading. In the above example, we have $P \vdash B$ sees $M:TBs \rightarrow T1 = \lfloor mB \rfloor$ in B and $P \vdash C$ sees $M:TCs \rightarrow T2 = \lfloor mC \rfloor$ in C, but not $P \vdash C$ sees $M:TBs \rightarrow T1 = \lfloor mB \rfloor$ in B, because M's definition in C overrides the one from B. Moreover, the lookup functions need not take into account the effects of access modifiers like `private` and `protected`, because JinjaThreads omits those.

I do not present the formal definitions for these lookup functions here, because I have taken them almost unchanged from Jinja [83]. They can be found in Appendix B.1.

2.1.2 Type system

The base type of a type T is T with all *Array* constructors stripped off:

$$base\text{-}type\, T = (case\, T\, of\, T'[] \Rightarrow base\text{-}type\, T' \mid \_ \Rightarrow T)$$

Types are valid (predicate *is-type*) iff all classes they refer to exist in the program and, in case of array types, their base type is not NT (see Figure 2.4). Array types with element type NT are an artefact of the formalisation, they do not occur in Java programs as there is no syntax for the type NT. Treating them as invalid types also avoids other problems, e.g., infinite ascending chains in the subtype relation (see below). *types P* denotes the set of all valid types for P.

Subtyping

In this section, I present subtyping on JinjaThreads types. The subclass relation $P \vdash \_ \leq^* \_$ is the reflexive and transitive closure of the direct

29

$$
\begin{aligned}
&\textit{is-type } P \quad \textit{Void} \quad = \textit{True} &&\textit{is-type } P \textit{ Boolean} = \textit{True} \\
&\textit{is-type } P \quad \textit{Integer} = \textit{True} &&\textit{is-type } P \quad \textit{NT} \quad = \textit{True} \\
&\textit{is-type } P \; (\textit{Class } C) = \textit{is-class } P \; C \\
&\textit{is-type } P \quad (T[]) \quad = \textit{is-type } P \; T \wedge \textit{base-type } T \neq \textit{NT} \\
\\
&\textit{types} \quad P \qquad\qquad = \{\, T.\ \textit{is-type } P \; T \,\}
\end{aligned}
$$

Figure 2.4: Valid types of a program

$$
\leq_{\text{REFL}}:\ P \vdash T \leq T \qquad
\leq_{\text{SUBCLS}}:\ \frac{P \vdash C \preceq^* D}{P \vdash \textit{Class } C \leq \textit{Class } D}
$$

$$
\leq_{\text{NULL}}:\ P \vdash \textit{NT} \leq \textit{Class } C \qquad
\leq_{\text{NULL}[]}:\ P \vdash \textit{NT} \leq T[]
$$

$$
\leq_{\text{OBJECT}}:\ P \vdash T[] \leq \textit{Class Object} \qquad
\leq_{\text{ARRAY}}:\ \frac{P \vdash T \leq T'}{P \vdash T[] \leq T'[]}
$$

Figure 2.5: The subtype relation

subclass relation $P \vdash \_ <^1 \_$. This induces a subtype relation $P \vdash \_ \leq \_$ on JinjaThreads types; Figure 2.5 shows the definition. The point-wise extension of $\leq$ to lists of types is written $[\leq]$.

The rules for subtyping follow Java, e.g., the array type constructor $\_[]$ is covariant ($\leq_{\text{ARRAY}}$). Subtyping is reflexive, transitive, and, if the subclass hierarchy is acyclic, antisymmetric.

The subtype relation has infinite chains, both decreasing and ascending ones. For example, $\leq_{\text{ARRAY}}$ gives in combination with $\leq_{\text{OBJECT}}$ and $\leq_{\text{NULL}[]}$:

$$
P \vdash \ldots \leq \textit{Class Object}[][] \leq \textit{Class Object}[] \leq \textit{Class Object}
$$
$$
P \vdash \textit{NT} \leq \textit{NT}[] \leq \textit{NT}[][] \leq \textit{NT}[][][] \leq \ldots
$$

However, every infinite ascending chain, as I show in §6.2.2, must contain invalid types. The bytecode verifier (§6.2.2) cannot deal with infinite ascending chains, which has been the motivation for disallowing arrays with $\textit{NT}$ as element type.

Figure 2.6 shows the Hasse diagram for the subtype relation for the following program declaration. Invalid types have been omitted.

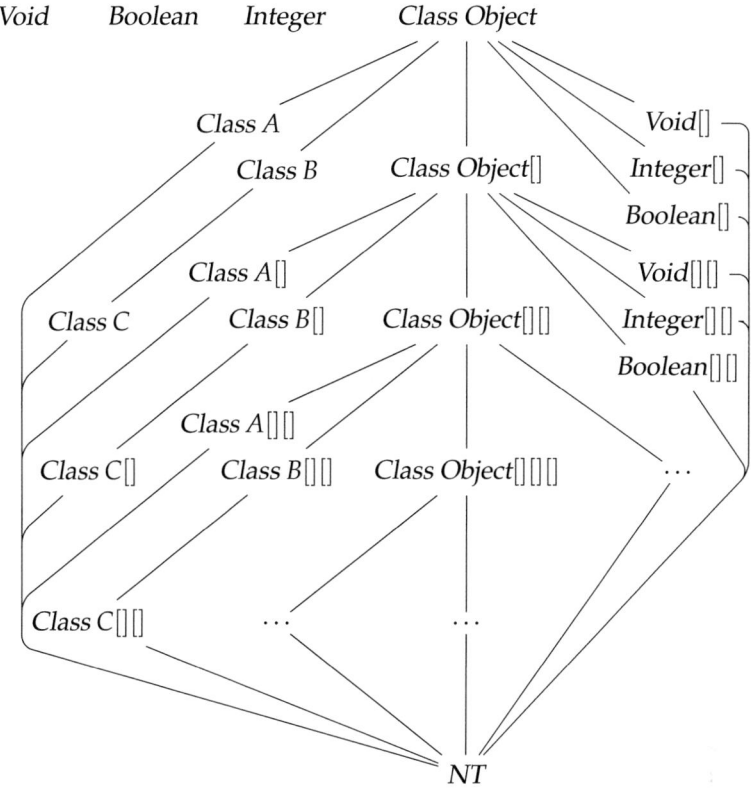

Figure 2.6: Hasse diagram for the subtype relation $P \vdash \_ \leq \_$ restricted to *types P* for the program P of four classes *Object, A, B,* and *C* where $P \vdash A <^1$ *Object,* $P \vdash B <^1$ *Object,* and $P \vdash C <^1 B$.

```
class Object {}
class A extends Object {}
class B extends Object {}
class C extends B {}
```

The left-hand side illustrates how the subclass relation is replicated for every number of array dimensions. The right-hand side shows that arrays of primitive types are subtypes of arrays of *Object* with one dimension less.

31

$$\text{WT}_{\text{BINOP}}: \quad \frac{P,E \vdash e_1 :: T_1 \qquad P,E \vdash e_2 :: T_2 \qquad P \vdash T_1 \text{ «}bop\text{» } T_2 :: T}{P,E \vdash e_1 \text{ «}bop\text{» } e_2 :: T}$$

$$\text{WT}_{\text{AASS}}: \quad \frac{P,E \vdash e_1 :: T[] \qquad P,E \vdash e_2 :: Integer \qquad P,E \vdash e_3 :: T' \qquad P \vdash T' \leq T}{P,E \vdash e_1[e_2] := e_3 :: Void}$$

$$\text{WT}_{\text{CALL}}: \quad \frac{P,E \vdash e :: T \qquad P,E \vdash es [::] Ts' \qquad class\text{-}of\, T = \lfloor C \rfloor \qquad P \vdash C \text{ sees } M:Ts{\rightarrow}T_r = meth \text{ in } D \qquad P \vdash Ts' [\leq] Ts}{P,E \vdash e.M(es) :: T_r}$$

$$\text{WT}_{\text{COND}}: \quad \frac{P,E \vdash e :: Boolean \qquad P,E \vdash e_1 :: T_1 \qquad P,E \vdash e_2 :: T_2 \qquad P \vdash lub\,(T_1,T_2) = T}{P,E \vdash if\,(e)\, e_1 \text{ else } e_2 :: T}$$

$$\text{WT}_{\text{THROW}}: \quad \frac{P,E \vdash e :: Class\, C \qquad P \vdash C \preceq^* Throwable}{P,E \vdash throw\, e :: Void}$$

$$\text{WT}_{\text{TRY}}: \quad \frac{P,E \vdash e_1 :: T \qquad P,E(V \mapsto Class\, C) \vdash e_2 :: T \qquad P \vdash C \preceq^* Throwable}{P,E \vdash try\, e_1\, catch(C\ V)\, e_2 :: T}$$

Figure 2.7: Selected typing rules for JinjaThreads source code

Type judgement

The type system for J is modelled as type judgements of the form $P,E \vdash e :: T$ where the environment E (of type $vname \rightharpoonup ty$, abbreviated as env) assigns types to local variables. $P,E \vdash es\,[::]\,Ts$ extends $P,E \vdash \_ :: \_$ pointwise to lists of expressions and types. Figure 2.7 shows a subset of the rules that exhibit the key features, Appendix B.6.2 lists the full set.

Analogous to the abstract syntax, where e_1 «bop» e_2 treats all 17 binary operators uniformly, WT$_{\text{BINOP}}$ applies to all binary operators – the judgement $P \vdash T_1$ «bop» $T_2 :: T$ captures the individual differences. It denotes that the binary operator bop takes arguments of types T_1 and T_2 and the result is of type T. Figure 2.8 shows some representative rules – the others are similar (Appendix B.2). WT/ for integer division is typical for integer operators. The equality operator requires the arguments'

WT/: $\qquad P \vdash Integer \ll/\gg Integer :: Integer$

WT==: $\qquad \dfrac{P \vdash T_1 \leq T_2 \vee P \vdash T_2 \leq T_1}{P \vdash T_1 \ll==\gg T_2 :: Boolean}$

WT&INT: $\qquad P \vdash Integer \ll\&\gg Integer :: Integer$

WT&BOOL: $\quad P \vdash Boolean \ll\&\gg Boolean :: Boolean$

Figure 2.8: Typing rules for the binary operators $/$, $==$, and $\&$

types to be comparable in the subtype relation (WT==), which imposes in particular equal types for primitive types. Overloaded operators like $\&$ and $|$ have one rule for each case (WT&INT and WT&BOOL). Unlike in Java, $+$ only operates on *Integer*s, not on *String*, because *String*s are not primitive in JinjaThreads.

Array cell assignment (WTAASS), like any other assignment, requires that the type of the right-hand side is a subtype of the left-hand side's.

Rule WTCALL deals with method calls. Since programs must explicitly declare native methods, it uniformly handles calls to native and non-native ones. It uses the partial function *class-of* T that returns the least class that is a supertype of T if $T \neq NT$. It is defined as

$$class\text{-}of\,(Class\,C) = \lfloor C \rfloor \qquad class\text{-}of\,(T[]) = \lfloor Object \rfloor \qquad (2.2)$$

and *None* for all other types. Hence, if the type T of the receiver is an array, method lookup starts in $C = Object$. Thus, all arrays inherit the methods from class *Object*.[7]

In WTCOND for conditionals, $P \vdash lub\,(T_1, T_2) = T$ denotes that T is a least upper bound (lub) for T_1 and T_2 w.r.t. subtyping. Note that

---

[7]The JLS [56, §6.4.5] requires that arrays inherit all methods from class *Object* except for *clone*. Arrays (type $T[]$) must override the *clone* from *Object* to (i) increase its visibility from `protected` to `public`, (ii) remove the checked exception `CloneNotSupportedException` from the signature, and (iii) specialize the return type from *Object* to $T[]$. As JinjaThreads neither models visibility nor checked exceptions, (i) and (ii) are irrelevant. However, JinjaThreads does not follow (iii) – which only the third edition of the JLS has introduced – because this special case would unnecessarily complicate definitions and proofs. Hence, JinjaThreads programs must explicitly cast the return value. For example, `int[] a; a = new int[1].clone();` becomes $\{a : Integer[]; a := Cast\,(Integer[])\,(new\,Integer[Val\,(Intg\,1)].clone([]))\}$ with an explicit cast.

lubs need not be unique at this point because P might be an ill-formed program declaration with cycles in the class hierarchy.

In rules WTTHROW and WTTRY for exception throwing and handling, the constraint $P \vdash C \leq^* Throwable$ enforces that only subclasses of $Throwable$ may be used as exceptions. WTTRY also illustrates the environment for local variables: The catch block implicitly declares the local variable V of type $Class\ C$ for the exception reference, which is modelled as the update of V in E in the premise for e_2. The constraint $P \vdash C \leq^* Throwable$ also ensures that the catch block refers to an existing class C because $Throwable$ is a system class which all well-formed programs must declare.

2.1.3 Native methods

Some methods that the standard Java API specifies cannot be implemented in Java syntax, e.g., $clone$ and $hashcode$ in class $Object$. If it were for the sequential part only, it would not be worth the effort to model native methods in JinjaThreads. However, calls to native methods implement most of Java's concurrency features, e.g., $wait$ in $Object$ and $start$ in $Thread$. Therefore, I added the infrastructure for including native methods in JinjaThreads.

A program must explicitly declare the native methods it uses, with $Native$ as method body (see §2.1.1). This allows the typing rules and method overriding to treat native methods like normal methods, see WTCALL for an example. However, the semantics only provides a fixed set of native methods, because native methods by definition cannot be implemented in JinjaThreads syntax and thus must be hard-wired. To that end, the judgement $C.M(Ts) :: T_r$ expresses that the semantics provides a native method M for class C with parameter types Ts and return type T_r. Well-formedness (§2.1.4) ensures that the semantics implements all methods that a program declares as native.

The sequential part defines only the two native methods $clone$ and $hashcode$ as follows, but I add more in §3.2.1:

$$Object.clone([]) :: Class\ Object$$
$$Object.hashcode([]) :: Integer \tag{2.3}$$

I defer the semantics of these native methods to the semantics section (§2.1.5).

2.1.4 Well-formedness

For most proofs, JinjaThreads programs must be well-formed. The well-formedness criteria fall in two categories: First, generic constraints such as acyclicity of the class hierarchy are independent of the concrete language. Second, language-specific constraints like well-typedness depend on the type of method bodies. To factor out the latter, the well-formedness test for programs takes a well-formedness test for method bodies as a parameter, ranged over by $wf\text{-}mb$:

type_synonym $'m\ wf\text{-}mdecl\text{-}test = 'm\ prog \Rightarrow cname \Rightarrow 'm\ mdecl \Rightarrow bool$

Generic well-formedess

The generic well-formedness predicates are shown in Figure 2.9. The function $classes$, which is the inverse to $Program$, returns the list of class declarations of a program. Hence, $map\ fst\ (classes\ P)$ computes the list of declared class names.

A program P is well-formed iff the system classes are as required (denoted by $wf\text{-}syscls\ P$), every class is declared only once, and all class declarations are well-formed. For the system classes, JinjaThreads requires class declarations for $Object$ and $Throwable$ and the latter must be a superclass of all system exceptions. This implicitly ensures that P declares all system exceptions.

A declaration of class C is well-formed (predicate $wf\text{-}cdecl$) iff all field and method declarations are well-formed (predicates $wf\text{-}fdecl$ and $wf\text{-}mdecl$), no field or method is declared twice, and if C is not $Object$, its direct superclass D exists and is no subclass of C (which rules out cycles in the subclass relation), and method overriding is contravariant in the parameters and covariant in the return type.

The predicate $wf\text{-}overriding$ checks the last constraint. The overriding method may have less specific parameter types and a more specific return type. Note that method overriding considers only method names, not signatures, i.e., there is no overloading.

The predicate $wf\text{-}mdecl$ checks that declared types are valid. For native methods, it checks that the semantics provides this method; for normal methods, it applies the language-specific well-formedness checker.

$wf\text{-}prog :: {}'m \; wf\text{-}mdecl\text{-}test \Rightarrow {}'m \; prog \Rightarrow bool$
$wf\text{-}prog \; wf\text{-}md \; P \longleftrightarrow wf\text{-}syscls \; P \wedge distinct \, (map \; fst \, (classes \; P)) \wedge$
$\qquad\qquad\qquad\qquad (\forall cd \in set \, (classes \; P). \; wf\text{-}cdecl \; wf\text{-}md \; P \; cd)$

$wf\text{-}syscls :: {}'m \; prog \Rightarrow bool$
$wf\text{-}syscls \; P \longleftrightarrow is\text{-}class \; P \; Object \wedge is\text{-}class \; P \; Throwable \wedge$
$\qquad\qquad\qquad (\forall C \in set \; sys\text{-}xcpts. \; P \vdash C \leq^* Throwable)$

$wf\text{-}cdecl :: {}'m \; wf\text{-}mdecl\text{-}test \Rightarrow {}'m \; prog \Rightarrow {}'m \; cdecl \Rightarrow bool$
$wf\text{-}cdecl \; wf\text{-}md \; P \; (C, D, fs, ms) \longleftrightarrow$
$\quad (\forall fd \in set \; fs. \; wf\text{-}fdecl \; P \; fd) \wedge distinct \, (map \; fst \; fs) \wedge$
$\quad (\forall md \in set \; ms. \; wf\text{-}mdecl \; wf\text{-}md \; P \; C \; md) \wedge distinct \, (map \; fst \; ms) \wedge$
$\quad (C \neq Object \longrightarrow is\text{-}class \; P \; D \wedge \neg \, P \vdash D \preceq^* C \wedge$
$\qquad\qquad\qquad (\forall md \in set \; ms. \; wf\text{-}overriding \; P \; D \; md))$

$wf\text{-}fdecl :: {}'m \; prog \Rightarrow fdecl \Rightarrow bool$
$wf\text{-}fdecl \; P \; (F, T, fm) \longleftrightarrow is\text{-}type \; P \; T$

$wf\text{-}overriding :: {}'m \; prog \Rightarrow cname \Rightarrow {}'m \; mdecl \Rightarrow bool$
$wf\text{-}overriding \; P \; D \; (M, Ts, T_r, m) \longleftrightarrow (\forall D' \; Ts' \; T'_r \; m'.$
$\quad P \vdash D \; sees \; M{:}Ts' {\rightarrow} T'_r = m' \; in \; D' \longrightarrow P \vdash Ts' \; [\leq] \; Ts \wedge P \vdash T_r \leq T'_r)$

$wf\text{-}mdecl :: {}'m \; wf\text{-}mdecl\text{-}test \Rightarrow {}'m \; option \; wf\text{-}mdecl\text{-}test$
$wf\text{-}mdecl \; wf\text{-}md \; P \; C \; (M, Ts, T_r, m) \longleftrightarrow$
$\quad set \; Ts \subseteq types \; P \wedge is\text{-}type \; P \; T_r \wedge$
$\quad (case \; m \; of \; Native \Rightarrow C.M(Ts) :: T_r$
$\qquad\quad | \; \lfloor mb \rfloor \Rightarrow wf\text{-}md \; P \; C \; (M, Ts, T_r, mb))$

Figure 2.9: Generic well-formedness constraints

$wf\text{-}J\text{-}mdecl :: J\text{-}mb \; wf\text{-}mdecl\text{-}test$
$wf\text{-}J\text{-}mdecl \; P \; C \; (M, Ts, T_r, (pns, body)) \longleftrightarrow$
$\quad |Ts| = |pns| \wedge distinct \; pns \wedge this \notin set \; pns \wedge$
$\quad (\exists T. \; P, [this \mapsto Class \; C, pns \, [\mapsto] \, Ts] \vdash body :: T \wedge P \vdash T \leq T_r) \wedge$
$\quad \mathcal{D} \; body \; \lfloor \{ this \} \cup set \; pns \rfloor$

$wf\text{-}J\text{-}prog = wf\text{-}prog \; wf\text{-}J\text{-}mdecl$

Figure 2.10: Well-formedness for JinjaThreads source code

type_synonym *J-state* $= heap \times locals$
type_synonym *locals* $= vname \rightharpoonup val$
type_synonym *heap* $= addr \rightharpoonup heap\text{-}entry$
datatype *heap-entry* $= Obj\ cname\ fields\ |\ Arr\ ty\ fields\ cells$
type_synonym *fields* $= vname \times cname \rightharpoonup val$
type_synonym *cells* $= val\ list$

Figure 2.11: Type definitions for the sequential state

Well-formed source code

Let me now turn to well-formedness for *J* programs (Figure 2.10). To that end, *wf-prog* gets instantiated with the checker *wf-J-mdecl* for *J* method declarations, abbreviated as *wf-J-prog*. I have taken the definition unchanged from Jinja [83]. It checks for

parameter names They must be equally many as parameter types, pairwise different and different from the *this* pointer.

typability The method body must be typable with a subtype of the declared return type.

definite assignment Definite assignment requires that during evaluation, whenever a local variable is read, it must have been assigned to before. The function $\mathcal{D}\ e\ A$ syntactically checks if e accesses only initialised variables if run from a state in which all variables in A have already been initialised. I have taken this test unchanged from Jinja with straightforward adaptations for the language extensions. Hence, I do not present the details here, Appendix B.6.3 shows the formal definition. For how it works, see [83].

2.1.5 Dynamic semantics

Having described the static semantics of *J*, I now turn to the dynamic semantics of the sequential subset.

State

The state (type *J-state*) is a pair of a heap (of type *heap*) for objects and arrays and a store for local variables (of type *locals*), see Figure 2.11. For now, the heap maps addresses to heap entries, which can either be objects or arrays.[8] Objects $Obj\,C\,fs$ store their class name C and a field table fs which maps pairs (F, D) to values. It is essential that the table's keys include the class D that declares the field F, because an object may have multiple fields of the same name. Arrays $Arr\,T\,fs\,cs$ have an element type T, a field table fs, and a list of cells cs each of which contains a value. The length of the cell list determines the array length. In Java, arrays inherit all fields of $Object$ [56, §6.4.5], so arrays need the field table for them. The declaring class is irrelevant in this field table, but I keep it for uniformity. For notation, h ranges over heaps, xs over local variables, and s over states. The functions hp and lcl extract the heap and the store from a state, respectively.

To simplify the semantics, JinjaThreads allocates one object for each system exception on the initial heap $start\text{-}heap$ at start-up time. The function $addr\text{-}of\text{-}sys\text{-}xcpt\,C$ returns the address of the preallocated object for the system exception C. As the exact definition is not relevant at the moment, I defer it to §4.1.

Statically, addresses have no type (cf. Figure 2.1). Dynamically, type information for an address (HOL type hty) consists of the class name or – if it is an array – of the type of its elements and its length. The accessor functions $ty\text{-}of$ and $array\text{-}length\text{-}of$ extract the type and array length.

$$\textbf{datatype } hty = ClassT\,cname \mid ArrayT\,ty\,nat$$

$$ty\text{-}of\,(ClassT\,C) = Class\,C \qquad ty\text{-}of\,(ArrayT\,T\,n) = T[]$$
$$array\text{-}length\text{-}of\,(ArrayT\,T\,n) = n$$

The function $typeof\text{-}addr :: heap \Rightarrow addr \rightharpoonup hty$ computes the type information from the heap:

$$
\begin{aligned}
typeof\text{-}addr\,h\,a = (&case\,h\,a\,of\,\lfloor Obj\,C\,\_\rfloor \Rightarrow \lfloor ClassT\,C\rfloor \\
&\mid\ \lfloor Arr\,T\,\_\,cs\rfloor \Rightarrow \lfloor ArrayT\,T\,|cs|\rfloor \\
&\mid\ None \Rightarrow None
\end{aligned}
\qquad (2.4)
$$

Then, $typeof_h$ extends $typeof$ to addresses accordingly:

$$
\begin{aligned}
typeof_h\,v = (&case\,v\,of\,Addr\,a \Rightarrow Option.map\,ty\text{-}of\,(typeof\text{-}addr\,h\,a) \\
&\mid\ \_ \Rightarrow typeof\,v)
\end{aligned}
$$

---

[8]In Chapter 4, I will revisit and change the heap model to accomodate different notions of concurrency.

CLONE:
$$\frac{new\text{-}Addr\,h = \lfloor a' \rfloor \qquad h' = h(a' := h\,a)}{P \vdash \langle a.clone([\,]), h \rangle \rightarrow_{nc} \langle Ret\text{-}Val\,a', h' \rangle}$$

CLONEF:
$$\frac{new\text{-}Addr\,h = None}{P \vdash \langle a.clone([\,]), h \rangle \rightarrow_{nc} \langle Ret\text{-}sys\text{-}xcpt\,OutOfMemory, h \rangle}$$

NCHASHC: $P \vdash \langle a.hashcode([\,]), h \rangle \rightarrow_{nc} \langle Ret\text{-}Val\,(Intg\,(hash\text{-}addr\,a)), h \rangle$

Figure 2.12: Semantics of native method calls in the sequential part

Native methods

I now turn to the semantics for native methods. The sequential language defines only two, namely *hashcode* and *clone* (2.3), but I add more in §3.2.1 for Java concurrency. Native method calls may either return a value v (denoted *Ret-Val v*) or the address a of an exception (written *Ret-Xcp a*). I abbreviate *Ret-Xcp (addr-of-sys-xcpt C)* as *Ret-sys-xcpt C*.

Native method calls execute in one step: $P \vdash \langle a.M(vs), h \rangle \rightarrow_{nc} \langle vx, h' \rangle$ denotes that calling M on address a with parameters vs and the heap h returns a value or exception address vx and the updated heap h'. Figure 2.12 shows the definition. The partial function *new-Addr* returns a fresh address for a given heap, if there is one, and *None* otherwise. CLONE copies the object at a to the fresh address a' in one go, CLONEF raises the *OutOfMemory* exception if all addresses are already in use. NCHASHC computes the object's hash using the function *hash-addr* :: $addr \Rightarrow word32$. Again, the concrete definitions for *new-Addr* and *hash-addr* are irrelevant until Chapter 4.

Binary operators

The evaluation of binary operators is defined via a partial function $binop :: bop \Rightarrow val \Rightarrow val \rightharpoonup bop\text{-}ret$, which returns either the evaluated value or the address of an exception.

$$\textbf{type\_synonym}\ bop\text{-}ret = val + addr$$

In case of type mismatches, it returns *None* to denote undefinedness. Essentially, it unpacks the values and applies the appropriate operator on *bool* or *word32*. Figure 2.13 shows the definitions for the binary

$$binop \quad / \quad (Intg\, i_1) \quad (Intg\, i_2) \; =$$
$$\lfloor if\, i_2 = 0 \; then\; Inr\, (addr\text{-}of\text{-}sys\text{-}xcpt\, ArithmeticException)$$
$$else\; Inl\, (Intg\, (i_1\, sdiv\, i_2))\rfloor$$
$$binop \;==\; \quad v_1 \qquad v_2 \quad = \lfloor Inl\, (Bool\, (v_1 = v_2))\rfloor$$
$$binop \; \& \; (Intg\, i_1) \; (Intg\, i_2) = \lfloor Inl\, (Intg\, (i_1\, AND\, i_2))\rfloor$$
$$binop \; \& \; (Bool\, b_1) \; (Bool\, b_2) = \lfloor Inl\, (Bool\, (b_1 \wedge b_2))\rfloor$$

Figure 2.13: Evaluation for the binary operators $/$, $==$, and $\&$

operators $/$, $==$, and $\&$, see Appendix B.2 for the others. Division $/$ (and analogously the remainder operation %) tests whether the divisor is 0, and if so, returns the preallocated *ArithmeticException*. Contrary to the typing rules in Figure 2.8, the equality test $==$ omits any (unnecessary) type checks, infeasible cases are mapped to $\lfloor Inl\, (Bool\, False)\rfloor$. Overloaded operators like $\&$ are defined for more than one combination of value constructors. *binop* $/$, *binop* $==$, and *binop* $\&$ return *None* for all value combinations not shown in Figure 2.13.

Small-step semantics

The core semantics for J is a small-step semantics written $P \vdash \langle e, s \rangle \rightarrow \langle e', s' \rangle$. I say that the expression e *reduces* in state s to e' and state s'. It is a standard small-step semantics with rules for subexpression reduction and exception propagation. An expression is *final*, i.e., fully reduced, when it is either a value *Val v* or a thrown exception *Throw a*.

For example, Figure 2.14 shows all rules for reducing method calls, which demonstrate the main ideas. For an extensive discussion, see [83]. The formal definition, with all extensions due to concurrency, can be found in Appendix B.6.5.

Rules RObj and RParam reduce the subexpressions of the call – $P \vdash \langle \_, \_ \rangle\, [\rightarrow]\, \langle \_, \_ \rangle$ lifts $P \vdash \langle \_, \_ \rangle \rightarrow \langle \_, \_ \rangle$ to parameter lists of expressions. If one of the subexpressions throws an exception, rules RObjX and RParamX propagate it. For the other expressions, similar rules exist for subexpressions that need to be evaluated. These rules also determine the order of evaluation: The object is evaluated before the parameters because RParam and RParamX are only applicable when the object is already a value.

ROBJ:
$$\frac{P \vdash \langle e, s \rangle \rightarrow \langle e', s' \rangle}{P \vdash \langle e.M(es), s \rangle \rightarrow \langle e'.M(es), s' \rangle}$$

RPARAM:
$$\frac{P \vdash \langle es, s \rangle [\rightarrow] \langle es', s' \rangle}{P \vdash \langle Val\, v.M(es), s \rangle \rightarrow \langle Val\, v.M(es'), s' \rangle}$$

ROBJX: $\quad P \vdash \langle Throw\, a.M(es), s \rangle \rightarrow \langle Throw\, a, s \rangle$

RPARAMX: $P \vdash \langle Val\, v.M(map\, Val\, vs\, @\, Throw\, a \cdot es), s \rangle \rightarrow \langle Throw\, a, s \rangle$

RCALLN: $\quad P \vdash \langle null.M(map\, Val\, vs), s \rangle \rightarrow \langle THROW\, NullPointer, s \rangle$

RCALL:
$$\frac{\begin{array}{c} typeof\text{-}addr\,(hp\, s)\, a\, = \lfloor hT \rfloor \\ P \vdash class\text{-}of'\, hT\, sees\, M{:}Ts{\rightarrow}T_r = \lfloor (pns, body) \rfloor\, in\, D \\ |vs| = |pns| \qquad |Ts| = |pns| \end{array}}{\begin{array}{c} P \vdash \langle addr\, a.M(map\, Val\, vs), s \rangle \rightarrow \\ \langle blocks\,(this \cdot pns)\,(Class\, D \cdot Ts)\,(Addr\, a \cdot vs)\, body, s \rangle \end{array}}$$

RNATIVE:
$$\frac{\begin{array}{c} typeof\text{-}addr\, h\, a = \lfloor hT \rfloor \\ P \vdash class\text{-}of'\, hT\, sees\, M{:}Ts{\rightarrow}T_r = Native\, in\, D \\ P \vdash \langle a.M(vs), h \rangle \rightarrow_{nc} \langle vx, h' \rangle \qquad e' = native\text{-}Ret2J\, vx \end{array}}{P \vdash \langle addr\, a.M(map\, Val\, vs), (h, xs) \rangle \rightarrow \langle e', (h', xs) \rangle}$$

Figure 2.14: Small-step semantics for reducing method calls

If the receiver evaluates to the null pointer *null*, the preallocated *NullPointer* exception is thrown (RCALLN), where *THROW C* abbreviates *Throw (addr-of-sys-xcpt C)*. *map Val vs* expresses that the parameter list has completely reduced to a list of values.

RCALL and RNATIVE are the main rules for calling a normal and native method, respectively. If the called method *M* for the receiver is not native, RCALL looks up the method definition in *P* and inlines the method body; the function *blocks Vs Ts vs e* surrounds *e* with local variable blocks for variables names *Vs* with types *Ts* and initial values *vs*. Dynamic inlining avoids the need for modelling the call stack explicitly; the local variable blocks ensure static binding for the *this* pointer and parameter names. Conversely, RNATIVE dispatches the call to the semantics for native methods. The function *native-Ret2J* injects the result *vx* into expressions as follows: *Val v* for return values *Ret-Val v* and *Throw a* for exception addresses *Ret-Xcp a*. Similar to the partial function *class-of* on *ty*, the total function *class-of'* on *hty* determines the class at which method lookup starts, i.e., *Object* for *ArrayT _ _* and *C* for *ClassT C*.

The semantics is strict in the sense that it gets stuck when values and types are not as expected, e.g., if the called method does not exist or requires a different number of parameters. The progress theorem (Theorem 2.1) shows that the type system rules out such cases.

Typically, the semantics of a program results from chaining together the individual steps of the semantics. However, as I aim for concurrency, I stop with the small-step semantics for now. Chapter 3 completes the semantics.

2.1.6   Type safety

In this section, I sketch the type safety proof for the sequential part of J. It takes the traditional form of two theorems, progress and preservation [180]. Progress expresses that any well-typed expression can reduce unless it is final. Preservation means that well-typed expressions reduce only to well-typed expressions whose type may only become more specific in the subtype relation. The proofs require the following invariants:

Conformance expresses that semantic objects conform to their syntactic description. A value v conforms to a type T (written $P, h \vdash v :\le T$) iff v's dynamic type is a subtype of T. This conformance notion naturally extends to list of values (written $P, h \vdash vs [:\le] Ts$), stores and environments (written $P, h \vdash xs (:\le) E$), objects, arrays, heaps (written $P \vdash h\surd$), and states (written $P, E \vdash s\surd$), see Appendix B.3 for the formal definitions. Conformance satisfies two essential properties: First, values read from a conformant state always conform to their declared type. Second, state updates preserve state conformance if the new values conform to the locations' types.

The typing rules from §2.1.2 are too strong to be invariant under reductions. For example, they rule out literal addresses in expressions, which arise naturally during reduction. To make them well-typed, the run-time type system [46] $P, E, h \vdash e : T$ takes the heap into account and relaxes various preconditions that are not invariant. For example, the subtyping condition in WTₐₐₛₛ may be violated during evaluation because e_1's element type may become more specific thanks to covariant

42

subtyping on arrays. The semantics throws an *ArrayStore* exception in that case. The details have been discussed at length elsewhere [46,83], so I do not repeat them here.

Now, progress holds under suitable conditions:

Theorem 2.1 (Progress). *If wf-J-prog P and $P, E, h \vdash e : T$ and $\mathcal{D} e \lfloor dom \, xs \rfloor$ and $P \vdash h\sqrt{}$ and $\neg$ final e, then $P \vdash \langle e, (h, xs) \rangle \rightarrow \langle e', s' \rangle$ for some e' and s'.*

Proof. The proof proceeds by induction on $P, E, h \vdash e : T$. Well-formedness ensures that method calls have the correct number of parameters; definite assignment checks that local variables are initialised when read; and heap conformance prevents field access from getting stuck if the accessed field has no value. □

The subject reduction theorem expresses that reductions preserve well-typedness. It is shown by induction on $P \vdash \langle e, s \rangle \rightarrow \langle e', s' \rangle$.

Theorem 2.2 (Subject reduction). *If wf-J-prog P and $P \vdash \langle e, s \rangle \rightarrow \langle e', s' \rangle$ and $P, E, hp \, s \vdash e : T$ and $P, E \vdash s\sqrt{}$, then there exists a T' such that $P, E, hp \, s' \vdash e' : T'$ and $P \vdash T' \leq T$.*

Preservation also requires the following preservation lemmata for all other invariants, i.e. definite assignment and conformance. Again, their proofs are by induction on the reduction.

Lemma 2.1 (Preservation of definite assignment). *If wf-J-prog P and $P \vdash \langle e, s \rangle \rightarrow \langle e', s' \rangle$ and $\mathcal{D} e \lfloor dom \, (lcl \, s) \rfloor$, then $\mathcal{D} e' \lfloor dom \, (lcl \, s') \rfloor$.*

Lemma 2.2 (Preservation of conformance). *Let wf-J-prog P and $P \vdash \langle e, (h, xs) \rangle \rightarrow \langle e', (h', xs') \rangle$ and $P, E, h \vdash e : T$. If $P \vdash h\sqrt{}$, then $P \vdash h'\sqrt{}$. If $P, h \vdash xs \, (:\leq) \, E$, then $P, h' \vdash xs' \, (:\leq) \, E$.*

2.2 The JinjaThreads virtual machine

This section describes the JinjaThreads virtual machine language (§2.2.1), its operational semantics (§2.2.2), well-formedness (§2.2.3) and the type safety proof (§2.2.4). The bytecode language and the JinjaThreads virtual machine (VM) model Java bytecode and the Java VM according to the Java Virtual Machine Specification (JVMS) [103].

$$\textbf{type\_synonym } jvm\text{-}method = nat \times nat \times instr\ list \times ex\text{-}table$$
$$\textbf{type\_synonym } jvm\text{-}prog = jvm\text{-}prog\ prog$$

$$\textbf{type\_synonym } ex\text{-}table = ex\text{-}entry\ list$$
$$\textbf{type\_synonym } ex\text{-}entry = pc \times pc \times cname\ option \times pc \times nat$$

Figure 2.15: Method bodies in bytecode

2.2.1 The bytecode language

The bytecode language JVM reuses many concepts from source code. For program declarations, I only have to specify the type of method bodies to be plugged in for $'m$. Everything else remains unchanged, in particular, the lookup functions, subtyping and generic well-formedness.

A method body (msl, mxl, ins, xt) in the bytecode language (of type $jvm\text{-}method$, see Figure 2.15) consists of an instruction list ins, an exception table xt, the maximum stack length msl, and the number mxl of required registers, not counting the *this* pointer and parameters. Hence, a JVM program instantiates the type variable $'m$ with $jvm\text{-}method$. The lookup functions $instrs\text{-}of\ P\ C\ M$ and $ex\text{-}table\text{-}of\ P\ C\ M$ extract the instruction list and exception table for method M in class C from P.

The exception table xt is a list of exception table entries (f, t, Co, pc, d) where Co is either some class name $\lfloor C \rfloor$ or the special constant $Any = None$. The exception handler starting at the index pc in ins expects d elements on the stack. It handles exceptions that are raised by instructions in the interval from f inclusive to t exclusive. If Co is a class name $\lfloor C \rfloor$, it handles only those that are a subclass of C; if Co is Any, it handles all.

Any might seem redundant because all exceptions must be subclasses of $Throwable$, i.e., $\lfloor Throwable \rfloor$ could replace Any. However, I include Any for two reasons: First, the Java Virtual Machine specification (JVMS) [103, §4.7.3] also specifies such a "catch-all" value, which is meant for compiling `finally` blocks. Second, $\lfloor Throwable \rfloor$ and Any are interchangeable only if one can prove that all raised exceptions are subclasses of $Throwable$, which requires a type safety proof. Thanks to Any, the compiler verification (Chapter 5) can avoid the subject reduction and preservation proofs for the intermediate language by not relying on such invariants.

Table 2.2 shows the instruction set of the sequential JinjaThreads VM (HOL type $instr$). If not provided explicitly, operands are taken

instruction		description
$Load\ i$		load from register i
$Store\ i$		store into register i
$Push\ v$		push literal value v on stack
Pop		pop value from stack
Dup	*	duplicate top value on stack
$Swap$	*	swap top elements on stack
$BinOp\ bop$	‡	apply binary operator bop
$New\ C$		create object of class C
$NewArray\ T$	*	create array with element type T
$ALoad$	*	fetch array cell
$AStore$	*	set array cell
$ALength$	*	get length of array
$Getfield\ F\ C$		fetch field F declared in class C
$Putfield\ F\ C$		set field F declared in class C
$Checkcast\ T$	‡	ensure that value conforms to type T
$Instanceof\ T$	*	check if object is of type T
$Invoke\ M\ n$		invoke method M with n parameters
$Return$		return from method
$Goto\ i$		relative jump
$IfFalse\ i$		branch if top of stack is $Bool\ False$
$ThrowExc$		throw top of stack as exception

Table 2.2: Instructions of the sequential virtual machine

from the stack and results pushed onto the stack. §3.2.3 will add the instructions for multithreading. Similar to Table 2.1, ‡ marks instructions which have been generalised with respect to Jinja. Now, casts between arbitrary types are possible, and the two instructions for binary operators in Jinja have been combined into one that covers all 17 operators from JinjaThreads.

The instructions that Jinja does not feature are marked with *. Klein [79] has already modelled arrays and the instructions Dup and $Swap$ for stack manipulation for μJava. $Instanceof$ is a variation of $Checkcast$ that returns a $Boolean$ rather than throwing an exception if it fails.

In comparison to Java bytecode instructions, JinjaThreads unifies instructions that only differ on their operand types (e.g., aload and

type_synonym *jvm-state* $= addr\ option \times heap \times frame\ list$
type_synonym *frame* $= opstack \times registers \times cname \times mname \times pc$
type_synonym *opstack* $= val\ list$
type_synonym *registers* $= val\ list$
type_synonym *pc* $= nat$

Figure 2.16: Type definitions for the sequential VM state space

iload) in polymorphic ones (e.g., *Load*), but the instructions have not been simplified conceptually. Moreover, a few instructions for stack and register manipulation (e.g., dup2, iinc) have been omitted, but they can be simulated by existing ones or could be added easily. Neither does JinjaThreads include any instructions for omitted types such as byte and float nor advanced control flow instructions like tableswitch and jsr for subroutines.

2.2.2 Semantics

As with source code, I only present the VM up to executing single instructions and defer complete executions to §3.2.3. The model of the sequential JinjaThreads virtual machine (VM) covers its state space and the semantics of the bytecode language.

The state space

The state space is taken from the Jinja VM [83], Figure 2.16 shows the relevant type definitions: The state (xcp, h, frs) of type *jvm-state* consists of an exception flag xcp ($\lfloor a \rfloor$ corresponds to *Throw a* in *J* and *None* denotes none), a heap h (the same as in J) and a stack of call frames.

Each method executes in its own call frame (type *frame*). A call frame (stk, loc, C, M, pc) contains the operand stack stk, an array loc of registers for the *this* pointer, the parameters, and local variables, the class name C, the method name M, and the program counter pc. Although *registers* are modelled as lists, their length does not change during execution. In contrast, the size of the operand stack does change, but the maximum size is statically known.

A state is final iff the stack of call frames is empty.

$exec\text{-}instr\ (Invoke\ M'\ n)\ P\ h\ stk\ loc\ C\ M\ pc\ frs =$
$(let\ ps = rev\ (take\ n\ stk);\ r = stk_{[n]};\ Addr\ a = r;\ \lfloor hT \rfloor = typeof\text{-}addr\ h\ a$
$\quad in\ if\ r = Null\ then$
$\qquad \{\ (\lfloor addr\text{-}of\text{-}sys\text{-}xcpt\ NullPointer \rfloor, h, (stk, loc, C, M, pc) \cdot frs)\ \}$
$\quad else\ let\ (D, Ts, T_r, m) = method\ P\ (class\text{-}of'\ hT)\ M'$
$\qquad in\ case\ m\ of\ Native \Rightarrow$
$\qquad\qquad \{\ native\text{-}Ret2jvm\ n\ h'\ stk\ loc\ C\ M\ pc\ frs\ vx\,|\,vx\ h'.$
$\qquad\qquad (vx, h') \in exec\text{-}native\ P\ a\ M'\ ps\ h\ \}$
$\qquad | \ \lfloor (msl, mxl, ins, xt) \rfloor \Rightarrow$
$\qquad\qquad let\ fr' = (\lceil\rceil, r \cdot ps\ @\ replicate\ mxl\ undefined\text{-}Val, D, M', 0)$
$\qquad\qquad in\ \{\ (None, h, fr' \cdot (stk, loc, C, M, pc) \cdot frs)\ \})$

Figure 2.17: Single-step semantics of the *Invoke* instruction

The aggressive VM

I now turn to the semantics of JinjaThreads bytecode. Following the Jinja VM, the JinjaThreads VM is defined in a functional style.

The function *exec-instr* :: *instr* ⇒ *jvm-prog* ⇒ *heap* ⇒ *opstack* ⇒ *registers* ⇒ *cname* ⇒ *mname* ⇒ *pc* ⇒ *frame list* ⇒ *jvm-state set* defines the semantics of a single instruction. Given the instruction, the program, the heap, and the curried non-empty call stack, it produces a non-empty set of successor states by pattern-matching on the instruction. The complete definition for *exec-instr* can be found in Appendix B.7.3, which includes the adaptations for concurrency. Although *exec-instr* is deterministic for sequential JinjaThreads, it returns a set of successor states, because this will be convenient later for multithreading (§3.2.3) and the Java memory model (Chapter 4).

As an example, Figure 2.17 shows the definition for *Invoke*. If the receiver *r* is the null pointer, it throws a *NullPointer* exception; the old frame and call stack is reassembled such that exception handling can find the right handler. If not, let *a* denote the receiver address, *hT* its dynamic type information and *m* the method body that method lookup returns. If the call is native, i.e., *m* = *Native*, *exec-instr* delegates the call to the functional reimplementation *exec-native* of $P \vdash \langle \_.\_(\_),\_ \rangle \rightarrow_{\mathrm{nc}} \langle \_,\_ \rangle$. Similarly to *native-Ret2J*, the function *native-Ret2jvm* assembles the new state from the result. Otherwise, *exec-instr* prepares the new call frame *fr'* according to the method body (msl, mxl, ins, xt): Initially, the

47

$$
\begin{aligned}
&exec\ P\ (xcp,\quad h,\ [])\qquad\qquad\qquad\qquad = \emptyset \\
&exec\ P\ (None,\ h,\ (stk, loc, C, M, pc) \cdot frs) = \\
&\qquad\qquad\quad exec\text{-}instr\ (instrs\text{-}of\ P\ C\ M)_{[pc]}\ P\ h\ stk\ loc\ C\ M\ pc\ frs \\
&exec\ P\ (\lfloor a \rfloor,\quad h,\ fr \cdot frs)\qquad\qquad\quad = \{\,xcpt\text{-}step\ P\ a\ h\ fr\ frs\,\}
\end{aligned}
$$

Figure 2.18: Combining normal execution and exception handling in the VM

operand stack is empty; the registers contain the receiver (i.e., *this* pointer) and the parameters *ps* (which are in reverse order on the stack); *replicate mxl undefined-Val* fills the remaining registers with the dummy value *undefined-Val*.

Being functional rather than relational, *exec-instr* uses functional lookup operations like *method* whose specifications rely on Russell's ι-operator. For example,

$$
method\ P\ C\ M = \iota(D, Ts, T_r, meth).\ P \vdash C\ sees\ M{:}Ts{\rightarrow}T_r = meth\ in\ D
$$

If there is no such method, *method P C M* is unspecified.

This leads to an aggressive VM: As can be seen in Figure 2.17, *exec-instr* assumes that there are always sufficiently many operands of the right types on the stack, all methods and fields exist, etc. If not, the result is unspecified. The type safety proof (§2.2.4) shows that these cases cannot occur for well-formed programs (to be defined in §2.2.3).

The function *exec* :: *jvm-prog* $\Rightarrow$ *jvm-state* $\Rightarrow$ *jvm-state set* incorporates exception handling in the semantics (see Figure 2.18). The VM halts if the call stack is empty. If no exception is flagged, *exec* executes the next instruction via *exec-instr*. Otherwise, *xcpt-step* (definition in Appendix B.7.3) tries to find an exception handler in the top-most call frame fr that matches the flagged exception at address a. If one is found, the operand stack is trimmed to the size specified in the exception table entry, a is pushed on the operand stack, and the program counter is set to the start of the handler. Otherwise, it pops fr and rethrows a at the *Invoke* instruction of the previous call frame.

For convenience, there also is a relational view on *exec*:

$$
\frac{s' \in exec\ P\ s}{P \vdash s \rightarrow_{jvm} s'}
$$

$check\text{-}instr\ (Invoke\ M'\ n)\ P\ h\ stk\ loc\ C\ M\ pc\ frs =$
$(n < |stk| \land is\text{-}Ref\ stk_{[n]} \land$
$\quad (stk_{[n]} \neq Null \longrightarrow$
$\qquad (let\ ps = rev\ (take\ n\ stk);\ Addr\ a = stk_{[n]};\ \lfloor hT \rfloor = typeof\text{-}addr\ h\ a;$
$\qquad\quad C' = class\text{-}of'\ hT;\ (D, Ts, T_r, meth) = method\ P\ C'\ M'$
$\qquad in\ typeof\text{-}addr\ h\ a \neq None \land P \vdash C'\ has\ M' \land$
$\qquad\quad P, h \vdash ps\ [:\leq]\ Ts \land (meth = Native \longrightarrow D.M'\ (Ts) :: T_r))))$

Figure 2.19: Defensive checks for the *Invoke* instruction

The defensive VM

JinjaThreads also features a defensive VM that introduces additional type and sanity checks at run time. If they are violated, the defensive VM raises a type error. The function *execd* adds these checks on top of the aggressive VM *exec*.

$$\mathbf{datatype}\ {}'a\ type\text{-}error = TypeError \mid Normal\ {}'a$$

$$execd\ P\ s = if\ check\ P\ s\ then\ Normal\ (exec\ P\ s)\ else\ TypeError$$

The function *check* checks that the class and method in the top call frame exist and that the program counter and stack size are valid. Moreover, if an exception is flagged, it must be the address of an object on the heap and, if an exception handler in the current method matches, the stack must have at least as many elements as the handler expects. Otherwise, if no exception is flagged, *check* calls *check-instr* (with identical parameters as *exec-instr*) to check instruction-specific conditions. For example, Figure 2.19 shows the run-time checks for the *Invoke* instruction. It clearly parallels the definition of *exec-instr* in Figure 2.17. *is-Ref v* predicates that *v* is *Null* or some *Addr a*, and $P \vdash C\ has\ M$ abbreviates $\exists Ts\ T_r\ meth\ D.\ P \vdash C\ sees\ M:Ts \rightarrow T_r = meth\ in\ D$. When a native method is called, i.e., $m = Native$, *check-instr* checks that the semantics does implement the native method.

Again, there is also a relational view on the defensive VM:

$$\frac{\neg\ check\ P\ s}{P \vdash Normal\ s \rightarrow_{jvmd} TypeError} \qquad \frac{check\ P\ s \qquad s' \in exec\ P\ s}{P \vdash Normal\ s \rightarrow_{jvmd} Normal\ s'} \quad (2.5)$$

2.2.3 Well-typings

When executing bytecode, the JinjaThreads VM relies on the following assumptions: There are as many operands as needed and of the right types; registers are initialised before being read; the operand stack stays within the declared limit; the declared register number is correct; and the program counter always points to a valid instruction.

To prevent violations of these assumptions during execution, the bytecode must satisfy certain type constraints, similar to the typing rules for source code. Other than source code, bytecode does not declare the types of the registers and the stack elements. Hence, JinjaThreads models type information separately. This yields an abstract interpretation of the bytecode semantics with values being abstracted to types, similar to bytecode verification (§6.2.2).

Well-typings in JinjaThreads do not differ from Jinja in any essential way. Here, I therefore only sketch the main ideas and introduce the notation relevant for this thesis. For details, see [83].

Typings

A state type τ characterises a set of run-time states for one instruction by giving type information for the operand stack and registers. $\tau = None$ denotes that control flow cannot reach the instruction. Otherwise, say $\tau = \lfloor (ST, LT) \rfloor$, ST :: ty list gives the types for the elements on the operand stack and LT the types for the register contents. The elements of LT are either Err or $OK\ T$ for some type T :: ty. Err denotes that a register is unusable and its type is unknown, e.g., if it has not been initialised yet. For example, $\lfloor ([], [OK\ (Class\ C),\ Err]) \rfloor$ denotes that the stack is empty and there are two registers, register 0 holds a reference to an object of a subclass of C (or the $Null$ pointer), the second is unusable. A method type τs is a list of state types, one for each instruction. A program typing for P is a function Φ such that $\Phi\ C\ M$ is the method type for every method M in every class C of P.

A state type τ for an instruction i is a state well-typing iff i can execute safely in any state that τ characterises and τ is consistent with the successor instruction's state type (to be explained below). A method type τs is a method well-typing iff each of its state types is a state well-typing for its instruction.

$$app_i \ (Invoke\ M\ n, P, (ST, LT)) =$$
$$\quad n < |ST| \wedge$$
$$\quad (ST_{[n]} \neq NT \longrightarrow$$
$$\quad\quad (\exists C\ Ts\ T_r\ m\ D.\ class\text{-}of\ ST_{[n]} = \lfloor C \rfloor \wedge$$
$$\quad\quad\quad P \vdash C\ sees\ M{:}Ts{\rightarrow}T_r = m\ in\ D \wedge P \vdash rev\ (take\ n\ ST)\ [\leq]\ Ts)$$

$$eff_i \ (Invoke\ M\ n, P, (ST, LT)) =$$
$$\quad let\ T = ST_{[n]};\ \lfloor C \rfloor = class\text{-}of\ T;\ (\_,\_,T_r,\_) = method\ P\ C\ M$$
$$\quad in\ (T_r \cdot drop\ (n+1)\ ST, LT)$$

Figure 2.20: Applicability and effect for the *Invoke* instruction

Abstract interpretation of the semantics

Applicability *app* takes the checks of the defensive VM to the type level –
in a state well-typing, it defines when the instruction can execute safely.
It is split into *app_i* for normal and *xcpt-app* for exceptional execution.
Similar to *check-instr*, the function *app_i* checks the instruction-specific
preconditions. For example, Figure 2.20 shows the definition for the
Invoke instruction. It parallels *check-instr* from Figure 2.19 – except
for the check that the semantics implements native methods because
well-formedness ensures this already.

For exceptions, *is-relevant-class i P C* predicates that handlers for
class C might match some exception that instruction i raises. Using this
specification, *xcpt-app* statically approximates all handlers that might
match at run time. Among others, it checks that they do not expect more
stack elements than are currently on the stack.

Effect (function *eff*) simulates *exec* on the type level. Since *app*
has already checked the instructions preconditions, *eff*'s specification
is aggressive. It returns a list of pairs, each of which consists of the
successor program counter and the changed state type. Like *app*, *eff*
decomposes into *eff_i* for normal executions and *xcpt-eff* for jumping to
exception handlers. Note how *eff_i* closely follows *exec-instr*, e.g., by
comparing Figure 2.20 to Figure 2.17. Here, *eff_i* does not treat the case
when the receiver is *Null*, because *exec-instr* always raises an exception
in that case. Note how *eff_i* uses the return types in method signatures
as summary information for the call. In contrast to the semantics, it
deals with normal and native methods uniformly, because looking up
the method to retrieve the signature works uniformly.

51

Like *xcpt-app*, *xcpt-eff* determines via *is-relevant-class* all potential exception handlers and adds them as successors with the stack typing trimmed to the specified height.

Consistency formalises that the effects are consistent with the state types of the successor instructions. To that end, Jinja first lifts the subtype relation to state types, written $P \vdash \tau \leq' \tau'$. *OK* elements are ordered according to the subtype relation, *Err* becomes the new top element. For register types *LT*, this relation is extended pointwise to lists. For the stack typing *ST*, the relation is $P \vdash \_ [\leq] \_$. The least state type is *None*; on $\lfloor (ST, LT) \rfloor$, the order is componentwise. Now, consistency requires that the state type τ of the successor i' is greater than or equal to the state type that *eff* computes.

An example well-typing

For example, Figure 2.21 shows a method in class C that takes a single Integer parameter and returns an *Object*. The left column specifies the instruction list and all of the right-hand side is a well-typing. A state type is one single row of the table, it describes the situation before executing the instruction in the same row. Initially, the stack is empty and the registers contain the *this* pointer and the parameter. It loads the *this* pointer and calls the native method *clone* on it, which clones the this pointer. Note how the receiver type *Class C* on the stack is replaced with the declared return type *Class Object* of *clone*. Then, it stores the returned reference to the clone in register 1, reusing the former parameter register. Finally, it loads *this* again and returns it. The *Return* instruction is also the handler for the *OutOfMemory* exception that the call to *clone* may raise. In that case, the method returns the caught exception.

Control flow merges at *Return*: Normal execution linearly runs from the first to the last instruction. In the exceptional case, *Return* executes directly after *Invoke*. Hence, the normal effect of the second *Load* 0 and the exceptional effect of *Invoke* for the specified handler must both be $\leq'$-smaller than or equal to the state type for *Return*. They are

$$\lfloor \qquad\qquad [\textit{Class C}], [\textit{OK (Class C)}, \textit{OK (Class Object)}] \rfloor$$
$$\text{and} \quad \lfloor [\textit{Class OutOfMemory}], [\textit{OK (Class C)}, \textit{OK Integer}] \qquad \rfloor,$$

respectively. For the stack, *Object* is a superclass of C and *OutOfMemory*, so this is fine. In the register 1, *Integer* and *Class Object* have no common supertype, so it must be marked unusable, i.e., *Err*.

instruction list	stack	registers	
$Load\ 0$	$\lfloor($	$[], [OK\ (Class\ C), OK\ Integer]$	$)\rfloor$
$Invoke\ clone\ 0$	$\lfloor($	$[Class\ C], [OK\ (Class\ C), OK\ Integer]$	$)\rfloor$
$Store\ 1$	$\lfloor([Class\ Object],$	$[OK\ (Class\ C), OK\ Integer]$	$)\rfloor$
$Load\ 0$	$\lfloor($	$[], [OK\ (Class\ C), OK\ (Class\ Object)]])\rfloor$	
$Return$	$\lfloor([Class\ Object],$	$[OK\ (Class\ C), Err]$	$)\rfloor$

exception table:	$[(1, 2, \lfloor OutOfMemory \rfloor, 4, 0)]$
maximum stack length:	1
local registers:	0

Figure 2.21: Example of a method well-typing

Well-formedness

Method well-typings are only method-local. Rather than checking applicability and effect across method boundaries do they take the method signatures as summaries for method calls. Among others, well-formedness ensures that these summaries are indeed correct.

A method declaration $(M, Ts, T, \lfloor(msl, mxl, ins, xt)\rfloor)$ in class D is well-typed with respect to τs iff

(i) τs is a well-typing for the method,

(ii) all state types in τs contain only valid types, and respect the maximum stack length msl and the fixed number mxl of registers, and

(iii) τs satisfies the start condition, i.e., it is non-empty and the first state type $\tau s_{[0]}$ is $\le'$-greater than the abstraction of the initial state of the call frame. Remember from Figure 2.17 that in the initial state, the operand stack is empty and the registers contain the *this* pointer and parameters, the local variables are undefined. Its abstraction is $\lfloor([], OK\ (Class\ D) \cdot map\ OK\ Ts\ @\ replicate\ mxl\ Err)\rfloor$.

Note that without the start condition, the typing $replicate\ |ins|\ None$ would be a well-typing for any method declaration with non-empty instruction sequence, but then, the method may never be called, because the first instruction is marked unreachable (*None*).

A program typing Φ is a (program) well-typing for P iff every method M in every class C of P is well-typed with respect to $\Phi\ C\ M$. A JVM program P is well-formed (written *wf-jvm-prog* P) iff it satisfies the generic well-formedness constraints (Figure 2.9) and there is a program well-typing Φ for it.

This definition of well-formedness is not constructive, because it does not specify how to obtain the well-typing from the bytecode program. To that end, JinjaThreads contains a bytecode verifier (§6.2.2). It rephrases the abstract interpretation as a data flow analysis problem and computes a well-typing with Kildall's algorithm [78].

2.2.4 Type safety

Type safety for bytecode means that the assumptions of the VM are always met at run time. This is expressed most clearly as: The defensive VM never raises a type error when it executes a well-formed program P. Let Φ be the well-typing for P. Naturally, the proof requires a state invariant called conformance, written $P, \Phi \vdash s \surd$.

Conformance requires that the state type correctly abstracts the run-time state (xcp, h, frs), i.e.,

(i) if $xcp = \lfloor a \rfloor$ flags the exception at address a, a designates an object on the heap h whose class C is a subclass of *Throwable* and conforms to the exception specification in *xcpt-app* for the current instruction in the top-most call frame,

(ii) the heap conforms, i.e., $P \vdash h \surd$,

(iii) for all call frames (stk, loc, C, M, pc) in frs, C declares M, pc points to a reachable instruction and the contents of the operand stack stk and registers loc conform to the type that the well-typing $(\Phi\ C\ M)_{[pc]}$ specifies, and

(iv) all call frames except for the top-most one are halted at an *Invoke* instruction that calls a method whose static summary information, i.e. parameter types and return type, is compatible with the call frame above.

For a well-formed program and correct state, one can now show type safety:

Theorem 2.3 (Type safety). *Let Φ be a well-typing for P and $P, \Phi \vdash s\sqrt{}$. Then, the following statements hold:*

(a) The defensive VM does not raise a type error:

$$\neg\, P \vdash Normal\, s \rightarrow_{\text{jvmd}} TypeError$$

(b) Aggressive and defensive VM agree:

$$P \vdash s \rightarrow_{\text{jvm}} s' \text{ iff } P \vdash Normal\, s \rightarrow_{\text{jvmd}} Normal\, s'.$$

(c) Conformance is preserved: If $P \vdash s \rightarrow_{\text{jvm}} s'$, then $P, \Phi \vdash s'\sqrt{}$.

The proof for (a) and (c) proceeds by case distinction on the current instruction. (b) directly follows from (a) by construction of the defensive VM. (c) shows that *app* and *eff* are indeed abstract interpretations of the semantics.

2.3 Comparison with Jinja, Bali, and μJava

In this section, I compare the sequential part of JinjaThreads with its predecessors Jinja [83], Bali [11, 84, 135], and μJava [79, 85]. A goal in extending Jinja with concurrency was to reuse as much as possible from Jinja. Hence, I built on many of the fundamental concepts, although textually, almost every definition has undergone some adaptations. Here, I only present the conceptual changes.

Every valid Jinja program can be trivially converted into a valid JinjaThreads program; one merely needs to adapt it to the generalisations of expressions, instructions, and declarations of native methods and additional system exceptions. Beyond that, sequential JinjaThreads extends Jinja mainly in three respects: binary operators, arrays, and native methods.

Binary operators

Jinja and μJava support only the binary operators for equality $==$ and integer addition $+$. In [84], Bali covers the full range of binary operators in Java – except for string concatenation, but syntactically distinguishes the overloaded operators &, |, and ˆ. Binary operators always return a value, e.g., division by 0 yields 0 instead of throwing an *ArithmeticException*. Moreover, Bali declares, but does not correctly implement the operators &, |, ^, and >> that manipulate integers bit-wise.

JinjaThreads covers the same set of operators as Bali. While Jinja-Threads' predecessors use unbounded integers (type *int*), I changed them in JinjaThreads to 32-bit machine integers (type *word32*) from Isabelle's word library. Hence, I can draw on the functions from the Isabelle word library for correctly implementing the bit-wise operators – except for / and %. The latter are implemented manually, because the word library only defines division and remainder for unsigned words. Thus, the arithmetic operations follow the Java behaviour even in case of overflows. However, this comes at the expense of introducing various coercions between *word32*, *nat*, and *int* for array accesses. In bytecode, *BinOp* takes the operator as a parameter, thereby unifying the various Java bytecode instructions, which are available as abbreviations.

Like Bali, JinjaThreads defines typing rules for binary operators (Figure 2.8) and the semantics (Figure 2.13) to encapsulate binary operators from the rest of the language. Unlike Bali, JinjaThreads generalises these such that a binary operator may fail with an exception, e.g., division by 0.

Arrays

Both Bali and Klein's extension of μJava bytecode [79] model arrays, but they have been omitted in Jinja. JinjaThreads reintroduces arrays. Everything is standard except for the set *types P* of valid types. Bali allows arrays with *NT* as element type; infinite ascending chains do not matter as it does not model an executable bytecode verifier. Klein limits the maximum number of array dimensions such that *types P* is finite. The class file format for Java bytecode limits array dimensions to 255 [103, §4.8.1]. There is no such bound for Java source code, but the maximum number of array dimensions can be computed statically for any fixed program. Instead of formalising and verifying such a computation, I leave the number of array dimensions unbounded in JinjaThreads.

Arrays entail the following adaptations to Jinja: First, additional conversions with *class-of* and *class-of'* permit to uniformly reuse the lookup functions, which are defined only for class names, e.g., in method calls (Figure 2.7, WTCALL; Figure 2.14, RCALL; Figures 2.17 and 2.19). This way, *Object* may declare fields and methods freely, which all array types inherit [56, §6.4.5]. Bali and µJava disallow fields in class Object, because their heap model cannot handle fields in arrays [79, §6.2]. The JLS neither specifies any field in *Object*, nor does it forbid such. The implementation of *Object* in the Java standard library does not declare any fields, but user-defined implementations of *Object* may do so.

Second, JinjaThreads generalises casts to arbitrary types, not only classes as in Jinja and µJava. At the same time, I also introduce an *instanceof* operator which allows to test on reference types without resorting to exceptions.

Third, as all thrown exceptions must be objects (and not arrays), the type safety proof requires that *Throwable* replace *Object* as the root of the exception hierarchy (like in Bali). For example, WTTHROW and WTTRY (Figure 2.7) strengthen the check *is-class P C* with $P \vdash C \leq^*$ *Throwable*. In contrast, Klein's extension of µJava permits to throw arrays as exceptions.

Native methods

Native methods are new in JinjaThreads, none of its predecessors has included them. Although the semantics only implements two native methods, namely *hashcode* and *clone* in sequential JinjaThreads, native methods will be crucial for multithreading.

Unlike Java, calls to *clone* in *Object* omit the test whether the receiver object implements the *Cloneable* interface, because JinjaThreads does not model interfaces. Instead, *clone* always returns a copy of the receiver if there is enough memory left. Also, JinjaThreads does not specialize the return type of *clone* for arrays (see Footnote 7 on page 33).

Other changes

Apart from the above extensions, sequential JinjaThreads also changes the following aspects of Jinja: For source code, JinjaThreads only defines a small-step semantics, but no big-step semantics, because a big-step semantics cannot adequately express the interleaving of threads. Jinja defined both a big-step and small-step semantics and proved them equivalent. Bali and µJava source code define only a big-step semantics.

Moreover, following a change in the JLS from the second [55] to the third edition [56], the typing rule for the conditional operator ? : (in JinjaThreads written as *if* (e) e_1 *else* e_2) has changed: According to the second edition [55, §15.25], which Jinja follows, the subtype relation must relate e_1's type T_1 with e_2's type T_2, i.e., $P \vdash T_1 \leq T_2$ or $P \vdash T_2 \leq T_1$; then, the conditional's type is the larger one of T_1 and T_2. In the new edition [56, §15.25], T_1 and T_2 only need to have a lub, which is also the type of the conditional, cf. WTCOND (Figure 2.7). Although this change may seem negligible, it affects code extraction (§6.2.3) non-trivially.

Further, a local variable block $\{V: T = \lfloor v \rfloor ; e\}$ in source code contains an optional initialisation value v, in which execution also keeps track of V's value. Jinja omits the $= \lfloor v \rfloor$, but emulates it as $\{V : T; V := Val\, v; ; e\}$, i.e., an uninitialised block whose body starts with assignment to the variable. Adding the explicit initialisation simplifies the semantics and proofs, e.g., progress (Theorem 2.1) no longer requires a custom induction rule.

In bytecode, exception handling has changed a little: Following the JVMS [103, §4.7.3], exception tables may now contain the special value *Any* to handle all exceptions that are raised at the guarded instructions (cf. §2.2.1). This increase in expressiveness simplifies the compiler verification (Chapter 5).

When an instruction raises an exception, the Jinja VM immediately transfers control to the right exception handler, which may require to scan and pop an arbitrary large part of the call stack. In contrast, the JinjaThreads VM allows raised, but yet unhandled exceptions as intermediate states, and searches the exception handlers of one call frame at a time (cf. Figure 2.18). This simplifies some proofs, in particular the compiler verification (cf. Chapter 5), but, in turn, conformance must be strengthened to account for the new states (condition (i) in the conformance definition, §2.2.4, is new).

More importantly, with this approach, the defensive VM can easily check that the operand stack contains sufficiently many values, before it trims it to the length that the exception handler expects. In Jinja, this check is missing.

Multithreading is just one damn thing after, before, or simultaneous with another.

Andrei Alexandrescu

Interleaving semantics

In this chapter, I describe how to add Java-style multithreading to the semantics from Chapter 2 and prove type safety. A precursor to this work has been published in [107].

Multithreading in JinjaThreads comprises dynamic thread creation, synchronisation via monitors, the wait-notify mechanism, and thread interruption. To separate the semantics of these mechanisms and their implications for type safety from the low-level details of allowed compiler and run-time optimisations, I defer the Java Memory Model [56, §17.4] to Chapter 4. Instead, I use interleaving semantics with a single shared memory through which threads interact. JinjaThreads omits all timing-related features such as `Thread.sleep(long)` and `Object.wait(long)` because JinjaThreads does not model time. Neither does it include the deprecated methods `stop`, `suspend`, and `resume` in `Thread`, nor the library extensions in `java.util.concurrent` which are not an integral part of Java.

The challenges in this chapter are the following:

language-independent interleaving Since both source code and bytecode must implement the above multithreading features, they best share as much as possible of the formalisation. To that end, I first develop a generic framework for interleaving semantics (§3.1), which is parametrised by the semantics of individual threads.

reuse of the sequential semantics and proofs As the framework manages the multithreaded state and implements the multithreading features, I reuse the sequential semantics from Chapter 2 with as little adaptations as possible (§3.2.2 and §3.2.3). Consequently, I am able to reuse the type safety theorems of sequential JinjaThreads when

layer	source code	bytecode
5	interleaved small-step	
3	statements	call stacks
	&	exception handling
	expressions	single instruction
2	native methods	

Figure 3.1: Stack of semantics with interleaving

proving type safety for multithreaded JinjaThreads. Here again, I show how to share as much as possible between source code and bytecode. The stack of semantics in Figure 3.1 shows how source code and bytecode share native methods and the interleaving semantics. As it can be seen at the layer numbering, some layers are still missing. I add them in Chapter 4 on memory models.

characterisation of deadlocks Progress is non-trivial when threads can deadlock. Therefore, §3.3 formalises deadlock and refines progress such that it allows for deadlock. This again is designed to be independent of the language.

3.1 Framework for interleaving semantics

The framework for interleaving semantics manages the interleaving of individual threads. It separates the single-thread semantics from the burdens of multithreading: It manages the multithreaded state (§3.1.1), i.e., the locks, wait sets, the thread pool, and interrupts. At the same time, it isolates the local states of the threads from each other.

Interaction between individual threads and the interleaving semantics only happens through designated actions called thread actions (cf. §3.1.2). They allow the framework to be oblivious of thread-local states such that I can use it for both source and bytecode.

Apart from the interleaving semantics (§3.1.3), the framework also provides the infrastructure to lift predicates and invariants on states of single threads to multithreaded states (§3.1.4).

3.1.1 The multithreaded state

The multithreaded state consists of five components: the locks status, the thread pool, the shared heap, the wait sets, and the interrupts. In this section, I present each of them first before I assemble the multithreaded state.

Locks

Java-style locks are mutually exclusive and re-entrant, i.e., at most one thread may hold the lock at one time, but it can acquire it multiple times. Hence, a lock (of type $'t\ lock$) stores which thread holds it, and if so, how many times; $'t$ is the type variable for thread IDs. A natural choice for $'t\ lock$ is the HOL type $('t \times nat)\ option$. Then, $None$ denotes that the lock is not held by any thread, and $\lfloor (t, n) \rfloor$ means that the thread with ID t has acquired the lock $n + 1$ times. Instead of working directly with this type, I introduce the following operations on $'t\ lock$; Figure 3.2 shows their implementations.

$has\text{-}locks\ L\ t$	number of times t has acquired L
$may\text{-}lock\ L\ t$	test whether t may lock L
$lock\text{-}lock\ L\ t$	acquire L for t once
$unlock\text{-}lock\ L$	release L once
$acquire\text{-}lock\ L\ t\ n$	acquire L for t n times
$release\text{-}lock\ L\ t$	completely release L if t holds L

In the following, $has\text{-}lock\ L\ t$ is short-hand for $has\text{-}locks\ L\ t > 0$.

Note that some operations on locks should be partial. For example, $lock\text{-}lock\ \lfloor (t', n) \rfloor\ t$ only makes sense if $t' = t$. However, since HOL is a logic of total functions, I must define $lock\text{-}lock$ for $t' \neq t$, too. For simplicity, $lock\text{-}lock$ ignores t and increments t''s lock counter in that case, but any other implementation would be fine, too.[9] This choice allows to remove some preconditions from certain lemmata. For instance, if $has\text{-}lock\ L\ t$, then also $has\text{-}lock\ (acquire\text{-}lock\ L\ t'\ n)\ t$. Other implementations would require the precondition $t' = t$ or, equivalently, $may\text{-}lock\ L\ t'$.

The status of all locks is modelled as a function from lock identifiers (type variable $'l$) to locks. Anticipating code generation in Chapter 6, this

---

[9]I could also have left $lock\text{-}lock$ unspecified for that case using Isabelle's **specification** command. However, underspecification is detrimental to code generation (see §6.4).

$$has\text{-}locks \quad None \ t \quad = 0$$
$$has\text{-}locks \quad \lfloor (t',n) \rfloor \ t \quad = (if \ t = t' \ then \ n+1 \ else \ 0)$$

$$may\text{-}lock \quad None \ t \quad = True \qquad may\text{-}lock \lfloor (t',n) \rfloor \ t = (t = t')$$

$$lock\text{-}lock \quad None \ t \quad = \lfloor (t,0) \rfloor \qquad lock\text{-}lock \lfloor (t',n) \rfloor \ t = \lfloor (t',n+1) \rfloor$$

$$unlock\text{-}lock \ None \qquad = None$$
$$unlock\text{-}lock \lfloor (t,n) \rfloor \qquad = (if \ n = 0 \ then \ None \ else \lfloor (t,n-1) \rfloor)$$

$$acquire\text{-}lock \ L \ t \ 0 \qquad = L$$
$$acquire\text{-}lock \ L \ t \ (n+1) = acquire\text{-}lock \ (lock\text{-}lock \ L \ t) \ t \ n$$

$$release\text{-}lock \quad None \ t \quad = None$$
$$release\text{-}lock \lfloor (t',n) \rfloor \ t \quad = (if \ t' = t \ then \ None \ else \lfloor (t',n) \rfloor)$$

Figure 3.2: Implementation of lock operations

is actually not a function, but a FinFun (see §1.4.1). Thus, the status of all locks formally has type $'l \Rightarrow_f 't \ lock$, written $('l, 't) \ locks$. For this chapter, the almost constant nature of FinFun's is irrelevant, and the reader may think of them as ordinary functions – except for the omnipresent "f" in the notation.

Thread pool

The multithreaded semantics manages the threads and their local states in a thread pool. A thread pool ts is a map from thread IDs to thread-local states (type variable $'x$) of the following type.

$$\textbf{type\_synonym} \ ('l, 't, 'x) \ tpool = 't \rightharpoonup ('x \times 'l \ tr\text{-}locks)$$

Free thread IDs are mapped to $None$. If $ts \ t = \lfloor (x, ln) \rfloor$, then t identifies the thread whose local state is x (of type $'x$). For example, for the source code semantics, x stores the current expression and the store of local variables, i.e., $'x$ gets instantiated with $expr \times locals$. In bytecode, $'x$ consists of the exception flag and the call stack.

The thread pool also stores for every thread a multiset ln of temporarily released locks, which I also model as a FinFun:

$$\textbf{type\_synonym} \ 'l \ tr\text{-}locks = 'l \Rightarrow_f nat$$

For example, when a Java thread suspends itself to a wait set, it temporarily releases the lock on the associated monitor. Upon removal from the wait set, it must reacquire the lock before it can continue (see §3.2.1 for the details of the mechanism). Recall the notation for FinFuns from §1.4.1: $K^f\ 0$ denotes the empty multiset, and $(K^f\ 0)(l :=_f 2)$, e.g., is the multiset which only contains l twice.

The multithreaded semantics keeps track of which locks have been thus released and how many times the thread had acquired them before. Moreover, the thread continues to execute only after it has reacquired its temporarily released locks. Since the multithreaded semantics implements all this (§3.1.3), , the single-threaded semantics need neither remember how many times the lock had been acquired, nor reacquire it explicitly afterwards.

Wait sets

Java offers wait sets as an alternative to busy waiting. Threads may suspend themselves to the wait set of a monitor where they remain until another thread notifies or interrupts them.

JinjaThreads does not model wait sets explicitly. Rather, it stores for every thread its wait set status:

$$\textbf{type\_synonym}\ ('w, 't)\ \textit{wait-sets} = 't \rightharpoonup 'w\ \textit{wait-set-status}$$

where $'w$ wait-set-status consists of the values $InWS\,w$, WS-Notified, and WS-WokenUp, and $'w$ represents the type of wait set identifiers. The wait set of a monitor $w :: 'w$ contains all threads whose wait status is $\lfloor InWS\,w \rfloor$. The predicate waiting wo tests whether the wait set status $wo :: 'w$ wait-set-status option is of the form $\lfloor InWS\,w' \rfloor$, i.e., the associated thread is in a wait set.

Figure 3.3 shows the different values for a thread's wait set status and their transitions as an automaton. Initially, after the thread has been spawned, its wait set status is None, i.e., the thread is not in any wait set. Normal execution takes place in that state (dotted arrow). The thread can suspend itself to a wait set with ID w (status $\lfloor InWS\,w \rfloor$). When another thread notifies or wakes up the thread (dashed lines), the latter's status changes to $\lfloor WS\text{-}Notified \rfloor$ or $\lfloor WS\text{-}WokenUp \rfloor$, respectively. From either of them, it leaves the wait set cycle and returns to the normal state None by processing the notification or wake-up, respectively. If the thread has

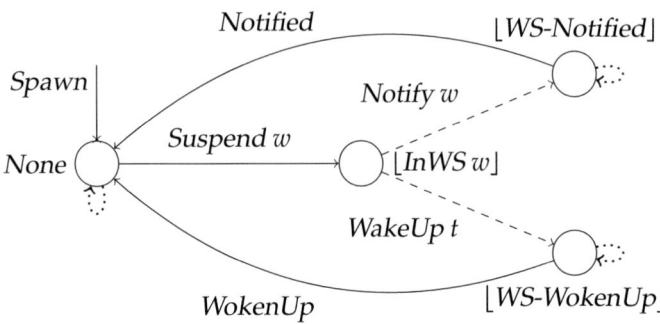

Figure 3.3: Wait sets, notification, and interruption

temporarily released some locks when it suspended itself to the wait set, it must reacquire them in states $\lfloor WS\text{-}Notified \rfloor$ and $\lfloor WS\text{-}WokenUp \rfloor$ (dotted arrow). Following the JLS [56, §17.8], reacquisition precedes processing the removal from the wait set, i.e., notification or wake-up, although the order is semantically irrelevant.

This only illustrates the purpuse of the different wait set status. I define the semantics and the interaction with locks formally in §3.1.3.

Interrupts

Java threads interrupt each other by invoking the *interrupt* method in class *Thread*. When running normally, the interrupted thread must actively query its interrupt status to take notice of the interrupt. However, if it is in a wait set at the time of interruption, it is removed from the wait set. When it is joining on a thread, it aborts joining. In both cases, it raises an *InterruptedException*.

The interleaving semantics stores the pending interrupts in a set of thread IDs, i.e., a thread t is interrupted iff t is in this set.

$$\textbf{type\_synonym } 't\ intrs = {'t}\ set$$

The multithreaded state

A multithreaded state $(ls, (ts, h), ws, is)$ consists of locks ls, a thread pool ts, the shared memory h, the wait set status ws, and the interrupts is.

thread t1	thread t2

```
synchronized (f) {          synchronized (g) {
  synchronized (g) {          t1.interrupt();
    synchronized (f) {      }
      g.wait();
}}}
```

Figure 3.4: Two threads with locks, wait sets, and interrupts

type_synonym $('l,'t,'x,'h,'w)$ $state =$
$$('l,'t)\ locks \times (('l,'t,'x)\ tpool \times 'h) \times ('w,'t)\ wait\text{-}sets \times 't\ intrs$$

The multithreaded semantics leaves the shared memory $h :: 'h$ uninterpreted, it just passes h between the threads. The projection functions *locks*, *thr*, *shr*, *wset*, and *intrs* return the locks, the thread pool, the shared memory, the wait sets, and the pending interrupts of a state, respectively.

For example, consider Figure 3.4 with two threads t1 and t2. Suppose t1 executes first until it enters the wait set of monitor g and then t2 executes until is has interrupted t1. Suppose further that f references an object at address f, and similarly for g. Then, this state is represented by the tuple $(ls, (ts, h), ws, is)$ where

$ls = [f \mapsto_f (t1, 1), g \mapsto_f (t2, 0)]$, i.e., threads t1 and t2 hold the locks f and g twice and once, respectively; all other locks are free.

$ts = [t1 \mapsto (\ldots, (K^f\ 0)(g :=_f 1)), t2 \mapsto (\ldots, K^f\ 0)]$, i.e., the thread pool stores the thread-local states (omitted) and the temporarily released locks. Thread t1 has temporarily released the lock on g which it had held once before. Thread t2 has not temporarily released any locks.

$h = [f \mapsto Obj \ldots, g \mapsto Obj \ldots, t1 \mapsto Obj\ Thread \ldots, t2 \mapsto Obj\ Thread \ldots]$, i.e., the shared heap contains the objects referenced by f and g, and the objects associated with threads t1 and t2.

$ws = [t1 \mapsto WS\text{-}WokenUp]$, i.e., an interrupt has removed thread t1 from g's wait set.

$is = \{t1\}$, i.e., only thread t1 has a pending interrupt.

3.1.2 Thread actions

The framework manages the multithreaded state, but the single-threaded semantics needs to query and manipulate that state. To keep them separated, the latter must not directly access that state. Instead, it uses a thread action to spawn a new thread, to acquire a lock, to wake another thread, etc., which provides a clear and restricted interface to access and update the multithreaded state. Thus, I can decompose proofs about the multithreaded semantics to the level of threads, because interaction between threads can only happen via thread actions (and the shared memory).

Reductions in the single-threaded semantics carry a thread action as label, i.e., I will adapt the sequential semantics from Chapter 2 accordingly (§3.2). When the interleaving semantics picks a reduction, it changes the multithreaded state according to the thread action. Note that these actions are the only means of "communication" between the two levels. Since this is unidirectional, the interleaving semantics can transfer information to the single-threaded semantics only by picking one reduction that the latter offers. Hence, the single-threaded semantics must anticipate in its reductions all possible answers it is willing to accept from the interleaving semantics.

Syntax of thread actions

Thread actions are composed of multiple basic thread actions (BTA). The framework implements 17 different BTAs, which can be split in five groups. Figure 3.5 shows the type definitions.

Locking *Lock* acquires a lock once for the current thread t – no other thread may hold the lock. *Unlock* releases it once, provided t is holding it. *Release* temporarily releases the lock if t holds it, and has no effect otherwise. *UnlockFail* tests whether t does not hold a lock, i.e., unlocking it would fail. There is no counterpart to *UnlockFail* for testing whether a thread holds a lock. This can be simulated by [*Unlock*, *Lock*], because the interleaving semantics picks a reduction only if the current state satisfies the precondition of *all* BTAs of the thread action.

datatype *lock-act* = *Lock* | *Unlock* | *UnlockFail* | *Release*

datatype *('t, 'x, 'h) new-thread-act* = *Spawn 't 'x 'h* | *ThreadEx 't bool*

datatype *'t condition-act* = *Join 't* | *Yield*

datatype *('t, 'w) wait-set-act* =
  Suspend 'w | *Notify 'w* | *NotifyAll 'w* | *WakeUp 't* | *Notified* | *WokenUp*

datatype *'t intr-act* = *Intr 't* | *ClearIntr 't* | *IsIntrd 't bool*

Figure 3.5: Type definitions for basic thread actions

Thread creation *Spawn t x h* spawns a new thread with ID t and initial local state x. There must not yet be a thread with ID t. Later (§3.1.4), it will be convenient to remember the shared heap h at spawn time. *ThreadEx t b* tests whether there is a thread with ID t in the thread pool, where $b :: bool$ denotes the result.

Condition actions *Join t* joins on thread t, i.e., t must have terminated before. *Yield* causes the current thread to pause temporarily and allow other threads to execute. *Yield* is only relevant for schedulers (§6.3.2).

Wait sets *Suspend w* inserts the current thread into the wait set w, any previous assignment is lost. *Notify w* (*NotifyAll w*) wakes up one (all) of the threads in the wait set w, their wait set status becomes $\lfloor WS\text{-}Notified \rfloor$ (see Figure 3.3). If w is empty, no thread is woken up. *WakeUp t* changes t's wait set status to $\lfloor WS\text{-}WokenUp \rfloor$, if it has been in a wait set before. Otherwise, nothing happens.

Notified and *WokenUp* label reductions that process the notification and wake-up for the thread that has been notified or woken up.

Interruption *Intr t* adds t to the set of interrupted threads; *ClearIntr t* removes it. *IsIntrd t b* tests whether the set of interrupted threads contains t, i.e., whether t has a pending interrupt; $b :: bool$ denotes the result.

To remember the lock on which BTAs for locking operate, they are arranged in a FinFun *las :: 'l lock-acts* such that the BTAs for lock l are listed in $las_f\ l$. In summary, a thread action consists of a FinFun for the BTAs for locks and one list for each of the other groups.

type_synonym $'l$ *lock-acts* $= 'l \Rightarrow_f$ *lock-act list*

type_synonym $('l,'t,'x,'h,'w,'o)$ *thread-action* $=$
$\quad 'l$ *lock-acts* $\times ('t,'x,'h)$ *new-thread-act list* $\times 't$ *condition-act list* $\times$
$\quad ('t,'w)$ *wait-set-act list* $\times 't$ *intr-act list* $\times 'o$ *list*

Since thread actions are used as labels for the reductions, they include a sixth component of type $'o$ *list* for further extensions (§4.3.2). The projection functions $\langle ta \rangle_l$, $\langle ta \rangle_t$, $\langle ta \rangle_c$, $\langle ta \rangle_w$, $\langle ta \rangle_i$, and $\langle ta \rangle_o$ extract from the thread action ta the BTAs for locks, thread creation, conditions, wait sets, interrupts, and the extension part, respectively.

All BTAs of a thread action are executed in a single reduction; if there is at least one BTA in the thread action of a reduction whose precondition is not met, the interleaving semantics does not select the reduction. Thus, a single-thread semantics can affect and query multiple parts of the multithreaded state in one step by composing BTAs. Since every BTA (except *Release*) affects only one part of the state, the interleaving semantics remains flexible and the proofs simple.

For example, in Java, a call to the *wait* method must test that the thread t has not been interrupted and that it holds the lock l associated with the receiver object, release the latter, and suspend t to the associated wait set w. This can be expressed by the following thread action:

$$((K^f [])(l :=_f [Unlock, Lock, Release]),$$
$$[], [], [Suspend\ w], [IsIntrd\ t\ False], \ldots)$$

As this notation is cumbersome to read and write, I use a list-like notation for thread actions, with lock identifiers added to lock BTAs. The Isabelle parser and pretty printer are set up such that they automatically convert it into the corresponding thread action. Hence, the above thread action is written as

$$(\!|Unlock{\rightarrow}l, Lock{\rightarrow}l, Release{\rightarrow}l, Suspend\ w, IsIntrd\ t\ False, \ldots |\!)$$

Let's now examine how the thread action achieves its goal. First, $Unlock{\rightarrow}l, Lock{\rightarrow}l$ checks that the current thread holds l without effectively changing the lock status. Then, $Release{\rightarrow}l$ releases l and $Suspend\ w$ adds the thread to the wait set. $IsIntrd\ t\ False$ tests that the thread t has no pending interrupt.

Note that the order of BTAs of the same group (and lock identifier) is important. For example, $(\!|Lock{\rightarrow}l, Unlock{\rightarrow}l|\!)$ does not alter the lock

$$upd\text{-}L :: {'}t\ lock \Rightarrow {'}t \Rightarrow lock\text{-}act \Rightarrow {'}t\ lock$$
$$upd\text{-}L\ L\ t\ Lock \qquad = lock\text{-}lock\ L\ t$$
$$upd\text{-}L\ L\ t\ Unlock \qquad = unlock\text{-}lock\ L$$
$$upd\text{-}L\ L\ t\ UnlockFail = L$$
$$upd\text{-}L\ L\ t\ Release \qquad = release\text{-}lock\ L\ t$$

$$upd\text{-}Ls :: {'}t\ lock \Rightarrow {'}t \Rightarrow lock\text{-}act\ list \Rightarrow {'}t\ lock$$
$$upd\text{-}Ls\ L\ t\ [] \qquad\qquad = L$$
$$upd\text{-}Ls\ L\ t\ (la \cdot las) \qquad = upd\text{-}Ls\ (upd\text{-}L\ L\ t\ la)\ t\ las$$

$$upd\text{-}locks :: ({'}l, {'}t)\ locks \Rightarrow {'}t \Rightarrow {'}l\ lock\text{-}acts \Rightarrow ({'}l, {'}t)\ locks$$
$$(upd\text{-}locks\ ls\ t\ las)_f\ l\ = upd\text{-}Ls\ (ls_f\ l)\ t\ (las_f\ l)$$

Figure 3.6: Update functions of the lock status for lock BTAs

state either, but checks that no other thread holds l. Conversely, BTAs of different groups are unordered, even though the $(\!|\ldots|\!)$ notation might conjure up the illusion of a total ordering.

Semantics of thread actions

The semantics for BTAs follows their division in groups. For each group, there are update functions for the affected parts of the multithreaded states and predicates to check the preconditions.

Lock actions For lock BTAs, Figure 3.6 shows the update functions of the lock status. The function $upd\text{-}L$ maps lock BTAs to the operations on locks from §3.1.1. Note that $UnlockFail$ does not change the lock because this BTA only queries the lock status. The functions $upd\text{-}Ls$ and $upd\text{-}locks$ lift this function to lists of lock BTAs for a single lock and to FinFuns for all locks, respectively.

The preconditions for the lock actions are shown in Figure 3.7. These functions exactly follow the pattern for the update functions: $ok\text{-}L$ translates single BTAs to operations on locks, $ok\text{-}Ls$ lifts $ok\text{-}L$ to lists, and $ok\text{-}locks$ checks all lists in the lock FinFun of a thread action simultaneously. Note how $ok\text{-}Ls\ L\ t\ (la \cdot las)$ updates the lock L such that checking the remaining BTAs las takes the effect of the first BTA la on L into account.

Since the locks that a thread has temporarily released are stored separately from the lock status, there are update functions for that part,

$ok\text{-}L :: {}'t\ lock \Rightarrow {}'t \Rightarrow lock\text{-}act \Rightarrow bool$
$ok\text{-}L\ L\ t\ Lock \qquad\ = may\text{-}lock\ L\ t$
$ok\text{-}L\ L\ t\ Unlock \qquad = has\text{-}lock\ L\ t$
$ok\text{-}L\ L\ t\ UnlockFail = \neg\ has\text{-}lock\ L\ t$
$ok\text{-}L\ L\ t\ Release \qquad = True$

$ok\text{-}Ls :: {}'t\ lock \Rightarrow {}'t \Rightarrow lock\text{-}act\ list \Rightarrow bool$
$ok\text{-}Ls\ L\ t\ [] \qquad\qquad = True$
$ok\text{-}Ls\ L\ t\ (la \cdot las) \quad\ = ok\text{-}L\ L\ t\ la \wedge ok\text{-}Ls\ (upd\text{-}L\ L\ L\ t\ la)\ t\ las$

$ok\text{-}locks :: ({}'l, {}'t)\ locks \Rightarrow {}'t \Rightarrow {}'l\ lock\text{-}acts \Rightarrow bool$
$ok\text{-}locks\ ls\ t\ las \qquad = (\forall l.\ ok\text{-}Ls\ (ls_f\ l)\ t\ (las_f\ l))$

Figure 3.7: Preconditions for lock BTAs

$upd\text{-}trl :: nat \Rightarrow {}'t\ lock \Rightarrow {}'t \Rightarrow lock\text{-}act \Rightarrow nat$
$upd\text{-}trl\ n\ L\ t\ Release \quad = n + has\text{-}locks\ L\ t$
$upd\text{-}trl\ n\ L\ t\ \_ \qquad\qquad = n$

$upd\text{-}trls :: nat \Rightarrow {}'t\ lock \Rightarrow {}'t \Rightarrow lock\text{-}act\ list \Rightarrow nat$
$upd\text{-}trls\ n\ L\ t\ [] \qquad\quad = n$
$upd\text{-}trls\ n\ L\ t\ (la \cdot las) = upd\text{-}trls\ (upd\text{-}trl\ n\ L\ t\ la)\ (upd\text{-}L\ L\ t\ la)\ t\ las$

$upd\text{-}TRL :: {}'l\ tr\text{-}locks \Rightarrow ({}'l, {}'t)\ locks \Rightarrow {}'t \Rightarrow {}'l\ lock\text{-}acts \Rightarrow {}'l\ tr\text{-}locks$
$(upd\text{-}TRL\ ln\ ls\ t\ las)_f\ l = upd\text{-}trls\ (ln_f\ l)\ (ls_f\ l)\ t\ (las_f\ l)$

Figure 3.8: Update functions for temporarily released locks

too (Figure 3.8), which follow the same pattern. Remember that for a fixed lock ID, the state of the temporarily released locks is just the number of times the thread had held it.

Thread creation actions For thread creation BTAs, the functions $upd\text{-}thr$ and $upd\text{-}thrs$ update the thread pool (Figure 3.9). Spawned threads are stored under their thread ID with the initial state given in the BTA and no temporarily released locks. The predicates $ok\text{-}thr$ and $ok\text{-}thrs$ check the preconditions (Figure 3.10), i.e., t is a free thread ID for $Spawn\ t\ x\ m$, and b in $ThreadEx\ t\ b$ expresses whether t is not a free thread ID. Thread IDs are free iff they are not in the domain of the thread pool map.

$upd\text{-}thr :: (\mathit{'l}, \mathit{'t}, \mathit{'x})\ tpool \Rightarrow (\mathit{'t}, \mathit{'x}, \mathit{'h})\ new\text{-}thread\text{-}act \Rightarrow (\mathit{'l}, \mathit{'t}, \mathit{'x})\ tpool$
$upd\text{-}thr\ ts\ (Spawn\ t\ x\ m) \quad = ts(t \mapsto (x, \mathrm{K^f}\ 0))$
$upd\text{-}thr\ ts\ (ThreadEx\ t\ b) \quad = ts$

$upd\text{-}thrs ::$
$\quad (\mathit{'l}, \mathit{'t}, \mathit{'x})\ tpool \Rightarrow (\mathit{'t}, \mathit{'x}, \mathit{'h})\ new\text{-}thread\text{-}act\ list \Rightarrow (\mathit{'l}, \mathit{'t}, \mathit{'x})\ tpool$
$upd\text{-}thrs\ ts\ [] \qquad\qquad\qquad = ts$
$upd\text{-}thrs\ ts\ (nt \cdot nts) \qquad\quad = upd\text{-}thrs\ (upd\text{-}thr\ ts\ nt)\ nts$

Figure 3.9: Update functions for thread creation BTAs

$free\text{-}thread\text{-}id :: (\mathit{'l}, \mathit{'t}, \mathit{'x})\ tpool \Rightarrow \mathit{'t} \Rightarrow bool$
$free\text{-}thread\text{-}id\ ts\ t \qquad\qquad = (ts\ t = None)$

$ok\text{-}thr :: (\mathit{'l}, \mathit{'t}, \mathit{'x})\ tpool \Rightarrow (\mathit{'t}, \mathit{'x}, \mathit{'h})\ new\text{-}thread\text{-}act \Rightarrow bool$
$ok\text{-}thr\ ts\ (Spawn\ t\ x\ m) \quad = free\text{-}thread\text{-}id\ ts\ t$
$ok\text{-}thr\ ts\ (ThreadEx\ t\ b) \quad = (b \neq free\text{-}thread\text{-}id\ ts\ t)$

$ok\text{-}thrs :: (\mathit{'l}, \mathit{'t}, \mathit{'x})\ tpool \Rightarrow (\mathit{'t}, \mathit{'x}, \mathit{'h})\ new\text{-}thread\text{-}act\ list \Rightarrow bool$
$ok\text{-}thrs\ ts\ [] \qquad\qquad\qquad = True$
$ok\text{-}thrs\ ts\ (nt \cdot nts) \qquad\quad = ok\text{-}thr\ ts\ nt \wedge ok\text{-}thrs\ (upd\text{-}thr\ ts\ nt)\ nts$

Figure 3.10: Preconditions for thread creation BTAs

Note that *Spawn t x m* has the same precondition as *ThreadEx t False*, which seems redundant at first sight. However, this redundancy simplifies the theorems and proofs because *Spawn* BTAs cannot override existing threads. Hence, I do not have to formalise that a thread action tests whether a thread *t* exists before it spawns *t*.

Condition actions Condition actions do not affect the multithreaded state. Hence, there are no update functions, but only predicates for the preconditions, see Figure 3.11. A thread *t* successfully joins on the thread *t'* iff

- *t'* has not yet been started, i.e., *thr s t = None*, or

- *t'* is not the executing thread itself, *t'* has been fully evaluated, not temporarily released any locks and is not in any wait set.

71

locale *final-thread* = fixes *final* :: $'x \Rightarrow bool$

$ok\text{-}cond$ :: $('l, 't, 'x, 'h, 'w)$ $state \Rightarrow 't \Rightarrow 't$ $condition\text{-}act \Rightarrow bool$
$ok\text{-}cond\ s\ t\ (Join\ t')$ =
   case thr s t' of None $\Rightarrow$ *True*
                | $\lfloor (x, ln) \rfloor \Rightarrow t \neq t' \wedge final\ x \wedge ln = K^f\ 0 \wedge wset\ s\ t' = None$
$ok\text{-}cond\ s\ t\ Yield$ = *True*

$ok\text{-}conds$ :: $('l, 't, 'x, 'h, 'w)$ $state \Rightarrow 't \Rightarrow 't$ $condition\text{-}act\ list \Rightarrow bool$
$ok\text{-}conds\ s\ t\ cas$ = $(\forall ca \in set\ cas.\ ok\text{-}cond\ s\ t\ ca)$

Figure 3.11: Predicates for condition actions

The predicate *final* on the thread-local state determines if t' has been fully evaluated. For modularity, *final* is an implicit parameter to *ok-cond* which source code and bytecode will instantiate (§3.2.2 and §3.2.3). In Isabelle, I use the locale declaration to hide the *final* parameter.

    The predicate *ok-conds* lifts *ok-cond* to lists *cas*. As there is no update function, it merely conjoins the preconditions of all actions in *cas*.

Wait set actions   For updating the wait sets, I define the relation $t \vdash ws = wa \Rightarrow ws'$ where t denotes the executing thread, ws and ws' the original and successor wait sets, and wa the wait set action to be executed. Unlike the other update functions, it is a relation, because *Notify w* non-deterministically picks one thread t' from the wait set.[10] The rules in Figure 3.12 implement the wait set automaton from Figure 3.3. For *Notify w*, the update relation removes one arbitrary thread t' from w if there is any. In contrast, *WakeUp t'* is deterministic as it removes t' from any wait set it has been suspended to. The BTAs *Notified* and *WokenUp* reset t''s wait set status to *None* for normal execution.

    As before, I lift $\_ \vdash \_ = \_ \Rightarrow \_$ to lists of BTAs. To that end, I define the reflexive, transitive closure r^{***} :: $'a \Rightarrow 'b\ list \Rightarrow 'a \Rightarrow bool$ of a ternary relation r :: $'a \Rightarrow 'b \Rightarrow 'a \Rightarrow bool$ as

$$r^{***}\ a\ [\,]\ a \qquad \frac{r^{***}\ a\ bs\ a' \qquad r\ a'\ b\ a''}{r^{***}\ a\ (bs\ @\ [b])\ a''}$$

---

[10]I model this as a non-deterministic relation rather than an underspecified function, using, e.g., Hilbert's choice operator, because the code generator cannot deal with this kind of underspecification (§6.4).

$$t \vdash ws = Suspend\, w \Rightarrow ws(t \mapsto InWS\, w)$$

$$\frac{ws\, t' = \lfloor InWS\, w \rfloor}{t \vdash ws = Notify\, w \Rightarrow ws(t' \mapsto WS\text{-}Notified)} \qquad \frac{\forall t'.\, ws\, t' \neq \lfloor InWS\, w \rfloor}{t \vdash ws = Notify\, w \Rightarrow ws}$$

$$t \vdash ws = NotifyAll\, w \Rightarrow$$
$$\lambda t.\, if\, ws\, t = \lfloor InWS\, w \rfloor\, then\, \lfloor WS\text{-}Notified \rfloor\, else\, ws\, t$$

$$\frac{ws\, t' = \lfloor InWS\, w \rfloor}{\begin{array}{c} t \vdash ws = WakeUp\, t' \Rightarrow \\ ws(t' \mapsto WS\text{-}WokenUp) \end{array}} \qquad \frac{\forall w.\, ws\, t' \neq \lfloor InWS\, w \rfloor}{t \vdash ws = WakeUp\, t' \Rightarrow ws}$$

$$t \vdash ws = Notified \Rightarrow ws(t := None) \qquad t \vdash ws = WokenUp \Rightarrow ws(t := None)$$

Figure 3.12: Update relation for wait sets

Then, $t \vdash \_ \, [=\_\Rightarrow] \, \_$ is the reflexive, transitive closure of $t \vdash \_ \, =\_\Rightarrow \, \_$, i.e., the former folds the latter over a list of wait set actions.

Unlike the other BTAs, the ones for wait sets do not have individual preconditions on the state. Rather, $\lfloor Notified \rfloor$ and $\lfloor WokenUp \rfloor$ characterise reductions of t that are meant to process notifications and interruptions. The predicate $ok\text{-}wsets$ formalises that such reductions require the wait set status to be $\lfloor WS\text{-}Notified \rfloor$ and $\lfloor WS\text{-}WokenUp \rfloor$, respectively, and all other reductions require the wait set status to be $None$.

> $ok\text{-}wsets\, ws\, t\, was =$
> $\quad if\, Notified \in set\, was\, then\, ws\, t = \lfloor WS\text{-}Notified \rfloor$
> $\quad else\, if\, WokenUp \in set\, was\, then\, ws\, t = \lfloor WS\text{-}WokenUp \rfloor$
> $\quad else\, ws\, t = None$

In particular, the rules for $\_ \vdash \_ = Notified \Rightarrow \_$ and $\_ \vdash \_ = WokenUp \Rightarrow \_$ in Figure 3.12 are applicable unconditionally.

Interrupt actions Figure 3.13 defines the update functions $upd\text{-}int$ and $upd\text{-}ints$ and predicates $ok\text{-}intr$ and $ok\text{-}intrs$ for interrupt actions. The interleaving semantics merely manages the set of interrupts, but it attaches no specific behaviour to them, nor does it impose any form of

$upd\text{-}int :: {}'t\ intrs \Rightarrow {}'t\ intr\text{-}act \Rightarrow {}'t\ intrs$
$upd\text{-}int\ is\ (Intr\ t) \qquad = is \cup \{t\}$
$upd\text{-}int\ is\ (ClearIntr\ t) = is - \{t\}$
$upd\text{-}int\ is\ (IsIntrd\ t\ b) \quad = is$

$upd\text{-}ints :: {}'t\ intrs \Rightarrow {}'t\ intr\text{-}act\ list \Rightarrow {}'t\ intrs$
$upd\text{-}ints\ is\ [] \qquad\qquad = is$
$upd\text{-}ints\ is\ (ia \cdot ias) \qquad = upd\text{-}ints\ (upd\text{-}int\ is\ ia)\ ias$

$ok\text{-}intr :: {}'t\ intrs \Rightarrow {}'t\ intr\text{-}act \Rightarrow bool$
$ok\text{-}intr\ is\ (IsIntrd\ t\ b) \quad = (b = (t \in is))$
$ok\text{-}intr\ is\ (Intr\ t) \qquad\quad = True$
$ok\text{-}intr\ is\ (ClearIntr\ t) \ = True$

$ok\text{-}intrs :: {}'t\ intrs \Rightarrow {}'t\ intr\text{-}act\ list \Rightarrow bool$
$ok\text{-}intrs\ is\ [] \qquad\qquad\quad = True$
$ok\text{-}intrs\ is\ (ia \cdot ias) \qquad = ok\text{-}intr\ is\ ia \wedge ok\text{-}intrs\ (upd\text{-}int\ is\ ia)\ ias$

Figure 3.13: Update functions and predicates for interruption BTAs

access control. Note that *Intr* and *ClearIntr* have no preconditions, they can change the interrupts of any thread, even non-existing ones. *IsIntrd* tests for pending interrupts similar to *ThreadEx* for thread existence.

As all BTAs in a thread action must be checked and executed in one step, it is straight-forward to implement a compare-and-swap operation on the interrupt status: For example, $(IsIntrd\ t\ True, ClearIntr\ t)$ checks that t is interrupted and clears it atomically.

Thread actions Now, I combine all the update functions and predicates for basic thread actions into a single one for thread actions. *ok-ta* checks the preconditions of all five groups, and *upd-ta* combines the update functions, except for *upd-TRL*, which the interleaving semantics will apply directly when it updates the thread-local state.

$ok\text{-}ta :: ({}'l,{}'t,{}'x,{}'h,{}'w)\ state \Rightarrow {}'t \Rightarrow ({}'l,{}'t,{}'x,{}'h,{}'w,{}'o)\ thread\text{-}action \Rightarrow bool$
$ok\text{-}ta\ s\ t\ ta = ok\text{-}locks\ (locks\ s)\ t\ \langle ta \rangle_l \wedge ok\text{-}thrs\ (thr\ s)\ \langle ta \rangle_t \wedge$
$\qquad\qquad ok\text{-}conds\ s\ t\ \langle ta \rangle_c \wedge ok\text{-}wsets\ (wset\ s)\ t\ \langle ta \rangle_w \wedge \qquad (3.1)$
$\qquad\qquad ok\text{-}intrs\ (intrs\ s)\ \langle ta \rangle_i$

$upd\text{-}ta :: ('l,'t,'x,'h,'w)\ state \Rightarrow 't \Rightarrow ('l,'t,'x,'h,'w,'o)\ thread\text{-}action$
$\Rightarrow ('l,'t,'x,'h,'w)\ state$

$$\frac{ls' = upd\text{-}locks\ ls\ t\ \langle ta \rangle_l \qquad ts' = upd\text{-}thrs\ ts\ \langle ta \rangle_t}{t \vdash ws\ [=\langle ta \rangle_w \Rightarrow]\ ws' \qquad is' = upd\text{-}ints\ is\ \langle ta \rangle_i}$$
$$upd\text{-}ta\ (ls,(ts,h),ws,is)\ t\ ta\ (ls',(ts',h),ws',is')$$

Design considerations

I have designed the basic thread actions such that each depends on and affects only one part of the state, if possible. This also guided the partitioning of the multithreaded state into five components. I store locks separately from threads because all threads need to access them. The locks that a thread has released temporarily, however, are local to the thread and thus stored together with its local state in the thread pool. As *Notify* and *WakeUp* modify the wait set status of other threads, the wait set status is split off the thread pool in a separate map. The interrupt status of a thread is like a global variable that all threads can access and modify. Thus, it could also have been part of the shared heap, which the single-threaded semantics manages. However, I model it explicitly in the interleaving semantics because interruption is relevant for deadlocks (see §3.3).

The multithreaded state must satisfy simultaneously the preconditions of all BTAs of which a thread action is composed. This is a powerful means to the single thread semantics to express preconditions for certain reductions. In fact, it is more expressive than what I need for Java threads. For example, no thread simultaneously joins on a thread and spawns a new thread. Thus, I am free to define the semantics of combining BTAs such that proofs are as modular and simple as possible. For example, the preconditions of the different parts of a thread action are checked independently on the original state (3.1).

3.1.3 Interleaving semantics

In this section, I put everything together that I have defined so far to obtain the interleaving semantics in the framework. It takes the single-threaded semantics as a parameter $r :: ('l,'t,'x,'h,'w,'o)\ semantics$ which source and bytecode will instantiate accordingly (§3.2).

$$\text{NORMAL} \quad \frac{\begin{array}{c} thr\ s\ t = \lfloor (x, \mathsf{K}^{\mathsf{f}}\ 0) \rfloor \qquad t \vdash (x, shr\ s) -ta\rightarrow (x', h') \\ ok\text{-}ta\ s\ t\ ta \qquad upd\text{-}ta\ s\ t\ ta\ (ls', (ts', h), ws', is') \\ s' = (ls', (ts'(t \mapsto (x', upd\text{-}TRL\ ls\ t\ (\mathsf{K}^{\mathsf{f}}\ 0)\ \langle ta\rangle_1)), h'), ws', is') \end{array}}{s -t{:}ta\rightarrow s'}$$

$$\text{ACQUIRE} \quad \frac{\begin{array}{c} thr\ s\ t = \lfloor (x, ln) \rfloor \qquad ln \neq \mathsf{K}^{\mathsf{f}}\ 0 \\ \neg\ waiting\ (wset\ s\ t) \qquad may\text{-}acquire\text{-}TRL\ (locks\ s)\ t\ ln \end{array}}{s -t{:}(\mathsf{K}^{\mathsf{f}}\ [],[],[],[],[], acq\text{-}events\ ln)\rightarrow upd\text{-}acq\ s\ t\ x\ ln}$$

Figure 3.14: Reductions in the interleaving semantics

type_synonym $('l, 't, 'x, 'h, 'w, 'o)$ *semantics* $=$
$'t \Rightarrow 'x \times 'h \Rightarrow ('l, 't, 'x, 'h, 'w, 'o)$ *thread-action* $\Rightarrow 'x \times 'h \Rightarrow bool$

In Isabelle, the locale *multithreaded-base* fixes the parameters *final* (inherited from *final-thread*), r, and *acq-events*:

locale *multithreaded-base* $=$ *final-thread* $+$
    fixes $r :: ('l, 't, 'x, 'h, 'w, 'o)$ *semantics* $(\_ \vdash \_ -\_\rightarrow \_)$ (3.2)
    and *acq-events* $:: 'l$ *tr-locks* $\Rightarrow 'o$ *list*

A single-step reduction $r\ t\ (x, h)\ ta\ (x', h')$ is written $t \vdash (x, h) -ta\rightarrow (x', h')$. It denotes that the thread with ID t can atomically reduce in the thread-local state x with shared heap h to the thread-local state x' with the new heap h' with thread action ta.

The last parameter *acq-events* of the locale produces the label (i.e., the sixth component of a thread action) for when a thread reacquires its temporarily released locks. Although these labels only become relevant in Chapter 4, I include them in the formalisation now such that I do not have to adapt the definitions later.

Figure 3.14 shows the definition of the atomic steps of the interleaving semantics *redT* (with syntax $s -t{:}ta\rightarrow s'$). The reductions of the interleaving semantics carry the ID t of the executing thread and the executed thread action ta as label.

NORMAL injects the atomic steps of the threads into the interleaving semantics. Given a thread t with local state x and without any temporarily released locks ($\mathsf{K}^{\mathsf{f}}\ 0$), if t can reduce with the shared heap *shr s* to x' and h' with thread action ta, the interleaving semantics tests whether

ta's preconditions are met and, if so, applies ta's effects to the state. In this new state, it updates t's local state to x' and its temporarily released locks, and the shared heap to h', which yields the successor state.

The other rule ACQUIRE reacquires the locks ln that a thread has temporarily released. Suppose t is a thread which has temporarily released some locks, i.e., $ln \neq K^f 0$, and is not in a wait set, i.e., $\neg waiting (wset\, s\, t)$. The predicate $may\text{-}acquire\text{-}TRL :: ('l, 't)\ locks \Rightarrow 't \Rightarrow 'l\ tr\text{-}locks \Rightarrow bool$ tests whether t may acquire all of its temporarily released locks.

$$may\text{-}acquire\text{-}TRL\ ls\ t\ ln = (\forall l.\ ln_f\ l > 0 \longrightarrow may\text{-}lock\ ls\ t\ l)$$

If so, $acquire\text{-}TRL :: ('l, 't)\ locks \Rightarrow 't \Rightarrow 'l\ tr\text{-}locks \Rightarrow ('l, 't)\ locks$ updates the lock state accordingly.

$$(acquire\text{-}TRL\ ls\ t\ ln)_f\ l = acquire\text{-}lock\ (ls_f\ l)\ t\ (ln_f\ l)$$

This produces the multithreaded state

$$(acquire\text{-}TRL\ (locks\ s)\ t\ ln, ((thr\ s)(t \mapsto (x, K^f\ 0)), shr\ s),$$
$$wset\ s, intrs\ s)$$

which I abbreviate as $upd\text{-}acq\ s\ t\ x\ ln$. Note that t's multiset of temporarily released locks is now empty. This reduction step carries as label the thread ID and a thread action without any BTAs, but the third parameter $acq\text{-}events$ of the locale determines the last component of the thread action – I will define it in §4.3.2.

Reductions in the reflexive and transitive closure $redT^{***}$ of the interleaving semantics are written as $s - ttas\rightarrow^* s'$. The list $ttas$, which has the type $('t \times ('l, 't, 'x, 'h, 'w, 'o)\ thread\text{-}action)\ list$, collects all the labels, i.e., thread ID and thread action, of the individual steps.

A thread is final iff its local state is $final$, its multiset of temporarily released locks is empty, and its wait set status is $None$, i.e., neither is it in a wait set, nor has it been removed from one without having processed the removal. $final\text{-}threads\ s$ denotes the set of all final threads in the multithreaded state s. s itself is final (written $mfinal\ s$) iff all threads are final.

$$\frac{thr\ s\ t = \lfloor (x, K^f\ 0) \rfloor \qquad final\ x \qquad wset\ s\ t = None}{t \in final\text{-}threads\ s}$$

$$mfinal\ s = (dom\ (thr\ s) \subseteq final\text{-}threads\ s)$$

The locale *multithreaded-base* imposes no assumptions on its parameters, but for the interleaving semantics to work correctly, the single-threaded semantics must be well-behaved. The locale *multithreaded* collects the most fundamental constraints.

locale *multithreaded* = *multithreaded-base* +
  assumes *final-no-red*: $[\![t \vdash (x,h) -ta\rightarrow (x',h'); \ final \ x]\!] \Longrightarrow False$
  and *Spawn-heap*:
    $[\![t \vdash (x,h) -ta\rightarrow (x',h'); \ Spawn \ t'' \ x'' \ h'' \in set \ \langle ta \rangle_t]\!] \Longrightarrow h'' = h'$

final-no-red expresses that *final* states are final, i.e., they cannot reduce any further. For proofs, it is convenient to remember the shared heap at the time when a thread is spawned (see §3.1.4 and §5.1.3). The assumption *Spawn-heap* imposes that the shared heap in the BTAs indeed remembers the shared heap at spawn time.

final-no-red also implies that *mfinal* states are final:

Lemma 3.1. *If mfinal s, then there are no t, ta, s' such that s −t:ta→ s'.*

3.1.4 Infrastructure for well-formedness constraints

Many theorems about the single-threaded semantics impose constraints on the state. For example, subject reduction (Theorem 2.2) requires conformance of the state, and progress (Theorem 2.1) requires definite assignment and heap conformance. For type safety, one must show that the semantics preserves these constraints (Lemmata 2.2 and 2.1 for state conformance and definite assignment, respectively). I now define the machinery to transfer such constraints and their preservation lemmata to the multithreaded semantics at little cost.

Thread-local predicates

Suppose that the predicate $Q :: {}'t \Rightarrow {}'x \Rightarrow {}'h \Rightarrow bool$ denotes such a constraint. The operator $\uparrow\_\uparrow$ lifts Q to a predicate of type $({}'l, {}'t, {}'x) \ tpool \Rightarrow {}'h \Rightarrow bool$ on the thread pool and shared heap such that $\uparrow Q \uparrow$ imposes Q on all threads in the thread pool.

$$\uparrow Q \uparrow ts \ h = (\forall t. \ case \ ts \ t \ of \ None \Rightarrow True \mid \lfloor (x, ln) \rfloor \Rightarrow Q \ t \ x \ h)$$

In the case of definite assignment, e.g., $Q = (\lambda t \ (e, xs) \ h. \ \mathcal{D} \ e \ \lfloor dom \ xs \rfloor)$, since the definite assignment check $\mathcal{D}$ (§2.1.4) only depends on the

locale *lifting-wf* = *multithreaded* +
  fixes $Q :: 't \Rightarrow 'x \Rightarrow 'h \Rightarrow bool$
  assumes *preserves-red*: $[\![t \vdash (x,h) -ta\rightarrow (x',h'); Q\ t\ x\ h]\!] \Longrightarrow Q\ t\ x'\ h'$
  and *preserves-Spawn*:
    $[\![t \vdash (x,h) -ta\rightarrow (x',h'); Q\ t\ x\ h; Spawn\ t''\ x''\ h' \in set\ \langle ta \rangle_t]\!]$
    $\Longrightarrow Q\ t''\ x''\ h'$
  and *preserves-other*:
    $[\![t \vdash (x,h) -ta\rightarrow (x',h'); Q\ t\ x\ h; Q\ t''\ x''\ h]\!] \Longrightarrow Q\ t''\ x''\ h'$

Figure 3.15: Definition of locale *lifting-wf*

thread-local state, which has type *expr* × *locals* in source code. Then, $\uparrow Q \uparrow\ ts\ h$ denotes that all threads in the thread pool *ts* assign to all local variables before they are used provided that all variables in the thread's local store have already been initialised.

To transfer the preservation lemma to the multithreaded state, I define the locale *lifting-wf* (see Figure 3.15). It fixes the constraint Q and assumes that

1. single-thread reductions preserves Q (*preserves-red*),

2. Q holds for new threads at the time of creation (*preserves-Spawn*), and

3. Q is preserved even if another thread, which also satisfies Q, changes the shared heap in a reduction (*preserves-other*).

Under these assumptions, the interleaving semantics preserves $\uparrow Q \uparrow$.

Lemma 3.2 (Preservation for $\uparrow\_\uparrow$). *Let* $\uparrow Q \uparrow\ (thr\ s)\ (shr\ s)$. *If* $s -t{:}ta\rightarrow s'$ *or* $s -ttas\rightarrow^* s'$, *then* $\uparrow Q \uparrow\ (thr\ s')\ (shr\ s')$, *too.*

Reconsider the definite assignment example. Lemma 2.1 discharges the first assumption of *lifting-wf*. As a spawned thread executes the *run* method of the associated *Thread* object, the well-formedness constraints for source code (§2.1.4) ensure *preserves-Spawn*. The last assumption *preserves-other* is vacuous for $\mathcal{D}$ because $\mathcal{D}$ does not depend on the heap.

Thread-local predicates with additional data

Some predicates on the thread level also need additional data, which is thread-specific, but invariant, e.g., a typing environment for the local store. I model such extra invariant data as maps from thread IDs to some type $'i$. Now, let $Q :: 'i \Rightarrow 't \Rightarrow 'x \Rightarrow 'h \Rightarrow bool$ also include the invariant data. The operator $\Uparrow Q \Uparrow$ lifts Q to thread pools similar to $\uparrow\_\uparrow$.

$$\Uparrow Q \Uparrow I \, ts \, h =$$
$$(\forall t. \, case \, ts \, t \, of \, None \Rightarrow True \mid \lfloor (x, ln) \rfloor \Rightarrow \exists i. \, I \, t = \lfloor i \rfloor \wedge Q \, i \, t \, x \, h)$$

where $I :: 't \rightharpoonup 'i$ is a map to invariant data. Such a map I is well-formed with respect to the thread pool ts (written $ts \vdash_i I$) iff their domains are equal.

In the case of state conformance from §2.1.6, for example, I stores the typing environment E for the thread's local store. Hence, the constraint is $\lambda E \, t \, (e, xs) \, h. \, P, E \vdash (h, xs) \sqrt{}$.

Let $I(nts \rightsquigarrow Q)$ denote the extension of I with invariant data for threads spawned in nts. For all $Spawn \, t \, x \, h \in set \, nts$, $I(nts \rightsquigarrow Q)$ updates I at t to $\varepsilon i. \, Q \, i \, t \, x \, h$.

$$
\begin{aligned}
I(&& [] \rightsquigarrow Q) &= I \\
I(\, Spawn \, t \, x \, h \cdot nts \rightsquigarrow Q) &= (I(t \mapsto \varepsilon i. \, Q \, i \, t \, x \, h))(nts \rightsquigarrow Q) && (3.3) \\
I(ThreadEx \, t \, b \cdot nts \rightsquigarrow Q) &= I(nts \rightsquigarrow Q)
\end{aligned}
$$

For labels $ttas$ of the reflexive and transitive closure $\_ - \_ \rightarrow^* \_$, let $I(ttas \, [\rightsquigarrow] \, Q)$ denote the extension

$$I(concat \, (map \, (\lambda(t, ta). \, \langle ta \rangle_t) \, ttas) \rightsquigarrow Q).$$

The term $map \, (\lambda(t, ta). \, \langle ta \rangle_t) \, ttas$ extracts all thread creation BTAs from $ttas$, $concat$ combines them in one list. The extension preserves well-formedness of maps to invariant data.

Lemma 3.3. *Suppose* $thr \, s \vdash_i I$. *If* $s - t{:}ta \rightarrow s'$, *then* $thr \, s' \vdash_i I(\langle ta \rangle_t \rightsquigarrow Q)$. *If* $s - ttas \rightarrow^* s'$, *then* $thr \, s' \vdash_i I(ttas \, [\rightsquigarrow] \, Q)$.

Equation 3.3 shows why it is necessary to remember the shared heap in $Spawn$ actions. $\_(\_ \rightsquigarrow Q)$ must know the heap at spawn time to choose the right invariant data, because it may depend on the heap at creation time. Since the transitive, reflexive closure discards the heaps of intermediate steps, I must store it in the thread actions.[11]

Similarly to *lifting-wf*, the locale *lifting-inv* collects the assumptions for lifting the preservation theorems. The main difference is that *lifting-inv* existentially quantifies over the invariant data for spawned threads. In fact, *lifting-wf* is just the special case of *lifting-inv* with the constraint instantiated to $\lambda\_.\ Q$.

locale *lifting-inv* = *multithreaded* +
  fixes $Q :: 'i \Rightarrow 't \Rightarrow 'x \Rightarrow 'h \Rightarrow bool$
  assumes $[\![t \vdash (x, h) -ta\rightarrow (x', h');\ Q\ i\ t\ x\ h]\!] \Longrightarrow Q\ i\ t\ x'\ h'$
  and $[\![t \vdash (x, h) -ta\rightarrow (x', h');\ Q\ i\ t\ x\ h;\ Spawn\ t''\ x''\ h' \in set\ \langle ta \rangle_t]\!]$
    $\Longrightarrow \exists i''.\ Q\ i''\ t''\ x''\ h'$
  and $[\![t \vdash (x, h) -ta\rightarrow (x', h');\ Q\ i\ t\ x\ h;\ Q\ i''\ t''\ x''\ h]\!] \Longrightarrow Q\ i''\ t''\ x''\ h'$

Analogous to Lemma 3.2, the next lemma shows that these assumptions are sufficient for the interleaving semantics preserving $\Uparrow Q \Uparrow$.

Lemma 3.4 (Preservation for $\Uparrow\_\Uparrow$). *Suppose that* $\Uparrow Q \Uparrow I\ (thr\ s)\ (shr\ s)$.

  (i) If $s -t{:}ta\rightarrow s'$, *then* $\Uparrow Q \Uparrow I(\langle ta \rangle_t \rightsquigarrow Q)\ (thr\ s')\ (shr\ s')$.

  (ii) If $s -ttas\rightarrow^* s'$, *then* $\Uparrow Q \Uparrow I(ttas\ [\rightsquigarrow]\ Q)\ (thr\ s')\ (shr\ s')$.

General invaraints

The above machinery works only for constraints that depend on the thread-local state and the shared heap only, but some lemmata need to impose constraints on the complete state. I have not developed any setup for such cases, but deal with them on a per-case basis. Nevertheless, I define a predicate *invariant* to succinctly express preservation for arbitrary ternary relations r and sets of states *invar*, i.e., that *invar* is r-closed:

$$invariant\ r\ invar = (\forall a\ b\ a'.\ a \in invar \longrightarrow r\ a\ b\ a' \longrightarrow a' \in invar)$$

Lemma 3.5. *Let* $a \in invar$ *and* invariant r invar. *If* $r\ a\ b\ a'$ *or* $r^{***}\ a\ bs\ a'$, *then* $a' \in invar$.

---

[11] Alternatively, one might try to choose the invariant data for spawned heaps w.r.t. to some underspecified intermediate heap. In that case, transitivity of $\_ -\_\rightarrow^*\_$ does not carry over to extensions because the possible intermediate heaps may change. But with the above approach, $I(nts\ @\ nts'\rightsquigarrow Q) = I(nts\rightsquigarrow Q)(nts'\rightsquigarrow Q)$ holds.

3.2   Multithreading in JinjaThreads

The framework for interleaving semantics from the previous section leaves the single-threaded semantics abstract. In this section, I define the single-threaded semantics for source code (§3.2.2) and bytecode (§3.2.3), which are adaptations and extensions of the sequential semantics from §2.1.5 and §2.2.2, respectively. They describe the full behaviour of a single thread, including all synchronisation and communication with other threads, e.g., via thread actions. Hence, I present how to implement Java concurrency in terms of thread actions. The multithreaded semantics of source code and bytecode specialises the framework for interleaving semantics with the respective single-threaded semantics. Since Java provides most synchronisation as native methods, I define them first (§3.2.1) such that source code and bytecode can share their implementation.

3.2.1   Native methods for synchronisation

This section concentrates on the multithreading features that Java provides via method calls. I implement them as native methods, reusing the formalism for native methods in sequential JinjaThreads from §2.1.3 and §2.1.5.

Signatures   I add to the signatures for native methods from (2.3) the signatures shown in Figure 3.16. The first group of four are the methods of *Thread* for (i) spawning (*start*), (ii) joining on (*join*), (iii) interrupting (*interrupt*), and (iv) testing for interruption (*isInterrupted*) of a thread.

The second group of methods consists of static methods in class *Thread* in Java. Since JinjaThreads lacks static methods, I moved them to class *Object* such that they can be called from every method via the *this* pointer.[12] They all operate on the current thread: *currentThread* returns the associated object, *interrupted* checks and clears the interrupt status, and *yield* advises the scheduler to schedule other threads if possible.

The last group declares *Object*'s methods for the wait-notify-mechanism.

---

[12]To ensure that this change does not affect method lookup, the method names *currentThread*, *interrupted*, and *yield* internally use characters that do not occur in normal Java method names.

$Thread.start([]) :: Void$
$Thread.join([]) :: Void$
$Thread.interrupt([]) :: Void$
$Thread.isInterrupted([]) :: Boolean$

$Object.currentThread([]) :: Class\ Thread$
$Object.interrupted([]) :: Boolean$
$Object.yield([]) :: Void$

$Object.wait([]) :: Void$
$Object.notify([]) :: Void$
$Object.notifyAll([]) :: Void$

Figure 3.16: Signatures of native methods for Java concurrency

Recording thread interaction Before I present the semantics for the new native methods, I define the sixth component (of type $'o\ list$ in the interleaving semantics) of thread actions, although they will become relevant only in Chapter 4. During this chapter, they may be safely ignored. I introduce them now to include them in the semantics rules such that I do not have to change them later on.

The JinjaThreads semantics instantiate $'o$ to the HOL type *event*, which records the heap operations and synchronisation events of a thread; Table 3.1 describes the elements. Although some of the synchronisation events are similar to BTAs, I keep them separate such that thread interactions for implementing correct interleaving are clearly distinguished from synchronisation that is relevant for the memory model. For example, *SUnlock* represents the effects of releasing a lock on the shared memory; these are independent of how often a thread actually releases the lock using *Unlock* or *Release* BTAs. For a detailed discussion, see §4.3.1 and §4.3.2.

Well-formedness Concurrency needs three additional system exceptions. Hence, I append *IllegalThreadState*, *IllegalMonitorState*, and *InterruptedException* to *sys-xcpts* from Equation 2.1. Consequently, generic well-formedness requires that every program declares them as subclasses of *Throwable* (cf. Figure 2.9). Moreover, *wf-syscls P* now also requires that P declare the class *Thread*, and *wf-cdecl* demands that

	event	description
heap	*Read a al v*	read *v* from member *al* of address *a*
	Write a al v	write *v* to member *al* of address *a*
	Allocate a hT	allocate address *a* for type information *hT*
	New-Obj a C	abbreviation for *Allocate a* (*ClassT C*)
	New-Arr a T n	abbreviation for *Allocate a* (*ArrayT T n*)
synchronisation	*TStart t*	spawn thread *t*
	TJoin t	join thread *t*
	SLock a	acquire lock *a* at least once
	SUnlock a	release lock *a* at least once
	TIntr t	interrupt thread *t*
	TIntrd t	determine that the thread *t* has been interrupted
	Extern a M vs v	call to external method *M* on *a* with parameters *vs* and return value *v*, e.g., for printing

Table 3.1: Events record memory and synchronisation operations of a thread

Thread declare a *run* method without parameters and with return type *Void*, i.e.,

$$C = Thread \longrightarrow (\exists m. \ (run, [], Void, m) \in set \ ms)$$

is added conjunctively to *wf-cdecl wf-md P* (*C, D, fs, ms*) in Figure 2.9.

Semantics   To implement the new native methods, I extend the semantics for native methods $P, t \vdash \langle a.M(vs), h \rangle \ -ta\rightarrow_{nc} \langle va, h' \rangle$. Note that the semantics now takes the thread ID *t* of the executing thread as an additional parameter and carries a thread action *ta* as label. The former rules from Figure 2.12 are adapted accordingly. They also take the thread ID, but ignore it; their thread action label only records the heap interaction (see §4.1.2 for details), i.e., it is of the form $\langle\!| \ldots |\!\rangle$ where ... is a list of *events*.

Now, I must also specify how source code and bytecode instantiate type variables in the interleaving semantics. Addresses (HOL type *addr*) identify locks (type variable *'l*) and wait sets (*'w*), because every object has one monitor and one wait set. The heap becomes the shared memory (*'h*). For thread IDs (*'t*), I use the opaque type *thread-id* with the operations *a2t :: addr* $\Rightarrow$ *thread-id* and *t2a :: thread-id* $\Rightarrow$ *addr* for now – later, thread IDs and addresses will be the same (§4.2, §4.3.2). $a2t$ converts addresses of objects of (subclasses of) *Thread* into their associated thread ID, and $t2a$ is $a2t$'s left inverse on addresses at which such objects may be allocated.[13] I defer instantiating the thread-local state ($'x$) because it differs between source code and bytecode.

The JLS specifies the native methods from Figure 3.16 only incompletely or not at all. Hence, I relied on the Java API [76] and, in case the JLS and API are ambiguous, on test runs of the Java HotSpot VM, version 1.6.0_22. The latter cases are marked as such.

Figure 3.17 shows the rules for the native methods of *Thread*, all of which carry the preconditions $typeof\text{-}addr\ h\ a\ =\ \lfloor ClassT\ C\rfloor$, $P \vdash C \preceq^*$ *Thread*, and – except for STARTFAIL and JOININTR – $t' = a2t\ a$. I have omitted them for conciseness.

Rule START spawns a new thread which is associated with the receiver object. The new thread is to execute the *run* method of the receiver object. Since both source code and bytecode build on the semantics of native methods, START cannot include the concrete initial state of the new thread in the *Spawn* BTA, because their state representations differ. Instead, it specifies to execute (without parameters) the *run* method that class C sees with receiver object a. The semantics for source code and bytecode has to convert this into the state representation as required. If the thread has already been started, STARTFAIL raises an *IllegalThreadState* exception.

The *join* method waits for the receiver thread to terminate, so JOIN includes the basic thread action *Join* t' where $t' = a2t\ a$. However, the API specifies that *join* first has to test whether the current thread t has not been interrupted. Otherwise, it raises an *InterruptedException* (JOININTR). Note that the interleaving semantics picks the reductions JOIN or JOININTR only if their thread action's precondition is satisfied. In particular, if t' is not *final* and t is not interrupted, the call to *join* gets stuck until either t' terminates or t gets interrupted.

Although the implementation of class *Thread* in Sun's and Oracle's JDK SE 6 declares (and has always declared in previous versions) the methods *start* and *join* as synchronized, neither the JLS nor the API require this. Hence, none of the rules for *start* and *join* includes *Lock* and *Unlock* actions, because such synchronisation would erroneously hide data races, which the Java memory model in §4.3 is about.

---

[13]This restriction may seem overly complicated, because any object may be allocated at any address in the current heap model (see §2.1.5). However, it is relevant for more elaborated ones, e.g., when addresses store the thread's ID that allocated it.

START: $\quad P, t \vdash \langle a.start([]), h \rangle - (\!|Spawn\ t'\ (C, run, a)\ h, TStart\ t'|\!) \rightarrow_{nc}$
$\quad\quad\quad \langle Ret\text{-}Val\ Unit, h \rangle$

STARTFAIL: $\quad P, t \vdash \langle a.start([]), h \rangle - (\!|ThreadEx\ (a2t\ a)\ True|\!) \rightarrow_{nc}$
$\quad\quad\quad \langle Ret\text{-}sys\text{-}xcpt\ IllegalThreadState, h \rangle$

JOIN: $\quad P, t \vdash \langle a.join([]), h \rangle - (\!|Join\ t', IsIntrd\ t\ False, TJoin\ t'|\!) \rightarrow_{nc}$
$\quad\quad\quad \langle Ret\text{-}Val\ Unit, h \rangle$

JOININTR: $\quad P, t \vdash \langle a.join([]), h \rangle - (\!|IsIntrd\ t\ True, ClearIntr\ t, TIntrd\ t|\!) \rightarrow_{nc}$
$\quad\quad\quad \langle Ret\text{-}sys\text{-}xcpt\ InterruptedException, h \rangle$

INTR: $\quad P, t \vdash \langle a.interrupt([]), h \rangle$
$\quad\quad\quad - (\!|ThreadEx\ t'\ True, WakeUp\ t', Intr\ t', TIntr\ t'|\!) \rightarrow_{nc}$
$\quad\quad\quad \langle Ret\text{-}Val\ Unit, h \rangle$

INTRINEX: $\quad P, t \vdash \langle a.interrupt([]), h \rangle - (\!|ThreadEx\ t'\ False|\!) \rightarrow_{nc}$
$\quad\quad\quad \langle Ret\text{-}Val\ Unit, h \rangle$

ISINTRDT: $\quad P, t \vdash \langle a.isInterrupted([]), h \rangle - (\!|IsIntrd\ t'\ True, TIntrd\ t'|\!) \rightarrow_{nc}$
$\quad\quad\quad \langle Ret\text{-}Val\ (Bool\ True), h \rangle$

ISINTRDF: $\quad P, t \vdash \langle a.isInterrupted([]), h \rangle - (\!|IsIntrd\ t'\ False|\!) \rightarrow_{nc}$
$\quad\quad\quad \langle Ret\text{-}Val\ (Bool\ False), h \rangle$

Figure 3.17: Semantics of native methods of class *Thread*. All rules additionally have the premises *typeof-addr h a* $= \lfloor ClassT\ C \rfloor$, $P \vdash C \leq^* Thread$, and – except for STARTFAIL and JOININTR – $t' = a2t\ a$.

When a thread interrupts another thread t' through the *interrupt* method (INTR), t' is removed from any wait set (BTA *WakeUp* t') and its interrupt status is set (BTA *Intr* t'), if t' already exists as a thread in the thread pool (BTA *ThreadEx* t' *True*). However, if t' is merely a *Thread* object which has not yet been started, the call to *interrupt* has no effect (INTRINEX). The *isInterrupted* method returns the interrupt status of the receiver thread $t' = a2t\ a$ (ISINTRDT and ISINTRDF).

Figure 3.18 shows the rules for static native methods of *Thread*. A call to *currentThread* returns the address of the object associated with the current thread (CURRTH). It uses the function *t2a* to convert the thread ID t into the address of the associated object. The *interrupted* method returns and clears the interrupt status of the executing thread (INTRDT

86

CURRTH: $P, t \vdash \langle a.currentThread([\,]), h \rangle - (\!|\,|\!) \to_{nc}$
$\langle Ret\text{-}Val\,(Addr\,(t2a\,t)), h \rangle$

INTRDT: $P, t \vdash \langle a.interrupted([\,]), h \rangle$
$- (\!|IsIntrd\,t\,True, ClearIntr\,t, TIntrd\,t|\!) \to_{nc}$
$\langle Ret\text{-}Val\,(Bool\,True), h \rangle$

INTRDF: $P, t \vdash \langle a.interrupted([\,]), h \rangle - (\!|IsIntrd\,t\,False|\!) \to_{nc}$
$\langle Ret\text{-}Val\,(Bool\,False), h \rangle$

YIELD: $P, t \vdash \langle a.yield([\,]), h \rangle - (\!|Yield|\!) \to_{nc} \langle Ret\text{-}Val\,Unit, h \rangle$

Figure 3.18: Static native methods of *Thread*, implemented as methods of *Object*

and INTRDF). Calling *yield* simply emits the BTA *Yield* (YIELD), which tells the scheduler to schedule another thread.

The rules for *wait*, *notify*, and *notifyAll* are more complicated (Figure 3.19). I start with *notify* and *notifyAll*. A call to either of them first tests via $Unlock \to a$, $Lock \to a$ whether the current thread has locked the receiver object's monitor a, without changing a's lock state. If so, it emits the BTA *Notify a* or *NotifyAll a*, respectively (NTF and NTFALL). Otherwise, $UnlockFail \to a$ checks that the thread does not hold the lock; rules NTFFAIL and NTFALLFAIL then raise an *IllegalMonitorState* exception.

I now explain the rules for *wait* from Figure 3.19 by going through Figure 3.20. It shows the individual steps to execute the call to *wait* as state transitions. Every state is defined by four relevant components which the legend at the bottom explains. The transitions are labelled by the rules that generate them – solid lines are t's steps, dashed lines denote reductions of other threads. From the three inital states at the top, the transitions lead to what the call returns, i.e., *Unit* or a system exception. Note how the transitions from the initial state in the centre step through the wait set automaton from Figure 3.3.

If the thread does not hold the lock on a (top left state), WAITFAIL raises an *IllegalMonitorState* exception. If t does hold the lock, *wait* tests whether t has a pending interrupt.[14] If so (top right state), WAITINTRD1 clears it and raises an *InterruptedException*.

---

[14]Neither the JLS [56, Ch. 17.8] nor the Java API [76] specify whether *wait* first tests for interrupts or for the lock on the monitor. JinjaThreads follows the HotSpot VM, which tests for the lock state first.

NTF: $P, t \vdash \langle a.notify([\,]), h \rangle - (\!|Unlock{\rightarrow}a, Lock{\rightarrow}a, Notify\ a|\!) {\rightarrow}_{nc}$
$\langle Ret\text{-}Val\ Unit, h \rangle$

NTFFAIL: $P, t \vdash \langle a.notify([\,]), h \rangle - (\!|UnlockFail{\rightarrow}a|\!) {\rightarrow}_{nc}$
$\langle Ret\text{-}sys\text{-}xcpt\ IllegalMonitorState, h \rangle$

NTFALL: $P, t \vdash \langle a.notifyAll([\,]), h \rangle$
$- (\!|Unlock{\rightarrow}a, Lock{\rightarrow}a, NotifyAll\ a|\!) {\rightarrow}_{nc}$
$\langle Ret\text{-}Val\ Unit, h \rangle$

NTFALLFAIL: $P, t \vdash \langle a.notifyAll([\,]), h \rangle - (\!|UnlockFail{\rightarrow}a|\!) {\rightarrow}_{nc}$
$\langle Ret\text{-}sys\text{-}xcpt\ IllegalMonitorState, h \rangle$

WAITFAIL: $P, t \vdash \langle a.wait([\,]), h \rangle - (\!|UnlockFail{\rightarrow}a|\!) {\rightarrow}_{nc}$
$\langle Ret\text{-}sys\text{-}xcpt\ IllegalMonitorState, h \rangle$

WAITINTRD1: $P, t \vdash \langle a.wait([\,]), h \rangle$
$- (\!|Unlock{\rightarrow}a, Lock{\rightarrow}a,$
$IsIntrd\ t\ True, ClearIntr\ t, TIntrd\ t|\!) {\rightarrow}_{nc}$
$\langle Ret\text{-}sys\text{-}xcpt\ InterruptedException, h \rangle$

WAIT: $P, t \vdash \langle a.wait([\,]), h \rangle$
$- (\!|Suspend\ a, Unlock{\rightarrow}a, Lock{\rightarrow}a, Release{\rightarrow}a,$
$IsIntrd\ t\ False, SUnlock\ a|\!) {\rightarrow}_{nc}$
$\langle Ret\text{-}Unchanged, h \rangle$

WAITNTFD: $P, t \vdash \langle a.wait([\,]), h \rangle - (\!|Notified|\!) {\rightarrow}_{nc} \langle Ret\text{-}Val\ Unit, h \rangle$

WAITINTRD2: $P, t \vdash \langle a.wait([\,]), h \rangle - (\!|WokenUp, ClearIntr\ t, TIntrd\ t|\!) {\rightarrow}_{nc}$
$\langle Ret\text{-}sys\text{-}xcpt\ InterruptedException, h \rangle$

Figure 3.19: Semantics of the native methods *wait*, *notify*, and *notifyAll*

Otherwise, the thread is in the top state in the centre, i.e., t holds the lock on a, it has not temporarily released any locks, its wait set status is *None* and it is not interrupted. Then, WAIT suspends t to a's wait set and temporarily releases all locks on a. Whether t will be interrupted or notified determines whether *wait* should return normally or raise an *InterruptedException*. As this is still indeterminate at this point of time, I extend the return values for native method calls with the special token *Ret-Unchanged*, which WAIT returns. The semantics of *Ret-Unchanged*

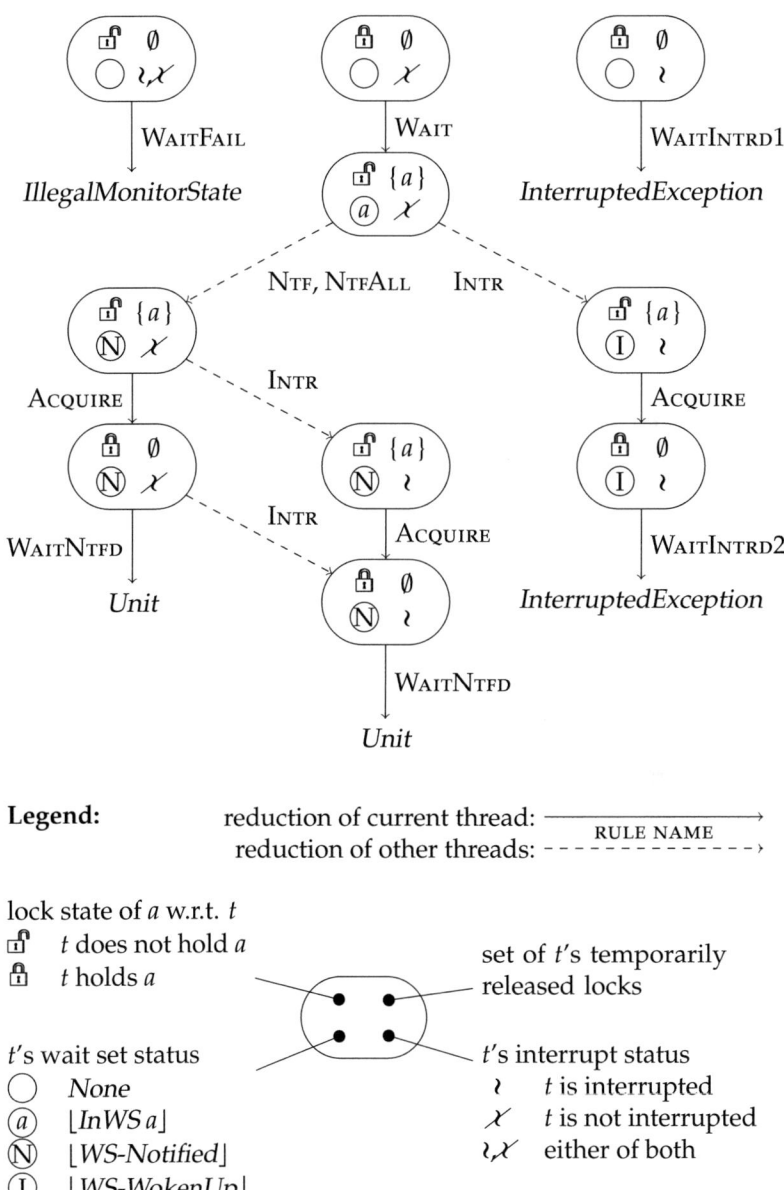

Legend: reduction of current thread: ——RULE NAME——→
reduction of other threads: - - - - - - - - - - - →

lock state of a w.r.t. t
🔓 t does not hold a
🔒 t holds a

set of t's temporarily released locks

t's wait set status
○ None
ⓐ ⌊InWS a⌋
Ⓝ ⌊WS-Notified⌋
Ⓘ ⌊WS-WokenUp⌋

t's interrupt status
ι t is interrupted
✗ t is not interrupted
ι,✗ either of both

Figure 3.20: Steps for t executing a call to *wait* on object a

is that the thread's next step should be to call the same method with the same parameters once more. This allows to effectively split the call to *wait* into two steps. Since WAIT suspends t to the wait set a, the interleaving semantics expects t to process its removal from the wait set in its next reduction, which must be tagged with the BTA *Notified* and *WokenUp*, respectively.

However, the interleaving semantics only picks one of t's reductions after it has been removed from the wait set and reacquired the locks on a. Hence, when another thread calls *notify* or *notifyAll* on a, or *interrupt* on t, t is removed from the wait set a (cf. Figure 3.3).[15] Note that this determines the result of the call to *wait*. Now, t's next step is to reacquire the locks on a. There is no need to add a rule for that to t's semantics because ACQUIRE of the interleaving semantics takes care of this.

Next, the second call to *wait* must process t's removal from the wait set, which WAITNTFD and WAITINTRD2 implement. The latter also clears t's interrupt status as required by the JLS [56, §17.8.1]. Note that another thread may interrupt t after t is has been notified, but before WAITNTFD processes t's removal. In that case, the call to *wait* returns normally and t's interrupt status is still set.

Interaction of interruption and notification JinjaThreads follows the JLS on the interaction between interruption and notification. Suppose the thread t in a wait set a is notified and interrupted "simultaneously". Then, it may either return normally with its interrupt status set, or raise an *InterruptedException*. In the second case, the notification must not be lost, i.e., all other threads in the wait set must return with an *InterruptedException* or one of them gets notified.

JinjaThreads meets this requirement as follows: Notifications use the BTA *Notify* or *NotifyAll*, interrupts use *WakeUp* (INTR). Hence, the interleaving semantics remembers how a thread has been removed in the wait set status $\lfloor WS\text{-}Notified \rfloor$ and $\lfloor WS\text{-}WokenUp \rfloor$, respectively (cf. Figures 3.3 and 3.20). This already determines whether WAITNTFD or WAITINTRD2 will process the removal, i.e., whether *wait* returns normally or throws an *InterruptedException*. In particular, WAITNTFD and WAITINTRD2 do not depend on the interrupt status at the time when they execute.

---

[15]If a's wait set contains multiple threads, the interleaving semantics may pick a thread different from t to be removed upon the call to *notify*.

Otherwise, if they did and the two wait set states $\lfloor WS\text{-}Notified \rfloor$ and $\lfloor WS\text{-}WokenUp \rfloor$ were merged, notifications could be lost. Suppose, for example, two threads t_1 and t_2 are in a wait set w and another thread calls $notify$ on a, which removes t_1. While t_1 waits to reacquire the locks on a, another thread interrupts t_1 (the INTR transistions from left to centre in Figure 3.20). In the above scenario, these states would be merged with the ones on the right. Hence, when t_1 processes its removal, its interrupt status has been set, i.e., it raises an $InterruptedException$. But now, the notification is lost, because t_2 remains in the wait set. This violates the above requirement.

The JLS also requires that any implementation must determine an order over the concurrent notification and interruption – which does not have to be consistent with other orderings – and behave accordingly [56, §17.8.1]. In JinjaThreads, the interleaving of threads automatically defines an order on notifications (BTA $Notify$ and $NotifyAll$) and interrupts (BTA $WakeUp$) from different threads which is consistent with all other orderings. If a single thread could issue notifications and interrupts in one step, these would be ordered by their position in the thread action. For example, $\langle\!\langle Notify\ a, WakeUp\ t\rangle\!\rangle$ orders the notification before the interrupt, and in $\langle\!\langle WakeUp\ t, Notify\ a\rangle\!\rangle$, the interrupt precedes the notification.

3.2.2 Source code

In the previous section, I have implemented native methods that deal with most of Java concurrency. Now, I define the single-threaded semantics for concurrency and extend the source code language J with synchronized statements. With this semantics, I instantiate the interleaving semantics from §3.1.3 to obtain J's interleaving semantics.

Adaptations to sequential JinjaThreads

Similarly to the semantics for native methods in the previous section, the semantics $P, t \vdash \langle e, (h, xs)\rangle - ta \rightarrow \langle e', (h', xs')\rangle$ of single threads for J adapts the small step semantics $P \vdash \langle e, (h, xs)\rangle \rightarrow \langle e', (h', xs')\rangle$. First, it takes the thread ID t as a parameter. Second, every reduction is labelled by a thread action. None of the existing rules – except for RNATIVE for native methods – issues BTAs of their own. Instead, rules for subexpression reduction propagate the label, and all others carry the empty thread action $(\emptyset)$.[16] For example, ROBJ and RCALLN now are as follows; the additions are highlighted in grey.

ROBJ:
$$\frac{P, t \vdash \langle e, s \rangle - ta \rightarrow \langle e', s' \rangle}{P, t \vdash \langle e.M(es), s \rangle - ta \rightarrow \langle e'.M(es), s' \rangle}$$

RCALLN: $P, t \vdash \langle null.M(es), s \rangle - (\emptyset) \rightarrow \langle THROW\ NullPointer, s \rangle$

Beyond the above changes, I have to adapt the rule RNATIVE for native method calls to the changes in §3.2.1 as follows:

RNATIVE:
$$\frac{\begin{array}{c} typeof\text{-}addr\ h\ a = \lfloor hT \rfloor \\ P \vdash class\text{-}of'\ hT\ sees\ M{:}Ts{\rightarrow}T_r = Native\ in\ D \\ P, t \vdash \langle a.M(vs), h \rangle - ta \rightarrow_{nc} \langle vx, h' \rangle \qquad ta' = native\text{-}TA2J\ P\ ta \\ e' = native\text{-}Ret2J\ (addr\ a.M(map\ Val\ vs))\ vx \end{array}}{P, t \vdash \langle addr\ a.M(map\ Val\ vs), (h, xs) \rangle - ta' \rightarrow \langle e', (h', xs) \rangle}$$

Remember that native-Ret2J converts the returned value or exception into J syntax. To deal with the new return token Ret-Unchanged, it now takes another parameter of type expr that it returns for Ret-Unchanged and ignores otherwise. Moreover, the local state of newly spawned threads in the thread action ta of the native call must be adapted to the state representation in J. To that end, native-TA2J P ta applies the conversion function native-BTA2J P to all local states (C, M, a) of all Spawn BTAs in ta. native-BTA2J P (C, M, a) looks up the parameter-less method M for class C and wraps its body in a block for the this pointer initialised to a, similarly to the rule RCALL for method calls. It leaves the local store undefined for all variables.

$$\begin{aligned} native\text{-}BTA2J\ &P\ (C, M, a) = \\ &let\ (D, \_, \_, m) = method\ P\ C\ M;\ \lfloor (\_, body) \rfloor = m \\ &in\ (\{this{:}\ Class\ D = \lfloor Addr\ a \rfloor; body\}, empty)) \end{aligned} \qquad (3.4)$$

The synchronized statement

Java has only a single statement for concurrency, namely synchronized. Everything else is provided as native methods, see §3.2.1. Hence, I

---

[16]Except for rules that access the heap, i.e., object and array allocation, field and array cell access. These rules record their accesses in the sixth component using the heap events from Table 3.1. As these only become relevant in Chapter 4, I discuss them there.

expression	description
$sync\ (e_1)\ e_2$	lock monitor e_1 for executing block e_2
$insync\ (a)\ e$	execute block e while having locked monitor a

Table 3.2: Expressions for synchronized statements

extend the abstract syntax of J (see Table 2.1) with the expressions shown in Table 3.2.

$sync\ (e_1)\ e_2$ models Java's synchronized statements, as specified in [56, §14.19]. It acquires the monitor e_1 first, then executes e_2, and finally releases the monitor. To remember that a synchronized statement has already acquired the monitor, I use the expression $insync\ (a)\ e$ instead of $sync\ (addr\ a)\ e$, which is not part of the input language. JinjaThreads does not model synchronized methods explicitly, because they are syntactic sugar for ordinary methods with their whole body inside a synchronized statement.

There is only one typing rule WTSYNC for $sync\ (\_)\ \_$ statements.

$$\text{WTSYNC:}\quad \frac{P,E \vdash e_1 :: T_1 \qquad \textit{is-refT}\ T_1 \qquad T_1 \neq NT \qquad P,E \vdash e_2 :: T}{P,E \vdash sync\ (e_1)\ e_2 :: T}$$

The monitor expression e_1 must have a reference type, but not NT. The return type of $sync\ (e_1)\ e_2$ is e_2's type. Similar to $try\ \_\ catch(\_\ \_)\ \_$, $sync\ (e_1)\ e_2$ generalises the synchronized statement to arbitrary expressions,. This is necessary to treat synchronized methods – which may return a value – as syntactic sugar for $sync\ (this)\ \_$ around their body. As $insync\ (\_)\ \_$ must not occur in programs, there is no typing rule for it.

Figure 3.21 shows the new reduction rules for synchronized blocks. RSYNC1 reduces the monitor subexpression. If the monitor subexpression becomes $null$, a $NullPointer$ exception is raised (RSYNCN). If an exception is raised while reducing the monitor subexpression, RSYNCX propagates the same exception. If the monitor subexpression reduces to some monitor address a, the thread can only reduce further by acquiring the lock on a. In that case, RLOCK rewrites the $sync\ (addr\ a)\ e$ expression to $insync\ (a)\ e$ to remember that the lock has been granted. Then, RSYNC2 executes the body. Once it has become a value or raised an

RSYNC1: $$\frac{P,t \vdash \langle e_1, s\rangle -ta\rightarrow \langle e_1', s'\rangle}{P,t \vdash \langle sync\ (e_1)\ e_2, s\rangle -ta\rightarrow \langle sync\ (e_1')\ e_2, s'\rangle}$$

RSYNCN: $P,t \vdash \langle sync\ (null)\ e, s\rangle -\langle\!\langle\rangle\!\rangle\rightarrow \langle THROW\ NullPointer, s\rangle$

RSYNCX: $P,t \vdash \langle sync\ (Throw\ a)\ e, s\rangle -\langle\!\langle\rangle\!\rangle\rightarrow \langle Throw\ a, s\rangle$

RLOCK: $P,t \vdash \langle sync\ (addr\ a)\ e, s\rangle$
$-\langle\!\langle Lock\rightarrow a, SLock\ a\rangle\!\rangle\rightarrow \langle insync\ (a)\ e, s\rangle$

RSYNC2: $$\frac{P,t \vdash \langle e, s\rangle -ta\rightarrow \langle e', s'\rangle}{P,t \vdash \langle insync\ (a)\ e, s\rangle -ta\rightarrow \langle insync\ (a)\ e', s'\rangle}$$

RUNLCK: $P,t \vdash \langle insync\ (a)\ (Val\ v), s\rangle$
$-\langle\!\langle Unlock\rightarrow a, SUnlock\ a\rangle\!\rangle\rightarrow \langle Val\ v, s\rangle$

RUNLCKX: $P,t \vdash \langle insync\ (a)\ (Throw\ a'), s\rangle$
$-\langle\!\langle Unlock\rightarrow a, SUnlock\ a\rangle\!\rangle\rightarrow \langle Throw\ a', s\rangle$

Figure 3.21: Semantics of synchronized blocks

exception, RUNLCK and RUNLCKX unlock the monitor, and return the value or propagate the exception, respectively.

Note that it is not necessary to explicitly release (and later reacquire) the monitor a when the body e of $insync\ (a)\ e$ calls $wait$ on a. The basic thread action $Release$ in WAIT and temporarily released locks in the interleaving semantics (cf. ACQUIRE) take care of this.

Interleaving semantics

In §3.2.1, I have already specified how the type variables in the interleaving semantics get instantiated for JinjaThreads source code and bytecode. Now, I fill in the missing details for thread-local states and the parameters of the locales. For J, the local state (type variable $'x$) consists of an expression and the local store, i.e., $expr \times locals$.

To instantiate the locale $multithreaded\text{-}base$ (3.2), I need some glue to adjust the parameter grouping, which is the price for not changing the original Jinja small-step semantics to syntactically match the format of the framework for interleaving.[17] *J-final* and *J-red P*, defined below, instantiate the parameters *final* and *r*. Since events are irrelevant for this chapter, I defer the definition of *acq-events* to Chapter 4.

$$J\text{-}final = (\lambda(e,xs).\ final\ e)$$
$$J\text{-}red\ P = (\lambda t\ ((e,xs),h)\ ta\ ((e',xs'),h').$$
$$P,t \vdash \langle e,(h,xs)\rangle -ta\rightarrow \langle e',(h',xs')\rangle)$$

By instantiating the locale, I also specialize the definitions in it. To distinguish them from the original definitions, I prefix them with *J.*, e.g., *J.redT* denotes *redT* with the above parameter instantiations. As *J-red* takes an additional parameter *P* for the program declaration, the specialised versions also take such a parameter if necessary, e.g., *J.redT P*. Analogous to §3.1.3, I write $P \vdash s -t:ta\rightarrow s'$ for a single step in the interleaving semantics *J.redT P*, and $P \vdash s -ttas\rightarrow^* s'$ for the reflexive and transitive closure $(J.redT\ P)^{***}$.

Lemma 3.6.
J-final and J-red P are well-formed with respect to the interleaving semantics.

Proof. I must show the assumptions of the locale *multithreaded* (cf. §3.1.3). *final-no-red* follows by case analysis of the rules. *Spawn-heap* holds by induction on the small step semantics and case analysis on the semantics for native methods. □

Start state

The start state *J-start P C M vs* for program *P* has exactly one thread *start-tID* with thread-local state

$$(blocks\ (this \cdot pns)\ (Class\ D \cdot Ts)\ (Null \cdot vs)\ body, empty)$$

where $(D, Ts, \_, \lfloor (pns, body) \rfloor) = method\ P\ C\ M$. Hence, *start-tID* is about to execute the non-native method *M* in class *C* with parameters *vs*.

---

[17]Modelling the interleaving semantics after the single-threaded semantics would have been no better alternative. Then, the interleaving semantics would be cluttered with glue code for splitting and composing pairs, because the thread local state would consist of two parts that I would have to store together to avoid additional invariants.

Setting the *this* pointer to *Null* simulates a static method.[18] The initial heap *start-heap* has preallocated a *Thread* object for *start-tID* and objects for all system exceptions. There are no locks held or temporarily released, all wait sets are empty and there are no interrupts. Formally:

$$J\text{-}start\ P\ C\ M\ vs =$$
$$(let\ (D, Ts, \_, m) = method\ P\ C\ M;\ \lfloor (pns, body) \rfloor = m$$
$$e = blocks\ (this \cdot pns)\ (Class\ D \cdot Ts)\ (Null \cdot vs)\ body$$
$$in\ (\mathrm{K}^{\mathrm{f}}None, ([start\text{-}tID \mapsto ((e, empty), \mathrm{K}^{\mathrm{f}}\ 0)], start\text{-}heap), empty, \emptyset))$$

A start state as specified by P, C, M, and vs is well-formed (written *wf-start P C M vs*) iff C sees a non-native method M and the parameters vs conform to M's parameter types in the *start-heap*.

3.2.3 Bytecode

In this section, I extend the single-threaded semantics for JinjaThreads bytecode to concurrency. As I use the interleaving semantics from §3.1 for bytecode, too, this section follows the same line as the previous for source code.

Adaptations to the sequential JinjaThreads VM

As the multithreading features are mostly hidden in native methods (§3.2.1), which source code and bytecode implement similarly, I adapt the JinjaThreads VM analogously to what I did for J:

1. The semantics functions *exec-native*, *exec-instr*, and *exec* now take the thread ID as parameter and return a set of pairs of thread action and successor state rather than just a set of successor states.

2. *native-Ret2jvm* also handles the return token *Ret-Unchanged*.

---

[18]Calling *Thread*'s static native methods like *yield* from the start method M becomes more complicated, because *Var this.yield*([]) (as §3.2.1 suggests) raises a *NullPointer* exception. Instead, they must be invoked on some other object. In practice, this is negligible since it only applies to the start method and the converter from Java to JinjaThreads (§6.5) wraps a method for bootstrapping around the actual main method. The same applies to the initial state for bytecode (§3.2.3).

$exec\text{-}instr\ (Invoke\ M'\ n)\ P\ t\ h\ stk\ loc\ C\ M\ pc\ frs =$
$(let\ ps = rev\ (take\ n\ stk);\ r = stk_{[n]};\ Addr\ a = r;\ \lfloor hT \rfloor = typeof\text{-}addr\ h\ a$
$\quad in\ if\ r = Null\ then$
$\qquad \{\ (\ \emptyset,\ \lfloor addr\text{-}of\text{-}sys\text{-}xcpt\ NullPointer \rfloor,h,(stk,loc,C,M,pc)\cdot frs)\ \}$
$\qquad else\ let\ (D,Ts,T_r,m) = method\ P\ (class\text{-}of'\ hT)\ M'$
$\qquad\quad in\ case\ m\ of\ Native \Rightarrow$
$\qquad\qquad \{\ (native\text{-}TA2jvm\ P\ ta,$
$\qquad\qquad\quad native\text{-}Ret2jvm\ n\ h'\ stk\ loc\ C\ M\ pc\ frs\ vx\ )\ |ta\ vx\ h'.$
$\qquad\qquad\quad (\ ta,\ vx,h') \in exec\text{-}native\ P\ t\ a\ M'\ ps\ h\ \}$
$\qquad\qquad |\ \lfloor (msl,mxl,ins,xt) \rfloor \Rightarrow$
$\qquad\qquad\quad let\ fr' = ([],r\cdot ps\ @\ replicate\ mxl\ undefined\text{-}Val,D,M',0)$
$\qquad\qquad\quad in\ \{\ (\ \emptyset,\ None,h,fr'\cdot(stk,loc,C,M,pc)\cdot frs)\ \})$

$exec\ P\ t\ (xcp,\quad h,\ []) \qquad\qquad\qquad\qquad = \emptyset$
$exec\ P\ t\ (None,h,(stk,loc,C,M,pc)\cdot frs) =$
$\qquad\qquad\qquad exec\text{-}instr\ (instrs\text{-}of\ P\ C\ M)_{[pc]}\ P\ t\ h\ stk\ loc\ C\ M\ pc\ frs$
$exec\ P\ t\ (\lfloor a \rfloor,\quad h,\ fr\cdot frs) \qquad\qquad\quad = \{\ (\ \emptyset,\ xcpt\text{-}step\ P\ a\ h\ fr\ frs\ )\ \}$

Figure 3.22: Adaptations to the single-step semantics for the VM

3. Analogous to *native-BTA2J*, the function *native-BTA2jvm* constructs the initial states of spawned threads. Then, the conversion function *native-TA2jvm P ta* applies *native-BTA2jvm P* to all spawned threads in *ta*.

$native\text{-}BTA2jvm\ P\ (C,M,a) =$
$\quad let\ (D,\_\,\_,m) = method\ P\ C\ M;\ \lfloor (mxs,mxl,ins,xt) \rfloor = m$
$\quad in\ (None,[([],Addr\ a\cdot replicate\ mxl\ undefined\text{-}Val,D,M,0)]))$

Figure 3.22 shows the updated definitions from Figures 2.17 and 2.18. I highlighted the additions in grey, everything else remains unchanged. In the same way, I adapt the defensive VM *execd P t s* and the relational views (notation $P, t \vdash s - ta \rightarrow_{jvm} s'$ and $P, t \vdash s - ta \rightarrow_{jvmd} s'$, respectively) to include the thread ID and the thread action.

instruction	description
MEnter	acquire lock on monitor
MExit	release lock on monitor

Table 3.3: Instructions for monitors

exec-instr MEnter P t h stk loc C M frs =
$(let\ v \cdot stk' = stk; Addr\ a = v$
$\ in\ if\ v = Null\ then$
$\quad \{\, (\langle\!\langle\rangle\!\rangle, \lfloor addr\text{-}of\text{-}sys\text{-}xcpt\ NullPointer\rfloor, h, (stk, loc, C, M, pc) \cdot frs)\,\}$
$\ else\ \{\, (\langle\!\langle Lock{\rightarrow}a, SLock\ a\rangle\!\rangle, None, h, (stk', loc, C, M, pc + 1) \cdot frs)\,\})$

exec-instr MExit P t h stk loc C M frs =
$(let\ v \cdot stk' = stk; Addr\ a = v$
$\ in\ if\ v = Null\ then$
$\quad \{\, (\langle\!\langle\rangle\!\rangle, \lfloor addr\text{-}of\text{-}sys\text{-}xcpt\ NullPointer\rfloor, h, (stk, loc, C, M, pc) \cdot frs)\,\}$
$\quad else$
$\qquad \{\, (\langle\!\langle Unlock{\rightarrow}a, SUnlock\ a\rangle\!\rangle, None, h, (stk', loc, C, M, pc + 1) \cdot frs),$
$\qquad\ (\langle\!\langle UnlockFail{\rightarrow}a\rangle\!\rangle, \lfloor addr\text{-}of\text{-}sys\text{-}xcpt\ IllegalMonitorState\rfloor,$
$\qquad\ h, (stk, loc, C, M, pc) \cdot frs)\,\})$

Figure 3.23: Semantics of the instructions for monitors

Instructions for monitors

Table 3.3 lists the new instructions *MEnter* and *MExit* for monitors. They are the bytecode equivalent of *sync* (_) _ blocks; they lock and unlock, respectively, the monitor whose address is at the top of the stack. Figure 3.23 defines their semantics.

If the value v on top of the stack is *Null*, they both raise a *NullPointer* exception. Otherwise, *MEnter* acquires the lock with the thread action $\langle\!\langle Lock{\rightarrow}a, SLock\ a\rangle\!\rangle$ where a is the address that v denotes. Note that the source code semantics uses the same thread action (RLOCK). *MExit* unlocks the monitor a with the thread action $\langle\!\langle Unlock{\rightarrow}a, SUnlock\ a\rangle\!\rangle$ just like RUNLCK. Unlike *sync* (_) _, locking and unlocking need not be structured in bytecode, i.e., *MEnter* and *MExit* need not come in pairs. Hence, *MExit* may also fail with an *IllegalMonitorState* exception if the current thread does not hold the monitor.

98

$$app_i\ (MEnter, P, (T \cdot ST, LT)) = is\text{-}refT\ T$$
$$app_i\ (MExit,\ \ P, (T \cdot ST, LT)) = is\text{-}refT\ T$$

$$eff_i\ (MEnter, P, (T \cdot ST, LT)) = (ST, LT)$$
$$eff_i\ (MExit,\ \ P, (T \cdot ST, LT)) = (ST, LT)$$

Figure 3.24: Applicability and effect for *MEnter* and *MExit*

For the well-typings and the bytecode verifier, Figure 3.24 defines the abstract interpretation of *MEnter* and *MExit* on the level of types (see §2.2.3). For both instructions, applicability requires that the stack is non-empty and the top element is a reference type, and the effect is dropping the top element.

Interleaving semantics

Bytecode instantiates the interleaving semantics twice, once for the aggressive VM and once for the defensive. The type variables are the same as for *J* – except for the thread-local states. For both the aggressive and defensive VM, a thread-local state consists of the exception flag and the call stack. Such a thread-local state is *jvm-final* iff the call stack is empty. Then, *jvm-exec P* and *jvm-execd P* instantiate parameter *r* of the locale *multithreaded-base* for the aggressive and defensive VM, respectively. Like for *J-red*, they require some glue to adjust the parameter grouping.

$$jvm\text{-}final = (\lambda(xcp, frs).\ frs = [])$$

$$jvm\text{-}exec\ P = (\lambda t\ ((xcp, frs), h)\ ta\ ((xcp', frs'), h').$$
$$P, t \vdash (xcp, h, frs)\ -ta \rightarrow_{jvm} (xcp', h', frs'))$$

$$jvm\text{-}execd\ P = (\lambda t\ ((xcp, frs), h)\ ta\ ((xcp', frs'), h').$$
$$P, t \vdash Normal\ (xcp, h, frs) -ta \rightarrow_{jvmd}$$
$$Normal\ (xcp', h', frs'))$$

Note that *jvm-execd* turns the defensive VM into a strict VM as it no longer raises *TypeErrors*, but just gets stuck. Nevertheless, I keep referring to it as the defensive VM in the following. The reason for dropping *TypeError* is that I can avoid duplications by using the same representation for thread-local states for both the aggressive and defensive VM.

For example, I can use the same state invariants for both VMs. In §3.3.5, I discuss how this simplification affects the type safety theorem.

For the definitions in the locale *multithreaded-base*, I use the prefixes *jvm.* and *jvmd.* to mark the versions of the aggressive and defensive VM, respectively. I write $P \vdash s -t:ta \rightarrow_{jvm} s'$ for $jvm.redT\ P\ s\ (t,ta)\ s'$, $P \vdash s -t:ta \rightarrow_{jvmd} s'$ for $jvmd.redT\ P\ s\ (t,ta)\ s'$, and $P \vdash s -ttas \rightarrow^*_{jvm} s'$ ($P \vdash s -ttas \rightarrow^*_{jvmd} s'$) for the reflexive and transitive closure of $jvm.redT\ P$ ($jvmd.redT\ P$).

Lemma 3.7. *jvm-final with either jvm-exec P or jvm-execd P are well-formed with respect to the interleaving semantics.*

Proof. I show the assumptions of the locale *multithreaded* for the parameter instantiations *jvm-final, jvm-exec P* and *jvm-final, jvm-execd P*. *final-no-red* follows by unfolding the definitions and *exec P t* $(xcp, h, [])$ being the empty set (see Figure 3.22). *Spawn-heap* holds by case analysis on emptiness of the call stack, the exception flag, the current instruction and the native method that is being called. □

Start state

The initial state *jvm-start P C M vs* of the JVM is the same as for J, except for the thread-local state of *start-tID*, which is

$$(None, [([], Null \cdot vs @ replicate\ mxl\ undefined\text{-}Val, D, M, 0)])$$

where $(D, \_, \_, \lfloor (mxs, mxl, ins, xt) \rfloor) = method\ P\ C\ M$, i.e., no exception is flagged and the VM is about to execute the first instruction of method M in D. Like in *J-start P C M vs*, no lock is held, all wait sets are empty, there are no interrupts, and *start-heap* has preallocated objects for *start-tID* and the system exceptions.

3.3 Deadlock and type safety

For sequential languages, type safety is typically expressed as the syntactic properties progress and preservation (see §2.1.6). Progress means that every well-formed and well-typed expression can be reduced unless it has already been fully evaluated, i.e., the semantics is not missing any reduction rules. Full evaluation is determined by a syntactic predicate *final*. Preservation requires that reductions preserve well-typedness and well-formedness. In §3.1.4, I have shown how to transfer preservation proofs from single threads to the interleaving semantics, i.e., they do not pose a problem. Deadlocks, however, can break the progress property.

Therefore, I formally define the concept of deadlock (§3.3.1, §3.3.2) and prove progress up to deadlock (§3.3.3) for the interleaving semantics. For the latter, I identify sufficient conditions on the single-threaded semantics. Hence, source code and bytecode can reuse the progress theorem by discharging these conditions (§3.3.4, §3.3.5).

Although progress typically identifies allowed stuck states syntactically, I formalise deadlock (and thus the allowed stuck states) semantically for two reasons. First, I want the formalisation to be shared between source code and bytecode, but any syntactic characterisation necessarily depends on the thread-local state representation. Second, deadlock typically involves several threads, i.e., a syntactic characterisation would have to examine all of them together. Hence, not only is there no easy syntactic characterisation, but any such would also break the abstraction of the interleaving semantics. Instead, I define deadlocks by looking at the possible thread actions of all threads. In principle, one could derive syntactic conditions from this definition by analysing the single-thread semantics, but I have not done so.

3.3.1 Deadlock as a state property

A system is said to be in deadlock iff all threads are waiting for something that will never occur. In operating systems, deadlock of processes has four preconditions on resource usage: mutual exclusion, hold and wait, circular waiting, and no preemption (see, e.g., [134]). In the interleaving semantics, there are four "resources" that a thread can wait for: acquiring a lock, termination of another thread, being removed from a wait set, and interruption. Since all of them are implemented as BTAs, I can formally define deadlock solely in terms of the reductions of a thread – independent of the concrete language.

Consider, for example, the schedules in Figure 3.25. On the left-hand side, in Figure 3.25a, thread t_1 acquires the lock l_1, then thread t_2 acquires the lock l_2. To continue, t_2 needs the lock l_1, too, so the $Lock{\to}l_1$ is postponed. However, t_1 requests the lock l_2, which t_2 is holding. Hence, both threads are in deadlock. In the centre (Figure 3.25b), t_3 waits for t_4's termination, but t_4 suspends itself to the wait set w. Hence, both t_3

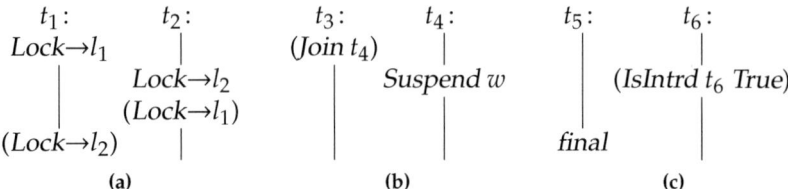

Figure 3.25: Three schedules with two threads each that lead to deadlock

and t_4 are in deadlock, because there is no thread left to notify t_4. The right-hand side (Figure 3.25c) shows a similar example with interruption. t_6 waits for being interrupted, but t_5 terminates without doing so. Thus, t_6 is deadlocked.

In the interleaving semantics, things are a bit more tricky than in the above examples, because threads can atomically request any number of locks and join on other threads. Moreover, they can wait for different events non-deterministically. In Java, for example, the `Thread.join()` method either waits for the receiver thread to terminate or for the executing thread to be interrupted.

To get a hold on this, I first define for what a thread may wait in deadlock. The function $waits\ ta\ ::\ ('l + 't + 't)\ set$ extracts all the resources for which the executing thread may be waiting, i.e., all the locks it acquires, the threads it joins on, and the threads which must be interrupted. Formally:

$$waits\ ta =$$
$$\{ l.\ Lock \in set\ (\langle ta \rangle_{lf}\ l) \} \uplus \{ t.\ Join\ t \in set\ \langle ta \rangle_c \} \uplus intr\text{-}waits\ \langle ta \rangle_i$$

where $\uplus$ is disjoint union and $intr\text{-}waits\ \langle ta \rangle_i$ is the set of thread IDs t for which $\langle ta \rangle_i$ contains an element $IsIntrd\ t\ True$ which is not preceeded by $Intr\ t$ or $ClearIntr\ t$. The last constraint removes interrupt checks whose result does not depend on the initial interrupt state, but is determined by the preceeding interrupt actions. Consider, for example,

$$intr\text{-}waits\ (\!|IsIntrd\ t\ True, ClearIntr\ t|\!) = \{ t \} \tag{3.5}$$
$$intr\text{-}waits\ (\!|Intr\ t, IsIntrd\ t\ True|\!) \quad = \emptyset \tag{3.6}$$

The thread action in (3.5) tests whether t has been interrupted and, if so, clears the interrupt status. Hence, it waits for t being interrupted.

$$\text{MW}_{\text{LOCK}}: \quad \frac{\textit{has-lock}\,((\textit{locks}\,s)_f\,l)\,t' \qquad t' \neq t \qquad t' \in T}{\textit{must-wait}\,s\,t\,(\textit{Inl}\,l)\,T}$$

$$\text{MW}_{\text{JOIN}}: \quad \frac{\textit{not-final-thread}\,s\,t' \qquad t' \in T}{\textit{must-wait}\,s\,t\,(\textit{Inr}\,(\textit{Inl}\,t'))\,T}$$

$$\text{MW}_{\text{INTR}}: \quad \frac{\textit{all-final-except}\,s\,T \qquad t' \notin \textit{intrs}\,s}{\textit{must-wait}\,s\,t\,(\textit{Inr}\,(\textit{Inr}\,t'))\,T}$$

Figure 3.26: Thread t must wait for resource w indefinitely

In (3.6), however, the test *IsIntrd t True* holds vacuously because *Intr t* sets the interrupt flag right before the test.

Note that I do not care about actions for unlocking, thread creation and thread existence, wait sets and not being interrupted for the following reasons:

unlocking Only a thread itself would be able to remedy the missing lock, not others.

thread creation In Java, spawning a thread either succeeds or raises an exception, i.e., it cannot deadlock.

wait sets A thread in a wait set cannot do anything to be removed. *ok-wsets* only distinguishes normal execution from processing the removal from a wait set. Waiting threads will be dealt with specifically.

non-interruption For the interleaving semantics, non-interruption is dual to interruption, i.e., I could treat both uniformly, but in Java, threads can only wait for being interrupted.

The predicate *must-wait s t w T* determines that in state s, the thread t will wait indefinitely for resource $w :: \text{'}l + \text{'}t + \text{'}t$ under the assumption that all threads in T are already deadlocked. Figure 3.26 shows the formal definition. The thread t must wait forever for the lock l (case $w = \textit{Inl}\,l$), if l is held by another thread t' which is deadlocked (MW$_{\text{LOCK}}$). The join on another thread t' fails forever (case $w = \textit{Inr}\,(\textit{Inl}\,t')$), if the thread t' is not final and already deadlocked (MW$_{\text{JOIN}}$). The predicate *not-final-thread s t* denotes that t exists, but is not final, i.e., $t \in \textit{dom}\,(\textit{thrs}\,s)$

103

$deadlock\ s =$
$(\forall t\ x.\ thr\ s\ t = \lfloor(x, K^f\ 0)\rfloor \wedge \neg final\ x \wedge wset\ s\ t = None$
$\quad \longrightarrow t \vdash (x, shr\ s)\ \wr \wedge$
$\qquad \forall W.\ t \vdash (x, shr\ s)\ W\wr \longrightarrow \exists w \in W.\ must\text{-}wait\ s\ t\ w\ (dom\ (thr\ s)) \wedge$
$(\forall t\ x\ ln.\ thr\ s\ t = \lfloor(x, ln)\rfloor \wedge ln \neq K^f\ 0 \wedge \neg waiting\ (wset\ s\ t)$
$\quad \longrightarrow \exists l.\ ln_f\ l > 0 \wedge must\text{-}wait\ s\ t\ (Inl\ l)\ (dom\ (thr\ s))) \wedge$
$(\forall t\ x.\ thr\ s\ t = \lfloor(x, K^f\ 0)\rfloor$
$\quad \longrightarrow wset\ s\ t \neq \lfloor WS\text{-}Notified\rfloor \wedge wset\ s\ t \neq \lfloor WS\text{-}WokenUp\rfloor)$

Figure 3.27: Formal definition of *deadlock*

and $t \notin final\text{-}threads\ s$. Note that *not-final-thread s t* negates the precondition of *Join* (see Figure 3.11) except for $t \neq t'$, which is irrelevant here. A thread waits indefinitely for t' being interrupted (case $w = Inr\ (Inr\ t')$, MWINTR), if t' is not interrupted, but all non-deadlocked threads are final – expressed by the predicate *all-final-except*.

$$all\text{-}final\text{-}except\ s\ T = \{t.\ not\text{-}final\text{-}thread\ s\ t\} \subseteq T$$

With these preparations, I can now formally define deadlock, see Figure 3.27. First, I introduce two abbreviations: $t \vdash (x, h)\ \wr$ denotes that t can reduce in the local state x and heap h with some thread action *ta* such that *ta* is not contradictory in itself, i.e., there is a multithreaded state s such that *ok-ta s t ta*. For example, $(\!|Lock{\rightarrow}l, UnlockFail{\rightarrow}l|\!)$ and $(\!|Intr\ t, IsIntrd\ t\ False|\!)$ are contradictory. The predicate $t \vdash (x, h)\ W\wr$ denotes that t can reduce in state (x, h) with a thread action *ta* such that $W = waits\ ta$. It abstracts t's reductions to the resources W it waits for.

Then, a multithreaded state s is in deadlock (written *deadlock s*) iff

(i) every non-final thread t that is ready to execute, say $thr\ s\ t = \lfloor(x, K^f\ 0)\rfloor$ and $wset\ s\ t = None$, can reduce, and no matter how it might reduce, it must wait indefinitely, and

(ii) every thread with temporarily released locks that is not in a wait set must wait indefinitely on one of these, and

(iii) for every thread which has not temporarily released any locks, its wait set status is neither $\lfloor WS\text{-}Notified\rfloor$ nor $\lfloor WS\text{-}WokenUp\rfloor$.

The first condition is the default case: $t \vdash (x, shr\ s)\ \wr$ ensures that the thread is not just stuck, i.e., universal quantification on W does not hold vacuously. For *must-wait*, I consider all threads as deadlocked (i.e., $T = dom\ (thr\ s)$), because the system as a whole is supposed to be in deadlock. Note that quantifying over all W with $t \vdash (x, shr\ s)\ W \wr$ allows a thread to non-deterministically wait for different "resources". The second condition accounts for acquisition of temporarily released locks. Since it is the interleaving semantics that performs the acquisition (ACQUIRE), but not the single threads, I need an extra case for that. The last condition ensures that there is no thread which has been removed from a wait set and has already reacquired the released locks, but has not yet processed the removal internally. Note that there is no condition for threads in wait sets, because they are automatically deadlocked when there is no thread to remove them.

For simplicity, I do not require that there is at least a thread which is not final. Hence, every *mfinal* state is also in *deadlock*.

Lemma 3.8. *States in deadlock are stuck, i.e., if $s -t{:}ta \to s'$, then $\neg$ deadlock s.*

3.3.2 Deadlock for threads

The previous section defines when all threads are in deadlock. However, some threads may already be in deadlock while others keep running. In this section, I define deadlock for single threads and prove that this notion generalises deadlock as a state property.

Figure 3.28 defines the set *deadlocked* of threads in deadlock coinductively. Note that coinductivity naturally captures that a thread is not deadlocked iff one can deduce in finitely many steps that it is not. Hence, finitely many steps (of other threads) suffice to allow the thread under consideration to continue. This definition considers the set of threads to be closed with respect to the outside, i.e., one cannot add a spinning thread to the system, which would "undeadlock" again all waiting threads.

Rules DACTIVE and DACQUIRE are very similar to conditions (i) and (ii) of *deadlock*, respectively. The only difference is the set of threads that *must-wait* takes: Instead of all threads, it now consists of deadlocked and final ones. The last rule DWAIT expresses that a waiting thread is deadlocked if all other threads are either final or *deadlocked* themselves (which includes *waiting*).[19]

---

[19] Remember that I do not model spurious wake-ups from wait sets. Otherwise, a waiting thread would never be deadlocked, because it could always be woken up spuriously.

$$\text{DACTIVE:} \quad \frac{thr\,s\,t = \lfloor(x,\mathrm{K^f}\,0)\rfloor \qquad wset\,s\,t = None \qquad t \vdash (x,shr\,s)\wr}{\forall W.\; t \vdash (x,shr\,s)\; W \wr \longrightarrow \exists w \in W.\; must\text{-}wait\,s\,t\,w\;(deadlocked\,s \cup final\text{-}threads\,s)}{t \in deadlocked\,s}$$

$$\text{DACQUIRE:} \quad \frac{thr\,s\,t = \lfloor(x,ln)\rfloor \qquad \neg\,waiting\,(wset\,s\,t) \qquad ln_{\mathrm{f}}\,l > 0}{\quad must\text{-}wait\,s\,t\,(Inl\,l)\,(deadlocked\,s \cup final\text{-}threads\,s)}{t \in deadlocked\,s}$$

$$\text{DWAIT:} \quad \frac{thr\,s\,t = \lfloor(x,ln)\rfloor}{waiting\,(wset\,s\,t) \qquad all\text{-}final\text{-}except\,s\,(deadlocked\,s)}{t \in deadlocked\,s}$$

Figure 3.28: Coinductive definition of the set of threads in deadlock

Rule DWAIT completely differs from condition (iii): The latter disallows the wait set status $\lfloor WS\text{-}Notified \rfloor$ and $\lfloor WS\text{-}WokenUp \rfloor$, which is implicit in *deadlocked* because there is no introduction rule for these cases. Recall that *deadlock* imposes no constraints on waiting threads, since they are implicitly included there.

Remember from §1.4.3 that (co)inductives predicates are defined as the fixed point of the associated functional and that this functional must be monotone. For *deadlocked*, I therefore must show that *must-wait* and *all-final-except* are monotone, because *deadlocked* is passed as a parameter to them.

Lemma 3.9 (Monotonicity of *all-final-except* and *must-wait*). *Let* $T \subseteq T'$. *If all-final-except* $s\,T$, *then all-final-except* $s\,T'$. *If must-wait* $s\,t\,w\,T$, *then must-wait* $s\,t\,w\,T'$.

Consider Figure 3.29 for an example of different deadlock situations. Suppose there are six threads which at the moment can reduce with the thread actions shown on the left-hand side. If there are multiple thread actions, then there is one reduction for each. Suppose further that no thread is waiting and that the i-th thread holds the lock l_i. The graph on the right-hand side shows which thread is waiting to obtain a lock held by another thread. Then, threads III and VI are waiting for each other without other reduction options. Clearly, both of them are deadlocked. Although I and II are also waiting for each other, they are not deadlocked

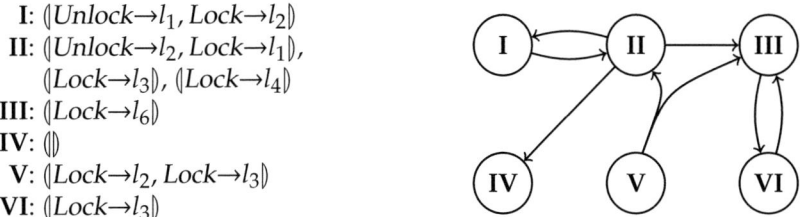

I: $\langle Unlock{\rightarrow}l_1, Lock{\rightarrow}l_2\rangle$
II: $\langle Unlock{\rightarrow}l_2, Lock{\rightarrow}l_1\rangle$,
    $\langle Lock{\rightarrow}l_3\rangle$, $\langle Lock{\rightarrow}l_4\rangle$
III: $\langle Lock{\rightarrow}l_6\rangle$
IV: $\langle\rangle$
V: $\langle Lock{\rightarrow}l_2, Lock{\rightarrow}l_3\rangle$
VI: $\langle Lock{\rightarrow}l_3\rangle$

Figure 3.29: Example with deadlocked threads

at the moment: II has two more reduction options. Waiting on lock l_3 will be in vain, because III is deadlocked. However, IV is not waiting for any resource, hence II may still hope to obtain the lock l_4 some time. Hence, I is not in deadlock either, as II might release l_2 afterwards. Since thread actions must be executed atomically, we may not interleave the thread actions of I and II, i.e., first unlock both l_1 and l_2 and then lock l_2 and l_1 again. Note that V is waiting simultaneously for II and III, because $V \vdash {}_{-} \{ Inl\, l_2, Inl\, l_3 \}\, \wr$. Since III is already in deadlock, so is V. Clearly, IV is not deadlocked. If its wait set status is *None*, the empty thread action $\langle\rangle$ is possible. Otherwise, it is $\lfloor WS\text{-}Notified\rfloor$ or $\lfloor WS\text{-}WokenUp\rfloor$, but then IV is not deadlocked by definition. Now, suppose thread IV is in a wait set. Then, all threads are deadlocked, because every thread except IV is waiting for some other thread to release a lock, and the only thread that could be reduced (i.e., IV) is waiting for some other thread waking it up.

Next, I show that *deadlocked* leads to the same characterisation of states in deadlock as *deadlock*. Let *deadlock′ s* denote that all non-final threads are deadlocked, i.e.,

$$deadlock' \ s = (\forall t.\ not\text{-}final\text{-}thread\ s\ t \longrightarrow t \in deadlocked\ s)$$

Theorem 3.1. *deadlock s iff deadlock′ s.*

Proof. From left to right: Suppose *deadlock s* and *not-final-thread s t*. Then, $t \in deadlocked\ s$ by coinduction with the set of *not-final-threads* as the coinduction invariant. In the coinduction step, I must show that any t' with *not-final-thread s t′* satisfies the assumptions of one of *deadlocked*'s introduction rules – with *deadlocked s* replaced by $\{ t.\ not\text{-}final\text{-}thread\ s\ t \} \cup deadlocked\ s$. DACTIVE and DACQUIRE follow from the assumption *deadlock s*, because they differ from their counterparts in the definition of *deadlock* only in the sets of thread IDs passed to *must-wait.* But they are equal in that case for the coinduction invariant, because

$$\{\, t.\ \textit{not-final-thread } s\ t\,\} \cup \textit{deadlocked } s \cup \textit{final-threads } s = \textit{dom} \,(\textit{thr } s)$$

As *all-final-except s* ($\{\, t.\ \textit{not-final-thread } s\ t\,\} \cup \textit{deadlocked } s$) holds vacuously, the case for DWAIT is trivial.

For the other direction, suppose $t' \in \textit{deadlocked } s$ for all t' such that *not-final-thread s t'*. All three conditions of *deadlock* trivially hold for final threads t, so suppose *not-final-thread s t*. Hence, $t \in \textit{deadlocked } s$. From this, conditions (i) and (ii) in the definition of *deadlock* directly follow by monotonicity of *must-wait* (Lemma 3.9). The last condition (iii) holds because *deadlocked*'s definition excludes threads with the forbidden wait set status. □

Given the thread-wise predicate about deadlock, I strengthen Lemma 3.8 to the following lemma, which is proven by case analysis on $s -t{:}ta{\rightarrow} s'$ and $t \in \textit{deadlocked } s$. Lemma 3.8 then directly follows with Theorem 3.1.

Lemma 3.10. *Every thread in deadlock is stuck, i.e., if $s -t{:}ta{\rightarrow} s'$, then $t \notin \textit{deadlocked } s$.*

Since I am considering now deadlocks of individual threads, execution may continue even if some threads are deadlocked. Still, threads in deadlock should remain deadlocked; otherwise, the deadlock definition would be flawed. However, deadlock preservation requires that the single-threaded semantics is well-behaved:

1. The changes of the shared heap by the executing threads must not deprive a deadlocked thread of all of its reduction options. Otherwise, it would be stuck and therefore no longer deadlocked, since deadlock explicitly excludes stuck threads.

2. Such changes must not enable new reduction options which would undeadlock it, either.

Locale *preserve-deadlocked* collects these assumptions (Figure 3.30). It fixes a set *wf-states* of well-formed states only for which the preservation requirements have to hold. The first assumption expresses that the interleaving semantics *redT* preserves *wf-states*. The other two

locale *preserve-deadlocked* $=$ *multithreaded* $+$
   fixes *wf-states* :: $('l, 't, 'x, 'h, 'w)$ *state set*
   assumes *invariant redT wf-states*
   and $[\![s \in \textit{wf-states}; \, s -t':ta \rightarrow s'; \, thr \, s \, t = \lfloor(x, K^f \, 0)\rfloor; \, t \vdash (x, shr \, s)\,\wr]\!]$
      $\Longrightarrow t \vdash (x, shr \, s')\,\wr$
   and $[\![s \in \textit{wf-states}; \, s -t':ta \rightarrow s'; \, thr \, s \, t = \lfloor(x, K^f \, 0)\rfloor;$
      $t \vdash (x, shr \, s') \, W'\,\wr]\!] \Longrightarrow \exists W \subseteq W'. \, t \vdash (x, shr \, s) \, W \wr$

Figure 3.30: Locale *preserve-deadlocked* collects the requirements for preservation of deadlock

assumptions express exactly the requirements from above. Note the covariance in the set W in the last assumption: Since $t \vdash \_ W \wr$ expresses that one of t's reduction requires *all* resources in W, changes in the heap may only increase W. Under these assumptions, the following holds:

Lemma 3.11 (Preservation of deadlock). *Let $s \in$ wf-states. If $s -t:ta \rightarrow s'$ or $s -ttas \rightarrow^* s'$, then deadlocked $s \subseteq$ deadlocked s'.*

Proof. If $s -t:ta \rightarrow s'$, the proof proceeds by case analysis on *redT*. In either case NORMAL and ACQUIRE, suppose $t' \in$ *deadlocked s*. I show $t' \in$ *deadlocked s'* by coinduction with *deadlocked s* as coinduction invariant. In the coinductive step, case analysis on $t' \in$ *deadlocked s* yields the interesting cases DACTIVE and DACQUIRE; the case DWAIT contradicts the assumption $s -t:ta \rightarrow s'$. In both former cases, the reduction from s to s' preserves *must-wait*. For DACTIVE, the assumptions of *preserve-deadlocked* relate $t' \vdash (x,\_) \wr$ and $t' \vdash (x,\_) \_\wr$ between *shr s* and *shr s'*, respectively.

The case $s -ttas \rightarrow^* s'$ follows from $s -t:ta \rightarrow s'$ by induction; the locale's first assumption reestablishes the induction invariant $s \in$ *wf-states* in the inductive step. □

3.3.3 Progress up to deadlock

Recall that I have formalised deadlocks to obtain a progress result for the interleaving semantics. In this section, I prove the following theorem and present the assumptions about $\_ \vdash \_ - \_ \rightarrow \_$ on which it depends.

Theorem 3.2 (Progress up to deadlock). *Let $s \in$ wf-states. If $\neg$ deadlock s, then there are t, ta, and s' such that $s -t:ta \rightarrow s'$.*

109

locale $progress = multithreaded +$
  fixes $wf\text{-}states :: ('l, 't, 'x, 'h, 'w)\ state\ set$
  assumes $invariant\ redT\ wf\text{-}states$
  and $wf\text{-}stateD: s \in wf\text{-}states \Longrightarrow ok\text{-}locks\text{-}thr\ s \wedge ok\text{-}wset\text{-}final\ s$
  and $progress: [\![s \in wf\text{-}states;\ thr\ s\ t = \lfloor (x, K^f\ 0) \rfloor;\ \neg\ final\ x]\!]$
            $\Longrightarrow \exists ta\ x'\ h'.\ t \vdash (x, shr\ s) - ta \rightarrow (x', h')$
  and $wf\text{-}ta:$
    $[\![s \in wf\text{-}states;\ thr\ s\ t = \lfloor (x, K^f\ 0) \rfloor;\ t \vdash (x, shr\ s) - ta \rightarrow (x', h')]\!]$
    $\Longrightarrow \exists s'.\ ok\text{-}ta\ s'\ t\ ta$
  and $wf\text{-}red:$
    $[\![s \in wf\text{-}states;\ thr\ s\ t = \lfloor (x, K^f\ 0) \rfloor;\ \neg\ waiting\ (wset\ s\ t);$
    $t \vdash (x, shr\ s) - ta \rightarrow (x', h')]\!]$
    $\Longrightarrow \exists ta'\ x''\ h''.\ t \vdash (x, shr\ s) - ta' \rightarrow (x'', h'') \wedge$
                $(ok\text{-}ta\ s\ t\ ta' \vee ok\text{-}ta'\ s\ t\ ta' \wedge waits\ ta' \subseteq waits\ ta)$
  and $Suspend\text{-}not\text{-}final:$
    $[\![s \in wf\text{-}states;\ thr\ s\ t = \lfloor (x, K^f\ 0) \rfloor;\ \neg\ waiting\ (wset\ s\ t);$
    $t \vdash (x, shr\ s) - ta \rightarrow (x', h');\ Suspend\ w \in set\ \langle ta \rangle_w]\!] \Longrightarrow \neg\ final\ x'$
  and $Wakeup\text{-}waits:$
    $[\![s \in wf\text{-}states;\ thr\ s\ t = \lfloor (x, K^f\ 0) \rfloor;\ t \vdash (x, shr\ s) - ta \rightarrow (x', h');$
    $Notified \in set\ \langle ta \rangle_w \vee WokenUp \in set\ \langle ta \rangle_w]\!] \Longrightarrow waits\ ta = \emptyset$

Figure 3.31: Definition of locale *progress*

Theorem 3.2 requires certain assumptions about the single-threaded semantics, which I collect in the locale *progress*, see Figure 3.31. Like *preserve-deadlocked*, it fixes a set *wf-states* of well-formed states that is closed under reductions. *wf-stateD* ensures that well-formed states satisfy two invariants: Only existing threads hold the locks (*ok-locks-thr s*) and all threads in *dom* (*wset s*) exist in *thr s* with their local state not being final (*ok-wset-final s*). Together with the other constraints, the latter invariant ensures that threads which have been removed from a wait set are able to process the removal.

The assumption *progress* expresses the usual progress condition for single threads: Every thread in any well-formed state whose local state is not final can reduce.

The remaining assumptions restrict the single-thread semantics such that irreducible multithreaded states are final or in deadlock. *wf-ta* ensures that the thread action of any reduction is not contradictory in itself.

Similar to progress expressing that no reduction rule is missing for well-typed terms, *wf-red* formalises that the reduction rules are able to generate all thread actions that are needed. *ok-ta'* formalises that *ta*'s conditions are met except for BTAs which are allowed to cause deadlock. It is like *ok-ta* (3.1) with the following modifications:[20]

- *ok-Ls* stops checking the lock preconditions when it encounters the first *Lock* BTA for l that t cannot acquire – though it does enforce the preconditions of *Unlock* and *UnlockFail* prior to this *Lock* BTA. For example, take $ta = \langle\!|Lock{\rightarrow}l, Unlock{\rightarrow}l, Unlock{\rightarrow}l|\!\rangle$. Then, *ok-ta'* requires that t already holds the lock l once, or that it cannot acquire the lock l.[21]

- *ok-intr* ignores conditions of BTAs of the form *IsIntrd _ True*.

- *ok-cond s t* (*Join t'*) is always *True*.

Thus, *wf-red* requires that every thread which is ready to execute, say with thread action *ta*, can reduce with thread action *ta'* such that either the current state s already meets *ta'*'s preconditions, or s meets them except for BTAs that are allowed to deadlock, but in the latter case, it must not add anything it is waiting for in *ta'* compared to *ta*.

Assumption *Suspend-not-final* demands that a thread be not final after it has suspended itself to a wait set, i.e., it can later process its removal.

The last one *Wakeup-waits* requires that while processing the removal from a wait set, the thread does not execute BTAs which may cause deadlock. Although the interleaving semantics could deal with such BTAs, I disallow them, because they would complicate the deadlock formalisation and proofs unnecessarily, and neither source code nor bytecode semantics uses this.

Under these assumptions, Theorem 3.2 holds.

---

[20]Technically, to implement the modifications, I have defined predicates *ok-Ls'*, *ok-intr'*, and *ok-cond'* that *ok-ta'* uses. As these modifications are obvious, I omit their presentation.

[21]*ok-Ls* stops checking at *Lock*s instead of skipping them (like *ok-intr* and *ok-cond* do for *IsIntrd _ True* and *Join _*) because *Lock* changes the lock status, i.e., checking the conditions of subsequent lock BTAs would be meaningless.

Proof of Theorem 3.2. As s is not in deadlock, by definition (Figure 3.27), there must be a thread, say $thr\, s\, t = \lfloor (x, ln) \rfloor$, such that

(a) t is not waiting, $ln = K^f\, 0$, not *final* x, and either not $t \vdash (x, shr\, s)\, \wr$ or there is a set W such that $t \vdash (x, shr\, s)\, W\, \wr$ and t need not wait for any $w \in W$, or

(b) t is not waiting, $ln \neq K^f\, 0$, and it need not wait for any of the locks in ln, or

(c) $ln = K^f\, 0$ and t's wait set status is $\lfloor WS\text{-}Notified \rfloor$ or $\lfloor WS\text{-}WokenUp \rfloor$.

I show for each case that t can take a step next.

In case (a), *progress* postulates a reduction $t \vdash (x, shr\, s) - ta \rightarrow (\_, \_)$. *wf-ta* ensures that the thread actions of any reduction is not contradictory in itself, in particular *ta* is not. Hence, $t \vdash (x, shr\, s)\, \wr$ by definition. With (a), let W be such that $t \vdash (x, shr\, s)\, W\, \wr$ and t need not wait for any $w \in W$. Again by definition, there is a reduction $t \vdash (x, shr\, s) - ta' \rightarrow (\_, \_)$ with $W = waits\, ta'$. By *wf-red*, there is another reduction $t \vdash (x, shr\, s) - ta'' \rightarrow (x', h')$ such that either (i) *ok-ta s t ta''*, or (ii) *ok-ta' s t ta''* and *waits ta''* $\subseteq$ *waits ta'*. In case (i), I am done by NORMAL, because *upd-ta* is a right-total relation. In case (ii), by choice of *ta'*, all $w \in waits\, ta'' \subseteq waits\, ta'$ meet their precondition. Hence, *ok-ta' s t ta''* implies *ok-ta s t ta''*, and I am back at case (i).

In case (b), the reduction directly follows with ACQUIRE.

In case (c), t must process its removal from a wait set. By *wf-stateD*, *ok-wset-final s*, in particular not *final* x. By the same argument as in case (a), there is a reduction $t \vdash (x, shr\, s) - ta'' \rightarrow (x', h')$ such that *ok-ta s t ta''* or *ok-ta' s t ta''*. If *ok-ta' s t ta''*, $\langle ta'' \rangle_w$ contains *Notified* or *WokenUp* due to t's wait set status. By *Wakeup-waits*, *waits ta''* $= \emptyset$, i.e., *ok-ta' s t ta''* and *ok-ta s t ta''* coincide. Thus, NORMAL yields the desired reduction. $\square$

3.3.4 Type safety for source code

With the above preparations in place, I now prove type safety for *J.redT P* (Theorem 3.3). Thereby, I reuse the type safety proof for the sequential subset from §2.1.6.

Theorem 3.3 (Type safety). *Let wf-J-prog P and wf-start P C M vs. If $P \vdash J\text{-}start\, P\, C\, M\, vs - ttas \rightarrow^* s$ such that $\neg P \vdash s - t' : ta' \rightarrow s'$ for any t', ta', s', then for every thread t in s, say $thr\, s\, t = \lfloor ((e, xs), ln) \rfloor$,*

(i) *if* $e = Val\, v$, *then* $ln = K^f\, 0$ *and* $P, shr\, s \vdash v :\leq T$ *where*

$$(start\text{-}ETs\, P\, C\, M)(ttas\, [\leadsto]\, P, \_,\_ \vdash \_,\_ \sqrt{})\, t = \lfloor (E, T) \rfloor$$

and start-ETs $P\, C\, M$ *is the initial map* $[start\text{-}tID \mapsto (empty, T_r)]$ *where* T_r *is* M's *return type.*

(ii) *if* $e = Throw\, a$, *then* $ln = K^f\, 0$ *and typeof-addr* $(shr\, s)\, a = \lfloor ClassT\, C \rfloor$ *for some* C *such that* $P \vdash C \leq^* Throwable,$

(iii) *otherwise,* $t \in J.deadlocked\, P\, s.$

In any case, t *has an associated* Thread *object at address* $t2a\, t$ *in shr* $s.$

Let me first review the type safety statement. Suppose we run the non-native method M of class C with the correct number of parameters vs of the correct types, and this halts in state s. Then, all threads of s either (i) have terminated normally with a return value v which conforms to the return type of the thread's initial method, which is M for $t = start\text{-}tID$ and run otherwise, or (ii) have terminated abnormally with an exception a which refers to an object of a subclass of *Throwable*, or (iii) are deadlocked. In particular, this also shows that synchronized blocks cannot get stuck because the thread does not hold the lock on the monitor. Note that type safety does not state anything about non-terminating program runs. These are uninteresting, because they are obviously not stuck, but do not return anything either.

In the remainder of this section, I develop the invariant necessary to ultimately prove Theorem 3.3 via progress and preservation. I always assume that P is well-formed, i.e., *wf-J-prog* P.

For progress, I have already discussed in §3.3.3 that it does not suffice to show that every non-final thread can reduce in the single-threaded semantics – the interleaving semantics may not be able to execute the reduction, because the current state violates the thread action's precondition. In locale *progress* (Figure 3.31), I have collected sufficient conditions to lift a single-threaded progress property to the interleaving semantics (Theorem 3.2). Now, I show that *J-red* P satisfies these conditions. Remember that the locale *progress* restricts the assumptions about the single-threaded semantics to a set *wf-states* of well-formed states that all reductions of the interleaving semantics must preserve. Hence, I first develop what the well-formedness constraints for J are.

$$\text{WTrtSync:} \quad \frac{P,E,h \vdash e_1 : T_1 \qquad \textit{is-refT } T_1 \qquad P,E,h \vdash e_2 : T}{P,E,h \vdash \textit{sync } (e_1)\, e_2 : T}$$

$$\text{WTrtInsync:} \quad \frac{\textit{typeof-addr } h\, a \neq None \qquad P,E,h \vdash e : T}{P,E,h \vdash \textit{insync } (a)\, e : T}$$

Figure 3.32: Run-time typing rules for synchronized blocks

Thread-local well-formedness constraints

The progress theorem for single threads (Theorem 2.1) requires that (i) the expression is type correct, (ii) it passes the definite assignment check, and (iii) the heap conforms. Subject reduction (Theorem 2.2) shows preservation for (i), but additionally requires that the local store conforms. Lemmata 2.1 and 2.2 show preservation of definite assignment and conformance, respectively.

First of all, I must adapt these proofs to the changes and extensions from the previous section. In particular, I add typing rules for $sync\ (\_)\ \_$ blocks to the run-time type system (see Figure 3.32). The rule WTrtSync replaces WTsync for $sync\ (e_1)\ e_2$ and drops the constraint $T_1 \neq NT$, because e_1 may evaluate to $null$ during reduction. There is now a rule WTrtInsync for $insync\ (a)\ e$ blocks, because Rlock introduces them in reductions. It requires the monitor address to be allocated and the body to be run-time typable. With these rules, proving the cases for $sync\ (\_)\ \_$ blocks in progress and subject reduction follows the standard pattern. Since $sync\ (\_)\ \_$ blocks involve neither the local store nor the heap, preservation of definite assignment and conformance is not affected.

Moreover, subject reduction now additionally requires that the ID of the executing thread has an associated thread object, because calling $currentThread$ returns its address (CurrTh). Thread conformance $P,h \vdash t \sqrt{_t}$ captures this as it predicates that $typeof\text{-}addr\ h\ (t2a\ t) = \lfloor ClassT\ C \rfloor$ for some C such that $P \vdash C \leq^* Thread$. Consequently, the subject reduction theorem now is as follows. Again, additions with respect to 2.2 are highlighted in grey.

Theorem 3.4 (Subject reduction). *If wf-J-prog P, and* $P, t \vdash \langle e,s \rangle - ta \rightarrow \langle e',s' \rangle$, *and* $P,E, hp\ s \vdash e : T$, *and* $P,E \vdash s\sqrt{}$, *and* $P, hp\ s \vdash t\ \sqrt{_t}$, *then there is a* T' *such that* $P,E, hp\ s' \vdash e' : T'$ *and* $P \vdash T' \leq T$.

Naturally, *wf-states* must impose all these thread-local constraints. In §3.1.4, I have developed the infrastructure for lifting such predicates and preservation theorems to the interleaving semantics. For definite assignment, the lifted predicate is $\uparrow \lambda t\ (e, xs)\ h.\ \mathcal{D}\ e\ \lfloor dom\ xs \rfloor \uparrow$, written $\uparrow \mathcal{D} \uparrow$. Conformance and typability depend on a typing environment E and the initial type T of the expression, which do not change during reduction. Hence, I model them as invariant data in a combined predicate. Let $P, (E, T), t \vdash (e, xs), h \sqrt{}$ denote

$$\exists T'.\ P, E, h \vdash e : T' \wedge P \vdash T' \leq T \wedge P, E \vdash (h, xs)\sqrt{} \wedge P, h \vdash t \sqrt{}_t \qquad (3.7)$$

Then, $P, \_ \vdash \_, \_ \Uparrow \sqrt{\Uparrow}$ lifts $P, \_, \_ \vdash \_, \_ \sqrt{}$ to multithreaded states using the lifting infrastructure from §3.1.4:

$$P, ETs \vdash ts, h \Uparrow \sqrt{\Uparrow} = \Uparrow P, \_, \_ \vdash \_, \_ \sqrt{\Uparrow}\ ETs\ ts\ h$$

A heap h' *extends* h (written $h \unlhd h'$) iff h' allocates at least all addresses that h does, and types and array lengths of entries in h are unchanged in h'.[22] Heap extension abstracts from changes to data in object fields and array cells during reductions:

Lemma 3.12. *If $P, t \vdash \langle e, (h, xs) \rangle -ta \rightarrow \langle e', (h', xs') \rangle$, then $h \unlhd h'$. If $P \vdash s -t{:}ta \rightarrow s'$ or $P \vdash s -ttas \rightarrow^* s'$, then $shr\ s \unlhd shr\ s'$.*

As conformance and the run-time type system only rely on type information in the heap, they are monotone with respect to heap extensions:

Lemma 3.13. *Let $h \unlhd h'$. If $P, h \vdash v :\leq T$, then $P, h' \vdash v :\leq T$. If $P, E, h \vdash e : T$, then $P, E, h' \vdash e : T$. If $P, h \vdash t \sqrt{}_t$, then $P, h' \vdash t \sqrt{}_t$.*

Lemma 3.14 (Preservation of definite assignment, typability and conformance). *Suppose $P \vdash s -t{:}ta \rightarrow s'$.*

(i) *If $\uparrow \mathcal{D} \uparrow\ (thr\ s)\ (shr\ s)$, then $\uparrow \mathcal{D} \uparrow\ (thr\ s')\ (shr\ s')$.*

(ii) *If $P, ETs \vdash thr\ s, shr\ s \Uparrow \sqrt{\Uparrow}$, let $ETs' = ETs(\langle ta \rangle_t \rightsquigarrow P, \_, \_ \vdash \_, \_ \sqrt{})$. Then $P, ETs' \vdash thr\ s', shr\ s' \Uparrow \sqrt{\Uparrow}$.*

Proof. By Lemmata 3.2 and 3.3, it suffices to discharge the assumptions of locales *lifting-wf* and *lifting-inv* from §3.1.4 for $\uparrow \mathcal{D} \uparrow$ and $P, \_ \vdash \_, \_ \Uparrow \sqrt{\Uparrow}$, respectively.

---

[22]Heap extension has already been formalised in Jinja [82], but is not described in [83].

115

The first assumption of each follows from the preservation theorems for single threads (Theorem 3.4 and Lemmata 2.1 and 2.2, adapted to concurrency) except for thread conformance. Thread conformance is preserved because it is monotone with respect to heap extensions (Lemma 3.13) and reductions only extend the heap (Lemma 3.12).

The second assumption requires that the initial state of spawned threads satisfy the conditions $\mathcal{D}$ and (3.7), respectively. Thread conformance holds because $t2a$ is the left-inverse to $a2t$ for addresses of objects of subclasses of *Thread*. For the rest, *native-BTA2J* builds the initial state from the method body of the *run* method, which must exist by well-formedness. Hence, its declaration meets J's method well-formedness constraints (Figure 2.10), from which the desired constraints follow.

The third assumption imposes that changes to the heap by other threads preserve the constraints. Since $\mathcal{D}$ does not depend on the heap, this holds trivially for (i). For (ii), such changes are only heap extensions by Lemma 3.12 with respect to which conformance and typability are monotone (Lemma 3.13). □

Inter-thread well-formedness constraints

Unfortunately, these constraints do not suffice to discharge the assumption *wf-red* of *progress*. It demands that if there is a reduction, then there is always a feasible one – except for deadlocking reductions due to *Lock*, *Join*, and *IsIntrd _ True*. For most reductions with BTAs, there are other reductions with negated preconditions such that one of them is always feasible. For example, START and STARTFAIL complement each other, and so do INTRDT and INTRDF. However, if a thread's local state does not conform to the multithreaded state, *wf-red* may be violated in two cases:

1. The lock status assigns less locks to a thread than its *insync* (_) _ blocks remember. In that case, RUNLCK and RUNLCKX try to unlock a monitor that is not held, but there is no reduction with *UnlockFail*.

2. The wait set status is ⌊*WS-Notified*⌋ or ⌊*WS-WokenUp*⌋, but the next reduction is not a native call to *wait*. Hence, the semantics cannot issue thread actions with *Notified* or *WokenUp*, respectively.

For both cases, I introduce additional constraints that the reductions in $J.redT\,P$ preserve.

For case 1, I define a function $\mathcal{I} :: expr \Rightarrow addr \Rightarrow nat$ such that $\mathcal{I} \, e \, a$ counts the *insync* $(a) \_$ subexpressions in e for any monitor address a. I write *has-$\mathcal{I}$ e* if $\mathcal{I} \, e$ is not 0 everywhere, i.e., e contains at least one *insync* $(\_) \_$ subexpression. Then, the invariant *lock-conf ls ts* expresses that for all thread IDs t,

(i) if t does not exist, it holds no locks, i.e., if *ts t* $=$ *None*, then $\neg$ *has-lock* $(ls_f \, a) \, t$ for all monitor addresses a, and

(ii) if t does exist, its *insync* $(\_) \_$ subexpressions exactly remember its locks, i.e., if *ts t* $= \lfloor ((e, xs), ln) \rfloor$, then $\mathcal{I} \, e \, a =$ *has-locks* $(ls_f \, a) \, t +$ $ln_f \, a$ for all a. Note that *lock-conf* must add t's temporarily released locks $(ln_f \, a)$ to the locks t actually holds (*has-locks* $(ls_f \, a) \, t$), because the *insync* $(a) \_$ blocks remain when a call to *wait* on a temporarily releases the locks on a.

However, preservation of *lock-conf* requires another invariant. Consider, for example, RSYNCN and suppose that e has an *insync* $(a) \_$ subexpression. Then, $\mathcal{I}$ (*sync* (*null*) e) $a > 0$ and $\mathcal{I}$ (*THROW NullPointer*) $a =$ 0, but a's lock state does not change. Hence, if the original state satisfies *lock-conf*, the successor state will not. The problem here is that e contains an *insync* $(\_) \_$ block although execution has not yet reached it.

To disallow such cases, I define the predicate *ok-$\mathcal{I}$ e* which ensures that *insync* $(\_) \_$ subexpressions occur only in subexpressions in which the next reduction will take place. Figure 3.33 shows the definition. For expressions with subexpressions, the definition follows a common pattern; all subexpressions must satisfy *ok-$\mathcal{I}$*, too, and if *has-$\mathcal{I}$* for any subexpression, then all subexpressions which are evaluated before must be a value. The predicate *is-Val e* expresses that e is of the form *Val v*. For example, if *has-$\mathcal{I}$ e_2* in e_1 «*bop*» e_2, then e_1 must be a value, because e_1 is evaluated before e_2. Control expressions allow *insync* $(\_) \_$ blocks only for the currently evaluated subexpression; for example, in e_1;; e_2, only for e_1. The loop *while* (e_1) e_2 does not allow them in either e_1 or e_2 because the semantics immediately rewrites it to *if* (e_1) e_2;; *while* (e_1) e_2 *else unit*, which would duplicate any *insync* $(\_) \_$ subexpression. The auxiliary function *has-$\mathcal{I}$s es* checks whether *has-$\mathcal{I}$ e* holds for some $e \in set \, es$.

Lemma 3.15. *If* $\neg$ *has-$\mathcal{I}$ e, then ok-$\mathcal{I}$ e.*

Proof. By induction on e. □

117

$$
\begin{aligned}
&\text{ok-}\mathcal{I}\ (new\ C) &&= True \\
&\text{ok-}\mathcal{I}\ (new\ T[e]) &&= \text{ok-}\mathcal{I}\ e \\
&\text{ok-}\mathcal{I}\ (e\ instanceof\ T) &&= \text{ok-}\mathcal{I}\ e \\
&\text{ok-}\mathcal{I}\ (Cast\ T\ e) &&= \text{ok-}\mathcal{I}\ e \\
&\text{ok-}\mathcal{I}\ (Val\ v) &&= True \\
&\text{ok-}\mathcal{I}\ (e_1\ «bop»\ e_2) &&= \text{ok-}\mathcal{I}\ e_1 \wedge \text{ok-}\mathcal{I}\ e_2 \wedge (\text{has-}\mathcal{I}\ e_2 \longrightarrow \text{is-Val}\ e_1) \\
&\text{ok-}\mathcal{I}\ (Var\ V) &&= True \\
&\text{ok-}\mathcal{I}\ (V := e) &&= \text{ok-}\mathcal{I}\ e \\
&\text{ok-}\mathcal{I}\ (e_1[e_2]) &&= \text{ok-}\mathcal{I}\ e_1 \wedge \text{ok-}\mathcal{I}\ e_2 \wedge (\text{has-}\mathcal{I}\ e_2 \longrightarrow \text{is-Val}\ e_1) \\
&\text{ok-}\mathcal{I}\ (e_1[e_2] := e_3) &&= \text{ok-}\mathcal{I}\ e_1 \wedge \text{ok-}\mathcal{I}\ e_2 \wedge \text{ok-}\mathcal{I}\ e_3 \\
&&&\quad \wedge (\text{has-}\mathcal{I}\ e_2 \longrightarrow \text{is-Val}\ e_1) \wedge (\text{has-}\mathcal{I}\ e_3 \longrightarrow \text{is-Val}\ e_1 \wedge \text{is-Val}\ e_2) \\
&\text{ok-}\mathcal{I}\ (e.length) &&= \text{ok-}\mathcal{I}\ e \\
&\text{ok-}\mathcal{I}\ (e.F\{D\}) &&= \text{ok-}\mathcal{I}\ e \\
&\text{ok-}\mathcal{I}\ (e_1.F\{D\} := e_2) &&= \text{ok-}\mathcal{I}\ e_1 \wedge \text{ok-}\mathcal{I}\ e_2 \wedge (\text{has-}\mathcal{I}\ e_2 \longrightarrow \text{is-Val}\ e_1) \\
&\text{ok-}\mathcal{I}\ (e.M(es)) &&= \text{ok-}\mathcal{I}\ e \wedge \text{ok-}\mathcal{I}s\ es \wedge (\text{has-}\mathcal{I}s\ es \longrightarrow \text{is-Val}\ e) \\
&\text{ok-}\mathcal{I}\ \{V: T = vo; e\} &&= \text{ok-}\mathcal{I}\ e \\
&\text{ok-}\mathcal{I}\ (e_1;; e_2) &&= \text{ok-}\mathcal{I}\ e_1 \wedge \neg\,\text{has-}\mathcal{I}\ e_2 \\
&\text{ok-}\mathcal{I}\ (if\ (e)\ e_1\ else\ e_2) &&= \text{ok-}\mathcal{I}\ e \wedge \neg\,\text{has-}\mathcal{I}\ e_1 \wedge \neg\,\text{has-}\mathcal{I}\ e_2 \\
&\text{ok-}\mathcal{I}\ (while\ (e_1)\ e_2) &&= \neg\,\text{has-}\mathcal{I}\ e_1 \wedge \neg\,\text{has-}\mathcal{I}\ e_2 \\
&\text{ok-}\mathcal{I}\ (throw\ e) &&= \text{ok-}\mathcal{I}\ e \\
&\text{ok-}\mathcal{I}\ (try\ e_1\ catch(C\ V)\ e_2) &&= \text{ok-}\mathcal{I}\ e_1 \wedge \neg\,\text{has-}\mathcal{I}\ e_2 \\
&\text{ok-}\mathcal{I}\ (sync\ (e_1)\ e_2) &&= \text{ok-}\mathcal{I}\ e_1 \wedge \neg\,\text{has-}\mathcal{I}\ e_2 \\
&\text{ok-}\mathcal{I}\ (insync\ (a)\ e) &&= \text{ok-}\mathcal{I}\ e \\
&\text{ok-}\mathcal{I}s\ [] &&= True \\
&\text{ok-}\mathcal{I}s\ (e \cdot es) &&= \text{ok-}\mathcal{I}\ e \wedge (\text{has-}\mathcal{I}s\ es \longrightarrow \text{is-Val}\ e)
\end{aligned}
$$

Figure 3.33: Definition of ok-$\mathcal{I}$

Like with the other thread-local well-formedness conditions, I lift ok-$\mathcal{I}$ to multithreaded states, written $\uparrow$ok-$\mathcal{I}\uparrow$, and show preservation with the locale *lifting-wf*.

Lemma 3.16 (Preservation of ok-$\mathcal{I}$ and $\uparrow$ok-$\mathcal{I}\uparrow$).

(i) *If* $P, t \vdash \langle e, s \rangle -ta\rightarrow \langle e', s' \rangle$ *and* ok-$\mathcal{I}$ *e, then* ok-$\mathcal{I}$ *e'.*

(ii) *If* $P \vdash s -t{:}ta\rightarrow s'$ *and* $\uparrow$ok-$\mathcal{I}\uparrow$ (*thr s*) (*shr s*),
     then $\uparrow$ok-$\mathcal{I}\uparrow$ (*thr s'*) (*shr s'*).

Proof. Case (i) by induction on the semantics. Isabelle proves all cases automatically except for non-native method calls (RCALL). In that case, the body *body* of the called method is well-typed because P is well-formed. Well-typed expressions have no *insync* (_) _ subexpressions because there is no typing rule for them. Hence, $ok\text{-}\mathcal{I}$ *body* by Lemma 3.15.

Case (ii) by Lemma 3.2 and instantiating the locale *lifting-wf* (Figure 3.15). Case (i) discharges the first assumption, and the same argument as for RCALL in the proof of (i) shows the second assumption. The third is vacuous because $ok\text{-}\mathcal{I}$ does not depend on the heap. □

Now, I am finally able to prove preservation of *lock-conf*.

Lemma 3.17 (Preservation of *lock-conf*). *Let lock-conf* $(locks\, s)(thr\, s)$ *and* $\uparrow ok\text{-}\mathcal{I}\uparrow$ $(thr\, s)$ $(shr\, s)$. *If* $P \vdash s - t{:}ta \rightarrow s'$, *then lock-conf* $(locks\, s')(thr\, s')$.

Proof. By case analysis on the interleaving semantics. In case ACQUIRE, t's local state remains unchanged and therefore $\mathcal{I}$, too. Moreover, *upd-acq* correctly acquires all of t's temporarily released locks, because no other thread holds any of them by ACQUIRE's last assumption. Since the temporarily released locks *ln* are reset to K^f 0, the sum of $ln_f\, a$ and *has-locks* $((locks\, s)_f\, a)\, t$ remains the same for all locks a. Moreover, other threads are not affected at all.

In case NORMAL, I have $P, t \vdash \langle e, (shr\, s, xs)\rangle - ta \rightarrow \langle e', (shr\, s', xs')\rangle$ where $thr\, s\, t = \lfloor((e, xs), \mathsf{K}^f\, 0)\rfloor$ and $thr\, s'\, t = \lfloor((e', xs'), ln')\rfloor$ for some ln'. Hence, $ok\text{-}\mathcal{I}\, e$. Induction on the small-step semantics (and case analysis for native method calls) shows that $\mathcal{I}\, e'\, a$ is equal to $\mathcal{I}\, e\, a$ plus the number of $Lock \rightarrow a$ and less the number of $Unlock \rightarrow a$ BTAs in $\langle ta \rangle_{lf}\, a$. But this change is exactly how *upd-locks* and *upd-TRL* change the sum of t's locks and temporarily released locks on a, respectively (by induction on $\langle ta \rangle_{lf}\, a$ with the assumption $ok\text{-}Ls\, ((locks\, s)_f\, a)\, t\, (\langle ta \rangle_{lf}\, a)$). Hence, lock conformance holds for t in s'. As all lock actions' preconditions are satisfied, the reduction does not affect locks and local states of threads other than t, so lock conformance holds for them in s', too. Having inspected all existing threads, I am left with newly spawned threads t'. Condition (1) in *lock-conf*'s definition ensures that t' does not hold any lock. By the same argument as in the proof of Lemma 3.16, t''s initial expression e satisfies $\neg\, has\text{-}\mathcal{I}\, e$, because it is the body of the *run* method. Since t' has not temporarily released any locks by construction (cf. Figure 3.9), lock conformance also holds for t' in s'. □

I now turn to the second way in which *J-red* may violate *wf-red*. In principle, I could pursue the same path as for lock conformance and require that whenever a thread's wait set status is not *None*, its next reduction will be a call to the native method *wait*, and show preservation. However, formalising the native-call-to-*wait* invariant is tedius and preservation proofs are no easier. Instead, I define an invariant that is independent of the local state and that I can reuse for the bytecode type safety proof in §3.3.5.

Given a set I of well-formed multithreaded states, *ok-Suspend I* restricts I to states in which the local states of all threads with wait set status other than *None* have resulted from a former reduction whose thread action contains a *Suspend* BTA. Formally (in locale *multithreaded-base*):

$$ok\text{-}Suspend\ I =$$
$$\{s.\ s \in I\ \wedge$$
$$(\forall t \in dom\ (wset\ s).\ \exists s_0 \in I.\ \exists s_1 \in I.\ \exists ttas\ x_0\ ta\ x\ w\ ln\ ln'.$$
$$s_0 -t:ta\rightarrow s_1 \wedge s_1 -ttas\rightarrow^* s \wedge thr\ s_0\ t = \lfloor(x_0, \mathrm{K}^\mathrm{f}\ 0)\rfloor \wedge$$
$$t \vdash (x_0, shr\ s_0) -ta\rightarrow (x, shr\ s_1) \wedge Suspend\ w \in set\ \langle ta\rangle_\mathrm{w} \wedge$$
$$ok\text{-}ta\ s_0\ t\ ta \wedge thr\ s_1\ t = \lfloor(x, ln)\rfloor \wedge thr\ s\ t = \lfloor(x, ln')\rfloor)\}$$

Then, *ok-Suspend* preserves preservation of invariants by definition.

Lemma 3.18 (Preservation of *ok-Suspend*). *If invariant redT I, then invariant redT (ok-Suspend I).*

Type safety

Finally, I define the set *J-wf-states P* of well-formed states for the type safety proof as

$$J.ok\text{-}Suspend\ P\ \{s.\ \exists ETs.\ P, ETs \vdash thr\ s, shr\ s \Uparrow\surd\Uparrow \wedge \uparrow\mathcal{D}\uparrow\ (thr\ s)\ (shr\ s) \wedge$$
$$\uparrow ok\text{-}I\uparrow\ (thr\ s)\ (shr\ s) \wedge lock\text{-}conf\ (locks\ s)\ (thr\ s)\}$$

Lemma 3.19. *J-red P satisfies the assumptions of progress for well-formed states J-wf-states P. Formally: progress J-final (J-red P) (J-wf-states P).*

Proof. I proof the assumptions of locale *progress* (Figure 3.31) as follows. Invariance of *J-wf-states* follows from Lemmata 3.14, 3.16, 3.17, and 3.18. The well-formedness condition *ok-locks-thr* directly follows from *lock-conf* because this is just case (i) in *lock-conf*'s definition. *ok-wset-final* follows from *J.ok-Suspend* and the assumption *Suspend-not-final*, which I discharge below. *progress* is just the progress theorem

2.1, adapted for concurrency. Inductions on the small-step semantics show the assumptions *wf-ta*, *Suspend-not-final*, and *Wakeup-waits*.

Now, only *wf-red* remains to be shown. By $s \in$ *J-wf-states P*, if t's wait set status is not *None*, t's last reduction must have issued a *Suspend* BTA in a state with a heap which the current heap *shr s* extends. Induction on this reduction shows that t can now reduce with basic thread actions $(\!|Notified|\!)$ and $(\!|WokenUp|\!)$ as necessary.

So suppose *wset s t* $=$ *None*. Without loss of generality, assume $\neg$ *ok-ta' s t ta*. Proof by induction over the small-step semantics. The interesting cases are RUNLCK and RNATIVE.

In case RUNLCK, $\mathcal{I}$ *(insync (a)* _*)* $a > 0$, i.e., by lock conformance, t holds the lock a. Thus, unlocking a is possible, i.e., *ok-ta' s t ta* holds.

In case RNATIVE, the proof proceeds by case analysis of the semantics for native methods. For each case with a non-trivial thread action, one must manually provide the alternative reduction. I present JOIN as an example: From $\neg$ *ok-ta' s t ta*, I obtain $t \in$ *intrs s*, because *ok-ta'* does not check the precondition of *Join* to allow for deadlocks. Hence, JOININTR is possible. $\square$

Corollary 3.1. *Let* $s \in$ *J-wf-states P be not in deadlock. Then, there are t, ta, and s' such that* $P \vdash s -t\!:\!ta\!\rightarrow s'$.

Proof. This is Theorem 3.2 with Lemma 3.19 discharging the locale assumptions. $\square$

The initial state *J-start P C M vs* satisfies all these well-formedness constraints.

Lemma 3.20. *If wf-J-prog P and wf-start P C M vs, then J-start P C M vs* $\in$ *J-wf-states P.*

Finally, I am able to prove type safety.

Proof of Theorem 3.3. By Lemma 3.20, *J-start P C M vs* $\in$ *J-wf-states P*. Since *J-wf-states P* is closed under reductions, $s \in$ *J-wf-states P*, too. Hence, $s \in$ *J.deadlock P* by Corollary 3.1, which subsumes all *mfinal* states. If e is *final*, cases (i) and (ii) follow from s being well-formed. Otherwise, Theorem 3.1 yields case (iii). The associated thread object exists because $s \in$ *J-wf-states P* implies thread conformance. $\square$

Preservation of deadlocks

In §3.3.2, the locale *preserve-deadlocked* established conditions on the single-threaded semantics such that threads in deadlock remain in deadlock, even when other threads keep executing. Now, I show that *J-red P* satisfies these conditions with *J-wf-states P* as the set of well-formed states.

Lemma 3.21. *J-red P meets the assumptions of locale preserve-deadlocked (Figure 3.30), i.e., preserve-deadlocked J-final (J-red P) (J-wf-states P).*

Proof. The first assumption is identical to the first in *progress* and therefore holds by the same argument as in Lemma 3.19. The assumptions *progress* and *wf-ta* of *progress* imply preservation of $P, t \vdash \_ \wr$ (second assumption in *preserve-deadlocked*). The thrid assumption follows from the next lemma, because $P \vdash s -t':ta \rightarrow s'$ implies $shr\, s \trianglelefteq shr\, s'$. □

Lemma 3.22. *Suppose $P, t \vdash \langle e, (h', xs) \rangle -ta \rightarrow \langle e', s' \rangle$. If $P, E, h \vdash e : T$ for some h such that $h \trianglelefteq h'$, $P \vdash h\sqrt{}$, and $P, h \vdash t \sqrt{}_t$, then there exist ta', e'', s'' such that $P, t \vdash \langle e, (h, xs) \rangle -ta' \rightarrow \langle e'', s'' \rangle$ and waits $ta' = $ waits ta.*

Proof. By induction on the small step semantics. Well-typedness of e in h and heap conformance ensure that field access and method lookup still succeed, heap extension ensures that the same methods (in particular native ones) are called. □

Preservation of deadlock now follows from Lemmata 3.11 and 3.21.

Theorem 3.5 (Preservation of deadlock). *Suppose $s \in$ J-wf-states P. If $P \vdash s -t:ta \rightarrow s'$ or $P \vdash s -ttas \rightarrow^* s'$, then J.deadlocked $P\, s \subseteq$ J.deadlocked $P\, s'$.*

3.3.5 Type safety for bytecode

In this section, I show type safety for well-typed bytecode. The approach is the same as for source code (§3.3.4), namely (i) identify necessary additional invariants, and (ii) prove the assumptions of locale *progress*. Instead of presenting the steps in detail once more, I focus on the similarities with and differences from source code. In this section, I always assume that Φ is a well-typing for P.

Theorem 3.6 (Type safety). *Let P be well-formed with well-typing Φ and the start state jvm-start $P\, C\, M\, vs$ be well-formed.*

(a) *The aggressive VM runs until all threads have terminated or are deadlocked. Formally:*
   If $P \vdash$ jvm-start $P\ C\ M\ vs\ -ttas \rightarrow^*_{jvm} s$ such that $\neg P \vdash s\ -t{:}ta \rightarrow_{jvm} s'$
   for any t, ta, s', then for every thread t in s, say $thr\ s\ t = \lfloor((xcp, frs), ln)\rfloor$,

   (i) $P, \Phi \vdash t{:}(xcp, shr\ s, frs) \surd$, *and*

   (ii) *if $frs \neq [\,]$ or $ln \neq K^f\ 0$, then $t \in$ jvm.deadlocked $P\ s$.*

(b) *Aggressive and defensive VM commute. Formally:*
   $P \vdash$ *jvm-start $P\ C\ M\ vs\ -ttas \rightarrow^*_{jvm} s$ iff*
   $P \vdash$ *jvm-start $P\ C\ M\ vs\ -ttas \rightarrow^*_{jvmd} s$.*

Compare this statement of type safety to the one for the sequential VM (Theorem 2.3). Theorem 2.3(a) showed that the sequential defensive VM never raises a type error. However, the multithreaded VM *jvm-execd* cannot raise such type errors by construction because of the following drawbacks of modelling type errors: On the one hand, I could have adjoined *TypeError* to the thread-local state of the defensive VM, but as I have argued in §3.2.3, I then cannot reuse the proof invariants for the defensive and aggressive VM. On the other hand, a single thread raising a type error could halt the whole VM with a type error. However, this does not fit the structure of the interleaving semantics because a single thread cannot abort the execution of other threads.

Hence, I cannot express absence of type errors directly, but I show progress (Lemma 3.27) instead. This is equivalent to the absence of type errors for individual steps, because type errors and normal reductions exclude each other in the defensive VM, see (2.5). Yet, Theorem 3.6 is slightly weaker than 2.3 for type errors, because the former does not exclude the case in which one thread is stuck at a type error and another thread runs for ever.

Parts 3.6(a)(i) and 3.6(b) express the remaining two parts of Theorem 2.3, where $P, \Phi \vdash \_{:}\_\surd$ strengthens $P, \Phi \vdash \_\surd$ to include thread conformance (see below).

Let me now turn to the proof of Theorem 3.6. Both the theorem and its proof are in structure similar to type safety for source code (Theorem 3.3). First, I describe the necessary well-formedness constraints *jvm-wf-states $P\ \Phi$* on the multithreaded states. Then, I prove that *jvm.redT P* and *jvmd.redT P* preserve them and the start state *jvm-start $P\ C\ M\ vs$* satisfies them, and that they are sufficient to discharge the assumptions of locale *progress*. The actual proof of Theorem 3.6 follows the same line as the one for Theorem 3.3, so I do not repeat it here.

Well-formedness constraints

Just like *J-wf-states* P, *jvm-wf-states* P Φ includes all well-formedness constraints of the sequential type safety proof, i.e., state conformance. Due to the new native method *currentThread*, single-threaded preservation now additionally requires thread conformance. Hence, I strengthen bytecode conformance to include thread conformance

$$P, \Phi \vdash t{:}s\sqrt{} = P, \Phi \vdash s\sqrt{} \wedge P, snd\, s \vdash t\, \sqrt{}_t \tag{3.8}$$

and lift it to thread pools with the infrastructure from §3.1.4.

$$P, \Phi \vdash (ts, h)\, \uparrow\sqrt{}\uparrow = \uparrow\lambda t\, (xcp, frs)\, h.\, P, \Phi \vdash t{:}(xcp, h, frs)\sqrt{}\uparrow ts\, h$$

Then, I define *jvm-wf-states* P Φ as

$$jvm.ok\text{-}Suspend\, P\, \{\, s.\, P, \Phi \vdash (thr\, s, shr\, s)\, \uparrow\sqrt{}\uparrow \wedge$$
$$ok\text{-}locks\text{-}thr\, (locks\, s)\, (thr\, s)\, \}$$

Let me compare *jvm-wf-states* with *J-wf-states*. Using the language-independent invariant transformer *ok-Suspend*, they both ensure that wait set status and thread-local states agree. Note that it is irrelevant whether *jvm-wf-states* uses *jvm.ok-Suspend* or *jvmd.ok-Suspend*. They both yield the same set because aggressive and defensive VM commute for conformant states (see Lemma 3.23 below). Also, they both include the thread-local well-formedness constraints lifted to multithreaded states with $\uparrow\_\uparrow$ and $\Uparrow\_\Uparrow$.

In contrast, *J-wf-states* and *jvm-wf-states* differ on the inter-thread well-formedness constraints. The latter requires only *ok-locks-thr*, because locale *progress* does so. In particular, no constraints on the locks are necessary, because unlike *sync* (_) _ blocks, unlocking a monitor with *MExit* may fail (see Figure 3.23).

Proof of type safety

Now, I present the key lemmata for proving the JinjaThreads VM type safe.

Lemma 3.23. *Aggressive and defensive VM commute.*

(i) Let $P, \Phi \vdash t{:}s\sqrt{}$. Then

$$P, t \vdash Normal\, s - ta \rightarrow_{jvmd} Normal\, s\ iff\ P, t \vdash s - ta \rightarrow_{jvm} s'.$$

(ii) Let $P, \Phi \vdash (thr\, s, shr\, s) \uparrow\!\sqrt{}\!\uparrow$. Then

$$P \vdash s - t{:}ta \rightarrow_{jvmd} s'\ iff\ P \vdash s - t{:}ta \rightarrow_{jvm} s'.$$

Proof. Case (i) adapts Theorem 2.3 (b) to include thread ID and thread actions. I extend the proof to cover the new native methods and monitor instructions.

For (ii), either direction proceeds by case analysis of the reduction. Case ACQUIRE is trivial because it does not depend on the single-threaded semantics. Case NORMAL follows from (i). □

The next lemma shows that the VM does not get stuck. Together with Lemma 3.23, it strengthens absence of type errors (Theorem 2.3 (a)) in that the defensive VM may not get stuck.

Lemma 3.24 (Progress). *Let $P, \Phi \vdash t{:}(xcp, h, frs)\sqrt{}$ and $frs \neq []$. Then, there are ta and s' such that $P, t \vdash (xcp, h, frs) - ta \rightarrow_{jvm} s'$.*

Next, I turn to the preservation lemmata.

Lemma 3.25 (Preservation of conformance). *If $P, \Phi \vdash (thr\, s, shr\, s) \uparrow\!\sqrt{}\!\uparrow$ and $P \vdash s - t{:}ta \rightarrow_{jvm} s'$, then $P, \Phi \vdash (thr\, s', shr\, s') \uparrow\!\sqrt{}\!\uparrow$.*

Proof. It suffices to discharge the assumptions of locale *lifting-wf* from §3.1.4. Single-threaded preservation (assumption 1) needs to extend the sequential type safety proof (Theorem 2.3 (c)) for the new native methods and monitor instructions.

The argument for spawned threads (assumption 2) follows the one for non-native method calls. By construction, the initial state of a new thread is just one call frame for the parameter-less *run* method with program counter 0. Condition (iii) of method well-typings ensures that the frame conforms to the well-typing.

Preservation for another thread t changing the heap (assumption 3) falls in two parts. t's reduction itself preserves heap conformance (condition (ii) in the definition of $P, \Phi \vdash \_\sqrt{}$) and extends the heap. As all other conformance conditions (exceptions, call frames, thread) are monotone with respect to heap extensions, conformance is preserved. □

Lemma 3.26 (Preservation of *jvm-wf-states*). $P \vdash \_ - \_:\_ \to_{jvm} \_$ *and* $P \vdash$ $\_ - \_:\_ \to_{jvmd} \_$ *preserve jvm-wf-states* P Φ.

Proof. Note that *redT* preserves *ok-locks-thr* independent of the single-threaded semantics (proof by case analysis). Then, for the aggressive VM, preservation follows from preservation of conformance (Lemma 3.25) and preservation of *ok-Suspend* (Lemma 3.18).

By Lemma 3.23, Lemma 3.25 also holds for the defensive VM. As noted above, I would have obtained the same set if *jvm-wf-states*'s used *jvmd.ok-Suspend*. Therefore, preservation for the defensive VM follows with Lemma 3.18. □

Lemma 3.27. *The aggressive and the defensive VM satisfy the assumption of progress for well-formed states jvm-wf-states* P Φ.

Proof. I only sketch the proof for the defensive VM. For the aggressive VM, I reuse the results for the defensive VM and Lemma 3.23. Invariance of *jvm-wf-states* P Φ follows from Lemma 3.26. Assumption *wf-stateD* holds because *jvm-wf-states* P Φ explicitly requires *ok-locks-thr s* and *jvm.ok-Suspend* P enforces *ok-wset-final s* like for *J*. Lemma 3.24 discharges *progress*. Assumptions *wf-red*, *Suspend-not-final* and *Wakeup-waits* are shown by case analysis whether an exception is flagged and which instruction executes next. For *wf-red*, other than in Theorem 3.3 for RUNLCK, the case for *MExit* is straightforward because *MExit* may fail with an *IllegalMonitorState* exception. □

Lemma 3.28. *The initial state is well-formed, i.e., if wf-start P C M vs, then jvm-start P C M vs* $\in$ *jvm-wf-states* P Φ.

Deadlock preservation

Preservation of deadlocks for the JinjaThreads VM is analogous to *J*, Lemma 3.29 corresponds to Lemma 3.21. The proof for the defensive VM is analogous, too, where Lemma 3.30 replaces Lemma 3.22.

Lemma 3.29. *For well-formed states jvm-wf-states* P Φ, *exec P and execd P satisfy the assumptions of locale preserve-deadlocked.*

Lemma 3.30. *Let* $P, t \vdash Normal\ (xcp, h', frs) -ta \to_{jvmd} Normal\ s'$ *and* $P \vdash h' \sqrt{}$. *If* $P, \Phi \vdash t:(xcp, h, frs) \sqrt{}$ *for some h such that* $h \trianglelefteq h'$, *then there exist* ta' *and* s'' *such that* $P, t \vdash Normal\ (xcp, h, frs) -ta' \to_{jvmd} Normal\ s''$ *and* *waits* $ta' \subseteq$ *waits* ta.

Hence, preservation of deadlock again follows with Lemma 3.11. Since aggressive and defensive VM commute, preservation also extends to the aggressive VM.

Theorem 3.7 (Preservation of deadlock). *Suppose $s \in jvm\text{-}wf\text{-}states\ P\ \Phi$.*

(i) *If $P \vdash s -t{:}ta\rightarrow_{jvmd} s'$ or $P \vdash s -ttas\rightarrow^*_{jvmd} s'$, then $jvmd.deadlocked\ P\ s \subseteq jvmd.deadlocked\ P\ s'$.*

(ii) *If $P \vdash s -t{:}ta\rightarrow_{jvm} s'$ or $P \vdash s -ttas\rightarrow^*_{jvm} s'$, then $jvm.deadlocked\ P\ s \subseteq jvm.deadlocked\ P\ s'$.*

3.4 Related work

3.4.1 Formalisations of Java and Java bytecode

Formalisations of (aspects of) sequential Java and Java bytecode abound in the literature, many of which study Java features that Jinja and JinjaThreads omit (cf. §7.4). Hartel and Moreau [67] provide a good overview, Alves-Foss [7] has collected many early works. Most closely related to JinjaThreads are its predecessors Jinja, Bali and μJava for sequential Java, see §2.3 for a detailed comparison.

Most formalisations cover either only Java source code or only Java bytecode. One notable exception is the semantics by Stärk et al. [166] for a subset of Java source code and bytecode in terms of abstract state machines, for which they prove subject reduction. Recently, Grunwald et al. [59] extended it to Java generics. However, they use neither machine support for the semantics nor for checking their proofs.

For concurrent Java, AtomicJava [51] by Flanagan et al. models most Java source code features except inheritance and exception handling. They use it to show that their non-standard type system ensures atomicity.

There are much more formalisations for multithreaded Java bytecode. First, Liu and Moore [104] report on an executable model M6 of the KVM, a JVM implementation for embedded devices, in ACL2, which covers all aspects of the Connected Limited Device Configuration (CLDC) specification [41]. Like JinjaThreads, their VM semantics implements native methods from the CLDC standard library, in particular to deal with reflection, class loading and concurrency. Since they model only the JVM, the implementations for the native methods manipulate the

127

VM state directly. In contrast, JinjaThreads encapsulates the semantics (and signatures) of native method calls such that both source code and bytecode can reuse it. They aim for verifying small Java programs [105,122] and JVM implementations with respect to the JVMS. Thus, they do not define a type system for bytecode nor prove type safety. The M6 models bytecode much closer to the JVMS than JinjaThreads does, e.g., the M6 explicitly models the constant pool and string literals. Like its predecessor, JinjaThreads abstracts from such technical details.

Second, Bicolano [121] serves as the basis for the proof carrying code infrastructure in the Mobius project [13]. It provides a comprehensive model for CLDC except for concurrency and class loading in Coq, which includes the class file format. In BicolanoMT, Huisman and Petri [70] extend Bicolano with interleaving concurrency. By using the extension framework by Czarnik and Schubert [42], they do not need to change the sequential Bicolano semantics at all. In contrast, JinjaThreads adds the semantics of *MEnter* and *MExit* instructions to the single-threaded semantics and clutters all rules with thread actions. Conversely, JinjaThreads uses the same interleaving semantics for source code and bytecode whereas the BicolanoMT extension is tightly tied to the bytecode language.

Third, Belblidia and Debbabi present a formal small-step semantics for multithreaded Java bytecode [20]. Like JinjaThreads, they have a semantics for threads in isolation and a second layer which manages the threads and receives basic thread actions, which they call labels, from them. In contrast to the JinjaThreads interleaving framework, at most one basic thread action can be issued at a time. Their single-threaded semantics already takes care of the locks, which are stored in the shared memory, i.e., they only have actions for creating, killing, blocking, and notifying threads. Yet, neither do they model the wait-notify mechanism, nor thread interruption; the second layer uses the block and notify actions to keep track of which threads are ready for execution. Like the M6 and Bicolano, they only give the semantics, but no type system and no proofs. In JinjaThreads, the framework semantics manages the complete multithreaded state which includes the locks, wait sets, and interrupts. This isolates them from one another and alleviates individual threads from the burdens of multithreading. By allowing multiple basic thread actions in a single reduction step, single threads can combine basic thread actions as building blocks for more complex behaviour, while each basic thread action still has simple semantics.

Forth, JavaFAN by Farzan et al. [48, 47] is a formal analyser for Java source and bytecode in Maude, see §6.6 for details. Although they provide formal semantics for both source code and bytecode, these are unconnected.

Apart from the ones mentioned above, I know of two other large-scale formalisations of sequential Java bytecode. First, Barthe et al. [14, 15] built a JVM similar to the sequential JinjaThreads VM in Coq, which covers the JavaCard platform. They show type safety for type-correct bytecode similar to Theorem 2.3.

Second, Atkey [9] has developed an executable JVM in Coq, which encodes the checks of the defensive VM as dependent types. He argues that this simplifies large-scale proofs against the JVM because they no longer need to show that these checks cannot fail.

3.4.2 Type safety proofs and deadlocks

There are only few type safety proofs for multithreaded languages like Java. However, often only subject reduction is shown, which eliminates the need to deal with deadlocks.

In [58], Grossman reports on type-based data race detection for multithreaded Cyclone – a type safe variant of C. In the type safety proof, he shows the progress property that no well-typed thread can get "badly stuck". A thread is badly stuck iff it either is final and still holds some locks or it would not be able to reduce any further even if it could acquire an arbitrary additional lock. Together with subject reduction, type safety follows, i.e., all threads reachable from a well-typed thread via reductions are not badly stuck. Like *deadlocked* in JinjaThreads, badly stuck is defined semantically. In general, being deadlocked is stronger than being badly stuck because the latter does not involve the aspect of circular waiting.

Goto et al. [57] also prove type safety for a multithreaded calculus with a weak memory model. Their progress statement only applies to a thread if it is not about to execute a synchronisation statement, which is a crude syntactic approximation of deadlock. Progress with this restriction no longer guarantees that the semantics is not missing any rule. For instance, it holds even for an operational semantics without any rules for synchronized statements.

There are also approaches to prevent potential deadlocks through type systems, which also must formalise deadlock. For example, Suenaga and Kobayashi [169] propose a calculus with thread creation, interrupts and synchronisation via structured locking. They assign to each syntactic occurrence of a lock a unique level tag. Their type system remembers bounds on the level of acquired locks in effect labels and ensures deadlock freedom by requiring that locks must be acquired in ascending order, which breaks the circular waiting condition. Their deadlock formalisation is purely syntactic: A set of threads is in deadlock iff every "reducible" subexpression of the thread's expressions is a synchronisation statement which has to acquire a lock which is already held. For JinjaThreads, such a syntactic characterisation could be obtained from the semantic definition of *deadlock*, but I have not done so. However, this cannot express that some threads are in deadlock while others are still active like *deadlocked* does. This unnecessarily weakens their type safety statement.

3.4.3 Large-scale programming language formalisations

Beyond Java, there are several other large-scale formalisations of programming languages in proof assistants. Foster and Vytiniotis [52] have formalised the core of FeatherweightJava [71] in Isabelle/HOL. Later, Delaware et al. [45] formalised FeatherweightJava with various extensions in Coq.

There are also substantial formalisations of C and C++, which are predecessors to Java. Based on Jinja, Wasserrab et al. [178] have formalised multiple inheritance in C++ and proven it type-safe. Ramananandro et al. [148, 149] have translated this semantics to Coq and extended it with concrete memory layouts and object construction and destruction. Norrish [131–133] has formalised large parts of the C and C++ language in HOL. Krebbers and Wiedijk [90] are working on formalising the full C99 standard. They aim to correctly capture the low-level intricacies of C while keeping the semantics relatively easy to use. Schirmer [158, 159] developed the SIMPL framework for sequential imperative languages in Isabelle/HOL and embeds a subset of C. As he concentrates on verifying programs, he devises an operational and axiomatic semantics where the latter is sound and complete with respect to the former.

Compiler verifications also come with formalised semantics, see §5.7 for a discussion.

Más extraño y más puro que todo hrön *es a veces el* ur: *la cosa producida por sugestión, el objeto educido por la esperanza.*

Jorge Luis Borges, *Tlön, Uqbar, Orbis Tertius; Ficciones*

Memory models

Zappa Nardelli et al. demand that a specification for a multiprocessor or programming-language memory model "be integrated with the semantics of the rest of the system (describing the behaviour of the processor instructions or of the phrases of the programming language). Memory models are typically presented in isolation, and this makes it all to easy to gloss over important details." [181] Hitherto, this criticism has applied to Java and the JMM, too [8,38,69]. In this chapter, I address this problem by linking the JinjaThreads semantics from Chapter 3 with the JMM. Moreover, I study whether this connection sustains the DRF guarantee, type safety, and the Java security architecture.

To that end, I parametrise the semantics from Chapter 3 over the memory model (MM) first (§4.1). Thus, the definitions and theorems from Chapter 3 are in fact the special case for sequential consistency (§4.2). The main contributions of this chapter then revolve around the JMM:

- a formal link between multithreaded Java and the JMM (§4.3.2),
- proofs of the DRF guarantee (§4.3.3) and consistency of the JMM (§4.3.4), and
- a proof that the JMM provides only a notion of type safety weaker than sequential consistency and an example that the JMM compromises Java's security guarantees (§4.3.5).

Technically, the challenges in this chapter are the following:

abstract over the memory model Chapters 2 and 3 define the semantics in terms of the concrete heap representation from §2.1.5. To support different memory models, I abstract over the implementation. To that end, I identify a set of kernel operations for shared memory together with their properties and adapt the definitions and proofs. These operations are flexible enough to cover sequential consistency and the JMM.

link JinjaThreads with the JMM Implementing the kernel operations does not suffice for the JMM, because its axiomatic rules decide a posteriori whether an execution is allowed. Therefore, I connect the operational semantics for source code and bytecode with the JMM by associating statements and instructions with their JMM events, i.e., the events from Table 3.1 that I asked the reader to ignore during Chapter 3.

prove the DRF guarantee and consistency of the JMM The JMM and the DRF guarantee have been formalised before [8, 69], but unconnected to a single-threaded semantics. To bridge the gap, I identify the assumptions of the DRF proof and show that the single-threaded semantics satisfy them. Although these assumptions are intuitive, discharging them surprisingly requires a subject reduction proof for non-speculative executions. Initialisations turn out to be the main complication. In particular, I construct sequentially consistent executions for a given prefix.

For consistency, I show that the JMM allows all sequentially consistent executions of *all* well-formed programs and, therefore, every well-formed program has at least one legal behaviour. To my knowledge, this is the the first consistency proof for the JMM.

4.1 The heap as a module

So far, I have only sketched how JinjaThreads models the heap in §2.1.5. In fact, JinjaThreads models the heap as a module with abstract operations and provides implementations for sequential consistency and the Java memory model. In this section, I introduce the module and its operations (§4.1.1) and show how the semantics and proofs use it (§4.1.2). In §4.1.3, I discuss some design decisions for the module.

In Chapters 2 and 3, addresses and thread IDs have been taken from the opaque types *addr* and *thread-id*, respectively. The JMM and code generation (§6.3.1) require more concrete types. Since Isabelle does not support type refinement, these types are actually type variables *'addr* and $'t$ in JinjaThreads. Hence, all previous definitions that depend on addresses or thread IDs are in fact polymorphic. For example, the real types for values (Figure 2.1) and J programs (Figure 2.3) are $'addr\ val$ and $'addr\ J\text{-}prog$, respectively. From now on, I write such types with these type parameters.

4.1.1 Abstract operations and their properties

In this section, I define the module's interface and present the properties of the abstract operations. As one would expect from a module's interface, the type variable $'heap$ generalises the type $heap$ for heaps such that the concrete implementations in §4.2 and §4.3 can instantiate $'heap$ as needed.

In Figure 4.1, the locale declaration $heap\text{-}base$ fixes the abstract heap operations. Locale $heap$ specifies how they affect type information and array lengths that the heap stores.[23] I now explain the intended meaning of the individual operations.

The functions $a2t$ and $t2a$ convert between addresses and thread IDs; I have already introduced them in §3.2.1. Since addresses and thread IDs are now type variables, I must fix the conversion functions as locale parameters, because different MMs might implement them differently. Assumption $a2t\text{-}inverse$ states that $t2a$ is the left-inverse of $a2t$ on addresses at which objects of subclasses of $Thread$ may be allocated. It ensures that the native method $currentThread$ correctly returns the address of the current thread (CURRTH).

The parameter $typeof\text{-}addr$ replaces the constant defined in Equation (2.4). From a heap, it extracts type information for addresses, which also includes the length of arrays.

The other operations manipulate the heap. The constant $empty\text{-}heap$ denotes the heap which has no objects allocated. The operation $alloc$ allocates a new object of the given class or an array of the given element type and size, respectively. It returns the updated heap h', and the

---

[23]The locale $heap$ both fixes a parameter P and imposes assumptions, which deviates from the general rule of separating these steps (§1.4.2). However, $heap$ only needs P to know about valid types and subtyping. Actually, $heap\text{-}base$ should fix P, but this is impossible, because the compiler verification in Chapter 5 refers to definitions in $heap\text{-}base$ for the source code and the compiled program at the same time. Although these definitions are provably equal, the locale mechanism and the HOL type system do not allow to conveniently combine them. As all definitions go into $heap\text{-}base$ and theorems are not affected, $heap$ fixes P and the declarations in $heap\text{-}base$ explicitly have P as an additional parameter when necessary.

datatype $loc = Field\ vname\ cname \mid Cell\ nat$

locale $heap\text{-}base =$
    fixes $a2t :: 'addr \Rightarrow 't$ and $t2a :: 't \Rightarrow 'addr$
    and $typeof\text{-}addr :: 'heap \Rightarrow 'addr \rightharpoonup hty$
    and $empty\text{-}heap :: 'heap$
    and $alloc :: 'heap \Rightarrow hty \Rightarrow 'heap \times ('addr\ option)$
    and $read :: 'heap \Rightarrow 'addr \Rightarrow loc \Rightarrow 'addr\ val \Rightarrow bool$
    and $write :: 'heap \Rightarrow 'addr \Rightarrow loc \Rightarrow 'addr\ val \Rightarrow 'heap \Rightarrow bool$

locale $heap = heap\text{-}base + $ fixes $P :: 'm\ prog$
    assumes $a2t\text{-}inverse:$
        $[\![typeof\text{-}addr\ h\ a = \lfloor ClassT\ C \rfloor;\ P \vdash C \leq^* Thread]\!]$
        $\implies t2a\ (a2t\ a) = a$
    and $alloc\text{-}type:$
        $[\![alloc\ h\ hT = (h', \lfloor a \rfloor);\ is\text{-}htype\ P\ hT]\!]$
        $\implies typeof\text{-}addr\ h'\ a = \lfloor hT \rfloor$
    and $alloc\text{-}hext:$ $alloc\ h\ hT = (h', ao) \implies h \trianglelefteq h'$
    and $write\text{-}hext:$ $write\ h\ a\ al\ v\ h' \implies h \trianglelefteq h'$

Figure 4.1: Locales *heap-base* and *heap* declare the heap module's interface

allocated address $\lfloor a \rfloor$ – or *None* if the allocation fails, e.g., due to insufficient memory. If the allocation succeeds, a's type information in h' must be correct – provided that the allocated type is valid (*alloc-type*); *is-htype* $P\ hT$ abbreviates *is-type* P (*ty-of* hT).

The predicates *read* and *write* model access to the heap. The member $al :: loc$ specifies which field ($al = Field\ F\ D$) or array cell ($al = Cell\ n$) of an address should be accessed. An address a and a member al identify a location (a, al). Given the current heap h and a location (a, al), *read* $h\ a\ al$ models (as a predicate) the set of values that memory may return. Similarly, writing to a location in the heap (*write* $h\ a\ al\ v\ h'$) non-deterministically updates the heap. Allocations and write access must be implemented such that they extend the heap ($h \trianglelefteq h'$), i.e., type information grows monotonically.

$$h \trianglelefteq h' = typeof\text{-}addr\ h \subseteq_m typeof\text{-}addr\ h'$$

Type safety requires further assumptions (Figure 4.2); in particular, the values that memory returns must conform to the type. This requires the

locale $conf\text{-}base = heap\text{-}base +$
fixes $hconf :: 'heap \Rightarrow bool$ and $P :: 'm\ prog$

locale $conf = conf\text{-}base + heap +$
assumes $hconf\ empty\text{-}heap$
and $[\![alloc\ h\ hT = (h', ao);\ hconf\ h;\ is\text{-}htype\ P\ hT]\!] \implies hconf\ h'$
and $[\![write\ h\ a\ al\ v\ h';\ hconf\ h;\ P,h \vdash a\text{-}al : T;\ P,h \vdash v :\leq T]\!]$
$\implies hconf\ h'$
and $[\![typeof\text{-}addr\ h\ a = \lfloor hT \rfloor;\ hconf\ h]\!] \implies is\text{-}htype\ P\ hT$

locale $conf\text{-}progress = conf +$
assumes $[\![hconf\ h;\ P,h \vdash a\text{-}al : T]\!] \implies \exists v.\ read\ h\ a\ al\ v$
and $[\![hconf\ h;\ P,h \vdash a\text{-}al : T;\ P,h \vdash v :\leq T]\!] \implies \exists h'.\ write\ h\ a\ al\ v\ h'$

locale $conf\text{-}read = conf +$
assumes $[\![read\ h\ a\ al\ v;\ hconf\ h;\ P,h \vdash a\text{-}al : T]\!] \implies P,h \vdash v :\leq T$

locale $typesafe = conf\text{-}progress + conf\text{-}read$

Figure 4.2: Locales for heap conformance

notion of the type of a location. Let $P,h \vdash a\text{-}al : T$ denote that the location (a, al) is supposed to store values that conform to type T. Formally:

$$\frac{typeof\text{-}addr\ h\ a = \lfloor hT \rfloor \qquad P \vdash class\text{-}of'\ hT\ has\ F{:}T\ (fm)\ in\ D}{P,h \vdash a\text{-}Field\ F\ D : T}$$

$$\frac{typeof\text{-}addr\ h\ a = \lfloor ArrayT\ T\ n' \rfloor \qquad n < n'}{P,h \vdash a\text{-}Cell\ n : T}$$

Now, consider the locales in Figure 4.2 in detail. Locale *conf-base* fixes the predicate *hconf* for heap conformance as parameter, which abstracts heap conformance $\_ \vdash \_\sqrt{}$ from §2.1.6. Locale *conf* assumes that the empty heap conforms and all heap-manipulating operations preserve heap conformance – if only valid types are allocated and type-conforming values written. Moreover, heap conformance must ensure that the dynamic types of all addresses are valid, too.

Following the division in progress and preservation, the actual assumptions for type safety are split in two groups. Locale *conf-progress*

135

collects the progress assumptions, i.e., for a conformant heap and valid member of an address, we must always be able to read some value from that member and write any type-conforming value to it. Conversely, subject reduction requires that reading from memory always returns type-conforming values, expressed in locale *conf-read*. Locale *typesafe* combines all these assumptions. This completes the specification of the heap module.

4.1.2 Adaptations to semantics and proofs

Before I discuss the design considerations in §4.1.3, I present how to adapt the definitions, theorems, and proofs in Chapter 3 to the heap module.

The language definitions are not affected at all, because the heap module only affects the dynamic semantics. Neither is the framework for interleaving semantics, since it is oblivious of the heap representation. The instantiations themselves for source code and bytecode differ slightly, as the type variable for the heap $'h$ is specialised to the type variable $'heap$ instead of the concrete type *heap*.

The abstract heap necessitates many syntactic adaptations in the specification of and proofs about the single-threaded semantics. Although locales are invaluable in syntactically hiding the heap operations, some details still change. For example, heap conformance no longer depends on the program P *inside* the locale, because P is one of its parameters and it would be nonsensical to clutter the formalisation with unnecessary applications of heap conformance to P. Accordingly, its syntax changes from $P \vdash h\sqrt{}$ to $hconf\ h$.Nevertheless, the definitions and theorems as presented in Chapter 3 are still machine-checked – to obtain them, one merely instantiates the generalised versions from this chapter with sequential consistency as defined in §4.2. I omit to list these generalisations as they are straightforward.

The definitions from Chapter 3 that depend on the heap are distributed over the locales *heap-base* and *conf-base* as follows:[24] Definitions that involve heap conformance go into *conf-base*, whereas *heap-base* collects

---

[24]Language-specific proof invariants (such as run-time well-typedness and bytecode conformance) demand specialised types for program declarations (such as $'addr\ J$-*prog* and $'addr\ jvm$-*prog*, respectively, instead of $'m\ prog$). Since the type variable $'m$ of the locale parameter P cannot be instantiated inside the locale due to HOL restrictions, I replicate the locale hierarchy from Figures 4.1 and 4.2 and constrain $'m$ as necessary. As this is only a technical issue, I do not distinguish these copies in the presentation.

	theorem	description	locale
source code	L 3.6	assumptions of *multithreaded*	*heap-base*
	T 3.3	type safety	*typesafe*
	T 3.4	subject reduction	*conf-read*
	L 3.12	heap extension	*heap*
	L 3.13	heap extension monotonicity	*heap*
	L 3.14(i)	preservation of definite assignment	*heap-base*
	L 3.14(ii)	preservation of conformance	*conf-read*
	L 3.16	preservation of *ok-I*	*heap-base*
	L 3.17	preservation of lock conformance	*heap-base*
	L 3.19	assumptions of *progress*	*typesafe*[a]
	C 3.1	multithreaded progress	*typesafe*
	L 3.20	well-formedness of the initial state	*conf*
	L 3.21	assumptions of *preserve-deadlocked*	*typesafe*
	L 3.22	preservation of reductions	*conf-progress*
	T 3.5	deadlock preservation	*typesafe*
bytecode	L 3.7	assumptions of *multithreaded*	*heap-base*
	T 3.6	type safety	*typesafe*
	L 3.23	aggressive & defensive VM commute	*conf-base* + *heap*[b]
	L 3.24	single-threaded progress	*conf-progress*
	L 3.25	preservation of conformance	*conf-read*
	L 3.26	preservation of *jvm-wf-states*	*conf-read*
	L 3.27	assumptions of *progress*	*typesafe*[a]
	L 3.28	well-formedness of the initial state	*conf*
	L 3.29	assumptions of *preserve-deadlocked*	*typesafe*
	L 3.30	preservation of execution options	*conf-progress*
	T 3.7	deadlock preservation	*typesafe*

[a]Locale *progress* assumes preservation of *wf-states*, which requires *conf-read*. Therefore, L 3.19 and L 3.27 are in the stronger locale *typesafe*. For the progress assumptions *progress* and *wf-red*, the assumptions of locale *conf-progress* suffice.

[b]L 3.23 requires $\Phi \vdash t{:}s\sqrt{}$, which is defined in *conf-base* because it imposes heap conformance. However, the proof does not depend on heap conformance, but only requires the *heap* assumptions. Therefore, it lives in a locale of its own that combines *heap* with *conf-base*.

Table 4.1: Distribution of lemmata (L), theorems (T), and corollaries (C) from §3.2, §3.3.4, and §3.3.5 over the locales from Figures 4.1 and 4.2

the others that only depend on the heap and its operations. The latter are the vast majority and include all semantics definitions. The former consist only of proof invariants; they no longer take the program P as an explicit parameter, because the locale already fixes it. For example, bytecode conformance is now written as $\Phi \vdash t{:}s\sqrt{}$ instead of $P, \Phi \vdash t{:}s\sqrt{}$.

For the theorems, the distribution is more complicated. Table 4.1 assigns the lemmata and theorems from §3.2, §3.3.4, and §3.3.5 to the locales according to the following rules: Theorems whose preconditions do not depend on heap conformance are provable under the assumptions of locale *heap*. Locale *heap-base* collects those that do not depend on the heap at all. Single-reduction preservation lemmata that require heap conformance go into *conf* – except for subject reduction, which requires *conf-read*. Single-reduction progress theorems are provable in *conf-progress*. Combinations of subject reduction and progress such as the type safety theorems live in *typesafe*. Accordingly, the proofs of these lemmata and theorems are adapted to use the assumptions of the respective locales.

Beyond these easy changes in syntax, there are also the following non-trivial adaptations. First, I construct the start heap *start-heap* with the preallocated *Thread* object and system exceptions from the primitive heap operations as follows: The constant *start-data* :: ′*heap* × ′*addr list* × *bool* preallocates the start heap using *alloc*, Figure 4.3 shows the definition. It consists of the start heap *start-heap*, the list of preallocated addresses *start-addrs* and the flag *start-ok* to indicate whether all allocations have succeeded. Then, the start thread's ID *start-tID* is the thread ID associated with the preallocated *Thread* object, and *addr-of-sys-xcpt C* retrieves the right address for preallocated system exceptions from *start-addrs*. For the start state being well-formed, all allocations must have succeeded.

Second, the semantics rules for accessing members of objects and arrays now use the abstract heap operations. Figures 4.4 and 4.5 show the semantics of reading and updating a field of an object or array for source code and bytecode, respectively. Note that the thread action records the reading and writing. The semantics for array cells are similar and can be found in the Appendices B.6.5 and B.7.3.

Third, I must change the implementations for the native methods *hashcode* and *clone* (Figure 2.12). Note that the other native methods (Figure 3.16) do not manipulate the heap and can thus be left untouched (Figures 3.17, 3.18, and 3.19). For *hashcode*, I use Isabelle's type classes to safely overload the function *hash-addr*.

$start\text{-}data = (let\ init\ (h, as, b)\ C = if\ b\ then$
$\qquad\qquad let\ (h', ao) = alloc\ h\ (ClassT\ C)$
$\qquad\qquad in\ case\ ao\ of\ None \Rightarrow (h', as, False)$
$\qquad\qquad\qquad |\ \lfloor a \rfloor \Rightarrow (h', as\ @\ [a], True)$
$\qquad\qquad else\ (h, as, False)$
$\qquad in\ foldl\ init\ (empty\text{-}heap, [], True)\ (Thread \cdot sys\text{-}xcpts))$

$(start\text{-}heap, start\text{-}addrs, start\text{-}ok) = start\text{-}data$

$start\text{-}tID = a2t\ (hd\ start\text{-}addrs)$

$addr\text{-}of\text{-}sys\text{-}xcpt = the \circ map\text{-}of\ (zip\ (Thread \cdot sys\text{-}xcpts)\ start\text{-}addrs)$

$wf\text{-}start\ P\ C\ M\ vs \longleftrightarrow$
$\qquad (\exists Ts\ T\ meth\ D.\ P \vdash C\ sees\ M:Ts{\rightarrow}T = \lfloor meth \rfloor\ in\ D\ \wedge$
$\qquad\qquad P, start\text{-}heap \vdash vs\ [:\leq]\ Ts\ \wedge\ start\text{-}ok)$

Figure 4.3: The bootstrap process constructs the start heap

$$\text{R}_{\text{FACC}}: \quad \frac{read\ h\ a\ (Field\ F\ D)\ v}{\begin{array}{l} P, t \vdash \langle addr\ a.F\{D\}, (h, xs)\rangle \\ -(\!| Read\ a\ (Field\ F\ D)\ v|\!) \rightarrow \langle Val\ v, (h, xs)\rangle \end{array}}$$

$$\text{R}_{\text{FASS}}: \quad \frac{write\ h\ a\ (Field\ F\ D)\ v\ h'}{\begin{array}{l} P, t \vdash \langle addr\ a.F\{D\} := Val\ v, (h, xs)\rangle \\ -(\!| Write\ a\ (Field\ F\ D)\ v|\!) \rightarrow \langle unit, (h', xs)\rangle \end{array}}$$

Figure 4.4: Semantics of field access and field assignment

The former implementation of *clone* copies the complete object to a fresh address (C_LONE) in one step. This is no longer feasible, because the heap operations allow to access only one member at a time. Therefore, I define a copy operation *copy-mems a a' als h obs h'* that copies one by one a list of members *als* from address *a* and heap *h* to address *a'*. The resulting heap is *h'*. Like for ordinary field access, *obs* records the memory accesses. Then, based on the receiver's type, the rules for *clone* (i) allocate a new object or array according to the receiver's type, (ii) compute the list of members to copy from the program declaration, and (iii) copy them using *copy-mems*. The lengthy formal definition can be found in Appendix B.4.2.

$exec\text{-}instr\,(Getfield\,F\,D)\,P\,t\,h\,stk\,loc\,C\,M\,pc\,frs =$
$(let\,v \cdot stk' = stk;\;Addr\,a = v$
$\quad in\;if\,v = Null\;then$
$\qquad \{\,(\langle\!\langle\rangle\!\rangle, \lfloor addr\text{-}of\text{-}sys\text{-}xcpt\,NullPointer\rfloor, h, (stk, loc, C, M, pc) \cdot frs)\,\}$
$\qquad else$
$\qquad\quad \{\,(\langle\!\langle Read\,a\,(Field\,F\,D)\,v'\rangle\!\rangle, None, h, (v' \cdot stk', loc, C, M, pc + 1) \cdot frs)$
$\qquad\quad |\,v'.\;read\,h\,a\,(Field\,F\,D)\,v'\,\})$

$exec\text{-}instr\,(Putfield\,F\,D)\,P\,t\,h\,stk\,loc\,C\,M\,pc\,frs =$
$(let\,v \cdot r \cdot stk' = stk;\;Addr\,a = r$
$\quad in\;if\,r = Null\;then$
$\qquad \{\,(\langle\!\langle\rangle\!\rangle, \lfloor addr\text{-}of\text{-}sys\text{-}xcpt\,NullPointer\rfloor, h, (stk, loc, C, M, pc) \cdot frs)\,\}$
$\qquad else$
$\qquad\quad \{\,(\langle\!\langle Write\,a\,(Field\,F\,D)\,v\rangle\!\rangle, None, h', (stk', loc, C, M, pc + 1) \cdot frs)$
$\qquad\quad |\,h'.\;write\,h\,a\,(Field\,F\,D)\,v\,h'\,\})$

Figure 4.5: Semantics of *Getfield* and *Putfield*

4.1.3 Design considerations

Like JinjaThreads as a whole reuses as many concepts of Jinja as possible, the heap module attempts to naturally abstract from the concrete heap representation. Jinja has already defined abstractions over the heap representation such as $typeof_h$; the heap module carries this one step further. First, it defines a kernel set of operations that permit to completely separate the semantics from the heap implementation. Then, it re-implements the existing abstractions in terms of these operations. When this was not possible, e.g., for heap conformance, I turned the abstraction into a parameter of the model.

It was more difficult to identify usable assumptions about the operations on which the proofs rest. To do so, I started to convert representation-dependent pieces of the main theorems for source code (progress, preservation, subject reduction) to use the heap module. Thereby, I examined the facts known in the proof context, which led me to the above assumptions. On the level of values, they are deliberately weak to allow for different memory models. For example, allocation must only return some address which has the correct type in the updated heap. However, there is no constraint that the address must be fresh or that it has not been typable in the original heap. Similarly, reading from and writing to the heap need only be defined for conformant heaps.

In contrast to values, JinjaThreads assumes that heap operations never mess up type information, i.e., the heap is only ever extended and typable addresses never change their type. Some proofs, e.g., the compiler verification in Chapter 5, rely on this even for non-conforming heaps. Therefore, the assumptions in *heap* must hold for any heap, not just conforming ones. Such a distinction can also be found in the specification of the JMM: The JMM guarantees only weak semantics for values, but requires sequential consistency for types.

The locale hierarchy mirrors JinjaThreads' proof structure. Distributing the assumptions over different locales has two advantages over combining them in a single one. First, as Table 4.1 shows, I can identify which assumptions a theorem really depends on. Second, one of the implementations for the JMM (§4.3.2) does not satisfy the locale *conf-read* – and therefore neither *typesafe*. Thanks to the modularity, I can still use all theorems in *conf-progress* and its anchestor theories for proofs about the JMM.

Finally, let me motivate why reading and writing are non-deterministic, but allocation is not. Since the JMM abstracts from implementation details like caches in processors and optimisations in compilers, non-deterministic reading models their effects. Writing is also non-deterministic for reasons of symmetry and because other MM formalisations [34] use non-deterministic writing instead of reading. However, I model allocation as a function such that bootstrapping can functionally construct the start heap from the empty heap (see Figure 4.3). If allocation was non-deterministic, too, I could not have fully specified the initial heap, which would complicate code generation. Moreover, a functional specification does not need progress assumptions like in locale *conf-progress*. Nevertheless, there are no fundamental obstacles to non-deterministic allocation and it would have elegantly solved other issues, see §4.3.6.

4.2 Sequential consistency

Under sequential consistency [93], a multithreaded program behaves as if every thread executes at a time and all threads immediately see all the writes of a thread. Interleaving semantics as presented in Chapter 3 captures sequential consistency. In this section, I introduce the implementation of the heap module from §4.1 for sequential consistency.

To distinguish types and definitions from the abstract ones, I prefix their names and decorate the notation with "sc", i.e., sc-heap for heap, sc-read for read, $\_,\_ \vdash_{sc} \_ :\leq \_$ for $\_,\_ \vdash \_ :\leq \_$, etc. I use the same scheme to refer to definitions in the locales heap-base and conf-base that the interpretation specialises.

For the purpose of code generation (§6.3.1), I use natural numbers as addresses. Then, the heap representation is defined as in Figure 2.11 and sc-typeof-addr like typeof-addr in Equation 2.4. The implementation of the abstract operations follows Jinja's heap model, I have only extracted them from different parts of the semantics. The interesting operations are reading, writing and heap conformance: sc-read h a al v holds iff in the heap h, member al of address a stores the value v. Similarly, sc-write h a al v h' requires that a is allocated in h and h' is h where a's member al is updated to v. The heap h conforms (written $P \vdash_{sc} h\sqrt{}$) iff for all allocated objects and arrays, their type T is valid, the field map stores type-conforming values for all fields that P declares for T, and – for arrays – all array cells store type-conforming values. The formal definitions of all operations can be found in Appendix B.3.1.

Theorem 4.1. *Sequential consistency satisfies all assumptions of the heap module for any input program.*

$$typesafe\ sc\text{-}a2t\ sc\text{-}t2a\ sc\text{-}typeof\text{-}addr\ sc\text{-}empty\text{-}heap$$
$$(sc\text{-}allocate\ P)\ sc\text{-}read\ sc\text{-}write\ (P \vdash_{sc} \_\sqrt{})\ P$$

Corollary 4.1. *JinjaThreads source code and bytecode are type safe under sequential consistency.*

4.3 Java memory model

In this section, I first motivate the JMM and explain its central concepts (§4.3.1), in more detail than in §1.1. Next, I formalise the JMM and connect it to the JinjaThreads semantics (§4.3.2). Then, I prove modularly that it provides the DRF guarantee (§4.3.3) and is consistent (§4.3.4). Further, I show that JMM only provides a weaker from of type safety and compromises security (§4.3.5). Finally, I discuss the formalisation and the proofs (§4.3.6). A preliminary version of this section has been published in [112].

4.3.1 Informal explanation

In §1.1, I have briefly motivated the need for the JMM already. Now, I delve deeper into how the JMM works.

Since the JMM must ensure that compilers can implement Java on a variety of hardware with different MMs efficiently, it reduces concrete thread operations to the events from Table 3.1, which are called inter-thread actions in JMM terminology:

- reading (*Read*) from, writing (*Write*) to and initialising (*Allocate*)[25] locations on the heap – with the abbreviations *New-Obj* and *New-Arr*,
- locking (*SLock*) and unlocking (*SUnlock*) a monitor,
- interrupting (*TIntr*) a thread and observing that it has been interrupted (*TIntrd*),[26]
- spawning (*TStart*) of and joining (*TJoin*) on a thread, and
- external actions (*Extern*) – for I/O, for example.

Additionally, the JMM requires that events *TInit* and *TFinish* mark the start and termination of a thread, respectively.

This way, the JMM is independent from syntax and implementation techniques. It nevertheless gets a global view on how a given program works algorithmically and on how its threads interact, and uses this to determine the set of legal behaviours. Note that the JMM falls in two parts: First, the JMM provides the strong model of sequential consistency for allocation, type information, and array lengths. In JinjaThreads, the JMM heap module implementations deal with them. Second, axiomatic rules determine a posteriori whether a given execution is an allowed (legal) behaviour of a given program. I model this part as additional layers on top of the interleaving semantics.

---

[25]Technically, the JMM defines an initialisation action that initialises only a single location. JinjaThreads uses one event per memory allocation that initialises *all* members of the allocated address. This way, allocation events keep track of allocated addresses whereas JMM initialisation actions would not if the allocated object or array contains no members, e.g., an array of length 0. Note that the special treatment of allocations in the JMM (see below) ensures that this deviation does not matter semantically.

[26]The JMM does not mention the events *TIntr* and *TIntrd* for thread interruption although its specification requires them.

143

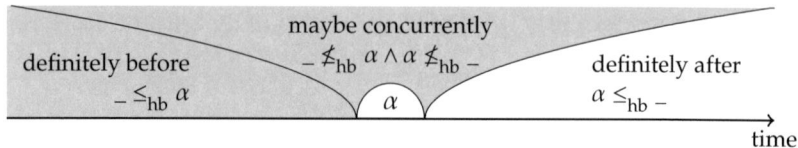

definitely before $-\leq_{hb} \alpha$

maybe concurrently $-\nleq_{hb} \alpha \wedge \alpha \nleq_{hb} -$

α

definitely after $\alpha \leq_{hb} -$

time

Figure 4.6: Happens-before provides a notion of time relative to a given event α. If α is a *Read*, it may see *Write* events in the grey area.

In such an execution, the events of a single thread are totally ordered by the sequence in which they would occur according to the single-threaded semantics, the so-called program order (notation $\leq_{po}$). Being consistent with this total order, the happens-before order $\leq_{hb}$ provides a notion of time relative to a given event. As Figure 4.6 illustrates, it partitions the other events of the execution into three groups: those that must have happened before it, those that must happen after it, and those that may happen concurrently. Synchronisation events, which are all events except for external actions and reads from and writes to non-volatile locations, introduce happens-before relationships between events of different threads. Hence, whenever α's thread cannot deduce – using only allowed means of synchronisation – that an event β of another thread must have happened before or will happen after α, then α and β may happen concurrently. This permits compilers and hardware to freely reorder independent statements of a thread without synchronisation in between.

Since the JMM is independent from a concrete language and sequential semantics, it is custom to write examples such as in Figure 4.7a in a simple imperative language rather than to obfuscate the point by irrelevant Java details. In this language, thread-local variables start with "r", e.g., r1, r2, whereas x, y, etc. denote shared locations. In examples, vertical rules separate the threads, and the thread in column i has ID t_i. Above the threads, the initial values of shared locations and any necessary declarations are given. In Figure 4.15 below, I show how to translate the above example to Java.

Sequential consistency does not allow the result r1 == 2 and r2 == 1 for Figure 4.7a, but the JMM does, because multi-core processors allow it, too. From a single-threaded perspective, l. 1 and l. 2 in the thread on the left are independent. Hence, one core might execute the write in l. 2 while l. 1 is still waiting for the memory controller to answer its request for x. While such an early execution is transparent to sequential

144

initially: x = y = 0;

1: r1 = x;	3: r2 = y;
2: y = 1;	4: x = 2;

(a)

1: $(t_1, Read\ x\ 2)$ 3: $(t_2, Read\ y\ 1)$

2: $(t_1, Write\ y\ 1)$ 4: $(t_2, Write\ x\ 2)$

(b)

Figure 4.7: Example program with data races [115, Fig. 1] (a) and its JMM execution for the result r1 == 2, r2 == 1 (b)

initially: x = y = 0;

1: r1 = x;	3: r2 = y;
2: y = r1;	4: x = r2;

1: $(t_1, Read\ x\ 42)$ 3: $(t_2, Read\ y\ 42)$

2: $(t_1, Write\ y\ 42)$ 4: $(t_2, Write\ x\ 42)$

Figure 4.8: Example of the value 42 appearing out of thin air [115, Fig. 2]

programs, the thread on the right can pierce the veil. In this situation, the second core reads 1 for y in l. 3 from their shared cache and then writes to x. If memory has not yet returned x's value, the first core uses the new value 2 instead – and the unexpected result becomes real.

Figure 4.7b shows how executions are depicted. The threads are abstracted to events – labelled with the thread ID – and orders. Solid arrows represent program order, transitive relationships are not shown. Dotted arrows used in later examples denote synchronisation (synchronises-with relationships, see §4.3.2 for the formal definition). The dashed arrows denote the flow of values from writes to reads; an execution assigns to each read event the write event it sees. The JMM requires that a read sees a write that happens before or may happen concurrently (grey area in Figure 4.6), i.e., the write must not happen after the read.

The execution shown in Figure 4.7b results in r1 == 2 and r2 == 1. As there is no synchronisation, happens-before coincides with program order. Hence, l. 1 and l. 2 may happen "concurrently" with l. 3 and l. 4. Therefore, l. 1 and l. 3 are allowed to see the writes from l. 4 and l. 2, respectively. In particular, the thread on the left is not allowed to deduce that l. 3 must have already executed from the fact that l. 1 reads the value 2 from l. 4, because there is no synchronisation involved.

If only happens-before constrains visibility of write events, values may appear out of thin air. Consider, e.g., the program and its execution in Figure 4.8, adapted from [115, Fig. 2]. The reads in ll. 1 and 3 may see the writes in ll. 4 and 2, respectively, as they may happen concurrently. If both writes write 42, both reads may read 42, although the program cannot normally produce 42. Hence, 42 appears out of thin air, as the happens-before constraints do not forbid this.

For type safety and security guarantees, it is vital that values do not appear out of thin air [145]. Otherwise, malicious code could exploit this to forge a pointer to an object to which it must not gain access or which it can then access in a type-unsafe fashion. To preclude this, the JMM adds a causality condition: Reads that see concurrent writes must be committed, i.e., there must be a justifying execution that writes the same value, but the read event sees a write that happens before it. This causality condition distinguishes the JMM from memory models of other languages like ADA, where concurrent reads and writes immediately result in the behaviour being undefined. In the above example, causality forbids r1 == 42 because no execution can produce the value 42 without having both reads see the concurrent writes. The important thing to note is that at the basis of any sequence of justifying executions, there is one in which all reads see writes that happen before them.

This is where initialisations come into play. The JMM assumes that all locations are initialised to their default value at the start of the execution. By definition, these initialisations happen before any other event. Thus, there is always at least one suitable write that happens before a given read, which ensures that a basis for justifying executions exists. Remember that program-order is consistent with happens-before. Hence, initialisations precede all other events of the same thread in program order, too, although they correspond to allocations that occur in the midst of an execution. Figure 4.9b shows an example. Thread t_1 generates the events as shown from top to bottom, but the allocation in l. 3 precedes all others in program order and happens before order.

The requirement that a heap location is conceptually initialised at the start (instead of when it is allocated) has been one of the main complications in the proofs – which previous formalisations have omitted [8, 69]. Since initialisation events originate from dynamic allocation, I must consider complete executions, which may be infinite, instead of finite prefixes – at least for the single-threaded semantics. Consider, e.g., the program and one of its executions in Figure 4.9. Remember from above that the initialisation for the field f of the object created in l. 3 at location a happens before all other events, although the single-

class A { field f:int; }	initially: x = y = null;
1: r1 = x;	5: r4 = y;
2: if (r1 != null) r2 = r1.f;	6: x = r4;
3: r3 = new A();	
4: y = r3;	

(a)

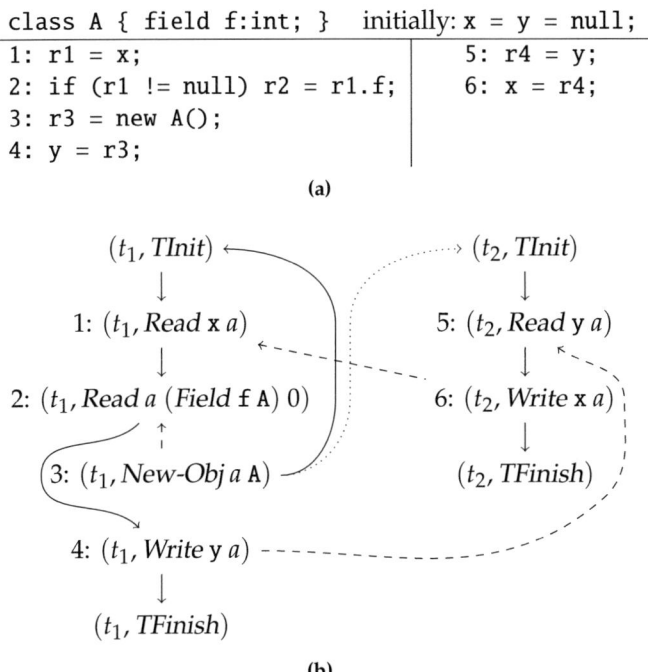

(b)

Figure 4.9: Program with an execution in which the read in l. 2 sees the initialisation from l. 3, which occurs later in the program text

threaded semantics executes it after ll. 1 and 2. Now take the prefix of this execution up to l. 2. If $(t_1, New\text{-}Obj\ a\ A)$ was not part of the prefix, the prefix would be ill-formed because l. 2 sees no write. Hence, prefixes must include the initialisation events. As the single-threaded semantics produces initialisation events only at allocations, I must run the program to completion, because it is undecidable at intermediate states whether all initialisation events have been collected. Thus, the formalisation must deal with infinite executions.

The technical complexity of the JMM makes it very hard to decide what the legal behaviours of a program are. Numerous subtleties, some of which the examples in this chapter illustrate, and the fact that legality can only be decided for whole programs complicate this further. Consequently, one cannot expect the average Java programmer to reason

147

layer	source code		bytecode
7	Java memory model		
6	complete interleavings		
5	interleaved small-step		
4	thread start & finish events		
3	statements & expressions	call stacks	
		exception handling	
		single instruction	
2	native methods		
1	heap operations		

Figure 4.10: Stack of semantics with the JMM

about the JMM. The DRF guarantee relieves the average programmer from this burden. If all thread communication is explicit in the program, Java maintains the illusion of sequential consistency. I prove that the JMM does provide the DRF guarantee in §4.3.3.

4.3.2 Formal definition

The JMM formalisation extends the stack of semantics from Figure 3.1 as shown in Figure 4.10; there are four new layers (shaded). In the single-threaded semantics, the JMM implements the heap module in two different ways (layer 1) and inserts the events for thread start and finish (layer 4). On top of the stack, I define complete interleavings of a program (layer 6) from which the axiomatic JMM (layer 7) selects the legal executions. The JMM also introduces a native method for printing on layer 2, but does not affect the sequential semantics (layer 3) or the interleaving semantics themselves (layer 5). The rest of this section traverses the stack from bottom to top and presents the new layers and changes, respectively.

The heap module: JMM implementation 1

An implementation of the heap module must define operations for values and types, but the weak semantics of the JMM only applies to values.

Recall that checked type casts, virtual method calls, and reading the length of an array are not part of the events. According to the JLS, reading types and array lengths must always return the correct data [56, §17.4.5].[27] Hence, type information also needs a "memory model".

In this implementation, I adopt sequential consistency for types, i.e., allocation determines the type information of the allocated address and distributes this information immediately to all threads. Hence, on the level of types, this approach is the same as in §4.2. Although being straightforward, it suffers from some drawbacks that I discuss below.

Technically, the heap h reduces to a map from addresses to their type information, i.e. $h :: 'addr \rightharpoonup hty$. Then, an address is fresh in the heap h iff h contains no type information for it. Since type information grows monotonically (as JinjaThreads does not model garbage collection), a fresh address has not been allocated before and will never be allocated once more afterwards.

With this heap implementation in mind, the module implementation is then straightforward: Thread IDs are identified with addresses, the empty heap is the empty map $empty$, allocation picks an arbitrary fresh address, and jmm-$typeof$-$addr$ is map lookup. Any value can be read at any time, i.e., jmm-$read$ is constantly $True$; writing does not change the heap. The heap conforms iff all allocated addresses have valid types. The formal definitions can be found in Appendix B.3.2.

Like "sc" for sequential consistency, I prefix or decorate the declarations in the heap locales with "jmm" to refer to their JMM instantiation.

Lemma 4.1. *The JMM heap implementation 1 satisfies the assumptions of the locale* conf-progress *and its anchestors.*

$$conf\text{-}progress\ jmm\text{-}a2t\ jmm\text{-}t2a\ jmm\text{-}typeof\text{-}addr\ jmm\text{-}empty\text{-}heap$$
$$jmm\text{-}allocate\ jmm\text{-}read\ jmm\text{-}write\ (P \vdash_{jmm} \_\sqrt{})\ P$$

Although this heap implementation is simple and straightforward, it does *not* satisfy the assumption of locale *conf-read*, because *jmm-read* allows to read arbitrary values, even non-type-conforming ones. Hence, subject reduction fails. The DRF guarantee shows that correctly synchronised programs, i.e., without data races, are type safe (§4.3.3), but correct synchronisation is undecidable. Programs with data races, however,

---

[27] Although the JLS specifies that every array has a final field `length` [56, §6.4.5] that stores its length, the JMM treats array lengths specially [56, §17.4.5].

```
class A { void f() {} }     initially: x = y = null;
1: r1 = x;                      4: r2 = y;
2: if (r1 != null) r1.f();      5: x = r2;
3: y = new A();
```

Figure 4.11: A program where dynamic dispatch requires type information that is not yet available

may have type-unsafe executions of two kinds. Both exploit that the type of an address is only determined upon allocation, but not when it is first used.

First, when the type of an address is not yet known, the source code semantics or defensive VM get stuck whereas the aggressive VM behaves in an undefined way. For example, the JMM allows that l. 1 in Figure 4.11 reads the address a of the object allocated in l. 3 via the detour of the second thread, because an optimising compiler might move l. 3 before l. 1. However, the semantics does not anticipate such optimisations, but executes the program as it is. Hence, when l. 2 executes the call to f on a, the source code semantics gets stuck, because a's type is still undefined (i.e., *typeof-addr h a = None*). So does the defensive VM, and the aggressive VM calls an unspecified method.

Second, reading an address before its type is determined may also compromise subject reduction. The program in Figure 4.12 has a legal execution where x, y and r2 reference an Integer object, although the program is type correct if it declares them of type String. For a detailed derivation of this execution, see §4.3.5. This is an artefact of the JMM as I am not aware of any optimisation that would produce such a result. In this example, the problem is again that l. 3 reads an address a that has not yet been allocated. Then, l. 4 non-deterministically chooses the type of the object to allocate – note that b can be either false (initial value) or true (assignment in l. 9). Since the object has already been stored in r2 of type String, the second alternative results in a non-conforming state, i.e., type safe is broken.

A temptingly simple measure would be to restrict reading such that only allocated addresses may be read from memory. However, the semantics then would miss some legal JMM behaviours, because this restriction prohibits reordering with memory allocations. For example, reconsider the program in Figure 4.11 with l. 2 removed. The JMM

initially: `b = false; x = y = null;`

1: r1 = y;	3: r2 = x;	9: b = true;
2: x = r1;	4: if (b)	
	5: r3 = new Integer();	
	6: else	
	7: r2 = new String();	
	8: y = r2;	

Figure 4.12: A program with a legal execution where r2 of type `String` references an `Integer` object

allows `r1 ==` y at the end of the modified program, because compilers are allowed to reorder the independent statements in ll. 1 and 3. However, the semantics could not produce this result because the read in l. 1 always happens before the allocation in l. 3, i.e., it could not return the address to be allocated.

The heap module: JMM implementation 2

To address the above type safety problems, I define the following alternative implementation of the heap module – see Appendix B.3.2 for the formal definitions. It is motivated by the insight that the core of the above problems is that the type of an address is only determined upon allocation, but not when it is first used. This model exposes the communication channel of type information between threads to the memory model while the previous one hides it (see below for an example).

Now, it is the address and not the heap that stores type information for the address. Hence, an address consists of its type information (HOL type *hty*) and a sequence number to distinguish objects of the same type.

$$\textbf{datatype } addr = Address\ hty\ nat$$

The type and array length of an address is the information stored in the address – provided that it refers to a valid type.[28] In particular, type information for every address is available from the start. Hence, the

---

[28]This restriction is necessary for the last assumption of locale *conf*. Since I want *typeof-addr* to not depend on the heap, *typeof-addr* may only assign types to addresses that refer to a valid type. Note that this is possible as *alloc-type* of locale *heap* is restricted to valid types.

programs in Figures 4.11 and 4.12 are unproblematic, because with this implementation,

(i) the defensive checks only ensure type correctness, but no longer test on the referenced object having been allocated, and

(ii) the allocations in ll. 5 and 7 always return different addresses.

Now that I have stripped type information off the shared heap, it only needs to remember which addresses are fresh for allocation. Hence, the heap (type *jmm'-heap*) maps type information (type *hty*) to the number of objects of that type that have already been allocated. Allocation then merely increments that number and uses the former value as sequence number for the new address. All heaps conform. Moreover, I also restrict the read operation to require that the value must be type-conforming. This way, this implementation satisfies all assumptions of the heap module. To distinguish it from the previous implementation, I call this implementation JMM' and use "jmm'" as prefix and decoration of the operations and derived definitions.

Theorem 4.2. *The JMM heap implementation 2 satisfies all assumptions of the heap module for any input program.*

$$\textit{typesafe jmm'-a2t jmm'-t2a jmm'-typeof-addr jmm'-empty-heap}$$
$$\textit{jmm'-read jmm'-write jmm'-hconf P}$$

The JMM' heap implementation suffers from two disadvantages compared to the first one. First, since type information partitions the address space, each read or write of an address value not only transfers a pointer value as on standard hardware, but simultaneously does so for the complete run-time type information of the object it references. From an implementation point of view, this is unrealistic.

Second, restricting the read operation to type correct values effectively makes the heap implementation type safe "by definition." Unlike for JMM heap implementation 1, I conjecture that this restriction does not exclude any legal JMM behaviour. The causality constraints should ensure that an execution which reads non-type-conforming values has no sequence of justifying executions. I have not attempted a formal proof yet, but if this is shown in the future, then the restriction may be dropped.

Let me now demonstrate how this heap implementation exposes the hidden communication channel of type information. Consider the

initially: x = 0; y = null;

1: r1 = x; 2: r2 = (r1 == 0 ? new A() : new B()); 3: y = r2;	4: x = 1;	5: r3 = y; 6: r4 = r3.f();

Figure 4.13: Example for implicit communication via type information

program in Figure 4.13. Suppose that classes A and B inherit from some class C which declares a method f(). Under implementation 1, the allocation in l. 2 returns the same address value, no matter whether A or B is allocated. Still, dynamic dispatch at l. 6 tells the thread on the right about the left thread's local variable r1. However, from the point of view of events, the thread on the right only reads an address (in fact the same value in both cases), but behaves differently. Heap implementation 2 allocates A's objects at different addresses than B's. Hence, the value that l. 5 reads completely determines the call target in l. 6. Analogously, threads can communicate through array lengths instead of types, see Figure 4.30 for an example. This is why implementation 2 allocates arrays of different lengths at distinct addresses.

External actions as observable behaviour

For the JMM, an observable behaviour of a program execution consists of a subset of the external actions that is consistent with happens before order and synchronisation order [56, §17.4.9]. This models what the user or other programs may observe without looking at the internal state of the JVM. However, the single-threaded semantics for source code and bytecode do not yet generate external actions. To remedy this, I add a native method *print* to class *Object* that generates intermediate output.

$$Object.print([Integer]) :: Void$$

$$P, t \vdash \langle a.print(vs), h \rangle - (\!| Extern\ a\ print\ vs\ Unit|\!) \rightarrow_{nc} \langle Ret\text{-}Val\ unit, h \rangle \quad (4.1)$$

to attach observable behaviour to the examples of this chapter, one assumes that all variables are output at the end of the program.

Intermediate output is only relevant for constraining the semantics of non-terminating executions, because in case of termination, one could augment the final state with observations of intermediate states. However, there is no such final state in non-terminating ones.

Associating statements and instructions with events

The JMM determines which values a read may return by assigning writes to reads. Synchronisation can restrict (and even enlarge [2,115]) this set of possible values. For that, the JinjaThreads semantics produce events that record memory accesses and synchronisation. Now, I return to the semantics of native methods and source code from §3.2.1 and §3.2.2, respectively, to explain the events that they generate. The bytecode instructions generate the same events as their source code equivalents.

First, reconsider the native methods of class *Thread* from Figure 3.17. The generated events follow exactly the JMM specification [56]. Successfully spawning a thread generates the appropriate *TStart* event. However, no event occurs when spawning fails, because only successful spawns synchronise with the first action of the started thread [56, §17.4.4].

Similarly, interrupting a thread t (INTR) synchronises with the observation that t has been interrupted (JOININTR, ISINTRDT, INTRDT, WAITINTRD1, WAITINTRD2), i.e., INTR produces the event *TIntr t*, the latter rules generate *TIntrd t*. Asymmetrically, clearing t's interrupt status (JOININTR, INTRDT, WAITINTRD1, WAITINTRD2), does not synchronise with the observation that t is not interrupted (ISINTRDF, INTRDF, WAIT), i.e., no event records that. Also, interrupting a thread that has not yet been started has no effect (INTRINEX).

A call to *wait* unlocks the monitor and reacquires the locks after notification. Hence, WAIT (Figure 3.19) generates the event *SUnlock*. Remember that the interleaving semantics already ensures mutual exclusion via thread actions as explained in Chapter 3. Since *SUnlock* only serves to identify synchronisation points for the memory model, one event *SUnlock* suffices, although WAIT may release the monitor multiple times.

When the thread reacquires the lock, ACQUIRE (Figure 3.14) generates the corresponding event *SLock* via the locale parameter *acq-events*, which I have left unspecified in the presentation so far. Source code and bytecode both instantiate *acq-events* such that *acq-events ln* computes a list of *SLock* events for all temporarily released locks in *ln*.

Only the *clone* method generates multiple events in a single reduction (see Appendix B.4.2), namely an allocation for the cloned object or array and *Read* and *Write* for all members that it copies.

The source code semantics generates three kinds of events: First, *sync* (_) _ produces *SLock* and *SUnlock* events (RLOCK, RUNLCK, and RUNLCKX in Figure 3.21). Second, access to members of an object are recorded in *Read* and *Write* events, see, e.g., RFACC and RFASS in Figure 4.4. Third, memory allocation via *new C* and *new T*[_] generates events *New-Obj_ C* and *NewArray_ T _*, respectively.

Thread start and finish events

Remember that the JMM requires that events mark the start and termination of every thread (notation *TInit* and *TFinish*, respectively). In JinjaThreads, layer 4 on the stack of semantics implements this generically as a semantics transformer in the context *multithreaded-base* from §3.1.3. Remember that r :: $('l, 't, 'x, 'h, 'w, 'o)$ *semantics* with notation $t \vdash (x, h) -ta\rightarrow (x', h')$ is the single-threaded semantics and the predicate *final* :: $'t \Rightarrow bool$ characterises final states. The transformer pairs every thread's local state (type $'x$) with its status (HOL type *status* with elements *Pre-Start*, *Running*, and *Finished*) and extends r to sf.r with notation $t \vdash ((s, x), h) -ta\rightarrow_{\text{sf}} ((s', x'), h')$ as follows:

SFINIT: $\quad t \vdash ((\textit{Pre-Start}, x), h) - (\textit{TInit}) \rightarrow_{\text{sf}} ((\textit{Running}, x), h)$

SFRUN: $\quad \dfrac{t \vdash (x, h) -ta\rightarrow (x', h')}{t \vdash ((\textit{Running}, x), h) -\textit{pair-Pre-Start ta}\rightarrow_{\text{sf}} ((\textit{Running}, x'), h')}$

SFFINISH: $\quad \dfrac{\textit{final } x}{t \vdash ((\textit{Running}, x), h) - (\textit{TFinish}) \rightarrow_{\text{sf}} ((\textit{Finished}, x), h)}$

Threads are initially marked as *Pre-Start*. They must transition to *Running* – which generates the start event *TInit* (SFINIT) – before they can execute according to r (SFRUN). The conversion function *pair-Pre-Start ta* pairs the initial states of spawned threads in *ta* with *Pre-Start* such that their first reduction generates the event *TInit* via SFINIT.[29] After the

---

[29]Technically, the type of events *event* and its abstraction $'o$ do not contain the events *TInit* and *TFinish*. Instead, I extend $'o$ to $'o$ *sf* where

$$\textbf{datatype } 'o \textit{ sf} = \textit{Event } 'o \mid \textit{TInit} \mid \textit{TFinish}$$

In the presentation, I identify $'o$ and $'o$ *sf* and omit the coercion *Event*. In particular, *pair-Pre-Start ta* implicitly injects events in $\langle ta \rangle_o$ to $'o$ *sf* and *sf.acq-events* = *map Event* ∘ *acq-events* replaces *acq-events*.

thread has terminated as predicated by *final*, SFFINISH adds the *TFinish* event.

Analogously, *sf.final* replaces *final* where

$$sf.final\ (s, x) \longleftrightarrow s = Finished \wedge final\ x$$

I will use the prefix "*sf.*" to refer to semantics that have been transformed this way, e.g., *sf.J-red* and *J.sf.redT*.

Lemma 4.2. *If r and final satisfy the well-formedness conditions of the interleaving semantics (locale* multithreaded*), so do sf.r and sf.final.*

$$\frac{multithreaded\ final\ r\ acq\text{-}events}{multithreaded\ sf.final\ sf.r\ sf.acq\text{-}events}$$

Complete interleavings

The JMM suggests to execute all threads in isolation and to determine a posteriori the legal executions in terms of their traces of events. Unfortunately, the events from §4.3.1 are insufficient to correctly implement the JLS, because the JLS (and the Java API) introduce other communication channels between threads. For example, consider the program in Figure 4.14 in which two threads race for spawning the same thread. Suppose both reads in ll. 3 and 5 see the write at l.2. Then, either l. 4 or l. 6 must throw an *IllegalThreadState* exception, but not both. Hence, both l. 4 and l. 6 must be allowed to fail in some executions. Thus, the two right-most threads may just start, read the address of the *Thread* object (then fail with the exception, but no event records that), and then finish. Hence, if each thread were run in isolation, they both would be allowed to fail, too. Since this contradicts the specification of the *start* method, there is a covert communication channel.

For the `start` method, the JMM specifies synchronisation only between a successful call and the first action of the spawned thread [56, §17.4.4]. A JVM implementation might add additional synchronisation, but my semantics must not, since such synchronisation might eliminate data races from programs, i.e., it could wrongly certify programs with data races as DRF. Therefore, the JinjaThreads semantics generates no synchronisation events when *start* fails (STARTFAIL).

Hence, threads cannot execute in isolation, as the JMM suggests. Instead, I employ the interleaving semantics from §3.1 to compute

initially: x = null;		
1: r1 = new Thread();	3: r2 = x;	5: r3 = x;
2: x = r1;	4: r2.start();	6: r3.start();

Figure 4.14: Thread spawn as an implicit communication channel

their interleavings. This way, I reuse the infrastructure for mutual exclusion for locks and managing the monitor wait sets, notifications and interrupts. The single-threaded semantics for source code and bytecode are $sf.J\text{-}red\ P$ and $sf.jvm\text{-}exec\ P$, respectively, i.e., the semantics from Chapter 3 augmented with thread start and finish actions from layer 4.

A complete interleaving E is a possibly infinite list[30] of pairs of thread ID and event. The relation $s \Downarrow E$ characterises all complete interleavings E that start in the state s, which I define as

$$s \Downarrow E \longleftrightarrow (\exists ttas.\ s \downarrow ttas \wedge E = concat\ (map\ events\ ttas)) \qquad (4.2)$$

where $events\ (t, ta) = map\ (\lambda e.\ (t, e))\ \langle ta \rangle_0$ pairs all events in ta with the thread ID t, and $s \downarrow ttas$ collects the list of thread actions labelled with the thread ID as follows:

$$\frac{s \not\rightarrow}{s \downarrow []}\ \text{STOP} \qquad \frac{s -t:ta\rightarrow s' \qquad s' \downarrow ttas}{s \downarrow (t, ta) \cdot ttas}\ \text{STEP}$$

where $\_ \not\rightarrow$ characterises stuck states in the interleaving semantics.

Note that the detour via a list of thread actions is necessary. If I defined $s \Downarrow E$ directly with the above coinductive rules STOP and STEP (i.e., prepending $events\ (t, ta)$ to E instead of consing), I could derive every trace E for a state s that can perform an infinite sequence of reductions without events, i.e., $\langle ta \rangle_0 = []$, because it would be impossible to prove that E was not a trace (see also the example on coinductive definitions in §1.4.3). My approach works fine since $(t, ta) \cdot E$ is productive and concatenating the infinite list of empty lists yields $[]$.

---

[30]Isabelle's default type for lists $'a\ list$ models only finite lists. Therefore, I have developed a theory of possibly infinite lists (HOL type $'a\ llist$) [110] based on the codatatype construction by Paulson [142]. For clarity of presentation, I use the same notation for operations on $'a\ list$ and $'a\ llist$ (e.g., $\_ \cdot \_$, $\_ @ \_$, and $concat$) and omit the coercions between the two types, although Isabelle distinguishes the former and requires the latter.

The start state (Figure 4.3) has preallocated *start-tID*'s *Thread* object and the system exceptions. Hence, I prefix the complete interleavings with the appropriate initialisation events *start-events*:

$$start\text{-}events =$$
$$(start\text{-}tID, TInit) \cdot map \ (\lambda(C, a). \ (start\text{-}tID, New\text{-}Obj \ a \ C))$$
$$(zip \ (Thread \cdot sys\text{-}xcpts) \ start\text{-}addrs)$$

For the JMM, a program P always comes with a fixed start state, i.e., let *start-state* refer to either *J-start* $P\,C\,M\,vs$ or *jvm-start* $P\,C\,M\,vs$.[31] Then, the JMM identifies a program with the set $\mathcal{E}$ of complete interleavings that start in *start-state*, prefixed with *start-events*. Formally:

$$\mathcal{E} = \{ \ start\text{-}events @ E \ | \ E. \ start\text{-}state \Downarrow E \ \}$$

$\mathcal{E}$ contains many ill-formed executions, because read operations may read arbitrary values, even not type-conforming ones under heap implementation 1 that no write operation of the program can ever produce. Since such executions have no write-seen function, the rules on layer 7 discard them.

Let me now present an example of $\mathcal{E}$ in detail. Figure 4.15 shows a Java implementation of the example in Figure 4.7. There is a bootstrapping thread t_0 that creates and spawns the two threads t_1 and t_2 whose *run* methods contain the code from the example. Since JinjaThreads does not model static fields, the shared locations x and y are represented by the fields of a container class C.

All complete interleavings start with the following events that represent t_0's main method up to the first call to *start*, abbreviated as as:

$$start\text{-}events @$$
$$[(t_0, New\text{-}Obj \ a_0 \ C),$$
$$(t_0, New\text{-}Obj \ a_1 \ (T1)), (t_0, Write \ a_1 \ (Field \ c \ T1) \ a_0),$$
$$(t_0, New\text{-}Obj \ a_2 \ (T2)), (t_0, Write \ a_2 \ (Field \ c \ T2) \ a_0), (t_0, TStart \ (a2t \ a_1))]$$

i.e., t_0 allocates the objects for the container and the two threads at locations a_0 to a_2 and executes *T1*'s and *T2*'s constructors. Remember that the allocations initialise the fields with default values, i.e., 0 for x and y declared in *C*, and *Null* for c declared in *T1* and *T2*.

---

[31]Since *start-events* already contains *start-tID*'s *TInit*, I assume that the initial thread-local state for *start-tID* is paired with *Running*.

```
class T0 {
  public static void main(String[] args) {
    C c = new C();
    Thread t1 = new T1(c);
    Thread t2 = new T2(c);
    t1.start();
    t2.start();
} }

class T1 extends Thread {
  C c;
  T1(C c) { this.c = c; }
  public void run() { C c = this.c; int r1 = c.x; c.y = 1; }
}

class T2 extends Thread {
  C c;
  T2(C c) { this.c = c; }
  public void run() { C c = this.c; int r2 = c.y; c.x = 2; }
}

class C { int x, y; }
```

Figure 4.15: Java implementation for the example in Figure 4.7

Thread t_1 has three structurally different traces depending on the kind of value that reading **this**.c stores in the local variable c, namely:

1. $[TInit, Read\ a_1\ (Field\ c\ T1)\ (Addr\ a), Read\ a\ (Field\ x\ C)\ v,$
   $Write\ a\ (Field\ y\ C)\ 1, TFinish],$
2. $[TInit, Read\ a_1\ (Field\ c\ T1)\ Null, TFinish],$ and
3. $[TInit, Read\ a_1\ (Field\ c\ T1)\ w],$

where a is an arbitrary address, v is an arbitrary value, and w is either *Unit* or an integer or boolean value. In the first form, the address a from the *Read* is then used to access the fields x and y of the referenced container. In the second, t_1 reads *Null*, so the subsequent field access raises the preallocated *NullPointer* exception and the thread immediately terminates. In the last case, w is type-incorrect, so the semantics gets stuck upon the next field access, i.e., there is no *TFinish*. Under implementation 2, the last case is impossible, and v must be an integer value if $a = a_0$,

159

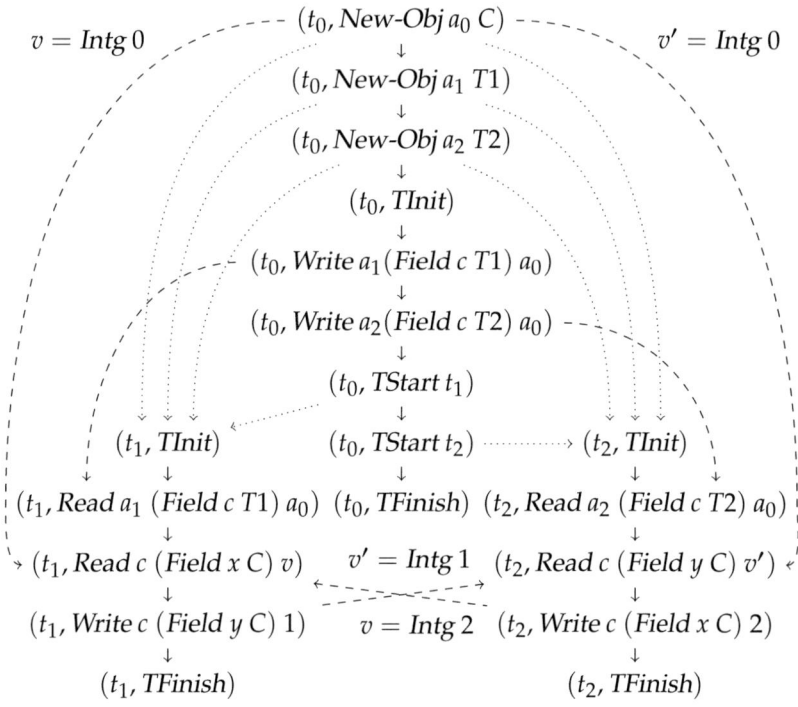

Figure 4.16: Well-formed executions for the program in Figure 4.15 where $t_1 = a2t\,a_1$ and $t_2 = a2t\,a_2$

because it forbids reads to return type-incorrect values. Thread t_2 has the same traces with x and y exchanged.

The complete interleavings in $\mathcal{E}$ for this program all start with αs and then interleave the threads. Of these, the JMM considers only those as well-formed that originate from the first form with $a = a_0$, $v \in \{\,Intg\,0, Intg\,2\,\}$ for t_1 and $v \in \{\,Intg\,0, Intg\,1\,\}$ for t_2. In particular, the unexpected behaviour from Figure 4.7 is well-formed. In terms of the JMM, all these interleavings collapse to four well-formed executions as shown in Figure 4.16 (where I have omitted the bootstrap events for clarity – except for t_0's initial event that is relevant for determining what happens before what). The write-seen arrows are labelled with conditions for which they apply. All well-formed executions are legal in this example.

Definition of the Java memory model

Now, I formally derive the orders of the JMM from a complete interleaving $E \in \mathcal{E}$. As this core of the JMM has been formalised before [8,69], I keep this section brief; for the intuition behind the concepts, see [8,56,69,115].

Since an event can occur multiple times in E, I use the index in E to assign a unique identifier to an event, i.e., $\mathcal{A}_E = \{\alpha.\ \alpha < |E|\}$ denotes the set of events for E. In the following, I identify an event with its index, i.e., I write α instead of $E_{[\alpha]}$ when it is clear from the context. A read event is an event of the form $(t, Read\ a\ al\ v)$, it reads from location (a, al) the value v; $\mathcal{R}_E$ denotes the set of read events of E. A write event is either a write $(t, Write\ a\ al\ v)$ or an initialisation $(t, Allocate\ a\ hT)$, $\mathcal{W}_E$ denotes the set of write events in E. A write event $\alpha \in \mathcal{W}_E$ writes to location (a, al) (is a write to (a, al)) iff $\alpha = (\_, Write\ a\ al\ \_)$, or $\alpha = (\_, Allocate\ a\ hT)$ and al is a member of hT, i.e., (i) if $al = Field\ F\ D$, then $P \vdash class\text{-}of'\ hT\ has\ F:\_\ (\_)\ in\ D$, and (ii) if $al = Cell\ n$, then $hT = ArrayT\ \_\ n'$ such that $n < n'$. I say that α accesses location (a, al) iff α is a read or write event that reads from or writes to (a, al), respectively. $locs\ P\ E\ \alpha$ denotes the set of locations that $\alpha \in \mathcal{R}_E \cup \mathcal{W}_E$ accesses; $locs\ P\ E\ \alpha = \emptyset$ for $\alpha \in \mathcal{A}_E - (\mathcal{R}_E \cup \mathcal{W}_E)$.

For $\alpha \in \mathcal{W}_E$, $value\text{-}written\ P\ E\ \alpha\ (a, al)$ denotes the value that α writes to location (a, al) – allocation events write default values ($Intg\ 0$, $Bool\ False$, and $Null$, respectively) for all allocated members; normal writes $Write$ store the value written themselves; it is undefined if α does not write to (a, al).

A member al is volatile (written $is\text{-}volatile\ P\ al$) iff $al = Field\ F\ D$ and P declares field F in D as volatile. A read or write α is volatile iff α reads from or writes to a volatile member of a location. Note that array cells are never volatile by definition [56, §8.3.1.4].

A complete interleaving E already provides the induced total order $\leq^E\ =\ \leq|_{\mathcal{A}_E}$ over $\mathcal{A}_E$, where $R|_A$ restricts the binary relation R to elements from A and $\leq$ is the standard order on natural numbers.

Since the JMM requires initialisation events (i.e. $Allocate$) to be ordered before the threads' initial events, I introduce the (total) execution order $\leq^E_{eo}$ on $\mathcal{A}_E$:

$$\alpha \leq^E_{eo} \alpha' \longleftrightarrow (\text{if } init_E\ \alpha \text{ then } \neg init_E\ \alpha' \vee \alpha \leq^E \alpha' \text{ else } \neg init_E\ \alpha' \wedge \alpha \leq^E \alpha')$$

where $init_E\ \alpha$ predicates that α is an initialisation event in E, i.e., $E_{[\alpha]} = (\_, Allocate\ \_\ \_)$.

161

$$(t, SUnlock\ a) \rightsquigarrow_{sw} (t', SLock\ a)$$
$$(t, Write\ a\ al\ v) \rightsquigarrow_{sw} (t', Read\ a\ al\ v')$$
$$(t, New\text{-}Obj\ a\ C) \rightsquigarrow_{sw} (t', Read\ a\ al\ v)$$
$$(t, TStart\ t') \rightsquigarrow_{sw} (t', TInit)$$
$$(t, TFinish) \rightsquigarrow_{sw} (t', TJoin\ t)$$
$$(t, Allocate\ a\ hT) \rightsquigarrow_{sw} (t', TInit)$$
$$(t, TIntr\ t'') \rightsquigarrow_{sw} (t', TIntrd\ t'')$$

Figure 4.17: Release-acquire pairs

The program order $\leq_{po}^{E}$ restricts $\leq_{eo}^{E}$ to events of the same thread. The synchronisation order $\leq_{so}^{P,E}$ restricts $\leq_{eo}^{E}$ to synchronisation events. Synchronisation events are the initialisation events (*Allocate*), reads from and writes to volatile locations, locking (*SLock*) and unlocking (*SUnlock*), thread spawns (*TStart*) and joins (*TJoin*), thread start (*TInit*) and finish events (*TFinish*), and the interruption events *TIntr* and *TIntrd*. The synchronises-with order $\leq_{sw}^{P,E}$ restricts $\leq_{so}^{P,E}$ to release-acquire pairs of events. (α, α') is a release-acquire pair (notation $\alpha \rightsquigarrow_{sw} \alpha'$, definition in Figure 4.17) iff

(i) α unlocks a monitor and α' locks the same monitor,
(ii) α writes to a location that α' reads,[32]
(iii) α spawns a thread whose start action is α',
(iv) α is the finish event of the thread on which α' joins,
(v) α is an initialisation event and α' is a thread start event, or
(vi) α interrupts a thread t and α' observes that t has been interrupted.

The happens-before order $\leq_{hb}^{P,E}$ is the transitive closure of $\leq_{po}^{E}$ and $\leq_{sw}^{P,E}$.

An execution (E, ws) consists of a complete interleaving E and a write-seen function ws that assigns to every read event in $\mathcal{A}_E$ the write event it sees. This yields the JMM notion of an execution [56, §17.4.6] as $(\mathcal{E}, \mathcal{A}_E, \leq_{po}^{E}, \leq_{so}^{P,E}, ws, value\text{-}written\ P\ E, \leq_{sw}^{P,E}, \leq_{hb}^{P,E})$.

An execution is well-formed (written $P \vdash (E, ws)\sqrt{}$) iff every thread has a thread start event that $\leq^{E}$-precedes its other events except for initialisation events (denoted *ok-init E*) and for all read events $\alpha \in \mathcal{R}_E$ to some location (a, al),

---

[32]I do not need to restrict writes and reads to volatiles explicitly like the JMM does [56, §17.4.4], because the synchronisation order already imposes this.

162

W1 $ws\ \alpha$ writes to (a, al), i.e., $ws\ \alpha \in \mathcal{W}_E$ and $(a, al) \in locs\ P\ E\ (ws\ \alpha)$,

W2 α reads the value $value\text{-}written\ E\ (ws\ \alpha)\ (a, al)$,

W3 $\alpha \not\leq_{hb}^{P,E} ws\ \alpha$,

W4 for all write events β to (a, al), if $ws\ \alpha \leq_{hb}^{P,E} \beta \leq_{hb}^{P,E} \alpha$, then $\beta = ws\ \alpha$, and

W5 if α is a volatile read, then $\alpha \not\leq_{so}^{P,E} ws\ \alpha$ and for all write actions β to (a, al), if $ws\ \alpha \leq_{so}^{P,E} \beta \leq_{so}^{P,E} \alpha$, then $\beta = ws\ \alpha$.

E is well-formed iff $P \vdash (E, ws) \surd$ for some ws.

These conditions correspond to the JMM well-formedness conditions 1 (each read sees a write to the same location), 4 ($\leq_{hb}^{P,E}$ consistency) and 5 ($\leq_{so}^{P,E}$ consistency for volatiles) in [56, §17.4.7]. (E, ws) meets conditions 2 ($\leq_{hb}^{P,E}$ is a partial order) and 3 (intra-thread consistency) by construction.

The JMM constrains $\leq_{so}^{P,E}$ to be an ω-order for well-formed executions. As Aspinall and Ševčík [8] already noted, in an infinitely running program, infinitely many allocation events for volatile fields synchronise with thread start events, which violates this constraint, i.e., the JMM would allow no behaviour at all. To remedy this, I drop this constraint. Note that $\leq^E$ is of order at most ω by construction, hence $\leq_{so}^{P,E}$ is of order at most $\omega + \omega$ by definition.

Lemma 4.3. *If $E \in \mathcal{E}$, then ok-init E.*

A legal execution is a well-formed execution (E, ws) that is justified by a sequence of justifying executions $(E_i, ws_i, C_i, \varphi_i)_i$, where C_i are the sets of committed events and the event renaming functions φ_i inject the committed events of E_i into E's events. The definition in Figure 4.18 uses the following notation: *inj-on f A* expresses that the function f is injective on the set A; $\alpha\ \varphi_i^{-1}(R)\ \alpha'$ iff $\varphi_i\ \alpha\ R\ \varphi_i\ \alpha'$ for a binary relation R; $\varphi_{i+1}^{-1}(\alpha)$ abbreviates $\varepsilon\alpha'.\ \alpha' \in C_{i+1} \wedge \varphi_{i+1}\ \alpha' = \alpha$; $(t, e) \simeq (t', e')$ iff $t = t'$ and the events e and e' are identical except for the values they write or read.

The constraints are exactly the JMM legality conditions 1 to 7 and 9 [56, §17.4.8] with explicit renaming of events plus basic requirements for commit sequences and event renamings. I omit condition 8 for two reasons: First, it relies on the transitive reduction of $\leq_{hb}^{P,E_i}$, which need

$$P \vdash (E, ws) \text{ justified-by } (E_i, ws_i, C_i, \varphi_i)_i \longleftrightarrow$$
$$(\forall i.\ P \vdash (E_i, ws_i) \sqrt{}) \wedge$$
$$(\forall i.\ \text{inj-on } \varphi_i\ \mathcal{A}_{E_i} \wedge (\forall \alpha \in C_i.\ E_{i[\alpha]} \simeq E_{[\varphi_i\ \alpha]})) \wedge (\forall i.\ C_i \subseteq \mathcal{A}_{E_i}) \wedge$$
$$C_0 = \emptyset \wedge (\forall i.\ \varphi_i\ {}'C_i \subseteq \varphi_{i+1}\ {}'C_{i+1}) \wedge \mathcal{A}_E = \bigcup_i \varphi_i\ {}'C_i \wedge$$
$$(\forall i.\ \leq_{\text{hb}}^{P,E_i}\Big|_{C_i} = \varphi_i^{-1}(\leq_{\text{hb}}^{P,E})\Big|_{C_i}) \wedge (\forall i.\ \leq_{\text{so}}^{P,E_i}\Big|_{C_i} = \varphi_i^{-1}(\leq_{\text{so}}^{P,E})\Big|_{C_i}) \wedge$$
$$(\forall i.\ \forall \alpha \in \mathcal{W}_{E_i} \cap C_i.\ \forall (a, al) \in \text{locs } P\ E\ (\varphi_i\ \alpha).$$
$$\quad \text{value-written } P\ E_i\ \alpha\ (a, al) = \text{value-written } P\ E\ (\varphi_i\ \alpha)\ (a, al)) \wedge$$
$$(\forall i.\ \forall \alpha \in \mathcal{R}_{E_i} \cap C_i.\ \varphi_{i+1}\ (ws_{i+1}\ (\varphi_{i+1}^{-1}\ (\varphi_i\ \alpha))) = ws\ (\varphi_i\ \alpha)) \wedge$$
$$(\forall i.\ \forall \alpha \in \mathcal{R}_{E_{i+1}}.\ \varphi_{i+1}\ \alpha \in \varphi_i\ {}'C_i \vee ws_{i+1}\ \alpha \leq_{\text{hb}}^{P,E_{i+1}} \alpha) \wedge$$
$$(\forall i.\ \forall \alpha \in \mathcal{R}_{E_{i+1}} \cap C_{i+1}.$$
$$\quad \varphi_{i+1}\ \alpha \in \varphi_i\ {}'C_i \vee \{\varphi_{i+1}\ (ws_{i+1}\ \alpha), ws\ (\varphi_{i+1}\ \alpha)\} \subseteq \varphi_i\ {}'C_i) \wedge$$
$$(\forall i.\ \forall \alpha \in \mathcal{A}_{E_i}.\ \forall \alpha' \in C_i.\ \forall a\ M\ vs\ v.$$
$$\quad E_{i[\alpha]} = \text{Extern } a\ M\ vs\ v \longrightarrow \alpha \leq_{\text{hb}}^{P,E_i} \alpha' \longrightarrow \alpha \in C_i)$$

$$P, \mathcal{E} \vdash (E, ws) \text{ legal} \longleftrightarrow E \in \mathcal{E} \wedge P \vdash (E, ws) \sqrt{} \wedge$$
$$(\exists (E_i, ws_i, C_i, \varphi_i)_i.\ P \vdash (E, ws) \text{ justified-by } (E_i, ws_i, C_i, \varphi_i)_i \wedge$$
$$(\forall i.\ E_i \in \mathcal{E}))$$

Figure 4.18: Legality constraints for the justification $(E_i, ws_i, C_i, \varphi_i)_i$ for the execution (E, ws)

not exists for infinite executions. Second, Torlak et al. [171] have shown that it is irrelevant for all JMM test cases.

I am not going to explain the constraints in detail, as others have done so already [8, 69]. As §4.3.1 explains, they serve to ban values appearing out of thin air, but §4.3.5 shows that they fail to do so.

4.3.3 The data race freedom guarantee

Remember that the JMM promises that correctly synchronised programs behave as if they were executed under sequential consistency. In this section, I recapitulate the definitions and identify the assumptions of this guarantee. Then, I show that source code and bytecode indeed satisfy these assumptions.

The proof of the DRF guarantee extends over all layers of the semantics stack (Figure 4.10). Hence, the challenge consists of adequately decomposing the proof and distributing it over the layers such that each proof is as abstract as possible. This way, I prove the DRF guarantee for both JMM heap implementations and for both source code and bytecode (Theorem 4.6) almost simultaneously. To that end, I extend the locales for the heap module (§4.1) and the multithreaded semantics (§3.1.3) with additional operations and assumptions. It is crucial that these assumptions respect the abstraction of the layer, i.e., they only refer to notions of the layer or below, but not above. For example, assumptions about the heap implementation must not mention JMM executions.

Therefore, this section focuses on what these assumptions are and how to formalise them. The transition from the global behaviour (executions and complete interleavings) to the individual steps of the small-step semantics is the most difficult one, because it must translate global notions into state invariants. Sometimes, this is not directly possible: for example, levels 5 and below generalise the happens-before order to the execution order, because happens-before is hard to express as a state invariant.

To derive and motivate the low-level assumptions from those on higher levels, the presentation starts with the proofs on the JMM level and then descends the stack of semantics, similar to backward-style reasoning.

The DRF guarantee

In this section, I formally state the DRF guarantee and prove it. Two events of an execution are conflicting if they are read or write events to the same location with at least one being a write event. Two conflicting events constitute a data race if they are not ordered by happens-before, i.e., may happen concurrently.

An execution (E, ws) is sequentially consistent (SC) iff every read event $\alpha \in \mathcal{R}_E$ sees the most recent write event, i.e. $ws\, \alpha \leq_{eo}^E \alpha$, and $\beta \leq_{eo}^E ws\, \alpha$ or $\alpha \leq_{eo}^E \beta$ for all write events β to the location that α reads from.[33]

A program is correctly synchronised (data race free) iff none of its SC executions contains a data race. Formally: Whenever $E \in \mathcal{E}$, $P \vdash (E, ws)\sqrt{}$

---

[33]The JMM only requires that $\leq_{po}^E$ is extended to a total order over all events of all threads to determine most recent writes [56, §17.4.3]. Aspinall and Ševčík [8] showed that, to respect mutual exclusion of locks, the total order must also extend $\leq_{so}^{P,E}$. My execution order $\leq_{eo}^E$ extends both by construction.

and (E, ws) is SC, then $\alpha \leq_{hb}^{P,E} \alpha'$ or $\alpha' \leq_{hb}^{P,E} \alpha$ for all conflicting events $\alpha, \alpha' \in \mathcal{A}_E$.

For the DRF guarantee, it is important that only SC executions must not contain a data race. Otherwise, it would fail its purpose because the programmer would have to understand the whole JMM to see whether her program is correctly synchronised and the DRF guarantee applies to it.

My proof of the DRF guarantee (Theorem 4.3) adapts the others' [8, 69, 115] to deal with memory allocation and initialisations (see §4.3.6 for a discussion). The key idea in all of them is that in a DRF program, a well-formed execution (E, ws) is SC if every read sees a write that happens before it (Lemma 4.4) – then, the legality constraints ensure that all legal executions are SC.

Lemma 4.4 (DRF lemma [8, Lemma 2]). *Let $\mathcal{E}$ be correctly synchronised and $E \in \mathcal{E}$ such that $P \vdash (E, ws) \sqrt{}$. If $ws\,\alpha \leq_{hb}^{P,E} \alpha$ for every read α in $\mathcal{R}_E$, then (E, ws) is sequentially consistent.*

To exploit correct synchronisation in a proof of this lemma by contradiction (see below), one first obtains a SC execution (E', ws') from (E, ws) as follows: E' starts like E until the first non-SC read α in E and continues sequentially consistently from there on. Then, it suffices to find a data race between α, $ws\,\alpha$, and $ws'\,\alpha$ in E'. For the latter, I use Lemma 4.6 (see below) to transfer happens-before relationships between E and E' on their common prefix. The proof therefore rests on two assumptions on the set of complete interleavings $\mathcal{E}$:

D1 For every sequentially-consistent prefix of a well-formed execution (E, ws) with $E \in \mathcal{E}$, there is a complete interleaving $E' \in \mathcal{E}$ with the same prefix and a write seen-function ws' such that $P \vdash (E', ws') \sqrt{}$ and (E', ws') is SC. If E immediately continues with a read after the prefix, E' also continues with a read from the same location.

D2 Every execution $E \in \mathcal{E}$ initialises every location at most once.

The first assumption ensures that E' as required in the proof of Lemma 4.4 does exist, the second is a standard well-formedness condition. Below, I prove that source code and bytecode satisfy these.

From the DRF lemma, the DRF guarantee (Theorem 4.3) follows. I omit its proof since it closely follows [8, Theorem 1].

Theorem 4.3 (DRF guarantee). *If the program P is correctly synchronised and (E, ws) a legal execution, then (E, ws) is sequentially consistent.*

To prove Lemma 4.4, I need two more lemmata about happens-before:

Lemma 4.5. *Let ok-init E and $\alpha, \alpha' \in \mathcal{A}_E$ such that $init_E\, \alpha$ and $\neg init_E\, \alpha'$. Then $\alpha \leq^{P,E}_{hb} \alpha'$.*

Proof. Let ι be the initial event *TInit* of α''s thread. By definition, $\alpha \leq^{P,E}_{sw} \iota \leq^{E}_{po} \alpha'$. $\qquad\square$

Lemma 4.6 (happens-before prefix lemma). *Let E and E' be two complete interleavings such that their first n events differ only in the values read or written, and let $\alpha, \alpha' < n$. If ok-init E' and $\alpha \leq^{P,E}_{hb} \alpha'$, then $\alpha \leq^{P,E'}_{hb} \alpha'$.*

Proof. By induction on the transitive closure of $\alpha \leq^{P,E}_{hb} \alpha'$. In the base case, $\alpha \leq^{E}_{po} \alpha'$ or $\alpha' \leq^{P,E}_{sw} \alpha'$. By unfolding the definitions, $\alpha \leq^{E'}_{po} \alpha'$ or $\alpha \leq^{P,E'}_{sw} \alpha'$ follows. Hence, $\alpha \leq^{P,E'}_{hb} \alpha'$.

In the induction step, I may assume $\alpha, \alpha'' < n$, and $\alpha \leq^{P,E}_{hb} \alpha'$, and $\alpha' \leq^{E}_{po} \alpha''$ or $\alpha' \leq^{P,E}_{sw} \alpha''$, and the induction hypothesis if $\alpha' < n$, then $\alpha \leq^{P,E'}_{hb} \alpha'$. I must show that $\alpha \leq^{P,E'}_{hb} \alpha''$.

If $\neg init_E\, \alpha'$ or $init_E\, \alpha''$, then $\alpha' \leq^{E} \alpha''$ by definition of $\leq^{E}_{eo}$, because $\alpha' \leq^{E}_{eo} \alpha''$ follows from either $\alpha' \leq^{E}_{po} \alpha''$ or $\alpha' \leq^{P,E}_{sw} \alpha''$. Since $\alpha'' < n$, also $\alpha' < n'$ and the induction hypothesis applies. Moreover, $\alpha' \leq^{E'}_{po} \alpha''$ or $\alpha' \leq^{P,E'}_{sw} \alpha''$ follow from $\alpha' \leq^{E}_{po} \alpha''$ or $\alpha' \leq^{P,E}_{sw} \alpha''$ as in the base case. Therefore, $\alpha \leq^{P,E'}_{hb} \alpha''$.

Otherwise, I have $init_E\, \alpha'$ and $\neg init_E\, \alpha''$. Then, $init_E\, \alpha$ follows from $init_E\, \alpha'$ by induction on $\alpha \leq^{P,E}_{hb} \alpha'$. Since $\alpha, \alpha'' < n$ and E's and E'''s first n actions only differ in the values read or written, $init_{E'}\, \alpha$ and $\neg init_{E'}\, \alpha''$, too. Hence $\alpha \leq^{P,E'}_{hb} \alpha''$ by Lemma 4.5. $\qquad\square$

Now, I am ready to prove the DRF lemma.

Proof of Lemma 4.4. By contradiction. Suppose that (E, ws) is not SC. Note that $\leq^{E}_{eo}$ is well-founded by construction. Let $\alpha \in \mathcal{R}_E$ be the $\leq^{E}_{eo}$-minimal read event from some location (a, al) such that $ws\, \alpha$ is not the most recent write for α in E. By assumption, $ws\, \alpha \leq^{P,E}_{hb} \alpha$. Moreover, there is a write event $\beta \in \mathcal{W}_E$ to (a, al) such that $\beta \not\leq^{P,E}_{hb} ws\, \alpha$, $\alpha \not\leq^{P,E}_{hb} \beta$, and $\beta \leq^{E}_{eo} \alpha$ – otherwise, $ws\, \alpha$ would be the most recent write for α.

167

Then, $\neg init_E\ \beta$, as otherwise $\neg init_E\ (ws\ \alpha)$, because E initialises every location at most once, and therefore $\beta \leq_{hb}^{P,E} ws\ \alpha$ by Lemma 4.5. I show that $ws\ \alpha \leq_{hb}^{P,E} \beta$, which violates the happens-before consistency condition W4 of ws being well-formed. If $init_E\ (ws\ \alpha)$, then $ws\ \alpha \leq_{hb}^{P,E} \beta$ by Lemma 4.5. So, suppose $\neg init_E\ (ws\ \alpha)$. With $\neg init_E\ \beta$, both β and $ws\ \alpha$ occur before α in E, i.e., $\beta, ws\ \alpha \leq^{E} \alpha$. By requirement D1, I obtain a well-formed execution (E', ws') that starts with E up to α and continues SC, with α being a read from (a, al) in E'. As $\beta, ws\ \alpha \in \mathcal{A}_{E'}$ are conflicting and (E', ws') is SC, $\beta \leq_{hb}^{P,E'} ws\ \alpha$ or $ws\ \alpha \leq_{hb}^{P,E'} \beta$. By Lemma 4.6, $\beta \leq_{hb}^{P,E} ws\ \alpha$ or $ws\ \alpha \leq_{hb}^{P,E} \beta$, but $\beta \nleq_{hb}^{P,E} ws\ \alpha$. □

Note that Lemma 4.6 (and Lemma 4.4 and Theorem 4.3 which build on it) requires that *all* initialisation events synchronise with thread start events, i.e., they are synchronisation events. For example, consider the program and two of its well-formed interleavings in Figure 4.19. Both interleavings share the prefix $[(t_1, TInit), (t_1, \text{initialise } x), (t_2, TInit)]$. If only initialisations for volatile locations synchronised with thread start events (as Manson suggested [114]), $(t_1, \text{initialise } x)$ would not synchronize with $(t_2, TInit)$, i.e., there would not be such a dotted arrow in Figure 4.19. For E_1, we would still get $(t_1, \text{initialise } x) \leq_{hb}^{P,E_1} (t_2, TInit)$, because

$$(t_1, \text{initialise } x) \leq_{po}^{E_1} (t_1, \text{New-Obj } a\ C) \leq_{sw}^{P,E_1} (t_2, TInit)$$

and $(t_1, \text{New-Obj } a\ C)$ writes (initialises) the volatile member *Field v C*. However, for E_2, not $(t_1, \text{initialise } x) \leq_{hb}^{P,E_2} (t_2, TInit)$.

As all initialisation events synchronise with *TInit* events, I may subsume initialisation events in a single allocation event. Otherwise, I would have had to separate the event for initialising ordinary members from the one for volatiles. This would have complicated the model and therefore the proofs as well.

At most one initialisation

Above, I have shown the DRF guarantee under two assumptions on the set $\mathcal{E}$ of complete interleavings. In the remainder of this section, I discharge them for source code and bytecode by descending the stack of semantics (Figure 4.10) and adapting the assumptions. They act like an

```
class C {                    t₁ initialises x = 0;
   volatile int v;    | 1: r1 = x;          | 4: x = 1;
}                     | 2: if (r1 == 0)     |
                      | 3:    r2 = new C();  |
```

E_1: $[(t_1, TInit), (t_1, \text{initialise } x), (t_2, TInit), (t_1, Read\ x\ 0),$
$(t_1, New\text{-}Obj\ a\ C), (t_2, Write\ x\ 1), (t_1, TFinish), (t_2, TFinish)]$

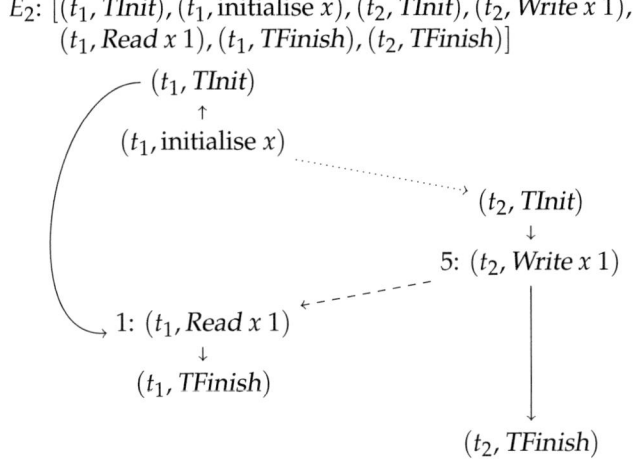

E_2: $[(t_1, TInit), (t_1, \text{initialise } x), (t_2, TInit), (t_2, Write\ x\ 1),$
$(t_1, Read\ x\ 1), (t_1, TFinish), (t_2, TFinish)]$

Figure 4.19: Two well-formed complete interleavings for the program at the top

169

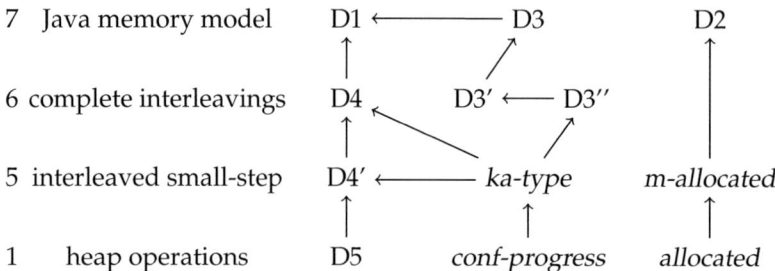

Figure 4.20: Assumptions of the DRF guarantee and their decomposition over the stack of semantics

interface between the levels and ensure that I can share the proofs for all layers that source code and bytecode share.

To help the reader follow the proofs, Figure 4.20 shows how the assumptions D1 and D2 evolve and assigns them to the level of the semantics. The arrows are stylised implications, i.e., the assumption at its source discharges the one at the target. Where multiple arrows point to one assumption, the conjunction of the sources imply the target. For example, assumptions D4 and D3 together discharge D1. The assumptions *ka-type*, *m-allocated*, and *allocated* extend the heap module by new operations; hence, I have phrased them as separate locales instead of additional assumptions. Layer 4 is not shown, because layer 4 is irrelevant for the assumptions that level 5 makes. Layer 3 and 2 are the core of the semantics where the crucial parts of the assumptions are discharged. Their assumptions about the heap module are listed at layer 1.

I start with assumption D2 that every execution initialises a location at most once. Remember that allocation events initialise locations. When an allocation returns an address, it was fresh before, but afterwards, it is allocated, i.e., not fresh. Hence, it suffices to prove that the semantics correctly keeps track of all memory allocations in the events.

To discharge D2 on the level of interleaving semantics, I extend the locale *multithreaded* with a parameter *allocated* $:: {}'h \Rightarrow {}'addr\ set$ that returns the set of allocated addresses (locale *m-allocated* in Figure 4.21). Its specification requires that for every single-thread reduction $t \vdash (x, h) -ta\rightarrow (x', h')$

(i) the set of allocated addresses never shrinks, i.e., *allocated h* $\subseteq$ *allocated h'*,

(ii) $\langle ta \rangle_0$ contains an allocation event for address a iff $a \in$ *allocated h'* and $a \notin$ *allocated h*, and

(iii) $\langle ta \rangle_0$ contains at most one allocation event per address.

Thus, the concept of allocated addresses reduces the global property of at most one initialisation to a property of single reductions.

To prove that *start-events* correctly records the allocations of the *start-heap*, I relate *allocated* also with the abstract heap operations. This way, the proofs about *start-events* and that the single-threaded semantics satisfy the assumptions of *m-allocated* do not depend on the concrete heap implementation. Locale *allocated*, from which *m-allocated* inherits, formalises these additional assumptions (Figure 4.21):

(i) the empty heap *empty-heap* has no allocated addresses,

(ii) if successful, allocation updates the heap h to h' such that the returned address a is allocated in h', but not in h, and the other addresses' allocation status remains unchanged, and

(iii) writing to a location and failed allocations leave the set of allocated addresses unchanged.[34]

The JMM heap implementations instantiate *allocated* with

$$dom \circ jmm\text{-}typeof\text{-}addr \quad \text{and} \quad \lambda h. \{ Address\ hT\ n \,|\, hT\ n.\ n < h\ hT \},$$

respectively. Both meet the assumptions of *allocated*.

Under these assumptions, it is routine to show that *start-events* exactly records the allocations for the start heap *start-heap* and that the sequential semantics of source code and bytecode meet *m-allocated*'s assumptions. This concludes the proof of D2.

Lemma 4.7 (Assumption D2). *In locale m-allocated, every execution $E \in \mathcal{E}$ initialises every location at most once.*

---

[34]I do not need any assumption for *read* because reading cannot change the heap, i.e., it does not affect *allocated* by construction.

locale *allocated-base* $=$ *heap-base* $+$ fixes *allocated* $::$ *'heap* $\Rightarrow$ *'addr set*

locale *allocated* $=$ *allocated-base* $+$ *heap* $+$
 assumes *allocated empty-heap* $= \emptyset$
 and *alloc h hT* $= (h', \lfloor a' \rfloor)$
   $\Longrightarrow$ *allocated h'* $= \{a'\} \cup$ *allocated h* $\wedge$ *a'* $\notin$ *allocated h*
 and *alloc h hT* $= (h',$ *None*$) \Longrightarrow$ *allocated h'* $=$ *allocated h*
 and *write h a al v h'* $\Longrightarrow$ *allocated h'* $=$ *allocated h*

locale *m-allocated* $=$ *allocated* $+$ *mthr: multithreaded* $+$
 assumes $t \vdash (x, h)$ $-ta{\rightarrow}$ $(x', h') \Longrightarrow$ *allocated h* $\subseteq$ *allocated h'*
 and $[\![t \vdash (x, h)$ $-ta{\rightarrow}$ $(x', h');$ *Allocate a hT* $\in$ *set* $\langle ta \rangle_o]\!]$
   $\Longrightarrow a \in$ *allocated h'* $\wedge a \notin$ *allocated h*
 and $[\![t \vdash (x, h)$ $-ta{\rightarrow}$ $(x', h');$ $a \in$ *allocated h'*$;$ $a \notin$ *allocated h* $]\!]$
   $\Longrightarrow \exists hT.$ *Allocate a hT* $\in$ *set* $\langle ta \rangle_o$
 and $[\![t \vdash (x, h)$ $-ta{\rightarrow}$ $(x', h');$ $\langle ta \rangle_{o[i]} =$ *Allocate a hT*$;$ $i < |\langle ta \rangle_o|;$
  $\langle ta \rangle_{o[j]} =$ *Allocate a hT'*$;$ $j < |\langle ta \rangle_o|]\!] \Longrightarrow i = j$

Figure 4.21: Locales formalising the set of allocated addresses

Sequential consistency coinductively

For the DRF guarantee, assumption D1 remains to be shown. However, the JMM definition of SC is not amenable to the coinductive definition of $\_ \downarrow \_$ as it relies on the notions of write-seen function and most recent write, which are only defined for complete interleavings. Therefore, I introduce a coinductive version of SC and prove that it adequately models SC.

A snapshot of a sequentially consistent heap (snapshot heap) H is a finite map from locations to values. The function *mrw P h* α updates the snapshot heap H if α is a write or initialisation action, else leaves H unchanged. The function *mrws P* folds *mrw P* over lists of events. An event list αs is sequentially consistent (SC') for the snapshot heap H (denoted $P, H \vdash \alpha s \sqrt{}_{\text{sc}}$) iff

$$\frac{}{P, H \vdash [] \sqrt{}_{\text{sc}}}$$

$$\frac{P, mrw\ P\ H\ \alpha \vdash \alpha s \sqrt{}_{\text{sc}} \qquad \alpha = Read\ a\ al\ v \Longrightarrow H\ (a, al) = \lfloor v \rfloor}{P, H \vdash \alpha \cdot \alpha s \sqrt{}_{\text{sc}}}$$

i.e., the empty list is SC' for all snapshot heaps, and $\alpha \cdot as$ is SC' for H iff as is SC' for the updated snapshot heap $mrw\ P\ H\ \alpha$ and if α reads the value v from a location (a, al), then the snapshot heap H must store v at (a, al).

The next theorem shows that $P, empty \vdash {}_-\sqrt{}_{sc}$ and sequential consistency are equivalent under the following assumption:

D3 Initialisations precede reads in E. If $\alpha \in \mathcal{R}_E$ reads from some location (a, al), then there is a write event $\beta \in \mathcal{W}_E$ such that $\beta \leq^E \alpha$, $init_E\ \beta$, and $(a, al) \in locs\ P\ E\ \beta$.

Thus, I can use coinduction to show an execution being SC.

Theorem 4.4. *Let ok-init E.*

(i) *If E initialises every location at most once (assumption D2) and $P, empty \vdash E\sqrt{}_{sc}$, then there is a ws such that $P \vdash (E, ws)\sqrt{}$ and (E, ws) is SC.*

(ii) *If initialisations precede reads in E (assumption D3) and $P \vdash (E, ws)\sqrt{}$ and (E, ws) is SC, then $P, empty \vdash E\sqrt{}_{sc}$.*

Proof. (i): Set $ws\ \alpha$ to be the most recent write for $\alpha \in \mathcal{R}_E$ to location (a, al). $P, empty \vdash E\sqrt{}_{sc}$ ensures that there is a write event for every read, D2 guarantees the existence of the most recent one.[35] Then, (E, ws) is SC by definition.

For $P \vdash (E, ws)\sqrt{}$, only condition W2 of well-formedness, i.e., α reads *value-written* $E\ (ws\ \alpha)\ (a, al)$, is interesting. Let as be the prefix of E up to α. From $P, empty \vdash E\sqrt{}_{sc}$, I obtain that $mrws\ P\ empty\ as\ (a, al) = \lfloor v \rfloor$ and α reads the value v. Since $ws\ \alpha$ is the most recent write for α in E, assumption D2 and $P, empty \vdash E\sqrt{}_{sc}$ ensure that $ws\ \alpha < \alpha$. Hence, *value-written* $E\ (ws\ \alpha)\ (a, al) = v$ holds.

(ii): Suppose $P \vdash (E, ws)\sqrt{}$ and (E, ws) is SC. Let $\alpha \in \mathcal{R}_E$ read v from location (a, al), and let as denote the prefix of E up to α. Since initialisations precede reads in E, the most recent write $ws\ \alpha$ precedes α, i.e. $ws\ \alpha \leq^E \alpha$. Well-formedness condition W2 of $P \vdash (E, ws)\sqrt{}$ yields that $v = $ *value-written* $E\ (ws\ \alpha)\ (a, al)$. Since $ws\ \alpha$ is the most recent write for α and $ws\ \alpha \leq^E \alpha$, I also have $mrws\ P\ empty\ as\ (a, al) = \lfloor v \rfloor$. As this holds for all reads α, $P, empty \vdash E\sqrt{}_{sc}$ follows by coinduction. $\square$

---

[35] Assumption D2 is necessary. For example, suppose that E initialises some location (a, al) infinitely often, but there is no *Write a al* _. Then, a read of the default value in E from (a, al) would be SC', but not SC, because none of the initialisations is most recent.

Corollary 4.2. *Let unique initialisations precede reads (assumptions D2 and D3) and ok-init E. Then, $P, empty \vdash E\sqrt{}_{sc}$ iff there is a ws such that $P \vdash (E, ws)\sqrt{}$ and (E, ws) is SC.*

This equivalence holds only if the initialisation of any location (a, al) occurs before the first read from (a, al) in the complete interleaving. For example, the complete interleaving

$$E = [(t, TInit), (t, Read\, a\, (Cell\, 0)\, 0), (t, New\text{-}Arr\, a\, Integer\, 1)]$$

is SC for $ws\, 1 = 2$, but not SC', i.e. $\neg P, empty \vdash E\sqrt{}_{sc}$. The problem is real: Figure 4.9 shows a (non-SC) execution of a type-correct program that violates assumption D3: The initialisation of $(a, Field\, F\, D)$ in l. 3 occurs after the read in l. 2. Thus, in order to exploit this equivalence, I show that initialisations precede reads in SC' prefixes of a complete interleaving:

D3' If a complete interleaving $E \in \mathcal{E}$ has an SC' prefix as followed by a read from (a, al), as initialises (a, al).

Lemma 4.8. *Assumption D3' implies D3 for all $E \in \mathcal{E}$ that are SC'.*

Initialisations precede reads

Next, I tackle D3' by decomposing it into smaller assumptions that no longer refer to complete interleavings, but only to single reductions in the small-step semantics – similar to what I did for assumption D2 above. At the same time, I prove it for a more general class of prefixes such that I can reuse this assumption when proving consistency in §4.3.4.

A heap record $\mathcal{H}$ is a function from locations to sets of values – it records all values that have been written to a location. Similar to mrw, if α is a write or initialisation event, the function $uhr\, P\, \mathcal{H}\, \alpha$ adds the written value(s) to the heap record $\mathcal{H}$, else it leaves $\mathcal{H}$ unchanged. The function $uhrs\, P$ folds $uhr\, P$ over lists of events. An event list as is non-speculative with respect to the heap record $\mathcal{H}$ (denoted $P, \mathcal{H} \vdash as\sqrt{}_{ns}$) iff for any read event α in as from any location (a, al), α reads a value that has been written to (a, al) in as before α or that has already been in $\mathcal{H}\, (a, al)$. Formally:

$$\overline{P, \mathcal{H} \vdash [\,]\sqrt{}_{ns}}$$

$$\frac{P, uhr\, P\, \mathcal{H}\, \alpha \vdash as\sqrt{}_{ns} \qquad \alpha = Read\, a\, al\, v \implies v \in \mathcal{H}\, (a, al)}{P, \mathcal{H} \vdash \alpha \cdot as\sqrt{}_{ns}}$$

A prefix of a complete interleaving is non-speculative iff its list of events is non-speculative with respect to the empty heap record $\lambda\_. \emptyset$.

A snapshot heap H fits to a heap record $\mathcal{H}$ iff whenever H stores a value for a location (a, al), then $\mathcal{H}(a, al)$ contains that value.

Lemma 4.9. *If αs is SC' for H and H fits to $\mathcal{H}$, then αs is non-speculative with respect to $\mathcal{H}$.*

Corollary 4.3. *An SC' prefix of a complete interleaving is non-speculative.*

This corollary shows that it suffices to prove the following assumption D3'' instead of D3'.

D3'' If a complete interleaving $E \in \mathcal{E}$ has a non-speculative prefix αs followed by a read from (a, al), αs initialises (a, al).

To discharge D3'', it suffices to show that (i) the program cannot make up addresses and (ii) it accesses only the declared fields of objects and cells within the bounds of the array. Then, since the prefix does not speculate, the read can only access an existing member of an address that has been allocated before. Since allocation initialises all fields and array cells, the member therefore must have been initialised.

For (i), I introduce the concept of known addresses. Let $ka :: \,'t \Rightarrow \,'x \Rightarrow \,'addr\ set$ be another locale parameter which returns the set of addresses that a given thread stores in its local state. A thread learns an address a in an event list αs iff αs contains a read event $Read \_\_ (Addr\ a)$ or an allocation $Allocate\ a \_$, i.e., it either reads the address from some location or allocates it. The function $learns\ \alpha s$ computes the set of learnt addresses from αs. The single-threaded semantics does not invent addresses iff ka satisfies the assumptions of locale ka in Figure 4.22.

In detail, after any reduction step, a thread may only know addresses which it has known before or learnt in this step. Also, a spawned thread may only know those addresses that the spawning thread knows.[36] Conversely, known addresses restrict the heap interactions of a thread as follows: It must only read from members of known addresses and whenever it writes an address to a location, it must know the address. Note the asymmetry between reads and writes. It suffices to restrict the

---

[36]I could relax this assumption such that the spawned thread may also know addresses that the spawning thread is learning in the reduction. However, this is irrelevant for JinjaThreads and the above form is simpler.

locale *ka-base* = *multithreaded-base* + fixes *ka* :: $'t \Rightarrow 'x \Rightarrow 'addr\ set$

locale *ka* = *m-allocated* + *ka-base* +
  assumes $t \vdash (x,h) -ta\rightarrow (x',h') \implies ka\ t\ x' \subseteq ka\ t\ x \cup learns\ \langle ta \rangle_o$
  and $[\![t \vdash (x,h) -ta\rightarrow (x',h');\ Spawn\ t'\ x''\ h'' \in set\ \langle ta \rangle_t]\!]$
    $\implies ka\ t'\ x'' \subseteq ka\ t\ x$
  and $[\![t \vdash (x,h) -ta\rightarrow (x',h');\ Read\ a\ al\ v \in set\ \langle ta \rangle_o]\!] \implies a \in ka\ t\ x$
  and $[\![t \vdash (x,h) -ta\rightarrow (x',h');\ \langle ta \rangle_{o[i]} = Write\ a\ al\ (Addr\ a');\ i < |\langle ta \rangle_o|]\!]$
    $\implies a' \in ka\ t\ x \cup learns\ (take\ i\ \langle ta \rangle_o)$

Figure 4.22: Locale *ka* formalises that threads do not invent addresses

reads to members at known addresses, but not the writes, because it cannot read from such locations. Moreover, *ka* allows to write an address that has just been learnt, but not to read from one of its members. The *clone* implementation requires the former because it copies (i.e., reads and writes) all locations of the object, which may contain arbitrary (unknown) addresses as values. Technically, it would be fine to immediately read from a learnt address, but this would unnecessarily complicate the proofs.

The concept of known addresses naturally extends to multithreaded states and the interleaving semantics. A state s knows the addresses $\bigcup_{t \in dom\ (thr\ s)} ka\ t\ (fst\ (the\ (thr\ s\ t)))$, written as *kas s*.

Lemma 4.10. *Let* $s -t{:}ta\rightarrow s'$ *in locale ka. Then* $kas\ s' \subseteq kas\ s \cup learns\ \langle ta \rangle_o$. *If Read a al v* $\in set\ \langle ta \rangle_o$, *then* $a \in kas\ s$.

Let the *recorded addresses addrs* $\mathcal{H}$ be the set of all addresses in the heap record $\mathcal{H}$, i.e., $addrs\ \mathcal{H} = \{\, a.\ \exists a'\ al.\ Addr\ a \in \mathcal{H}\ (a, al)\,\}$. Then, the interleaving semantics preserves the invariant that all known or recorded addresses are allocated for non-speculative executions. The proof goes by case analysis of the reduction and induction on the prefixes of $\langle ta \rangle_o$. It requires that *acq-events* only generates synchronisation events.

Lemma 4.11. *Let* $s -t{:}ta\rightarrow s'$ *in locale ka such that* $P, \mathcal{H} \vdash \langle ta \rangle_o \sqrt{}_{ns}$. *If* $kas\ s \cup addrs\ \mathcal{H} \subseteq allocated\ (shr\ s)$, *then*

$$kas\ s' \cup addrs\ (uhrs\ P\ \mathcal{H}\ \langle ta \rangle_o) \subseteq allocated\ (shr\ s').$$

Now, I can prove that non-speculative prefixes allocate addresses before they read from their locations, which is part (i) of proving D3''.

locale *ka-type* $=$ *ka* $+$
  fixes $Q :: {}'t \Rightarrow {}'x \Rightarrow {}'heap \Rightarrow bool$
  assumes $t \vdash (x, h) -ta \rightarrow (x', h') \Longrightarrow h \unlhd h'$
  and $[\![s -t{:}ta \rightarrow s'; \ {\uparrow}Q{\uparrow} \ (thr \ s) \ (shr \ s); \ P \vdash \mathcal{H} ::\leq shr \ s; \ P, \mathcal{H} \vdash \langle ta \rangle_o \surd_{ns}]\!]$
    $\Longrightarrow {\uparrow}Q{\uparrow} \ (thr \ s') \ (shr \ s') \wedge P \vdash uhrs \ P \ \mathcal{H} \ \langle ta \rangle_o ::\leq shr \ s'$
  and $[\![t \vdash (x, h) -ta \rightarrow (x', h'); \ Q \ t \ x \ h; \ Read \ a \ al \ v \in set \ \langle ta \rangle_o]\!]$
    $\Longrightarrow \exists T. \ P, h \vdash a{\cdot}al : T$
  and $[\![t \vdash (x, h) -ta \rightarrow (x', h'); \ Q \ t \ x \ h; \ Allocate \ a \ hT \in set \ \langle ta \rangle_o]\!]$
    $\Longrightarrow typeof{-}addr \ h' \ a = \lfloor hT \rfloor$

Figure 4.23: Locale *ka-type* combines known addresses with type information

Let *start-$\mathcal{H}$* denote the start heap record *uhrs* P ($\lambda\_.\ \emptyset$) *start-events*, and define *events'* $(t, ta) = \langle ta \rangle_o$ to extract events from a reduction label.

Lemma 4.12. *In locale ka, let start-state $-ttas \rightarrow^* s$ and $s -t{:}ta \rightarrow s'$ with Read a al $v \in$ set $\langle ta \rangle_o$ such that*

$$P, \lambda\_.\ \emptyset \vdash start\text{-}events \ @ \ concat \ (map \ events' \ ttas) \surd_{ns}.$$

Suppose kas start-state $\subseteq$ allocated start-heap. Then, either

(i) a is preallocated, i.e., Allocate a hT $\in$ set start-events for some hT, or

(ii) some reduction has allocated a, i.e., there are t', ta', and hT such that $(t', ta') \in$ set ttas and Allocate a hT $\in$ set $\langle ta' \rangle_o$.

Proof. If $a \in$ *allocated start-heap*, then (i) holds by construction of *start-heap*. So suppose $a \notin$ *allocated start-heap*. Let αs abbreviate *concat* (*map events' ttas*). Since allocations write default values, which are never addresses, *addrs start-$\mathcal{H}$* $= \emptyset$ by definition of *start-events*. Therefore, *kas* $s \cup$ *addrs* (*uhrs* P *start-$\mathcal{H}$* αs) $\subseteq$ *allocated* (*shr* s) by Lemma 4.11 and induction on *start-state $-ttas \rightarrow^* s$*. In particular, I have $a \in$ *allocated* (*shr* s), because $a \in$ *kas* s by Lemma 4.10. Since $a \notin$ *allocated start-heap*, induction on *start-state $-ttas \rightarrow^* s$* yields (ii) using the assumptions of locale *m-allocated*. $\qquad\qquad\square$

Let me now return to part (ii) of obligation D3″, namely to show that the location being read is a declared field or a cell within the bounds of an array. The proof approach combines known addresses with conformance

177

and heap extension. Conformance of a heap record $\mathcal{H}$ with respect to a heap h, written $P \vdash \mathcal{H} ::\leq h$, denotes that all values in $\mathcal{H}$ conform to the location's type, i.e.,

$$P \vdash \mathcal{H} ::\leq h \longleftrightarrow (\forall a\,al.\ \forall v \in \mathcal{H}\ (a,al).\ \exists T.\ P,h \vdash a\cdot al : T \wedge P,h \vdash v :\leq T)$$

Locale *ka-type* in Figure 4.23 formally connects the three notions, where the new parameter Q abstracts over language-specific conformance conditions:

- Type information grows monotonically.

- Reductions with non-speculative events preserve conformance of states and heap records.

- Any reduction that starts in a conforming state reads only locations that have a type.

- After an allocation event, the address' type information agrees with the event's.

For source code, Q is instantiated to the invariant for subject reduction (Theorem 3.4) from Equation 3.7, i.e., $Q\ t\ (e,xs)\ h = \exists E\ T.\ P,(E,T),t \vdash (e,xs),h\ \sqrt{}$. For bytecode, Q is bytecode conformance from Equation 3.8, i.e., $Q\ t\ (xcp,frs)\ h = P,\Phi \vdash t{:}(xcp,h,frs)\sqrt{}$.

The locale parameter *ka* is implemented as follows. For source code, *J.ka* $t\ (e,xs)$ consists of the addresses that (i) occur in e or *ran xs*, or (ii) are preallocated (*set start-addrs*), or (iii) *t2a t* returns. The latter two are necessary, because JinjaThreads preallocates the system exceptions – for example, *throw null* reduces to *THROW NullPointer*, but *addr-of-sys-xcpt NullPointer* need not be known before and is not learnt – and *currentThread* returns the address of t's *Thread* object. Accordingly, in bytecode, *jvm.ka* includes the exception flag when set, all addresses in local registers and the operand stack in any call frame, and the preallocated addresses and *t2a t*. Then, source code and bytecode satisfy the assumptions of locale *ka-type* for well-formed programs.[37]

---

[37]For bytecode, this proof assumes that *undefined-Val* is no address, because this value initialises the registers of call frames (see Figure 3.22). Theoretically, I could have defined *jvm.ka* such that it ignores inaccessible registers in call frames as determined by the bytecode verifier. Then, this assumption would not be needed. However, this would severely complicate the proofs in two ways. First, since bytecode satisfies the assumptions

The next lemma shows that locale *ka-type* implies assumption D3″. Hence, initialisations precede reads in non-speculative prefixes of complete interleavings and Theorem 4.4 and Corollary 4.2 are applicable.

Lemma 4.13 (Assumption D3″). *In locale* ka-type, *let* P *be well-formed,* $\uparrow Q \uparrow$ (thr start-state) start-heap, *kas start-state* $\subseteq$ *allocated start-heap, and* $P \vdash$ start-$\mathcal{H}$ $::\leq$ start-heap. *If* $E \in \mathcal{E}$, $E_{[i]} =$ Read a al v *with* $i < |E|$, *and* $P, \lambda\_. \emptyset \vdash$ take i (map snd E) $\sqrt{}_{ns}$, *then there is a* $j < i$ *such that* $E_{[j]}$ *initialises* (a, al).

Proof. Since $E \in \mathcal{E}$, there is *ttas* such that *start-state* $\downarrow$ *ttas* and $E =$ *start-events* @ *concat* (map events ttas). Since $i < |E|$, I can split *ttas* such that *ttas* = *ttas′* @ $(t, ta) \cdot ttas″$, and Read a al $v \in$ set $\langle ta \rangle_0$, and |concat (map events ttas′)| $< i$. Then, there are s and $s′$ such that *start-state* $-ttas′ \rightarrow^* s$ and $s - t{:}ta \rightarrow s′$. Since non-speculative prefixes of executions preserve conformance, (a, al) is typable in *shr s*, i.e., P, shr $s \vdash$ $a{\cdot}al : T$ for some T. It suffices to show that there is an event Allocate a hT in *start-events* or *ttas′* such that *typeof-addr* (shr s) $a = \lfloor hT \rfloor$, because P, shr $s \vdash a{\cdot}al : T$ then implies that Allocate a hT initialises (a, al).

By Lemma 4.12, the address a has been allocated before, i.e., either in *start-events* or in *ttas′*. If Allocate a $hT \in$ set *start-events*, then *typeof-addr start-heap* $a = \lfloor hT \rfloor$, and therefore *typeof-addr* (shr s) $a = \lfloor hT \rfloor$ since *start-heap* $\unlhd$ *shr s*. Otherwise, *ttas′* = *ttas** @ $(t^*, ta^*) \cdot ttas^{**}$ for some *ttas**, t^*, ta^*, and *ttas*** such that Allocate a $hT \in$ set $\langle ta^* \rangle_0$ for some hT. Hence, there are states s^* and s^{**} such that *start-state* $-ttas^* \rightarrow^* s^*$, $s^* - t^*{:}ta^* \rightarrow s^{**}$, and $s^{**} -ttas^{**} \rightarrow^* s$. By assumption of *ka-type*, I obtain *typeof-addr* (shr s^{**}) $= \lfloor hT \rfloor$ and therefore *typeof-addr* (shr s) $a = \lfloor hT \rfloor$ since shr $s^{**} \unlhd$ shr s. $\qquad\square$

Sequentially consistent completions

Now, only assumption D1 remains to be shown, i.e., sequentially consistent prefixes of well-formed executions can be completed sequentially consistently. To that end, I construct a sequentially consistent completion

---

of locale *ka* only for conformant states, *ka* must already fix the conformance predicate Q from *ka-type* and restrict its assumptions to conformant states. Consequently, all proofs in *ka* are burdened with conformance. Second, discharging the assumptions of *ka* for bytecode requires to exploit conformance. As can be seen in the bytecode type safety proof of Jinja and JinjaThreads, good automation is hard to achieve for bytecode conformance.

$scc\ s\ H$ that starts with a multithreaded state s and a snapshot heap H. I define scc by corecursion as follows:

$$scc\ s\ H = (\ \textit{if}\ \exists t\ ta\ s'.\ s -t{:}ta\to s'$$
$$\textit{then let}\ (t, ta, s') = \varepsilon(t, ta, s').\ s -t{:}ta\to s' \wedge P, H \vdash \langle ta\rangle_o \sqrt{}_{sc}$$
$$\textit{in}\ (t, ta) \cdot scc\ s'\ (mrws\ P\ H\ \langle ta\rangle_o)$$
$$\textit{else}\ [])$$

In order to prove anything about $scc\ s\ H$, I must make sure that the predicate to the ε-operator is satisfiable for all reachable configurations. Hence, I presume for now the following:

D4 The interleaving semantics satisfies the cut-and-update property for the start state $start\text{-}state$ and the start snapshot heap $start\text{-}H = mrws\ P\ empty\ start\text{-}events$.

The $cut\text{-}and\text{-}update\ property$ (C&U) for s and H (denoted $C\&U\ s\ H$) denotes the following. Let the state s' be reachable from s via an SC′ prefix of a complete interleaving, say $s -ttas\to^* s'$ such that $P, H \vdash concat\ (map\ events'\ ttas) \sqrt{}_{sc}$, and let H' denote the updated snapshot heap $mrws\ P\ H\ (concat\ (map\ events'\ ttas))$. Then, for every reduction $s' -t'{:}ta'\to s''$ from s', there are ta'', s''' such that (i) $s' -t'{:}ta''\to s'''$, (ii) $P, H' \vdash \langle ta''\rangle_o \sqrt{}_{sc}$, and (iii) $P, H' \vdash \langle ta'\rangle_o \approx \langle ta''\rangle_o$ (to be explained in a moment).

Conditions (i) and (ii) predicate that all reachable, non-stuck states can reduce with events $\langle ta''\rangle_o$ that are SC′ w.r.t. the current snapshot heap H'; they suffice to prove that scc does compute an SC′ interleaving (Lemma 4.15). In condition (iii), $P, H' \vdash as \approx as'$ denotes that two event lists as and as' consist of the same events up to the first SC′ inconsistent read in as (if any) and as' continues with a read from the same location. With condition (iii), given a complete interleaving that is SC′ up to a read α, I can cut the interleaving after α, replace α with a read of the most recent value, and continue the interleaving SC′.

Lemma 4.14 (Preservation of C&U). *If $C\&U\ s\ H$, $s -t{:}ta\to s'$, and $P, H \vdash \langle ta\rangle_o \sqrt{}_{sc}$, then $C\&U\ s'\ (mrws\ P\ H\ \langle ta\rangle_o)$.*

Proof. This holds by definition of C&U because every state that is reachable via SC′ executions from s' is also reachable via SC′ exeuctions from s by prefixing the SC′ reduction $s -t{:}ta\to s'$. □

Under assumption D4, scc computes an SC' execution (Lemma 4.15). By the equivalence of SC and SC' (Theorem 4.4), I then discharge the main assumption of the DRF proof (Theorem 4.5).

Lemma 4.15.
If $C\&U\, s\, H$, then $s \downarrow scc\, s\, H$ and $P, H \vdash concat\,(map\; events'\,(scc\, s\, H))\,\sqrt{}_{sc}$.

Theorem 4.5 (SC completion). *Let $E \in \mathcal{E}$, $P \vdash (E, ws)\sqrt{}$, (E, ws) be SC up to a read event $(t, Read\, a\, al\, v)$, say $E = E_1 @ (t, Read\, a\, al\, v) \cdot E_2$ with ws α being the most recent write for all reads $\alpha \in \mathcal{A}_{E_1}$. Then, there are E_3, v', and ws' such that $E^* := E_1 @ (t, Read\, a\, al\, v') \cdot E_3 \in \mathcal{E}$, $P \vdash (E^*, ws')\sqrt{}$, and (E^*, ws') is SC.*

Proof of Lemma 4.15. I show $s \downarrow scc\, s\, H$ by coinduction with $C\&U\, s\, H$ as the coinduction invariant. If s is stuck, then $scc\, s\, H = []$ and I am done by STOP. Otherwise, conditions (i) and (ii) of C&U ensure that the predicate to Hilbert's choice is satisfiable. Hence, it does pick an SC' reduction step $s -t{:}ta\rightarrow s'$ and updates H to $H' := mrws\, P\, H\, \langle ta \rangle_0$. Note how this mimics STEP. Since SC' reductions preserve C&U (Lemma 4.14), and the reduction is SC', $C\&U\, s'\, H'$ holds, too. This concludes the coinductive step.

For $P, H \vdash concat\,(map\; events'\,(scc\, s\, H))\,\sqrt{}_{sc}$, the standard coinduction rule is too weak because $concat$ is unproductive for any number of consecutive reductions without events. Hence, I derive a custom coinduction rule for $\_,\_ \vdash \_\sqrt{}_{sc}$ (Lemma 4.16 below), which allows to defer the next step if one decreases in a well-founded relation. Taking as measure the length of the maximal prefix of $scc\, s\, H$ for which $\langle ta \rangle_0$ consists of empty lists, I show $P, H \vdash concat\,(map\; events'\,(scc\, s\, H))\,\sqrt{}_{sc}$ with the invariant $C\&U\, s\, H$ like above. □

Lemma 4.16 (Strong coinduction rule for $\_,\_ \vdash \_\sqrt{}_{sc}$). *Let $(R_q)_q$ be a family of sets over snapshot heaps and lists of events indexed over a type with a well-founded order $\prec$. Suppose that for all q and $(H, \alpha s) \in R_q$, either $\alpha s = []$, or there is a q' with $q' \prec q$ and $(H, \alpha s) \in R_{q'}$, or αs can be split in $\alpha s'$ and $\alpha s''$ such that $\alpha s' \neq []$ and $P, H \vdash \alpha s'\,\sqrt{}_{sc}$ and if $\alpha s'$ is finite, there is a q' such that $(mrws\, P\, H\, \alpha s', \alpha s'') \in R_{q'}$ or $P, mrws\, P\, H\, \alpha s' \vdash \alpha s''\,\sqrt{}_{sc}$. If $(H^*, \alpha s^*) \in R_{q^*}$ for some q^*, then $P, H^* \vdash \alpha s^*\,\sqrt{}_{sc}$.*

Proof. By well-founded induction on $\prec$, I prove that the union R of all R_q satisfies the following: For all $(H, \alpha s) \in R$, either $\alpha s = []$, or αs can

181

be split in as' and as'' such that $as' \neq []$ and $P, H \vdash as' \sqrt{}_{sc}$ and if as' is finite, $(mrws\ P\ H\ as', as'') \in R$ or $P, mrws\ P\ H\ as' \vdash as'' \sqrt{}_{sc}$. This proof follows the same pattern as for the strong coinduction rule in §1.4.3.

Then, I show $P, H^* \vdash as^* \sqrt{}_{sc}$ by coinduction on $P, \_ \vdash \_ \sqrt{}_{sc}$ with coinduction invariant $(H^*, as^*) \in R$. □

Proof of Theorem 4.5. Construct E_3 as follows: First, identify the reduction $s -t:ta\rightarrow s'$ that generates $(t, Read\ a\ al\ v)$. Let E'_1 be the prefix of E up to *events* (t, ta) exclusively, which is also a prefix of E_1. Since all reads in E_1 (and thus E'_1) see the most recent write, E'_1 is SC' by Theorem 4.4. Since C&U holds for the start state and the start snapshot heap and SC' reductions preserve C&U (Lemma 4.14), C&U holds for s and $H_1 = mrws\ P\ empty\ E'_1$, too. Hence, by C&U, there are ta' and s'' such that $s -t:ta'\rightarrow s''$, $P, H_1 \vdash \langle ta'\rangle_0 \sqrt{}_{sc}$, and $P, H_1 \vdash \langle ta\rangle_0 \approx \langle ta'\rangle_0$. From the latter, I know that $\langle ta\rangle_0$ and $\langle ta'\rangle_0$ are the same up to the read *Read a al v* in $\langle ta\rangle_0$ (exclusively), which is *Read a al v'* in ta' for the SC'-correct value v'. Now, choose E_3 to be the rest of $\langle ta'\rangle_0$ followed by *concat* (*map events* (*scc s* (*mrws P H_1 $\langle ta'\rangle_0$*))).

With Lemma 4.15, I get that E^* is SC' and $E^* \in \mathcal{E}$. Theorem 4.4 yields the required ws'. □

Corollary 4.4. *Every well-formed program has a well-formed, sequentially consistent execution.*

Proof. Set $E = start\text{-}events\ @\ concat$ (*map events* (*scc s H*)). Then, $E \in \mathcal{E}$ and $P, empty \vdash E \sqrt{}_{sc}$ by Lemma 4.15 and definition of $\mathcal{E}$ and *start-events*. By Theorem 4.4, there is a ws such that $P \vdash (E, ws) \sqrt{}$ and (E, ws) is SC. □

Cut and update

For the DRF guarantee, it remains to show that the interleaving semantics satisfies C&U for the start state (assumption D4). Similar to initialisations preceding reads, I generalise this property to non-speculative prefixes and reading any previously written value, not only the most recent one. Thus, I can reuse the proof for consistency in §4.3.4.

Formally, the sequential semantics has the generalised cut-and-update property (gC&U) for a state s and heap record $\mathcal{H}$ iff for all states s' reachable from s in the interleaving semantics with non-speculative events as and any reduction $t \vdash (x, shr\ s') -ta\rightarrow (x', h')$ of any thread t in s' with *ok-ta* s' t ta, whenever $\langle ta\rangle_{0[i]} = Read\ a\ al\ v$ for some $i < |\langle ta\rangle_0|$ such that P, $uhrs\,P\,\mathcal{H}\ as \vdash take\,i\,\langle ta\rangle_o\,\sqrt{}_{ns}$ and for any value $v' \in uhrs\,P\,\mathcal{H}\ (as\,@\ take\,i\,\langle ta\rangle_o)\ (a, al)$, there is a reduction $t \vdash (x, shr\,s')\ -ta' \to (x'', h'')$ such that $ok\text{-}ta\ s'\ t\ ta'$, $i < |\langle ta'\rangle_o| \leq |\langle ta\rangle_o|$, $\langle ta'\rangle_{o[i]} = Read\ a\ al\ v'$, and $take\,i\,\langle ta\rangle_o = take\,i\,\langle ta'\rangle_o$.

Intuitively, gC&U allows to cut a complete interleaving at any read event in its non-speculative prefix and replace it with a read from the same location that reads any value which has previously been written to that location. This might seem overly complicated, but I cannot require that the updated read reads any arbitrary value, because I want the DRF guarantee to hold for both JMM implementations of the abstract heap model. In particular, the second allows to read only type-correct values. Since non-speculative executions preserve conformance, gC&U holds for any abstract heap model that always allows to read all type-correct values, see Lemma 4.18 below. If I were able to drop this conformance restriction on the read operation in JMM heap implementation 2, I could simply require that every read in every state can be cut and arbitrarily updated, which would considerably simplify the proofs.

Lemma 4.17 (gC&U implies C&U). *If P is well-formed, the single-threaded semantics satisfies gC&U for start-state and start-$\mathcal{H}$, and kas start-state $\subseteq$ allocated start-heap, and $\uparrow Q \uparrow$ (thr start-state) start-heap, then it also satisfies C&U for start-state and start-H.*

Proof. Suppose $start\text{-}state\ -ttas\to^* s$ and $s\ -t{:}ta\to s'$ such that $P, start\text{-}H \vdash concat\ (map\ events'\ ttas)\,\sqrt{}_{sc}$. Let $as = concat\ (map\ events'\ ttas)$ and $H = mrws\,P\ start\text{-}H\ as$. I must show that there are ta' and s'' such that $s\ -t{:}ta' \to s''$, $P, H \vdash \langle ta'\rangle_o\,\sqrt{}_{sc}$, and $P, H \vdash \langle ta\rangle_o \approx \langle ta'\rangle_o$.

If $s\ -t{:}ta \to s'$ originates from ACQUIRE, $\langle ta\rangle_o$ contains no read by definition of $acq\text{-}events$. Hence, ta and s' themselves serve as witnesses.

Otherwise, $t \vdash (x, shr\,s)\ -ta\to (x', shr\,s')$ for some thread in s by NORMAL. By Lemma 4.9, $P, start\text{-}\mathcal{H} \vdash as\sqrt{}_{ns}$, i.e., gC&U allows to cut and update t's reductions in state s. Then, construct $\langle ta'\rangle_o$ iteratively as follows: Start with $ta' = ta$ and consider the first event in $\langle ta'\rangle_o$. If it is an event reading not the most recently written value (according to the snapshot heap H), change the reduction to the most recently written value using gC&U, then continue with the new reduction for the next event. Otherwise, update the snapshot heap H for the event and consider the next event. This process terminates after at most $|\langle ta\rangle_o|$ iterations because gC&U bounds the length of the replacement events $\langle ta'\rangle_o$ to that length. The reduction thus obtained serves as witness.

183

The key step in the iteration is to show that H stores a most recently written value at all. I show similar to Lemma 4.13 that $start\text{-}state\ -ttas\rightarrow^*$ s initialises the location. This ensures that H does store some value v for the location and – since H fits to $\mathcal{H} = uhrs\ P\ start\text{-}\mathcal{H}$ as – $\mathcal{H}$ has recorded v, too. Hence, gC&U ensures that I can cut and update the reduction as described. □

Now, it remains to show that both source code and bytecode satisfy gC&U, i.e.,

D4' The interleaving semantics satisfies gC&U for $start\text{-}state$ and $start\text{-}\mathcal{H}$.

Although D4' is tedious to prove for the layers 2 to 5, from the $clone$ method to the source code semantics and defensive VM, these proofs do not pose any interesting challenges. To abstract over both JMM heap implementations, they make the following assumption about the implementation, which both implementations satisfy by definition:

D5 The heap implementation allows to read any type-correct value, i.e., whenever $hconf\ h$ and $P,h \vdash a\cdot al : T$ and $P,h \vdash v :\le T$, then $read\ h\ a\ al\ v$.

This assumption is stronger than progress because it allows to read any type-correct value. Since gC&U involves only non-speculative prefixes of executions, locale $ka\text{-}type$ ensures that these preserve conformance of the heap and the heap record. Therefore, any value that gC&U requires to be read conforms to its type. Thus, I am finally able to conclude that the DRF guarantee holds for source code and bytecode.

Lemma 4.18. *In locale ka-type and under assumption D5, the sequential semantics for source code (bytecode) satisfies gC&U for the start state J-start P C M vs (jvm-start P C M vs) and start-$\mathcal{H}$ provided that (i) P is well-formed, (ii) wf-start P C M vs, and (iii) the parameters vs only refer to preallocated addresses, if at all.*

Theorem 4.6. *The DRF guarantee holds for source code and bytecode.*
If the start state satisfies the conditions of Lemma 4.18 and P is correctly synchronised, then every legal execution is SC.

4.3.4 Consistency

In the previous section, I have shown that the JMM allows solely sequentially consistent behaviour for correctly synchronised programs. This proves that the JMM is strong enough to disallow certain undesired behaviours. Conversely, consistency requires that the JMM be not too strong in that for some programs it does not allow any behaviour at all. In this section, I prove that the JMM does assign some legal behaviour to every *well-formed* program, not only to correctly synchronised ones. In particular, I show that any sequentially consistent execution is legal. This is not trivial because in programs with data races, the most recent write for a read need not happen before it. Hence, these data races must be justified.

Theorem 4.7. *Every well-formed source code and bytecode program has a sequentially consistent execution. Every sequentially consistent execution is legal.*

Like in the previous section, I have identified assumptions on the interfaces between different layers of the semantics such that I can conduct the proofs as abstractly as possible. In fact, this section only relies on the properties of the single-threaded semantics from the previous section. All theorems are on the level of the interleaving semantics or on higher ones. Like in §4.3.3, I start at the JMM level with assumptions about complete interleavings and then discharge these assumptions in the levels below.

At the JMM level, the assumptions are now

C1 For every sequentially consistent prefix of a well-formed execution (E, ws) with $E \in \mathcal{E}$, there is a complete interleaving $E' \in \mathcal{E}$ with the same prefix and a write seen function ws' such that (i) $P \vdash (E', ws') \sqrt{}$, (ii) for all read actions $r \in \mathcal{A}_{E'}$, if r is in the prefix, then $ws'\ r = ws\ r$ else $ws'\ r \leq_{\mathrm{hb}}^{P,E}\ r$, and (iii) if E continues with an event α directly after the prefix, E' continues with the same α, except that if α is a read, it may read a different value.

C2 If a well-formed execution has an SC prefix αs followed by a read from (a, al), αs initialises (a, al).

D2 Every execution initialises every location at most once.

Assumption C1 expresses that I can cut any execution after an SC prefix and continue such that every read in the continuation sees a write that happens before. The second assumption C2 is similar to D3' with SC' replaced by SC. Assumptions C2 and D2 ensure that for well-formed executions with an SC prefix followed by a read α, (i) a most recent write α' exists for α with $\alpha' < \alpha$, and (ii) if a write α^* happens before α, then $\alpha^* < \alpha$, too.

Theorem 4.8. *Under assumptions C1, C2, and D2, every SC execution is legal.*

Proof. Let $E \in \mathcal{E}$ such that $P \vdash (E, ws) \checkmark$ and (E, ws) is SC. I must justify (E, ws) by a justifying sequence $(E_i, ws_i, C_i, \varphi_i)_i$. For $i \leq |E|$, choose some (E_i, ws_i) with the following properties:

- $E_i \in \mathcal{E}$
- $P \vdash (E_i, ws_i) \checkmark$
- $i \leq |E_i|$
- $take\ (i-1)\ E = take\ (i-1)\ E_i$
- Suppose $i > 0$. If $E_{[i-1]} = Read\ a\ al\ v$, then $E_{i[i-1]} = Read\ a\ al\ v'$ for some v', else $E_{[i-1]} = E_{i[i-1]}$.
- For all read events $j \in \mathcal{A}_{E_i}$, if $j < i-1$ then $ws_i\ j = ws\ j$, else $ws_i\ j \leq_{\mathrm{hb}}^{P,E_i} j$.

Assumption C1 ensures that such (E_i, ws_i) exist. Set $C_i = \{ j.\ j < i \}$, i.e., (E_i, ws_i) commits the first i events.

For $i > |E|$, set $E_i = E$ and $ws_i = ws$ and $C_i = \mathcal{A}_E$. Then, the sequence $(E_i, ws_i, C_i, \varphi_i)_i$ justifies (E, ws) where all renamings φ_i are the identity.

To illustrate how $(E_i, ws_i, C_i, \varphi_i)_i$ justifies reads which see writes that do not happen before, consider the following program where the write in l. 1 races with the read in l. 2.

$$\frac{\text{initially: x = 0;}}{\text{1: x = 1;}\ |\ \text{2: r = x;}} \qquad (P)$$

Figure 4.24 shows the executions for the two complete interleavings where the thread t_1 on the left executes before the one on the right (t_2). I wish to justify the SC execution shown in Figure 4.24a. Suppose that we are about to commit the read event, i.e., $i = 5$. Figure 4.24b shows (E_4, ws_4) where the grey area contains all committed events.

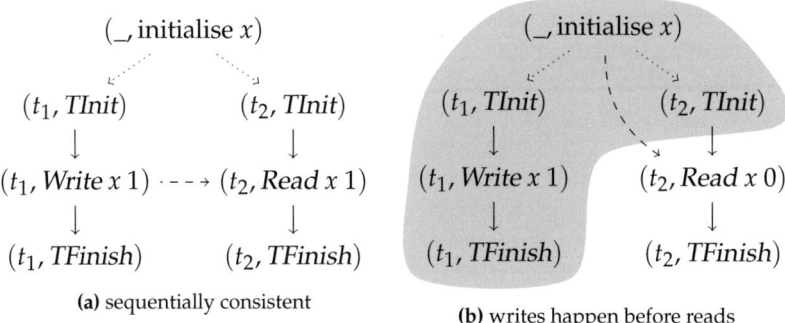

(a) sequentially consistent

(b) writes happen before reads

Figure 4.24: Two executions of the complete interleavings $[(\_, \text{initialise } x), (t_1, \text{TInit}), (t_1, \text{Write } x \ 1), (t_1, \text{TFinish}), (t_2, \text{TInit}), (t_2, \text{Read } x \ v), (t_2, \text{TFinish})]$ for (a) $v = 1$ and (b) $v = 0$ for the program (P)

The JMM justification rules allow the write-seen function (dashed arrows) to change only for reads that the previous justifying execution has committed for the first time. Since (E_5, ws_5) commits the read, it must still see the allocation as there are no other writes that happen before the read. Thus, Figure 4.24b also shows (E_5, ws_5). In the next step, (E_6, ws_6) may change the read such that it sees the write, i.e., Figure 4.24a shows (E_6, ws_6). At the same time, it also commits the last event $(t_2, \text{TFinish})$.

This offset explains why the specification of (E_i, ws_i) mostly refers to $i - 1$. However, one cannot shift the whole sequence by one because the JMM requires that (E_0, ws_0) has not yet committed any events.

The proof that $(E_i, ws_i)_i$ justifies (E, ws) is tedious and largely uninteresting, except for the case where the $i - 1$-th event in E reads from a write w that does not happen before. In that case, (E_i, ws_i) changes the write from $ws_{i-1} \ i$ to $ws \ i$. The legality conditions require that (E_i, ws_i) has already commited both of them, i.e., $ws_{i-1} \ i < i$ and $ws \ i < i$. As noted above, assumptions C2 and D2 ensure this, because $ws \ i$ is the most recent write and $ws_{i-1} \ i$ happens before i. □

Corollary 4.5. *Under assumptions D2, D3', D4, C1, and C2, every program has a legal execution.*

Proof. By Corollary 4.4, it has a well-formed SC execution. By Theorem 4.8, this execution is legal. □

Next, I show that source code and bytecode satisfy assumptions C1 and C2. Note that the latter is equivalent to D3' by Theorem 4.4, i.e., Lemma 4.13 discharges it.

Assumption C1 is structured similarly to D1. Thus, I construct a witness execution by corecursion similar to scc, but choose ta such that reads in $\langle ta \rangle_0$ see writes that happen before them. Since assumptions C2 and D2 ensure that such writes precede the reads in the execution, the prefix up to the read is non-speculative and thus gC&U ensures that such a witness exists. Here, the crucial step is to show that such a write exists. Note that the initialisation exists by assumption D3" and happens before the read by Lemma 4.5. Then, the $\leq_{eo}$-maximal write to the location that happens before the read serves as witness. Since the proof structure is similar to sequentially consistent completions (Lemmata 4.14 and 4.15, Theorem 4.5), I omit the details.

4.3.5 Type safety

For the JMM heap implementations, I have claimed in §4.3.2 that only the second leads to a type-safe language. In this section, I substantiate this claim and discuss the relation between type safety and values appearing out of thin air.

First, note that for correctly synchronised programs, the DRF guarantee applies (§4.3.3). Hence, all of their executions are sequentially consistent, and analoguous to the type safety proof of sequential consistency, one can show type safety for them. However, the JMM assigns semantics to *all* Java programs such that type safety and Java's security promises hold unconditionally.

Now, reconsider the program in Figure 4.12, which Figure 4.25a repeats. Figures 4.25b to Figure 4.25e show the justifying executions for the type unsafe execution in Figure 4.25e under the JMM heap implementation 1. The shaded areas contain the committed events.

The trick is to justify the address of the *Integer* object allocated in l. 5 as an out-of-thin-air value for the data races on x and y. These races have the same pattern as in Figure 4.8, where the JMM is sufficiently strong to disallow out-of-thin-air values. However, in Figure 4.25a, this cycle occurs only if the then branch (l. 5) executes. The justification first executes the else branch (l. 7) until both data races on x and y are committed (Figures 4.25b to 4.25d). Then, the branches are switched (Figure 4.25e) and the address a keeps being passed between the two data races as an out-of-thin-air value. The then branch could then do almost anything – in the example, it allocates an *Integer* object. The allocation strategy of the JMM heap implementation 1 uses the same address as the allocation in l. 7 has used in previous executions. Hence, the locations x and y of type *String* now point to an *Integer* object, which is type-unsafe.

Note that this problem is not specific to the allocation strategy of the first heap implementation. A similar example can be conceived for any given strategy that allows to allocate objects of different types at the same address. JMM heap implementation 2 circumvents this issue, because *Integer* and *String* objects have distinct address spaces.

However, tying addresses to their dynamic type information only treats the symptoms, not the cause. First, the type safety statement under the JMM heap implementation 2 is weaker than for sequential consistency from §4.2, because *jmm'-typeof-addr* no longer encodes which addresses are allocated. For example, bytecode type safety (Theorem 3.6) states that if a thread terminates with a raised exception a, then *typeof-addr* $h\ a = \lfloor ClassT\ C \rfloor$ such that $P \vdash C \leq^* \textit{Throwable}$ in the final heap h. Under sequential consistency, this expresses that a refers to an allocated object. Although this theorem literally holds for any legal execution of the JMM with heap implementation 2, too, *typeof-addr* $h\ a = \lfloor ClassT\ C \rfloor$ no longer implies that a has been allocated during the execution. For example, Figure 4.26 shows a slight modification of Figure 4.25a. A justification analogous to Figure 4.25 allows the execution where r1, r2, x, and y all contain the address that the allocation in l. 5 would return, but without executing l. 5. Thus, this model assumes that all objects already "exist" at the start of the execution, allocation merely picks an "unsed" one.

Second, another variation of this program (Figure 4.27) shows how to break the out-of-thin-air guarantee of the JMM. It changes ll. 5 and 7 such that they allocate an array of the same type and length. Then, no heap implementation would be able to disallow x and y pointing to the object allocated in l. 5. Although the out-of-thin-air guarantee is not clearly defined, such a forged pointer could be used to break Java's security features, which rely on this guarantee. Imagine l. 5 allocaes the char array that is to store the contents f a *String* object. By using malicious code like this, an attacker could obtain a reference to modify the string's contents, but Java's security features "depend upon *String*s being perceived as truly immutable" [56, §17.5].

initially: b = false; x = y = null;

| 1: r1 = y;
2: x = r1; | 3: r2 = x;
4: if (b)
5:   r3 = new Integer();
6: else
7:   r2 = new String();
8: y = r2; | 9: b = true; |

(a) Program (repeated from Figure 4.12)

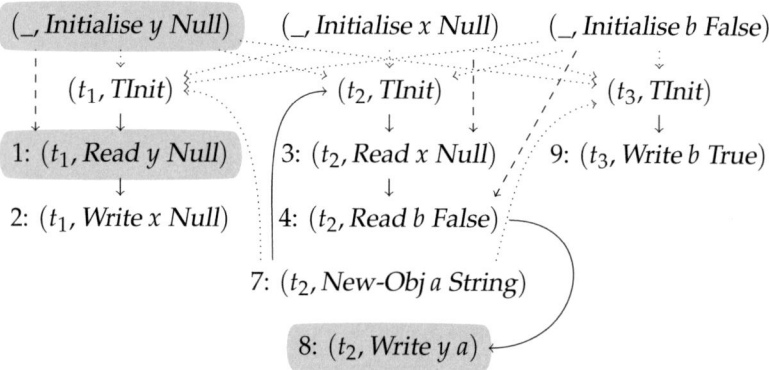

(b) Initial execution in which every write happens before the read that sees it. Commit the writes to and read from location y.

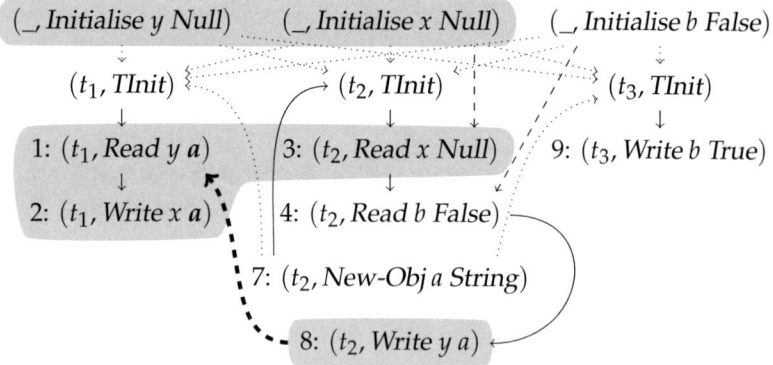

(c) Change the read of y in l. 1 to see the write in l. 8, commit the writes to and read from location x.

Figure 4.25: Justifying executions for the type-unsafe one of the program in (a)

190

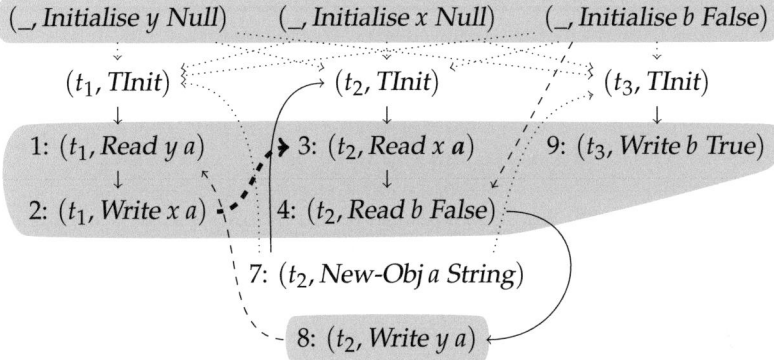

(d) Change the read of x in l. 3 to see the write in l. 2, commit the writes to and read from location b.

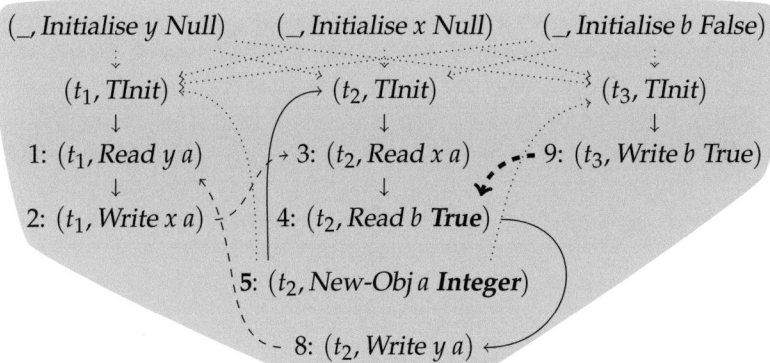

(e) Change the read of b in l. 4 to see the write in l. 9, which switches the if's branches such that l. 5 allocates an *Integer* instead of a *String*; commit all remaining events.

Figure 4.25: Justifying executions for the type-unsafe one of the program in (a)

```
                 initially: b = false; x = y = null;
1: r1 = y;   3: r2 = x;                          8: b = true;
2: x = r1;   4: if (!b)
             5:    r2 = new Exception();
             6: y = r2;
             7: throw r2;
```

Figure 4.26: A program that the JMM allows to terminate with a raised, but unallocated exception

```
                 initially: b = false; x = y = null;
1: r1 = y;   3: r2 = x;                          9: b = true;
2: x = r1;   4: if (b)
             5:    r3 = new char[2];
             6: else
             7:    r2 = new char[2];
             8: y = r2;
```

Figure 4.27: Variation of Figure 4.25a

This example shows that the out-of-thin-air guarantee is too weak to support the Java's security architecture [54]. However, this is only a theoretical example, because I do not know of any optimisation in a compiler, a JVM, nor in hardware that could lead to such behaviour. Hence, this should be considered a deficiency of the JMM specification.

4.3.6 Discussion

The JMM formalisation

Lessons learnt. The formalisation in §4.3.2 shows how to connect a Java semantics with the JMM, which has been missing in the literature [8,38,69]. The main insight is that event traces of isolated threads do not suffice to obey the JLS and Java API. Figures 4.13 and 4.14 present examples of hidden communication channels in Java that the JMM inter-thread actions do not capture – although the examples only use Java features that the JMM mentions. In my model, the basic thread actions are the only communication channel between the interleaving semantics and the different threads. With the JMM heap implementation 2, the shared state remembers only what addresses are fresh. Hence, BTAs suffice to expose all communication channels for the features that JinjaThreads models.[38]

Most obviously, the JMM misses events for thread interrupts. It predicates that Thread.interrupt "synchronises-with the point where any other thread [...] determines that [the thread] has been interrupted" [56, §17.4.4], but there are no designated events for neither thread interruption nor "that point". Hence, I have added the synchronisation events *TIntr* and *TIntrd*. Their duals for non-interruption *ClearIntr* and *IsIntrd_False* only exist as BTAs for the interleaving semantics. Similarly, the API of class Thread requires the existence of BTAs to query a thread's state, e.g., *ThreadEx*. Thus, a comprehensive model of Java concurrency has to include such BTAs. Previous JMM formalisations [8, 34, 69] did without these, because they omitted interruption and wait sets, but a realistic formalisation like JinjaThreads cannot.

The interesting question was which of these new BTAs should become events that participate in synchronisation and happens-before order. I follow the original JMM in that only *TIntr* synchronises with *TIntrd*. In particular, BTAs do not occur in complete interleavings, and therefore, they do not synchronise with any event and need not be committed or justified. Hence, they do not affect the writes that a read may see. I consider this sensible, because I have found it very hard to construct programs that can exploit such additional synchronisation to avoid data races. Typically, other schedules exhibit races in such programs.

Figure 4.28 shows an exception to this. The read in l. 6 executes only if the left thread has spawned x before l. 4 executes, which happens after the write to y in l. 1. Yet, l. 1 does not happen before l. 6 according to the JMM, because l. 4 does not generate any synchronisation event. Hence, the program is not correctly synchronised according to my definitions.

However, there are alternative definitions for data races that do not depend on the happens-before order to approximate time. More intuitively, two conflicting events race iff in some complete interleaving, they are adjacent, i.e., no event occurs between them, and the location is

---

[38]There is still a covert channel via *hashcode*, because JinjaThreads implements *hashcode* in terms of the overloaded function *hash-addr* :: '*addr* ⇒ *int*. Hence, a thread can infer how many objects of a given type have already been allocated globally by allocating a new one and taking its hash code. The easiest way to close this channel is to decouple *hashcode*'s implementation from the concrete addresses; Liu and Moore [104], e.g., implement *hashcode* such that it always returns 0. Note that this covert channel exists in commercial JVMs, too, and poses problems for security analyses [123].

initially: `x = new Thread(); y = 0`	
`1: y = 1;`	`3: try {`
`2: x.start();`	`4:    x.start();`
	`5: } catch (IllegalThreadStateException e) {`
	`6:    r = y;`
	`7: }`

Figure 4.28: The race on `Thread.start` does not eliminate the data race on y

not marked volatile. For simple models of happens-before, both definitions are equivalent [32], but not for Java with implicit communication channels between threads.

The program in Figure 4.28 would be correctly synchronised under the alternative definition, because there is no sequentially consistent interleaving with adjacent conflicting events. I argue that it is correct to not consider this program as correctly synchronised, because thread spawns are a degenerate form of synchronisation, and compilers should not need to respect such forms. In [32], Boehm and Adve have a similar problem with `trylock` in C++. They restore the equivalence by allowing `trylock` to fail spuriously. Analogously, one could tweak the *start* method to fail spuriously, but this would violate the semantics (see the example in Figure 4.14).

Under JMM heap implementation 1, I interleave the execution to obtain sequential consistency for types. This solves the problem of finding a fresh address for memory allocation, as the shared memory stores which addresses are fresh. However, complete interleavings introduce a global notion of time, which typical implementations in concurrent hardware do not provide.

The JMM heap implementation 2 actually does not need to broadcast type information at all, because it partitions the address space by type and array length like in [75], i.e, an address carries complete type information. Still, the interleaving needs to communicate (via shared state) which addresses are fresh. With an allocation operation that non-deterministically returns any address of the correct type, and with the BTAs as additional events, one could eliminate the complete interleaving; new rules at the JMM layer then would ensure that every addresses is allocated at most once. I have not followed this path because I would have had to reimplement all the management facilities that the interleaving framework already provides. Moreover, the proofs via state invariants and preservation theorems rely on the globla notion of time, although the JMM order relations do not when the constrain the possible writes for a read.

Faithfulness of the semantics Aspinall and Ševčík [8] suggested to weaken legality to enable more optimisation without sacrificing the DRF guarantee. Since my proof on the JMM level follows theirs, it also works for their weaker notion of legality. I have not formally checked that JinjaThreads validates all JMM test cases by Pugh et. al. [144]. Torlak et. al. [171] have shown that the original JMM does not validate test cases 19 and 20, but the fix by Aspinall and Ševčík [8] does. Since none of the test cases uses dynamic allocation, spawning nor interruption of threads, nor wait and notify, my formalisation should perform equivalent to the original JMM. With the fix by Aspinall and Ševčík, my formalisation should also validate test cases 19 and 20.

Alas, there are two corner cases where JinjaThreads does not model all allowed behaviours. Remember from Chapter 3 that I do not model spurious wake-ups, which the JLS permits. However, this opens a communication channel between a call to *notify* and *wait* that can erroneously make programs correctly synchronised. Figure 4.29 shows an example. There are only two conflicting events, namely the write in l. 1 conflicts with the read in l. 8. If spurious wake-ups are impossible, the following argument shows that l. 1 always happens before l. 8, i.e., there is no data race. The read in l. 8 executes only if the right-hand thread wakes up from the call to *wait* in l. 6. In the absence of spurious wake-ups, only *notify* in l. 3 can cause this. Hence, the reacquisition of the monitor m when *wait* returns happens after the unlock in l. 4, which itself happens after l. 1 by program order. However, suppose the thread on the right wakes up spuriously in l. 6. Then, the execution where the thread on the right runs before the one on the left is sequentially consistent, but the conflicting ll. 1 and 8 are not related by happens-before, i.e., the program is incorrectly synchronised. Note that "the Java coding practice of using *wait* only within loops that terminate only when some logical condition that the thread is waiting for holds" [56, §17.8.1] eliminates this problem. If this advice is followed, spurious wake-ups obscure deadlocks, because they replace deadlocks by busy waiting (see Figure 7.2 in §7.4 for such a potential deadlock in Java's class initialisation procedure [56, §17.4.2]).

```
             initially: m = new Object(); x = 0;
1: x = 1;                    5: synchronized (m) {
2: synchronized (m) {        6:    m.wait();
3:    m.notify();            7: }
4: }                         8: r = x;
```

Figure 4.29: Incorrectly synchronised program due to spurious wake-ups

The second corner case arises from inadequate atomicitiy of execution steps. The interleaving semantics executes every step of the single-threaded semantics atomically, which includes calls to native methods. For *clone*, this assumption is unrealistic. Sun and OpenJDK JVMs allow threads to concurrently manipulate the object that is being cloned. To see this, I ran the following test. One thread clones an object with 1000 volatile fields of type **int** while another changes the first and the last field. Volatility ensures that the program is correctly synchronised and the DRF guarantee applies. Then, cloning is observed as not atomic if the first field of the clone stores the original value, but not the last field. Depending on the hardware and JVM, I observed non-atomicity between 270 and 2.5k times out of 10M. Hence, JinjaThreads's *clone* implementation should be replaced by a better one.

Technical changes to the JMM   First, for the DRF guarantee, *all* initialisation events must be synchronisation events, not only those for volatile locations, which follows Aspinall and Ševčík [8]. In contrast to them, I do not need a special initialisation thread (which might run infinitely in the case of an infinite execution), but assign to initialisation events the thread's ID which created the object. This change is relevant for the final field semantics extension to the JMM, which requires to know which thread created which object [56, §17.5.1].

Second, happens-before for the `wait` method arises not only from the associated unlock and lock events [56, §17.4.5], but calling `interrupt` on the waiting thread synchronises with throwing the *InterruptedException*, too. When a thread in a wait set is both interrupted and notified, the JinjaThreads semantics always respects happens-before, although the JLS does not require this [56, §17.8.1] – see the discussion in §3.2.1.

Third, I do not model thread divergence events. The JMM introduces them to "model how a thread may cause all other threads to stall and fail to make progress" [56, §17.4.2]. My construction achieves the same via the coinductive definition of $\_ \downarrow \_$ and concatenation of event lists in Equation 4.2.

Finally, JinjaThreads models neither final fields nor class initialisation nor finalisation. Hence, I do not model that part of the JMM, either [56, §17.5, §12.4.2, §12.6.1.1] – see §7.4 for how this could be included.

The data race freedom guarantee

Insights The DRF guarantee for Java (§4.3.3) has been formalised before [8, 69] – in fact, I employ the same key ideas for the proof on the JMM level. The novel aspects are that

- JinjaThreads' JMM formalisation covers dynamic allocation with explicit allocation events and infinite executions, and

- I identify the assumptions of the DRF guarantee on the single-threaded semantics and discharge them for source code and byte-code.

The key insights are the following:

1. The new events for interruption and different kinds of synchronisation do not affect the DRF proof. This suggests that other means of synchronisation that JinjaThreads does not cover, e.g. atomics in `java.util.concurrent`, do not affect it either.

2. One must find better ways to handle initialisations, as the JMM way severely complicates the proofs. One option is to omit initialisations completely. Instead, a read is allowed to not see any write event if no write to that location has happened before and the value read is the default value. The default value is uniquely defined when types partition the address space as explained above.

3. The equivalence of SC and SC′ (Corollary 4.2) shows that the treatment of initialisations is irrelevant for the DRF guarantee. Hence, one is not constrained when searching for better ways.

Insight 3 a posteriori justifies Aspinall's and Ševčík's simpler approach of considering finite prefixes for the purpose of formalising the DRF guarantee [8]. However, it is still insufficient when dealing with the full

JMM. For example, the JMM allows the execution in Figure 4.9, but not some of its prefixes.

Similarly, my DRF proof shows that it would be safe to globally restrict read operations to type-conforming values – for correctly synchronised programs. Subject reduction and preservation proofs would become significantly easier. However, it would disallow some legal executions of programs with data races such as Figure 4.9.

Technical considerations My proof of Theorem 4.3 differs from [8, 69, 115] mainly in the proof of the DRF Lemma 4.4. I adapt the others' in two respects to deal with explicit initialisations.

First, the others topologically sort $\leq_{\text{po}}^{E}$ [115] or $\leq_{\text{hb}}^{P,E}$ [8, 69] first to obtain $\leq_{\text{eo}}^{E}$, and then take $\left\{ \beta.\ \beta \leq_{\text{eo}}^{E} \alpha \right\}$ as the prefix for the sequentially consistent execution. I omit the sorting and use the induced total order $\leq^{E}$ (rather than $\leq_{\text{eo}}^{E}$), which does not move initialisation events to the program start.

Second, Manson et al. [115] and Huisman and Petri [69] require a sequentially consistent completion E'; so do I. However, the former ignore that different initialisation events in the suffix might change the $\leq_{\text{hb}}^{P,-}$ relation on the prefix. The latter note this problem, but add an axiom that $\leq_{\text{hb}}^{P,-}$ remain unchanged. I circumvent the issue by using $\leq^{E}$ instead of $\leq_{\text{eo}}^{E}$. Hence, $\leq_{\text{hb}}^{P,-}$ on the prefix becomes independent of later initialisations (Lemma 4.6). Aspinall and Ševčík [8] completely avoid it by restricting their model to finite prefixes of executions.

Initialisations also complicate the construction of sequentially consistent completions. I failed to construct them directly, as due to the special treatment of initialisations, ill-formed programs might not have such, see the example below. Hence, I would need appropriate constraints that the semantics preserves, but the JMM notion of execution is unsuitable for preservation proofs. Instead, I proved that sequential consistency with respect to happens-before is the same as for interleaving semantics – if initialisations do not interfere (Corollary 4.2).[39] Being operational, interleaving semantics is much more amenable to reduction invariants and their preservation proofs than the JMM. While it is still challenging

---

[39]Interestingly, Batty et al. [16, §4] found that initialisations of atomics cause problems in the DRF proof for C++11, too.

initially: $x = 0$

1: print a.length;	3: r1 = x;
2: x = 1;	4: new int[r1];

(a)

(b)

Figure 4.30: An ill-formed program (a) and its execution (b) with a sequentially consistent prefix (grey area) followed by a read (l. 3) that cannot be cut, updated, and completed sequentially consistently.

to show properties about *scc*, most proofs follow the well-known pattern of preservation.

The program in Figure 4.30a demonstrates that ill-formed programs can have sequentially consistent prefixes of executions which cannot be cut, updated, and completed sequentially consistently.[40] Note that the program is ill-formed only because it literally constains an address. However, such a program could well occur as an intermediate state while executing a well-formed program.

In the execution in Figure 4.30b, the read in l. 3 sees the write from l. 2, but the most recent write would be the initialisation of location x. Suppose that l. 3 is scheduled after l. 1, but before l. 2, as indicated by the grey area. Then, the prefix up to l. 1 is sequentially consistent, but has no sequentially consistent completion when l. 3 executes next. If l. 3 is updated to read the initial value 0, then l. 4 allocates an array of length

---

[40] For simplicity, this example abstracts from the type checks that cause the semantics to get stuck.

199

0 at address a, but l. 1 has already output a's array length as 1. This violates the JLS that array lengths are always correct [56, §17.4.5]. Note that this problem only arises for JMM heap implementation 1, because 2 uses different addresses for arrays of different lengths.

In this example, the problem is that t_1 literally contains the address a that the allocation of the other thread t_2 returns. The proof of the DRF guarantee relies on the fact that a thread only knows an address if it has allocated it itself or it has read it from memory.

Consistency, type safety and out-of-thin-air values

To the best of my knowledge, consistency of the JMM has never been proven formally before. Although the proof itself is unsurprising, consistency is not obvious, because legality is a collection of axiomatic constraints. In particular, it only succeeds because my formalisation omits legality constraint 8 (§4.3.2). Aspinall and Ševčík [8] have already noted this inconsistency. Consistency and the DRF guarantee show the following:

(i) Every program has some legal behaviour (Corollary 4.5), i.e., the JMM constraints are not contradictory.

(ii) The JMM is indeed weaker than sequential consistency, because it allows all SC executions. Together with the introductory example in Figure 4.7, the JMM is strictly weaker.

(iii) For correctly synchronised programs, the JMM is *equivalent* to sequential consistency.

Banning values that appear out of thin air has been an important concern during the last decade – Pugh [145] first noticed the need to ban such values and Manson et al. [115] expand on the issue. The recent standard C++11 bans out of thin air values, too, although informally [72, §29.3.10]. Nevertheless, it is still unclear what actually constitutes a value appearing out of thin air and no formal definition has been found to date. However, one can narrow down this notion from its motivation, namely Java's type safety and security promises.

Ševčík [160, 161] proves a weak form of out-of-thin-air guarantee: If a program has no means of constructing a value, such a value will never appear in any legal execution. For example, if a program never allocates an object of a class C, then no legal execution may contain a pointer to a C object. But this guarantee is too weak to ensure Java's security promises and type safety, as my examples in §4.3.5 shows. Partitioning the address space by run-time type information rescues type safety, but is nothing more than a quick fix. A real solution is still missing.

4.4 Related work

4.4.1 Memory models and data race freedom

A lot of work has been devoted to hardware MMs, see [3] for an overview. Here, I focus on programming language MMs, which are looser than hardware MMs (and therefore harder to design), because they should be efficiently implementable on various hardware and allow as many compiler optimisations as possible, but nevertheless should be defined unambiguously.

Huisman and Petri [69] have formalised the JMM and the proof of the DRF guarantee in Coq. They have already noted that initialisations break the proof, but added an axiom to avoid the problem. They set out at the abstract level of threads in isolation, without connection to an operational semantics.

Aspinall and Ševčík [8] have formalised parts of the JMM relevant for the DRF guarantee and proved the latter in Isabelle/HOL — which I have found very helpful in extending the DRF guarantee proof. Since they omit dynamic allocation, they need to consider only finite prefixes of executions. This simplifies their proofs considerably, as they do not need to assume that sequentially consistent completion of executions exist. They do not provide an intra-thread semantics, either. Instead, they model a program as an unspecified predicate that checks whether a trace of memory accesses and synchronisation operations represents a valid execution of the thread. This does not suffice to model the hidden communication channels between threads that the JLS specifies (see the examples in Figures 4.13 and 4.14).

For a kernel language, Cenciarelli et al. [38] define an interleaving small-step semantics that generates configuration structures of events which an axiomatic theory constrains. On paper, they show that they only generate behaviours that the JMM allows, but it is unknown whether they produce every allowed behaviour and whether their model satisfies the DRF guarantee.

Torlak et al. [171] developed a model checker for axiomatic memory models. Using whole-program analysis, they derive JMM executions from small Java programs that are restricted to a small (finite) number of heap locations and finite state; loops are unrolled. Thus, their algorithm can compute all inter-thread actions and memory allocations in advance. They focus on checking small test cases rather than providing a full semantics and proofs.

Jagadeesan et al. [75] define an operational semantics for weak MMs with speculative computations similar to the JMM. Instead of validating executions a posteriori, their semantics explicitly encodes permitted reorderings and speculation. Yet, their model is neither machine-checked nor comparable to the JMM for programs with data races and synchronisation. Although they claim that their model bans values out of thin air, the modified example from §4.3.5 also exhibits the out of thin air value in their semantics.

Boyland [34] formalises in Twelf a semantics for a simple language with allocation, synchronisation, volatiles, thread spawns and joins, which may raise an error upon a data race. He shows that a program never raises such errors iff it is data-race free in the JMM sense. For programs with data races, the semantics misses many behaviours that the JMM allows, e.g., reorderings as in Figures 4.7 and 4.9, whereas my semantics deals with the full JMM.

The standard C++11 [72] considers programs with data races ill-formed and assigns undefined semantics to them, but offers finer shades of synchronisation than Java. Boehm and Adve [32] describe the MM and prove the DRF guarantee for programs which use only strong synchronisation primitives. They show that such programs are characterised more intuitively as never having conflicting events adjacent in any interleaving. For the JMM, this equivalence does not hold since threads can communicate without introducing happens-before relationships (§4.3.6). Batty et al. [16, 17] have formalised the MM with a focus on rigorously defining the semantics, and proved correct some compilation schemes for synchronisation primitives to assembly code.

Ševčík et al. [163] have verified the CompCert compiler backend with respect to the formal MM for x86 processors by Sewell et al. [164], which is the first formal correctness proof for an optimising compiler backend with respect to a weak MM. They expose the x86-TSO model in a C-like programming language, which is considerably stronger than the JMM and also provides a DRF guarantee.

Various type systems exist to statically ensure that programs are data race free, i.e., the DRF guarantee applies. Flanagan and Abadi [49] came up with an object calculus and a type system with dependent types to ensure that data races in accessing object members cannot occur. Object members are annotated with locks' names, the type system ensures that accessing a member is only possible if the specified lock is held by the thread. An appropriate subject reduction theorem shows soundness. Flanagan and Freund [50] translated this calculus to full Java bytecode and implemented it in the rccjava tool. In [58], Grossman extends their approaches to multithreaded Cyclone, which is a type safe variant of C (see §3.4.2).

4.4.2 Abstract heap modules

As part of the CompCERT project, Leroy and Blazy [100] have formalised a heap model for a subset of sequential C. Similar to my approach, they use Coq's module system [40] to separate the axiomatic specification from a concrete implementation. Their module signatures consists of the four operations *alloc, free, load,* and *store,* and two predicates $\_ \vDash \_$ and $\mathcal{B}$ on validity of block references and their bounds, respectively. Their JinjaThreads counterparts are *alloc, read, write,* and *allocated,* respectively. Since JinjaThreads has no garbage collection, *free* has no counterpart. And $\mathcal{B}$ is remotely similar to the information that *typeof-addr* and $P, \_ \vdash \_ \cdot \_ : \_$ encode. The four operations are all partial functions, i.e., implementations must be deterministic. Although JinjaThreads has similar operations, the assumptions are different. Leroy and Blazy's memory module aims to simplify the formal verification of program transformations. Hence, their assumptions mostly describe the interplay between allocations, loads and stores on the level of values. In contrast, most assumptions in JinjaThreads deal with type information. They also implement one concrete representation that distantly resembles Jinja's heap representation, which has been the basis for §4.2.

Ramananandro et al. [148] verify object layout algorithms for C++ multiple inheritance. They use a concrete low-level memory implementation and abstract over the concrete object layout in terms of a module. Its operations compute offsets to the *this* pointer for fields and casts and must satisfy 26 constraints. They prove that two layout algorithms satisfy these constraints and that an implementation of a high-level heap model similar to one by Wasserrab et al. [178] based on these operations

203

is sound. JinjaThreads has no low-level implementation of the heap, but the heap module is sufficiently abstract that such an implementation could be shown correct. Then, it would be interesting to show that the low-level implementation is correct with respect to the current high-level implementation.

4.4.3 Modular formalisations

Other theorem provers provide facilities for modular reasoning similar to Isabelle, e.g., Coq [40] and PVS [141]. Since modular developments are consequently ubiquituous, I only list works with a special emphasis on modularity and programming languages. Wasserrab and Lohner [176] decompose the definition and verification of program slicing and checking for non-interference into locales. Like the heap module and the single-threaded semantics in JinjaThreads, they use different interpretations of the locales to easily share definitions and proofs.

Delaware et al. [45] take modularisation to another level. They formalised FeatherweightJava [71] with various language extensions in Coq in the style of product lines. Extensions are modelled as features that can be plugged together to obtain different languages. To that end, they equip all definitions with variation points, i.e., parameters of the modules. Like in JinjaThreads, assumptions about the parameters separate the modules such that the proofs are module-local and theorems compose. While JinjaThreads employs this concept only for the semantics stack, Delaware et al. focus on syntactic language extensions. It would be interesting to see whether their rigorous approach scales to JinjaThreads to separate the extensions of Chapters 3 and 4 from the previous ones.

Poetry is what gets lost in translation.

Robert Frost

5

Compiler

JinjaThreads' compiler from source code to bytecode bridges the gap between the two languages; its correctness proof shows that both fit together.[41] More precisely, in this chapter, I extend Jinja's non-optimising compiler [83, §5] to JinjaThreads and prove that it is

type-preserving It compiles well-formed source code into well-formed bytecode (Theorem 5.14).

semantics-preserving If the source program terminates or diverges or deadlocks, then so does the compiled program and vice versa (Theorem 5.17). In any case, the intermediate output is the same and all terminated threads have terminated in the same way (normally or by throwing a certain exception). In particular, source code and compiled code have the same set of legal executions under the JMM (Theorem 5.18).

DRF-preserving The compiled program is correctly synchronised iff the source code is (Corollary 5.4).

The proof for type preservation follows Jinja's, because JinjaThreads only extends the Jinja language. In contrast, concurrency changes the semantics drastically and, therefore, pervades the proofs, too. The challenges of semantic preservation are the following:

compiling `synchronized` blocks is nontrivial in three ways: First, the source code semantics remembers in a *sync* (_) _ block the monitor address whereas bytecode must cache it in a local register. Second,

---

[41] A preliminary version of this chapter has been published in [111].

unlike the bytecode instructions for monitors *MEnter* and *MExit*, synchronized blocks enforce structured locking of monitors, i.e., unlocking never fails in source code. Hence, the compiler verification must prove that *MExit* never fails in compiled programs. Third, the monitor must also be unlocked when an exception abruptly terminates the block. To that end, the compiler adds an exception handler to ensure this.

small-step semantics As JinjaThreads only defines a small-step semantics, I cannot verify the compiler against the big-step semantics as Jinja does. This is much harder, because the verification must deal with intermediate states and incomparable granularity of atomic steps. Moreover, on the state representation level, the VM uses explicit call stacks, which would be implicit in the big-step semantics. In contrast, the small-step semantics dynamically inlines method calls, i.e., there is no call stack at all.

interleavings, deadlocks and nontermination While sequential programs are typically deterministic, there are many ways in which threads can interleave. The compiler verification must address this, because nondeterminism precludes the standard approach of modelling nontermination as "no behaviour", and deadlocks are a new form of behaviour. To separate these concerns from sequential challenges, I prove that the compiler preserves the behaviour of single threads that is observable to other threads. Since this includes synchronisation and heap access, I conveniently deal with interleavings and deadlock on the abstract level of the interleaving framework, which both source code and bytecode instantiate.

The JMM plays only a minor role in the verification, because the compiler does not optimise. Consequently, DRF preservation follows easily from semantic preservation, because it preserves the set of complete interleavings (§5.1.4).

To deal with nondeterminism, I follow a bisimulation approach (§5.1). As notion of bisimulation, I use delay bisimulation with explicit divergence, which is sufficiently strong to preserve deadlocks and nontermination and to support thread-local reasoning. Bisimulation also addresses the granularity of atomic steps, because it allows the compiler to introduce or eliminate internal computation steps that other threads cannot observe.

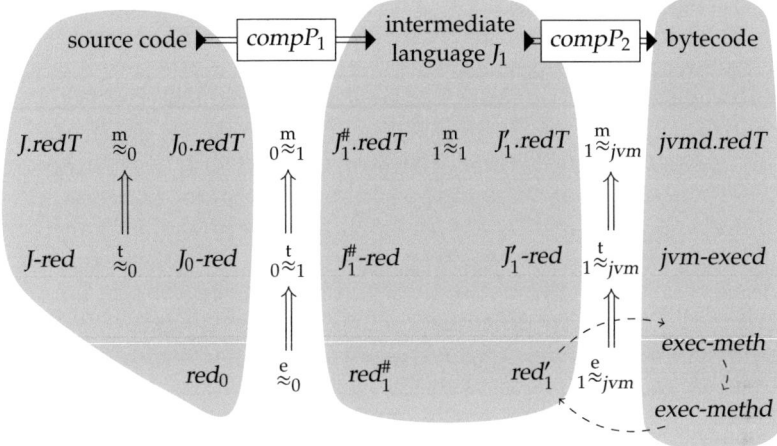

Figure 5.1: Structure of the compiler (top row) and its verification. Each column corresponds to a semantics or bisimulations ($\approx$), the rows represent different levels (m = multithreaded, t = single-threaded, e = expressions). The grey areas group the semantics by the language that they belong to.

JinjaThreads' compiler *J2JVM* operates in two stages: The first stage $compP_1$ allocates local variables to registers (§5.3), the second $compP_2$ generates the bytecode instructions (§5.4). Figure 5.1 shows its structure and the different semantics that the verification involves.

Although there is just one intermediate language J_1, the verification spans five different semantics: For source code, I first (§5.2) develop a small-step semantics J_0 that makes call stacks explicit like in bytecode and prove it bisimilar to the source code semantics from §3.2.2. To deal with the difficulty that *MExit* can fail, there are two semantics for the intermediate language: J_1' allows *sync* (_) _ blocks to fail upon unlocking, whereas $J_1^{\#}$ does not. For bytecode, I choose the defensive VM because it gets stuck in ill-formed states. The aggressive VM would carry on with undefined behaviour, which the source code semantics cannot simulate.[42]

---

[42]Sometimes, the defensive VM gets stuck earlier than the source code semantics. To avoid problems in the simulation proof, I take a detour via a semi-aggressive VM *exec-meth* and exploit that the defensive and aggressive VM commute (Theorem 3.6). See §5.4.3 for

The main verification effort is on the level of expressions and statements (last row in Figure 5.1), which contains all execution steps of a single thread except for calls to and returns from non-native methods. The bisimulation relations on this level are marked with "e". The next group of semantics lifts the expression level semantics to call stacks and adds method calls and returns. This level (marked with "t") corresponds to the single-threaded semantics *J-red* and *jvm-execd* for source code and bytecode, respectively. Finally, the multithreaded semantics models the full behaviour for multithreaded programs. In all languages, this is the interleaving semantics instantiated with the appropriate single-threaded semantics. The legality constraints of the JMM, which reside even higher in the stack of semantics, are not affected because the compiler preserves the set of complete interleavings (§5.1.4).

5.1 Semantic preservation via bisimulation

In this section, I define semantic preservation (§5.1.1), introduce delay bisimulations with explicit divergence as proof tool (§5.1.2), and show how preservation for single threads extends to the interleaving semantics (§5.1.3) and the JMM (§5.1.4).

5.1.1 Semantic preservation

Semantic preservation aims to show that semantic properties established on the source code also hold for the target code and vice versa. Such properties or specifications, e.g., a safety property like no null pointer exceptions, are typically modelled as predicates on the traces of observable behaviour, i.e., the sequence of observable steps of a program execution, or on the sets of possible traces (for nondeterministic programs). Thus, a correct compiler *Comp* must ensure that the (sets of) traces of the source program P and of the compiled program *Comp P* are equal.

Formally, *Comp* preserves the semantics of P iff the following holds: Let s_1 and s_2 be the initial states for P and *Comp P*, respectively. For every execution of P that starts in s_1 and terminates in s_1', there must be an execution of *Comp P* from s_2 to s_2' such that both the executions'

---

details.

traces and the observable data in s_1' and s_2' (such as the result values or exceptional termination) are the same. For every infinite execution of P that starts in s_1, $Comp\ P$ has an infinite execution with the same trace that starts in s_2. Conversely, every execution of $Comp\ P$ from s_2 must be matched that way by one of P from s_1.

From a specification point of view, only the second direction is essential. The interleaving semantics and the memory model only specify the set of allowed behaviours, of which the implementation $Comp\ P$ may pick any (non-empty) subset. Still, I show both directions for two reasons.

The main reason is that semantics properties on sets of traces such as possibilistic security properties [118] require both directions. The compiled code must not miss any observable nondeterministic choice, neither may it introduce additional observable behaviour. Some atomic high-level statements are translated into a sequence of simple instructions, which allow more interleavings. A correct compiler must ensure that these new interleavings do not lead to new behaviours. Conversely, some constructs (like exception handling) are atomic in the compiled code, but require many steps in the source code semantics. Although the compiled code has consequently less interleavings, no observable behaviour must be missed. Being part of the Quis Custodiet project [147], JinjaThreads serves as the semantics basis for verifying concurrent information flow control algorithms, e.g., for possibilistic non-interference [53]. Hence, to transfer such results between source code and bytecode, it is essential that verification covers both directions.

On the technical level, a second reason is that the interleaving framework defines deadlocks in terms of the semantics (§3.3) whose preservation requires both directions, too.

Regarding schedulers, semantic preservation is possibilistic: The source and compiled program may have different behaviour under a *fixed* scheduler whose strategy depends on unobservable steps. Under a round-robin scheduler, e.g., the number of unobservable steps between two observable ones influences the interleaving. Since a compiler changes this number, source code and bytecode may have different behaviours under this scheduler. In this sense, semantic preservation means: If there is a scheduler for P such that s_1 produces trace t and either terminates in s_1' or runs infinitely, then there is also a scheduler for $Comp\ P$ such that s_2 produces trace t and either ends in s_2' or runs infinitely, respectively.

5.1.2 Simulation properties

For semantic preservation, I must show trace equivalence for the source code and the compiled code. To do this, it is standard to show bisimilarity. The latter implies trace equivalence and can be shown by inspecting individual steps of execution instead of whole program executions. For the verification, I have chosen delay bisimilarity [1, 119] augmented with explicit divergence [27], because multithreaded states are delay bisimilar with explicit divergence if each of their threads is so. As this notion is transitive, I can decompose the compiler into smaller transformations and verify each on its own. Transitivity ensures that the overall compiler is correct, too.

In this setting, programs define labelled transition systems (LTS) whose states are the program states and whose labels constitute the observable behaviour. I write $s \stackrel{tl}{\rightarrowtriangle} s'$ for a single transition (move), i.e., execution step in the small-step semantics, from state s to state s' with transition label tl. Both the semantics $t \vdash \_ - \_ \rightarrow \_$ of an individual thread t and the interleaving semantics $\_ - \_:\_ \rightarrow \_$ fit into this format. A predicate $\tau\text{-move } s \ tl \ s'$ determines whether the transition $s \stackrel{tl}{\rightarrowtriangle} s'$ is unobservable to the outside world, i.e., other threads for the single-threaded semantics and other processes and the user for the multithreaded semantics. Such transitions are called silent or τ-moves. Since their labels are irrelevant, I don't keep track of them and write $s \stackrel{\tau}{\rightarrowtriangle} s'$ for $\exists tl. \ s \stackrel{tl}{\rightarrowtriangle} s' \wedge \tau\text{-move } s \ tl \ s'$. Moreover, $\_ \stackrel{\tau}{\rightarrowtriangle}^+ \_$ denotes the transitive closure of $\_ \stackrel{\tau}{\rightarrowtriangle} \_$, and $\_ \stackrel{\tau}{\rightarrowtriangle}^* \_$ the reflexive and transitive closure. A state s can diverge (denoted $s \stackrel{\tau}{\rightarrowtriangle} \infty$) iff an infinite sequence of τ-moves starts in s. A visible move $s \stackrel{tl}{\twoheadrightarrow} s'$ consists of a finite sequence of τ-moves followed by an observable transition, i.e., $s \stackrel{tl}{\twoheadrightarrow} s'$ abbreviates $\exists s''. \ s \stackrel{\tau}{\rightarrowtriangle}^* s'' \wedge s'' \stackrel{tl}{\rightarrowtriangle} s' \wedge \neg \tau\text{-move } s'' \ tl \ s'$.

In this chapter, I often have states, labels, reductions, and the like for two or more programs and semantics. To keep the notation simple and clear, I will usually index variables, arrows, etc. with numbers to assign them to one of them, i.e., $'x_1, s_1, t \vdash \_ - \_ \rightarrow_1 \_$, etc. for the first, $'x_2, s_2, t \vdash \_ - \_ \rightarrow_2 \_$, etc. for the second and so on.

A delay bisimulation (with explicit divergence) consists of two binary relations $\approx$ and $\sim$ on states and transition labels, respectively, that satisfy the simulation diagrams in Figure 5.2:

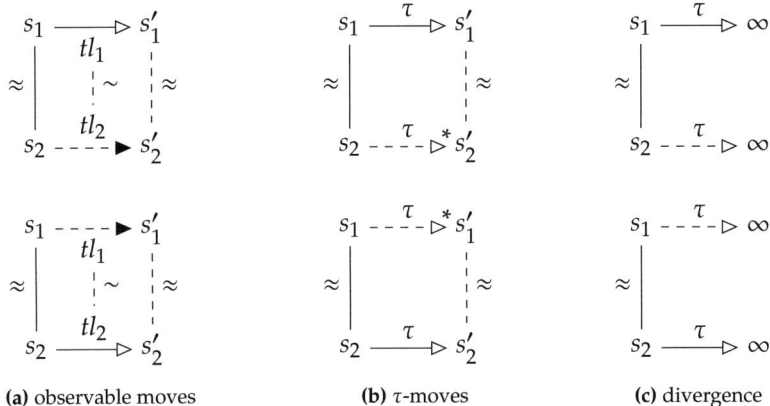

(a) observable moves   (b) τ-moves   (c) divergence

Figure 5.2: Simulation diagrams for delay bisimulations with explicit divergence. Solid lines denote assumptions, dashed lines conclusions.

(a) An observable move is simulated by a visible move such that $\approx$ relates the resulting states and $\sim$ relates the transition labels.

(b) A τ-move is simulated by a finite (possibly empty) sequence of τ-moves such that $\approx$ relates the resulting states.

(c) $\approx$ relates only states of which either both or none can diverge.

Locale *dbisim-div* in Figure 5.3 formalises this notion.

Two programs, i.e., transition systems, are (delay) bisimilar (with explicit divergence) iff there exists a delay bisimulation with explicit divergence for them that relates their start states. A special case of delay bisimulation is strong bisimulation [120] where every move is simulated by exactly one move. When $\sim$ is obvious from the context, I sometimes omit it and refer to $\approx$ as a delay bisimulation.

Note that condition (b) does not imply condition (c) because of the classic infinite stuttering problem. Infinitely many τ-moves may be simulated by no move at all.

Figure 5.4 shows two LTSs with states $\{s_1, s_1', s_1''\}$ and $\{s_2, s_2', s_2''\}$, respectively, and a delay bisimulation with explicit divergence $(\approx, \sim)$ between them. The upper LTS with start state s_1 can delay arbitrarily long the decision whether to diverge or to produce the observable transition with label tl_1, whereas the lower LTS, whose start state is s_2, must decide immediately. Nevertheless, they are delay bisimilar with

type_synonym $('s, 't)$ $lts = {}'s \Rightarrow {}'tl \Rightarrow {}'s \Rightarrow bool$
type_synonym $('s_1, 's_2)$ $bisim = {}'s_1 \Rightarrow {}'s_2 \Rightarrow bool$

locale $dbisim\text{-}base =$
   fixes $\twoheadrightarrow_1 :: ('s_1, 'tl_1)$ lts and $\twoheadrightarrow_2 :: ('s_2, 'tl_2)$ lts
   and $\approx :: ('s_1, 's_2)$ $bisim$ and $\sim :: ('tl_1, 'tl_2)$ $bisim$
   and $\tau\text{-}move_1 :: ('s_1, 'tl_1)$ lts and $\tau\text{-}move_2 :: ('s_2, 'tl_2)$ lts

locale $dbisim\text{-}div = dbisim\text{-}base +$
   assumes $simulation1 : [\![s_1 \approx s_2;\ s_1 \xrightarrow{tl_1}_1 s_1';\ \neg\, \tau\text{-}move_1\ s_1\ tl_1\ s_1']\!]$
     $\implies \exists tl_2\ s_2'.\ s_2 \xrightarrow{tl_2}_2 s_2' \land s_1' \approx s_2' \land tl_1 \sim tl_2$
   and $simulation2 : [\![s_1 \approx s_2;\ s_2 \xrightarrow{tl_2}_2 s_2';\ \neg\, \tau\text{-}move_2\ s_2\ tl_2\ s_2']\!]$
     $\implies \exists tl_1\ s_1'.\ s_1 \xrightarrow{tl_1}_1 s_1' \land s_1' \approx s_2' \land tl_1 \sim tl_2$
   and $simulation\text{-}\tau1 : [\![s_1 \approx s_2;\ s_1 \xrightarrow{\tau}_1 s_1']\!] \implies \exists s_2'.\ s_2 \xrightarrow{\tau}{}^*_2 s_2' \land s_1' \approx s_2'$
   and $simulation\text{-}\tau2 : [\![s_1 \approx s_2;\ s_2 \xrightarrow{\tau}_2 s_2']\!] \implies \exists s_1'.\ s_1 \xrightarrow{\tau}{}^*_1 s_1' \land s_1' \approx s_2'$
   and $bisim\text{-}diverge : s_1 \approx s_2 \implies s_1 \xrightarrow{\tau}_1 \infty \longleftrightarrow s_2 \xrightarrow{\tau}_2 \infty$

locale $dbisim\text{-}final = dbisim\text{-}base +$
   fixes $final_1 :: {}'s_1 \Rightarrow bool$ and $final_2 :: {}'s_2 \Rightarrow bool$
   assumes $final_1\text{-}simulation :$
     $[\![s_1 \approx s_2;\ final_1\ s_1]\!] \implies \exists s_2'.\ s_2 \xrightarrow{\tau}{}^*_2 s_2' \land s_1 \approx s_2' \land final_2\ s_2'$
   and $final_2\text{-}simulation :$
     $[\![s_1 \approx s_2;\ final_2\ s_2]\!] \implies \exists s_1'.\ s_1 \xrightarrow{\tau}{}^*_1 s_1' \land s_1' \approx s_2 \land final_1\ s_1'$

Figure 5.3: Locale $dbisim\text{-}div$ formalises the notion of delay bisimulations with explicit divergence; locale $dbisim\text{-}final$ defines preservation of final states

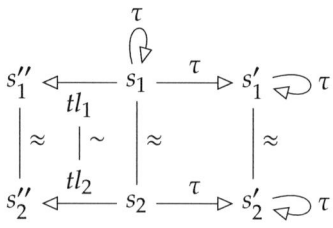

Figure 5.4: Example of a delay bisimulation with explicit divergence that is not a well-founded delay bisimulation

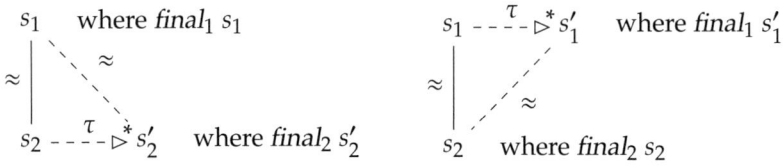

Figure 5.5: Simulation diagrams for preservation of final states

explicit divergence because divergence (Figure 5.2c) is a trace property and thus independent of the visited states.

A delay bisimulation $(\approx, \sim)$ preserves final states iff whenever one of the related states is final, then the other can reach a final state via τ-moves. Locale *dbisim-final* in Figure 5.3 formalises this notion, Figure 5.5 shows the simulation diagrams. Note that a delay bisimulation with explicit divergence preserves final states if finality coincides with being stuck. However, in general, not all stuck states are final. For example, deadlocked states in the multithreaded semantics are stuck, but not final – and so may type-incorrect states. Preservation of final states ensures that compiled programs whose source code terminates in a final state also terminate in a final state, and vice versa.

Lemma 5.1 (Transitivity of delay bisimulations). *Let $(\approx_1, \sim_1)$ and $(\approx_2, \sim_2)$ be delay bisimulations with explicit divergence. Then, their composition $(\approx_1 \circ \approx_2, \sim_1 \circ \sim_2)$ (denoted $(\approx_1, \sim_1) \circ_B (\approx_2, \sim_2)$) is also a delay bisimulation – where $\circ$ denotes relational composition, i.e., $x \; R \circ S \; z$ for binary relations R and S iff there is a y such that $x \; R \; y$ and $y \; S \; z$.*

If both $(\approx_1, \sim_1)$ and $(\approx_2, \sim_2)$ preserve final states, so does their composition.

Proof. Aceto et al. [1] showed this for delay bisimulations without explicit divergence, i.e., the simulation diagrams in (a) and (b) of Figure 5.2. The simulation diagrams in (c) are straightforward to prove.

For preservation of final states, suppose $s_1 \approx_1 \circ \approx_2 s_3$ and $final_1 \; s_1$. Hence, $s_1 \approx_1 s_2$ and $s_2 \approx_2 s_3$ for some s_2. By assumption, there is a s_2' with $s_2 \xrightarrow{\tau}^* s_2'$ and $s_1 \approx_1 s_2'$ and $final_2 \; s_2'$. By induction on $s_2 \xrightarrow{\tau}^* s_2'$ with invariant $s_2 \approx_2 s_3$, obtain s_3' such that $s_2' \approx s_3'$ and $s_3 \xrightarrow{\tau}^* s_3'$, using *simulation-τ1* in the inductive step. Since s_2' is $final_2$, there is an s_3'' with $s_3' \xrightarrow{\tau}^* s_3''$ and $s_2' \approx s_3''$ and $final_3 \; s_3''$. Then, $s_3 \xrightarrow{\tau}^* s_3''$ and $s_1 \approx_1 \circ_B \approx_2 s_3''$ and $final_3 \; s_3''$ by transitivity and definition, which

213

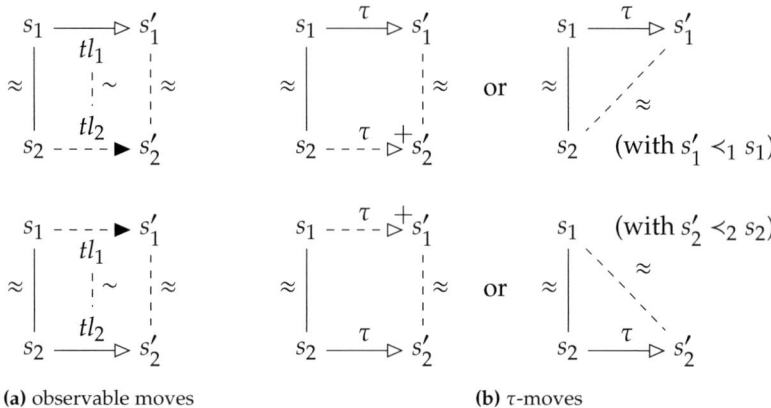

(a) observable moves (b) τ-moves

Figure 5.6: Simulation diagrams for well-founded delay bisimulations

concludes this direction. The other direction that starts from $final_3\ s_3$ follows by symmetry.[43] □

Explicit divergence violates the approach of inspecting individual steps of execution, because divergence consists of infinitely many steps. Hence, it is difficult to prove delay bisimilarity with explicit divergence directly. Instead, I adapt Leroy's notion of star simulation [97] as follows:

Let $\prec_1$ and $\prec_2$ be two well-founded binary relations on states. $(\approx, \sim)$ is a well-founded delay bisimulation iff it satisfies the simulation diagrams in Figure 5.6:

(a) Observable moves are simulated as in delay bisimulations with explicit divergence.

(b) A τ-move $s_i \xrightarrow{\tau}_i s_i'$ ($i \in \{1,2\}$) is either simulated by a finite *nonempty* sequence of τ-moves, or by no move at all. In the latter case, the τ-move being simulated must descend in $\prec_i$, i.e., $s_i' \prec_i s_i$.

Since $\prec_1$ and $\prec_2$ are well-founded, i.e., there are no infinitely decreasing chains, the infinite stuttering problem cannot occur. Proving well-founded delay bisimulation is easier than delay bisimulation with explicit divergence because all assumptions only involve a single transition.

---

[43]Proofs by symmetry in this chapter are not only a matter of presentation. I appeal to symmetry also in the Isabelle formalisation. This way, I had to write detailed proofs for only one direction.

The next lemma shows that well-founded delay bisimulation is at least as strong as delay bisimulation with explicit divergence, i.e., I can use the former whenever I need the latter.

Lemma 5.2. *Let $(\approx, \sim)$ be a well-founded delay bisimulation for $\prec_1$ and $\prec_2$. Then, $(\approx, \sim)$ is a delay bisimulation with explicit divergence.*

Proof. Since Figure 5.2a and Figure 5.6a are identical and Figure 5.6b trivially implies Figure 5.2b, only the simulation diagrams for divergence (Figure 5.2c) are interesting. The latter directly follow by coinduction on $s_i \xrightarrow{\tau}_i \infty$ ($i \in \{1, 2\}$) with $s_1 \approx s_2$ and $s_{3-i} \xrightarrow{\tau}_{3-i} \infty$ as coinduction invariant using the strengthened coinduction rule (see §1.4.3) with $\prec_{3-i}$ as well-founded order. □

The converse does not hold, as Figure 5.4 shows.[44] The relations $\approx$ and $\sim$ as shown form a delay bisimulation with explicit divergence and relate the start states s_1 and s_2. However, there is no well-founded delay bisimulation $(\approx', \sim')$ that relates states s_1 and s_2, because s_2 cannot simulate the τ-move $s_1 \xrightarrow{\tau}_1 s_1$ according to Figure 5.6b. Clearly, $\approx'$ cannot relate s_1 and s_2', because s_1 can produce the observable label tl_1 and s_2' cannot. This excludes the possibility on the left of Figure 5.6b. However, the right one is not feasible, either, as $s_1 \prec_1 s_1$ would violate well-foundedness of $\prec_1$.

The advantage of delay bisimulation with explicit divergence over well-founded delay bisimulation is that only the former is closed under composition (Lemma 5.1), but not the latter. Figure 5.7 shows three LTSs (solid, dashed, and dotted arrows) and two well-founded delay bisimulations (dashed and dotted lines) whose composition is no well-founded delay bisimulation, because there is no suitable well-founded relation $\prec_1'$ for the solid LTS. Suppose $\prec_1'$ were such. Then, for all $i > 0$, u_i can only simulate the τ-move $s_{2i-1} \xrightarrow{\tau} s_{2i}$ by staying at u_i, hence $s_{2i} \prec_1' s_{2i-1}$ by Figure 5.6b. But for all $j > 0$, u_{j+1}' is related to s_{2j} whose τ-move to s_{2j+1} it can only simulate by staying at u_{j+1}'. Hence, $s_{2j+1} \prec_1' s_{2j}$ by Figure 5.6b. Therefore, $s_{i+1} \prec_1' s_i$ for all i, i.e., $\prec_1'$ contains an infinite descending chain, which contradicts well-foundedness.

This example demonstrates only that well-founded delay bisimulations do not compose. It does not rule out that well-founded delay

---

[44]This example was found by Nitpick [30], a counter example generator for Isabelle/HOL, after several failed attempts of mine to prove equivalence (see §7.2).

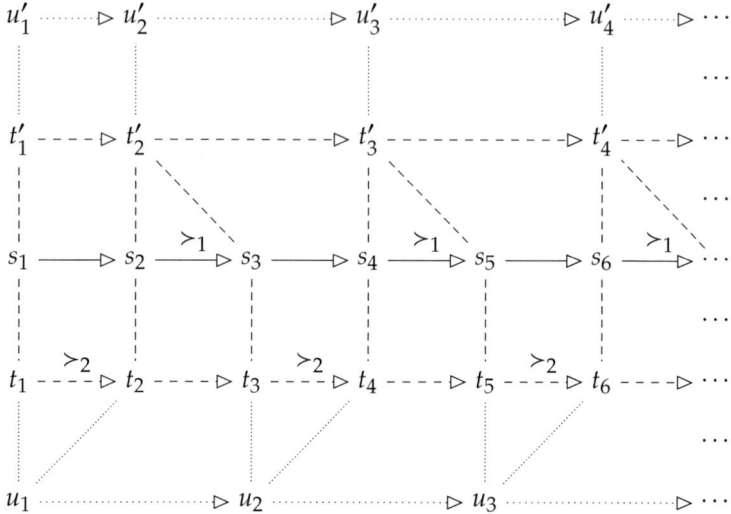

Figure 5.7: Three transition systems (solid, dashed, and dotted arrows) and two well-founded delay bisimulations (dashed and dotted lines) whose composition is no well-founded delay bisimulation for the solid and dotted transition systems. All transitions are τ-moves.

bisimilarity is transitive, because there may be delay bisimilarity relations other than the composition O_B for which a well-founded relation exists. I have not attempted to prove this, because directly composing bisimulation relations helps in breaking down the ultimate correctness result.

For this chapter, an execution ξ from a state s consists of the labels of a possibly infinite sequence of observable moves and – if these are only finitely many – the terminal state $\lfloor s \rfloor$ or the special symbol $None$ (written $\overset{\infty}{\to}$) for divergence. Formally, it is a possibly infinite list of labels where the constructor for the empty list carries a symbol, i.e., elements of the following codatatype:[45]

$$\textbf{codatatype} \quad ('a,'b)\ tllist \quad = []_{'b} \mid 'a \cdot ('a,'b)\ tllist$$
$$\textbf{type\_synonym}\ ('s,'tl)\ execution = ('tl,'s\ option)\ tllist$$

---

[45]Since Isabelle/HOL has no built-in codatatype support, I construct this type with the quotient package [77] as the quotient of $'a\ llist \times 'b$ through the equivalence relation $\{\,((xs,b),(ys,b')).\ xs = ys \wedge (lfinite\ ys \longrightarrow b = b')\,\}$ where $lfinite$ characterises finite lists.

$$\Downarrow\text{TERMINATE}: \quad \frac{s \xrightarrow{\tau}{}^* s' \qquad \forall tl\ s''.\ \neg s' \xrightarrow{tl} s''}{s \Downarrow []_{\lfloor s' \rfloor}} \qquad\qquad \Downarrow\text{DIVERGE}: \quad \frac{s \xrightarrow{\tau} \infty}{s \Downarrow []_{\xrightarrow{\infty}}}$$

$$\Downarrow\text{STEP}: \quad \frac{s \xrightarrow{tl} s' \qquad s' \Downarrow \xi}{s \Downarrow tl \cdot \xi}$$

Figure 5.8: Executions as traces of observable moves

Like for possibly infinite lists (see Footnote 30), I do not distinguish syntactically such lists from ordinary lists, except for the additional symbol of the empty list constructor. An execution ξ terminates in the state s iff ξ is finite and the empty list constructor in ξ carries the symbol $\lfloor s \rfloor$.

The predicate $s \Downarrow \xi$ characterises all executions ξ that start in s (Figure 5.8). If s can reach via τ-moves a stuck state s', then an execution terminates in s' ($\Downarrow$TERMINATE). If an infinite sequence of τ-moves starts in s, then an execution diverges ($\Downarrow$DIVERGE). If s can do a visible move with transition label tl to some state s', then s's executions include s''s prepended with tl ($\Downarrow$STEP).

Let $[\approx, \sim]$ denote the point-wise extension of $(\approx, \sim)$ to executions, i.e., $\sim$ holds point-wise for all list elements and $\approx$ for the terminal states, if any. In delay bisimilar transition systems with explicit divergence, related states have bisimilar executions, i.e., delay bisimulations imply semantic preservation.

Theorem 5.1 (Semantic preservation). *Let $(\approx, \sim)$ be a delay bisimulation with explicit divergence for the LTSs $(\twoheadrightarrow_1, \tau\text{-move}_1)$ and $(\twoheadrightarrow_2, \tau\text{-move}_2)$ and $s_1 \approx s_2$. Then, the following holds:*

(i) *Whenever $s_1 \Downarrow_1 \xi_1$, then $s_2 \Downarrow_2 \xi_2$ for some ξ_2 such that $\xi_1 [\approx, \sim] \xi_2$.*

(ii) *Whenever $s_2 \Downarrow_2 \xi_2$, then $s_1 \Downarrow_1 \xi_1$ for some ξ_1 such that $\xi_1 [\approx, \sim] \xi_2$.*

Proof sketch. It suffices to prove (i) because (ii) follows from (i) by symmetry. Since ξ_2 is existentially quantified in (i), I must first construct it explicitly by corecursion from s_1 and ξ_1 before showing $s_2 \Downarrow_2 \xi_2$ and $\xi_1 [\approx, \sim] \xi_2$ by coinduction. However, ξ_1 is only a trace of transition labels without the intermediate states. Since trace properties are strictly weaker than bisimulation properties, it is too weak to be used as coinduction invariant.

217

Therefore, I define a variant $\Downarrow'$ of $\Downarrow$ where $\Downarrow$STEP not only prepends the transition label, but also remembers the intermediate state, i.e.,

$$\Downarrow'\text{STEP}: \quad \frac{s \xrightarrow{tl} s' \qquad s' \Downarrow' \xi}{s \Downarrow' (tl,s') \cdot \xi}$$

Coinduction (with invariant $s \Downarrow \xi_1$) shows that there is a ξ_1' such that $s \Downarrow_1' \xi_1'$ and ξ is the projection of ξ_1' on the transition labels. Construct $\xi_2' = simulate\, s_2\, \xi_1'$ by corecursion as follows:

$$simulate\, s_2\, []_{\lfloor s_1' \rfloor} =$$
$$(let\, s_2' = \varepsilon s_2'.\, s_2 \xrightarrow{\tau}{}_2^* s_2' \wedge (\forall tl_2\, s_2''.\, \neg s_2' \xrightarrow{tl_2}{}_2 s_2'') \wedge s_1' \approx s_2'\, in\, []_{\lfloor s_2' \rfloor})$$

$$simulate\, s_2\, []_{\overrightarrow{\infty}} = []_{\overrightarrow{\infty}}$$

$$simulate\, s_2\, ((tl_1,s_1') \cdot \xi_1) =$$
$$(let\, (tl_2,s_2') = \varepsilon(tl_2,s_2').\, s_2 \xrightarrow{tl_2}{}_2 s_2' \wedge s_1' \approx s_2' \wedge tl_1 \sim tl_2$$
$$in\, (tl_2,s_2') \cdot simulate\, s_2'\, \xi_1)$$

Then, I prove by coinduction with invariant $s_1 \approx s_2$ and $s_1 \Downarrow' \xi_1'$ that $s \Downarrow_2' \xi_2'$ and that ξ_1' and ξ_2' are related point-wise by $\approx$ and $\sim$. Hence, choose ξ_2 to be the projection of ξ_2' to transition labels. $\qquad \square$

Theorem 5.2 (Preservation of final states). *Let $(\approx, \sim)$ preserve final states. Suppose $s_1 \Downarrow_1 \xi_1$ and $s_2 \Downarrow_2 \xi_2$ such that $\xi_1 [\approx, \sim] \xi_2$. Then, ξ_1 terminates in a $final_1$-state iff ξ_2 terminates in a $final_2$-state.*

5.1.3 Lifting simulations in the interleaving framework

The delay bisimulations for showing semantic preservation always relate multithreaded states. As I use the framework for interleaving semantics at all compilation stages, I uniformly lift delay bisimulations for single threads to multithreaded states. Thus, to show delay bisimilarity on the multithreaded level, it suffices to show delay bisimilarity for single threads plus some constraints that the lifting imposes.

A reduction in the multithreaded semantics is a τ-move (predicated by $m\tau$-move) iff it originates from a τ-move of the single-threaded semantics via NORMAL. In particular, reacquisition of temporarily released locks (rule ACQUIRE) is no τ-move, because another thread can observe the lock acquisition by no longer being able to acquire the lock.

First, I lift a relation on thread-local states and the shared heap to multithreaded states s_1 and s_2 as follows: Let $t \vdash (x_1, h_1) \approx (x_2, h_2)$ denote a bisimulation relation for thread t and $x_1 \overset{w}{\approx} x_2$ be a relation of thread-local states for threads in wait sets. This induces the following relation $s_1 \approx_m s_2$:

(i) Locks, wait sets and interrupts are equal in s_1 and s_2, i.e., $locks\, s_1 = locks\, s_2$, $wset\, s_1 = wset\, s_2$, and $intrs\, s_1 = intrs\, s_2$.

(ii) All threads in s_1 also exist in s_2 and vice versa, i.e., $dom\,(thr\, s_1) = dom\,(thr\, s_2)$.

(iii) For every thread in s_1 and s_2, say $thr\, s_1\, t = \lfloor(x_1, ln_1)\rfloor$ and $thr\, s_2\, t = \lfloor(x_2, ln_2)\rfloor$, the temporarily released locks are the same ($ln_1 = ln_2$), the thread-local states related ($t \vdash (x_1, shr\, s_1) \approx (x_2, shr\, s_2)$), and if t's wait set status is not $None$, $x_1 \overset{w}{\approx} x_2$.

(iv) All waiting threads exist, i.e., $dom\,(wset\, s_1) \subseteq dom\,(thr\, s_1)$.

(v) There are only finitely many threads, i.e., $finite\,(dom\,(thr\, s_1))$.

Let me now briefly review the constraints. Since threads can observe the status of locks, wait sets and interrupts and the existence of threads, equality in (i) and (ii) ensures that $\approx_m$-related states are indistinguishable to any of their threads. Constraint (iii) imposes the thread-local bisimulation on all thread states. The last condition $x_1 \overset{w}{\approx} x_2$ imposes stronger simulation properties on threads in wait sets, because the interleaving semantics does not allow a thread to execute τ-moves between its removal from the wait set and the (observable) reduction of processing the removal – with BTAs $Notified$ and $WokenUp$, respectively. Constraint (iv) ensures that spawned threads are not in a wait set, i.e., their thread-local states need not satisfy the stronger $\overset{w}{\approx}$ relation. Finally, the last constraint (v) ensures that $\approx_m$ preserves divergence.

To see that (v) is necessary, consider, e.g., two infinite pools of threads. In one of them, each thread only does a single τ-move $x_1 \overset{\tau}{\rhd}_1 x_1'$ before it terminates. In the other, all threads have terminated in state x_2. For the (well-founded) delay bisimulation between single threads that relates both x_1 and x_1' with x_2, constraints (i) to (iv) are satisfied, but the first

219

type_synonym $('l, 't, 'x, 'h, 'w, 'o)$ $\tau\text{-moves} =$
$\quad 'x \times 'h \Rightarrow ('l, 't, 'x, 'h, 'w, 'o)$ $thread\text{-}action \Rightarrow 'x \times 'h \Rightarrow bool$

locale $\tau\text{-multithreaded} = multithreaded +$
$\quad$ fixes $\tau\text{-move} :: ('l, 't, 'x, 'h, 'w, 'o)$ $\tau\text{-moves}$
$\quad$ assumes $\tau\text{-}ta\colon \tau\text{-move}\ (x, h)\ ta\ (x', h') \Longrightarrow ta = (\!\!|\!\!|)$
$\quad$ and $\tau\text{-}heap\colon [\![t \vdash (x, h) -ta\!\rightarrow (x', h');\ \tau\text{-move}\ (x, h)\ ta\ (x', h')]\!] \Longrightarrow h' = h$

Figure 5.9: Locale $\tau\text{-multithreaded}$ enforces that τ-moves are unobservable

thread pool can diverge (by executing one thread at a time), whereas the second is stuck. Hence, without constraint (v), $\approx_m$ would not be a delay bisimulation with explicit divergence.

The bisimulation $\_ \vdash \_ \approx \_$ for single threads also yields the relation on the thread actions as transition labels: $\vdash ta_1 \sim ta_2$ denotes that ta_1 and ta_2 are equal except for the parameters x_1, h_1 and x_2, h_2 to *Spawn t* BTAs which must satisfy $t \vdash (x_1, h_1) \approx (x_2, h_2)$, i.e, ta_1 and ta_2 may only differ in the initial states of spawned threads, which must be bisimilar.[46]

The above definition for $\approx_m$ is sensible. If $(t \vdash \_ \approx \_, \vdash \_ \sim \_)$ is a delay bisimulation with explicit divergence, then so is $\approx_m$. However, this requires additional assumptions that the communication channels through thread actions are respected; Figures 5.9 and 5.10 collect them.

Most importantly, a thread must not be able to observe the τ-moves of other threads. To that end, I require that τ-moves neither execute any BTAs, nor change the shared heap, which the locale $\tau\text{-multithreaded}$ formalises in Figure 5.9.

Second, since bisimilarity of threads comprises the shared heap, I require that heap changes preserve $\_ \vdash \_ \approx \_$, i.e., the heap changes by one thread must not break bisimilarity of other threads. Assumption *heap-change-preserve* of locale *m-dbisim-div* captures this formally: Let $t \vdash (x_1, h_1) \approx (x_2, h_2)$ be two bisimilar states with visible moves to (x'_1, h'_1) and (x'_2, h'_2), respectively, such that $t \vdash (x'_1, h'_1) \approx (x'_2, h'_2)$, i.e., the visible moves simulate each other. Then, for any thread t', whenever $t' \vdash (x^*_1, h_1) \approx (x^*_2, h_2)$ holds for the old heaps h_1 and h_2, $t' \vdash (x^*_1, h'_1) \approx (x^*_2, h'_2)$ must still hold for the updated heaps h'_1 and h'_2.

---

[46]This is the second place (besides lifting thread-local well-formedness conditons in §3.1.4) where storing the current heap in the BTA *Spawn* simplifies the definition, because $t \vdash \_ \approx \_$ relates pairs of thread-local states and the current heaps.

locale *m-dbisim-div* =
  r1 : *τ-multithreaded final₁ r₁ acq-events τ-move₁* +
  r2 : *τ-multithreaded final₂ r₂ acq-events τ-move₂* +
  fixes _ ⊢ _ ≈ _ :: $'t \Rightarrow ('x_1 \times 'h_1, 'x_2 \times 'h_2)$ *bisim* and $\overset{w}{\approx}$ :: $('x_1, 'x_2)$ *bisim*
  assumes *dbisim-div* $(r_1\ t)\ (r_2\ t)\ (t \vdash \_ \approx \_)\ (\vdash \_ \sim \_)$ *τ-move₁ τ-move₂*
  and *dbisim-final* $(r_1\ t)\ (r_2\ t)\ (t \vdash \_ \approx \_)\ (\vdash \_ \sim \_)$ *τ-move₁ τ-move₂*
      $(\lambda(x_1,h_1).\ final_1\ x_1)\ (\lambda(x_2,h_2).\ final_2\ x_2)$
  and *heap-change-preserve*:
    $\llbracket t \vdash (x_1,h_1) \approx (x_2,h_2);\ t \vdash (x'_1,h'_1) \approx (x'_2,h'_2);\ \vdash tl_1 \sim tl_2;$
    $\quad t \vdash (x_1,h_1) \xrightarrow{tl_1}_1 (x'_1,h'_1);\ t \vdash (x_2,h_2) \xrightarrow{tl_2}_2 (x'_2,h'_2);$
    $\quad t' \vdash (x_1^*,h_1) \approx (x_2^*,h_2)\rrbracket \implies t' \vdash (x_1^*,h'_1) \approx (x_2^*,h'_2)$
  and $\overset{w}{\approx}I$:
    $\llbracket t \vdash (x_1,h_1) \approx (x_2,h_2);\ t \vdash (x'_1,h'_1) \approx (x'_2,h'_2);\ \vdash tl_1 \sim tl_2;$
    $\quad t \vdash (x_1,h_1) \xrightarrow{tl_1}_1 (x'_1,h'_1);\ t \vdash (x_2,h_2) \xrightarrow{tl_2}_2 (x'_2,h'_2);$
    Suspend w $\in set\langle ta_1\rangle_w$; *Suspend w* $\in set\langle ta_2\rangle_w\rrbracket$
    $\implies (x'_1,h'_1) \overset{w}{\approx} (x'_2,h'_2)$
  and *simulation-$\overset{w}{\approx}1$*:
    $\llbracket t \vdash (x_1,h_1) \approx (x_2,h_2);\ x_1 \overset{w}{\approx} x_2;\ t \vdash (x_1,h_1) -ta_1\rightarrow_1 (x'_1,h'_1);$
    Notified $\in set\langle ta_1\rangle_w \lor$ *WokenUp* $\in set\langle ta_1\rangle_w\rrbracket$
    $\implies \exists ta_2\ x'_2\ h'_2.\ t \vdash (x_2,h_2) -ta_2\rightarrow_2 (x'_2,h'_2) \land$
    $\quad\quad\quad\quad t \vdash (x'_1,h'_1) \approx (x'_2,h'_2) \land \vdash ta_1 \sim ta_2$
  and *simulation-$\overset{w}{\approx}2$*:
    $\llbracket t \vdash (x_1,h_1) \approx (x_2,h_2);\ x_1 \overset{w}{\approx} x_2;\ t \vdash (x_2,h_2) -ta_2\rightarrow_2 (x'_2,h'_2);$
    Notified $\in set\langle ta_2\rangle_w \lor$ *WokenUp* $\in set\langle ta_2\rangle_w\rrbracket$
    $\implies \exists ta_1\ x'_1\ h'_1.\ t \vdash (x_1,h_1) -ta_1\rightarrow_1 (x'_1,h'_1) \land$
    $\quad\quad\quad\quad t \vdash (x'_1,h'_1) \approx (x'_2,h'_2) \land \vdash ta_1 \sim ta_2$
  and *Ex-final-inv*: $(\exists x_1.\ final_1\ x_1) \longleftrightarrow (\exists x_2.\ final_2\ x_2)$

Figure 5.10: Locale *m-dbisim-div* collects the necessary assumptions for $\approx_m$ being a delay bisimulation with explicit divergence

Third, $t \vdash \_ \approx \_$ must preserve final states for all t. This ensures that if a thread t in state s_1 successfully joins on another thread t' in one state (recall that successfulness is determined by t''s local state being final), then any $\approx_m$-bisimilar state s_2 can reach via τ-moves a bisimilar state s'_2 in which t''s local state is also final, i.e., t's join suceeds in s'_2, too.

Forth, the wait-notify mechanism requires that when a thread has been removed from its wait set, its very next step processes the removal. Therefore, $\approx_m$ enforces that threads in wait sets are related in $\overset{w}{\approx}$. The next three assumptions connect $\overset{w}{\approx}$ with the semantics. Assumption $\overset{w}{\approx}I$ expresses that whenever a thread suspends itself to a wait set, $\overset{w}{\approx}$ must relate the resulting states. Moreover (assumptions $simulation\text{-}\overset{w}{\approx}1$ and $simulation\text{-}\overset{w}{\approx}2$), $\overset{w}{\approx}$ is a "one-step" strong bisimulation for processing the removal from the wait set, i.e., whenever one of the related states can process a removal, so can the other (without any intervening τ-moves), but only $t \vdash \_ \approx \_$ needs to relate resulting states.

Last, for technical reasons, $m\text{-}dbisim\text{-}div$ requires that final states exist for either both single-threaded semantics or none. I discuss this assumption in more detail in Footnote 47 when I prove preservation for deadlocks (Theorem 5.4).

Under these assumptions, $\approx_m$ is a delay bisimulation with explicit divergence that preserves final states.

Theorem 5.3. *Under the assumptions of locale m-dbisim-div, $(\approx_m, \sim_m)$ is a delay bisimulation for r1.redT and r2.redT that preserves final states. Formally:*

(i) dbisim-div r1.redT r2.redT $\approx_m \sim_m$ r1.mτ-move r2.mτ-move
(ii) dbisim-final r1.redT r2.redT $\approx_m \sim_m$ r1.mτ-move r2.mτ-move
   r1.mfinal r2.mfinal

Proof. I show the simulation diagrams from Figures 5.2 and 5.5 for (i) and (ii), respectively. As before, it suffices to show just one direction of each diagram, because the other follows by symmetry.

For an observable move $s_1 -t{:}ta_1 \rightarrow_1 s'_1$ and $\approx_m$-bisimilar state s_2 (Figure 5.2a), if the move originates from ACQUIRE, s_2 can directly simulate it because $\approx_m$ ensures that the lock states of and t's temporarily released locks and wait set status in s_1 and s_2 are equal.

Otherwise (NORMAL), it originates from some observable move of t's semantics, say $t \vdash (x_1, shr\, s_1) -ta_1 \rightarrow_1 (x'_1, shr\, s'_1)$. Since $s_1 \approx_m s_2$, t exists in s_2 with local state x_2 such that $t \vdash (x_1, shr\, s_1) \approx (x_2, shr\, s_2)$

and – if t's wait set status is not $None$ – $x_1 \overset{w}{\approx} x_2$. If t's wait set status is $None$, bisimilarity of the single threads yields a visible move $t \vdash (x_2, shr\, s_2) \xrightarrow{ta_2}_2 (x'_2, h'_2)$ such that $t \vdash (x'_1, shr\, s'_1) \approx (x'_2, h'_2)$ and $\vdash ta_1 \sim ta_2$. Unfortunately, this does not directly translate into a visible move of the interleaving semantics, because ta_2's preconditions need not be met in s_2. In particular, if ta_2 joins on a thread t', i.e., $Join\, t' \in \langle ta_2 \rangle_c$, t' may be final in s_1, but need not be final in s_2. However, since $t' \vdash \_ \approx \_$ preserves final states, t' can silently reduce to a final state.

Hence, the simulating visible move consists of

- t's τ-moves,
- the silent reductions to final states of all threads ta_2 joins on, and
- t's observable move.

Proving that $\approx_m$ relates the resulting states s'_1 and s'_2 falls in five parts. First, the locks, wait sets, interrupts and domains of the thread pool are equal because τ-moves do not change them and the observable moves have identical thread actions except for the initial states of spawned threads. Second, t's thread-local states x'_1 and x'_2 are related as required – assumption $\overset{w}{\approx}I$ establishes $x'_1 \overset{w}{\approx} x'_2$ if $wset\, s'_1\, t \neq None$, which can only occur if ta_1 and ta_2 contain a $Suspend$ BTA. Third, $\vdash ta_1 \sim ta_2$ guarantees that local states of newly spawned threads are related – $dom\,(wset\, s_1) \subseteq dom(thr\, s_1)$ ensures that their wait set status is $None$, i.e., their local states need not be related in $\overset{w}{\approx}$. Forth, thanks to assumption $heap\text{-}change\text{-}preserve$, all other threads remain bisimilar. Fifth, finiteness of the thread pool is preserved because only finitely many threads can be spawned in a single step. The case for $wset\, s_1\, t \neq None$ is analogous except that assumption $simulation\text{-}\overset{w}{\approx}1$ yields the simulating move and t does no τ-moves before the observable move.

Simulating a τ-move (Figure 5.2b) is easy. It must originate from a τ-move in the single-threaded semantics, so there is a simulating sequence of τ-moves. Since none of them generates any thread action, NORMAL naturally injects them into the interleaving semantics.

To prove preservation of divergence, note that $\approx_m$ ensures that there are only finitely many threads. Induction on this finite set yields that the interleaving semantics can only diverge if one of its threads can diverge. Conversely, it obviously can diverge if one of the threads can (by coinduction). Putting these arguments together, $\approx_m$ preserves divergence.

223

For preservation of final states, remember that all threads in an *mfinal* state are final. So suppose $r1.mfinal\ s_1$ and $s_1 \approx_m s_2$. By induction on the (finite) set of threads in s_1, there is a state s_2' such that $s_2 \xrightarrow{\tau}\rhd_2^* s_2'$ and $s_1 \approx_m s_2'$ and $r2.mfinal\ s_2'$. In the inductive step, the next thread t can silently reduce to an appropriate final state because $t \vdash \_ \approx \_$ preserves final states. I combine them with the silent moves from the induction hypothesis to obtain the desired reductions. □

The proof of Theorem 5.3 motivates why I chose delay bisimulation instead of more common notions of bisimulation like weak bisimulation by Milner [120]. Milner allows observable moves to be simulated by a finite sequence of τ-moves, the observable move, and another finite sequence of τ-moves. However, there is no analogue of Theorem 5.3 for weak bisimulations, because the observable transition might suspend itself to a wait set, after which the interleaving semantics does not allow any additional τ-moves.

Theorem 5.4 (Preservation of deadlocks). *Under the assumptions of locale m-dbisim-div, $\approx_m$ preserves deadlocks. Let $s_1 \approx_m s_2$. If $t \in r1.deadlocked\ s_1$, then s_2 can reduce via τ-moves to some s_2' such that $s_1 \approx_m s_2'$ and $t \in r2.deadlocked\ s_2'$. Conversely, if $t \in r2.deadlocked\ s_2$, then s_1 can reduce via τ-moves to some s_1' such that $s_1' \approx_m s_2$ and $t \in r1.deadlocked\ s_1'$.*

Proof. By symmetry, it suffices to prove only one direction. So suppose $t \in r1.deadlocked\ s_1$. Since $\_ \vdash \_ \approx \_$ preserves final states, there is an s_2^* which is reachable via τ-moves from s_2 such that $s_1 \approx_m s_2^*$ and all $final_1$ threads in s_1 are $final_2$ in s_2^*, too (by induction on the finite set of threads). Since $\_ \vdash \_ \approx \_$ preserves divergence, a similar induction shows that there is an s_2' which is reachable via τ-moves from s_2^* such that $s_1 \approx_m s_2'$ and all threads in s_1 that cannot do any τ-move cannot do any in s_2' either.

Then, I prove $t \in r2.deadlocked\ s_2'$ by coinduction with invariant $t \in r1.deadlocked\ s_1$. In the coinductive step, I show by case analysis of $t \in r1.deadlocked\ s_1$ that each case suffices to prove the corresponding case for $t \in r2.deadlocked\ s_2'$.

For DACTIVE, this follows from the simulation for observable moves. Since t is deadlocked in s_1', it cannot do any τ-moves and, therefore, neither can it in s_2'. Hence, the visible move that simulates a move of t can only consist of the observable move, but no τ-moves. Therefore, $\approx_m$

preserves $t \vdash (\_, shr\, s)\, \wr$ and $t \vdash (\_, shr\, s)\, \_\wr$.[47] Since final threads in s_1 are final in s_2, too, and locks and wait sets are equal, *must-wait* is preserved, too. This concludes this case.

For the cases DACQUIRE and DWAIT, preservation of *must-wait* and *all-final-except* is straightforward by the choice of s'_2. Hence, they follow easily. $\qquad\qquad\qquad\qquad\qquad\qquad\qquad\qquad\qquad\qquad\qquad\qquad\qquad$ □

5.1.4 Semantic preservation for the Java memory model

Concerning semantic preservation for the JMM, the JLS only specifies that "an implementation is free to produce any code it likes, as long as all resulting executions of a program produce a result that can be predicted by the memory model" [56, §17.4], i.e., it takes the specification point of view (§5.1.1).

My bisimulation approach for semantic preservation ensures that both the source program and the compiled code have the same set of traces (Theorem 5.1). Since legality of executions only depends on the set of traces, a semantics-preserving compiler is correct for the JMM, too. However, the JMM and semantic preservation refer to different definitions of traces. The former does not distinguish between observable and silent moves, but includes all of them, whereas the latter only consists of observable moves. Fortunately, since τ-moves produce no events by assumption τ-*ta* in Figure 5.9, concatenating all events as in Equation 4.2 yields the same set of complete interleavings.

Lemma 5.3. $s \Downarrow E$ *iff* E *is of the form* $concat\ (map\ events\ E')$ *such that* $s \Downarrow E'$.

Corollary 5.1. *Two programs that are delay bisimilar with explicit divergence have the same set of legal executions.*

Since the JMM formalisation adds thread start and finish events to the single-threaded semantics (layer 4 in Figure 4.10) by a semantics

---

[47]Remember that $t \vdash (x, h)\, \wr$ expresses that t with local state x can reduce with a thread action *ta* which is not contradictory in itself. This is where the technical assumption *Ex-final-inv* from Figure 5.10 becomes relevant for preservation. It excludes the case in which some x_1 satisfies *final*$_1$, but *final*$_2$ is unsatisfiable. Hence, $\_ \vdash \_\wr_1$ allows *Join* BTAs in the underlying execution, but $\_ \vdash \_\wr_2$ does not, which compromises preservation. Note that the other assumptions do not exclude this case. Only preservation of final states involves *final*, but if x_1 is unreachable, $\_ \vdash \_ \approx \_$ need not relate x_1 to any x_2, i.e., preservation of final states would be trivially satisfied.

transformer, I lift τ-moves and delay bisimulations in the same way. For the former, $sf.\tau\text{-}move$ adapts $\tau\text{-}move$ to the changes in the thread-local states, but adds no additional τ-moves (assumption $\tau\text{-}ta$ in Figure 5.9). In particular, the reductions for start and final events are observable, because (i) other threads can observe through $Join$ BTAs that the thread has terminated, and (ii) the interleaving framework does not allow events for τ-moves.

$$\frac{\tau\text{-}move\ (x,h)\ ta\ (x',h')}{sf.\tau\text{-}move\ ((Running,x),h)\ (pair\text{-}Pre\text{-}Start\ ta)\ ((Running,x'),h')}$$

The lifted bisimulation $t \vdash \_ \approx_{\mathrm{sf}} \_$ is defined as follows:

$$
\begin{aligned}
& t \vdash ((s_1,x_1),h_1) \approx_{\mathrm{sf}} ((s_2,x_2),h_2) \longleftrightarrow \\
& \quad s_1 = s_2 \wedge t \vdash (x_1,h_1) \approx (x_2,h_2) \wedge \\
& \quad (s_2 = \textit{Finished} \longrightarrow \textit{final}_1\ x_1 \wedge \textit{final}_2\ x_2)
\end{aligned}
$$

Similarly, $\overset{\mathrm{w}}{\approx}_{\mathrm{sf}}$ transforms $\overset{\mathrm{w}}{\approx}$:

$$\frac{x_1 \overset{\mathrm{w}}{\approx} x_2}{(Running,x_1) \overset{\mathrm{w}}{\approx}_{\mathrm{sf}} (Running,x_2)}$$

Now, I can lift $t \vdash \_ \approx_{\mathrm{sf}} \_$ and $\overset{\mathrm{w}}{\approx}_{\mathrm{sf}}$ to multithreaded bisimilations just like $t \vdash \_ \approx \_$ and $\overset{\mathrm{w}}{\approx}$.

Lemma 5.4.

$$\frac{\begin{array}{c} m\text{-}dbisim\text{-}div\ \textit{final}_1\ r_1\ acq\text{-}events\ \tau\text{-}move_1 \\ \textit{final}_2\ r_2\ acq\text{-}events\ \tau\text{-}move_2\ (\_ \vdash \_ \approx \_)\ \overset{\mathrm{w}}{\approx} \end{array}}{\begin{array}{c} m\text{-}dbisim\text{-}div\ sf.\textit{final}_1\ sf.r_1\ sf.acq\text{-}events\ \tau\text{-}move_1 \\ sf.\textit{final}_2\ sf.r_2\ sf.acq\text{-}events\ \tau\text{-}move_2\ (\_ \vdash \_ \approx_{\mathrm{sf}} \_)\ \overset{\mathrm{w}}{\approx}_{\mathrm{sf}} \end{array}}$$

5.2 Explicit call stacks for source code

The verification of both compiler stages requires an explicit notion of call stacks in the states themselves. The small-step semantics for source code, however, dynamically inlines method calls (RCALL). Hence, I first define an alternative state representation and small-step semantics J_0 with explicit call stacks for the source code language (§5.2.1). Note that this does not affect the program declarations, i.e., the input language itself. Second, after having defined the observable transitions, I prove that the semantics with call stacks is delay bisimilar to the semantics without call stacks (§5.2.2).

5.2.1 State and semantics

On the call-stack level, local stores are irrelevant for the semantics; any free variable can be bound by an additional block. The rule for method calls RCALL and the start state J-start already do so for the $this$ pointer and the parameters. Hence, the thread-local state in J_0 consists only of a (non-empty) list of expressions, one for each method on the call stack. To encode non-emptiness in the HOL type, I model the local state as a pair of the head and tail of the call stack.

There are now three levels for the semantics. The expression level deals with the execution of expressions, i.e. method bodies. The call-stack level lifts the semantics for expressions to call stacks and handles calls and returns. This is also the semantics for a single thread. The interleaving semantics lifts this to concurrent programs as before.

To separate method calls and returns from the rest of the semantics, I introduce two auxiliary functions. First, the partial function $call\ e$ returns $\lfloor (a, M, vs) \rfloor$ whenever e is about to call the method M on address a with parameter values vs, and it is $None$ in all other cases. I say that e pauses at the call (a, M, vs) iff $call\ e = \lfloor (a, M, vs) \rfloor$, and e pauses at a call iff $call\ e \neq None$. Figure 5.11 shows the definition for $call$ where $is\text{-}addr\ e$ predicates that e is of the form $addr\ a$ and $is\text{-}Vals\ es$ denotes that es consists only of values, i.e., $es = map\ Val\ vs$ for some vs. Note that $call$ traverses the abstract syntax tree in exactly the same way as the small-step semantics $\_,\_ \vdash \langle\_,\_\rangle -\_\rightarrow \langle\_,\_\rangle$ does. When it finds a call of the form $addr\ a.M(map\ Val\ vs)$, it returns $\lfloor (a, M, vs) \rfloor$; otherwise, it descends into the subexpression that the small-step semantics evaluates next if there is any, else it returns $None$.

The second function $inline\ e_0\ e$ follows the same recursion pattern (Figure 5.12). If e pauses at a call, $inline\ e_0\ e$ replaces this call with e_0. Otherwise, $inline\ e_0\ e$ leaves e unchanged. Hence, $inline$ mimics the small-step semantics' dynamic inlining of method calls.

227

$$
\begin{aligned}
&call\ (new\ C) &&= None\\
&call\ (new\ T[e]) &&= call\ e\\
&call\ (e\ instanceof\ T) &&= call\ e\\
&call\ (Cast\ T\ e) &&= call\ e\\
&call\ (Val\ v) &&= None\\
&call\ (e_1\ \text{«}bop\text{»}\ e_2) &&= (if\ is\text{-}Val\ e_1\ then\ call\ e_2\ else\ call\ e_1)\\
&call\ (Var\ V) &&= None\\
&call\ (V := e) &&= call\ e\\
&call\ (e_1[e_2]) &&= (if\ is\text{-}Val\ e_1\ then\ call\ e_2\ else\ call\ e_1)\\
&call\ (e_1[e_2] := e_3) &&=\\
&\quad (if\ is\text{-}Val\ e_1\ then\ (if\ is\text{-}Val\ e_2\ then\ call\ e_3\ else\ call\ e_2)\ else\ call\ e_1)\\
&call\ (e.length) &&= call\ e\\
&call\ (e.F\{D\}) &&= call\ e\\
&call\ (e_1.F\{D\} := e_2) &&= (if\ is\text{-}Val\ e_1\ then\ call\ e_2\ else\ call\ e_1)\\
&call\ (e.M(es)) &&=\\
&\quad (if\ is\text{-}Val\ e\ then\\
&\qquad (if\ is\text{-}Vals\ es \wedge is\text{-}addr\ e\\
&\qquad\ then\ \lfloor(\iota a.\ e = addr\ a, M, \iota vs.\ es = map\ Val\ vs)\rfloor\ else\ calls\ es)\\
&\qquad else\ call\ e)\\
&call\ \{V: T = vo; e\} &&= call\ e\\
&call\ (e_1;;\ e_2) &&= call\ e_1\\
&call\ (if\ (e)\ e_1\ else\ e_2) &&= call\ e\\
&call\ (while\ (e_1)\ e_2) &&= None\\
&call\ (throw\ e) &&= call\ e\\
&call\ (try\ e_1\ catch(C\ V)\ e_2) &&= call\ e_1\\
&call\ (sync\ (e_1)\ e_2) &&= call\ e_1\\
&call\ (insync\ (a)\ e) &&= call\ e\\
&calls\ [] &&= None\\
&calls\ (e \cdot es) &&= (if\ is\text{-}Val\ e\ then\ call\ e\ else\ calls\ es)
\end{aligned}
$$

$$
\begin{aligned}
&no\text{-}call\ P\ h\ e =\\
&\quad (\forall a\ M\ vs.\ call\ e = \lfloor(a, M, vs)\rfloor \longrightarrow\\
&\qquad (\exists hT\ Ts\ T_r\ D.\ typeof\text{-}addr\ h\ a = \lfloor hT\rfloor \wedge\\
&\qquad\qquad P \vdash class\text{-}of'hT\ sees\ M{:}Ts{\rightarrow}T_r = Native\ in\ D))
\end{aligned}
$$

Figure 5.11: The partial function *call* computes which method *e* is about to call, if any; *no-call P h e* predicates that *e* is not about to call a non-native method.

$inline\ e_0\ (new\ C)$ $= new\ C$
$inline\ e_0\ (new\ T[e])$ $= new\ T[inline\ e_0\ e]$
$inline\ e_0\ (e\ instanceof\ T)$ $= (inline\ e_0\ e)\ instanceof\ T$
$inline\ e_0\ (Cast\ T\ e)$ $= Cast\ t\ (inline\ e_0\ e)$
$inline\ e_0\ (Val\ v)$ $= Val\ v$
$inline\ e_0\ (e_1\ «bop»\ e_2)$ $=$
$\quad (if\ is\text{-}Val\ e_1\ then\ e_1\ «bop»\ (inline\ e_0\ e_2)\ else\ (inline\ e_0\ e_1)\ «bop»\ e_2)$
$inline\ e_0\ (Var\ V)$ $= Var\ V$
$inline\ e_0\ (V := e)$ $= V := inline\ e_0\ e$
$inline\ e_0\ (e_1[e_2])$ $=$
$\quad (if\ is\text{-}Val\ e_1\ then\ e_1[inline\ e_0\ e_2]\ else\ (inline\ e_0\ e_1)[e_2])$
$inline\ e_0\ (e_1[e_2] := e_3)$ $=$
$\quad (if\ is\text{-}Val\ e_1\ then$
$\qquad (if\ is\text{-}Val\ e_2\ then\ e_1[e_2] := inline\ e_0\ e_3\ else\ e_1[inline\ e_0\ e_2] := e_3)$
$\quad else\ (inline\ e_0\ e_1)[e_2] := e_3)$
$inline\ e_0\ (e.length)$ $= (inline\ e_0\ e).length$
$inline\ e_0\ (e.F\{D\})$ $= (inline\ e_0\ e).F\{D\}$
$inline\ e_0\ (e_1.F\{D\} := e_2)$ $=$
$\quad (if\ is\text{-}Val\ e_1\ then\ e_1.F\{D\} := inline\ e_0\ e_2\ else\ (inline\ e_0\ e_1).F\{D\} := e_2)$
$inline\ e_0\ (e.M(es))$ $=$
$\quad (if\ is\text{-}Val\ e\ then$
$\qquad (if\ is\text{-}Vals\ es\ \wedge\ is\text{-}addr\ e\ then\ e_0\ else\ e.M(inlines\ e_0\ es))$
$\quad else\ (inline\ e_0\ e).M(es))$
$inline\ e_0\ \{V: T = vo; e\}$ $= \{V: T = vo; inline\ e_0\ e\}$
$inline\ e_0\ (e_1;; e_2)$ $= (inline\ e_0\ e_1);; e_2$
$inline\ e_0\ (if\ (e)\ e_1\ else\ e_2)$ $= if\ (inline\ e_0\ e)\ e_1\ else\ e_2$
$inline\ e_0\ (while\ (e_1)\ e_2)$ $= while\ (e_1)\ e_2$
$inline\ e_0\ (throw\ e)$ $= throw\ (inline\ e_0\ e)$
$inline\ e_0\ (try\ e_1\ catch(C\ V)\ e_2)$ $= try\ inline\ e_0\ e_1\ catch(C\ V)\ e_2$
$inline\ e_0\ (sync\ (e_1)\ e_2)$ $= sync\ (inline\ e_0\ e_1)\ e_2$
$inline\ e_0\ (insync\ (a)\ e)$ $= insync\ (a)\ (inline\ e_0\ e)$
$inlines\ e_0\ []$ $= []$
$inlines\ e_0\ (e \cdot es)$ $=$
$\quad (if\ is\text{-}Val\ e\ then\ (inline\ e_0\ e) \cdot es\ else\ e \cdot (inlines\ e_0\ es))$

Figure 5.12: The function $inline\ e_0\ e$ replaces the call that e is about to execute with e_0, if any, and leaves e unchanged otherwise.

$$\text{RED}_0: \quad \frac{P,t \vdash \langle e, (h, empty)\rangle -ta\rightarrow \langle e', (h', xs')\rangle \qquad no\text{-}call\ P\ h\ e}{P,t \vdash \langle e,h\rangle -ta\rightarrow_0^e \langle e',h'\rangle}$$

$$\text{R}_0\text{RED}: \quad \frac{P,t \vdash \langle e,h\rangle -ta\rightarrow_0^e \langle e',h'\rangle}{P,t \vdash \langle (e,es),h\rangle -ta\rightarrow_0^t \langle (e',es),h'\rangle}$$

$$\text{R}_0\text{CALL}: \quad \frac{\begin{array}{c} call\ e = \lfloor(a, M, vs)\rfloor \qquad typeof\text{-}addr\ h\ a = \lfloor hT\rfloor \\ P \vdash class\text{-}of'\ hT\ sees\ M{:}Ts{\rightarrow}T_r = \lfloor(pns, body)\rfloor\ in\ D \\ |vs| = |pns| \qquad |Ts| = |pns| \end{array}}{\begin{array}{c} P,t \vdash \langle (e,es),h\rangle -\langle\!\langle\rangle\!\rangle\rightarrow_0 \\ \langle (blocks\ (this{\cdot}pns)\ (Class\ D{\cdot}Ts)\ (Addr\ a{\cdot}vs)\ body, e{\cdot}es), h\rangle \end{array}}$$

$$\text{R}_0\text{RET}: \quad \frac{final\ e}{P,t \vdash \langle (e, e'\cdot es), h\rangle -\langle\!\langle\rangle\!\rangle\rightarrow_0^t \langle (inline\ e\ e', es), h\rangle}$$

Figure 5.13: Single-threaded source code semantics with explicit call stacks

The expression level semantics red_0 (notation $P,t \vdash \langle e,h\rangle -ta\rightarrow_0^e$ $\langle e',h'\rangle$) is the same as in J except for calling, see RED_0 in Figure 5.13.[48] To avoid redundancies, I do not define a new small-step semantics, but use the predicate $no\text{-}call\ P\ h\ e$ to filter out all reductions due to RCALL from $P,t \vdash \langle e, (h, xs)\rangle -ta\rightarrow \langle e', (h', xs')\rangle$. As Figure 5.11 shows, $no\text{-}call\ P\ h\ e$ holds iff whenever e pauses at a call, then the called method must be native. Note that red_0 discards the new local store xs' after the reduction – well-formedness ensures that xs' is always $empty$ (Corollary 5.2).

Figure 5.13 also shows the small-step semantics $J_0\text{-}red$ for the call-stack level (notation $P,t \vdash \langle (e,es),h\rangle -ta\rightarrow_0^t \langle (e',es'),h'\rangle$). It consists of all reductions of the expression level semantics red_0 for the top of the call stack (R_0RED). Additionally, it reintroduces the reductions for method calls that red_0 has filtered out (R_0CALL). Rather than dynamically inlining

---

[48]Technically, I must also adjust the thread-local state in $Spawn$ actions in ta. Formally, $\_,\_ \vdash \langle\_,\_\rangle -\_\rightarrow \langle\_,\_\rangle$ is parametrised over $native\text{-}TA2J\ P$. The definition of red_0 passes $native\text{-}TA2J_0\ P$ instead of $native\text{-}TA2J\ P$, where $native\text{-}TA2J_0\ P$ converts all local states (C, M, a) of $Spawn$ BTAs to

$let\ (D, \_, \_, m) = method\ P\ C\ M;\ \lfloor(\_, body)\rfloor = m\ in\ (\{this{:}\ Class\ C = \lfloor Addr\ a\rfloor\ ;\ body\}, [])$

In the remainder of this chapter, I omit this technical detail.

the method body, R_0CALL pushes the called method's body on top of the call stack and leaves the caller's expression unchanged. When a method returns, i.e., its expression is *final*, R_0RET replaces the call in the caller's expression with the return value or exception using *inline*. This assumes that every expression on the stack except the top one pauses at the method invocation. R_0RET has no counterpart in $\_, \_ \vdash \langle \_, \_ \rangle - \_ \rightarrow \langle \_, \_ \rangle$, because dynamic inlining turns returns into no-ops.

A state (e, es) in J_0 is final, written *final*$_0$ (e, es), iff *final e* and $es = []$. The start state J_0-*start P C M vs* has one thread *start-tID* with local state

$$(blocks\,(this \cdot pns)\,(Class\,D \cdot Ts)\,(Null \cdot vs)\,body, [])$$

where $(D, Ts, \_, \lfloor (pns, body) \rfloor]) = method\,P\,C\,M$.

Analogous to J, the multithreaded semantics $J_0.redT$ for J_0 is the interleaving semantics for the parameter instantiations *final*$_0$ and J_0-*red*.

I consider the following operations as observable moves: memory allocation, calls to native methods other than *hashcode* and *currentThread*, access and assignment to fields and array cells, reading array lengths, and synchronisation. In particular, since thread spawns, joining, interruption and the wait-notify mechanism are implemented as native methods, all of them are observable. Conversely, all control flow constructs, including exception throwing and handling, and local variable manipulation are only relevant to the thread that executes them, so these generate only τ-moves.

For simplicity of the formalisation, I define observability in terms of the state being reduced rather than the reduction itself. Hence, either all reductions of a thread in one thread-local state and heap are observable or none of them. As a consequence, the set of observable reductions is larger than necessary. For example, the array cell access *addr a*[*Val (Intg i)*] returns either the *i*-th array cell's content or fails with an *ArrayIndexOutOfBounds* exception. Thus, J and J_0 also treat throwing the *ArrayIndexOutOfBounds* exception as an observable move. Fortunately, a larger set of observable moves only strengthens the correctness result.

Formally, I define a predicate τ-*move* :: '*m prog* $\Rightarrow$ '*heap* $\Rightarrow$ '*addr expr* $\Rightarrow$ *bool* that identifies states in which τ-moves originate. Its definition can be found in Appendix B.6.6. Then, J-τ-*move* and J_0-τ-*move* determine the τ-moves for J and J_0, respectively, where

$$J\text{-}\tau\text{-}move\ P\ ((e, xs), h)\quad ta\ \_ \longleftrightarrow \tau\text{-}move\ P\ h\ e\ \wedge ta = (\!|\!|\!)$$
$$J_0\text{-}\tau\text{-}move\ P\ ((e_0, es_0), h_0)\ ta\ \_ \longleftrightarrow (\tau\text{-}move\ P\ h_0\ e_0 \vee final\ e_0) \wedge ta = (\!|\!|\!)$$

Lemma 5.5. *J and J_0 satisfy the assumptions of locale τ-multithreaded.*

$$\text{τ-multithreaded J-final } (J\text{-red } P) \text{ acq-events } J\text{-τ-move}$$
$$\text{τ-multithreaded final}_0 \ (J_0\text{-red } P) \text{ acq-events } J_0\text{-τ-move}$$

5.2.2 Semantic equivalence

Now, I show that J_0 is equivalent to J in the sense that a program is delay bisimilar to itself under the two semantics. Thus, I can verify the compiler against J_0 instead of J.

A variable V is free in the expression e (written $V \in fv\ e$) iff e contains a subexpression *Var V* that is not contained in a local-variable or catch block that declares V. The expression e is closed iff it contains no free variables, i.e., $fv\ e = \emptyset$. A call stack of expressions (e_0, es_0) is well-formed (notation $wf_0\ (e_0, es_0)$) iff e_0 is closed, and all expressions in es_0 are closed and pause at a call. Formally:

$$wf_0\ (e_0, es_0) \longleftrightarrow fv\ e_0 = \emptyset \wedge (\forall e \in set\ es_0.\ fv\ e = \emptyset \wedge call\ e \neq None)$$

Closedness rules out references to global variables.[49] Hence, it is irrelevant that J_0 executes method bodies in a local store that contains only *this* and the parameters (R_0CALL) while inlining method calls with blocks for *this* and the parameters in J adds them to the local store of the caller (RCALL).

Let *collapse* (e_0, es_0) abbreviate the expression to which inlining collapses the call stack, i.e., *collapse* $(e_0, es_0) = foldl\ inline\ e_0\ es_0$. Then, the delay bisimulation relation $\overset{t}{\approx}_0$ for single threads relates the J state $((e, xs), h)$ with $((e_0, es_0), h_0)$ iff xs is empty, the heaps are the same, (e_0, es_0) is well-formed, and (e_0, es_0) collapses to e. Formally:

$$\frac{wf_0\ (e_0, es_0)}{((collapse\ (e_0, es_0), empty), h) \overset{t}{\approx}_0 ((e_0, es_0), h)}$$

---

[49] Already in Jinja, closedness was crucial for the small-step semantics and its equivalence to the big-step semantics [83, §2.3.2, §2.4.1, §2.5]. Klein and Nipkow write: "we can only get away with this simple rule for method calls [for the small-step semantics] because there are no global variables in Java. Otherwise one could unfold a method body that refers to some global variable into a context that declares a local variable of the same name, which would essentially amount to dynamic variable binding." [83, §2.3.2].

Since both $J.redT$ and $J_0.redT$ are instances of the interleaving semantics, I lift $\overset{t}{\approx}_0$ to multithreaded states as described in §5.1.3. Let $\overset{m}{\approx}_0$ and $\sim_0$ denote the corresponding instance of $\approx_m$ and $\vdash\_ \sim \_$ where $(e, xs) \overset{w}{\approx} (e_0, es_0)$ iff $\neg\, final\; e_0$.

Theorem 5.5. *If wf-J-prog P, then $(\overset{t}{\approx}_0, \sim_0)$ is a delay bisimulation with explicit divergence for J-red P t and J_0-red P t.*

The proof requires a number of lemmata first.

Lemma 5.6. *If wf-J-prog P and $P, t \vdash \langle e, (h, xs)\rangle - ta\rightarrow \langle e', (h', xs')\rangle$, then fv $e' \subseteq$ fv e and dom $xs' \subseteq$ dom $xs \cup$ fv e*

Proof. By induction on $P, t \vdash \langle e, (h, xs)\rangle - ta\rightarrow \langle e', (h', xs')\rangle$. Method call (RCALL) is the interesting case. Since the call sees the method, say $P \vdash C$ sees $M{:}Ts{\rightarrow}T_r = \lfloor(pns, body)\rfloor$ in D, and P is well-formed, $P, E \vdash body :: T$ for $E = [this \mapsto Class\; C, pns\; [\mapsto]\; Ts]$ and some T (see Figure 2.10). Induction on $P, E \vdash body :: T$ yields fv $body \subseteq$ dom E. Hence, *blocks* $(this{\cdot}pns)$ $(Class\; D{\cdot}Ts)$ $(Addr\; a{\cdot}vs)$ *body* is closed. □

Corollary 5.2. *If wf-J-prog P and $P, t \vdash \langle e, (h, empty)\rangle - ta\rightarrow \langle e', (h', xs')\rangle$ and e is closed, then $xs' = empty$.*

Lemma 5.7. *If wf-J-prog P, then J_0-red P t preserves well-formedness.*

Proof. Let $P, t \vdash \langle(e_0, es_0), h\rangle - ta\rightarrow_0^t \langle(e_0', es_0'), h'\rangle$ and $wf_0\; (e_0, es_0)$. I show $wf_0\; (e_0', es_0')$ by case analysis of the reduction.

For R_0RED, Lemma 5.6 applies. For R_0CALL, the same argument as for method calls in Lemma 5.6 yields closedness of the new call frame. For R_0RET, fv $(inline\; e_0\; e) \subseteq$ fv $e_0 \cup$ fv e (provable by induction on e) yields fv $(inline\; e_0\; e) = \emptyset$. □

A call stack (e_0, es_0) is normalised iff $\neg\, final\; e_0$ or $es_0 = [\,]$, i.e., rule R_0RET is not applicable. The next lemma shows that J_0 can silently normalise any call stack; it is provable by induction on es_0.

Lemma 5.8. *For every call stack (e_0, es_0), there is a normalised call stack (e_0', es_0') such that collapse $(e_0, es_0) =$ collapse (e_0', es_0') and (e_0, es_0) silently reduces to (e_0', es_0').*

A normalised call stack (e_0, es_0) simulates reductions of the collapsed call stack $collapse\ (e_0, es_0)$ directly, i.e., without any additional τ-moves.

Lemma 5.9. *Let (e_0, es_0) be well-formed and normalised.*

(i) *If $P, t \vdash \langle e_0, (h, empty) \rangle -ta \rightarrow \langle e_0', (h', empty) \rangle$, then*
$$P, t \vdash \langle collapse\ (e_0, es_0), (h, empty) \rangle$$
$$-ta \rightarrow \langle collapse\ (e_0', es_0), (h', empty) \rangle$$

(ii) *If $P, t \vdash \langle collapse\ (e_0, es_0), (h, empty) \rangle -ta \rightarrow \langle e', (h', empty) \rangle$, then e' is of the form $collapse\ (e_0', es_0)$ and $P, t \vdash \langle e_0, (h, empty) \rangle -ta \rightarrow \langle e_0', (h', empty) \rangle$.*

Proof. Note that inlining the top of the call stack preserves well-formedness. Without loss of generality, $\neg\ final\ e_0$ – otherwise, $es_0 = []$ by normalisation and the lemma holds trivially. Then, each direction follows by induction on es_0 from the following generalised one-step versions for arbitrary e with $call\ e \neq None$:

(i) If $P, t \vdash \langle e_0, (h, empty) \rangle -ta \rightarrow \langle e_0', (h', empty) \rangle$, then
$$P, t \vdash \langle inline\ e_0\ e, (h, xs) \rangle -ta \rightarrow \langle inline\ e_0'\ e, (h', xs) \rangle.$$

(ii) If $P, t \vdash \langle inline\ e_0\ e, (h, xs) \rangle -ta \rightarrow \langle e', (h', xs') \rangle$, then $xs = xs'$ and e' is of the form $e' = inline\ e_0'\ e$ and $P, t \vdash \langle e_0, (h, empty) \rangle -ta \rightarrow \langle e_0', (h', empty) \rangle$.

Both of them are proved by induction on e. The only interesting case is when e is the call that *inline* replaces with e_0. Then, the local store in e_0's reduction must change from xs to $empty$ or vice versa. This follows from the next two easy lemmata (provable by induction) that Jinja uses to prove the big-step and small-step semantics equivalent [83, §2.5]:

(i) If $P, t \vdash \langle e, (h, xs) \rangle -ta \rightarrow \langle e', (h', xs') \rangle$, then $P, t \vdash \langle e, (h, xs_0 ++ xs) \rangle -ta \rightarrow \langle e', (h', xs_0 ++ xs') \rangle$.

(ii) If $P, t \vdash \langle e, (h, xs) \rangle -ta \rightarrow \langle e', (h', xs') \rangle$ and $fv\ e \subseteq W$, then $P, t \vdash \langle e, (h, xs \upharpoonright_W) \rangle -ta \rightarrow \langle e', (h', xs' \upharpoonright_W) \rangle$,

where $f \upharpoonright_A$ restricts the map f to A, i.e., $\lambda x.\ if\ x \in A\ then\ f\ x\ else\ None$, and $f ++ g$ abbreviates $\lambda x.\ case\ g\ x\ of\ None \Rightarrow f\ x \mid \lfloor y \rfloor \Rightarrow \lfloor y \rfloor$. $\qquad\square$

The next lemma shows that when e pauses at a call, J's next reduction is to replace the call by the method body.

Lemma 5.10. *Let call* $e = \lfloor (a, M, vs) \rfloor$ *and typeof-addr* $h\ a = \lfloor hT \rfloor$ *and* $P \vdash$ *class-of' hT sees* $M{:}Ts{\rightarrow}T_r = \lfloor (pns, body) \rfloor$ *in D and* $blks = blocks\ (this{\cdot}pns)\ (Class\ D{\cdot}Ts)\ (Addr\ a{\cdot}vs)\ body.$

(i) *If* $P, t \vdash \langle e, (h, xs) \rangle\ {-ta{\rightarrow}}\ \langle e', (h', xs') \rangle$, *then* $e' = inline\ blks\ e.$

(ii) *If* $|vs| = |pns|$ *and* $|Ts| = |pns|$,
then $P, t \vdash \langle e, (h, xs) \rangle\ {-ta{\rightarrow}}\ \langle inline\ blks\ e, (h', xs') \rangle.$

Proof of Theorem 5.5. By Lemma 5.2, it suffices to find two measures $\prec_1$ and $\prec_2$ for which $(\overset{t}{\approx}_0, \sim_0)$ is a well-founded delay bisimulation. Choose $\_\ \not{\prec}_1\ \_$, and $((e_0, es_0), h_0) \prec_2 ((e'_0, es'_0), h'_0)$ iff $|es_0| < |es'_0|$, i.e., only returns R_0RET from method calls (when the call stack shrinks) need not have a counterpart in J.

For the simulation diagrams from Figure 5.6, I distinguish three cases:

1. Calls of non-native methods. For J_0 simulating J, it normalises the call stack first (Lemma 5.8). Then, Lemma 5.9 shows that the top call frame of the normalised call stack can reduce using the call, and Lemma 5.10 decomposes the resulting expression as necessary for the simulation with R_0CALL. For the other direction, Lemma 5.10 shows that the expression in the top call frame could also inline the call and so can the collapsed call stack by Lemma 5.9.

2. Returns from a method call (R_0RET) are a no-op in J, but the call stack length decreases.

3. Otherwise, it is an expression-level reduction, for which J and J_0 use the same semantics; Lemma 5.9 shows that collapsing the call stack does not change the semantics. As with calls of non-native methods, J_0 first normalises the call stack.

In all cases, well-formedness of the new call stack holds by preservation (Lemma 5.7). □

Lemma 5.11. $(\overset{t}{\approx}_0, \sim_0)$ *preserves final states.*

Theorem 5.6. $(\overset{m}{\approx}_0, \sim_0)$ *is a delay bisimulation with explicit divergence for* $J.redT\ P$ *and* $J_0.redT\ P$ *that preserves final states.*

Proof. By Theorem 5.3, it suffices to discharge the assumptions of locale *m-dbisim-div*. Theorem 5.5 and Lemma 5.11 discharge the inherited locales. Since $\overset{t}{\approx}_0$ does not depend on the heap, *heap-change-preserve* holds trivially. For $\overset{w}{\approx}I$, case analysis and induction show that whenever J_0-*red* generates a *Suspend* BTA, the top call frame is not *final*. Since $\overset{w}{\approx}$ guarantees that the J_0 call stack is normalised, *simulation-$\overset{w}{\approx}1$* follows easily, because normalised call stacks simulate J's reductions without any additional τ-moves. Similarly, *simulation-$\overset{w}{\approx}2$* holds because J simulates observable moves of J_0 without τ-moves. Finally, *Ex-final-inv* holds trivially. □

Finally, I show that the bisimulation relation $\overset{m}{\approx}_0$ contains the well-formed start state.

Lemma 5.12. *If wf-J-prog P and wf-start P C M vs, then J-start P C M vs $\overset{m}{\approx}_0$ J_0-start P C M vs.*

5.3   Register allocation

The first stage of the compiler replaces variable names in expressions by indices into an array of registers. In this section, I present the intermediate language J_1 with syntax, well-formedness, and semantics (§5.3.1), the first compilation stage (§5.3.2), and the proof of its correctness (§5.3.3 and §5.3.4).

5.3.1   Intermediate language J_1

Syntax

The intermediate language J_1 retains the expressions from source code, but stores local variable values in an array of registers – like bytecode does. Hence, local variables in J_1 are no longer identified by their name, but by an index in the array. J_1 extends Jinja's intermediate language [83, §5.1] analogous to what J does in source code, of which I have already described the details in §2.3 and §3.2.2.

To avoid duplication, JinjaThreads parametrises the type of expressions $('a, 'b, 'addr)$ *exp* not only over the type of addresses $'addr$, but also over the variable names $'a$ and an annotation type $'b$ for *sync* $(\_)\_$ and *insync* $(\_)\_$ blocks. $'addr$ *expr* abbreviates $(vname, unit, 'addr)$ *exp* where *unit* is the HOL type of only one element $()$. Expressions in J_1 are of type

$(nat, nat, 'addr)$ exp (denoted $'addr\ expr_1$), i.e., variable names are natural numbers and $sync_i$ (_) _ and $insync_i$ (_) _ blocks are now annotated with $i :: nat.^{50}$ Following the JVMS [103, §7.14], the variable i will be used in bytecode to store the monitor address between the $MEnter$ and $MExit$ instructions that implement the monitor locking and unlocking.

The type of J_1 programs $'addr\ J_1\text{-}prog$ is $'addr\ expr_1\ prog$. Note that methods no longer declare parameter names because they have been replaced by numbers.

Well-formedness

J_1 requires a very specific layout of the registers, which $compP_1$ ensures. Register 0 holds the *this* pointer, the parameters occupy registers 1 to n where n is the number of parameters. Then, the local variables follow according to the nesting depth: If a block $\{i: T = vo; e\}$ is nested in k local variable or catch blocks or bodies of $sync\_$ (_) _, then $i = 1 + n + k$; and similarly for $try\ e\ catch(C\ i)\ e'$ and $sync_i\ (e)\ e'$. For example,

$$try\ e_1\ catch(C\ 3)\ (sync_4\ (\{4: T_1 = vo_1; e_2\}))\ \{5: T_2 = vo_2; e_3\})$$

is fine for a method with two parameters, but $\{3: T_1 = vo_1; \{5: T_2 = vo_2; e\}\}$, $\{4: T = vo; e\}$, and $\{3: T_1 = vo_1; \{2: T_2 = vo_2; e\}\}$ are not. Klein and Nipkow call this layout "an inverse de Bruijn numbering scheme" [83, §5.1.1]. The predicate $\mathcal{B}\ e\ n$ in Figure 5.14 enforces it where n denotes the starting number for the outermost blocks.

The typing rules for J_1 are almost identical to J. In $P, E \vdash_1 e :: T$, the program P has type $'addr\ J_1\text{-}prog$ and the environment E for local variables now is a list of types where the i-th element corresponds to variable i. The rule WT_1SYNC for $sync\_$ (_) _ blocks demonstrates all relevant changes:

$$WT_1SYNC: \quad \frac{is\text{-}refT\ T_1 \quad T_1 \neq NT \quad P, E\ @\ [Class\ Object] \vdash_1 e_2 :: T}{P, E \vdash_1 sync_j\ (e_1)\ e_2 :: T}$$

with $P, E \vdash_1 e_1 :: T_1$ as the top premise.

$P, E \vdash_1 \_ :: \_$ implicitly relies on the numbering scheme with $|E|$ as start index, as WT_1SYNC ignores the annotation variable j. Instead, it extends the environment for the monitor variable with the type $Class\ Object$.

---

^{50}Technically, they are annotated in J, too, namely with (). Hence, $sync\ (e)\ e'$ actually abbreviates $sync_{()}\ (e)\ e'$ and similarly for $insync\ (a)\ e$.

$$\mathcal{B}\ (new\ C)\ i \longleftrightarrow True$$
$$\mathcal{B}\ (new\ T[e])\ i \longleftrightarrow \mathcal{B}\ e\ i$$
$$\mathcal{B}\ (e\ instanceof\ T)\ i \longleftrightarrow \mathcal{B}\ e\ i$$
$$\mathcal{B}\ (Cast\ T\ e)\ i \longleftrightarrow \mathcal{B}\ e\ i$$
$$\mathcal{B}\ (Val\ v)\ i \longleftrightarrow True$$
$$\mathcal{B}\ (e_1\ «bop»\ e_2)\ i \longleftrightarrow \mathcal{B}\ e_1\ i \wedge \mathcal{B}\ e_2\ i$$
$$\mathcal{B}\ (Var\ j)\ i \longleftrightarrow True$$
$$\mathcal{B}\ (V := e)\ i \longleftrightarrow \mathcal{B}\ e\ i$$
$$\mathcal{B}\ (e_1[e_2])\ i \longleftrightarrow \mathcal{B}\ e_1\ i \wedge \mathcal{B}\ e_2\ i$$
$$\mathcal{B}\ (e_1[e_2] := e_3)\ i \longleftrightarrow \mathcal{B}\ e_1\ i \wedge \mathcal{B}\ e_2\ i \wedge \mathcal{B}\ e_3\ i$$
$$\mathcal{B}\ (e.length)\ i \longleftrightarrow \mathcal{B}\ e\ i$$
$$\mathcal{B}\ (e.F\{D\})\ i \longleftrightarrow \mathcal{B}\ e\ i$$
$$\mathcal{B}\ (e_1.F\{D\} := e_2)\ i \longleftrightarrow \mathcal{B}\ e_1\ i \wedge \mathcal{B}\ e_2\ i$$
$$\mathcal{B}\ (e.M(es))\ i \longleftrightarrow \mathcal{B}\ e\ i \wedge \mathcal{B}s\ es\ i$$
$$\mathcal{B}\ \{j: T = vo; e\}\ i \longleftrightarrow i = j \wedge \mathcal{B}\ e\ (i+1)$$
$$\mathcal{B}\ (e_1;;\ e_2)\ i \longleftrightarrow \mathcal{B}\ e_1\ i \wedge \mathcal{B}\ e_2\ i$$
$$\mathcal{B}\ (if\ (e)\ e_1\ else\ e_2)\ i \longleftrightarrow \mathcal{B}\ e\ i \wedge \mathcal{B}\ e_1\ i \wedge \mathcal{B}\ e_2\ i$$
$$\mathcal{B}\ (while\ (e_1)\ e_2) \longleftrightarrow \mathcal{B}\ e_1\ i \wedge \mathcal{B}\ e_2\ i$$
$$\mathcal{B}\ (throw\ e)\ i \longleftrightarrow \mathcal{B}\ e\ i$$
$$\mathcal{B}\ (try\ e_1\ catch(C\ j)\ e_2)\ i \longleftrightarrow \mathcal{B}\ e_1\ i \wedge i = j \wedge \mathcal{B}\ e_2\ (i+1)$$
$$\mathcal{B}\ (sync_j\ (e_1)\ e_2)\ i \longleftrightarrow \mathcal{B}\ e_1\ i \wedge i = j \wedge \mathcal{B}\ e_2\ (i+1)$$
$$\mathcal{B}\ (insync_j\ (a)\ e)\ i \longleftrightarrow i = j \wedge \mathcal{B}\ e\ (i+1)$$
$$\mathcal{B}s\ []\ i \longleftrightarrow True$$
$$\mathcal{B}s\ (e \cdot es)\ i \longleftrightarrow \mathcal{B}\ e\ i \wedge \mathcal{B}s\ es\ i$$

Figure 5.14: Definition of $\mathcal{B}$

Since the compiler introduces these monitor variables, no expression should access them. The predicate $\mathcal{S}\ e$ ensures this by checking that $i \notin fv\ e'$ for all subexpressions of e of the form $sync_i\ (\_)\ e'$ or $insync_i\ (a)\ e'$.[51]

The well-formedness conditions specific to J_1 are similar to J's (Figure 2.10). The constraints on parameter names have been dropped and the numbering scheme and no access to monitor variables are required. $\{..n\}$ denotes the set of natural numbers from 0 to n inclusive.

---

[51] In the definition of fv, I pretended that it is defined on $'addr\ expr$, but in reality it is defined on $('a, 'b, 'addr)\ exp$. Hence, it works on $'addr\ expr_1$, too. The same applies to $final$, $\mathcal{D}$, $inline$, and $ok\text{-}\mathcal{I}$.

$wf\text{-}J_1\text{-}mdecl\ P\ C\ (M, Ts, T_r, body) =$
$\quad (\exists T.\ P, Class\ C \cdot\ Ts \vdash_1 body :: T\ \wedge\ P \vdash T \leq T_r)\ \wedge$
$\quad \mathcal{D}\ body\ \lfloor\{..|Ts|\}\rfloor \wedge \mathcal{B}\ body\ (|Ts| + 1) \wedge \mathcal{S}\ body$

$wf\text{-}J_1\text{-}prog = wf\text{-}prog\ wf\text{-}J_1\text{-}mdecl$

Semantics

The state space of J_1 is already close to bytecode. The thread-local state is a list of call frames each of which consists of an expression and a fixed-size array of registers for the local variables.

On the expression level, the small-step semantics red_1 is now of the form $fail, P, t \vdash \langle e, (h, xs)\rangle -ta\rightarrow_1^e \langle e', (h', xs')\rangle$ where $P :: 'addr\ J_1\text{-}prog$ and $xs, xs' :: 'addr\ val\ list$. The new parameter $fail :: bool$ determines whether unlocking a monitor may fail.

The main difference between J_0 and J_1 is that J_1 handles local variables and synchronisation like bytecode.

In particular, $sync_i\ (addr\ a)\ e$ stores the monitor address a in the local variable i upon locking the monitor. Accordingly, when unlocking the monitor, $insync_i\ (a)\ e$ ignores a, but retrieves the monitor address from register i. Figure 5.15 shows the rules for synchronisation. Note that they explicitly check for the bounds of the register array. Compared to Figure 3.21, there are two new pairs of rules for unlocking: First, R_1UNLCKN and R_1UNLCKXN raise a *NullPointer* exception if the register $xs_{[i]}$ for the monitor stores the *Null* pointer instead of an address. Second, R_1UNLCKF and R_1UNLCKXF allow unlocking to non-deterministically fail with an *IllegalMonitorState* exception like *MExit* (see Figure 3.23). The switch $fail$ must be set to *True* to activate the latter.

$fail, P, t \vdash \langle e, (h, xs)\rangle -ta\rightarrow_1^e \langle e', (h', xs')\rangle$ differs from $P, t \vdash \langle \_, \_\rangle -\_\rightarrow \langle \_, \_\rangle$ in two further respects. First, the small-step semantics treats local variable blocks with initialisation, say $\{i: T = \lfloor v\rfloor; e\}$, like $\{i: T = None; i := Val\ v;; e\}$ and completely ignores uninitialised blocks. This ensures that J_1 and bytecode treat local variables identically. Second, there is no rule for calling non-native methods.

Instead, the semantics $J_1\text{-}red$ for single threads (notation $fail, P, t \vdash \langle((e, xs), exs), h\rangle -ta\rightarrow_1^t \langle((e', xs'), exs'), h'\rangle$) takes care of method calls and returns similar to $J_0\text{-}red$ – see Figure 5.16 for the definition. The conversion function $native\text{-}TA2J_1$ for thread actions is defined analogously to $native\text{-}TA2J$ and $native\text{-}TA2J_0$. $call_1$ differs from $call$ only for

R_1SYNC1:
$$\dfrac{fail, P, t \vdash \langle e_1, s \rangle - ta \rightarrow^e_1 \langle e'_1, s' \rangle}{fail, P, t \vdash \langle sync_i \,(e_1)\, e_2, s \rangle - ta \rightarrow^e_1 \langle sync_i \,(e'_1)\, e_2, s' \rangle}$$

R_1SYNCN:
$$\dfrac{i < |xs|}{\begin{array}{l} fail, P, t \vdash \langle sync_i \,(null)\, e, (h, xs) \rangle \\ \quad - (\!|\!\!|) \rightarrow^e_1 \langle THROW\ NullPointer, (h, xs[i := null]) \rangle \end{array}}$$

R_1SYNCX:
$$fail, P, t \vdash \langle sync_i \,(Throw\ a)\, e, s \rangle - (\!|\!\!|) \rightarrow^e_1 \langle Throw\ a, s \rangle$$

R_1LOCK:
$$\dfrac{i < |xs|}{\begin{array}{l} fail, P, t \vdash \langle sync_i \,(addr\ a)\, e, (h, xs) \rangle - (\!|Lock \rightarrow a, SLock\ a|\!) \rightarrow^e_1 \\ \quad \langle insync_i \,(a)\, e, (h, xs[i := Addr\ a]) \rangle \end{array}}$$

R_1SYNC2:
$$\dfrac{fail, P, t \vdash \langle e, s \rangle - ta \rightarrow^e_1 \langle e', s' \rangle}{fail, P, t \vdash \langle insync_i \,(a)\, e, s \rangle - ta \rightarrow^e_1 \langle insync_i \,(a)\, e', s' \rangle}$$

R_1UNLCKN:
$$\dfrac{xs_{[i]} = Null \qquad i < |xs|}{\begin{array}{l} fail, P, t \vdash \langle insync_i \,(a^*)\, (Val\ v), (h, xs) \rangle \\ \quad - (\!|\!\!|) \rightarrow^e_1 \langle THROW\ NullPointer, (h, xs) \rangle \end{array}}$$

R_1UNLCK:
$$\dfrac{xs_{[i]} = Addr\ a \qquad i < |xs|}{\begin{array}{l} fail, P, t \vdash \langle insync_i \,(a^*)\, (Val\ v), (h, xs) \rangle \\ \quad - (\!|Unlock \rightarrow a, SUnlock\ a|\!) \rightarrow^e_1 \langle Val\ v, (h, xs) \rangle \end{array}}$$

R_1UNLCKF:
$$\dfrac{fail \qquad xs_{[i]} = Addr\ a \qquad i < |xs|}{\begin{array}{l} fail, P, t \vdash \langle insync_i \,(a^*)\, (Val\ v), (h, xs) \rangle - (\!|UnlockFail \rightarrow a|\!) \rightarrow^e_1 \\ \quad \langle THROW\ IllegalMonitorState, (h, xs) \rangle \end{array}}$$

R_1UNLCKXN:
$$\dfrac{xs_{[i]} = Null \qquad i < |xs|}{\begin{array}{l} fail, P, t \vdash \langle insync_i \,(a^*)\, (Throw\ a'), (h, xs) \rangle \\ \quad - (\!|\!\!|) \rightarrow^e_1 \langle THROW\ NullPointer, (h, xs) \rangle \end{array}}$$

R_1UNLCKX:
$$\dfrac{xs_{[i]} = Addr\ a \qquad i < |xs|}{\begin{array}{l} fail, P, t \vdash \langle insync_i \,(a^*)\, (Throw\ a'), (h, xs) \rangle \\ \quad - (\!|Unlock \rightarrow a, SUnlock\ a|\!) \rightarrow^e_1 \langle Throw\ a', (h, xs) \rangle \end{array}}$$

R_1UNLCKXF:
$$\dfrac{fail \qquad xs_{[i]} = Addr\ a \qquad i < |xs|}{\begin{array}{l} fail, P, t \vdash \langle insync_i \,(a^*)\, (Throw\ a')\, (h, xs) \rangle - (\!|UnlockFail \rightarrow a|\!) \rightarrow^e_1 \\ \quad \langle THROW\ IllegalMonitorState, (h, xs) \rangle \end{array}}$$

Figure 5.15: Reduction rules for synchronized blocks in J_1

R_1RED:
$$\frac{fail, P, t \vdash \langle e, (h, xs)\rangle - ta \rightarrow_1^e \langle e', (h', xs')\rangle}{\begin{array}{c} fail, P, t \vdash \langle ((e, xs), exs), h\rangle -native\text{-}TA2J_1\ P\ ta \rightarrow_1^t \\ \langle ((e', xs'), exs), h'\rangle \end{array}}$$

R_1CALL:
$$\frac{\begin{array}{c} call_1\ e = \lfloor (a, M, vs)\rfloor \qquad typeof\text{-}addr\ h\ a = \lfloor hT\rfloor \\ P \vdash class\text{-}of'\ hT\ sees\ M{:}Ts{\rightarrow}T = \lfloor body\rfloor\ in\ D \\ |vs| = |Ts| \qquad e' = blocks_1\ 0\ (Class\ D \cdot Ts)\ body \\ xs' = Addr\ a \cdot vs\ @\ replicate\ (max\text{-}vars\ body)\ undefined\text{-}Val \end{array}}{fail, P, t \vdash \langle ((e, xs), exs), h\rangle - \lparen\!\rparen \rightarrow_1^t \langle ((e', xs'), (e, xs) \cdot exs), h\rangle}$$

R_1RET:
$$\frac{final\ e}{\begin{array}{c} fail, P, t \vdash \langle ((e, xs), (e', xs') \cdot exs), h\rangle - \lparen\!\rparen \rightarrow_1^t \\ \langle ((inline\ e\ e', xs'), exs), h\rangle \end{array}}$$

Figure 5.16: Reduction rules for call stacks in J_1

blocks. Initialised blocks never pause at a call, since the semantics first "uninitialises" them.

$$call_1\ (\{i{:}\ T = vo; e\}) = (if\ vo = None\ then\ call_1\ e\ else\ None)$$

Note that R_1CALL initialises the registers of the new call frame just like *exec-instr* does in Figure 3.22. The function *max-vars* computes the maximum depth of nested local variables including the variables for *sync_* (_) _ blocks. Analogous to *blocks*, *blocks$_1$ n Ts body* wraps *body* in uninitialised blocks for local variables n to $n + |ts| - 1$ with types Ts.

Setting *fail* to *False* or *True* yields two different semantics of J_1, to which I refer as $J_1^\#$ and J_1', respectively; J_1 refers to both. Similarly, I sometimes omit the *fail* parameter from the semantics and instead decorate them with ' or #, e.g., $J_1^\#$-*red* and $\_,\_\vdash \langle\_,\_\rangle - \_ \rightarrow_1^{t'} \langle\_,\_\rangle$.

Like for source code, the multithreaded semantics $J_1^\#.redT$ and $J_1'.redT$ are the interleaving semantics instantiated with $J_1^\#$-*red* and J_1'-*red*, respectively. A J_1 thread is final, written J_1-*final* $((e, xs), exs)$, iff *final e* and $exs = []$. The start state J_1-*start P C M vs* has one thread *start-tID* with local state

$$((blocks_1\ 0\ (Class\ D \cdot Ts)\ (Null \cdot vs)\ body,$$
$$Null \cdot vs\ @\ replicate\ (max\text{-}vars\ body)\ undefined\text{-}Val), [])$$

where $(D, Ts, \_, \lfloor body\rfloor) = method\ P\ C\ M$.

$$compE_1\ (Var\ V) \qquad\qquad = Var\ (index\ Vs\ V)$$
$$compE_1\ Vs\ \{V\colon T = vo;\ e\} = \{|Vs|\colon T = vo;\ compE_1\ (Vs\,@\,[V])\ e\}$$
$$compE_1\ Vs\ (sync\ (e_1)\ e_2) =$$
$$\qquad sync_{|Vs|}\ (compE_1\ Vs\ e_1)\ (compE_1\ (Vs\,@\,[fresh\text{-}vname\ Vs])\ e_2)$$
$$compE_1\ Vs\ (insync\ (a)\ e) =$$
$$\qquad insync_{|Vs|}\ (a)\ (compE_1\ (Vs\,@\,[fresh\text{-}vname\ Vs])\ e)$$

Figure 5.17: Register allocation $compE_1$ for local variables, blocks, and synchronisation

On the level of single threads, $J_1^{\#}$ and J_1' are not bisimilar, because unlocking a monitor can non-deterministically fail in J_1', but not in $J_1^{\#}$. Below, I will use $J_1^{\#}$ for proving the first compiler stage correct and J_1' for the second. Then, I will show that under suitable conditions, $J_1^{\#}$ and J_1' coincide on the multithreaded level.

To identify τ-moves, J_1 defines a predicate $\tau\text{-move}_1$ similar to $\tau\text{-move}$. Like for $call$ vs. $call_1$, the only difference is that red_1 may silently "uninitialise" initialised blocks first.

$$\tau\text{-move}_1\ P\ h\ \{i\colon T = vo;\ e\} \longleftrightarrow vo \neq None \vee \tau\text{-move}_1\ P\ h\ e \vee final\ e$$

J_1-τ-move lifts $\tau\text{-move}_1$ to call stacks:

$$J_1\text{-}\tau\text{-move}\ P\ (((e, xs), exs), h)\ ta\ \_ \longleftrightarrow (\tau\text{-move}_1\ P\ h\ e \vee final\ e) \wedge ta = (\!|\!|)$$

Lemma 5.13. *$J_1^{\#}$ and J_1' satisfy the assumptions of locale τ-multithreaded.*

$$\tau\text{-multithreaded}\ J_1\text{-final}\ (J_1^{\#}\text{-red}\ P)\ acq\text{-events}\ J_1\text{-}\tau\text{-move}$$
$$\tau\text{-multithreaded}\ J_1\text{-final}\ (J_1'\text{-red}\ P)\ acq\text{-events}\ J_1\text{-}\tau\text{-move}$$

5.3.2 Compilation stage 1

Jinja already contains a compiler $compE_1$ from $'addr\ expr$ to $'addr\ expr_1$, i.e., for method bodies. It assigns registers to variables [83, §5.2] in the following order: first the *this* pointer, then the method parameters, and finally local variables ordered by block nesting level. While traversing the expression, $compE_1$ keeps track of the list of variables Vs declared on the path from the root of the expression to the current subexpression and replaces variables V by their index in Vs (written $index\ Vs\ V$), i.e., the position of the last occurrence of V in Vs. Figure 5.17 shows an excerpt of its definition, the full definition can be found in Appendix B.9.2.

For $sync\ (e_1)\ e_2$ blocks, $compE_1$ reserves the register $|Vs|$ to hold the monitor address. To shift the registers in e_2 by 1, it appends a fresh variable name $fresh\text{-}vname\ Vs$ to Vs. Freshness (i.e., $fresh\text{-}vname\ Vs \notin set\ Vs$) ensures that it does not hide any variables in surrounding blocks.

Jinja defines an operator $compP$ to lift compilation at the level of expressions to whole programs [83, §5.4]. I have straightforwardly adapted it to JinjaThreads programs (see Appendix B.9.1). The compiler from source code to intermediate language

$$compP_1 = compP\ (\lambda C\ M\ Ts\ T\ (pns, body).\ compE_1\ (this \cdot pns)\ body)$$

applies $compE_1$ to all method bodies.

For example, consider the following method declaration in Java, whose body is $([f], sync\ (Var\ f)\ (Var\ this.m([])))$ in abstract syntax:

```
int foo(Object f) { synchronized(f) { return this.m(); } }
```

This compiles to $sync_2\ (Var\ 1)\ (Var\ 0.m([]))$.

5.3.3 Preservation of well-formedness

Jinja's proof of $compP_1$ generating well-formed programs sets the ground for JinjaThreads'. Extending it is straightforward except for two aspects:

First, JinjaThreads additionally requires that registers for monitors be not accessed, i.e., condition $\mathcal{S}\ body$. The next lemma (provable by induction) shows that $compE_1$ ensures this. The interesting cases $sync\ (e_1)\ e_2$ and $insync\ (a)\ e$ rely on $fresh\text{-}vname\ Vs$ being fresh for Vs.

Lemma 5.14. *If $fv\ e \subseteq set\ Vs$, then $\mathcal{S}\ (compE_1\ Vs\ e)$.*

Second, preservation of well-typedness requires the stronger induction on the structure of expressions instead of usual induction on the derivation of the typing judgement:

Lemma 5.15 ([83, Lem. 5.5.]). *If wf-prog $wf\text{-}md\ P$ and $P, [Vs\ [\mapsto]\ Ts] \vdash e :: T$ and $|Ts| = |Vs|$, then $compP_1\ P, Ts \vdash_1 compE_1\ Vs\ e :: T$.*

Proof. By induction on e. The interesting new case is $sync\ (e_1)\ e_2$. From $P, [Vs \mapsto] Ts] \vdash sync\ (e_1)\ e_2 :: T$, there is a $T_1 \neq NT$ such that $is\text{-}refT\ T_1$, $P, [Vs \mapsto] Ts] \vdash e_1 :: T_1$, and $P, [Vs \mapsto] Ts] \vdash e_2 :: T$ by rule inversion. By induction hypothesis, $compP_1\ P, Ts \vdash_1 compE_1\ Vs\ e_1 :: T_1$. For e_2, it does not suffice to apply the induction hypothesis directly, because this would give $compP_1\ P, Ts \vdash_1 compE_1\ Vs\ e_2 :: T$, instead of

$$compP_1\ P, Ts\ @\ [Class\ Object] \vdash_1 compE_1\ (Vs\ @\ [fresh\text{-}vname\ Vs])\ e_2 :: T$$

as required by WT_1SYNC. This is also the reason why the standard induction rule for $P, [Vs \mapsto] Ts] \vdash e :: T$, which Jinja uses, is too weak for this proof. Instead, since $fresh\text{-}vname\ Vs$ is fresh,

$$P, [Vs\ @\ [fresh\text{-}vname\ Vs]\ [\mapsto]\ Ts\ @\ [Class\ Object]] \vdash e_2 :: T$$

follows from $[\![P, E \vdash e :: T;\ E \subseteq_m E']\!] \Longrightarrow P, E' \vdash e :: T$ (provable by rule induction) – and the induction hypothesis applies. $\square$

The remaining language-specific well-formedness constraints hold like in Jinja. Hence, preservation of well-formedness follows.

Theorem 5.7. *If wf-J-prog P, then wf-J$_1$-prog (compP$_1$ P).*

5.3.4 Semantic preservation

Semantic preservation for the intermediate language falls in two parts. First, I prove that P and $compP_1\ P$ are delay bisimilar under the semantics J_0 and $J_1^{\#}$. Second, I show that unlocking a monitor in $compP_1\ P$ never fails, i.e., $J_1^{\#}$ and J_1' give the same semantics to $compP_1\ P$ in spite of J_1''s additional reductions R_1UNLCKF and R_1UNLCKXF.

Semantic preservation for *compE$_1$*

J_0 and $J_1^{\#}$ only differ in the treatment of local variables. Hence, the thread features and arrays that JinjaThreads adds to Jinja do not introduce anything essentially new for the verification. Still, extending the old correctness proof (which uses a big-step semantics) requires substantial changes:

(i) The delay bisimulation between J_0 and $J_1^{\#}$ must now relate not only initial and final states, but also all intermediate states.

(ii) Since J_0 and $J_1^\#$ consist of a stack of semantics, the delay bisimulation at one layer composes language-specific constraints and bisimilulation relations from the level below (see Figure 5.1), and so do I compose the proofs.

(iii) I must now also show that the small-step reductions preserve the language-specific constraints that the bisimulation proof relies on.

Although the simulations are now much finer and covers both directions, the key ideas for the correctness proof [83, §5.5] are still sufficient.

In detail, the bisimulation relation $_0\overset{e}{\approx}_1$ at the level of expressions is naturally the heart of the correctness proof, because the translation's core is at this level. $_0\overset{t}{\approx}_1$ extends $_0\overset{e}{\approx}_1$ to call stacks; $_0\overset{m}{\approx}_1$ lifts $_0\overset{t}{\approx}_1$ to the interleaving semantics as described in §5.1.3. Hence, I want to prove that $_0\overset{t}{\approx}_1$ satisfies the assumptions of locale m-$dbisim$-div.

Most of these assumptions are simulation properties of the following form: Given two related states, if either can reduce in a given way, then the other can also reduce correspondingly such that the resulting states are related again. These properties can be derived from Theorem 5.8 (forward direction) and Theorem 5.9 (backward direction) in Figure 5.18, which I now discuss in detail.

Consider the assumptions of the theorems first. The central relation $Vs \vdash (e_0, xs_0) \approx (e_1, xs_1)$ fully encapsulates the relation between (e_0, xs_0) and (e_1, xs_1). The others, i.e., $fv\ e_0 \subseteq set\ Vs$ and $|Vs| + max\text{-}vars\ e_1 \le |xs_1|$ and $\mathcal{D}\ e_0\ \lfloor dom\ xs_0 \rfloor$, are only language-specific constraints that involve either of them. To improve proof automation, there are separate preservation lemmata for the latter. Consequently, only $Vs \vdash (e_0', xs_0') \approx (e_1', xs_1')$ appears in the conclusion. In detail, $Vs \vdash (e_0, xs_0) \approx (e_1, xs_1)$ predicates that

(a) the initialised local variables are the same, i.e., $xs_0 \subseteq_m [Vs\ [\mapsto]\ xs_1]$,

(b) e_1 adheres to the numbering scheme for variables, i.e., $\mathcal{B}\ e_1\ |Vs|$,

(c) for all $insync_i\ (a)$ _ subexpressions of e_1, xs_1 stores $Addr\ a$ in register i, and

(d) e_0 and e_1 are identical except for (i) variable names which are resolved according to the compilation scheme and (ii) local variable blocks where xs_1 may store the initialisation's value of e_0 and the

245

Theorem 5.8. *Let wf-J-prog P and $Vs \vdash (e_0, xs_0) \approx (e_1, xs_1)$.*
Let $fv\, e_0 \subseteq set\, Vs$ and $|Vs| + max\text{-}vars\, e_1 \leq |xs_1|$.
Suppose that $P, t \vdash \langle e_0, (h, xs_0) \rangle - ta_0 \to_0^e \langle e_0', (h', xs_0') \rangle$.
Then, there are ta_1, e_1', and xs_1' such that $Vs \vdash (e_0', xs_0') \approx (e_1', xs_1')$ and the
following hold:

(i) *If $\tau\text{-move}_0\, P\, h\, e_0$, then $h' = h$ and $ta_1 = \langle\!\langle\rangle\!\rangle$ and $\langle e_1, (h, xs_1) \rangle$ reduces*
in $J_1^{\#}$ with at least one τ-move to $\langle e_1', (h', xs_1') \rangle$.

(ii) *If $\neg\, \tau\text{-move}_0\, P\, h\, e_0$ and $call\, e_0 \neq None$ and $call_1\, e_1 \neq None$, then*
$\neg\, \tau\text{-move}_1\, (compP_1\, P)\, h\, e_1$ and $compP_1\, P, t \vdash \langle e_1, (h, xs_1) \rangle - ta_1 \to_1^{e\#}$
$\langle e_1', (h', xs_1') \rangle$ and ta_0 is $_0\!\overset{t}{\approx}_1$-bisimilar to native-TA2J$_1$ $(compP_1\, P)\, ta_1$.

(iii) *Otherwise, there are e_1'' and xs_1'' such that $\langle e_1, (h, xs_1) \rangle$ reduces in $J_1^{\#}$ with*
(possibly no) τ-moves to $\langle e_1'', (h, xs_1'') \rangle$ and $\neg\, \tau\text{-move}_1\, (compP_1\, P)\, h\, e_1''$
and $compP_1\, P, t \vdash \langle e_1'', (h, xs_1'') \rangle - ta_1 \to_1^{e\#} \langle e_1', (h', xs_1') \rangle$ and ta_0 is $_0\!\overset{t}{\approx}_1$-
bisimilar to native-TA2J$_1$ $(compP_1\, P)\, ta_1$.

Theorem 5.9. *Let wf-J-prog P and $Vs \vdash (e_0, xs_0) \approx (e_1, xs_1)$.*
Let $fv\, e_0 \subseteq set\, Vs$ and $|Vs| + max\text{-}vars\, e_1 \leq |xs_1|$ and $\mathcal{D}\, e_0\, \lfloor dom\, xs_0 \rfloor$.
Suppose that $compP_1\, P, t \vdash \langle e_1, (h, xs_1) \rangle - ta_1 \to_1^{e\#} \langle e_1', (h', xs_1') \rangle$.
Then, there are ta_0, e_0', and xs_0' such that $Vs \vdash (e_0', xs_0') \approx (e_1', xs_1')$ and the
following hold:

(i) *If $\tau\text{-move}_1\, (compP_1\, P)\, h\, e_1$, then $h' = h$ and $ta_0 = \langle\!\langle\rangle\!\rangle$ and $\langle e_0, (h, xs_0) \rangle$*
reduces in J_0 with τ-moves to $\langle e_0', (h', xs_1') \rangle$. If this involves no τ-moves,
then $cnt\text{-}IB\, e_1' < cnt\text{-}IB\, e_1$.

(ii) *If $\neg\, \tau\text{-move}_1\, (compP_1\, P)\, h\, e_1$ and $call\, e_0 \neq None$ and $call_1\, e_1 \neq None$,*
then $\neg\, \tau\text{-move}_0\, P\, h\, e_0$ and $P, t \vdash \langle e_0, (h, xs_0) \rangle - ta_0 \to_0^e \langle e_0', (h', xs_0') \rangle$
and ta_0 is $_0\!\overset{t}{\approx}_1$-bisimilar to native-TA2J$_1$ $(compP_1\, P)\, ta_1$.

(iii) *Otherwise, there are e_0'' and xs_0'' such that $\langle e_0, (h, xs_0) \rangle$ reduces in J_0*
with (possibly no) τ-moves to $\langle e_0'', (h, xs_0'') \rangle$ and $\neg\, \tau\text{-move}_0\, P\, h\, e_0''$ and
$P, t \vdash \langle e_0'', (h, xs_0'') \rangle - ta_0 \to_0^e \langle e_0', (h', xs_0') \rangle$ and ta_0 is $_0\!\overset{t}{\approx}_1$-bisimilar to
native-TA2J$_1$ $(compP_1\, P)\, ta_1$.

Figure 5.18: Simulation theorems on the expression level for compilation stage 1

246

block is uninitialised in e_1. Such differences in initialisations may only occur in subexpressions that the semantics reduces next. Moreover, the other subexpressions must not contain $insync\_$ $(\_)$ $\_$ blocks, i.e., $\neg\, has\text{-}I\, \_$.

Note that I need not require (c) for $sync$ $(\_)$ $\_$ expressions, because they have not yet stored the monitor address in the registers.

The language-specific constraints are similar to Jinja's correctness proof. First, to ensure that register allocation succeeds, $fv\, e_0 \subseteq set\, Vs$ expresses that Vs captures all free variables in e. Second, $|Vs| + max\text{-}vars\, e_1 \leq |xs_1|$ guarantees that xs_1 is large enough to hold all local variables during execution. The third constraint $\mathcal{D}\, e_0\, \lfloor dom\, xs_0 \rfloor$ only appears in Theorem 5.9 and is new compared to Jinja. It ensures that J_0 does not get stuck when looking up a local variable in xs_0. This is necessary because $J_1^{\#}$ does not distinguish initialised and uninitialised variables.

Now, turn to the conclusions. Case (i) corresponds to the τ-move simulation diagrams for well-founded delay bisimulations in Figure 5.6b. Theorem 5.8 always proves the left column, i.e., $J_1^{\#}$ simulates every τ-move in J_0 by at least one τ-move. In contrast, J_1 deinitialises local variable blocks before it executes the block's body (see §5.3.1), which has no counterpart in J_0. Hence, Theorem 5.9(i) allows J_0 to stall when the number of initialised blocks decreases – the measure $cnt\text{-}IB\, e_1$ counts the initialised blocks in e_1.

Case (iii) corresponds to the visible moves simulating observable moves (Figure 5.6a). Case (ii) is the special case when both e_0 and e_1 pause at a call. In that case, no τ-moves may precede the simulating move. Remember that $simulation\text{-}\overset{w}{\approx}1$ and $simulation\text{-}\overset{w}{\approx}2$ of locale $m\text{-}dbisim\text{-}div$ require this for processing the removal from a wait set. Both cases require the thread actions to be bisimilar, i.e., identical except for thread-local states of spawned threads, which must be $_0\overset{t}{\approx}_1$-related. This is what well-formedness (premise $wf\text{-}J\text{-}prog\, P$) is necessary for. Bisimilarity (defined below) involves definite assignment and no free variables.

Both theorems are proven by induction on the derivation of the reduction. The only interesting cases are for local variables and synchronisation blocks, but Jinja's notions of hidden and unmodified variables [83, §5.5] suffice for that. Again, it is essential that $fresh\text{-}vname\, Vs$ is fresh.

247

Now, it is clear what the bisimulation relations should be. Remember that the expressions in J_0 call frames are closed, i.e., $Vs = []$ and $xs_0 = empty$. Hence,

$$e_0 \; {}_0\overset{e}{\approx}_1 (e_1, xs_1) \longleftrightarrow$$
$$[] \vdash (e_0, empty) \approx (e_1, xs_1) \land fv\, e_0 = \emptyset \land \mathcal{D}\, e_0 \lfloor \emptyset \rfloor \land max\text{-}vars\, e_1 \leq |xs_1|$$

Lifting to single threads is straightforward. The heaps must be the same, the call stacks must be ${}_0\overset{e}{\approx}_1$-related pointwise, and all call frames except the top pause at a call.

$$((e_0, es_0), h_0) \; {}_0\overset{t}{\approx}_1 (((e_1, xs_1), exs_1), h_1) \longleftrightarrow$$
$$h_0 = h_1 \land e_0 \; {}_0\overset{e}{\approx}_1 (e_1, xs_1) \land |es_0| = |exs_1| \land$$
$$(\forall (e_0', (e_1', xs_1')) \in set\,(zip\, es_0\; exs_1).$$
$$e_0' \; {}_0\overset{e}{\approx}_1 (e_1', xs_1') \land call\, e_0' \neq None \land call_1\, e_1' \neq None)$$

For ${}_0\overset{m}{\approx}_1$, I take $\approx_m$ from §5.1.3 instantiated with ${}_0\overset{t}{\approx}_1$ and ${}_0\overset{w}{\approx}_1$, where

$$(e_0, es_0) \; {}_0\overset{w}{\approx}_1 ((e_1, xs_1), exs_1) \longleftrightarrow call\, e_0 \neq None \land call_1\, e_1 \neq None,$$

i.e., threads in wait sets must pause at a call.

Lemma 5.16. *Let wf-J-prog P. ${}_0\overset{t}{\approx}_1$ is a delay bisimulation with explicit divergence for J_0-red P t and $J_1^{\#}$-red $(compP_1\, P)$ t.*

Proof. Since J_0 and J_1 have similar call-stack semantics (Figures 5.13 and 5.16), it follows easily with Theorems 5.8 and 5.9 that ${}_0\overset{t}{\approx}_1$ is a well-founded delay bisimulation with well-founded relations $<_0$ and $<_1$, where

$$(e_0', es_0') <_0 (e_0, es_0) \qquad \longleftrightarrow False$$
$$((e_1', xs_1'), exs_1') <_1 ((e_1, xs_1), exs_1) \longleftrightarrow cnt\text{-}IB\, e_1' < cnt\text{-}IB\, e_1$$

From this, the statement follows by Lemma 5.2. $\qquad\qquad\square$

Theorem 5.10. *Let wf-J-prog P. ${}_0\overset{m}{\approx}_1$ is a delay bisimulation with explicit divergence for $J_0.redT\, P$ and $J_1^{\#}.redT\,(compP_1\, P)$ that preserves final states.*

Proof. It suffices to show that the assumptions of locale *m-dbisim-div* are met. Lemma 5.16 discharges the first. Preservation of final states and heap changes is trivial, because (i) finality is invariant under $_0\approx_1^t$ and (ii) $_0\approx_1^t$ only imposes equality on the heaps, but does not otherwise depend on it. $\approx^w I$ is provable by induction and case analysis, whereas *simulation-*$\approx^w 1$ and *simulation-*$\approx^w 2$ follow from case (ii) of Theorems 5.8 and 5.9. $\square$

Lemma 5.17. *If wf-J-prog P and wf-start P C M vs, then*

$$J\text{-}start\ P\ C\ M\ vs\ _0\approx_1^m\ J_1\text{-}start\ (compP_1\ P)\ C\ M\ vs.$$

Equivalence of $J_1^\#$ and J_1'

The compiler verification has to show that unlocking a monitor in compiled code never fails. The intermediate language is the right place for this, because its semantics already stores the monitor address in the registers like bytecode, but the syntax still enforces the structured locking discipline.

I prove that $J_1^\#.redT\ P$ and $J_1'.redT\ P$ are the same for a multithreaded state s_1 in which the lock state agrees with the *insync_* (_) _ subexpressions of the threads. Agreement (notation *lock-conf*$_1$) is defined analogously to *lock-conf* in §3.3.4. In such a state, $J_1'.redT\ P$ never picks R_1UNLCKF nor R_1UNLCKXF, because the precondition of the thread action $(UnlockFail\rightarrow a)$ is violated. $J_1^\#.redT\ P$ preserves *lock-conf*$_1$ under the following condition (notation 🔒_ √) that for every call frame (e_1, xs_1) of every thread,

(i) for all subexpressions *insync$_i$* (a) e_1' of e_1, xs_1 stores *Addr a* in register i and e_1' does not modify register i and

(ii) *ok-I* e_1, i.e., all *insync_* (_) _ subexpressions of e_1 lie on one path from the root in e_1's abstract syntax tree (see Figure 3.33).

Hence, I define $_1\approx_1^m$ as follows:

$$s_1\ _1\approx_1^m\ s_1' \longleftrightarrow s_1 = s_1' \wedge lock\text{-}conf_1\ (locks\ s_1)\ (thr\ s_1) \wedge 🔒\ s_1\ \sqrt{}$$

Theorem 5.11. *If wf-J_1-prog P, then $_1\overset{m}{\approx}_1$ is a strong bisimulation for $J_1^{\#}.redT\,P$ and $J_1'.redT\,P$.*

Corollary 5.3. *If wf-J_1-prog P, then $_1\overset{m}{\approx}_1$ is a delay bisimulation with explicit divergence for $J_1^{\#}.redT\,P$ and $J_1'.redT\,P$ that preserves final states.*

Lemma 5.18. *If wf-J_1-prog P and wf-start $P\,C\,M\,vs$, then*

$$J_1\text{-start } P\,C\,M\,vs\ _1\overset{m}{\approx}_1\ J_1\text{-start } P\,C\,M\,vs.$$

5.4 Code generation

The first stage has already replaced variable names by register numbers. The second stage $compP_2$ now completes the translation in that it generates the bytecode instructions and exception tables for the expressions (§5.4.1). In this section, I show preservation of well-typedness (§5.4.2) and semantics (§5.4.3) for $compP_2$.

5.4.1 Compilation stage 2

The second stage of the compiler translates expressions into instruction lists (function $compE_2 :: {}'addr\ expr_1 \Rightarrow {}'addr\ instr\ list$) and exception tables (function $compxE_2 :: {}'addr\ expr_1 \Rightarrow pc \Rightarrow nat \Rightarrow ex\text{-}table$). $compP_2$ lifts $compE_2$ and $compxE_2$ to programs using $compP$ and computes the maximum stack size $max\text{-}stack$ and register size using $max\text{-}vars$.

$compP_2 = compP\ compMb_2$

$compMb_2\ C\ M\ Ts\ T\ body =$
$\quad (let\ ins = compE_2\ body\ @\ [Return];\ xt = compxE_2\ body\ 0\ 0$
$\quad in\ (max\text{-}stack\ body, max\text{-}vars\ body, ins, xt))$

For JinjaThreads, I have extended Jinja's $compE_2$ and $compxE_2$ to $sync_i\ (e_1)\ e_2$ expressions, on which I focus in this section. For details on the others, see [83, §5.3] and Appendix B.9.3.

The translation of a $sync_i\ (e_1)\ e_2$ expression to bytecode must ensure that the monitor is unlocked even if an unhandled exception occurs in e_2. An exception handler, which applies to *all* exceptions, needs to do this. Thus, the instructions for $sync_i\ (e_1)\ e_2$ are

$compE_2 \; e_1 \; @ \; [Dup, Store \; i, MEnter] \; @$
$compE_2 \; e_2 \; @ \; [Load \; i, MExit, Goto \; 4] \; @ \; [Load \; i, MExit, ThrowExc]$

First, the monitor expression e_1 is evaluated, its result on the stack duplicated and stored in register i; $MEnter$ locks the monitor. Then, the block e_2 is executed, the monitor address loaded back from register i and the monitor unlocked. $Goto$ 4 jumps to the instruction after the exception handler that follows. The handler also loads the monitor address, unlocks the monitor and rethrows the caught exception whose address is still on top of the stack.

Since the exception tables contain absolute program counters and stack depth, $compxE_2$ takes the current program counter pc and stack depth d as parameters. For $sync_i \; (e_1) \; e_2$, $compxE_2$ appends to the exception tables for e_1 and e_2 the entry $(pc_1, pc_2, Any, pc_2 + 3, d)$ where $pc_1 = pc + |compE_2 \; e_1| + 3$ and $pc_2 = pc_1 + |compE_2 \; e_2|$. Hence, the entry matches all exceptions that e_2's instructions raise. Since it is placed at the end, it does not take precedence over exception handlers in e_2.

Reconsider the compilation example in §5.3.2. $compE_2$ compiles the method body $sync_2 \; (Var \; 1) \; (Var \; 0.m([]))$ to

$[Load \; 1, Dup, Store \; 2, MEnter, Load \; 0, Invoke \; m \; 0, Load \; 2, MExit,$
$Goto \; 4, Load \; 2, MExit, ThrowExc, Return]$

with exception table $[(4, 6, Any, 9, 0)]$.

As I have already discussed in §2.2.1, Any is important for the verification, although $\lfloor Throwable \rfloor$ would also do in theory. Since the latter only applies to subclasses of $Throwable$, the bisimulation relation would have to ensure that only such exceptions are ever raised. This would pull in the complete type safety proof of the JVM and therefore severly complicate the proof.

5.4.2 Preservation of well-formedness

To show that $compP_2$ preserves well-formedness, Jinja defines a type compiler that computes a well-typing for the generated bytecode [83, §5.9]. Since JinjaThreads' extensions for arrays and synchronisation naturally fit in the compilation scheme, I only present the final theorem – see the formalisation [106] for the full details.

Theorem 5.12. *If wf-J$_1$-prog P, then wf-jvm-prog P.*

251

5.4.3 Semantic preservation

The translation from the intermediate language to bytecode is the most complicated one. It flattens the tree structure of expressions to a linear list of instructions. Exception handlers are registered in exception tables. synchronized blocks are implemented by *MEnter* and *MExit* instructions and an exception handler.

To show delay bisimilarity, I first must define which VM transitions are unobservable, i.e., τ-moves. Exception handling and the following instructions generate only τ-moves: *Load, Store, Push, Pop, Dup, Swap, BinOp, Checkcast, Instanceof, Goto, IfFalse, ThrowExc,* and *Return.* Additionally, *Invoke* generates a τ-move only if the called method is non-native or one of the native methods *hashcode* or *currentThread*.

Like between J_0 and $J_1^{\#}$, the key to correctness is delay bisimilarity on the expression level, on which I focus in this section. Calling and returning from methods works similarly in J_1' and the JVM, the laborious, but uninteresting proof lifts delay bisimilarity. The multithreaded level is the interleaving semantics in both semantics. Hence, I leverage Theorem 5.3 once more to show delay bisimilarity for J_1' and the JVM.

For the expression level, I take a detour via two new bytecode semantics *exec-meth* and *exec-methd* that differ from the VM in when they get stuck (see Figure 5.1). A single step of execution is written $chk, P, ins, xt, t \vdash \langle (stk, loc, pc, xcp), h \rangle - ta \rightarrow^{e}_{jvm} \langle (stk', loc', pc', xcp'), h' \rangle$: If the exception flag *xcp* is *None*, it denotes that the sanity check *chk* succeeds (see below), *pc* points to an instruction in *ins* and (stk', loc', pc', xcp') describes a possible successor state of executing instruction $ins_{[pc]}$ with stack *stk* and registers *loc* according to *exec-instr*; *ta* is the corresponding thread action. If the exception flag is set, it denotes that *xt* contains an exception handler at *pc'* that applies and no stack underflow occurs. Since I am at the expression level, the step must not change the length of the call stack, i.e., neither return from a method nor call a non-native method.

The parameter *chk* controls when the semantics gets stuck. For *exec-meth*, *chk* ensures that the stack does not underflow and that jumps only go to program counters between 0 and $|pc|$ inclusive. Since it is stricter than the aggressive VM, steps in *exec-meth* are preserved when I enlarge the instruction list at either end and extend the stack at the bottom. The inductive cases in the simulation proof rely on this. But it is not as strict as *exec-methd*, where *chk* performs all checks of *check-instr*.

Since *exec-meth* gets stuck only when red'_1 is also stuck, I use *exec-meth* for simulating red'_1's reductions.

For the other direction, I use *exec-methd*, because it gets stuck more often than red'_1. For *ThrowExc*, e.g., *check-instr* requires that the thrown exception is a subclass of *Throwable*, but red'_1 does not. Hence, *exec-methd* cannot simulate red'_1 unless the bisimulation relation excludes such cases, e.g., by requiring bytecode conformance. But this would further complicate the proofs which are already tedious. Conversely, red'_1 cannot simulate *exec-meth* because the former gets stuck, e.g., when trying to access a field of an integer, but the latter carries on with undefined behaviour.

As the generated bytecode is well-formed (Theorem 5.12), *exec-methd* simulates *exec-meth* for conformant states and preserves bytecode conformance. Note that conformance does not complicate proofs any more at this level of abstraction, because I do not have to unfold its definition for individual instructions. This closes the circle of simulations. In principle, it should be possible to define *chk* such that the bytecode semantics gets stuck whenever red'_1 does. Since this appears to be very tedious, error-prone and sensitive to even small changes, I have not attempted to do so.

Note that this detour only affects the semantics, not the bisimulation relation $1\overset{e}{\approx}_{jvm}$. As before, $1\overset{e}{\approx}_{jvm}$ consists of two parts, (i) a relation between J_1 call frames and JVM expression-level states and (ii) well-formedness conditions of the states that the semantics preserve individually. The relation $P, e, h \vdash (e_1, xs_1) \approx (stk, loc, pc, xcp)$ relates a J_1 call frame (e_1, xs_1) (expression and local variables) to a JVM expression-level state (stk, loc, pc, xcp) for a heap h that is the same for both. P only defines the class hierarchy, whereas the expression $e :: 'addr\ expr_1$ compiles to the instruction list $ins = compE_2\ e$ and $xt = compxE_2\ e\ 0\ 0$. The inductive definition for $\approx$ mirrors the reduction rules of red'_1 and relates a partially evaluated expression e_1 with the corresponding stack stk and registers loc, and the instruction position pc in the compiled code.

Figure 5.19 shows some representative rules from the inductive definition. The single rule B_1 for all expressions exploits that the last instruction in a compiled expression always puts its result value on top of the stack. Unfortunately, this does not extend to exceptions, because bytecode does not propagate exceptions from subexpressions, but uses exception tables. Hence, $\approx$ contains separate exception propagation rules for every expression, similar to B_2. Still, it abstracts from computed

$B_1:$ $\quad P, e, h \vdash (Val\ v, xs) \approx ([v], xs, |compE_2\ e|, None)$

$B_2:$ $\quad \dfrac{P, e_1, h \vdash (Throw\ a, xs) \approx (stk, loc, pc, \lfloor a \rfloor)}{P, sync_i\ (e_1)\ e_2, h \vdash (Throw\ a, xs) \approx (stk, loc, pc, \lfloor a \rfloor)}$

$B_3:$ $\quad \dfrac{P, e_2, h \vdash (e, xs) \approx (stk, loc, pc, xcp)}{\begin{array}{c} P, sync_i\ (e_1)\ e_2, h \vdash (insync_i\ (a)\ e, xs) \approx \\ (stk, loc, |compE_2\ e_1| + 3 + pc, xcp) \end{array}}$

$B_4:$ $\quad P, sync_i\ (e_1)\ e_2, h \vdash (sync_i\ (Val\ v)\ e_2, xs) \approx$
$([v], xs[i := v], |compE_2\ e_1| + 2, None)$

Figure 5.19: Example introduction rules for the relation $\approx$

values and addresses of thrown exceptions and only requires that they are the same in both states. Moreover, rules like B_3 for all subexpressions of all expressions embed bisimilar states for the subexpression into the context of the larger expression, thereby shifting the stack and instruction pointer as necessary. Finally, the definition contains a rule for every bytecode instruction and corresponding J_1 state. For example, B_4 relates the J_1 state which next acquires the monitor's lock to the intermediate JVM state after executing the *Store i* instruction that stores the monitor address. Although J_1' and the JVM operate on the local variable array in the same way, the bisimulation relation must not require that xs and loc be equal, because they differ in such intermediate states like in B_4, which R_1LOCK skips.

The bisimulation relation $_1\overset{e}{\approx}_{jvm}$ specialises this relation to complete call frames as follows:

$$\dfrac{\begin{array}{c} P \vdash C\ sees\ M:Ts \to T = \lfloor body \rfloor\ in\ D \\ P, blocks_1\ 0\ (Class\ D \cdot Ts)\ body, h \vdash (e_1, xs_1) \approx (stk, loc, pc, xcp) \\ max\text{-}vars\ e_1 \leq |xs_1| \end{array}}{P, h \vdash (e_1, xs_1)\ _1\overset{e}{\approx}_{jvm}\ (xcp, stk, loc, C, M, pc)}$$

The main simulation theorems at the expression level are similar in structure to Theorems 5.8 and 5.9. Their proofs consist of a huge induction on the relation and case analysis of the reductions. Control constructs like conditionals and loops, which are compiled to (conditional) jumps, are verified like in sequential Jinja.

The bisimulation relation $_1\overset{t}{\approx}_{jvm}$ for single threads lifts $_1\overset{e}{\approx}_{jvm}$ to call stacks. Although great care is required to ensure that everything fits together, the construction and its verification just reuses the ideas from the first compilation stage. Hence, I conclude that the second stage is correct, too.

Theorem 5.13 (Correctness of stage 2). *In locale conf-read, suppose that wf-J_1-prog P. Then,*

(i) $_1\overset{t}{\approx}_{jvm}$ *is a delay bisimulation with explicit divergence for J'_1-red P t and the defensive VM jvm-execd (compP$_2$ P) t.*

(ii) $_1\overset{m}{\approx}_{jvm}$ *is a delay bisimulation with explicit divergence for J'_1.redT P and jvmd.redT (compP$_2$ P) that preserves final states.*

Lemma 5.19. *If wf-J_1-prog P and wf-start P C M vs, then*

$$J_1\text{-start } P\ C\ M\ vs\ _1\overset{m}{\approx}_{jvm}\ jvm\text{-start } (compP_2\ P)\ C\ M\ vs.$$

5.5 Complete compiler

In the previous sections, I have shown that all relations in Figure 5.1 are delay bisimulations with explicit divergence. Now, it remains to compose these results for the full compiler $J2JVM = compP_2 \circ compP_1$.

Preservation of well-formedness follows immediately from Theorems 5.7 and 5.12.

Theorem 5.14. *If wf-J-prog P, then wf-jvm-prog (J2JVM P).*

For semantic preservation, let $(_J\approx_{jvm}, _J\sim_{jvm})$ be the composition of all multithreaded delay bisimulations, i.e.,

$$(_J\approx_{jvm}, _J\sim_{jvm}) = \overset{m}{\approx}_0 \text{O}_B\ _0\overset{m}{\approx}_1 \text{O}_B\ _1\overset{m}{\approx}_1 \text{O}_B\ _1\overset{m}{\approx}_{jvm}$$

Lemmata 5.12, 5.17, 5.18, and 5.19 show that $_J\approx_{jvm}$ relates the start states. And Lemma 5.1 composes the bisimulation theorems 5.6, 5.10, 5.13 and Corollary 5.3 to obtain the main correctness theorem 5.16.

Theorem 5.15. *If wf-J-prog P and wf-start P C M vs, then*

$$J\text{-start } P\ C\ M\ vs\ _J\approx_{jvm}\ jvm\text{-start } (J2JVM\ P)\ C\ M\ vs.$$

255

Theorem 5.16. *In locale conf-read, if wf-J-prog P, then $(_J\approx_{jvm}, _J\sim_{jvm})$ is a delay bisimulation with explicit divergence that preserves final states.*

$$dbisim\text{-}div\ (J.redT\ P)\ (jvmd.redT\ (J2JVM\ P))\ _J\approx_{jvm}\ _J\sim_{jvm}$$
$$(J.m\tau\text{-}move\ P)\ (jvm.m\tau\text{-}move\ (J2JVM\ P))$$

$$dbisim\text{-}final\ (J.redT\ P)\ (jvmd.redT\ (J2JVM\ P))\ _J\approx_{jvm}\ _J\sim_{jvm}$$
$$(J.m\tau\text{-}move\ P)\ (jvm.m\tau\text{-}move\ (J2JVM\ P))$$
$$J.mfinal\ jvm.mfinal$$

All proofs have been conducted independently of the heap module implementation in various locales. Since $_1\approx_{jvm}^t$ imposes bytecode conformance on the JVM state to show that *exec-meth* and *exec-methd* are equivalent, Theorem 5.16 holds for all heap implementations that satisfy *conf-read*. These are sequential consistency (§4.2, Theorem 4.1) and JMM heap implementation 2 (§4.3.2, Theorem 4.2).

Since $_J\approx_{jvm}$ decomposes into the relations for each stage, I now can break down correctness in terms of bisimilarity to concrete executions ξ, i.e., trace equivalence, using the Theorems 5.1 and 5.2 about semantic preservation. As before, I decorate the semantics arrows with J and jvmd to refer to the definition with the parameters appropriately instantiated.

Theorem 5.17 (Correctness). *Let wf-J-prog and wf-start $P\ C\ M\ vs$.*

(a) *Let $P \vdash J\text{-}start\ P\ C\ M\ vs \Downarrow_J \xi$. Then, there is a ξ' such that $J2JVM\ P \vdash jvm\text{-}start\ (J2JVM\ P)\ C\ M\ vs \Downarrow_{jvmd} \xi'$ and $\xi\ [_J\approx_{jvm}, _J\sim_{jvm}]\ \xi'$. In particular:*

    (i) *If ξ terminates in s and $J.mfinal\ s$, then ξ' terminates in the jvm-final state mexception s.*

    (ii) *If ξ deadlocks in state s, then ξ' deadlocks in some s', too.*

    (iii) *If ξ diverges or runs infinitely, so does ξ'.*

(b) *Let $J2JVM\ P \vdash jvm\text{-}start\ (J2JVM\ P)\ C\ M\ vs \Downarrow_{jvmd} \xi'$. Then there is a ξ such that $P \vdash J\text{-}start\ P\ C\ M\ vs \Downarrow_J \xi$ and $\xi\ [_J\approx_{jvm}, _J\sim_{jvm}]\ \xi'$. In particular:*

    (i) *If ξ' terminates in s' and $jvm.mfinal\ s'$, then ξ terminates in some s such that $J.mfinal\ s$ and $s' = mexception\ s$.*

    (ii) *If ξ' deadlocks in state s', then ξ deadlocks in some s, too.*

    (iii) *If ξ' diverges or runs infinitely, so does ξ.*

In any case, ξ and ξ' produce the same sequence of events, i.e., map events $\xi = $ map events ξ' – in particular, the same output.

256

Proof outline. Case (a) states that every execution of the source code has a corresponding execution of the bytecode, and case (b) states the converse. The main statements directly follows from Theorems 5.1 and 5.2.

The subcases (i) to (iii) only specialise this statement to the concrete bisimulation. For a final J state s, the function *mexception s* extracts the correct exception flag for every thread in s, i.e., *None* for normal termination and $\lfloor a \rfloor$ if the exception at address a caused the abrupt termination.

Preservation of deadlocks in subcase (ii) does not follow directly, because I have defined deadlock in terms of the semantics of single threads, not the interleaved semantics that the bisimulation is about. However, Theorem 5.4 shows that $\overset{m}{\approx}_0$, $_0\overset{m}{\approx}_1$, and $_1\overset{m}{\approx}_{jvm}$ preserve deadlocks. For $_1\overset{m}{\approx}_1$, it is easy to show that the semantics for $J_1^{\#}$ and J_1' differ only in states that cannot be in deadlock. Hence, $_1\overset{m}{\approx}_1$ preserves deadlocks, too. Since s and s' are stuck by construction of ξ and ξ', there are no τ-moves that Theorem 5.4 would allow, i.e., s and s' are both deadlocked. □

While the above theorem correctly describes semantic preservation for sequential consistency, the JMM adds a few layers that are not yet reflected. First, the events for thread start and finish (layer 4) are missing. However, §5.1.4 explains how to extend the bisimulation relations $\overset{m}{\approx}_0$, $_0\overset{m}{\approx}_1$, and $_1\overset{m}{\approx}_{jvm}$ to handle them (Lemma 5.4). It is also straightforward to show that I can extend $_1\overset{m}{\approx}_1$ accordingly. Hence, Theorem 5.16 has an analogue for the JMM stack of semantics. Second, the layers 6 and 7 for complete interleavings and legality of executions not yet covered. By Corollary 5.1, delay bisimiliarity enforces that the complete interleavings of P and *J2JVM P* are the same. Thus, so are the legal executions.

Theorem 5.18. *Let wf-J-prog P and wf-start P C M vs. Then, (E, ws) is a legal execution of P with start state J-start P C M vs iff (E, ws) is a legal execution of J2JVM P with start state jvm-start $(J2JVM P)$ C M vs.*

Corollary 5.4. *Let wf-J-prog P and wf-start P C M vs. Then, P is correctly synchronised iff J2JVM P is.*

5.6 Discussion

Concurrency poses three challenges to verifying a compiler: (i) nondeterministic interleaving, (ii) different granularity of atomic operations between source and bytecode, and (iii) memory models for optimisations. In this chapter, I have addressed (i) and (ii).

For nondeterminism, I use bisimulation instead of forward simulation, in which only the compiled program simulates the source program. For bisimulation, it does not suffice to merely show the other direction, but some subtleties arise: First, neither the source nor the compiled program may carry on if the other gets stuck, e.g., due to type errors. In JinjaThreads, the source code semantics is a small-step semantics, whereas the VM is an abstract state machine. Both naturally contain different type checks, only a full type system and type safety proof at every stage would ensure bisimilarity. By using both the aggressive and defensive VM in the simulation proofs, I only need a single type safety proof for bytecode which ensures that both VMs are equivalent for verified bytecode. Therefore, the compiler verification only holds for type-safe heap implementations such as JMM heap implementation 2. In particular, the proofs do not hold for JMM heap implementation 1.

Second, the bisimulation must relate all states that are reachable from *either* initial state. Ordinary simulations do not have to relate intermediate states in the compiled code which the source code skips. This substantially increases the size of the bisimulation relation and consequently the number of cases the simulation proofs have to consider.

For example, several statements such as *sync* (_) _ generate multiple instructions. Hence, a single observable step in the source code program is decomposed into a number of silent steps and one observable step in between. Conversely, exceptions slowly propagate up in source code whereas the VM directly jumps to the exception handler.

The interleaving semantics, which I use at all stages, allows to decompose the multithreaded case to single threads, where shared memory accesses and synchronisation must be observable. Hence, I do not have to worry about interleavings in the main correctness proofs themselves. However, this approach also restricts the allowed optimisations to thread-local ones, because observable behaviour must not be changed. Consequently, I cannot exploit the additional flexibility that the JMM allows. For *J2JVM*, this is irrelevant because it just follows the recommendations in the JVMS [103, Ch. 7] and does not optimise at all. In fact, even Sun's javac compiler in Java 2 SE optimises only very little, but leaves this to the JIT compiler in the VM.

Classical compiler verifications only cover terminating executions, see, e.g., [83, 166]. My correctness result also extends to nontermination and deadlock. However, the standard (bi-)simulation approach with τ-moves cannot prove this, because infinitely many consecutive τ-moves might be simulated by no moves at all, which is known as the infinite stuttering problem. Instead, my notion of bisimulation explicitly includes divergence, but is nevertheless transitive unlike other approaches.

5.7 Related work

Compiler verification in general has been an active research topic for more than 40 years; see [44] for an annotated bibliography. Rittri [150] and Wand [174] first used bisimulations for compiler verification for a simple, parallel functional language. They showed that running the compiled code on a virtual machine is weakly bisimilar to the source code's denotational semantics, which ignores divergence.

Most closely related to JinjaThreads' compiler is naturally Jinja's [83, §5] which itself builds on Strecker's [167] for μJava as part of the VerifyCard project. They handle subsets of sequential JinjaThreads and are verified with respect to the big-step semantics.

More remotely, JinjaThreads' compiler is related to the one by Stärk et al. [166], which handles only sequential Java source code. As already pointed out in [83], they lack the formal rigour required for machine-checked proofs and their theorem does not imply preservation of non-terminating computations.

As for compiler verification for concurrent Java, Ševčík and Aspinall [162] report on verifying individual compiler optimisations w.r.t. the JMM. They show that (i) the JMM does not allow as many as intended by its designers for programs with data races, and (ii) all trace-preserving compilers are correct. However, their proofs are only on paper for a toy core language without almost all sequential Java features. Hecker [68] has verified two such transformations for the JMM in Isabelle/HOL.

Leroy's CompCert project [97–99] has been the most remarkable landmark in mechanised compiler verification recently. He has verified a complete compilation tool chain from a subset of C source code to PowerPC assembly language in Coq. CompCert focuses on low-level details and language features such as memory layout, register allocation and instruction selection. JinjaThreads's simulation diagrams for well-founded delay bisimulations are similar to CompCert's, but the latter only require the forward direction (the upper half of Figure 5.6) since CompCert's target language is deterministic.

As part of the Verisoft project, Leinenbach [96] has verified a non-optimising compiler from C0, a subset of C, directly to DLX assembler in Isabelle/HOL. Like CompCert, he focuses on low-level details and only proves a weak simulation theorem for sequential executions, but not for the backward direction.

Compiler correctness for concurrent programs is an active research under the aspect of memory models. Ševčík et al. [163] have extended parts of CompCert's backend to concurrency under the x86-TSO memory model (see §4.4.1). In [161], Ševčík studies what compiler optimisations are allowed under the DRF memory model, which provides only the DRF guarantee. Owens [140] and Batty et al. [16,17,154] verify the implementation of language primitives for synchronisation in assembly code for various hardware memory models. Lea [95] and McKenney and Silvera [117] have developed guidelines on how to implement the Java and C++ memory models in modern hardware. These works seem highly relevant for a potential future extension of JinjaThreads' compiler to machine code.

One challenge in the compiler verification was to prove that unlocking a monitor in bytecode never fails. My proof rests on the syntactic restrictions for the intermediate language. For arbitrary bytecode, Iwama and Kobayashi [73] propose to tag every object with a usage label which specifies a policy on how this object may be locked. A type system, for which they also give a type inference algorithm, guarantees that method implementations respect the usage tags, and the subject reduction theorem ensures soundness. It would be interesting to see whether their type system accepts the bytecode which *J2JVM* generates – since this would require a considerable extension of their language, I have not attempted to do so. If this held, I could avoid having two semantics of the intermediate language.

To tackle the same problem of proper lock acquisition and release, Laneve [94] presents an operational semantics and a type system for a slightly larger subset of Java bytecode which includes both synchronisation and the wait-notify mechanism. It enforces the structured locking principle that is known from Java source code. Moreover, the soundness proof gives that well-typed programs are free of *IllegalMonitorState* exceptions, even for calls to *wait* and *notify*. Unfortunately, this makes his type system unusable for the verification of JinjaThreads' compiler, because JinjaThreads allows calls to *wait* to fail like in Java.

One can't proceed from the informal to the formal by formal means.

Alan J. Perlis

JinjaThreads as a Java interpreter

Given the size and complexity of JinjaThreads, making sure that it faithfully models (a subset of) Java is non-trivial. Rushby [152] and Norrish [133] suggest three ways to address validation: (i) the social process of reviewing, publication, and reuse by others, (ii) challenging the specification by proving sanity theorems, and (iii) validation against a concrete implementation. JinjaThreads has gone all three ways to some extend. First, JinjaThreads continues the line of Bali, μJava, and Jinja. Hence, numerous publications in various venues [24, 79–87, 106, 107, 111–113, 126, 129, 130, 135–138, 146, 156–159, 167, 168] and its reuse in [37] support the claim of faithfulness. Type safety (Chapter 3) and in particular the compiler verification (Chapter 5) are excellent examples for the second. However, bugs may still hide in technical details that publications gloss over and in areas that sanity theorems fail to cover.

Therefore, this chapter takes the third route.[52] Using Isabelle's code generator, I obtain an executable interpreter, VM, and compiler from the formal definitions and validate the semantics by running Java test programs and comparing the results with Sun's reference implementation. To make the vast supply of Java programs available for testing, I also developed a translator Java2Jinja from Java to JinjaThreads abstract syntax (§6.5). By running these test cases, I found a bug in the implementation of binary operators (§6.5.2), which all previous proofs were unable to reveal. Although validation through testing can never prove the absence of errors, I am now confident that JinjaThreads faithfully models the Java subset that I claim.

---

[52]Excerpts of this chapter have been published in [113]. Although this is joint work with Lukas Bulwahn, this chapter presents only my work unless noted otherwise.

Another contribution beyond validation are the executable VM, bytecode verifier, and the compiler themselves, which I have automatically extracted from the formalisation. Under the assumption that Isabelle's code generator is correct, the extracted compiler is verified and the VM is type safe. In general, everything provable about the formalisation also applies to them. This is particularly important in the context of Quis Custodiet, which uses JinjaThreads to verify algorithms for enforcing information flow policies. Running the certified Java programs under the extracted VM ensures that the program behaves indeed as predicted by the static program analysis.

Efficiency of the extracted code matters for both validation through testing and running non-trivial programs, but JinjaThreads focuses on proofs and modularity. Hence, non-negligible complications in specifications and proofs for the sake of direct executability and efficiency were out of the question. In particular, only the compiler is directly executable, since it is written as a functional program. In §6.2 and §6.3, I demonstrate how to combine Isabelle's code extraction facilities (see §6.1 for an overview) such that (i) changes to the existing formalisation stay minimal and (ii) efficient implementations replace inefficient or even unexecutable ones. Empirical evidence shows that the VM is competitive in performance with another formalised JVM that has been designed for executability and efficiency from the start (§6.3.4).

From Bulwahn's and my experience, we have distilled simple guidelines on how to develop future formalisations with executability in mind (§6.4). Thus, JinjaThreads as a case study demonstrates that extracting efficient code from large developments is feasible – even if executability is of little concern in their design.

6.1 Isabelle code extraction facilities

In its most basic form, code extraction in Isabelle[53] converts functional programs in HOL into code in a functional programming language like Standard ML, Haskell, OCaml, and Scala. For example, Figure 6.1 shows

---

[53]In the recent Isabelle literature [61,62], the terms "code generation" and "generated code" refer to automatically obtaining (obtained) code in a functional programming language from formal specifications. To avoid ambiguities with the bytecode that JinjaThreads's compiler outputs, I use the older term "extraction" [22]. This must not be confused with Coq's extraction mechanism [102], which is based on the Curry-Howard isomorphism.

datatype *tree* = *Leaf* | *Node tree int tree*

fun *preorder* :: *tree* ⇒ *int list* **where**
   preorder Leaf = []
 | *preorder* (*Node l i r*) = *i* · *preorder l* @ *preorder r*

(a) Isabelle declaration of binary trees and preorder traversal

```
datatype tree = Leaf | Node of tree * IntInf.int * tree;
fun preorder Leaf = []
  | preorder (Node (l, i, r)) = i :: preorder l @ preorder r;
```

(b) Extracted ML code for *preorder*

```
data Tree = Leaf | Node Tree Integer Tree;
preorder :: Tree -> [Integer];
preorder Leaf = [];
preorder (Node l i r) = i : preorder l ++ preorder r;
```

(c) Extracted Haskell code for *preorder*

Figure 6.1: Preorder traversal for binary trees in Isabelle/HOL and the extracted code

the declaration of a binary tree datatype *tree* and a pre-order traversal *preorder* in Isabelle (a) and the extracted code in Standard ML (b) and Haskell (c). The extracted code directly mirrors the defining equations and uses the predefined types and operations for lists and integers.

It serves various purposes. It can be either interfaced and executed with other code (see the Java2Jinja tool in §6.5 for an example) or run in the theorem prover's process to assist the user in proving theorems. Examples for the latter are Isabelle's counter example generator Quickcheck [23,36] (§7.2), evaluation of ground terms [62], normalisation of HOL terms [5], and proof by normalisation [6].

6.1.1   The code generator

Isabelle's code generator [62] turns a set of equational theorems into a functional program with the same equational rewrite system, see Figure 6.1 for an example. As it builds on equational logic, the translation guarantees partial correctness by construction, because one could simulate every execution step in the functional language by rewriting with the corresponding equational theorem in the logic. Thus, every theorem also holds for any terminating execution of the code. For example, the type safety proof shows that the defensive VM as defined in Isabelle never gets stuck at a type error for programs that the bytecode verifier (§6.2.2) accepts. Thus, we can be sure that running verified bytecode never crashes the extracted JVM because of a type error, either.[54]

Since only equations matter, the user may easily refine programs and data without affecting her formalisation globally. Program refinement can separate code extraction issues from the rest of the formalisation. As any (executable) equational theorem suffices for code extraction, the user may *locally* derive new (code) equations to use upon code extraction. Hence, existing definitions and proofs remain unaffected, which has been crucial for JinjaThreads.

For example, consider the definition of the prefix relation *prefix* on lists in Figure 6.2. The code generator cannot use the original definition because it contains an existential quantifier which ranges over an infinite type. The user can prove the equations *prefix-code* that pattern-match on the list constructors [] and · such that the code generator uses them instead of the definition. Importantly, she does not touch the original definition, which might break some proofs.

For data refinement, she may replace constructors of a datatype by other constants and derive equations that pattern-match on these new (pseudo-)constructors. Neither need the new constructors be injective and pairwise disjoint, nor exhaust the type. Again, this is local as it affects only code extraction, but not the logical properties of the refined type. Thus, one cannot exploit inside the logic the type's new structure for code extraction. For example, the lower half of Figure 6.2 defines the pseudo-constructor *Lazy* for implementing lists lazily and states the appropriate code equation *prefix-Lazy* for *prefix*.

Only type constructors can be refined; some special types (such as $'a \rightharpoonup 'b$ for maps) must first be wrapped in an (isomorphic) type of their

---

[54] As equational logic has no notion of execution, the evaluation strategy of the target language still can cause abrupt or non-termination [22]. For example, the code for

definition $hd' :: 'a\ list \rightharpoonup 'a$ where $hd'\ xs = (let\ x = hd\ xs\ in\ if\ xs = []\ then\ None\ else\ \lfloor x \rfloor)$

raises a MATCH exception in ML when hd' is applied to the empty list, because ML's eager evaluation tries to compute $hd\ []$ although x is never used. In contrast, laziness in Haskell makes the definition work fine.

definition *prefix* :: *'a list* $\Rightarrow$ *'a list* $\Rightarrow$ *bool* where
$\quad$ *prefix xs ys* $\longleftrightarrow$ ($\exists zs.\ ys = xs \,@\, zs$)

lemma *prefix-code* [*code*]:
$\quad$ *prefix* [] *ys* $\longleftrightarrow$ *True* $\qquad$ *prefix* ($x \cdot xs$) [] $\longleftrightarrow$ *False*
$\quad$ *prefix* ($x \cdot xs$) ($y \cdot ys$) $\longleftrightarrow x = y \wedge$ *prefix xs ys*

definition *Lazy* :: (*unit* $\rightharpoonup$ *'a* $\times$ *'a list*) $\Rightarrow$ *'a list* where
$\quad$ *Lazy xs* = (*case xs* () *of None* $\Rightarrow$ [] | $\lfloor(x, xs')\rfloor \Rightarrow x \cdot xs$)

lemma *prefix-Lazy* [*code*]:
$\quad$ *prefix* (*Lazy xs*) (*Lazy ys*) =
$\quad\quad$ (*case xs* () *of None* $\Rightarrow$ *True*
$\quad\quad$ | $\lfloor(x, xs')\rfloor \Rightarrow$ (*case ys* () *of None* $\Rightarrow$ *False*
$\quad\quad\quad\quad$ | $\lfloor(y, ys')\rfloor \Rightarrow x = y \wedge$ *prefix xs' ys'*))

Figure 6.2: Program and data refinement for the prefix predicate on lists

own (e.g., (*'a, 'b*) *mapping*). Data refinement allows to implement them as associative lists or red-black trees.

6.1.2 The predicate compiler

The predicate compiler [21] translates specifications of inductive predicates, i.e., the introduction rules, into executable equational theorems for Isabelle's code generator. The translation is based on the notion of modes. A mode partitions the arguments into input and output. For a given predicate, the predicate compiler infers the set of possible modes such that all terms are ground during execution. Lazy sequences handle the non-determinism of inductive predicates. By default, the equations implement a Prolog-style depth-first execution strategy. Applying the predicate compiler to JinjaThreads' inductive definitions has initiated the following improvements by Bulwahn [113] over its initial description [21]:

First, mode annotations restrict the generation of code equations to modes of interest. This is necessary because the set of modes is exponential in the number of arguments of a predicate. Therefore, the space and time consumption of the underlying mode inference algorithm grows exponentially in that number; for all applications prior to JinjaThreads, this has never posed a problem. In case of many arguments (up to 15 in JinjaThreads), the plain construction of this set of modes burns up any available hardware resource. To sidestep this limitation, modes can now be declared and hence they are not inferred, but only checked to be consistent.

Second, he improved the compilation scheme: The previous one sequentially checked which of the introduction rules were applicable. Hence, the input values were repeatedly compared to the terms in the conclusion of each introduction rule by pattern matching. For large specifications, such as JinjaThreads' semantics (contains 89 rules), this naïve compilation made execution virtually impossible due to the large number of rules. To obtain an efficient code expression, he modified the compilation scheme to partition the rules by patterns of the input values first and then only compose the matching rules – this resembles similar techniques in Prolog compilers, such as clause indexing and switch detection. I report on the performance improvements due to this modification in §6.3.4.

Third, the predicate compiler now offers non-intrusive program refinement, i.e. the user can declare alternative introduction rules. For an example, see §6.3.1.

Fourth, the predicate compiler was originally limited to the restricted syntactic form of introduction rules. Bulwahn added some preprocessing that transforms definitions in predicate logic to a set of introduction rules [36]. For example, the predicate compiler now directly processes the definition of type-safe method overriding *wf-overriding* in Figure 2.9.

6.1.3 Data structures

Typically, definitions in proof assistants use standard HOL types for data structures instead of concrete implementations, e.g., $'a \rightharpoonup 'b$ instead of associative lists or red-black trees. This reduces clutter, because proofs need not deal with different representations of the map. Such maps occur in JinjaThreads source code as environment for typing judgements, the local store, and the heap in the SC implementation. For code extraction, however, this approach can lead to highly inefficient code or completely defy extraction (§6.3.4).

Isabelle's standard library provides associative lists and red-black trees as backing implementations for maps and sets via data refinement (§6.1.1), i.e., the code can treat sets and maps as data. As part of my work, I have generalised this concept to FinFuns [108, 109]. A FinFun is a function that is almost-everywhere constant. Via data refinement, it is implemented as an associative list that additionally stores the function's value outside the domain of the associative list. For example, a finite map would store the default value *None*, a finite set – modelled as a predicate – *False*, and complements of finite sets *True*. Since the FinFun type $'a \Rightarrow_f 'b$ contains only almost-everywhere constant functions, quantifiers and function equality are decidable. JinjaThreads uses FinFuns for managing the locks (§3.1.1) and storing lock BTAs in thread actions (§3.1.2).

Some operations remain unexecutable though, since data refinement does not enrich the refined type's structure. For example, iteration over a finite set remains unexecutable when the result depends on the order in which the iteration visits the elements. The Isabelle Collections Framework (ICF) [91, 92] (joint work with Peter Lammich) advocates dealing with refinement explicitly in the logic instead of hiding it in the code generator. Locales abstractly specify the operations, concrete implementations interpret them. This allows for executing truly underspecified functions. Additionally, the ICF provides more data structures (tries and hashing) and a uniform interface for accessing them. JinjaThreads uses the ICF for refining the non-deterministic interleaving semantics with a scheduler.

6.1.4 Locales and code extraction

Locales and code extraction do not (yet) go well together. As code extraction requires equational theorems in the (foundational) theory context, equational theorems that reside in the context of a locale cannot serve as code equations directly, but must be transferred into the theory context.[55] For a simple example, consider a locale L with one parameter p, one assumption $A\,p$ and one definition $f = \ldots$ that depends on p. Let g be a function in the theory context for which $A\,(g\,z)$ holds for all z. I want to generate code for f where p is instantiated to $g\,z$.

The Isabelle code generator tutorial [61] proposes interpretation and definition: One instantiates p by $g\,z$ and discharges the assumption with $A\,(g\,z)$, for arbitrary z. This yields the code equation $L.f\,(g\,z) = \ldots$, which is ill-formed because the left-hand side applies f to the non-constructor constant g. For code extraction, one must manually define a

---

[55]Similarly, the predicate compiler only operates on introduction rules in the theory context, i.e. the same restrictions and solutions apply.

new function f' by $f' z = L.f(g z)$ and derive $f' z = \ldots$ as code equation. This approach is unsatisfactory for two reasons: It requires to manually re-define all dependent locale definitions in the theory context (and for each interpretation), and the interpretation must be unconditional, i.e. $A(g z)$ must hold for all z. In JinjaThreads, the latter is often violated, e.g. $g z$ satisfies A only if z is well-formed.

To overcome these deficiencies, my new approach splits the locale L into two: L-base and L^*. L-base fixes the parameter p and defines f; L^* inherits from L-base, assumes $A\ p$, and contains the theorems and proofs from L. Since L-base makes no assumptions about p, the locale implementation exports the equation $f = \ldots$ in L-base as an unconditional equation L-base.$f\ p = \ldots$ in the theory context, which directly serves as code equation. For execution, I merely pass $g z$ to L-base.f. I use this scalable approach throughout JinjaThreads. Its drawback is that the existence of a model for f, as required for its definition, must not depend on L's assumptions; e.g., the termination argument of a general recursive function must not require L's assumptions. Many typical definitions (all in JinjaThreads) satisfy this restriction.

6.2 Static semantics

The static semantics fall into generic well-formedness constraints (Figure 2.9) and language-specific ones (Figure 2.10 and §2.2.3). In this section, I describe what is necessary to obtain an executable well-formedness checker for source code and bytecode.

6.2.1 Generic well-formedness

Generic well-formedness (Figure 2.9) poses little problems to code extraction. The direct subclass relation $P \vdash \_ <^1 \_$ and its reflexive transitive closure (RTC) $P \vdash \_ \leq^* \_$ and the subtype relation $P \vdash \_ \leq \_$ are inductive predicates that the predicate compiler preprocesses. So does it for *wf-overriding* thanks to Bulwahn's recent extensions in its preprocessor. Further, since all universal quantifiers are bound by lists, they pose no problem either. Hence, it is easy to extract code for *wf-prog*.

It is harder to see that the extracted code might not terminate for programs with cyclic class hierarchies. The subclass relation $P \vdash \_ \leq^* \_$ builds on the RTC and the prolog-style execution for RTC might loop in the hierarchy's cycle. Instead, I configure the code generator to use a tabled RTC by Berghofer [113, §2.3]. This ensures that querying $P \vdash \_ \preceq^* \_$ always terminates, i.e., wf-prog reliably detects cyclic class hierarchies.

Even less obvious, another source of non-termination hides in the order in which the various well-formedness constraints are executed. wf-prog calls wf-cdecl for all classes in P in the order in which they appear in P – and wf-cdecl checks that the current class is not part of a cycle in the class hierarchy (condition $\neg P \vdash D \preceq^* C$). Hence, when the other predicates of wf-cdecl are being executed, there still may be some undetected cycle in other parts of the hierarchy – in particular, superclasses may be part of that. But method lookup as used in wf-overriding recurses over the class hierarchy and – like the default setup for $P \vdash \_ \preceq^* \_$ – might not terminate. The simplest fix is to check acyclicity up-front. Hence, the code generator uses the following equation for wf-prog:

$$\textit{wf-prog wf-md } P \longleftrightarrow$$
$$\textit{acyclic-hierarchy } P \wedge \textit{wf-syscls } P \wedge$$
$$\textit{distinct } (\textit{map fst } P) \wedge (\forall cd \in \textit{set } (\textit{classes } P).\ \textit{wf-cdecl}' \textit{ wf-md } P\ cd)$$

$$\textit{acyclic-hierarchy } P \longleftrightarrow$$
$$(\forall(C, D, ms, fs) \in \textit{set } (\textit{classes } P).\ C \neq \textit{Object} \longrightarrow \neg P \vdash D \preceq^* C)$$

where wf-cdecl' differs from wf-cdecl only in that wf-cdecl' omits the acyclicity test $\neg P \vdash D \preceq^* C$.

Both sources of non-termination have already flawed Jinja's and μJava's bytecode verifiers. They are generally hard to track down, because HOL cannot reflect the notion of computation that is inherent in the extracted code. Hence, only extensive testing as I have done for JinjaThreads with Quickcheck (§7.2) and Java2Jinja (§6.5) can provide some level of confidence.

6.2.2 The bytecode verifier

The bytecode verifier has to check statically that every execution of the program meets at run-time the assumptions that the VM makes (§2.2.3). To that end, the JVMS [103] specifies a verification procedure that interprets bytecode methods abstractly. Like Jinja, JinjaThreads models the verification as a data flow analysis (DFA) using Klein's DFA framework [79]. The abstract values are state types, applicability app and effect eff implement the transfer functions (see §2.2.3). Hence, bytecode verification is to compute a solution to the data flow problem, using the summary information for methods, i.e. parameter and return types, from the program declaration. Any solution of the data flow analysis yields a consistent method-well typing. Since JinjaThreads only extends Jinja's bytecode verifier to the new instructions, I omit a detailed presentation and refer the interested reader to [83].

The DFA framework solves DFA problems using Kildall's worklist algorithm [78] under the following prerequisites that ensure correctness and termination: First, there is no infinitely ascending chain of valid types, all transfer functions are monotone and preserve validity of types. Second, the least upper bound of two abstract values is computable and a valid type.

Only proving the ascending chain condition (ACC, notation acc) and computing least upper bounds (lub) are novel. In Jinja, the set of valid types is finite, i.e., acyclicity of the class hierarchy ensures the ACC. JinjaThreads, however, contains infinitely many types due to unbounded array dimensions. In fact, as described in §2.1.2, the subtype relation does contain infinitely ascending chains. The key to proving ACC and computing lubs is that single inheritance in JinjaThreads allows to organise valid reference types other than NT in a tree rooted at $Class\ Object$ such that valid supertypes are exactly the transitive parents – see Figure 2.6 for the Hasse diagram. Hence, the distance from the root $Class\ Object$, i.e., the depth, is a measure on array and class types for subtyping. The function $inheritance\text{-}level\ P\ C$ recurses over P's class hierarchy to determine the number of superclasses of C; the acyclicity check ensures that the recursion always terminates. Then, the function $subtype\text{-}measure$ computes the depth in the tree.

$$
\begin{aligned}
subtype\text{-}measure\ P\ (Class\ C) &= inheritance\text{-}level\ P\ C \\
subtype\text{-}measure\ P\ (T[]) &= 1 + subtype\text{-}measure\ P\ T \\
subtype\text{-}measure\ P\ \_ &= 0
\end{aligned}
$$

$$
\begin{aligned}
&inheritance\text{-}level\ P\ C = \\
&\quad (if\ acyclic\ (P \vdash \_ <^1 \_) \wedge is\text{-}class\ P\ C \wedge C \neq Object \\
&\quad\ then\ let\ \lfloor (D, \_, \_) \rfloor = class\ P\ C\ in\ inheritance\text{-}level\ P\ D + 1 \\
&\quad\ else\ 0)
\end{aligned}
$$

Hence, subtyping on valid class and array types has no infinitely ascending chain. From this, it follows easily that subtyping on valid types has no such chain either.

Lemma 6.1. *If wf-prog wf-md P, then acc (types P) $(P \vdash \_ \leq \_)$.*

The above tree structure of the subtype relation also allows to extend Jinja's iterative algorithm for computing lubs on class names to valid types. If both types T_1 and T_2 are class or array types, start with T at T_1 and keep ascending in the tree until T is a supertype of T_2. Then, T is the lub of T_1 and T_2. Otherwise, the lub does not depend on the program and therefore can be hardwired.

Using Klein's DFA framework, I obtain an executable bytecode verifier to decide the bytecode-specific well-formedness constraints. Hence, *wf-jvm-prog* is executable.

In μJava, Klein [79] bounds the number of array dimensions by 255 as the JMVS does [103] due to syntactic restrictions of the class file format. Thus, the type universe is finite and the ascending chain condition reduces to acyclicity. Moreover, Klein's bytecode verifier computes sets of types instead of taking the least upper bound. Hence, he does not need to derive an executable lub implementation. The same would be possible for JinjaThreads, because one could compute a bound on the dimensions for every program. However, I conjecture that dealing with sets is less efficient than computing lubs. Moreover, type checking source code needs executable lubs anyway (§6.2.3).

6.2.3 Type inference for source code

Source code well-formedness (Figure 2.10) requires well-typedness of the method body. Hence, a well-formedness checker must include a type checker, but even type checking requires type inference. Consider, e.g., the typing judgement for assignment to array cells below, which repeats WTAAss from Figure 2.7.

$$\frac{P, E \vdash e_1 :: T[] \qquad P, E \vdash e_2 :: Integer \qquad P, E \vdash e_3 :: T' \qquad P \vdash T' \leq T}{P, E \vdash e_1[e_2] := e_3 :: Void}$$

When the predicate compiler compiles $\_, \_ \vdash \_ :: \_$, mode analysis must ensure that all variables are assigned to ground terms when the modes of the assumptions consider them as input. Type checking corresponds to the mode where all parameters are input, type inference assigns output to the expression type. Since P, E, e_1, e_2, and e_3 occur in input positions in the conclusion of WTAAss in either case, they pose no problem. However,

271

the first and third premise require T and T' to be ground for type checking. Hence, the predicate compiler can choose to either enumerate all pairs (T', T) for which the subtype relation $P \vdash T' \leq T$ holds, or infer e_1's and e_3's type and check for $P \vdash T' \leq T$, or any combination thereof. Note that in case $e_1[e_2] := e_3$ is type-incorrect, only the second option terminates always, because $Class\ Object\ (NT)$ has infinitely many subtypes (supertypes). To force the predicate compiler choose right, mode annotations allow only mode "everything input" for the subtype relation.

For type inference, the rule for the conditional operator $\_\ ?\ \_\ :\ \_$ in Java requires to compute the lub of the types of the second and third argument [56, §15.25]. As the declarative definition of the type system uses the declarative lub definition (WTcond), type inference (and thus type checking) is not executable. Therefore, I have parametrised $\_,\_\vdash\_::\_$ by the lub operation. The standard version takes the declarative lub predicate from §2.1.2, the one for code extraction the executable lub implementation of the bytecode verifier (§6.2.2). Then, I prove that both versions agree on acyclic class hierarchies rooted at $Object$, but I cannot refine the declarative definition because equality only holds under acyclicity. Since generic well-formedness ensures the precondition, $wf\text{-}J\text{-}mdecl$ can use the executable version.

After these preparations, well-formedness for source code no longer poses any difficulties for code extraction. Note that all the setup is transparent to the existing formalisation.

6.3 Interpreter and virtual machine

In this section, I describe the obstacles on the way to an executable source code interpreter and an executable virtual machine, and how to overcome them.

6.3.1 The single-threaded semantics

Memory model

For code extraction, I only use sequential consistency as heap module implementation (§4.2), because the legality constraints of the JMM are axiomatic and thus not executable. As sketched in Figure 2.11, sequential consistency models the heap as a partial function from addresses (natural

RPARAMX:
$$P, t \vdash \langle Val\ v.M(map\ Val\ vs\ @\ Throw\ a \cdot es), s \rangle \\ -\langle\!|\rangle \rightarrow \langle Throw\ a, s \rangle$$

RPARAMX$_2$:
$$\frac{is\text{-}Throws\ es}{P, t \vdash \langle Val\ v.M(es), s \rangle - \langle\!|\rangle \rightarrow \langle hd\ (dropWhile\ is\text{-}Val\ es), s \rangle}$$

Figure 6.3: Original and alternative introduction rule of the small-step semantics

numbers) to objects and arrays. Allocation must find a fresh address, i.e., one not in the heap's domain. Originally, this was defined via Hilbert's underspecified (and thus not executable) ε-operator as in (6.1). For code extraction, I had to change *new-Addr*'s specification to the least fresh address, replacing ε with *LEAST*. Then, I proved (6.2) and (6.3) to search for the least fresh address.

$$new\text{-}Addr\ h$$
$$= if\ (\exists a.\ h\ a = None)\ then \lfloor \varepsilon a.\ h\ a = None \rfloor\ else\ None \qquad (6.1)$$
$$new\text{-}Addr\ h = gen\text{-}new\text{-}Addr\ h\ 0 \qquad (6.2)$$
$$gen\text{-}new\text{-}Addr\ h\ n$$
$$= if\ (h\ n = None)\ then\ \lfloor n \rfloor\ else\ gen\text{-}new\text{-}Addr\ h\ (n+1) \qquad (6.3)$$

Small-step semantics

The small-step semantics $P, t \vdash \langle e, (h, xs) \rangle -ta \rightarrow \langle e', (h', xs) \rangle$ is another inductive predicate. The predicate compiler processes 84 of 88 introduction rules automatically. For the others, I must provide alternative introduction rules via program refinement. Figure 6.3 shows the rule RPARAMX for propagating the exception raised while evaluating the parameters, which is representative for the four. This rule violates the desired mode for executing the semantics because its execution would require pattern-matching against the term *map Val vs @ Throw a · es*. The remedy is to declare the alternative introduction rule RPARAMX$_2$: It replaces the problematic term by a fresh variable *es* and instead uses the guard *is-Throws es* with the following inductive definition.

$$is\text{-}Throws\ (Throw\ a \cdot es) \qquad \frac{is\text{-}Throws\ es}{is\text{-}Throws\ (Val\ v \cdot es)}$$

To obtain *Throw a* as the reduced expression, *dropWhile is-Val* removes *es*'s prefix of values until the head is the raised exception. To ensure that the alternative introduction rules replace the definitional ones in a complete manner, I have to prove the elimination rule that corresponds to the new introduction rules, a technically difficult, but conceptionally straightforward task.

Mode annotations for executing the small-step semantics are crucial. The abstraction of the heap module in the locale *heap-base* adds seven parameters to the small-step semantics in the theory context, which consequently allows a monstrous number of modes.

Virtual machine

The single-threaded VM poses no significant challenges for code extraction, because it is written as a functional program. Unfortunately, the code generator does not yet support set comprehensions over predicates such as *read* and *write*. Hence, I adapt the equations for accessing the heap like in Figure 4.5 to directly use their functional implementation produced by the predicate compiler.

6.3.2 Schedulers

Executing the interleaving semantics from Chapter 3 poses three problems:

1. The thread pool and the wait sets are modelled as functions of type $\_ \Rightarrow \_$ *option*. Neither quantifying over these maps' domains (e.g. to decide whether all threads have terminated) nor picking one of its elements (e.g. to remove an arbitrary thread from a wait set upon notification) are executable.

2. The state space of all possible interleavings is usually too large to be effectively enumerable. Therefore, one wants to pick one typical interleaving.

3. JinjaThreads programs that might not terminate should at least produce a prefix of the observable operations of such an infinite run.

To address the first, I previously [109] proposed to replace these maps with FinFuns, a generalisation of finite maps. Although quantification over the domain then becomes executable, it turned out that choosing an underspecified element remains unexecutable. I therefore use them only for lock management (§3.1.1). For the thread pool and the wait sets, I instead follow the approach of the Isabelle Collections Framework [92]. In the refined multithreaded state, I replace the concrete functions with modules, i.e., type variables and abstract operations that I specify in two locales. Picking an arbitrary element remains underspecified, but this is now explicit inside the logic, not HOL's metalogic. Before code extraction, I instantiate the locales with concrete data structure implementations like red-black trees and thus resolve the underspecification.

As to the second problem, I do not use the predicate compiler for $\_ -\_:\_\to \_$ and $\_ -\_\to^* \_$, as it would produce a depth-first search that enumerates all possible interleavings. The first few interleavings would be such that one thread executes completely (or until it blocks), then the next thread executes completely, etc. Interesting interleavings would occur only very much later – or never at all, if one of the preceding ones did not terminate. Instead, I let a scheduler pick the next thread at each step.

Formally, a scheduler consists of two operations (that I specify abstractly in two locales again): The function *schedule* takes the scheduler's state and the refined multithreaded state, and returns either a thread together with its next transition and the updated scheduler state, or *None* to denote that the execution has finished or is deadlocked. The other function *wakeup* chooses from a monitor's wait set the thread to be notified. In terms of these two functions, I define a deterministic, executable step function that updates the multithreaded state just like the non-deterministic interleaving semantics does. To obtain a complete interleaving as a potentially infinite trace, I corecursively unfold this step function. Then, I formally prove that this in fact yields an interleaving.

I have instantiated this specification with two concrete schedulers: a round-robin scheduler and a random scheduler based on a pseudo-random number generator. The most intricate problem is how to obtain (as a function) the thread's step from the (relational) small-step semantics, once the scheduler has decided which thread to execute. Fortunately, the semantics under SC is deterministic, if one considers only transitions whose preconditions are met by the current state. Thus, I use Bulwahn's executable version of Russell's definite descriptor [113].

Corecursive traces also solve the third problem. I instruct the code generator to implement possibly infinite lists lazily. For Haskell, this is the default; for the other target languages, data and program refinement provide an easy setup.

1 **datatype** $'m\ prog = Program\ 'm\ cdecl\ list$
2 **definition** $prog\text{-}impl\text{-}invar\ P'\ c\ s\ f\ m =$
   $(c = Mapping\ (class\ (Program\ P')) \wedge \dots)$
3 **typedef** $'m\ prog\text{-}impl = \{\,(P',c,s,f,m).\ prog\text{-}impl\text{-}invar\ P'\ c\ s\ f\ m\,\}$
   morphisms $impl\text{-}of\ Abs\text{-}prog$
4 **definition** $ProgDecl = Program \circ fst \circ impl\text{-}of$
5 **code_datatype** $ProgDecl$
6 **lemma** $[code]$: $class\ (ProgDecl\ P) = lookup\ (fst\ (snd\ (impl\text{-}of\ P)))$
7 **definition** $tabulate\ P' = Abs\text{-}prog\ (P', tab\text{-}class\ P', tab\text{-}subcls\ P', \dots)$
8 **lemma** $[code]$: $Program = ProgDecl \circ tabulate$
9 **fun** $compP\text{-}impl\ f\ (P,c,s,f,m) =$
   $(let\ P' = map\ (compC\ f)\ P\ in\ (P', tab\text{-}class\ P', s, f, tab\text{-}method\ P'))$
10 **definition** $compP'\ f = Abs\text{-}prog\ \circ compP\text{-}impl\ f \circ impl\text{-}of$
11 **lemma** $[code]$: $compP\ f\ (ProgDecl\ P) = ProgDecl\ (compP'\ f\ P)$

Figure 6.4: Tabulation for lookup functions and the subclass relation

6.3.3 Tabulation

An execution of a JinjaThreads program frequently checks type casts and performs method lookups. However, with the above setup, the semantics recomputes the subtype relation and lookup functions at every type cast and method call from scratch. Now, I show how to leverage program and data refinement to avoid such recomputations with only minimal changes to the formalisation itself. I precompute the subclass relation, field and method lookup (a standard technique for VMs) and store them in mappings – Isabelle's special-purpose type for maps, see §6.1.1. Figure 6.4 sketches the necessary steps.

Remember that a JinjaThreads program declaration wraps the list of class declarations in a type of its own (l. 1 in Figure 6.4, repeated from Figure 2.3).

First, I define the type $'m\ prog\text{-}impl$ (l. 3); the morphisms $impl\text{-}of$ and $Abs\text{-}prog$ translate between the new type and the set of its elements. Apart from the original program declaration (as a list P'), the elements (P',c,s,f,m) consist of mappings from class names to (i) the class declaration (c), (ii) the set of its superclasses (s), and (iii) two mappings for field and method lookup with field and method names as keys (f and m). The invariant $prog\text{-}impl\text{-}invar$ (l. 2) states that the mappings correctly tabulate the lookup functions and subclass relation. Then, I define (l. 4) and declare (l. 5) the new constructor $ProgDecl :: 'm\ prog\text{-}impl \Rightarrow 'm\ prog$ for data refinement, which (in the logic) only extracts the program declaration.

For the lookup functions, the subclass relation, and the associated constants that the predicate compiler has introduced, I next prove code equations that implement them via lookup in the respective mapping – see l. 6 for class declaration lookup. This program refinement suffices to avoid recomputing lookup functions and the subclass relation during execution.

However, the extracted code now expects the input program to come with the correctly precomputed mappings. Thus, I define $tabulate$ (l. 7) and auxiliary functions (not shown) that tabulate the lookup functions and subclass relation in these mappings for a given list P' of class declarations. Finally, I implement the former constructor $Program$ in terms of $tabulate$ and $ProgDecl$ (l. 8).

As the representation of programs has changed, I must also adapt the compiler. The function $compP\text{-}impl$ is $compP$'s analogon on the representation of type $'m\ prog\text{-}impl$ (l. 9). First, it compiles all classes and then rebuilds the tabulations for $class$ and $method$. Since compilation does not change the subclass relation or field lookup, their tabulations need not be recomputed. $compP'$ takes $compP\text{-}impl$ to the new type $'m\ prog\text{-}impl$ (l. 10). Finally, I derive the new code equation for $compP$ (l. 11).

6.3.4 Efficiency of the interpreter

Although I cannot expect the generated interpreter to be as efficient as an optimising JVM, to see whether it is suited to run small programs, I have evaluated it on a standard producer-buffer-consumer example; Appendix A contains the code. The producer thread allocates n objects and enqueues them in the ring buffer, which can store ten elements at the same time. Concurrently, the consumer thread dequeues n objects from the buffer. Table 6.1 lists the running times of the source code interpreter for different code generator setups. All tests ran on a Pentium DualCore E5300 2.6 GHz with 2GB RAM using MLton 20100608 and Ubuntu GNU/Linux 9.10. The figures are the average of four runs for each setup.

With the adaptations from §6.3.1 and §6.3.2 only, the code is unbearably slow (column 1). For $n = 100$, interpreting the program takes 38 min, i.e., 2,320.35 s. As the main bottleneck, I identified the naïve compilation scheme for the small-step semantics. Switching to the improved compilation scheme in the predicate compiler (§6.1.2) speeds up the

n	default setup	with indexing	almost strict	heap as RBT	tabu-lation
10	236.51	3.40	.12	.11	.09
100	2,320.35	31.03	1.71	.99	.86
1,000	—	—	579.76	9.84	8.67
10,000	—	—	—	91.77	81.73
100,000	—	—	—	1,394.93	1,280.62

Table 6.1: Timing (in seconds) for running the producer-consumer example (Appendix A) on n objects for different adjustments to the source code interpreter; — denotes timeout after 1 h

interpreter by two orders of magnitude (column 2). The definite descriptor ι that extracts the result configuration from the enumerations, strictly evaluates all branches. Hence, explicit laziness in the generated code is unnecessary. If I remove the most obvious constructions that enforce laziness from the code equations that were compiled under the improved scheme, a program run with $n = 100$ takes only 1.71 s (column 3).

As n increases, another bottleneck shows up: memory allocation (cf. §6.3.1). Since the heap is modelled as a function and writes as function updates, i.e., closures, finding the next fresh address takes time quadratic in the number of previous allocations. Thus, interpreting the example program is quadratic in n although the program itself only requires linearly many steps. To speed up allocation and read access, I implemented the heap module (§4.1.1) for sequential consistency a second time with efficient data structures from the ICF: The heap is now a red-black tree (RBT) with addresses as keys, the array cell list becomes an RBT with indices as keys, and tries implement the field tables. Combined with the other improvements, this already provides a decent interpreter (column 4): Run times grow linearly in n as expected. $n = 100,000$ is an outlier because memory consumption exceeds the two 2 GB of physical memory and garbage collection of the ML runtime environment runs frequently.

Finally, I also added tabulation (§6.3.3), where the mappings are for simplicity implemented as associative lists. Surprisingly, the speed-up (less than 15%) is modest. The reason might be the tiny class hierarchy of the example program for which lookup functions terminate quickly.

n	default setup	heap as RBT	tabu- lation	caching w/o tabulation	tabulation & caching
10	1.00	.03	.01	.02	.01
100	1.81	.11	.07	.07	.06
1,000	23.68	1.07	.70	.61	.62
10,000	—	10.97	7.07	6.21	6.29
100,000	—	109.90	71.12	62.36	63.05

Table 6.2: Timing (in seconds) for running the producer-consumer example (Appendix A) on n objects for different setups of the virtual machine; — denotes timeout after 1 h.

I also ran the tests with the code generated in Haskell (compiled with Glasgow Haskell Compiler 6.10.4) and OCaml (compiled to native code with OCaml 3.11.1). The Haskell code is about 50% slower than ML and the OCaml code takes between 2 and 5 times as much time as MLton. Nevertheless, the different adjustments to the interpreter affect the run times similarly to ML.

I have also compiled the example program with JinjaThreads' compiler and run it in the virtual machine. Table 6.2 shows the timings for the VM – again with different setups. Although the VM is much faster than the source code interpreter, the VM is still relatively slow under the default setup (column 1). Like for source code, switching to red-black trees helps (column 2). Tabulation (column 3) has a much greater effect (35% speed-up) on the VM, because the VM performs method lookup at every step to retrieve the next instruction to execute. Therefore, I implemented a second VM that caches the instruction list and exception table in the call frames. With the heap as RBT, this gains another 12% in performance over tabulation (column 4). Surprisingly, combining tabulation and caching slightly slows the VM down (column 5). Since the performance loss is not a constant, it is unlikely that building the lookup tables is the reason. Rather, I suspect that the more complicated type representation for JinjaThreads programs impairs MLton's optimiser, since the same effect is much stronger (20% slow-down) under PolyML 5.4.1, which optimises less aggressively.

Although the VM run-times are already decent (about one minute for 100,000 objects), the interpreter and VM are still far from a commercial VM: The Java HotSpot VM takes only 150 ms for 100,000 objects.

In [104], Lui and Moore test their JVM formalisation M6 in ACL2 on a simple parallel factorial algorithm. To compare my interpreter with theirs, I have converted the Java program to JinjaThreads with the Java2Jinja tool (§6.5). For computing 10! with five threads in parallel, the source code semantics takes 26.7 s and the VM just 0.2 s. The M6 takes 6.2 s when run in the ACL2 interpreter, version 2.7 with GNU CLISP 2.42. Hence, JinjaThreads and the M6 have comparable performance.

6.4 Guidelines for executable formalisations

From Bulwahn's and my experience with JinjaThreads, we have distilled the following guidelines to easily obtain executable formalisations in Isabelle/HOL.

Avoid Hilbert's ε-operator! Hilbert's choice cannot express under-specification adequately as, in HOL's model, its interpretation is fully specified. Partial correctness of the code generator guarantees that all evaluations in the functional language hold in every model. Thus, one cannot replace it by any implementing function that chooses one suitable value consistently and fixes the underspecified function to one concrete model. Instead, use one of the following options:

1. Change the definition to make the choice deterministic and imple-mentable, e.g., always pick the least element.

2. Use locales for intra-logical underspecification and instantiate the choice operator to a concrete implementation by locale interpreta-tion.

3. Switch to a relational description and prove the correctness for all values.

The first is least intrusive to the formalisation, but requires changes to the original specification. To execute the deterministic choice, one needs to run the predicate compiler on the choice property and use Bulwahn's executable definite descriptor for predicates [113], or implement a suitable search algorithm via program refinement. I use the former in the scheduler (§6.3.2) and the latter for memory allocation (§6.3.1).

The second is the most flexible option, but also tedious, as the locale does not automatically setup proof automation and lacks true polymorphism. I use this approach, e.g., to specify schedulers (§6.3.2). Care must be taken in combination with data refinement via the code generator, as the choice must not depend on the additional structure that the interpretation introduces.

The last option completely avoids underspecification, but relinquishes the functional implementation. For code extraction, one should either (i) apply the predicate compiler to obtain code that computes all possible implementations for the specification, or (ii) provide a functional implementation and show correctness (§6.3.2). For the latter, one must typically replace the involved types with others that have additional structure.

Structure locales wisely!   Modular specifications, i.e., locales, and code extraction do not (yet) go well together (see §6.1.4). To combine them, one best adheres to the following discipline: One locale *Sig* fixes the parameters' signatures and contains all definitions that depend on the parameters. Another locale *Spec* extends *Sig* and states the assumptions about the parameters; all proofs that depend on the assumptions go into *Spec*. For functions and inductive predicates of *Sig*, one feeds the equational theorems and introduction rules exported into the theory context to the code generator or predicate compiler, respectively. To obtain the (correctness) theorems, instantiate *Spec* and prove the assumptions. I have used this approach throughout JinjaThreads.

Annotate predicates with modes!   Mode annotations for predicates instruct the predicate compiler to generate only modes of interest, not all modes that its mode analysis can infer. They provide three benefits. First, if the predicate has many parameters, analysing all modes can quickly become computationally intractable (cf. §6.3.1) – in this case, they are necessary. Second, they ease maintenance and debugging as they fail immediately after adjustments: If changes in the development disable a mode of interest, an error message indicates which clauses are to blame. Without annotations, the missing mode might remain undiscovered until much later, which then complicates correcting errors. Third, some not annotated, but inferable modes might lead to generation of slow or non-terminating functions. By disallowing them, the predicate compiler cannot accidentally pick one of them when it compiles a subsequent predicate.

6.5 The translator Java2Jinja

Formalisations in the size of JinjaThreads require better validation than manually scrutinising the definitions and comparing them to the language specification. One way of validating the semantics is to execute test programs and check for the expected result. However, JinjaThreads' syntax is different from and only a subset of Java's.

Hence, to make the vast supply of Java programs available, Jonas Thedering, Antonio Zea, and I have developed the conversion tool Java2Jinja[56] as a plugin to the Eclipse IDE with the following modes of operation. First, it translates Java class hierarchies into JinjaThreads abstract syntax, emulating many unsupported Java features. Second, it provides a frontend to the well-formedness checker (§6.2), interpreter (§6.3), and compiler (§5.5) that I have extracted from the formalisation using Isabelle's code generator. Third, it can automatically run full test suites where command-line arguments and the expected output are provided as Java annotations in the programs.

Being implemented in Java and on top of the Eclipse Java Development Tools (JDT), the translator itself defies formal verification. The possibility for introducing errors is negligible for the subset of Java that JinjaThreads directly models, because the translations are minuscule. However, even small Java programs require some parts of the Java standard API which exceed this subset, e.g., class String. Therefore, Java2Jinja emulates these features with non-trivial, unverified transformations (§6.5.1), which possibly introduce errors. I have extensively tested Java2Jinja (§6.5.2), but this naturally cannot prove their absence. These threats could only be avoided if JinjaThreads was extended to support the missing features, which are mostly of sequential nature. However, this is beyond the scope of this work.

Figure 6.5 shows Java2Jinja's user interface. When the user invokes the conversion tool, e.g., using the new button Java2Jinja in the tool bar, which the mouse cursor points to, she can choose which main method to execute and specify parameters as needed. Then, the translated

---

[56]http://pp.info.uni-karlsruhe.de/projects/quis-custodiet/Java2Jinja/

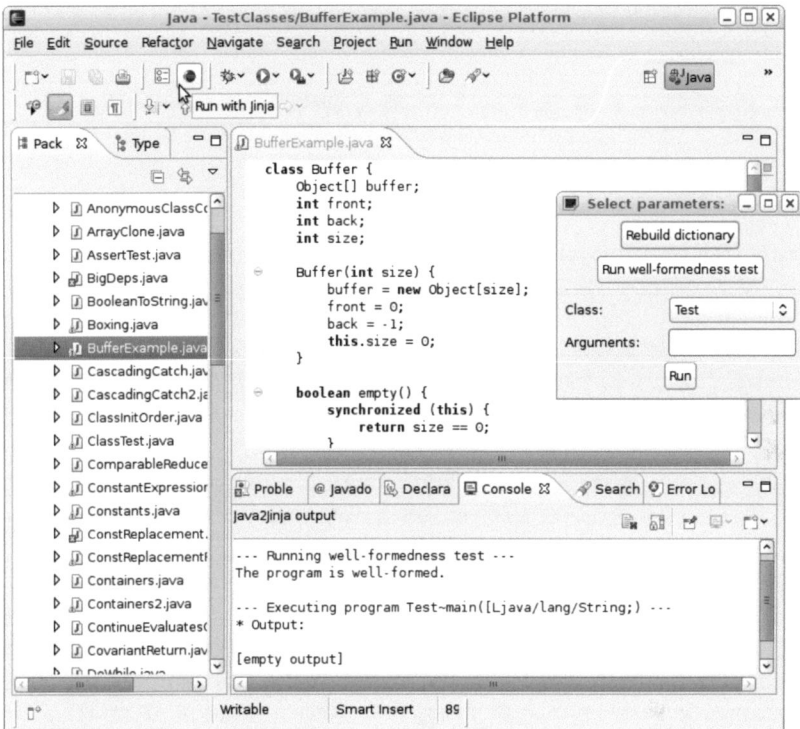

Figure 6.5: Java2Jinja in the Eclipse IDE for the producer-consumer example from Appendix A

program can be checked for well-formedness or executed in the extracted interpreter or VM – Java2Jinja prints the results in the console window (at the bottom).

Note that well-formedness checking is a sanity check for the translation being correct, not syntactic correctness of the Java source code. The JDT already catch such compiler errors. Nevertheless, JinjaThreads considers some well-formed Java programs to be ill-formed, because its definite assignment analysis (taken from Jinja) is less precise than the one that the JLS specifies [56, §16]. For example [56, §16], the following program passes Java's definite assignment test, but not Jinja-Threads', because the latter's analysis does not infer that the access to

283

k in the method call occurs only if both conditions are evaluated, i.e., k
is initialised.

`int k; if (v > 0 && (k = ...) >= 0) { System.out.println(k); }`

6.5.1 The translation

Although JinjaThreads syntax already covers a substantial part of Java,
lots of syntactic sugar and some imperative control structures are omitted.
Some of them could be easily added to the semantics, bloating the model
and especially proofs. Others would require substantial re-engineering.
Hence, Java2Jinja tries to emulate these as good as possible. In the
following, I briefly describe the translations.

Operators JinjaThreads misses the operator for string concatenation [56,
§15.18.1], unary ones [56, §15.15], postfix ones [56, §15.14], and compound
assignment ones [56, §15.26.2]. Java2Jinja replaces string concatenation
with `StringBuilder` as allowed by the JLS [56, §15.18.1.2]. Unary operators are emulated via their binary counterparts, e.g., -x becomes
$Val\,(Intg\,0)$ «$-$» $(Var\,x)$. Postfix operators are emulated using a fresh
local variable that remembers the former value. For example, y = x++;
becomes $y := \{\sim tmpVar\_0: Integer = None; \sim tmpVar\_0 := x;; x :=$
$Var\,\sim tmpVar\_0$ «$+$» $Val\,(Intg\,1);; Var\,\sim tmpVar\_0\}$. Here, the translation
exploits that Java identifiers never contain $\sim$ and that local variable
blocks in JinjaThreads may return a value. Compound assignments are
desugarized and fresh local variables store the computed parts of the
left-hand side (e.g., `f()` in `a[f()] += x;`) such that they are evaluated
only once.

Primitive types The primitive types **byte**, **short**, **char**, and **int** are all
mapped to *Integer*. This is sound since all Java operators automatically
promote these to **int**. There is no support for **long** or floating point values.
Auto-(un)boxing of supported primitive types [56, §5.1.7, §5.1.8] is
replaced by method calls of the appropriate classes, e.g., `Integer i = 0;` is
translated like `Integer i = Integer.valueOf(0);`. Conversions between
primitive types are either no-ops (widening [56, §5.1.2]) or extract the
required bits (narrowing [56, §5.1.3]). For example, `(char) x` becomes
`x & 65535`.

Control flow structures JinjaThreads only supports conditionals, while loops, and exceptions. Java's other statements for locally transferring control (switch, do-while loops, and for loops) are implemented with conditionals and while loops. Non-local transfer of control (break, continue, return) are implemented by throwing an exception and catching it again at the target. For finally clauses, Java2Jinja follows the JVMS' recommendation for compilation to bytecode [103, §7.13]. They are duplicated and inserted at the end of the try block and in an exception handler that catches all raised exceptions.

Methods Java2Jinja resolves overloaded methods and appends the method descriptor to the name [103, §4.3.3]. Lack of visibility constraints affects method resolution in that private methods should be resolved statically. Since JinjaThreads knows only dynamic dispatch, private methods are renamed uniquely such that dynamic and static dispatch agree. The same applies to invocations with super – if necessary, method signatures are duplicated and the dynamically dispatched version delegates to the statically dispatched. For example, in

```
class A { void g() { h(); }   private void h() { } }
class B extends A { void g() { super.g(); }   void h() { } }
```

g in A must call h of A and **super**.g() must disable dynamic dispatch for g and call A's method. Hence, h in A is renamed to A~h()V and there are two copies of A's method g: (i) A~g()V is called by **super**.g();, its body calls A~h()V. (ii) g()V delegates to A~g()V, B overrides it.

Abstract methods throw an UnsupportedOperationException. Native methods are translated to native JinjaThreads methods. If JinjaThreads does not provide an implementation (§2.1.3 and §3.2.1), the program is ill-formed and execution gets stuck when such a method is called.

Constructors and initialisation Like in Java bytecode, JinjaThreads allows objects to be allocated without executing their constructor. Java2Jinja inserts the constructor calls and default constructors as necessary. Instance initialisers [56, §8.6] and field initialisations [56, §8.3.2] are added to the constructors after the call of the super-constructor in the order they appear in the program text.

285

Static members and compile-time constants   Since JinjaThreads supports only non-static members, Java2Jinja introduces a singleton class that collects all static fields, methods and initialisers. Their names are prefixed by the fully qualified name of the declaring class to avoid ambiguities. Moreover, every object and array stores a reference to the singleton object in a field through which threads access these members. For simplicity, all static initialisers are executed before the main method of the program, which violates the official class initialisation procedure [56, §12.4]. Following the latter would require further substantial transformations of the program.

Nested classes   Java2Jinja provides limited support for nested classes in that it replaces them by ordinary top-level classes that store a reference to the enclosing instance if necessary. However, accessing fields and local variables of enclosing classes and methods is still experimental.

Generics   Type erasure removes all generics. Reflective type tokens such as <T> **void** f(Class<T> c) and multiple bounds are not supported.

Interfaces   Although interfaces are widely used in Java programs, they cannot be simulated in JinjaThreads and are therefore unsupported. In the special case where a class C inherits from *Object* and a single interface I, Java2Jinja turns I into a class and changes the class hierarchy such that I extends *Object* and C extends I. Since interfaces are another common source of ill-formedness of converted programs, Java2Jinja lists all problematic classes and interfaces during the translation as a warning message.

Standard API   Every Java program uses Java's standard API, e.g., the main method takes an array of Strings. To avoid that unnecessary parts are sucked in, Java2Jinja approximates the classes and their members that are actually needed and only translates these. Otherwise, irrelevant code would bloat the JinjaThreads code or possibly inhibit correct translation, because it might include unsupported Java code, e.g., heavy use of interfaces. It would also deteriorate performance, since (i) the well-formedness checker has to analyse more code, and (ii) initialisations before the main method starts take longer, because they allocate all string literals. The heuristics is sound except for initialisations. For example, Java2Jinja removes the field i from

```
class A { int i = 1 / 0;
  public static void main(String[] args) { new A(); } }
```

because it is not used. Hence, the translated program terminates normally whereas the Java program fails with an ArithmeticException.

Further, JinjaThreads also provides a customized version of the standard library classes derived from OpenJDK 6 [139]. Some native methods like System.arraycopy are implemented manually such that they are available in translated programs. Moreover, we have removed Unicode processing from String and Character and replaced the affected methods with those from CLDC [41] with ASCII support only. Unicode processing requires large character data tables that are initialised laziliy through class initialisation in Java. As Java2Jinja initialises all classes before the start of the program, the translated program would eagerly initialise all of them, which consumes prohibitive amounts of memory and time.

6.5.2 Validation

I have tested the semantics and translation thoroughly by executing numerous test cases from different sources. Although most bugs were caused by the translation, I also found one in the semantics: For division and remainder, JinjaThreads used the default implementation that Isabelle's Word library provides, but the JLS specifies them differently for negative divisors. Since both source code and bytecode use the very same operation, the compiler verification was not able to catch this bug.

In detail, I have used the following test cases:

- 59 hand-written programs for regression testing.

- Jacks [74], a suite of test cases designed to identify bugs in Java compilers. These tests identified only bugs in the translation. I use 136 cases out of 149 from the runtime section, the 13 remaining ones deal with binary compatibility, which does not apply to JinjaThreads. For 30 out of the 136, the translation fails or is incorrect. In detail, 11 cases inherently rely on unsupported features like native methods, interfaces, and floats; initialisation issues cause 4 failures; 13 cases exhibit bugs in the translation, in particular for nested classes. The remaining 2 cases require behaviour that the interpreter does not produce, e.g., it crashes instead of raising an *OutOfMemory* exception.

- Tests for the `java.lang.*` classes from OpenJDK 6 [139]. Since they test OpenJDK's implementation of the API, many rely on native methods or other Java features like Unicode that JinjaThreads does not implement. Hence, I found only 24 out of 184 test cases (13%) that Java2Jinja can correctly translate to JinjaThreads. One of these also exhibited the division and remainder bug mentioned above. Using JinjaThreads' compiler to bytecode and its VM for execution, all but four test cases terminated within minutes. These four are randomised test cases with a large number of iterations and use `System.arraycopy` frequently, which is particularly slow in JinjaThreads.

  I have also looked at OpenJDK tests for other packages. However, these typically use IO or the Java collections framework. Jinja-Threads does not model the former and the latter heavily uses interfaces. Therefore, they cannot be used.

Validation by executing translated test programs checks the translator and the semantics at the same time. Since the translation itself is very complex, failed test cases must be examined manually to see whether the translation or the semantics is buggy. In all but one case, it was the translation's fault. In principle, it is conceivable that bugs in the translation hide errors of the semantics. Since Java2Jinja directly translates the Java subset that JinjaThreads models, this possibility is negligible.

Therefore, I conclude that validation has been successful for the subset under examination. The numerous failures indicate that the model should cover more features such that less error-prone emulations are necessary (see §7.4 for more details). Although validation has tested the sequential semantics thoroughly, execution explores only a single schedule for a multithreaded program. Hence, this approach cannot prove that the semantics covers *all* allowed behaviours. For example, in §4.3.6, I have already mentioned two cases for which JinjaThreads does not model the full behaviour. Moreover, validation has not covered the JMM at all, because it is not executable. In conclusion, this is only a first step towards rigorous validation.

6.6 Related Work

Most closely related to JinjaThreads' well-formedness checker and compiler is Berghofer's and Strecker's work [24] on extracting a well-formedness checker and compiler for JinjaThreads' predecessor Bali. The former suffers from the very same termination problems that I have presented in §6.2, the latter is similar to JinjaThreads compiler except that it does not support exceptions. For an in-depth comparison, see §7.3.

Some formalisations of Java and the JVM in theorem provers are directly executable. First, the M6 by Lui and Moore [104, 105] models the JVM in ACL2 covering the CLDC specification; see §3.4.1 for details. Efficient execution was a major goal in its design. Thus, it is remarkable that JinjaThreads achieves similar performance although it focuses on simplifying proofs. Moore's and Porter's jvm2acl2 tool [122] translates Java bytecode into M6's representation. Since the M6 models Java bytecode quite closely to the JVMS, jvm2acl2 in fact translates only concrete to abstract syntax. JinjaThreads is far from such a point.

Second, Farzan et al. [48, 47] report on a formal semantics for Java source code and a virtual machine for Java bytecode in Maude. Maude's rewriting logic allows to execute programs in abstract syntax symbolically and analyse them using model-checking techniques. Their source code semantics covers about the same subset as JinjaThreads except for exceptions. For efficiency reasons, their semantics is based on continuations. This way, they bypass a major source of inefficiency from which JinjaThreads' source code interpreter suffers. For example, recursive methods enclose the statement to execute in more and more blocks for *this* and the parameters, and execution has to traverse them at every step of execution. Hence, executing

```
void recurse(int d) { if (d > 0) recurse(d - 1); }
```

in source code is quadratic in d. Continuation-based semantics keeps the next statement to execute at the outer-most level. Note that explicit call stacks in JinjaThreads bytecode also avoid the problem. Their VM follows a traditional style, but separates deterministic sequential instructions from non-deterministic multithreading to boost performance. They also implemented JavaFAN as a front-end to the semantics that takes Java source code or bytecode and converts it into abstract syntax. It is unclear whether JavaFAN tries to emulate missing features like Java2Jinja does. Moreover, they do not report on any attempt to validate their semantics or the translation. In an effort to cross-validate deduction rules of the Key system, Sasse [155] found and corrected several bugs in their source code semantics.

Third, Atkey [9] presents an executable JVM model in Coq. He concentrates on encoding defensive checks as dependent types, but does not provide any data about the efficiency.

The CCCP tool by Wasserrab [175] is similar to Java2Jinja. It translates C programs to CoreC++ [178], another descendant of Jinja, and executes them in the source code semantics. He also uses the tool for validating CoreC++.

Batty et al. [17] have implemented CPPMEM to explore their formalisation of the C++ memory model in Isabelle/HOL. It consists of two parts. First, a (manually written) symbolic execution engine generates sets of potential executions for a given (small) C++ program. Second, a checker that Isabelle's code generator has extracted from the formalisation prunes this set to the executions that the C++ memory model actually allows. The interpreter and VM that I have extracted implement sequential consistency; the axiomatic definition of the Java memory model is beyond the capabilities of Isabelle's code generator.

Code extraction in general is a well-established business, in particular extraction of functional implementations. In [116], Marić presents a formally verified implementation of a SAT solver in Isabelle/HOL. In the CeTA project, Thiemann and Sternagel [170] generate a self-contained executable termination checker for term rewrite systems. The Flyspeck project uses code extraction to compute the set of tame graphs [18, 127]. All these formalisations were developed with executability in mind. Complications in proofs to obtain an efficiently executable implementation were willingly taken and handling them are large contributions of these projects.

Code extraction in Coq [102] has been used in various developments, notably the CompCert compiler [99] and the certificate checkers in the MOBIUS project [13]. Like in Isabelle, functional specifications pose no intrinsic problems. Although code extraction is in principle possible for any Coq specification, mathematical theories can lead to "a nightmare in term of extracted code efficiency and readability" [102]. Hence, Coq's users, too, are facing the problem of how to extract (roughly) efficient code from specifications not aimed towards executability. ACL2 and PVS translate only functional implementations to Common Lisp.

The hardest thing is to go to sleep at night, when there are so many urgent things needing to be done. A huge gap exists between what we know is possible with today's machines and what we have so far been able to finish.

Donald Knuth

7

Discussion and Future Work

After hundreds of pages filled with formal definitions and technical details, this chapter takes a step back. Now, I contrast the efforts with the rewards (§7.1), comment on my experience as an Isabelle user (§7.2) and on how the advances in Isabelle influenced the formalisation (§7.3), compare JinjaThreads with Java (§7.4), and identify directions for future work (§7.5).

7.1 Efforts and rewards of a machine-checked formalisation

Efforts Building a formal model of a programming language in a theorem prover is a major investment. I have been working on JinjaThreads for five years, but not full-time. Not counting developing foundational libraries for Isabelle [108, 110], I estimate the net amount of time at three person years. It is difficult to exactly break down the figure to the individual parts, since I have worked on some of them in parallel. I had the first working version of the interleaving semantics (as described in [107] without thread interruption) and the type safety proof for source code after about four months. Extending it to bytecode took less than one month. The abstract heap module and the JMM formalisation with the proofs required about one year. The compiler was most laborious with more than one year. Since I worked on code extraction occasionally during the whole development, I am not able to give a figure for that. The remaining time has gone into refactoring the formalisation and extending the JinjaThreads language.

	defini-tions	lem-mata	lo-cales	LoC	Jinja LoC
shared infrastructure	158	397	10	5,690	1,808
interleaving semantics	91	406	11	5,140	—
source code + type safety	55	196	7	6,461	2,684[a]
bytecode + verifier	58	258	12	7,274	3,878
JMM + DRF	97	483	41	13,105	—
compiler + verification	139	1,398	30	34,024	4,112
code extraction	169	231	25	6,471	591
library extensions	19	220	0	1,947	292
DFA framework	62	268	6	3,948	3,835
total	848	3,857	142	84,060	17,200

[a]not counting the big-step semantics and the equivalence proof (2,052 LoC)

Table 7.1: Formalisation size of JinjaThreads in comparison with Jinja

Table 7.1 lists some figures that measure JinjaThreads' size: the number of definitions (including (co-)recursive and (co-)inductive ones), lemmata (including theorems and corollaries), locales, and the lines of Isabelle code. It breaks down the total figures into the various parts of JinjaThreads (cf. Figure 1.4). For comparison, the last column shows the lines of code (LoC) of the respective part of Jinja.

Since JinjaThreads covers a larger subset of Java than Jinja, it is, of course, larger. Source code and bytecode have roughly doubled in size to account for concurrency and arrays. Shared infrastructure has even tripled, but one third stems from native methods (1318 LoC) and binary operators (585 LoC). Here, it can be seen that reusing the interleaving semantics in source code and bytecode pays off, although I suppose that two monolithic semantics would have required less than twice the 5 kLoC of the framework. The benefit of reuse becomes much clearer for the JMM and the proofs about it. 10 kLoC out of the 13 kLoC are needed to formalise the JMM and the language-independent parts of the DRF guarantee and consistency. Only 3 kLoC fall upon discharging the final assumptions of the locales about the single-threaded semantics – and these 3 kLoC distribute roughly equally over native methods, source code, and bytecode. This shows that my design separates concurrency from single-threaded issues well.

The compiler verification offers a different picture – the transition from big-step to small-step semantics caused its size to explode. In detail, the bisimulation framework and lifting proofs (§5.1) require 4,237 LoC. Explicit call stacks in source code add another 2,068 LoC. However, the majority (18,231 LoC) is spent on the bisimulation relations and proofs for the individual compiler stages. In code generation, in particular, I have to deal with each inductive case manually. Specialised proof procedures might have been sensible here.

Code extraction refers to the extensions that were necessary to obtain the executable interpreter, VM, and compiler. In particular, it subsumes the formalisation of schedulers (§6.3.2). It is one order of magnitude larger than in Jinja, but offers another level of quality in two respects. First, Jinja used manual translations for unexecuable definitions like Hilbert's choice, whereas JinjaThreads does without. Second, Jinja does not care about efficiency, whereas I have demonstrated that the JinjaThreads VM is usable in practice.

On a Pentium DualCore 2.50 GHz running Ubuntu 10.04, Isabelle in single-threaded mode takes 1:55 h and 17 GB of memory to process the JinjaThreads sources, recheck all proofs, and extract the executable parts.

Rewards The investment in the formalisation starts to pay off fairly soon in various ways.

First, we can be sure that the proofs are correct with respect to the formal definitions, and that the formal definitions are at least type-checked. In particular, a series of false claims and their subsequent disproof – as has happened for the JMM [115, 38, 162, 171] – is impossible. Type-checking alone supports the formalisation tremendously, because obvious mistakes are caught early on. In addition, Isabelle provides some tools for finding bugs automatically (see §7.2 for details).

Furthermore, machine-support is fundamental for extending and adapting such a formal model, since proofs can be replayed automatically. JinjaThreads has evolved from Jinja gradually, adding feature after feature. In such a step, Isabelle determines which proofs need to be extended or changed and – most importantly – which ones I need not reconsider. Extending a pen-and-paper model requires to revisit *all* theorems and proofs, which is tedious and error-prone, because subtle interactions may be missed easily.

The ability to replay proofs was equally essential during the development of a single feature. After I had corrected a typo or conceptual error in a definition or theorem, Isabelle automatically rechecks the theorems that had already been adapted to the new feature. Often enough, such typos have erroneously rendered some proof cases trivial that in fact need some argument. A typical example is to inadvertently give two (different) variables the same name. The following typing rule for local variable blocks illustrates the problem:

$$\frac{is\text{-}type\ P\ T \qquad P, E(V \mapsto T) \vdash e :: T' \qquad case\ vo\ of\ None \Rightarrow True\ |\ \lfloor v \rfloor \Rightarrow \exists T''.\ typeof\ v = \lfloor T'' \rfloor \wedge P \vdash T'' \leq T}{P, E \vdash \{V : T = vo;\ e\} :: T'}$$

Following the format and naming conventions of the other rules (see Appendix B.6.2), one is tempted to write T instead of T' in the shaded positions, but T already denotes the type of the declared variable. Obviously, the corresponding inductive case of the theorem

$$\llbracket P, E \vdash e :: T;\ ran\ E \subseteq types\ P \rrbracket \implies is\text{-}type\ P\ T$$

becomes trivial with the typo.

In conclusion, mechanisation

(i) supports the process of formalising,

(ii) guarantees the absence of errors, and

(iii) eases reuse in other projects, because definitions can be easily adapted when necessary and Isabelle checks that everything fits together properly.

7.2 Experience: Working with Isabelle/HOL

In this section, I comment on my experience of formalising JinjaThreads with Isabelle/HOL and which features were particularly useful and which would have been desirable.

Essential Isabelle features

Essential Isabelle features for JinjaThreads are Isar, locales, and the high degree of built-in proof automation, on which I now comment in turn.

Almost all proofs in JinjaThreads are written in Isabelle's declarative proof language Isar [179, 25], see Figure 7.1 for an example. Proofs in Isar style tend to be a bit longer than imperative proof scripts and usually take more time to write, but the extra effort is not spent in vain. Since Isar follows the mathematical language of informal reasoning, Isar proofs are intelligible to non-experts. Being declarative, they typically make the line of argument explicit. Moreover, Isar proofs are more robust to adaptations than imperative proof scripts or hand-coded proof procedures, because when the proofs are replayed, (i) they break exactly where manual intervention is necessary, and (ii) being declarative, they record the exact intermediate statement, i.e., one need not guess what the proof state should have been. Therefore, Isar proofs are easier to maintain, which is a major concern in large formalisations like JinjaThreads. Such adaptations of existing proofs are triggered by new Isabelle releases (seven of which happened during the development of JinjaThreads) and changes to the formalisation itself.

Locales have proven essential in structuring the formalisation, as can be seen in Chapters 3, 4, and 5. Unfortunately, locale contexts are purely dynamic, i.e., whenever one switches from one locale to another, Isabelle discards the old and constructs the new from scratch. Since this involves to replay each previous declaration of the new context including all inherited locales, entering a locale context can take a few minutes. In fact, when Isabelle processes JinjaThreads, the peaks in memory consumption occur when it rebuilds such locale contexts.

Thanks to Isabelle's sophisticated procedures for proof automation, JinjaThreads does not need custom tactics, although theorem-specific tactics might drastically reduce some proof sizes, as Chlipala demonstrates in a case study in Coq [39]. Instead, I have focused on properly setting up proof automation, where simplification is the main workhorse. Unfortunately, Isar provides only little support for simplification steps, but favors natural deduction. Consequently, predicates should come with introduction and elimination rules to be used in Isar proofs and simplification rules for good automation. However, Isabelle's means of specification used to provide either the former (**(co)inductive**) or the

295

latter (**fun**). Upon my suggestion, Bulwahn extended the **inductive** package such that one can a posteriori derive rewrite rules for (co-)inductive predicates and sets. Since this feature has been available, I have defined most predicates and sets (co-)inductively and had Isabelle automatically derive simplification rules.

Sledgehammer [29, 33] runs automated theorem provers to discover a proof of a theorem. It is particularly useful for proof obligations about notions from libraries that the formalisation builds on, e.g., 32-bit integers and coinductive natural numbers. In such a case, Sledgehammer only needs to combine the right bunch of lemmata that the library provides. Since it identifies the relevant ones, this saves the user from the time-consuming task of becoming an expert for each library she uses. It is less effective for solving goals about what one is currently developing, though, because the lemma base is still largely incomplete, and the new lemmata are rarely simple consequences of others.

Counterexample generation

To support the user in exploratory stages, Isabelle provides two counterexample generators Quickcheck [23] and Nitpick [28, 30]. When the user enters a theorem she wants to prove, they automatically try to refute it and present a counterexample, if they succeed.

Quickcheck converts the putative statement into ML code via Isabelle's code generator, installs test data generators for the free variables, and executes the code. If the code returns *False*, the assignment to the free variables constitutes a counterexample. Quickcheck supported the development of JinjaThreads only little because it suffers from two drawbacks. First, the code generator must be able to process *all* definitions that the statement refers to. This restriction is severe, because early on, when the definitions still keep changing, most errors are to be found, but time is not spent on deriving executable equations for all constants unless one expects them to be in the final form. Moreover, proof invariants such as conformance involve universal or existential quantifiers, which cannot be executed. Second, until recently, it used to generate the test data randomly, which often misses the subtle cases. Now, Bulwahn changed Quickcheck to use exhaustive search [29, 36]. On the positive side, when it is applicable, Quickcheck is extremely fast. Even statements that involve complicated definitions are tested within seconds. In JinjaThreads, Quickcheck has spotted typos in definitions and statements, but none of the conceptual bugs in definitions; exhaustive testing might have changed the latter.

Nitpick follows a different approach. It converts the statement and all definitions and axioms it depends on into first-order relational logic (FORL) and calls a relational model finder. This way, it handles non-executable constructs and underspecification without further ado, but is limited by the complexity of the generated formula. Moreover, its performance is sensitive to the FORL encoding. Although sensible defaults are provided, Blanchette et al. [31] showed that manually tuning Nitpick's numerous parameters can boost performance.

In JinjaThreads, I applied Nitpick successfully for the bisimulations from §5.1, where it found the counterexample in Figure 5.4 after several attempts of mine to prove the equivalence of delay bisimulation with explicit divergence and well-founded delay bisimulations. However, Nitpick's output overwhelmed the model finder for any theorem that involves program declarations or the semantics. Conversely, Nitpick helped a lot in developing the library of coinductive lists [110], because it is able to find unintuitive counterexamples with infinite lists, which are out of Quickcheck's reach.

In conclusion, both Quickcheck and Nitpick work well for smallish developments, but they are of little help to identify intricate cases where things do not fit together in formalisations as large as JinjaThreads.

Suggestions for improvement

Despite the good support for developing formalisations, I found the following suggestions for further improvement.

Isabelle's support for coinductive datatypes, corecursive definitions and proofs by coinduction is poor. Coinductive datatypes still must be constructed manually like Paulson did 15 years ago [142]. The proof method for coinductive proofs lacks many of the conveniences of its inductive counterpart. Consequently, coinductive Isar proofs typically contain four steps of boilerplate code (the highlighted parts of the proof[57] in Figure 7.1). First, auxiliary variables for instantiated coinduction parameters are introduced (l. 3). Second, all assumptions are combined using HOL conjunction (instead of meta-conjunction that

---

[57] $tmap\ f\ g\ xs$ is the map operator for terminated coinductive lists. It applies f to all elements of xs and g to the symbol of the $[]\_$ constructor.

```
 1  lemma assumes s ⇊' ξ    shows s ⇊ tmap snd id ξ
 2  proof -
 3     def ξ' ≡ tmap snd id ξ
 4     with assms have ∃ξ. s ⇊' ξ ∧ ξ' = tmap snd id ξ by ...
 5     thus s ⇊ ξ'
 6     proof coinduct
 7        case (τRuns s ξ')
 8        then obtain ξ where s ⇊' ξ and ξ' = tmap snd id ξ by ...
 9        thus ?case by ...
10     qed
11  qed
```

Figure 7.1: Isar proof for the proof step $s \Downarrow' \xi \implies s \Downarrow tmap\ snd\ id\ \xi$ from Theorem 5.1. Boilerplate code is highlighted.

Isar proofs favor) and generalised using existential quantifiers (l. 4). Third, the goal is restated using the auxiliary variables (l. 5). After the subsequent application of the coinduction rule, every coinductive case unpacks the existential quantifiers and separates the assumptions again (l. 8). Thus, a five-line proof is bloated with six lines of boiler-plate code.

Another neglected issue is support for refactorings, e.g., (i) moving and renaming definitions and theorems, (ii) promoting subproofs to lemmata, (iii) changing the order of parameters or pretty-printing syntax for a function or predicate, and (iv) (un-)currying functions and predicates. While simple renamings can be achieved relatively easily with standard command-line tools and their support of regular expressions, changing the order of parameters is particularly tricky, because Isar proofs often refer to variables in theorems and proofs by position. In total, I have spent at least two months on such simple refactorings for the most pressing issues, but much remains to be done in this respect. In particular, JinjaThreads in its current state lacks consistent naming of constants, variables and theorems and much of the pretty syntax in this thesis. Fortunately, Ruegenberg [151] has recently implemented the Levity prototype for renaming definitions and theorems and moving the latter. I hope that this work continues and am looking forward to when such tool support is availabe in Isabelle's IDE.

298

7.3 From Java$^{\ell ight}$ to JinjaThreads

JinjaThreads is currently the result of 15 years of formalising Java in Isabelle/HOL, see §1.2 for the historic view. In this section, I look back to see what has made it into JinjaThreads and how new features of Isabelle offer new formalisation options.

Reuse is most obvious in Jinja's declaration infrastructure, lookup functions and generic well-formedness, which can be traced back to early versions of Bali [129]. Although the definitions have changed textually over time, JinjaThreads still benefits from the good choice of proven lemmata and setup for proof automation. Similarly, the sequential VM follows the well-engineered structure from μJava and Jinja. JinjaThreads's compiler inherits Jinja's and merely extends it to the new statements for arrays and synchronisation, and the same applies to the proof of type-preservation. However, the proof of semantic correctness merely exploits the same abstract ideas, but completely differs in all other respects, because it is now carried out against the concurrent small-step semantics instead of the sequential big-step semantics. Bytecode and the bytecode verifier also descend directly from μJava.

In contrast, the small-step semantics for source code is comparatively young, as Bali only defines a preliminary one and μJava none at all. Thus, in retrospect, Nipkow's and Oheimb's investment in Bali [129] keeps paying off. Still, it has taken more than a decade to achieve their goal of extending Bali with Java concurrency.

Among the numerous improvements in Isabelle, the effect of three on the formalisation deserves mentioning. The most obvious is the Isar language [179, 25] of human-readable proof, which I have discussed already in §7.2. Some parts of JinjaThreads go back to early parts of Bali and μJava and are therefore still written as imperative proof scripts.

Second come more powerful packages that reduce clutter in definitions and proofs. In detail, Krauss' packages for defining (partial) recursive functions [88,89] automate termination proofs or render them unnecessary and additionally derive custom rules for induction and case analysis. Even if the function is primitively recursive and therefore structural induction would suffice, proof automation often works better with custom rules, because the latter incorporates how other parameters change in recursive calls. With structural induction, proof automation often fails to discover these changes. For example, I use **fun** to define *ok-thrs* from Figure 3.10. The auxiliary lemma $\llbracket$*ok-thrs ts nts*; *Spawn t x h* $\in$

299

set nts $\rrbracket \implies ts \ t = None$ is proven automatically with the custom induction rule, but automation fails with structural induction on *nts*.[58]

The third aspect concerns code extraction. Jinja and its predecessors used the first version of Isabelle's code generator by Berghofer [22]. This has now been replaced by Haftmann's [62] and Bulwahn's predicate compiler [21]. The new version handles type classes, data refinement, and data type invariants, and compiles predicates inside the logic. In [92,109,113], I have explored these new possibilites for code extraction. JinjaThreads exploits them in the following ways. It rarely uses type classes – a widely-used Isabelle feature for type-safe overloading [63] – but naturally depends on them via the standard library. Data refinement and data type invariants [60] are essential to a posteriori replace unexecutable or inefficient data structures by more efficient ones, e.g., tabulation (§6.3.3).

Berghofer's code generator was already able to handle inductive definitions, but it performed the (non-trivial) transformations outside the LCF inference kernel [21]. The new predicate compiler computes a functional implementation for inductive definitions inside the logic and proves it correct. Apart from the increased confidence of correctness, all Isabelle tools can now be used to manipulate the functional interpreter. For example, JinjaThreads simplifies the code equations to improve performance (see §6.3.4). Moreover, an implementation of Russell's definite description operator using the functional interpreter [113] (§6.1.2) would require an extension of the code generator if compilation happened outside the logic.

In [24], Berghofer and Strecker report on the effort needed to extract μJava's well-formedness checker and compiler. They had to replace manually existential quantifiers like in *wf-J-mdecl*'s definition (Figure 2.10) with new predicates. Bulwahn has added a preprocessor to transform definitions in predicate logic to a set of introduction rules [113], such that this step is no longer necessary. Still, it is not advisable to invoke the preprocessor on *wf-J-mdecl*, because it applies the transformation too aggressively. Not only does it introduce such an inductive predicate for the existentially quantified subformula, but also for all the other constants,

---

[58] Alternatively, I could have defined *ok-thrs* inductively, like many of the other predicates (see the discussion in §7.2). **fun**'s induction rule is more versatile, because the induction rule from an inductive definition requires that the statement to prove contains *ok-thrs* as a premise. When proving simplification rules for such predicates, I can use only the former directly.

i.e., $\sqcup$, *distinct, set, $\mathcal{D}$*, and for the constants these depend on. To guide the preprocessor, I have promoted this subformula to a constant of its own, invoked it on the new constant, and replaced the subformula by the new constant in *wf-J-mdecl*'s code equation. Although this still requires manual intervention, it is a significant improvement over the state in 2003, because the user does not need to perform any of the conversions himself.

Apart from that, Berghofer and Strecker also face the problem that a definition is only (efficiently) executable under certain preconditions, but all calling contexts satisfy the precondition. In JinjaThreads, this concerns least upper bounds and the typing rules (§6.2.3). It is unfortunate that no satisfactory solution has been found to date. Since the code generator restricts invariants for data types to be first-order [60], they can only solve this problem in the most simple cases.

7.4 Comparison between Java and JinjaThreads

JinjaThreads is not Java – this becomes most obvious when one looks at all the transformations Java2Jinja needs to perform (§6.5.1) – but Jinja-Threads does not aim for a comprehensive model, anyway. Nevertheless, JinjaThreads covers the full range of concurrency features from the JLS. In particular, most thread features are accessed through native method calls like in Java. It is faithful except for spurious wake-ups and atomicity of *clone* (§4.3.6).

However, it misses a few concurrency issues from the Java standard API. Most prominent are the `java.util.concurrent` package and *Thread*'s methods `isAlive`, `holdsLock`, and `getState`. The former, a library of lock-free and thread-safe classes for synchronisation and exchanging data between threads, builds on an atomic compare-and-set (CAS) operation. In JinjaThreads, the CAS operation could be implemented directly as a native method that atomically reads and writes a volatile location.[59] Similarly, one could add the three methods of class *Thread*, too. `holdsLock` could be implemented directly via the following thread actions: $\langle Unlock{\rightarrow}a, Lock{\rightarrow}a\rangle$ when it returns *True*, and

---

[59]The `java.util.concurrent` classes define further CAS methods with weaker ordering constraints than volatile semantics. To model them, one has to define appropriate synchronisation events and extend the JMM accordingly. Since the proofs about the memory model hardly depend on the kind of synchronisation, this should not pose any big problems.

$(UnlockFail{\rightarrow}a)$ for $False$. However, isAlive requires another BTA for querying that a thread has not yet terminated (the dual to $Join$). getState necessitates further BTAs, e.g., for querying whether a thread is waiting in a wait set or joining on another thread. For the latter, the current implementation for $join$ no longer works. At present, if a (uninterrupted) thread t joins on thread t', but t' has not yet finished, then t is stuck at the call. In particular, the multithreaded state does not record the failed attempt, but t's state that getState returns changes from running to waiting. One could extend the interleaving semantics to record such failed attempts in the multithreaded state. However, getState's documentation disallows to use it for synchronisation purposes in the JMM sense. Hence, the same issues arise as for synchronisation via thread spawning (Figure 4.28).

As for sequential Java, numerous features are still missing, the following lists them. From the concurrency point of view, class initialisation, final fields, and finalisation are particularly interesting for the following reasons:

1. Classes must be initialised at most once even if multiple threads trigger initialisation concurrently. Interesting points are whether the initialisation procedure in the JLS [56, §12.4.2] in fact achieves this, and how one can model the allowed deviations from it [56, §12.4.3]. The latter affects whether a program is correctly synchronised, because threads can implicitly synchronise through class initialisation.

   For example, consider the two threads in Figure 7.2 with the classes and their static initialisers on the left. Class initialisation occurs in ll. 2 and 3, and both classes cause initialisation of the other. Note that the initialisation of B succeeds only when it is triggered by A's initialisation, because in that case, B's static initialiser reads the default value **false** for A.a as part of recursive class initialisation. Hence, l. 4 executes only if l. 2 executes before l. 3. There is only one potential data race, namely on x between l. 1 and l. 4 – accesses to the static members occurs only in static initialisers and therefore cannot participate in data races. Since initialisation involves locking and unlocking, l. 2 happens before (in the JMM sense) l. 3, and so does l. 1 before l. 4. Thus, there is no data race and the program is correctly synchronised. However, the JLS allows compilers and the JVM to remove unnecessary synchronisation for class initialisation [56, §12.4.3]. It is unclear whether this exception applies to the above

```
class A {                                initially: x = 0
    static boolean t = B.b;          1: x = 1;    3: new B();
    static boolean a = true;         2: new A();  4: r = x;
}
class B {
    static boolean b = true;
    static { if (A.a) throw new Error(); }
}
```

Figure 7.2: Synchronisation through and potential deadlock during class initialisation

example and whether the compiler must still ensure the semantics of synchronisation, i.e., whether ll. 3 and 4 must not be reordered.

Moreover, class initialisation according to the JLS [56, §12.4.2] may cause the program from Figure 7.2 to deadlock. If both threads simultaneously start to initialise A and B, respectively, each thread can end up in the other class' monitor, waiting to be notified. Since there is no other thread to wake them up, they are deadlocked.[60] This is a known defect of the class initialisation procedure, but no better solution is known [35]. If class initialisation is revised again, one could then use a suitable extension of JinjaThreads to prove the absence of deadlocks.

Class initialisation would require non-trivial changes to the semantics and the compiler verification. Liu and Moore [104] model class initialisation by switching their VM M6 into a designated state and executing the static initialiser like a static method in its own call frame. I guess that a similar approach might work for JinjaThreads, too.

2. For final fields, the JMM provides stronger guarantees than for ordinary ones [56, §17.5]. Since final fields are closely tied to constructors, one first must extend JinjaThreads with constructors,[61]

---

[60]Even if either of the threads wakes up spuriously, step 2 of the initialisation procedure immediately suspends the thread again. Hence, they should be considered deadlocked in that case, too. However, spurious wake-ups would remove the threads from the waits again, i.e., both threads would keep spinning in step 2. This is an example of how spurious wake-ups can obscure deadlocks.

[61]A good starting point would be Klein's work on constructors in μJava bytecode [79].

but it should then be straightforward to extend the JMM formalisation with final fields. However, final fields are designed to be used without synchronisation. In particular, writes to final fields need not happen before reads [56, §17.5.1] – otherwise, final fields would have synchronisation semantics like volatiles. Therefore, one must also revisit data-race freedom. Ideally, one would show that data races on final fields can only occur in programs that already contain another data race on some non-final field.[62] This would strenghten the DRF guarantee, because one would not need to consider final fields when checking data race freedom. If this does not hold, however, one should nevertheless exclude final fields from data races, because their usage should not expel programs from the DRF guarantee. However, one then has to check whether the DRF guarantee still holds.

3. Finalisation executes in separate finalisation threads for which the JMM defines separate visibility restrictions [56, §12.6.1.1]. It would be interesting to study which coding idioms for finalisers in fact yield DRF programs.

Note that exceptions are the only kind of non-local transfer of control in JinjaThreads source code. From the compiler perspective, it would be interesting to also include `break`, `continue`, `return`, because they interact with $sync\ (\_)\ \_$ blocks non-trivially. If one of the former causes such a block to terminate abruptly, the lock must be released like in the exceptional case, but bytecode provides no dedicated support like an exception handler table for that. More generally, `finally` blocks – which are missing, too – can intercept such transfer of control, execute arbitrary code and even redirect the flow of control. While it is well-known how to model such constructs semantically, e.g. [99, 135], the compiler and its verification would need substantial adaptations.

---

[62]The informal argument goes like this: Only the constructor assigns to final fields of an object, i.e., there are exactly two writes to a final field: the initialisation with the default value and the constructor's assignment, but they never conflict by definition. Since a conflicting read of the final field must occur in another thread, the thread must have learnt the object's address before. Hence, both threads must synchronise to pass the address without a data race. If the thread adheres to the coding discipline of not writing "a reference to the object being constructed in a place where another thread can see it before the object's constructor is finished" [56, §17.5], then the writes to the final field happen before the reads. It remains to be shown whether this informal argument can be made rigorous.

When one views JinjaThreads as an efficient, executable formalised interpreter and VM, the most pressing issues are static fields and methods, interfaces, the remaining primitive types, and primitive support for *String*s. Java^{light} has already covered the first two [135], but neither μJava nor Jinja have. Reintroducing them would be tedious, but uninteresting. The main obstacle for primitive types is that Isabelle lacks a formalisation of floating points at present, but existing solutions in other theorem provers should be easily portable [43,66,153]. Busenius [37] has included *String*s in his port of JinjaThreads to Coq.

Apart from the above, JinjaThreads also omits the following: method overloading, abstract classes and methods, throws clauses, auto-boxing, generics, nested classes, packages, access modifiers, class loaders, reflection, and the statements assert and switch.

7.5 Future work

The mainly negative results on the JMM – the original set of JMM events is insufficient to implement the Java API (§4.3.2), type safety hinges on all objects being in existence from the start (§4.3.5), security guarantees are compromised (§4.3.5) – immediately raise the question for future research: How can we do better? Since the JMM does not allow optimisations as intended [8,38,115,162,171], either, another revision seems necessary. However, it is unclear what out-of-thin-air values should be and how to characterise them formally. Analogously, it is currently unknown how to formally state and prove the security guarantees that the JMM is supposed to provide. Future work must address these questions and investigate how possible solutions restrict the compiler beyond the DRF model.

Although I have shown how to connect syntax and single-threaded semantics with the JMM, the solution is not completely satisfying, because interleaving semantics still occurs as an intermediate layer. It could be eliminated with two radical changes. First, the shared heap is reduced to carry no information at all – the allocation operation of the heap module returns non-deterministically any address, even if it might already be in use. Then, every thread executes in isolation. Second, the multithreaded semantics connects to single threads via their set of possible traces of thread actions and events. It imposes the global synchronisation order, ensures mutual exclusion of locks and freshness of allocations, keeps track of the wait sets and interrupts, etc. The JMM then matches reads and writes as before.

Since this amounts to a complete redesign, most proofs would need to be redone, because the preservation proofs rely on the global notion of time. However, such a change would free the way to re-introduce the (more intuitive) big-step semantics for single threads. It seems worthwhile to explore whether coinductive big-step operational semantics, which has recently become popular in the Coq community [101,124,125], offers an elegant approach for infinite executions for JinjaThreads, too.

The Quis custodiet project, in which JinjaThreads originates, suggests another direction for future work, namely extending JinjaThreads to full Java. Then, one could run safety-critical programs, which the verified IFC tool has certified, in an extracted VM such that the program behaviour definitely respects the semantics.

At the moment, the main show stoppers are interfaces, primitive types like **long** and **double**, and class initialisation. Interfaces only affect the type system, but not concurrency; since Bali models them, including them should not pose any deep problems. Neither would additional primitive types, as they are orthogonal to concurrency, but this would require to formalise floating-point arithmetic in Isabelle first. Class initialisation is a different matter, see the previous section for details.

The challenges in this scenario are (i) keeping the formal model tractable and (ii) tuning the extracted VM for efficiency. However, I would not expect any deep insights for Java as a programming language, since most features have already been studied in isolation.

Finally, if either direction is followed, validation of the model becomes even more important. My work in §6.5.2 is only a first step in this direction, since the scheduler produces only one single behaviour, and only for the sequentially consistent heap implementation. Hence, validation tests the sequential subset more thoroughly than multithreading. In particular, this approach cannot prove that some behaviour is erroneously disallowed due to the inherent non-determinism. To boost confidence in JinjaThreads as a model for Java, one can devise a tool that tests whether a given behaviour is allowed, or that enumerates all allowed behaviours of a program. Then, one could explore the full model, ideally interactively, albeit only for tiny programs due to the state space explosion. For sequential consistency, e.g., enumeration of all possible interleavings would be possible by using the predicate compiler for the interleaving semantics (see §6.3.2).

Studies serve for delight, for ornament and for ability. To spend too much time in studies is sloth, to use them too much for ornament is affectation; to make judgement wholly by their rules is the humour of a scholar.

Francis Bacon, *Essays*

8

Conclusion

My mechanised model of multithreaded Java spans from a realistic subset of Java source code and bytecode plus compiler via operational semantics for statements and instructions to the axiomatic Java memory model. I have shown type safety, consistency of the JMM, and the DRF guarantee, and verified the compiler. It is executable and has been tested thoroughly.

In this work, I have focused on studying the effects of concurrency in a *unified* model rather than in isolation such that important details cannot be missed easily. Tractability quickly becomes a major concern, modularity is the key to push the limits. I have demonstrated how to disentangle sequential aspects, concurrency features, and the memory model from each other, and the proofs show that JinjaThreads is indeed a usable model despite being sizeable.

Beyond the structuring principle and unified model, I also contributed to the analysis of individual facets. First, I have given a precise and formal definition of deadlock in terms of the single-threaded semantics. Hence, the type safety statement is stronger than previous ones which over-approximate deadlocks syntactically. Second, the compiler verification was the first for multithreaded Java. Although the proof technique is much more difficult than for sequential languages, it can be reused to verify translations between different program representations. Although the compiler literature often considers such translations obviously correct, this work shows once more [99] that formally proving them correct is non-trivial. Third, I have bridged the gap between Java and the Java memory model, and identified several subtle cases that the JMM misses. Via this link, I also proved the DRF guarantee and consistency, and discovered that the JMM in theory breaks Java's security architecture.

The DRF proof is not limited to Java, because it is largely independent of the Java-specific legality conditions. In fact, the key lemma 4.4 plays a similar role in other DRF guarantee proofs, e.g., [4,32]. They all postulate sequentially consistent completions of prefixes, which I have constructed formally for the first time and for a realistic language. For Java, this surprisingly requires a full type-safety proof, but this need not be a restriction for other languages. C and C++, e.g., assign such type-unsafe programs undefined semantics and exclude them from the guarantee.

For the Quis custodiet project, the formalisation of bytecode and the executable (sequentially consistent) VM are probably the most relevant parts. QC's analyses for information flow control operate on Java bytecode, so it is natural to verify them against the bytecode formalisation. The executable VM and the converter Java2Jinja are the first step towards a trusted environment for executing security-critical Java programs.

However, the analyses are sound only for sequential consistency, but not the JMM. Like for Java's security architecture, out-of-thin-air values compromise their soundness, too. For example, standard points-to analysis as used in VALSOFT/Joana and QC determines that r2 and r3 never alias for the program in Figure 4.27, but the JMM allows aliasing. Since the IFC algorithms build on this information, they, too, become unsound for programs with data races, although Hammer [64] and Giffhorn [53] claim that VALSOFT/Joana correctly over-approximates the weak semantics of the JMM. This is just another evidence that the specification of the JMM is flawed.

Beyond Quis custodiet, JinjaThreads is already used in other contexts, too. Busenius [37] has ported a preliminary version to Coq and extended it with generics and wildcards. He uses it as a target language for the verification of Expi2Java [10], a code generator for cryptographic protocols. He chose JinjaThreads "over other formalized Java fragments because of its comprehensiveness." [10, §6]. In the context of the CeTA project [170], Kochesser is using Java2Jinja and the compiler to convert Java programs into Jinja bytecode [personal communication], which is then fed to CeTA's termination and complexity analyser.

In the future, JinjaThreads could be used, e.g., to cross-validate other formal semantics for (concurrent) Java. For example, Trentelman [172] has verified some proof rules of the KeY tool [19], a verification tool for JavaCard programs, against Jinja's predecessor Bali. Continuing this effort, JinjaThreads could formally link different analyses tools like KeY with the IFC checker formalisation from the Quis custodiet project. In such a setting, the compiler verification becomes especially valuable because it permits to transfer results freely between source code (KeY) and bytecode (QC).

A

Producer-consumer example

This producer-consumer example program in JinjaThreads source code syntax has been used for benchmarking the interpreter and VM (§6.3.4).

Example n = Program (SystemClasses @ [ThreadC, StringC, IntegerC,
   BufferC, ProducerC n, ConsumerC n, TestC])

ProducerC n =
   ("Producer", Thread,
    [("buffer", Class "Buffer", (|volatile = False|))],
    [(run, [], Void, ⌊([],
       {"i" : Integer = ⌊Intg 0⌋ ;
         while (Var "i" «!=» Val (Intg (word-of-int n))) (
            Var "buffer"."put"([
               {"temp" : Class "Integer";
                 "temp" := new "Integer";;
                 Var "temp"."value"{} := "i";; Var "temp"}]);;
         "i" := Var i «+» Val (Intg 1))})⌋)])

ConsumerC n =
   ("Consumer", Thread,
    [("buffer", Class "Buffer", (|volatile = False|))],
    [(run, [], Void, ⌊([],
       {"i" : Integer = ⌊Intg 0⌋ ;
         while (Var "i" «!=» Val (Intg (word-of-int n)))
            {"o" : Class Object;
              "o" := Var "buffer"."get"([]);;
              "i" := Var i «+» Val (Intg 1)}})⌋)])

$BufferC =$
  ("Buffer", $Object$,
   [("buffer", $Class\ Object[]$, $(volatile = False)$),
   ("front", $Integer$, $(volatile = False)$),
   ("back", $Integer$, $(volatile = False)$),
   ("size", $Integer$, $(volatile = False)$)],
   [("constructor", $[Integer]$, $Void$, $\lfloor([$"size"$]$,
     "buffer" $:= new\ Class\ Object[Var$ "size"$]$; ;
     "front" $:= Val\ (Intg\ 0)$; ;
     "back" $:= Val\ (Intg\ -1)$; ;
     $Var\ this.$"size"$\{\} := Val\ (Intg\ 0))\rfloor)$,
   ("empty", $[]$, $Boolean$, $\lfloor([]$,
     $sync\ (Var\ this)\ (Var$ "size" «$==$» $Val\ (Intg\ 0)))\rfloor)$,
   ("full", $[]$, $Boolean$, $\lfloor([]$,
     $sync\ (Var\ this)\ (Var$ "size" «$==$» $(Var$ "buffer"$).length))\rfloor)$,
   ("get", $[]$, $Class\ Object$, $\lfloor([]$,
     $sync\ (Var\ this)\ ($
       $while\ (Var\ this.$"empty"$([]))$
         $try\ Var\ this.wait([])\ catch(InterruptedException$ "e"$)\ unit$; ;
       "size" $:= Var$ "size" «$-$» $Val\ (Intg\ 1)$; ;
       $\{$"result" $:\ Class\ Object$;
         "result" $:= Var$ "buffer"$[Var$ "front"$]$; ;
         "front" $:= Var$ "front" «$+$» $Val\ (Intg\ 1)$; ;
         $(if\ (Var$ "front" «$==$» Var "buffer"$.length)$
           "front" $:= Val\ (Intg\ 0)$
          $else\ unit)$; ;
         $Var\ this.notifyAll([])$; ;
         Var "result"$\}))\rfloor)$,
   ("put", $[Class\ Object]$, $Void$, $\lfloor([$"o"$]$,
     $sync\ (Var\ this)\ ($
       $while\ (Var\ this.$"full"$([]))$
         $try\ Var\ this.wait([])\ catch(InterruptedException$ "e"$)\ unit$; ;
       "back" $:= Var$ "back" «$+$» $Val\ (Intg\ 1)$; ;
       $(if\ (Var$ "back" «$==$» Var "buffer"$.length)$
         "back" $:= Val\ (Intg\ 0)$
       $else\ unit)$; ;
       Var "buffer"$[Var$ "back"$] := Var$ "o"; ;
       "size" $:= Var$ "size" «$+$» $Val\ (Intg\ 1)$; ;
       $Var\ this.notifyAll([])))\rfloor)])$

$TestC =$
  $(\text{"Test"}, Object, [],$
   $[(\text{"main"}, [Class \text{"String"}[]], Void, \lfloor ($
      $\{\text{"b"} : Class \text{"Buffer"};$
        $\text{"b"} := new \text{"Buffer"};;$
        $Var \text{"b"}.\text{"constructor"}([Val (Intg\ 10)]);;$
        $\{\text{"p"} : Class \text{"Producer"};$
          $Var \text{"p"} := new \text{"Producer"};;$
          $\{\text{"c"} : Class \text{"Consumer"};$
            $Var \text{"c"} := new \text{"Consumer"};;$
            $Var \text{"c"}.\text{"buffer"}\{\} := Var \text{"b"};;$
            $Var \text{"p"}.\text{"buffer"}\{\} := Var \text{"b"};;$
            $Var \text{"c"}.start([]);;\ Var \text{"p"}.start([])\}\}\})\rfloor)])$

$IntegerC =$
  $(\text{"Integer"}, Object, [(\text{"value"}, Integer, (volatile = False))], [])$

$StringC = (\text{"String"}, Object, [], [])$

$ThreadC =$
  $(Thread, Object, [],$
   $[(run, [], Void, \lfloor([], unit)\rfloor),$
    $(start, [], Void, Native), (join, [], Void, Native),$
    $(interrupt, [], Void, Native), (isInterrupted, [], Boolean, Native)])$

$SystemClasses =$
  $[ObjectC, ThrowableC, NullPointerC, ClassCastC, OutOfMemoryC,$
   $ArrayIndexOutOfBoundsC, ArrayStoreC, NegativeArraySizeC,$
   $ArithmeticC, IllegalMonitorStateC, IllegalThreadStateC,$
   $InterruptedC]$

$ObjectC =$
  $(Object, \text{""}, [],$
   $[(wait, [], Void, Native), (notify, [], Void, Native),$
    $(notifyAll, [], Void, Native), (hashcode, [], Integer, Native),$
    $(clone, [], Class\ Object, Native), (print, [Integer], Void, Native),$
    $(currentThread, [], Class\ Thread, Native),$
    $(interrupted, [], Boolean, Native), (yield, [], Void, Native)])$

$ThrowableC = (Throwable, Object, [], [])$

$NullPointerC = (NullPointer, Throwable, [], [])$

$ClassCastC = (ClassCast, Throwable, [], [])$

$OutOfMemoryC = (OutOfMemory, Throwable, [], [])$

$ArrayIndexOutOfBoundsC = (ArrayIndexOutOfBounds, Throwable, [], [])$

$ArrayStoreC = (ArrayStore, Throwable, [], [])$

$NegativeArraySizeC = (NegativeArraySize, Throwable, [], [])$

$ArithmeticC = (ArithmeticException, Throwable, [], [])$

$IllegalMonitorStateC = (IllegalMonitorState, Throwable, [], [])$

$IllegalThreadStateC = (IllegalThreadState, Throwable, [], [])$

$InterruptedC = (InterruptedException, Throwable, [], [])$

DON'T PANIC!
Douglas Adams, *The Hitchhiker's Guide to the Galaxy*

Formal definitions

This appendix contains the formal definitions for JinjaThreads source code and bytecode syntax and semantics. I have not repeated the interleaving framework from §3.1, because §3.1 already contains all unabridged definitions.

B.1 Declarations and lookup functions

Type declarations

datatype	$'addr\ val = Unit \mid Bool\ bool \mid Intg\ word32 \mid Null \mid Addr\ 'addr$
datatype	$ty = Void \mid Boolean \mid Integer \mid NT \mid Class\ cname \mid Array\ ty$
datatype	$hty = ClassT\ cname \mid ArrayT\ ty\ nat$
datatype	$'m\ prog = Program\ 'm\ cdecl\ list$
type_synonym	$'m\ cdecl = cname \times 'm\ class$
type_synonym	$'m\ class = cname \times fdecl\ list \times 'm\ option\ mdecl\ list$
type_synonym	$fdecl = vname \times ty \times fmod$
record	$fmod = volatile :: bool$
type_synonym	$'m\ mdecl = mname \times ty\ list \times ty \times 'm$

$$ty\text{-}of\,(ClassT\ C) = Class\ C \qquad ty\text{-}of\,(ArrayT\ T\ n) = T[]$$
$$array\text{-}length\text{-}of\,(ArrayT\ T\ n) = n$$

Lookup functions

class declarations	$classes\,(Program\ P) = P$
class declaration	$class\,(Program\ P) = map\text{-}of\ P$
valid class name	$is\text{-}class\ P\ C = (class\ P\ C \neq None)$

direct subclass relation

$$\frac{class\ P\ C = \lfloor (D, rest) \rfloor \qquad C \neq Object}{P \vdash C <^1 D}$$

subclass relation

$$P \vdash C \leq^* D = (\lambda C\ D.\ P \vdash C <^1 D)^{**}\ C\ D$$

valid types

$$
\begin{aligned}
&is\text{-}type\ P\ Void &&= True \\
&is\text{-}type\ P\ Boolean &&= True \\
&is\text{-}type\ P\ Integer &&= True \\
&is\text{-}type\ P\ NT &&= True \\
&is\text{-}type\ P\ (Class\ C) &&= is\text{-}class\ C \\
&is\text{-}type\ P\ (T[]) &&= is\text{-}type\ P\ T \wedge base\text{-}type\ T \neq NT
\end{aligned}
$$

$$types\ P = \{\ T.\ is\text{-}type\ P\ T\ \}$$

$$is\text{-}htype\ P\ hT = is\text{-}type\ P\ (ty\text{-}of\ hT)$$

base type

$$base\text{-}type\ T = (case\ T\ of\ T'[] \Rightarrow base\text{-}type\ T'\ |\ \_ \Rightarrow T)$$

method lookup

$$\_ \vdash \_\ sees\text{-}methods \_ ::$$

$$'m\ prog \Rightarrow cname \Rightarrow (mname \rightharpoonup (ty\ list \times ty \times 'm) \times cname) \Rightarrow bool$$

$$\frac{class\ P\ Object = \lfloor (D, fs, ms) \rfloor \qquad Mm = Option.map\ (\lambda m.\ (m, Object)) \circ map\text{-}of\ ms}{P \vdash Object\ sees\text{-}methods\ Mm}$$

$$\frac{class\ P\ C = \lfloor (D, fs, ms) \rfloor \quad C \neq Object \quad P \vdash D\ sees\text{-}methods\ Mm \qquad Mm' = Mm ++ (Option.map\ (\lambda m.\ (m, C)) \circ map\text{-}of\ ms)}{P \vdash C\ sees\text{-}methods\ Mm'}$$

where $\quad Option.map\ f\ None = None \qquad\qquad Option.map\ f\ \lfloor x \rfloor = \lfloor f\ x \rfloor$

$$P \vdash C\ sees\ M{:}Ts \rightarrow T = meth\ in\ D = \\ (\exists Mm.\ P \vdash C\ sees\text{-}methods\ Mm \wedge Mm\ M = \lfloor ((Ts, T, meth), D) \rfloor)$$

$$method\ P\ C\ M = (\iota(D, Ts, T, meth).\ P \vdash C\ sees\ M{:}Ts \rightarrow T = meth\ in\ D)$$

field lookup

$P \vdash F$ *has-fields* $FDTs ::$

$$'m\ prog \Rightarrow cname \Rightarrow ((vname \times cname) \times (ty \times fmod))\ list \Rightarrow bool$$

$$\frac{class\ P\ Object = \lfloor (D, fs, ms) \rfloor \quad FDTs = map\ (\lambda(F, T, fm).\ ((F, Object), (T, fm)))\ fs}{P \vdash Object\ has\text{-}fields\ FDTs}$$

$$\frac{class\ P\ C = \lfloor (D, fs, ms) \rfloor \quad C \neq Object \quad P \vdash D\ has\text{-}fields\ FDTs \quad FDTs' = map\ (\lambda(F, T, fm).\ ((F, C), (T, fm)))\ fs\ @\ FDTs}{P \vdash C\ has\text{-}fields\ FDTs'}$$

$P \vdash C\ has\ F{:}T\ (fm)\ in\ D =$
$\quad (\exists FDTs.\ P \vdash C\ has\text{-}fields\ FDTs \wedge map\text{-}of\ FDTs\ (F, D) = \lfloor (T, fm) \rfloor)$

$P \vdash C\ sees\ F{:}T\ (fm)\ in\ D = (\exists FDTs.\ P \vdash C\ has\text{-}fields\ FDTs \wedge$
$\quad map\text{-}of\ (map\ (\lambda((F, D), Tfm).\ (F, (D, Tfm)))\ FDTs)\ F = \lfloor (D, T, fm) \rfloor$

$fields\ P\ C = (\iota FDTs.\ P \vdash C\ has\text{-}fields\ FDTs)$

$field\ P\ C\ F = (\iota(D, T, fm).\ .\ P \vdash C\ sees\ F{:}T\ (fm)\ in\ D)$

$is\text{-}volatile\ P\ (Field\ F\ D) = volatile\ (snd\ (snd\ (field\ P\ D\ F)))$
$is\text{-}volatile\ P\ (Cell\ n) = False$

B.2 Binary operators

datatype $bop = == | != | < | <= | > | >= | + | - | * | / | \% |$
$\quad << | >> | >>> | \& | | | \hat{\ }$

Signatures

$$\frac{P \vdash T_1 \leq T_2 \vee P \vdash T_2 \leq T_1}{P \vdash T_1\ «==»\ T_2 :: Boolean} \qquad \frac{P \vdash T_1 \leq T_2 \vee P \vdash T_2 \leq T_1}{P \vdash T_1\ «!=»\ T_2 :: Boolean}$$

$P \vdash Integer\ «<»\ Integer :: Boolean \qquad P \vdash Integer\ «<=»\ Integer :: Boolean$

$P \vdash Integer\ «>»\ Integer :: Boolean \qquad P \vdash Integer\ «>=»\ Integer :: Boolean$

$P \vdash Integer\ «+»\ Integer :: Integer \qquad P \vdash Integer\ «-»\ Integer :: Integer$

$P \vdash Integer\ «*»\ Integer :: Integer \qquad P \vdash Integer\ «/»\ Integer :: Integer$

317

$$P \vdash Integer\,«\%»\,Integer :: Integer \qquad P \vdash Integer\,«<<»\,Integer :: Integer$$

$$P \vdash Integer\,«>>»\,Integer :: Integer \qquad P \vdash Integer\,«>>>»\,Integer :: Integer$$

$$P \vdash Integer\,«\&»\,Integer :: Integer \qquad P \vdash Boolean\,«\&»\,Boolean :: Boolean$$

$$P \vdash Integer\,«|»\,Integer :: Integer \qquad P \vdash Boolean\,«|»\,Boolean :: Boolean$$

$$P \vdash Integer\,«\hat{\,}»\,Integer :: Integer \qquad P \vdash Boolean\,«\hat{\,}»\,Boolean :: Boolean$$

Semantics

$$
\begin{aligned}
&binop \;==\quad v_1 \qquad\quad v_2 \qquad = \lfloor Inl\,(Bool\,(v_1 = v_2))\rfloor \\
&binop \;!=\quad\; v_1 \qquad\quad v_2 \qquad = \lfloor Inl\,(Bool\,(v_1 \neq v_2))\rfloor \\
&binop \;<\quad (Intg\,i_1)\;\;(Intg\,i_2) = \lfloor Inl\,(Bool\,(i_1 <_s i_2))\rfloor \\
&binop \;<=\;(Intg\,i_1)\;\;(Intg\,i_2) = \lfloor Inl\,(Bool\,(i_1 \leq_s i_2))\rfloor \\
&binop \;>\quad (Intg\,i_1)\;\;(Intg\,i_2) = \lfloor Inl\,(Bool\,(i_2 <_s i_1))\rfloor \\
&binop \;>=\;(Intg\,i_1)\;\;(Intg\,i_2) = \lfloor Inl\,(Bool\,(i_2 \leq_s i_1))\rfloor \\
&binop \;+\quad (Intg\,i_1)\;\;(Intg\,i_2) = \lfloor Inl\,(Bool\,(i_1 + i_2))\rfloor \\
&binop \;-\quad (Intg\,i_1)\;\;(Intg\,i_2) = \lfloor Inl\,(Bool\,(i_1 - i_2))\rfloor \\
&binop \;*\quad (Intg\,i_1)\;\;(Intg\,i_2) = \lfloor Inl\,(Bool\,(i_1 * i_2))\rfloor \\
&binop \;/\quad (Intg\,i_1)\;\;(Intg\,i_2) = \\
&\quad \lfloor if\,i_2 = 0\;then\;Inr\,(addr\text{-}of\text{-}sys\text{-}xcpt\;ArithmeticException) \\
&\qquad\qquad else\;Inl\,(Intg\,(i_1\;sdiv\,i_2))\rfloor \\
&binop \;\%\quad (Intg\,i_1)\;\;(Intg\,i_2) = \\
&\quad \lfloor if\,i_2 = 0\;then\;Inr\,(addr\text{-}of\text{-}sys\text{-}xcpt\;ArithmeticException) \\
&\qquad\qquad else\;Inl\,(Intg\,(i_1\;smod\,i_2))\rfloor \\
&binop \;\&\quad (Intg\,i_1)\;\;(Intg\,i_2) = \lfloor Inl\,(Intg\,(i_1\;AND\;i_2))\rfloor \\
&binop \;\&\quad (Bool\,b_1)\,(Bool\,b_2) = \lfloor Inl\,(Bool\,(b_1 \wedge b_2))\rfloor \\
&binop \;|\quad (Intg\,i_1)\;\;(Intg\,i_2) = \lfloor Inl\,(Intg\,(i_1\;OR\;i_2))\rfloor \\
&binop \;|\quad (Bool\,b_1)\,(Bool\,b_2) = \lfloor Inl\,(Bool\,(b_1 \vee b_2))\rfloor \\
&binop \;\hat{\,}\quad (Intg\,i_1)\;\;(Intg\,i_2) = \lfloor Inl\,(Intg\,(i_1\;XOR\;i_2))\rfloor \\
&binop \;\hat{\,}\quad (Bool\,b_1)\,(Bool\,b_2) = \lfloor Inl\,(Bool\,(b_1 \neq b_2))\rfloor \\
&binop \;<<\;(Intg\,i_1)\;\;(Intg\,i_2) = \lfloor Inl\,(Intg\,(i_1 << unat\,(i_2\;AND\;0x1f)))\rfloor \\
&binop \;>>\;(Intg\,i_1)\;\;(Intg\,i_2) = \lfloor Inl\,(Intg\,(i_1 >>> unat\,(i_2\;AND\;0x1f)))\rfloor \\
&binop >>>\,(Intg\,i_1)\;\;(Intg\,i_2) = \lfloor Inl\,(Intg\,(i_1 >> unat\,(i_2\;AND\;0x1f)))\rfloor \\
&binop \;\_\qquad\quad \_\qquad\qquad \_\qquad = None
\end{aligned}
$$

Auxiliary functions on *word32*:

$<_s, \leq_s$	signed comparisons
$+, -, *$	addition, subtraction, and multiplication
sdiv, smod	signed division and remainder
AND, OR, XOR	bitwise "and", "or", and "xor"
unat	unsigned interpretation of *word32* as *nat*
$<<, >>, >>>$	left shift, unsigned and signed right shift[63]

B.3 Heap module implementations

default values

$default\text{-}val :: ty \Rightarrow {}'addr\ val$
$default\text{-}val\ Void \quad = Unit \qquad\qquad default\text{-}val\ NT \qquad = Null$
$default\text{-}val\ Boolean = Bool\ False \qquad default\text{-}val\ (Class\ C) = Null$
$default\text{-}val\ Integer \; = Intg\ 0 \qquad\quad default\text{-}val\ (T[]) \qquad = Null$

conformance
$P, h \vdash v :\leq T \longleftrightarrow (\exists T'.\ typeof_h\ v = \lfloor T' \rfloor \wedge P \vdash T' \leq T)$
$P, h \vdash vs\ [:\leq]\ Ts \longleftrightarrow |vs| = |Ts| \wedge (\forall(v, T) \in set\ (zip\ vs\ Ts).\ P, h \vdash v :\leq T)$
$P, h \vdash xs\ (:\leq)\ E \longleftrightarrow (\forall V\ v.\ xs\ V = \lfloor v \rfloor \longrightarrow (\exists T.\ E\ V = \lfloor T \rfloor \wedge P, h \vdash v :\leq T))$
$P, E \vdash (h, xs)\surd \longleftrightarrow P, h \vdash xs\ (:\leq)\ E \wedge hconf\ h$

B.3.1 Sequential consistency

type of thread IDs (instantiates $'t$):
 type_synonym *thread-id* $= nat$

type of addresses (instantiates $'addr$):
 type_synonym *addr* $\quad = nat$

type of the heap (instantiates $'heap$):
 type_synonym *heap* $\qquad = addr \rightharpoonup heap\text{-}entry$
 datatype *heap-entry* $\quad = Obj\ cname\ fields\ |\ Arr\ ty\ fields\ cells$
 type_synonym *fields* $\qquad = vname \times cname \rightharpoonup addr\ val$
 type_synonym *cells* $\qquad = addr\ val\ list$

conversion between address and thread ID
 abbreviation *sc-a2t* $\quad = (\lambda a.\ a)$
 abbreviation *sc-t2a* $\quad = (\lambda t.\ t)$

---

[63]Note that the meaning of >> and >>> from Isabelle's word library is opposite to Java.

implementation of abstract heap operations

$sc\text{-}typeof\text{-}addr\,h\,a$ $= (case\,h\,a\,of\,\lfloor Obj\,C\,\_\rfloor \Rightarrow \lfloor ClassT\,C\rfloor$
$\qquad\qquad\qquad\qquad\qquad | \lfloor Arr\,T\,\_\,cs\rfloor \Rightarrow \lfloor ArrayT\,T\,|cs|\rfloor$
$\qquad\qquad\qquad\qquad\qquad | \,None \Rightarrow None)$

$sc\text{-}empty\text{-}heap$ $= empty$

$sc\text{-}allocate\,P\,h\,hT$ $=$
$\qquad (case\,new\text{-}Addr\,h\,of\,None \Rightarrow (h, None)$
$\qquad\qquad\qquad\qquad | \lfloor a\rfloor \Rightarrow (h(a \mapsto blank\,P\,hT)\,,\lfloor a\rfloor))$

$sc\text{-}read:$
$$\frac{h\,a = \lfloor Obj\,C\,fs\rfloor \qquad fs\,(F, D) = \lfloor v\rfloor}{sc\text{-}read\,h\,a\,(Field\,F\,D)\,v}$$

$$\frac{h\,a = \lfloor Arr\,T\,fs\,cs\rfloor \qquad fs\,(F, D) = \lfloor v\rfloor}{sc\text{-}read\,h\,a\,(Field\,F\,D)\,v}$$

$$\frac{h\,a = \lfloor Arr\,T\,fs\,cs\rfloor \qquad n < |cs|}{sc\text{-}read\,h\,a\,(Cell\,n)\,cs_{[n]}}$$

$sc\text{-}write:$
$$\frac{h\,a = \lfloor Obj\,C\,fs\rfloor \qquad h' = h(a \mapsto Obj\,C\,(fs((F, D) \mapsto v)))}{sc\text{-}write\,h\,a\,(Field\,F\,D)\,v\,h'}$$

$$\frac{h\,a = \lfloor Arr\,T\,fs\,cs\rfloor \qquad h' = h(a \mapsto Arr\,T\,(fs((F, D) \mapsto v))\,cs)}{sc\text{-}write\,h\,a\,(Field\,F\,D)\,v\,h'}$$

$$\frac{h\,a = \lfloor Arr\,T\,fs\,cs\rfloor \qquad h' = h(a \mapsto Arr\,T\,fs\,(cs[n := v]))}{sc\text{-}write\,h\,a\,(Cell\,n)\,v\,h'}$$

auxiliary definitions

$hash\text{-}addr$ $= word\text{-}of\text{-}int \circ int$

$new\text{-}Addr\,h$ $=$
$\qquad (if\,\exists a.\,h\,a = None\,then\,\lfloor LEAST\,a.\,h\,a = None\rfloor\,else\,None)$

$blank\,P\,(ClassT\,C)$ $= Obj\,C\,(init\text{-}fields\,(fields\,P\,C))$

$blank\,P\,(ArrayT\,T\,n)$ $=$
$\qquad Arr\,T\,(init\text{-}fields\,(fields\,P\,Object)\,(replicate\,n\,(default\text{-}val\,T))$

$init\text{-}fields$ $=$
$\qquad map\text{-}of \circ map\,(\lambda(FD, (T, fm)).\,(FD, default\text{-}val\,T))$

heap conformance

$P \vdash_{sc} h\surd$ $= (\forall ho \in ran\,h.\,P, h \vdash_{sc} ho\surd)$

$P, h \vdash_{sc} Obj\,C\,fs\surd$ $= is\text{-}class\,P\,C \wedge P, C, h \vdash_{sc} fs\surd$

$P, h \vdash_{sc} Arr\,T\,fs\,cs\surd$ $=$
$\qquad is\text{-}type\,P\,(T[]) \wedge P, Object, h \vdash_{sc} fs\surd \wedge (\forall v \in set\,cs.P, h \vdash_{sc} v :\preceq T)$

$P, C, h \vdash_{sc} fs\sqrt{}$ $=$
$(\forall\, F\, T\, fm\, D.\ P \vdash C\ has\ F{:}T\ (fm)\ in\ D \longrightarrow$
$(\exists v.\ fs\ (F, D) = \lfloor v \rfloor \wedge P, h \vdash_{sc} v :\leq T))$

B.3.2 The Java memory model

Version 1: Type information grows

thread IDs and addresses are unified, but remain unspecified
type of the heap (instantiates $'heap$):
    type_synonym $'addr\ jmm\text{-}heap = {'addr} \rightharpoonup hty$

conversion between address and thread ID
    abbreviation $jmm\text{-}a2t$ $= (\lambda a.\, a)$
    abbreviation $jmm\text{-}t2a$ $= (\lambda t.\, t)$

implementation of abstract heap operations
    $jmm\text{-}typeof\text{-}addr\ h\ a$ $= Option.map\ ty\text{-}of\ (h\ a)$
    $jmm\text{-}empty\text{-}heap$ $= empty$
    $jmm\text{-}allocate\ h\ hT$ $=$
        $(case\ jmm\text{-}new\text{-}Addr\ h\ of\ None \Rightarrow (h, None)$
                        $|\ \lfloor a \rfloor \Rightarrow (h(a \mapsto hT), \lfloor a \rfloor))$
    $jmm\text{-}read\ h\ a\ al\ v$ $= True$
    $jmm\text{-}write\ h\ a\ al\ v\ h'$ $= (h' = h)$

auxiliary definitions
    $jmm\text{-}new\text{-}Addr\ h$ $=$
        $(if\ \exists a.\ h\ a = None\ then\ \lfloor \varepsilon a.\ h\ a = None \rfloor\ else\ None)$

heap conformance
    $P \vdash_{jmm} h\sqrt{}$ $= (\forall hT \in ran\ h.\ is\text{-}htype\ P\ hT)$

Version 2: Addresses store type information

type of addresses (instantiates $'addr$):
    datatype $addr$ $= Address\ hty\ nat$

type of thread IDs (instantiates $'t$):
    type_synonym $thread\text{-}id = addr$

type of the heap (instantiates $'heap$):
    type_synonym $jmm'\text{-}heap = hty \Rightarrow nat$

conversion between address and thread ID
  abbreviation jmm'-$a2t$ $\quad = (\lambda a.\, a)$
  abbreviation jmm'-$t2a$ $\quad = (\lambda t.\, t)$

implementation of abstract heap operations:
  jmm'-$typeof$-$addr\ P\ h\ (Address\ hT\ n) =$
    $(if\ is\text{-}htype\ P\ hT\ then\ \lfloor hT \rfloor\ else\ None)$
  jmm'-$empty$-$heap$ $\quad = (\lambda hT.\, 0)$
  jmm'-$allocate\ h\ hT$ $\quad =$
    $(let\ n = h\ hT\ in\ (h(hT := n+1),\lfloor Address\ hT\ n \rfloor))$
  jmm'-$read\ P\ h\ a\ al\ v$ $\quad = (\forall T.\ P,h \vdash_{jmm'} a{\cdot}al : T \longrightarrow P,h \vdash_{jmm'} v :\leq T)$
  jmm'-$write\ h\ a\ al\ v\ h'$ $\quad = (h' = h)$

auxiliary definitions
  $hash$-$addr\ (Address\ hT\ n) = word\text{-}of\text{-}int\ (int\ n)$

heap conformance
  jmm'-$hconf\ h$ $\qquad\qquad = True$

B.4   Native methods

B.4.1   Signatures

$Thread.start(\lfloor\rfloor) :: Void$
$Thread.join(\lfloor\rfloor) :: Void$
$Thread.interrupt(\lfloor\rfloor) :: Void$
$Thread.isInterrupted(\lfloor\rfloor) :: Boolean$
$Object.wait(\lfloor\rfloor) :: Void$
$Object.notify(\lfloor\rfloor) :: Void$
$Object.notifyAll(\lfloor\rfloor) :: Void$
$Object.clone(\lfloor\rfloor) :: Class\ Object$
$Object.hashcode(\lfloor\rfloor) :: Integer$
$Object.currentThread(\lfloor\rfloor) :: Class\ Thread$
$Object.interrupted(\lfloor\rfloor) :: Boolean$
$Object.yield(\lfloor\rfloor) :: Void$
$Object.print(\lfloor Integer \rfloor) :: Void$

B.4.2 Semantics of method *clone*

copying one member:

$$copy\text{-}mem :: {}'addr \Rightarrow {}'addr \Rightarrow loc \Rightarrow {}'heap \Rightarrow ({}'addr, {}'t)\ event\ list \Rightarrow {}'heap \Rightarrow bool$$

$$\frac{read\ h\ a\ al\ v \qquad write\ h\ a'\ al\ v\ h'}{copy\text{-}mem\ a\ a'\ al\ h\ [Read\ a\ al\ v, Write\ a'\ al\ v]\ h'}$$

copying a list of members:

$$copy\text{-}mems :: {}'addr \Rightarrow {}'addr \Rightarrow loc\ list \Rightarrow {}'heap$$
$$\Rightarrow ({}'addr, {}'t)\ event\ list \Rightarrow {}'heap \Rightarrow bool$$

$$copy\text{-}mems\ a\ a'\ [\,]\ h\ [\,]\ h$$

$$\frac{copy\text{-}mem\ a\ a'\ al\ h\ \alpha s\ h' \qquad copy\text{-}mems\ a\ a'\ als\ h'\ \alpha s'\ h''}{copy\text{-}mems\ a\ a'\ (al \cdot als)\ h\ (\alpha s\ @\ \alpha s')\ h''}$$

cloning an object or array:

$$heap\text{-}clone :: {}'m\ prog \Rightarrow {}'heap \Rightarrow {}'addr$$
$$\Rightarrow {}'heap \Rightarrow (({}'addr, {}'t)\ event \times {}'addr)\ option \Rightarrow bool$$

$$\frac{typeof\text{-}addr\ h\ a = \lfloor hT \rfloor \qquad alloc\ h\ hT = (h', None)}{heap\text{-}clone\ P\ h\ a\ h'\ None}$$

$$\frac{\begin{array}{c} typeof\text{-}addr\ h\ a = \lfloor ClassT\ C \rfloor \\ alloc\ h\ (ClassT\ C) = (h', \lfloor a' \rfloor) \qquad P \vdash C\ has\text{-}fields\ FDTs \\ copy\text{-}mems\ a\ a'\ (map\ (\lambda((F, D), \_).\ Field\ F\ D)\ FDTs)\ h'\ \alpha s\ h'' \end{array}}{heap\text{-}clone\ P\ h\ a\ h''\ \lfloor (New\text{-}Obj\ a'\ C \cdot \alpha s, a') \rfloor}$$

$$\frac{\begin{array}{c} typeof\text{-}addr\ h\ a = \lfloor ArrayT\ T\ n \rfloor \\ alloc\ h\ (ArrayT\ T\ n) = (h', \lfloor a' \rfloor) \qquad P \vdash Object\ has\text{-}fields\ FDTs \\ als = map\ (\lambda((F, D), \_).\ Field\ F\ D)\ FDTs\ @\ map\ Cell\ [0..{<}n] \\ copy\text{-}mems\ a\ a'\ als\ h'\ \alpha s\ h'' \end{array}}{heap\text{-}clone\ P\ h\ a\ h''\ \lfloor (New\text{-}Arr\ a'\ T\ n \cdot \alpha s, a') \rfloor}$$

B.4.3 Semantics of native methods

native methods of class *Thread* (Figure 3.17):

$$\frac{\textit{typeof-addr } h \, a = \lfloor \textit{ClassT C} \rfloor \qquad P \vdash C \preceq^* \textit{Thread} \qquad t' = \textit{a2t a}}{P, t \vdash \langle a.start([\,]), h \rangle - (\!|\textit{Spawn } t' \, (C, run, a) \, h, \textit{TStart } t'|\!) \rightarrow_{nc} \langle \textit{Ret-Val Unit}, h \rangle}$$

$$\frac{\textit{typeof-addr } h \, a = \lfloor \textit{ClassT C} \rfloor \qquad P \vdash C \preceq^* \textit{Thread}}{P, t \vdash \langle a.start([\,]), h \rangle - (\!|\textit{ThreadEx } (\textit{a2t a}) \, \textit{True}|\!) \rightarrow_{nc}}{\langle \textit{Ret-sys-xcpt IllegalThreadState}, h \rangle}$$

$$\frac{\textit{typeof-addr } h \, a = \lfloor \textit{ClassT C} \rfloor \qquad P \vdash C \preceq^* \textit{Thread} \qquad t' = \textit{a2t a}}{P, t \vdash \langle a.join([\,]), h \rangle - (\!|\textit{Join } t', \textit{IsIntrd } t \, \textit{False}, \textit{TJoin } t'|\!) \rightarrow_{nc} \langle \textit{Ret-Val Unit}, h \rangle}$$

$$\frac{\textit{typeof-addr } h \, a = \lfloor \textit{ClassT C} \rfloor \qquad P \vdash C \preceq^* \textit{Thread}}{P, t \vdash \langle a.join([\,]), h \rangle - (\!|\textit{IsIntrd } t \, \textit{True}, \textit{ClearIntr } t, \textit{TIntrd } t|\!) \rightarrow_{nc}}{\langle \textit{Ret-sys-xcpt InterruptedException}, h \rangle}$$

$$\frac{\textit{typeof-addr } h \, a = \lfloor \textit{ClassT C} \rfloor \qquad P \vdash C \preceq^* \textit{Thread} \qquad t' = \textit{a2t a}}{P, t \vdash \langle a.interrupt([\,]), h \rangle - (\!|\textit{ThreadEx } t' \, \textit{True}, \textit{WakeUp } t', \textit{Intr } t', \textit{TIntr } t'|\!) \rightarrow_{nc}}{\langle \textit{Ret-Val Unit}, h \rangle}$$

$$\frac{\textit{typeof-addr } h \, a = \lfloor \textit{ClassT C} \rfloor \qquad P \vdash C \preceq^* \textit{Thread} \qquad t' = \textit{a2t a}}{P, t \vdash \langle a.interrupt([\,]), h \rangle - (\!|\textit{ThreadEx } t' \, \textit{False}|\!) \rightarrow_{nc} \langle \textit{Ret-Val Unit}, h \rangle}$$

$$\frac{\textit{typeof-addr } h \, a = \lfloor \textit{ClassT C} \rfloor \qquad P \vdash C \preceq^* \textit{Thread} \qquad t' = \textit{a2t a}}{P, t \vdash \langle a.isInterrupted([\,]), h \rangle - (\!|\textit{IsIntrd } t' \, \textit{True}, \textit{TIntrd } t'|\!) \rightarrow_{nc}}{\langle \textit{Ret-Val } (\textit{Bool True}), h \rangle}$$

$$\frac{\textit{typeof-addr } h \, a = \lfloor \textit{ClassT C} \rfloor \qquad P \vdash C \preceq^* \textit{Thread} \qquad t' = \textit{a2t a}}{P, t \vdash \langle a.isInterrupted([\,]), h \rangle - (\!|\textit{IsIntrd } t' \, \textit{False}|\!) \rightarrow_{nc} \langle \textit{Ret-Val } (\textit{Bool False}), h \rangle}$$

static native methods of class *Thread* as methods of class *Object* (Figure 3.18):

$$P, t \vdash \langle a.currentThread([\,]), h \rangle - (\!|\,|\!) \rightarrow_{nc} \langle \textit{Ret-Val } (\textit{Addr } (\textit{t2a } t)), h \rangle$$

$$P, t \vdash \langle a.interrupted([\,]), h \rangle - (\!|\textit{IsIntrd } t \, \textit{True}, \textit{ClearIntr } t, \textit{TIntrd } t|\!) \rightarrow_{nc}}{\langle \textit{Ret-Val } (\textit{Bool True}), h \rangle}$$

$$P, t \vdash \langle a.interrupted([\,]), h \rangle - (\!|IsIntrd\ t\ False|\!) \rightarrow_{nc} \langle Ret\text{-}Val\ (Bool\ False), h \rangle$$

$$P, t \vdash \langle a.yield([\,]), h \rangle - (\!|Yield|\!) \rightarrow_{nc} \langle Ret\text{-}Val\ Unit, h \rangle$$

native methods of class *Object* (Figures 2.12 and 3.19 and Equation 4.1):

$$\frac{heap\text{-}clone\ P\ h\ a\ h'\ None}{P, t \vdash \langle a.clone([\,]), h \rangle - (\!|\,|\!) \rightarrow_{nc} \langle Ret\text{-}sys\text{-}xcpt\ OutOfMemory, h' \rangle}$$

$$\frac{heap\text{-}clone\ P\ h\ a\ h'\ \lfloor (\alpha s, a') \rfloor}{P, t \vdash \langle a.clone([\,]), h \rangle - (K^f[\,], [\,], [\,], [\,], [\,], \alpha s) \rightarrow_{nc} \langle Ret\text{-}Val\ (Addr\ a'), h' \rangle}$$

$$P, t \vdash \langle a.hashcode([\,]), h \rangle - (\!|\,|\!) \rightarrow_{nc} \langle Ret\text{-}Val\ (Intg\ (hash\text{-}addr\ a)), h \rangle$$

$$P, t \vdash \langle a.notify([\,]), h \rangle - (\!|Unlock{\rightarrow}a, Lock{\rightarrow}a, Notify\ a|\!) \rightarrow_{nc} \langle Ret\text{-}Val\ Unit, h \rangle$$

$$P, t \vdash \langle a.notify([\,]), h \rangle - (\!|UnlockFail{\rightarrow}a|\!) \rightarrow_{nc}$$
$$\langle Ret\text{-}sys\text{-}xcpt\ IllegalMonitorState, h \rangle$$

$$P, t \vdash \langle a.notifyAll([\,]), h \rangle - (\!|Unlock{\rightarrow}a, Lock{\rightarrow}a, NotifyAll\ a|\!) \rightarrow_{nc}$$
$$\langle Ret\text{-}Val\ Unit, h \rangle$$

$$P, t \vdash \langle a.notifyAll([\,]), h \rangle - (\!|UnlockFail{\rightarrow}a|\!) \rightarrow_{nc}$$
$$\langle Ret\text{-}sys\text{-}xcpt\ IllegalMonitorState, h \rangle$$

$$P, t \vdash \langle a.wait([\,]), h \rangle - (\!|UnlockFail{\rightarrow}a|\!) \rightarrow_{nc} \langle Ret\text{-}sys\text{-}xcpt\ IllegalMonitorState, h \rangle$$

$$P, t \vdash \langle a.wait([\,]), h \rangle$$
$$- (\!|Unlock{\rightarrow}a, Lock{\rightarrow}a, IsIntrd\ t\ True, ClearIntr\ t, TIntrd\ t|\!) \rightarrow_{nc}$$
$$\langle Ret\text{-}sys\text{-}xcpt\ InterruptedException, h \rangle$$

$$P, t \vdash \langle a.wait([\,]), h \rangle$$
$$- (\!|Suspend\ a, Unlock{\rightarrow}a, Lock{\rightarrow}a, Release{\rightarrow}a,$$
$$IsIntrd\ t\ False, SUnlock\ a|\!) \rightarrow_{nc}$$
$$\langle Ret\text{-}Unchanged, h \rangle$$

$$P, t \vdash \langle a.wait([\,]), h \rangle - (\!|Notified|\!) \rightarrow_{nc} \langle Ret\text{-}Val\ Unit, h \rangle$$

$$P, t \vdash \langle a.wait([\,]), h \rangle - (\!|WokenUp, ClearIntr\ t, TIntrd\ t|\!) \rightarrow_{nc}$$
$$\langle Ret\text{-}sys\text{-}xcpt\ InterruptedException, h \rangle$$

$$P, t \vdash \langle a.print(vs), h \rangle - (\!|Extern\ a\ print\ vs\ Unit|\!) \rightarrow_{nc} \langle Ret\text{-}Val\ unit, h \rangle$$

aggressive functional implementation of native methods:

$exec\text{-}native :: 'm \ prog \Rightarrow 't \Rightarrow 'addr \Rightarrow mname \Rightarrow 'addr \ val \ list \Rightarrow 'heap$
$\qquad\qquad \Rightarrow ((('addr, 't, cname \times mname \times 'addr, 'heap, 'addr, ('addr, 't) \ event)$
$\qquad\qquad\quad thread\text{-}action \times 'addr \ native\text{-}ret \times 'heap) \ set$
$exec\text{-}native \ P \ t \ a \ M \ vs \ h =$
$(if \ M = wait \ then$
$\quad \{ \ ((\langle Unlock{\to}a, Lock{\to}a, IsIntrd \ t \ True, ClearIntr \ t, TIntrd \ t\rangle,$
$\qquad Ret\text{-}sys\text{-}xcpt \ InterruptedException, h),$
$\qquad (\langle Suspend \ a, Unlock{\to}a, Lock{\to}a, Release{\to}a, IsIntrd \ t \ False, SUnlock \ a\rangle,$
$\qquad Ret\text{-}Unchanged, h),$
$\qquad (\langle UnlockFail{\to}a\rangle, Ret\text{-}sys\text{-}xcpt \ IllegalMonitorState, h),$
$\qquad (\langle Notified\rangle, Ret\text{-}Val \ Unit, h),$
$\qquad (\langle WokenUp, ClearIntr \ t, TIntrd \ t\rangle, h, Ret\text{-}sys\text{-}xcpt \ InterruptedException) \ \}$
$else \ if \ M = notify \ then$
$\quad \{ \ ((\langle Notify \ a, Unlock{\to}a, Lock{\to}a\rangle, Ret\text{-}Val \ Unit, h),$
$\qquad (\langle UnlockFail{\to}a\rangle, Ret\text{-}sys\text{-}xcpt \ IllegalMonitorState, h) \ \}$
$else \ if \ M = notifyAll \ then$
$\quad \{ \ ((\langle NotifyAll \ a, Unlock{\to}a, Lock{\to}a\rangle, Ret\text{-}Val \ Unit, h),$
$\qquad (\langle UnlockFail{\to}a\rangle, Ret\text{-}sys\text{-}xcpt \ IllegalMonitorState, h) \ \}$
$else \ if \ M = clone \ then$
$\quad \{ \ (K^f \ [], [], [], [], [], \alpha s), Ret\text{-}Val \ a', h') \ | \ \alpha s \ a' \ h'. \ heap\text{-}clone \ P \ h \ a \ h' \ \lfloor(\alpha s, a')\rfloor \}$
$\quad \cup \{ \ ((\langle\rangle, Ret\text{-}sys\text{-}xcpt \ OutOfMemory, h') \ | \ h'. \ heap\text{-}clone \ P \ h \ a \ h' \ None \}$
$else \ if \ M = hashcode \ then \ \{ \ ((\langle\rangle, Ret\text{-}Val \ (Intg \ (hash\text{-}addr \ a)), h) \ \}$
$else \ if \ M = print \ then \ \{ \ ((\langle Extern \ a \ M \ vs \ Unit\rangle, Ret\text{-}Val \ Unit, h) \ \}$
$else \ if \ M = currentThread \ then \ \{ \ ((\langle\rangle, Ret\text{-}Val \ (Addr \ (a2t \ a)), h) \ \}$
$else \ if \ M = interrupted \ then$
$\quad \{ \ ((\langle IsIntrd \ t \ True, ClearIntr \ t, TIntrd \ t\rangle, Ret\text{-}Val \ (Bool \ True), h),$
$\qquad (\langle IsIntrd \ t \ False\rangle, Ret\text{-}Val \ (Bool \ False), h) \ \}$
$else \ if \ M = yield \ then \ \{ \ ((\langle Yield\rangle, Ret\text{-}Val \ Unit, h) \ \}$
$else \ let \ \lfloor hT \rfloor = typeof\text{-}addr \ h \ a$
$\quad in \ if \ P \vdash ty\text{-}of \ hT \leq Class \ Thread \ then \ let \ t_a = a2t \ a; Class \ C = ty\text{-}of \ hT \ in$
$\qquad if \ M = start \ then$
$\qquad\quad \{ \ ((\langle Spawn \ t_a \ (C, run, a) \ h, TStart \ t_a\rangle, Ret\text{-}Val \ Unit, h),$
$\qquad\qquad (\langle ThreadEx \ t_a \ True\rangle, Ret\text{-}sys\text{-}xcpt \ IllegalThreadState, h) \ \}$
$\qquad else \ if \ M = join \ then$
$\qquad\quad \{ \ ((\langle Join \ t_a, IsIntrd \ t \ False, TJoin \ t_a\rangle, Ret\text{-}Val \ Unit, h),$
$\qquad\qquad (\langle IsIntrd \ t \ True, ClearIntr \ t, TIntrd \ t\rangle,$
$\qquad\qquad Ret\text{-}sys\text{-}xcpt \ InterruptedException, h) \ \}$
$\qquad else \ if \ M = interrupt \ then$
$\qquad\quad \{ \ ((\langle ThreadEx \ t_a \ True, WakeUp \ t_a, Intr \ t_a, TIntr \ t_a\rangle, Ret\text{-}Val \ Unit, h),$
$\qquad\qquad (\langle ThreadEx \ t_a \ False\rangle, Ret\text{-}Val \ Unit, h) \ \}$

$else\ if\ M = isInterrupted\ then$
  $\{\,((\!\langle IsIntrd\ t_a\ False\rangle\!),Ret\text{-}Val\,(Bool\ False),h),$
    $((\!\langle IsIntrd\ t_a\ True,\ TIntrd\ t_a\rangle\!),Ret\text{-}Val\,(Bool\ True),h)\,\}$
  $else\,\{\,((\!\langle\rangle\!),undefined)\,\}$
$else\,\{\,((\!\langle\rangle\!),undefined)\,\})$

B.4.4 Observability

unobservable native methods calls: $\tau native :: cname \Rightarrow mname \Rightarrow bool$

$\tau native\ Object\ hashcode$ $\qquad\qquad \tau native\ Object\ currentThread$

B.5 Generic well-formedness

$sys\text{-}xcpts :: cname\ list$
$sys\text{-}xcpts = [NullPointer, ClassCast, ArithmeticException, OutOfMemory,$
         $ArrayIndexOutOfBounds, ArrayStore, NegativeArraySize,$
         $IllegalThreadState, IllegalMonitorState, InterruptedException]$

$wf\text{-}prog :: {}'m\ wf\text{-}mdecl\text{-}test \Rightarrow {}'m\ prog \Rightarrow bool$
$wf\text{-}prog\ wf\text{-}md\ P \longleftrightarrow wf\text{-}syscls\ P \wedge distinct\,(map\ fst\,(classes\ P)) \wedge$
         $(\forall cd \in set\,(classes\ P).\ wf\text{-}cdecl\ wf\text{-}md\ P\ cd)$

$wf\text{-}syscls :: {}'m\ prog \Rightarrow bool$
$wf\text{-}syscls\ P \longleftrightarrow is\text{-}class\ P\ Object \wedge is\text{-}class\ P\ Throwable \wedge is\text{-}class\ P\ Thread \wedge$
         $(\forall C \in set\ sys\text{-}xcpts.\ P \vdash C \leq^* Throwable)$

$wf\text{-}cdecl :: {}'m\ wf\text{-}mdecl\text{-}test \Rightarrow {}'m\ prog \Rightarrow {}'m\ cdecl \Rightarrow bool$
$wf\text{-}cdecl\ wf\text{-}md\ P\ (C, D, fs, ms) \longleftrightarrow$
  $(\forall fd \in set\ fs.\ wf\text{-}fdecl\ P\ fd) \wedge distinct\,(map\ fst\ fs) \wedge$
  $(\forall md \in set\ ms.\ wf\text{-}mdecl\ wf\text{-}md\ P\ C\ md) \wedge distinct\,(map\ fst\ ms) \wedge$
  $(C \neq Object \longrightarrow is\text{-}class\ P\ D \wedge \neg\ P \vdash D \leq^* C \wedge$
         $(\forall md \in set\ ms.\ wf\text{-}overriding\ P\ D\ md) \wedge$
  $(C = Thread \longrightarrow (\exists m.\ (run, [], Void,\ m) \in set\ ms))$

$wf\text{-}fdecl :: {}'m\ prog \Rightarrow fdecl \Rightarrow bool$
$wf\text{-}fdecl\ P\ (F, T, fm) \longleftrightarrow is\text{-}type\ P\ T$

$wf\text{-}overriding :: {}'m\ prog \Rightarrow cname \Rightarrow {}'m\ mdecl \Rightarrow bool$
$wf\text{-}overriding\ P\ D\ (M, Ts, T_r, m) \longleftrightarrow (\forall D'\ Ts'\ T'_r\ m'.$
  $P \vdash D\ sees\ M{:}Ts' {\rightarrow} T'_r = m'\ in\ D' \longrightarrow P \vdash Ts'\ [\leq]\ Ts \wedge P \vdash T_r \leq T'_r)$

$wf\text{-}mdecl :: 'm\ wf\text{-}mdecl\text{-}test \Rightarrow 'm\ option\ wf\text{-}mdecl\text{-}test$
$wf\text{-}mdecl\ wf\text{-}md\ P\ C\ (M, Ts, T_r, m) \longleftrightarrow$
$\quad set\ Ts \subseteq types\ P \wedge is\text{-}type\ P\ T_r \wedge$
$\quad (case\ m\ of\ Native \Rightarrow C.M(Ts) :: T_r$
$\qquad\quad | \lfloor mb \rfloor \Rightarrow wf\text{-}md\ P\ C\ (M, Ts, T_r, mb))$

B.6 Source code

B.6.1 Syntax

datatype $('a, 'b, 'addr)\ exp = new\ cname\ |\ new\ ty[('a, 'b, 'addr)\ exp]\ |$
$\quad Cast\ ty\ ('a, 'b, 'addr)\ exp\ |\ ('a, 'b, 'addr)\ exp\ instanceof\ ty\ |\ Val\ 'addr\ val\ |$
$\quad ('a, 'b, 'addr)\ exp\ «bop»\ ('a, 'b, 'addr)\ exp\ |\ Var\ 'a\ |$
$\quad 'a := ('a, 'b, 'addr)\ exp\ |\ ('a, 'b, 'addr)\ exp[('a, 'b, 'addr)\ exp]\ |$
$\quad ('a, 'b, 'addr)\ exp[('a, 'b, 'addr)\ exp] := ('a, 'b, 'addr)\ exp\ |\ ('a, 'b, 'addr)\ exp.length\ |$
$\quad ('a, 'b, 'addr)\ exp.vname\{cname\}\ |$
$\quad ('a, 'b, 'addr)\ exp.vname\{cname\} := ('a, 'b, 'addr)\ exp\ |$
$\quad ('a, 'b, 'addr)\ exp.mname(('a, 'b, 'addr)\ exp\ list)\ |$
$\quad \{'a : ty = 'addr\ val\ option;\ ('a, 'b, 'addr)\ exp\}\ |$
$\quad ('a, 'b, 'addr)\ exp;;\ ('a, 'b, 'addr)\ exp\ |$
$\quad if\ (('a, 'b, 'addr)\ exp)\ ('a, 'b, 'addr)\ exp\ else\ ('a, 'b, 'addr)\ exp\ |$
$\quad while\ (('a, 'b, 'addr)\ exp)\ ('a, 'b, 'addr)\ exp\ |\ throw\ ('a, 'b, 'addr)\ exp\ |$
$\quad try\ ('a, 'b, 'addr)\ exp\ catch(cname\ 'a)\ ('a, 'b, 'addr)\ exp\ |$
$\quad sync_b\ (('a, 'b, 'addr)\ exp)\ ('a, 'b, 'addr)\ exp\ |\ insync_b\ ('addr)\ ('a, 'b, 'addr)\ exp$

type_synonym $'addr\ expr\ \ \ = (vname, unit, 'addr)\ exp$
type_synonym $'addr\ J\text{-}mb\ \ \ = vname\ list \times 'addr\ expr$
type_synonym $'addr\ J\text{-}prog = 'addr\ J\text{-}mb\ prog$

B.6.2 Typing rules for expressions

$$\frac{is\text{-}class\ P\ C}{P, E \vdash new\ C :: Class\ C} \qquad \frac{P, E \vdash e :: Integer \qquad is\text{-}type\ P\ (T[])}{P, E \vdash new\ T[e] :: T[]}$$

$$\frac{P, E \vdash e :: T' \qquad P \vdash T \le T' \vee P \vdash T' \le T \qquad is\text{-}type\ P\ T}{P, E \vdash Cast\ T\ e :: T}$$

$$\frac{P, E \vdash e :: T' \qquad P \vdash T \le T' \vee P \vdash T' \le T \qquad is\text{-}type\ P\ T \qquad is\text{-}refT\ T}{P, E \vdash e\ instanceof\ T :: Boolean}$$

$$\frac{\textit{typeof } v = \lfloor T \rfloor}{P, E \vdash \textit{Val } v :: T} \qquad \frac{E\,V = \lfloor T \rfloor}{P, E \vdash \textit{Var } V :: T}$$

$$\frac{P, E \vdash e_1 :: T_1 \qquad P, E \vdash e_2 :: T_2 \qquad P \vdash T_1 \textit{ «bop» } T_2 :: T}{P, E \vdash e_1 \textit{ «bop» } e_2 :: T}$$

$$\frac{E\,V = \lfloor T \rfloor \qquad P, E \vdash e :: T' \qquad P \vdash T' \leq T \qquad V \neq \textit{this}}{P, E \vdash V := e :: \textit{Void}}$$

$$\frac{P, E \vdash e :: T[]}{P, E \vdash e.\textit{length} :: \textit{Integer}} \qquad \frac{P, E \vdash e_1 :: T[] \qquad P, E \vdash e_2 :: \textit{Integer}}{P, E \vdash e_1[e_2] :: T}$$

$$\frac{P, E \vdash e_1 :: T[] \qquad P, E \vdash e_2 :: \textit{Integer} \qquad P, E \vdash e_3 :: T' \qquad P \vdash T' \leq T}{P, E \vdash e_1[e_2] := e_3 :: \textit{Void}}$$

$$\frac{P, E \vdash e :: T \qquad \textit{class-of } T = \lfloor C \rfloor \qquad P \vdash C \textit{ sees } F{:}T' \ (\textit{fm}) \textit{ in } D}{P, E \vdash e.F\{D\} :: T'}$$

$$\frac{P, E \vdash e_1 :: T_1 \qquad \textit{class-of } T_1 = \lfloor C \rfloor}{P \vdash C \textit{ sees } F{:}T' \ (\textit{fm}) \textit{ in } D \qquad P, E \vdash e_2 :: T_2 \qquad P \vdash T_2 \leq T'}{P, E \vdash e_1.F\{D\} := e_2 :: \textit{Void}}$$

$$\frac{P, E \vdash e :: T \qquad P, E \vdash es \ [::] \ Ts'}{\textit{class-of } T = \lfloor C \rfloor \qquad P \vdash C \textit{ sees } M{:}Ts{\rightarrow}T_r = \textit{meth in } D \qquad P \vdash Ts' \ [\leq] \ Ts}{P, E \vdash e.M(es) :: T_r}$$

$$\frac{\textit{is-type } P\ T \qquad P, E(V \mapsto T) \vdash e :: T'}{\textit{case } vo \textit{ of None} \Rightarrow \textit{True} \mid \lfloor v \rfloor \Rightarrow \exists T''. \ \textit{typeof } v = \lfloor T'' \rfloor \wedge P \vdash T'' \leq T}{P, E \vdash \{V : T = vo; e\} :: T'}$$

$$\frac{P, E \vdash e_1 :: T_1 \qquad P, E \vdash e_2 :: T_2}{P, E \vdash e_1;; e_2 :: T_2}$$

$$\frac{P, E \vdash e :: \textit{Boolean} \qquad P, E \vdash e_1 :: T_1 \qquad P, E \vdash e_2 :: T_2 \qquad P \vdash \textit{lub}\,(T_1, T_2) = T}{P, E \vdash \textit{if } (e)\ e_1 \textit{ else } e_2 :: T}$$

$$\frac{P, E \vdash e_1 :: \textit{Boolean} \qquad P, E \vdash e_2 :: T}{P, E \vdash \textit{while } (e_1)\ e_2 :: \textit{Void}}$$

$$\frac{P,E \vdash e :: Class\,C \qquad P \vdash C \preceq^* Throwable}{P,E \vdash throw\,e :: Void}$$

$$\frac{P,E \vdash e_1 :: T \qquad P,E(V \mapsto Class\,C) \vdash e_2 :: T \qquad P \vdash C \preceq^* Throwable}{P,E \vdash try\,e_1\,catch(C\,V)\,e_2 :: T}$$

$$\frac{P,E \vdash e_1 :: T_1 \qquad is\text{-}refT\,T_1 \qquad T_1 \neq NT \qquad P,E \vdash e_2 :: T_2}{P,E \vdash sync\,(e_1)\,e_2 :: T_2}$$

$$P,E \vdash [\,]\,[::]\,[\,] \qquad \qquad \frac{P,E \vdash e :: T \qquad P,E \vdash es\,[::]\,Ts}{P,E \vdash e \cdot es\,[::]\,T \cdot Ts}$$

B.6.3 Definite Assignment

Hypersets: **type_synonym** $'a\ hyperset = 'a\ set\ option$

$$\begin{array}{ll}
None \sqcup\ B\ = None & None \sqcap\ B\ = B \\
A\ \sqcup None = None & A\ \sqcap None = A \\
\lfloor A \rfloor \sqcup \lfloor B \rfloor = \lfloor A \cup B \rfloor & \lfloor A \rfloor \sqcap \lfloor B \rfloor = \lfloor A \cap B \rfloor
\end{array}$$

$$\begin{array}{ll}
None \ominus a = None & a \in\in None = True \\
\lfloor A \rfloor \ominus a = \lfloor A - \{a\} \rfloor & a \in\in \lfloor A \rfloor = a \in A
\end{array}$$

Definitely assigned variables:

$$\begin{array}{ll}
\mathcal{A} :: ('a,'b,'addr)\ exp \Rightarrow 'a\ hyperset & \\
\mathcal{A}\,(new\,C) & = \lfloor \emptyset \rfloor \\
\mathcal{A}\,(new\,T[e]) & = \mathcal{A}\,e \\
\mathcal{A}\,(e\ instanceof\ T) & = \mathcal{A}\,e \\
\mathcal{A}\,(Cast\,T\,e) & = \mathcal{A}\,e \\
\mathcal{A}\,(Val\,v) & = \lfloor \emptyset \rfloor \\
\mathcal{A}\,(e_1\ \text{«}bop\text{»}\ e_2) & = \mathcal{A}\,e_1 \sqcup \mathcal{A}\,e_2 \\
\mathcal{A}\,(Var\,V) & = \lfloor \emptyset \rfloor \\
\mathcal{A}\,(V := e) & = \lfloor \{V\} \rfloor \sqcup \mathcal{A}\,e \\
\mathcal{A}\,(e_1[e_2]) & = \mathcal{A}\,e_1 \sqcup \mathcal{A}\,e_2 \\
\mathcal{A}\,(e_1[e_2] := e_3) & = \mathcal{A}\,e_1 \sqcup \mathcal{A}\,e_2 \sqcup \mathcal{A}\,e_3 \\
\mathcal{A}\,(e.length) & = \mathcal{A}\,e \\
\mathcal{A}\,(e.F\{D\}) & = \mathcal{A}\,e \\
\mathcal{A}\,(e_1.F\{D\} := e_2) & = \mathcal{A}\,e_1 \sqcup \mathcal{A}\,e_2 \\
\mathcal{A}\,(e.M(es)) & = \mathcal{A}\,e \sqcup \mathcal{A}s\,es \\
\mathcal{A}\,\{V : T = vo; e\} & = \mathcal{A}\,e \ominus V \\
\mathcal{A}\,(e_1;; e_2) & = \mathcal{A}\,e_1 \sqcup \mathcal{A}\,e_2
\end{array}$$

$$\begin{aligned}
&\mathcal{A}\ (if\ (e)\ e_1\ else\ e_2) &&= \mathcal{A}\ e \sqcup (\mathcal{A}\ e_1 \sqcap \mathcal{A}\ e_2)\\
&\mathcal{A}\ (while\ (e_1)\ e_2) &&= \mathcal{A}\ e_1\\
&\mathcal{A}\ (throw\ e) &&= None\\
&\mathcal{A}\ (try\ e_1\ catch(C\ V)\ e_2) &&= \mathcal{A}\ e_1 \sqcap (\mathcal{A}\ e_2 \ominus V)\\
&\mathcal{A}\ (sync_b\ (e_1)\ e_2) &&= \mathcal{A}\ e_1 \sqcup \mathcal{A}\ e_2\\
&\mathcal{A}\ (insync_b\ (a)\ e) &&= \mathcal{A}\ e
\end{aligned}$$

$$\begin{aligned}
&\mathcal{A}s :: ('a,'b,'addr)\ exp\ list \Rightarrow 'a\ hyperset\\
&\mathcal{A}s\ [] &&= \lfloor\emptyset\rfloor\\
&\mathcal{A}s\ (e \cdot es) &&= \mathcal{A}\ e \sqcup \mathcal{A}\ es
\end{aligned}$$

Definite assignment test:

$$\begin{aligned}
&\mathcal{D} :: ('a,'b,'addr)\ exp \Rightarrow 'a\ hyperset \Rightarrow bool\\
&\mathcal{D}\ (new\ C)\ A &&\longleftrightarrow True\\
&\mathcal{D}\ (new\ T[e])\ A &&\longleftrightarrow \mathcal{D}\ e\ A\\
&\mathcal{D}\ (e\ instanceof\ T)\ A &&\longleftrightarrow \mathcal{D}\ e\ A\\
&\mathcal{D}\ (Cast\ T\ e)\ A &&\longleftrightarrow \mathcal{D}\ e\ A\\
&\mathcal{D}\ (Val\ v)\ A &&\longleftrightarrow True\\
&\mathcal{D}\ (e_1\ \text{«}bop\text{»}\ e_2)\ A &&\longleftrightarrow \mathcal{D}\ e_1\ A \wedge \mathcal{D}\ e_2\ (A \sqcup \mathcal{A}\ e_1)\\
&\mathcal{D}\ (Var\ V)\ A &&\longleftrightarrow V \in\in A\\
&\mathcal{D}\ (V := e)\ A &&\longleftrightarrow \mathcal{D}\ e\ A\\
&\mathcal{D}\ (e_1[e_2])\ A &&\longleftrightarrow \mathcal{D}\ e_1\ A \wedge \mathcal{D}\ e_2\ (A \sqcup \mathcal{A}\ e_1)\\
&\mathcal{D}\ (e_1[e_2] := e_3)\ A &&\longleftrightarrow\\
&\qquad \mathcal{D}\ e_1 \wedge \mathcal{D}\ e_2\ (A \sqcup \mathcal{A}\ e_1) \wedge \mathcal{D}\ e_3\ (A \sqcup \mathcal{A}\ e_1 \wedge \mathcal{A}\ e_2)\\
&\mathcal{D}\ (e.length)\ A &&\longleftrightarrow \mathcal{D}\ e\ A\\
&\mathcal{D}\ (e.F\{D\})\ A &&\longleftrightarrow \mathcal{D}\ e\ A\\
&\mathcal{D}\ (e_1.F\{D\} := e_2)\ A &&\longleftrightarrow \mathcal{D}\ e_1\ A \wedge \mathcal{D}\ e_2\ (A \sqcup \mathcal{A}\ e_1)\\
&\mathcal{D}\ (e.M(es))\ A &&\longleftrightarrow \mathcal{D}\ e\ A \wedge \mathcal{D}s\ es\ (A \sqcup \mathcal{A}\ e)\\
&\mathcal{D}\ \{V : T = vo;\ e\} &&\longleftrightarrow\\
&\qquad (if\ vo = None\ then\ \mathcal{D}\ e\ (A \ominus V)\ else\ \mathcal{D}\ e\ (A \sqcup \lfloor\{V\}\rfloor))\\
&\mathcal{D}\ (e_1;;\ e_2)\ A &&\longleftrightarrow \mathcal{D}\ e_1\ A \wedge \mathcal{D}\ e_2\ (A \sqcup \mathcal{A}\ e_1)\\
&\mathcal{D}\ (if\ (e)\ e_1\ else\ e_2)\ A &&\longleftrightarrow \mathcal{D}\ e\ A \wedge \mathcal{D}\ e_1\ (A \sqcup \mathcal{A}\ e) \wedge \mathcal{D}\ e_2\ (A \sqcup \mathcal{A}\ e)\\
&\mathcal{D}\ (while\ (e_1)\ e_2)\ A &&\longleftrightarrow \mathcal{D}\ e_1\ A \wedge \mathcal{D}\ e_2\ (A \sqcup \mathcal{A}\ e_1)\\
&\mathcal{D}\ (throw\ e)\ A &&\longleftrightarrow \mathcal{D}\ e\ A\\
&\mathcal{D}\ (try\ e_1\ catch(C\ V)\ e_2)\ A &&\longleftrightarrow \mathcal{D}\ e_1\ A \wedge \mathcal{D}\ e_2(A \sqcup \lfloor\{V\}\rfloor)\\
&\mathcal{D}\ (sync_b\ (e_1)\ e_2)\ A &&\longleftrightarrow \mathcal{D}\ e_1\ A \wedge \mathcal{D}\ e_2\ (A \sqcup \mathcal{A}\ e_1)\\
&\mathcal{D}\ (insync_b\ (a)\ e)\ A &&\longleftrightarrow \mathcal{D}\ e\ A
\end{aligned}$$

$$\begin{aligned}
&\mathcal{D}s :: ('a,'b,'addr)\ exp\ list \Rightarrow 'a\ hyperset \Rightarrow bool\\
&\mathcal{D}s\ [] &&\longleftrightarrow True\\
&\mathcal{D}s\ (e \cdot es)\ A &&\longleftrightarrow \mathcal{D}\ e\ A \wedge \mathcal{D}\ es\ (A \sqcup \mathcal{A}\ e)
\end{aligned}$$

331

B.6.4 Well-formedness

wf-J-mdecl :: *'addr J-mb wf-mdecl-test*
wf-J-mdecl P C $(M, Ts, T_r, (pns, body)) \longleftrightarrow$
$|Ts| = |pns| \wedge$ *distinct pns* $\wedge$ *this* $\notin$ *set pns* $\wedge$
$(\exists T. P, [this \mapsto Class\ C, pns\ [\mapsto] Ts] \vdash body :: T \wedge P \vdash T \leq T_r) \wedge$
$\mathcal{D}\ body\ \lfloor \{this\} \cup set\ pns \rfloor$

wf-J-prog $=$ *wf-prog wf-J-mdecl*

B.6.5 Small-step semantics

Subexpression reduction rules

$$\frac{P, t \vdash \langle e, s \rangle -ta\rightarrow \langle e', s' \rangle}{P, t \vdash \langle new\ T[e], s \rangle -ta\rightarrow \langle new\ T[e'], s' \rangle}$$

$$\frac{P, t \vdash \langle e, s \rangle -ta\rightarrow \langle e', s' \rangle}{P, t \vdash \langle Cast\ T\ e, s \rangle -ta\rightarrow \langle Cast\ T\ e', s' \rangle}$$

$$\frac{P, t \vdash \langle e, s \rangle -ta\rightarrow \langle e', s' \rangle}{P, t \vdash \langle e\ instanceof\ T, s \rangle -ta\rightarrow \langle e'\ instanceof\ T, s' \rangle}$$

$$\frac{P, t \vdash \langle e_1, s \rangle -ta\rightarrow \langle e_1', s' \rangle}{P, t \vdash \langle e_1 \ll bop\gg e_2, s \rangle -ta\rightarrow \langle e_1' \ll bop\gg e_2, s' \rangle}$$

$$\frac{P, t \vdash \langle e_2, s \rangle -ta\rightarrow \langle e_2', s' \rangle}{P, t \vdash \langle Val\ v_1 \ll bop\gg e_2, s \rangle -ta\rightarrow \langle Val\ v_1 \ll bop\gg e_2', s' \rangle}$$

$$\frac{P, t \vdash \langle e, s \rangle -ta\rightarrow \langle e', s' \rangle}{P, t \vdash \langle V := e, s \rangle -ta\rightarrow \langle V := e', s' \rangle} \qquad \frac{P, t \vdash \langle e_1, s \rangle -ta\rightarrow \langle e_1', s' \rangle}{P, t \vdash \langle e_1[e_2], s \rangle -ta\rightarrow \langle e_1'[e_2], s' \rangle}$$

$$\frac{P, t \vdash \langle e_2, s \rangle -ta\rightarrow \langle e_2', s' \rangle}{P, t \vdash \langle Val\ v_1[e_2], s \rangle -ta\rightarrow \langle Val\ v_1[e_2'], s' \rangle}$$

$$\frac{P, t \vdash \langle e_1, s \rangle -ta\rightarrow \langle e_1', s' \rangle}{P, t \vdash \langle e_1[e_2] := e_3, s \rangle -ta\rightarrow \langle e_1'[e_2] := e_3, s' \rangle}$$

$$\frac{P,t \vdash \langle e_2,s \rangle -ta \rightarrow \langle e_2',s' \rangle}{P,t \vdash \langle Val\, v_1[e_2] := e_3, s \rangle -ta \rightarrow \langle Val\, v_1[e_2'] := e_3, s' \rangle}$$

$$\frac{P,t \vdash \langle e_3,s \rangle -ta \rightarrow \langle e_3',s' \rangle}{P,t \vdash \langle Val\, v_1[Val\, v_2] := e_3, s \rangle -ta \rightarrow \langle Val\, v_1[Val\, v_2] := e_3', s' \rangle}$$

$$\frac{P,t \vdash \langle e,s \rangle -ta \rightarrow \langle e',s' \rangle}{P,t \vdash \langle e.length, s \rangle -ta \rightarrow \langle e'.length, s' \rangle} \qquad \frac{P,t \vdash \langle e,s \rangle -ta \rightarrow \langle e',s' \rangle}{P,t \vdash \langle e.F\{D\}, s \rangle -ta \rightarrow \langle e'.F\{D\}, s' \rangle}$$

$$\frac{P,t \vdash \langle e_1,s \rangle -ta \rightarrow \langle e_1',s' \rangle}{P,t \vdash \langle e_1.F\{D\} := e_2, s \rangle -ta \rightarrow \langle e_1'.F\{D\} := e_2, s' \rangle}$$

$$\frac{P,t \vdash \langle e_2,s \rangle -ta \rightarrow \langle e_2',s' \rangle}{P,t \vdash \langle Val\, v_1.F\{D\} := e_2, s \rangle -ta \rightarrow \langle Val\, v_1.F\{D\} := e_2', s' \rangle}$$

$$\frac{P,t \vdash \langle e,s \rangle -ta \rightarrow \langle e',s' \rangle}{P,t \vdash \langle e.M(es), s \rangle -ta \rightarrow \langle e'.M(es), s' \rangle}$$

$$\frac{P,t \vdash \langle es,s \rangle\, [-ta \rightarrow]\, \langle es',s' \rangle}{P,t \vdash \langle Val\, v.M(es), s \rangle -ta \rightarrow \langle Val\, v.M(es'), s' \rangle}$$

$$\frac{P,t \vdash \langle e, (h, xs(V := vo))) \rangle -ta \rightarrow \langle e', (h', xs') \rangle}{P,t \vdash \langle \{V:T = vo; e\}, (h, xs) \rangle -ta \rightarrow \langle \{V:T = xs'\, V; e'\}, (h', xs'(V := xs\, V)) \rangle}$$

$$\frac{P,t \vdash \langle e_1,s \rangle -ta \rightarrow \langle e_1',s' \rangle}{P,t \vdash \langle e_1;; e_2, s \rangle -ta \rightarrow \langle e_1';; e_2, s' \rangle}$$

$$\frac{P,t \vdash \langle e,s \rangle -ta \rightarrow \langle e',s' \rangle}{P,t \vdash \langle if\, (e)\, e_1\, else\, e_2, s \rangle -ta \rightarrow \langle if\, (e')\, e_1\, else\, e_2, s' \rangle}$$

$$\frac{P,t \vdash \langle e,s \rangle -ta \rightarrow \langle e',s' \rangle}{P,t \vdash \langle throw\, e, s \rangle -ta \rightarrow \langle throw\, e', s' \rangle}$$

$$\frac{P,t \vdash \langle e_1,s \rangle -ta \rightarrow \langle e_1',s' \rangle}{P,t \vdash \langle try\, e_1\, catch(C\, V)\, e_2, s \rangle -ta \rightarrow \langle try\, e_1'\, catch(C\, V)\, e_2, s' \rangle}$$

$$\frac{P,t \vdash \langle e_1,s \rangle -ta \rightarrow \langle e_1',s' \rangle}{P,t \vdash \langle sync\, (e_1)\, e_2, s \rangle -ta \rightarrow \langle sync\, (e_1')\, e_2, s' \rangle}$$

$$\frac{P,t \vdash \langle e,s\rangle -ta\rightarrow \langle e',s'\rangle}{P,t \vdash \langle insync\ (a)\ e,s\rangle -ta\rightarrow \langle insync\ (a)\ e',s'\rangle}$$

$$\frac{P,t \vdash \langle e,s\rangle -ta\rightarrow \langle e',s'\rangle}{P,t \vdash \langle e\cdot es,s\rangle\ [-ta\rightarrow]\ \langle e'\cdot es,s'\rangle} \qquad \frac{P,t \vdash \langle es,s\rangle\ [-ta\rightarrow]\ \langle es',s'\rangle}{P,t \vdash \langle Val\ v\cdot es,s\rangle\ [-ta\rightarrow]\ \langle Val\ v\cdot es',s'\rangle}$$

Expression reduction rules

$$\frac{alloc\ h\ (ClassT\ C) = (h',\lfloor a\rfloor)}{P,t \vdash \langle new\ C,(h,xs)\rangle -\langle\!| New\text{-}Obj\ a\ C|\!\rangle\rightarrow \langle addr\ a,(h',xs)\rangle}$$

$$\frac{alloc\ h\ (ClassT\ C) = (h',None)}{P,t \vdash \langle new\ C,(h,xs)\rangle -\langle\!|\rangle\!\rightarrow \langle THROW\ OutOfMemory,(h',xs)\rangle}$$

$$\frac{i <_s 0}{P,t \vdash \langle new\ T[Val\ (Intg\ i)],s\rangle -\langle\!|\rangle\!\rightarrow \langle THROW\ NegativeArraySize,s\rangle}$$

$$\frac{0 \leq_s i \qquad alloc\ h\ (ArrayT\ T\ (nat\ (sint\ i))) = (h',\lfloor a\rfloor)}{\begin{array}{c}P,t \vdash \langle new\ T[Val\ (Intg\ i)],(h,xs)\rangle\\ -\langle\!| New\text{-}Arr\ a\ T\ (nat\ (sint\ i))|\!\rangle\rightarrow \langle addr\ a,(h',xs)\rangle\end{array}}$$

$$\frac{0 \leq_s i \qquad alloc\ h\ (ArrayT\ T\ (nat\ (sint\ i))) = (h',None)}{P,t \vdash \langle new\ T[Val\ (Intg\ i)],(h,xs)\rangle -\langle\!|\rangle\!\rightarrow \langle THROW\ OutOfMemory,(h',xs)\rangle}$$

$$\frac{typeof_{hp\ s}\ v = \lfloor T'\rfloor \qquad P \vdash T' \leq T}{P,t \vdash \langle Cast\ T\ (Val\ v),s\rangle -\langle\!|\rangle\!\rightarrow \langle Val\ v,s\rangle}$$

$$\frac{typeof_{hp\ s}\ v = \lfloor T'\rfloor \qquad \neg P \vdash T' \leq T}{P,t \vdash \langle Cast\ T\ (Val\ v),s\rangle -\langle\!|\rangle\!\rightarrow \langle THROW\ ClassCast,s\rangle}$$

$$\frac{typeof_{hp\ s}\ v = \lfloor T'\rfloor \qquad b \longleftrightarrow v \neq Null \wedge P \vdash T' \leq T}{P,t \vdash \langle Val\ v\ instanceof\ T,s\rangle -ta\rightarrow \langle Val\ (Bool\ b),s\rangle}$$

$$\frac{binop\ bop\ v_1\ v_2 = \lfloor Inl\ v\rfloor}{P,t \vdash \langle Val\ v_1\ \ll bop\gg\ Val\ v_2,s\rangle -\langle\!|\rangle\!\rightarrow \langle Val\ v,s\rangle}$$

$$\frac{binop\ bop\ v_1\ v_2 = \lfloor Inr\ a\rfloor}{P,t \vdash \langle Val\ v_1\ \ll bop\gg\ Val\ v_2,s\rangle -\langle\!|\rangle\!\rightarrow \langle Throw\ a,s\rangle}$$

$$\frac{lcl\,s\,V = \lfloor v \rfloor}{P,t \vdash \langle Var\,V,s \rangle - \langle\!\langle\rangle\!\rangle \rightarrow \langle Val\,v,s \rangle}$$

$$P,t \vdash \langle V := Val\,v,(h,xs) \rangle - \langle\!\langle\rangle\!\rangle \rightarrow \langle unit,(h,xs(V \mapsto v)) \rangle$$

$$P,t \vdash \langle null[Val\,v],s \rangle - \langle\!\langle\rangle\!\rangle \rightarrow \langle THROW\,NullPointer,s \rangle$$

$$\frac{typeof\text{-}addr\,(hp\,s)\,a = \lfloor ArrayT\,T\,n \rfloor \qquad i <_s 0 \vee sint\,i \geq int\,n}{P,t \vdash \langle Val\,v_1[Val\,v_2],s \rangle - \langle\!\langle\rangle\!\rangle \rightarrow \langle THROW\,ArrayIndexOutOfBounds,s \rangle}$$

$$\frac{typeof\text{-}addr\,h\,a = \lfloor ArrayT\,T\,n \rfloor}{0 \leq_s i \qquad sint\,i < int\,n \qquad read\,h\,a\,(Cell\,(nat\,(sint\,i)))\,v}{P,t \vdash \langle Val\,v_1[Val\,v_2],(h,xs) \rangle - \langle\!\langle Read\,a\,(Cell\,(nat\,(sint\,i)))\,v \rangle\!\rangle \rightarrow \langle Val\,v,(h,xs) \rangle}$$

$$P,t \vdash \langle null[Val\,v_2] := Val\,v_3,s \rangle - \langle\!\langle\rangle\!\rangle \rightarrow \langle THROW\,NullPointer,s \rangle$$

$$\frac{typeof\text{-}addr\,(hp\,s)\,a = \lfloor ArrayT\,T\,n \rfloor \qquad i <_s 0 \vee sint\,i \geq int\,n}{P,t \vdash \langle addr\,a[Val\,(Intg\,i)] := Val\,v_3,s \rangle \atop - \langle\!\langle\rangle\!\rangle \rightarrow \langle THROW\,ArrayIndexOutOfBounds,s \rangle}$$

$$\frac{typeof\text{-}addr\,(hp\,s)\,a = \lfloor ArrayT\,T\,n \rfloor}{0 \leq_s i \qquad sint\,i < int\,n \qquad typeof_{hp\,s}\,v_3 = \lfloor T' \rfloor \qquad \neg P \vdash T' \leq T}{P,t \vdash \langle addr\,a[Val\,(Intg\,i)] := Val\,v_3,s \rangle - \langle\!\langle\rangle\!\rangle \rightarrow \langle THROW\,ArrayStore,s \rangle}$$

$$\frac{typeof\text{-}addr\,h\,a = \lfloor ArrayT\,T\,n \rfloor \qquad 0 \leq_s i \qquad sint\,i < int\,n}{typeof_h\,v_3 = \lfloor T' \rfloor \qquad P \vdash T' \leq T \qquad write\,h\,a\,(Cell\,(nat\,(sint\,i)))\,v_3\,h'}{P,t \vdash \langle addr\,a[Val\,(Intg\,i)] := Val\,v_3,(h,xs) \rangle \atop - \langle\!\langle Write\,a\,(Cell\,(nat\,(sint\,i)))\,v_3 \rangle\!\rangle \rightarrow \langle unit,(h',xs) \rangle}$$

$$P,t \vdash \langle null.length,s \rangle - \langle\!\langle\rangle\!\rangle \rightarrow \langle THROW\,NullPointer,s \rangle$$

$$\frac{typeof\text{-}addr\,(hp\,s)\,a = \lfloor ArrayT\,T\,n \rfloor}{P,t \vdash \langle addr\,a.length,s \rangle - \langle\!\langle\rangle\!\rangle \rightarrow \langle Val\,(Intg\,(word\text{-}of\text{-}int\,(int\,n))),s \rangle}$$

$$P,t \vdash \langle null.F\{D\},s \rangle - \langle\!\langle\rangle\!\rangle \rightarrow \langle THROW\,NullPointer,s \rangle$$

$$\frac{read\,h\,a\,(Field\,F\,D)\,v}{P,t \vdash \langle addr\,a.F\{D\},(h,xs) \rangle - \langle\!\langle Read\,a\,(Field\,F\,D)\,v \rangle\!\rangle \rightarrow \langle Val\,v,(h,xs) \rangle}$$

$$P,t \vdash \langle null.F\{D\} := Val\,v_2,s \rangle - \langle\!\langle\rangle\!\rangle \rightarrow \langle THROW\,NullPointer,s \rangle$$

335

$$\frac{write\ h\ a\ (Field\ F\ D)\ v_2\ h'}{P,t \vdash \langle addr\ a.F\{D\} := Val\ v_2, (h, xs)\rangle - \langle\!|Write\ a\ (Field\ F\ D)\ v_2|\!\rangle \rightarrow \langle unit, (h', xs)\rangle}$$

$$P,t \vdash \langle null.M(es), s\rangle - \langle\!|\,|\!\rangle \rightarrow \langle THROW\ NullPointer, s\rangle$$

$$\frac{typeof\text{-}addr\ (hp\ s)\ a = \lfloor hT \rfloor \\ P \vdash class\text{-}of'\ hT\ sees\ M:Ts \rightarrow T_r = \lfloor (pns, body) \rfloor\ in\ D \\ |vs| = |pns| \qquad |Ts| = |pns|}{P,t \vdash \langle addr\ a.M(map\ Val\ vs), s\rangle \\ - \langle\!|\,|\!\rangle \rightarrow \langle blocks\ (this \cdot pns)\ (Class\ D \cdot Ts)\ (Addr\ a \cdot vs)\ body, s\rangle}$$

$$\frac{typeof\text{-}addr\ h\ a = \lfloor hT \rfloor \qquad P \vdash class\text{-}of'\ hT\ sees\ M:Ts \rightarrow T_r = Native\ in\ D \\ P,t \vdash \langle a.M(vs), h\rangle - ta \rightarrow_{nc} \langle vx, h'\rangle \\ ta' = native\text{-}TA2J\ P\ ta \qquad e' = native\text{-}Ret2J\ (addr\ a.M(map\ Val\ vs))\ vx}{P,t \vdash \langle addr\ a.M(map\ Val\ vs), (h, xs)\rangle - ta' \rightarrow \langle e', (h', xs)\rangle}$$

$$P,t \vdash \langle \{V: T = vo;\ Val\ v\}, s\rangle - \langle\!|\,|\!\rangle \rightarrow \langle Val\ v, s\rangle$$

$$P,t \vdash \langle Val\ v;;\ e_2, s\rangle - \langle\!|\,|\!\rangle \rightarrow \langle e_2, s\rangle \qquad P,t \vdash \langle if\ (true)\ e_1\ else\ e_2, s\rangle - \langle\!|\,|\!\rangle \rightarrow \langle e_1, s\rangle$$

$$P,t \vdash \langle if\ (false)\ e_1\ else\ e_2, s\rangle - \langle\!|\,|\!\rangle \rightarrow \langle e_2, s\rangle$$

$$P,t \vdash \langle while\ (e_1)\ e_2, s\rangle - \langle\!|\,|\!\rangle \rightarrow \langle if\ (e_1)\ e_2;;\ while\ (e_1)\ e_2\ else\ unit, s\rangle$$

$$P,t \vdash \langle throw\ null, s\rangle - \langle\!|\,|\!\rangle \rightarrow \langle THROW\ NullPointer, s\rangle$$

$$P,t \vdash \langle try\ Val\ v\ catch(C\ V)\ e_2, s\rangle - \langle\!|\,|\!\rangle \rightarrow \langle Val\ v, s\rangle$$

$$\frac{typeof\text{-}addr\ (hp\ s)\ a = \lfloor ClassT\ D \rfloor \qquad P \vdash D \leq^* C}{P,t \vdash \langle try\ Throw\ a\ catch(C\ V)\ e_2, s\rangle - \langle\!|\,|\!\rangle \rightarrow \langle \{V: Class\ C = \lfloor a \rfloor;\ e_2\}, s\rangle}$$

$$\frac{typeof\text{-}addr\ (hp\ s)\ a = \lfloor ClassT\ D \rfloor \qquad \neg P \vdash D \leq^* C}{P,t \vdash \langle try\ Throw\ a\ catch(C\ V)\ e_2, s\rangle - \langle\!|\,|\!\rangle \rightarrow \langle Throw\ a, s\rangle}$$

$$P,t \vdash \langle sync\ (null)\ e_2, s\rangle - \langle\!|\,|\!\rangle \rightarrow \langle THROW\ NullPointer, s\rangle$$

$$P,t \vdash \langle sync\ (addr\ a)\ e_2, s\rangle - \langle\!|Lock \rightarrow a, SLock\ a|\!\rangle \rightarrow \langle insync\ (a)\ e_2, s\rangle$$

$$P,t \vdash \langle insync\ (a)\ (Val\ v), s\rangle - \langle\!|Unlock \rightarrow a, SUnlock\ a|\!\rangle \rightarrow \langle Val\ v, s\rangle$$

Exception propagation rules

$$P, t \vdash \langle new \; T[Throw \; a], s \rangle - (\!|\!) \rightarrow \langle Throw \; a, s \rangle$$

$$P, t \vdash \langle Cast \; T \; (Throw \; a), s \rangle - (\!|\!) \rightarrow \langle Throw \; a, s \rangle$$

$$P, t \vdash \langle (Throw \; a) \; instanceof \; T, s \rangle - (\!|\!) \rightarrow \langle Throw \; a, s \rangle$$

$$P, t \vdash \langle Throw \; a \; «bop» \; e_2, s \rangle - (\!|\!) \rightarrow \langle Throw \; a, s \rangle$$

$$P, t \vdash \langle Val \; v_1 \; «bop» \; Throw \; a, s \rangle - (\!|\!) \rightarrow \langle Throw \; a, s \rangle$$

$$P, t \vdash \langle V := Throw \; a, s \rangle - (\!|\!) \rightarrow \langle Throw \; a, s \rangle$$

$$P, t \vdash \langle Throw \; a[e_2], s \rangle - (\!|\!) \rightarrow \langle Throw \; a, s \rangle$$

$$P, t \vdash \langle Val \; v_1[Throw \; a], s \rangle - (\!|\!) \rightarrow \langle Throw \; a, s \rangle$$

$$P, t \vdash \langle Throw \; a[e_2] := e_3, s \rangle - (\!|\!) \rightarrow \langle Throw \; a, s \rangle$$

$$P, t \vdash \langle Val \; v_1[Throw \; a] := e_3, s \rangle - (\!|\!) \rightarrow \langle Throw \; a, s \rangle$$

$$P, t \vdash \langle Val \; v_1[Val \; v_2] := Throw \; a, s \rangle - (\!|\!) \rightarrow \langle Throw \; a, s \rangle$$

$$P, t \vdash \langle Throw \; a.length, s \rangle - (\!|\!) \rightarrow \langle Throw \; a, s \rangle$$

$$P, t \vdash \langle Throw \; a.F\{D\}, s \rangle - (\!|\!) \rightarrow \langle Throw \; a, s \rangle$$

$$P, t \vdash \langle Throw \; a.F\{D\} := e_2, s \rangle - (\!|\!) \rightarrow \langle Throw \; a, s \rangle$$

$$P, t \vdash \langle Val \; v_1.F\{D\} := Throw \; a, s \rangle - (\!|\!) \rightarrow \langle Throw \; a, s \rangle$$

$$P, t \vdash \langle Throw \; a.M(es), s \rangle - (\!|\!) \rightarrow \langle Throw \; a, s \rangle$$

$$P, t \vdash \langle Val \; v.M(map \; Val \; vs \; @ \; Throw \; a \cdot es), s \rangle - (\!|\!) \rightarrow \langle Throw \; a, s \rangle$$

$$P, t \vdash \langle \{V : T = vo; \; Throw \; a\}, s \rangle - (\!|\!) \rightarrow \langle Throw \; a, s \rangle$$

$$P, t \vdash \langle Throw \; a; ; \; e_2, s \rangle - (\!|\!) \rightarrow \langle Throw \; a, s \rangle$$

$$P, t \vdash \langle if \; (Throw \; a) \; e_1 \; else \; e_2, s \rangle - (\!|\!) \rightarrow \langle Throw \; a, s \rangle$$

$$P, t \vdash \langle throw \; (Throw \; a), s \rangle - (\!|\!) \rightarrow \langle Throw \; a, s \rangle$$

$$P, t \vdash \langle sync \ (Throw \ a) \ e, s \rangle - (\!\!|\!\!)\!\!\rightarrow \langle Throw \ a, s \rangle$$

$$P, t \vdash \langle insync \ (a) \ (Throw \ a'), s \rangle - (\!|Unlock{\rightarrow}a, SUnlock \ a|\!) \rightarrow \langle Throw \ a', s \rangle$$

auxiliary functions

$blocks \ [] \qquad [] \qquad [] \qquad e = e$

$blocks \ (V \cdot Vs) \ (T \cdot Ts) \ (v \cdot vs) \ e = \{V \colon T = \lfloor v \rfloor; blocks \ Vs \ Ts \ vs \ e\}$

B.6.6 Observability

$\tau\text{-}move :: \ 'm \ prog \Rightarrow \ 'heap \Rightarrow \ 'addr \ expr \Rightarrow bool$

$\tau\text{-}move \ P \ h \ (new \ C) \qquad \longleftrightarrow False$

$\tau\text{-}move \ P \ h \ (new \ T[e]) \qquad \longleftrightarrow \tau\text{-}move \ P \ h \ e \vee is\text{-}Throw \ e$

$\tau\text{-}move \ P \ h \ (Cast \ T \ e) \qquad \longleftrightarrow \tau\text{-}move \ P \ h \ e \vee is\text{-}Throw \ e \vee is\text{-}Val \ e$

$\tau\text{-}move \ P \ h \ (e \ instanceof \ T) \qquad \longleftrightarrow \tau\text{-}move \ P \ h \ e \vee is\text{-}Throw \ e \vee is\text{-}Val \ e$

$\tau\text{-}move \ P \ h \ (Val \ v) \qquad \longleftrightarrow False$

$\tau\text{-}move \ P \ h \ (e_1 \ \text{«}bop\text{»} \ e_2) \qquad \longleftrightarrow \tau\text{-}move \ P \ h \ e_1 \vee is\text{-}Throw \ e \vee$
$\qquad is\text{-}Val \ e_1 \wedge (\tau\text{-}move \ P \ h \ e_2 \vee is\text{-}Throw \ e_2 \vee is\text{-}Val \ e_2)$

$\tau\text{-}move \ P \ h \ (Var \ V) \qquad \longleftrightarrow True$

$\tau\text{-}move \ P \ h \ (V := e) \qquad \longleftrightarrow \tau\text{-}move \ P \ h \ e \vee is\text{-}Throw \ e \vee is\text{-}Val \ e$

$\tau\text{-}move \ P \ h \ (e_1[e_2]) \qquad \longleftrightarrow \tau\text{-}move \ P \ h \ e_1 \vee is\text{-}Throw \ e_1 \vee$
$\qquad is\text{-}Val \ e_1 \wedge (\tau\text{-}move \ P \ h \ e_2 \vee is\text{-}Throw \ e_2)$

$\tau\text{-}move \ P \ h \ (e_1[e_2] := e_3) \qquad \longleftrightarrow \tau\text{-}move \ P \ h \ e_1 \vee is\text{-}Throw \ e_1 \vee$
$\qquad is\text{-}Val \ e_1 \wedge (\tau\text{-}move \ P \ h \ e_2 \vee is\text{-}Throw \ e_2 \vee$
$\qquad\qquad is\text{-}Val \ e_2 \wedge (\tau\text{-}move \ P \ h \ e_3 \vee is\text{-}Throw \ e_3))$

$\tau\text{-}move \ P \ h \ (e.length) \qquad \longleftrightarrow \tau\text{-}move \ P \ h \ e \vee is\text{-}Throw \ e$

$\tau\text{-}move \ P \ h \ (e.F\{D\}) \qquad \longleftrightarrow \tau\text{-}move \ P \ h \ e \vee is\text{-}Throw \ e$

$\tau\text{-}move \ P \ h \ (e_1.F\{D\} := e_2) \qquad \longleftrightarrow \tau\text{-}move \ P \ h \ e_1 \vee is\text{-}Throw \ e_1 \vee$
$\qquad is\text{-}Val \ e_1 \wedge (\tau\text{-}move \ P \ h \ e_2 \vee is\text{-}Throw \ e_2)$

$\tau\text{-}move \ P \ h \ (e.M(vs)) \qquad \longleftrightarrow \tau\text{-}move \ P \ h \ e \vee is\text{-}Throw \ e \vee$
$\qquad (\exists v. \ e = Val \ v \wedge (\tau\text{-}moves \ P \ h \ es \vee is\text{-}Throws \ es \vee is\text{-}Vals \ es \wedge (v = Null \vee$
$\qquad\qquad (\forall T \ C \ Ts \ T_r \ D. \ typeof_h \ v = \lfloor T \rfloor \longrightarrow class\text{-}of \ T = \lfloor C \rfloor \longrightarrow$
$\qquad\qquad\qquad P \vdash C \ sees \ M{:}Ts{\rightarrow}Tr = Native \ in \ D \longrightarrow \tau native \ D \ M))))$

$\tau\text{-}move \ P \ h \ \{V \colon T = vo; e\} \qquad \longleftrightarrow \tau\text{-}move \ P \ h \ e \vee is\text{-}Throw \ e \vee is\text{-}Val \ e$

$\tau\text{-}move \ P \ h \ (sync \ (e_1) \ e_2) \qquad \longleftrightarrow \tau\text{-}move \ P \ h \ e_1 \vee is\text{-}Throw \ e_1$

$\tau\text{-}move \ P \ h \ (insync \ (a) \ e) \qquad \longleftrightarrow \tau\text{-}move \ P \ h \ e$

$\tau\text{-}move \ P \ h \ (e_1;; e_2) \qquad \longleftrightarrow \tau\text{-}move \ P \ h \ e_1 \vee is\text{-}Throw \ e_1 \vee is\text{-}Val \ e_1$

$\tau\text{-}move \ P \ h \ (if \ (e_1) \ e_2 \ else \ e_3) \qquad \longleftrightarrow \tau\text{-}move \ P \ h \ e_1 \vee is\text{-}Throw \ e_1 \vee is\text{-}Val \ e_1$

$\tau\text{-}move \ P \ h \ (while \ (e_1) \ e_2) \qquad \longleftrightarrow True$

$\tau\text{-}move \ P \ h \ (throw \ e) \qquad \longleftrightarrow \tau\text{-}move \ P \ h \ e \vee is\text{-}Throw \ e \vee e = null$

$\tau\text{-}move \ P \ h \ (try \ e_1 \ catch(C \ V) \ e_2) \longleftrightarrow \tau\text{-}move \ P \ h \ e_1 \vee is\text{-}Throw \ e_1 \vee is\text{-}Val \ e_1$

τ-moves :: $'m$ prog $\Rightarrow$ $'heap \Rightarrow 'addr$ expr list $\Rightarrow$ bool

τ-moves P h $[]$ $\qquad\qquad\longleftrightarrow$ False

τ-moves P h $e \cdot es$ $\qquad\qquad\longleftrightarrow$ τ-move P h e $\vee$ is-Val e $\wedge$ τ-moves P h es

J-τ-move P $((e, xs), h)$ ta _ $\qquad\longleftrightarrow$ τ-move P h e $\wedge$ $ta = (\!|\!|)$

auxiliary functions: is-Throw $e \longleftrightarrow (\exists a.\ e = Throw\ a)$

B.7 Bytecode

B.7.1 Syntax

Instructions

datatype $'addr$ instr = Load nat | Store nat | Push $'addr$ val | Pop | Dup | Swap |
BinOp bop | New cname | NewArray ty | ALoad | AStore | ALength |
Getfield vname cname | Putfield vname cname | Checkcast ty | Instanceof ty |
Invoke mname nat | Return | Goto int | IfFalse int | ThrowExc |
MEnter | MExit

Program declarations

type_synonym $'addr$ jvm-method = nat $\times$ nat $\times$ $'addr$ instr list $\times$ ex-table

type_synonym $'addr$ jvm-prog = $'addr$ jvm-method prog

type_synonym ex-table = ex-entry list

type_synonym ex-entry = pc $\times$ pc $\times$ cname option $\times$ pc $\times$ nat

B.7.2 Applicability and effect

datatype $'a$ err = Err | OK $'a$

type_synonym ty_i = ty list $\times$ ty err list

ok-val $(OK\ T) = T$

the-Array $(T[]) = T$

Effect

successor instructions under normal execution:

succs :: $'addr$ instr $\Rightarrow ty_i \Rightarrow pc \Rightarrow pc$ list

succs $(Load\ i)$ $\qquad \tau\ pc = [pc + 1]$

succs $(Store\ i)$ $\qquad \tau\ pc = [pc + 1]$

succs $(Push\ v)$ $\qquad \tau\ pc = [pc + 1]$

$$
\begin{array}{ll}
succs\ Pop & \tau\ pc = [pc + 1] \\
succs\ Dup & \tau\ pc = [pc + 1] \\
succs\ Swap & \tau\ pc = [pc + 1] \\
succs\ (BinOp\ bop) & \tau\ pc = [pc + 1] \\
succs\ (New\ C) & \tau\ pc = [pc + 1] \\
succs\ (NewArray\ T) & \tau\ pc = [pc + 1] \\
succs\ ALoad & \tau\ pc = (if\ (fst\ \tau)_{[1]} = NT\ then\ []\ else\ [pc + 1]) \\
succs\ AStore & \tau\ pc = (if\ (fst\ \tau)_{[2]} = NT\ then\ []\ else\ [pc + 1]) \\
succs\ ALength & \tau\ pc = (if\ (fst\ \tau)_{[0]} = NT\ then\ []\ else\ [pc + 1]) \\
succs\ (Getfield\ F\ D) & \tau\ pc = [pc + 1] \\
succs\ (Putfield\ F\ D) & \tau\ pc = [pc + 1] \\
succs\ (Checkcast\ T) & \tau\ pc = [pc + 1] \\
succs\ (Instanceof\ T) & \tau\ pc = [pc + 1] \\
succs\ (Invoke\ M\ n) & \tau\ pc = (if\ (fst\ \tau)_{[n]} = NT\ then\ []\ else\ [pc + 1]) \\
succs\ Return & \tau\ pc = [] \\
succs\ (Goto\ i) & \tau\ pc = [nat\ (int\ pc + i)] \\
succs\ (IfFalse\ i) & \tau\ pc = [pc + 1, nat\ (int\ pc + i)] \\
succs\ ThrowExc & \tau\ pc = [] \\
succs\ MEnter & \tau\ pc = (if\ (fst\ \tau)_{[0]} = NT\ then\ []\ else\ [pc + 1]) \\
succs\ MExit & \tau\ pc = (if\ (fst\ \tau)_{[0]} = NT\ then\ []\ else\ [pc + 1])
\end{array}
$$

effect of instructions:

$$
\begin{array}{ll}
eff_i :: {}'addr\ instr \times {}'m\ prog \times ty_i \Rightarrow ty_i \\
eff_i\ (Load\ i, P, ST, LT) & = (\text{ok-val}\ LT_{[i]} \cdot ST, LT) \\
eff_i\ (Store\ i, P, T \cdot ST, LT) & = (ST, LT[i := OK\ T]) \\
eff_i\ (Push\ v, P, ST, LT) & = (the\ (typeof\ v) \cdot ST, LT) \\
eff_i\ (Pop\ v, P, T \cdot ST, LT) & = (ST, LT) \\
eff_i\ (Dup, P, T \cdot ST, LT) & = (T \cdot T \cdot ST, LT) \\
eff_i\ (Swap, P, T_1 \cdot T_2 \cdot ST, LT) & = (T_2 \cdot T_1 \cdot ST, LT) \\
eff_i\ (BinOp\ bop, P, T_1 \cdot T_2 \cdot ST, LT) & = ((\iota T.\ P \vdash T_1\ \text{«}bop\text{»}\ T_2 :: T) \cdot ST, LT) \\
eff_i\ (New\ C, P, ST, LT) & = (Class\ C \cdot ST, LT) \\
eff_i\ (NewArray\ T, P, T' \cdot ST, LT) & = (T[] \cdot ST, LT) \\
eff_i\ (ALoad, P, T_1 \cdot T_2 \cdot ST, LT) & = (\text{the-Array}\ T_2 \cdot ST, LT) \\
eff_i\ (AStore, P, T_1 \cdot T_2 \cdot T_3 \cdot ST, LT) & = (ST, LT) \\
eff_i\ (ALength, P, T \cdot ST, LT) & = (Integer \cdot ST, LT) \\
eff_i\ (Getfield\ F\ D, P, T \cdot ST, LT) & = (fst\ (snd\ (field\ P\ D\ F)) \cdot ST, LT) \\
eff_i\ (Putfield\ F\ D, P, T_1 \cdot T_2 \cdot ST, LT) & = (ST, LT) \\
eff_i\ (Checkcast\ T, P, T' \cdot ST, LT) & = (T \cdot ST, LT) \\
eff_i\ (Instanceof\ T, P, T' \cdot ST, LT) & = (Boolean \cdot ST, LT)
\end{array}
$$

$$eff_i \, (Invoke \, M \, n, P, ST, LT) \quad =$$
$$\quad (let \, \lfloor C \rfloor = class\text{-}of \, ST_{[n]}; \, (\_, \_, T_r, \_) = method \, P \, C \, M$$
$$\quad in \, (T_r \cdot drop \, (n+1) \, ST, LT))$$
$$eff_i \, (Goto \, i, P, ST, LT) \quad\quad\quad = (ST, LT)$$
$$eff_i \, (IfFalse \, i, P, T \cdot ST, LT) \quad = (ST, LT)$$
$$eff_i \, (MEnter \, i, P, T \cdot ST, LT) \quad = (ST, LT)$$
$$eff_i \, (MExit \, i, P, T \cdot ST, LT) \quad = (ST, LT)$$

relevant classes for exception handlers

$binop\text{-}relevant\text{-}class :: bop \Rightarrow 'm \, prog \Rightarrow cname \Rightarrow bool$
$binop\text{-}relevant\text{-}class \, / \quad\quad P \, C \longleftrightarrow P \vdash ArithmeticException \preceq^* C$
$binop\text{-}relevant\text{-}class \, \% \quad\quad P \, C \longleftrightarrow P \vdash ArithmeticException \preceq^* C$
$binop\text{-}relevant\text{-}class \, \_ \quad\quad P \, C \longleftrightarrow False$

$is\text{-}relevant\text{-}class :: 'addr \, instr \Rightarrow 'm \, prog \Rightarrow cname \Rightarrow bool$
$is\text{-}relevant\text{-}class \, (BinOp \, bop) \quad P \, C \longleftrightarrow binop\text{-}relevant\text{-}class \, P \, C$
$is\text{-}relevant\text{-}class \, (Getfield \, F \, D) \, P \, C \longleftrightarrow P \vdash NullPointer \preceq^* C$
$is\text{-}relevant\text{-}class \, (Putfield \, F \, D) \, P \, C \longleftrightarrow P \vdash NullPointer \preceq^* C$
$is\text{-}relevant\text{-}class \, (Checkcast \, T) \quad P \, C \longleftrightarrow P \vdash ClassCast \preceq^* C$
$is\text{-}relevant\text{-}class \, (New \, C) \quad\quad P \, C \longleftrightarrow P \vdash OutOfMemory \preceq^* C$
$is\text{-}relevant\text{-}class \, ThrowExc \quad\quad P \, C \longleftrightarrow True$
$is\text{-}relevant\text{-}class \, Invoke \, M \, n \quad P \, C \longleftrightarrow True$
$is\text{-}relevant\text{-}class \, (NewArray \, T) \, P \, C \longleftrightarrow$
$\quad P \vdash OutOfMemory \preceq^* C \vee P \vdash NegativeArraySize \preceq^* C$
$is\text{-}relevant\text{-}class \, ALoad \quad\quad\quad P \, C \longleftrightarrow$
$\quad P \vdash ArrayIndexOutOfBounds \preceq^* C \vee P \vdash NullPointer \preceq^* C$
$is\text{-}relevant\text{-}class \, AStore \quad\quad P \, C \longleftrightarrow P \vdash ArrayIndexOutOfBounds \preceq^* C \vee$
$\quad P \vdash ArrayStore \preceq^* C \vee P \vdash NullPointer \preceq^* C$
$is\text{-}relevant\text{-}class \, ALength \quad\quad P \, C \longleftrightarrow P \vdash NullPointer \preceq^* C$
$is\text{-}relevant\text{-}class \, MEnter \quad\quad P \, C \longleftrightarrow$
$\quad P \vdash IllegalMonitorState \preceq^* C \vee P \vdash NullPointer \preceq^* C$
$is\text{-}relevant\text{-}class \, MExit \quad\quad\quad P \, C \longleftrightarrow$
$\quad P \vdash IllegalMonitorState \preceq^* C \vee P \vdash NullPointer \preceq^* C$
$is\text{-}relevant\text{-}class \, \_ \quad\quad\quad\quad P \, C \longleftrightarrow False$

$is\text{-}relevant\text{-}entry :: 'm \, prog \Rightarrow 'addr \, instr \Rightarrow pc \Rightarrow ex\text{-}entry \Rightarrow bool$
$is\text{-}relevant\text{-}entry \, P \, i \, pc \, (f, t, Co, h, d) \longleftrightarrow$
$\quad (case \, Co \, of \, Any \Rightarrow True \mid \lfloor C \rfloor \Rightarrow is\text{-}relevant\text{-}class \, i \, P \, C) \wedge f \leq pc \wedge pc < t$

$relevant\text{-}entries :: 'm \, prog \Rightarrow 'addr \, instr \Rightarrow pc \Rightarrow ex\text{-}table \Rightarrow ex\text{-}table$
$relevant\text{-}entries \, P \, i \, pc = filter \, (is\text{-}relevant\text{-}entry \, P \, i \, pc)$

$xcpt\text{-}class\ Any = Class\ Throwable$
$xcpt\text{-}class\ \lfloor C \rfloor = Class\ C$

$xcpt\text{-}eff :: \text{'}addr\ instr \Rightarrow \text{'}m\ prog \Rightarrow pc \Rightarrow ty_i \Rightarrow ex\text{-}table \Rightarrow (pc \times ty_i\ option)\ list$
$xcpt\text{-}eff\ i\ P\ pc\ (ST, LT)\ xt =$
$\quad map\ (\lambda(f, t, Co, h, d).\ (h, \lfloor (xcpt\text{-}class\ Co \cdot drop\ (|ST| - d)\ ST, LT) \rfloor))$
$\quad\quad (relevant\text{-}entries\ P\ i\ pc)$

$norm\text{-}eff :: \text{'}addr\ instr \Rightarrow \text{'}m\ prog \Rightarrow pc \Rightarrow ty_i \Rightarrow (pc \times ty_i\ option)\ list$
$norm\text{-}eff\ i\ P\ pc\ \tau = map\ (\lambda pc'.\ (pc', \lfloor eff_i\ (i, P, \tau) \rfloor))\ (succs\ i\ \tau\ pc)$

$eff :: \text{'}addr\ instr \Rightarrow \text{'}m\ prog \Rightarrow pc \Rightarrow ex\text{-}table \Rightarrow ty_i\ option \Rightarrow (pc \times ty_i\ option)\ list$
$eff\ i\ P\ pc\ xt\ None = []$
$eff\ i\ P\ pc\ xt\ \lfloor \tau \rfloor\quad = norm\text{-}eff\ i\ P\ pc\ xt\ @\ xcpt\text{-}eff\ i\ P\ pc\ \tau\ xt$

Applicability

$app_i :: \text{'}addr\ instr \times \text{'}m\ prog \times pc \times nat \times ty \times ty_i \Rightarrow bool$
$app_i\ (Load\ i, P, pc, msl, T_r, ST, LT) \quad\quad\quad\quad \longleftrightarrow$
$\quad i < |LT| \wedge LT_{[i]} \neq Err \wedge |ST| < msl$
$app_i\ (Store\ i, P, pc, msl, T_r, T \cdot ST, LT) \quad\quad\quad \longleftrightarrow i < |LT|$
$app_i\ (Push\ v, P, pc, msl, T_r, ST, LT) \quad\quad\quad\quad \longleftrightarrow$
$\quad |ST| < msl \wedge typeof\ v \neq None$
$app_i\ (Pop, P, pc, msl, T_r, T \cdot ST, LT) \quad\quad\quad\quad \longleftrightarrow True$
$app_i\ (Dup, P, pc, msl, T_r, T \cdot ST, LT) \quad\quad\quad\quad \longleftrightarrow |ST| + 1 < msl$
$app_i\ (Swap, P, pc, msl, T_r, T_1 \cdot T_2 \cdot ST, LT) \quad\quad \longleftrightarrow True$
$app_i\ (BinOp\ bop, P, pc, msl, T_r, T_1 \cdot T_2 \cdot ST, LT) \quad \longleftrightarrow (\exists T.\ P \vdash T_1\ \text{«}bop\text{»}\ T_2 :: T)$
$app_i\ (New\ C, P, pc, msl, T_r, ST, LT) \quad\quad\quad\quad \longleftrightarrow is\text{-}class\ P\ C \wedge |ST| < msl$
$app_i\ (NewArray\ T, P, pc, msl, T_r, Integer \cdot ST, LT) \longleftrightarrow is\text{-}type\ P\ (T[])$
$app_i\ (ALoad, P, pc, msl, T_r, Integer \cdot T \cdot ST, LT) \quad \longleftrightarrow T \neq NT \longrightarrow is\text{-}Array\ T$
$app_i\ (AStore, P, pc, msl, T_r, T_1 \cdot T_2 \cdot T_3 \cdot ST, LT) \quad \longleftrightarrow$
$\quad T_2 = Integer \wedge (T_3 \neq NT \longrightarrow is\text{-}Array\ T_3)$
$app_i\ (ALength, P, pc, msl, T_r, T \cdot ST, LT) \quad\quad\quad \longleftrightarrow T = NT \vee is\text{-}Array\ T$
$app_i\ (Getfield\ F\ C, P, pc, msl, T_r, T \cdot ST, LT) \quad\quad \longleftrightarrow$
$\quad (\exists T_f\ fm.\ P \vdash C\ sees\ F{:}T_f\ (fm)\ in\ C \wedge P \vdash T \leq Class\ C)$
$app_i\ (Putfield\ F\ C, P, pc, msl, T_r, T_1 \cdot T_2 \cdot ST, LT) \quad \longleftrightarrow$
$\quad (\exists T_f\ fm.\ P \vdash C\ sees\ F{:}T_f\ (fm)\ in\ C \wedge P \vdash T_2 \leq Class\ C \wedge P \vdash T_1 \leq T_f)$
$app_i\ (Checkcast\ T, P, pc, msl, T_r, T' \cdot ST, LT) \quad\quad \longleftrightarrow is\text{-}type\ P\ T$
$app_i\ (Instanceof\ T, P, pc, msl, T_r, T' \cdot ST, LT) \quad\quad \longleftrightarrow is\text{-}type\ P\ T \wedge is\text{-}ref\ T\ T'$
$app_i\ (Invoke\ M\ n, P, pc, msl, T_r, ST, LT) \quad\quad\quad \longleftrightarrow$
$\quad n < |ST| \wedge$
$\quad (ST_{[n]} \neq NT \longrightarrow (\exists C\ D\ Ts\ T\ m.\ class\text{-}of\ ST_{[n]} = \lfloor C \rfloor \wedge$
$\quad\quad P \vdash C\ sees\ M{:}Ts{\rightarrow}T = m\ in\ D \wedge P \vdash rev\ (take\ n\ ST)\ [\leq]\ Ts))$

$app_i\ (Return, P, pc, msl, T_r, T \cdot ST, LT)$ $\longleftrightarrow P \vdash T \le T_r$
$app_i\ (Goto\ i, P, pc, msl, T_r, ST, LT)$ $\longleftrightarrow 0 \le int\ pc + i$
$app_i\ (IfFalse\ i, P, pc, msl, T_r, Boolean \cdot ST, LT)$ $\longleftrightarrow 0 \le int\ pc + i$
$app_i\ (ThrowExc, P, pc, msl, T_r, T \cdot ST, LT)$ $\longleftrightarrow$
$\quad\quad T = NT \vee (\exists C.\ T = Class\ C \wedge P \vdash C \le^* Throwable)$
$app_i\ (MEnter, P, pc, msl, T_r, T \cdot ST, LT)$ $\longleftrightarrow is\text{-}refT\ T$
$app_i\ (MExit, P, pc, msl, T_r, T \cdot ST, LT)$ $\longleftrightarrow is\text{-}refT\ T$
$app_i\ (\_, P, pc, msl, T_r, ST, LT)$ $\longleftrightarrow False$

$xcpt\text{-}app :: {}'addr\ instr \Rightarrow {}'m\ prog \Rightarrow pc \Rightarrow nat \Rightarrow ex\text{-}table \Rightarrow ty_i \Rightarrow bool$
$xcpt\text{-}app\ i\ P\ pc\ msl\ xt\ \tau =$
$\quad\quad (\forall (f, t, Co, h, d) \in set\ (relevant\text{-}entries\ P\ i\ pc\ xt).$
$\quad\quad\quad (case\ Co\ of\ Any \Rightarrow True \mid \lfloor C \rfloor \Rightarrow is\text{-}class\ P\ C) \wedge d < |fst\ \tau| \wedge d < msl)$

$app :: {}'addr\ instr \Rightarrow {}'m\ prog \Rightarrow nat \Rightarrow ty \Rightarrow nat \Rightarrow nat \Rightarrow ex\text{-}table \Rightarrow ty_i\ option$
$\quad\quad \Rightarrow bool$
$app\ i\ P\ msl\ T_r\ pc\ mpc\ xt\ None \longleftrightarrow True$
$app\ i\ P\ msl\ T_r\ pc\ mpc\ xt\ \lfloor \tau \rfloor \longleftrightarrow$
$\quad\quad app_i\ (i, P, msl, T_r, \tau) \wedge xcpt\text{-}app\ i\ P\ pc\ msl\ xt\ \tau \wedge$
$\quad\quad (\forall (pc', \tau') \in set\ (eff\ i\ P\ pc\ xt\ \lfloor \tau \rfloor).\ pc' < mpc)$

B.7.3 The virtual machine

Semantics of instructions

$exec\text{-}instr\ (Load\ n)\ P\ t\ h\ stk\ loc\ C\ M\ pc\ frs =$
$\{ (\langle\!\langle\rangle\!\rangle, (None, h, (loc_{[n]} \cdot stk, loc, C, M, pc + 1) \cdot frs)) \}$

$exec\text{-}instr\ (Store\ n)\ P\ t\ h\ stk\ loc\ C\ M\ pc\ frs =$
$\{ (\langle\!\langle\rangle\!\rangle, (None, h, (tl\ stk, loc[n := hd\ stk], C, M, pc + 1) \cdot frs)) \}$

$exec\text{-}instr\ (Push\ v)\ P\ t\ h\ stk\ loc\ C\ M\ pc\ frs =$
$\{ (\langle\!\langle\rangle\!\rangle, (None, h, (v \cdot stk, loc, C, M, pc + 1) \cdot frs)) \}$

$exec\text{-}instr\ Pop\ P\ t\ h\ stk\ loc\ C\ M\ pc\ frs =$
$\{ (\langle\!\langle\rangle\!\rangle, (None, h, (tl\ stk, loc, C, M, pc + 1) \cdot frs)) \}$

$exec\text{-}instr\ Dup\ P\ t\ h\ stk\ loc\ C\ M\ pc\ frs =$
$\{ (\langle\!\langle\rangle\!\rangle, (None, h, (hd\ stk \cdot stk, loc, C, M, pc + 1) \cdot frs)) \}$

$exec\text{-}instr\ Swap\ P\ t\ h\ stk\ loc\ C\ M\ pc\ frs =$
$\{ let\ v_1 \cdot v_2 \cdot stk' = stk\ in\ (\langle\!\langle\rangle\!\rangle, (None, h, (v_2 \cdot v_1 \cdot stk', loc, C, M, pc + 1) \cdot frs)) \}$

$exec\text{-}instr\ (BinOp\ bop)\ P\ t\ h\ stk\ loc\ C\ M\ pc\ frs =$
$\{\ let\ v_2 \cdot\ v_1 \cdot stk' = stk;\ \lfloor va \rfloor = binop\ bop\ v_1\ v_2$
$\quad in\ case\ va\ of\ Inl\ v \Rightarrow (\langle\!\langle\rangle\!\rangle, (None, h, (v \cdot stk', loc, C, M, pc + 1) \cdot frs))$
$\qquad\qquad\qquad\ \mid Inr\ v \Rightarrow (\langle\!\langle\rangle\!\rangle, (\lfloor a \rfloor, h, (stk, loc, C, M, pc) \cdot frs))\ \}$

$exec\text{-}instr\ (New\ C')\ P\ t\ h\ stk\ loc\ C\ M\ pc\ frs =$
$\{\ let\ (h', ao) = alloc\ h\ (ClassT\ C')$
$\quad in\ case\ ao\ of\ None \Rightarrow$
$\qquad\qquad (\langle\!\langle\rangle\!\rangle, (\lfloor addr\text{-}of\text{-}sys\text{-}xcpt\ OutOfMemory \rfloor, h', (stk, loc, C, M, pc) \cdot frs))$
$\qquad \mid \lfloor a \rfloor \Rightarrow (\langle\!\langle New\text{-}Obj\ a\ C' \rangle\!\rangle, (None, h', (Addr\ a \cdot stk, loc, C, M, pc + 1) \cdot frs))\ \}$

$exec\text{-}instr\ (NewArray\ T)\ P\ t\ h\ stk\ loc\ C\ M\ pc\ frs =$
$\{\ let\ Intg\ si \cdot stk' = stk;\ i = nat\ (sint\ si)$
$\quad in\ if\ si <_s 0\ then$
$\qquad\ (\langle\!\langle\rangle\!\rangle, (\lfloor addr\text{-}of\text{-}sys\text{-}xcpt\ NegativeArraySize \rfloor, h, (stk, loc, C, M, pc) \cdot frs))$
$\qquad else\ let\ (h', ao) = alloc\ h\ (ArrayT\ T\ i)$
$\qquad\qquad in\ case\ ao\ of\ None \Rightarrow$
$\qquad\qquad\qquad (\langle\!\langle\rangle\!\rangle, (\lfloor addr\text{-}of\text{-}sys\text{-}xcpt\ OutOfMemory \rfloor, h', (stk, loc, C, M, pc) \cdot frs))$
$\qquad\qquad\quad \mid \lfloor a \rfloor \Rightarrow$
$\qquad\qquad\qquad (\langle\!\langle New\text{-}Arr\ a\ T\ i \rangle\!\rangle, (None, h', (Addr\ a \cdot stk', loc, C, M, pc + 1) \cdot frs))\ \}$

$exec\text{-}instr\ ALoad\ P\ t\ h\ stk\ loc\ C\ M\ pc\ frs =$
$(let\ Intg\ i \cdot v \cdot stk' = stk;\ Addr\ a = v;\ idx = nat\ (sint\ i);$
$\quad \lfloor hT \rfloor = typeof\text{-}addr\ h\ a;\ len = array\text{-}length\text{-}of\ hT$
$\quad in\ if\ v = Null\ then$
$\qquad \{\ (\langle\!\langle\rangle\!\rangle, (\lfloor addr\text{-}of\text{-}sys\text{-}xcpt\ NullPointer \rfloor, h, (stk, loc, C, M, pc) \cdot frs))\ \}$
$\qquad else\ if\ i <_s 0 \vee int\ len \leq sint\ i\ then$
$\qquad\quad \{\ (\langle\!\langle\rangle\!\rangle, (\lfloor addr\text{-}of\text{-}sys\text{-}xcpt\ ArrayIndexOutOfBounds \rfloor,$
$\qquad\qquad h, (stk, loc, C, M, pc) \cdot frs))\ \}$
$\qquad else\ \{\ (\langle\!\langle Read\ a\ (Cell\ idx)\ v' \rangle\!\rangle, (None, h, (v' \cdot stk', loc, C, M, pc + 1) \cdot frs)) \mid v'.$
$\qquad\quad read\ h\ a\ (Cell\ idx)\ v'\ \})$

exec-instr AStore P t h stk loc C M pc frs =
$(let\, v_2 \cdot\, Intg\, i \cdot v_1 \cdot stk' = stk;\ Addr\, a = v_1;\ idx = nat\,(sint\, i);$
$\quad \lfloor hT \rfloor = typeof\text{-}addr\, h\, a;\ len = array\text{-}length\text{-}of\, hT;\ T[] = ty\text{-}of\, hT;$
$\quad \lfloor T' \rfloor = typeof_h\, v_2;$
$\ in\ if\, v_1 = Null\ then$
$\qquad \{\,(\langle\!\langle\rangle\!\rangle, (\lfloor addr\text{-}of\text{-}sys\text{-}xcpt\, NullPointer \rfloor, h, (stk, loc, C, M, pc) \cdot frs))\,\}$
$\quad else\ if\, i <_s 0 \vee int\, len \leq sint\, i\ then$
$\qquad \{\,(\langle\!\langle\rangle\!\rangle, (\lfloor addr\text{-}of\text{-}sys\text{-}xcpt\, ArrayIndexOutOfBounds \rfloor,$
$\qquad\qquad h, (stk, loc, C, M, pc) \cdot frs))\,\}$
$\quad else\ if\, P \vdash T' \leq T\ then$
$\qquad \{\,(\langle\!\langle Write\, a\,(Cell\, idx)\, v_2 \rangle\!\rangle, (None, h', (stk', loc, C, M, pc + 1) \cdot frs)) \mid h'.$
$\qquad write\, h\, a\,(Cell\, idx)\, v_2\, h'\,\}$
$\quad else\,\{\,(\langle\!\langle\rangle\!\rangle, (\lfloor addr\text{-}of\text{-}sys\text{-}xcpt\, ArrayStore \rfloor, h, (stk, loc, C, M, pc) \cdot frs))\,\})$

exec-instr ALength P t h stk loc C M pc frs =
$\{\,(\langle\!\langle\rangle\!\rangle, let\, v \cdot stk' = stk;\ Addr\, a = v;\ \lfloor hT \rfloor = typeof\text{-}addr\, a;$
$\qquad len = array\text{-}length\text{-}of\, hT$
$\quad in\ if\, v = Null\ then$
$\qquad\quad (\lfloor addr\text{-}of\text{-}sys\text{-}xcpt\, NullPointer \rfloor, h, (stk, loc, C, M, pc) \cdot frs)$
$\qquad else\ (None, h, (word\text{-}of\text{-}int\,(int\, len) \cdot stk', loc, C, M, pc + 1) \cdot frs))\,\}$

exec-instr (Getfield F D) P t h stk loc C M pc frs =
$(let\, v \cdot stk' = stk;\ Addr\, a = v$
$\ in\ if\, v = Null\ then$
$\qquad \{\,(\langle\!\langle\rangle\!\rangle, (\lfloor addr\text{-}of\text{-}sys\text{-}xcpt\, NullPointer \rfloor, h, (stk, loc, C, M, pc) \cdot frs))\,\}$
$\quad else$
$\qquad \{\,(\langle\!\langle Read\, a\,(Field\, F\, D)\, v' \rangle\!\rangle, (None, h, (v' \cdot stk', loc, C, M, pc + 1) \cdot frs)) \mid v'.$
$\qquad read\, h\, a\,(Field\, F\, D)\, v'\,\})$

exec-instr (Putfield F D) P t h stk loc C M pc frs =
$(let\, v \cdot r \cdot stk' = stk;\ Addr\, a = r$
$\ in\ if\, r = Null\ then$
$\qquad \{\,(\langle\!\langle\rangle\!\rangle, (\lfloor addr\text{-}of\text{-}sys\text{-}xcpt\, NullPointer \rfloor, h, (stk, loc, C, M, pc) \cdot frs))\,\}$
$\quad else$
$\qquad \{\,(\langle\!\langle Write\, a\,(Field\, F\, D)\, v \rangle\!\rangle, (None, h', (stk', loc, C, M, pc + 1) \cdot frs)) \mid h'.$
$\qquad write\, h\, a\,(Field\, F\, D)\, v\, h'\,\})$

exec-instr (Checkcast T) P t h stk loc C M pc frs =
$\{\,(\langle\!\langle\rangle\!\rangle, let\, \lfloor T' \rfloor = typeof_h\,(hd\, stk)$
$\quad in\ if\, P \vdash T' \leq T\ then\ (None, h, (stk, loc, C, M, pc + 1) \cdot frs)$
$\qquad else\ (\lfloor addr\text{-}of\text{-}sys\text{-}xcpt\, ClassCast \rfloor, h, (stk, loc, C, M, pc) \cdot frs))\,\}$

345

exec-instr (*Instanceof T*) *P t h stk loc C M pc frs* =
{ ((∅), *let v · stk'* = *stk*; ⌊*T'*⌋ = *typeof$_h$ v*
    in (*None, h,* (*Bool* (*v ≠ Null ∧ P* ⊢ *T'* ≤ *T*) *· stk', loc, C, M, pc* + 1) *· frs*)) }

exec-instr (*Invoke M'* *n*) *P t h stk loc C M pc frs* =
(*let ps* = *rev* (*take n stk*); *r* = *stk$_{[n]}$*; *Addr a* = *r*; ⌊*hT*⌋ = *typeof-addr h a*
  in if r = *Null then*
        { ((∅), (⌊*addr-of-sys-xcpt NullPointer*⌋ *, h,* (*stk, loc, C, M, pc*) *· frs*)) }
      else let (*D, Ts, T$_r$, m*) = *method P* (*class-of'* *hT*) *M'*
          in case m of Native ⇒
                { (*native-TA2jvm P ta, native-Ret2jvm n h' stk loc C M pc frs vx*)
                  | *ta vx h'.* (*ta, vx, h'*) ∈ *exec-native P t a M' ps h* }
              | ⌊(*msl, mxl, ins, xt*)⌋ ⇒
                  let fr' = ([], *r · ps @ replicate mxl undefined-Val, D, M',* 0)
                  in { ((∅), (*None, h, fr'* *·* (*stk, loc, C, M, pc*) *· frs*)) })

exec-instr Return P t h stk loc C M pc frs =
{ ((∅), *if frs* = [] *then* (*None, h,* [])
      else let v = *hd stk*; (*stk', loc', C', M', pc'*) *· frs'* = *frs*;
            (_, *Ts,* _, _) = *method P C M*
          in (*None, h,* (*v · drop* (|*Ts*| + 1) *stk', loc', C', M', pc'* + 1) *· frs'*)) }

exec-instr (*Goto i*) *P t h stk loc C M pc frs* =
{ ((∅), (*None, h,* (*stk, loc, C, M, nat* (*int pc* + *i*)) *· frs*)) }

exec-instr (*IfFalse i*) *P t h stk loc C M pc frs* =
{ ((∅), *let pc'* = *if hd stk* = *Bool False then nat* (*int pc* + *i*) *else pc* + 1
      in (*None, h,* (*stk, loc, C, M, pc'*) *· frs*)) }

exec-instr ThrowExc P t h stk loc C M pc frs =
{ ((∅), *let v ·* _ = *stk*; *Addr a* = *v*;
          xp = *if v* = *Null then* ⌊*addr-of-sys-xcpt NullPointer*⌋ *else* ⌊*a*⌋
          in (*xp, h,* (*stk, loc, C, M, pc*) *· frs*)) }

exec-instr MEnter P t h stk loc C M frs =
(*let v · stk'* = *stk*; *Addr a* = *v*
  in if v = *Null then*
        { ((∅), (⌊*addr-of-sys-xcpt NullPointer*⌋ *, h,* (*stk, loc, C, M, pc*) *· frs*)) }
      else { ((⌊*Lock→a, SLock a*⌋), (*None, h,* (*stk', loc, C, M, pc* + 1) *· frs*)) })

$exec\text{-}instr\ MExit\ P\ t\ h\ stk\ loc\ C\ M\ frs =$
$(let\ v \cdot stk' = stk;\ Addr\ a = v$
$\ in\ if\ v = Null\ then$
$\qquad \{\,((\!|\!|),(\lfloor addr\text{-}of\text{-}sys\text{-}xcpt\ NullPointer\rfloor,h,(stk,loc,C,M,pc)\cdot frs))\,\}$
$\quad else\ *$
$\qquad \{\,((\!|Unlock{\rightarrow}a,SUnlock\ a|\!),(None,h,(stk',loc,C,M,pc+1)\cdot frs)),$
$\qquad\quad ((\!|UnlockFail{\rightarrow}a|\!),(\lfloor addr\text{-}of\text{-}sys\text{-}xcpt\ IllegalMonitorState\rfloor,$
$\qquad\qquad\qquad\qquad h,(stk,loc,C,M,pc)\cdot frs))\,\})$

Exception handling

$matches\text{-}ex\text{-}entry :: {}'m\ prog \Rightarrow cname \Rightarrow pc \Rightarrow ex\text{-}entry \Rightarrow bool$
$matches\text{-}ex\text{-}entry\ P\ C\ pc\ (f,t,Co,pc',d) \longleftrightarrow$
$\qquad f \leq pc \wedge pc < t \wedge (case\ Co\ of\ Any \Rightarrow True \mid \lfloor C'\rfloor \Rightarrow P \vdash C \preceq^* C')$

$match\text{-}ex\text{-}table :: {}'m\ prog \Rightarrow cname \Rightarrow pc \Rightarrow ex\text{-}entry \Rightarrow (pc \times nat)\ option$
$match\text{-}ex\text{-}table\ P\ C\ pc\ [] = None$
$match\text{-}ex\text{-}table\ P\ C\ pc\ (ex \cdot xt) =$
$\qquad (if\ matches\text{-}ex\text{-}entry\ P\ C\ pc\ ex\ then\ \lfloor snd\ (snd\ (snd\ ex))\rfloor$
$\qquad\ else\ match\text{-}ex\text{-}table\ P\ C\ pc\ xt)$

$xcpt\text{-}step :: {}'addr\ jvm\text{-}prog \Rightarrow {}'addr \Rightarrow {}'heap \Rightarrow {}'addr\ frame \Rightarrow {}'addr\ frame\ list$
$\qquad\qquad\quad \Rightarrow ({}'addr, {}'heap)\ jvm\text{-}state$
$xcpt\text{-}step\ P\ a\ h\ (stk,loc,C,M,pc)\ frs =$
$\qquad (case\ match\text{-}ex\text{-}table\ P\ (cname\text{-}of\ h\ a)\ pc\ (ex\text{-}table\text{-}of\ P\ C\ M)\ of$
$\qquad\quad None \Rightarrow (\lfloor a\rfloor,h,frs)$
$\qquad \mid \lfloor(pc',d)\rfloor \Rightarrow (None,h,(Addr\ a \cdot drop\ (|stk| - d)\ stk,loc,C,M,pc')\cdot frs))$

auxiliary functions:
$cname\text{-}of\ h\ a = (let\ \lfloor hT\rfloor = typeof\text{-}addr\ h\ a;\ Class\ C = ty\text{-}of\ hT\ in\ C)$

$ex\text{-}table\text{-}of\ P\ C\ M =$
$\qquad (let\ (\_,\_,\_,meth) = method\ P\ C\ M;\ \lfloor(\_,\_,\_,xt)\rfloor = meth\ in\ xt)$

$instrs\text{-}of\ P\ C\ M =$
$\qquad (let\ (\_,\_,\_,meth) = method\ P\ C\ M;\ \lfloor(\_,\_,ins,\_)\rfloor = meth\ in\ ins)$

Single-threaded semantics

$exec\ P\ t\ (xcp,\quad h,[]) \qquad\qquad\qquad = \emptyset$
$exec\ P\ t\ (None,h,(stk,loc,C,M,pc)\cdot frs) =$
$\qquad\qquad\qquad exec\text{-}instr\ (instrs\text{-}of\ P\ C\ M)_{[pc]}\ P\ t\ h\ stk\ loc\ C\ M\ pc\ frs$
$exec\ P\ t(\lfloor a\rfloor,\quad h,fr\cdot frs) \qquad\qquad = \{\,((\!|\!|),xcpt\text{-}step\ P\ a\ h\ fr\ frs)\,\}$

B.7.4 Observability

τ-instr :: 'm prog $\Rightarrow$ 'heap $\Rightarrow$ 'addr opstack $\Rightarrow$ 'addr instr $\Rightarrow$ bool

τ-instr P h stk (Load i) $\longleftrightarrow$ True

τ-instr P h stk (Store i) $\longleftrightarrow$ True

τ-instr P h stk (Push v) $\longleftrightarrow$ True

τ-instr P h stk Pop $\longleftrightarrow$ True

τ-instr P h stk Dup $\longleftrightarrow$ True

τ-instr P h stk Swap $\longleftrightarrow$ True

τ-instr P h stk (BinOp bop) $\longleftrightarrow$ True

τ-instr P h stk (New C) $\longleftrightarrow$ False

τ-instr P h stk (NewArray T) $\longleftrightarrow$ False

τ-instr P h stk ALoad $\longleftrightarrow$ False

τ-instr P h stk AStore $\longleftrightarrow$ False

τ-instr P h stk ALength $\longleftrightarrow$ False

τ-instr P h stk (Getfield F D) $\longleftrightarrow$ False

τ-instr P h stk (Putfield F D) $\longleftrightarrow$ False

τ-instr P h stk (Checkcast T) $\longleftrightarrow$ True

τ-instr P h stk (Instanceof T) $\longleftrightarrow$ True

τ-instr P h stk (Invoke M n) $\longleftrightarrow$ $n < |stk| \wedge$
  $(stk_{[n]} = Null \vee$
    $(\forall T\ Ts\ T_r\ D.\ typeof\text{-}addr\ h\ (the\text{-}Addr\ stk_{[n]}) = \lfloor T \rfloor \longrightarrow$
      $P \vdash class\text{-}of'\ T\ sees\ M{:}Ts{\rightarrow}T_r = Native\ in\ D \longrightarrow \tau native\ D\ M))$

τ-instr P h stk Return $\longleftrightarrow$ True

τ-instr P h stk (Goto i) $\longleftrightarrow$ True

τ-instr P h stk (IfFalse i) $\longleftrightarrow$ True

τ-instr P h stk ThrowExc $\longleftrightarrow$ True

τ-instr P h stk MEnter $\longleftrightarrow$ False

τ-instr P h stk MExit $\longleftrightarrow$ False

τjvm :: 'addr jvm-prog $\Rightarrow$ ('addr, 'heap) jvm-state $\Rightarrow$ bool

$\tau jvm\ P\ (xcp, h, []) = False$

$\tau jvm\ P\ (xcp, h, (stk, loc, C, M, pc) \cdot frs) =$
  $(let\ (\_,\_,\_, meth) = method\ P\ C\ M;\ \lfloor(\_,\_, ins, xt)\rfloor = meth$
   $in\ pc < |ins| \wedge (xcp = None \longrightarrow \tau\text{-}instr\ P\ h\ stk\ stk_{[pc]}))$

$jvm\text{-}\tau\text{-}move\ P\ ((xcp, frs), h)\ ta\ \_ \longleftrightarrow \tau jvm\ P\ (xcp, h, frs) \wedge ta = \langle\!\langle\rangle\!\rangle$

auxiliary function: $the\text{-}Addr\ (Addr\ a) = a$

B.8 The Java memory model

type_synonym $JMM\text{-}event = nat$
type_synonym $('addr,'t)\ execution = ('t \times ('addr,'t)\ event\ sf)\ llist$

$\mathcal{A}\_ :: ('addr,'t)\ execution \Rightarrow JMM\text{-}event\ set$
$\mathcal{A}_E = \{\alpha.\ \alpha < |E|\}$

$$is\text{-}write\ (Allocate\ a\ hT) \qquad is\text{-}write\ (Write\ a\ al\ v)$$

$\mathcal{W}\_ :: ('addr,'t)\ execution \Rightarrow JMM\text{-}event\ set$
$\mathcal{W}_E = \left\{\alpha.\ \alpha \in \mathcal{A}_E \wedge is\text{-}write\ (snd\ E_{[\alpha]})\right\}$

$\mathcal{R}\_ :: ('addr,'t)\ execution \Rightarrow JMM\text{-}event\ set$
$\mathcal{R}_E = \left\{\alpha.\ \alpha \in \mathcal{A}_E \wedge (\exists a\ al\ v.\ snd\ E_{[\alpha]} = Read\ a\ al\ v)\right\}$

$init\_ :: ('addr,'t)\ execution \Rightarrow JMM\text{-}event \Rightarrow bool$
$init_E\ \alpha \longleftrightarrow (\exists a\ hT.\ snd\ E_{[\alpha]} = Allocate\ a\ hT)$

Synchronisation events

$$\frac{is\text{-}volatile\ P\ al}{sync\text{-}event\ P\ (Read\ a\ al\ v)} \qquad \frac{is\text{-}volatile\ P\ al}{sync\text{-}event\ P\ (Write\ a\ al\ v)}$$

$$sync\text{-}event\ P\ (Allocate\ a\ hT) \qquad sync\text{-}event\ P\ (TStart\ t)$$

$$sync\text{-}event\ P\ (TJoin\ t) \qquad sync\text{-}event\ P\ (SLock\ a)$$

$$sync\text{-}event\ P\ (SUnlock\ a) \qquad sync\text{-}event\ P\ (TIntr\ t)$$

$$sync\text{-}event\ P\ (TIntrd\ t) \qquad sync\text{-}event\ P\ TInit \qquad sync\text{-}event\ P\ TFinish$$

$sync\text{-}events :: 'm\ prog \Rightarrow ('addr,'t)\ execution \Rightarrow JMM\text{-}event\ set$
$sync\text{-}events\ P\ E = \left\{\alpha.\ \alpha \in \mathcal{A}_E \wedge sync\text{-}event\ P\ (snd\ E_{[\alpha]})\right\}$

Accessed locations

$$(a, al) \in locs'\ P\ (Read\ a\ al\ v) \qquad (a, al) \in locs'\ P\ (Write\ a\ al\ v)$$

$$\frac{P \vdash class\text{-}of'\ hT\ has\ F\text{:}T_f\ (fm)\ in\ D}{(a, Field\ F\ D) \in locs'\ P\ (Allocate\ a\ hT)}$$

$$\frac{n < n'}{(a, Cell\ n) \in locs'\ P\ (New\text{-}Arr\ a\ T\ n')}$$

$locs :: {}'m\ prog \Rightarrow ({}'addr, {}'t)\ execution \Rightarrow ({}'addr \times loc)\ set$
$locs\ P\ E\ \alpha = locs'\ P\ (snd\ E_{[\alpha]})$

$loc\text{-}default :: {}'m\ prog \Rightarrow hty \Rightarrow loc \Rightarrow {}'addr\ val$
$loc\text{-}default\ P\ (ClassT\ C)\ (Field\ F\ D) =$
$\quad default\text{-}val\ (fst\ (the\ (map\text{-}of\ (fields\ P\ C)\ (F, D))))$
$loc\text{-}default\ P\ (ArrayT\ T\ n)\ (Field\ F\ D) =$
$\quad default\text{-}val\ (fst\ (the\ (map\text{-}of\ (fields\ P\ Object)\ (F, Object))))$
$loc\text{-}default\ P\ (ArrayT\ T\ n)\ (Cell\ n') = default\text{-}val\ T$

$value\text{-}written'\ P\ (Allocate\ a\ hT)\ al = loc\text{-}default\ P\ hT\ al$
$value\text{-}written'\ P\ (Write\ a\ al\ v)\ al' = (if\ al = al'\ then\ v\ else\ undefined)$

$value\text{-}written\ P\ E\ \alpha\ (a, al) = value\text{-}written'\ P\ (snd\ E_{[\alpha]})\ al$

Orders

release-acquire pairs:

$$(t, SUnlock\ a) \rightsquigarrow_{\text{sw}} (t', SLock\ a) \qquad (t, Write\ a\ al\ v) \rightsquigarrow_{\text{sw}} (t', Read\ a\ al\ v')$$

$$(t, New\text{-}Obj\ a\ C) \rightsquigarrow_{\text{sw}} (t', Read\ a\ al\ v) \qquad (t, TStart\ t') \rightsquigarrow_{\text{sw}} (t', TInit)$$

$$(t, TFinish) \rightsquigarrow_{\text{sw}} (t', TJoin\ t) \qquad (t, Allocate\ a\ hT) \rightsquigarrow_{\text{sw}} (t', TInit)$$

$$(t, TIntr\ t'') \rightsquigarrow_{\text{sw}} (t', TIntrd\ t'')$$

induced total order: $\qquad \leq^E = \leq|_{\mathcal{A}_E}$
execution order:
$\quad \alpha \leq^E_{\text{eo}} \alpha' \longleftrightarrow (if\ init_E\ \alpha\ then\ \neg init_E\ \alpha' \vee \alpha \leq^E \alpha'\ else\ \neg init_E\ \alpha' \wedge \alpha \leq^E \alpha')$
program order: $\qquad\qquad\qquad \alpha \leq^E_{\text{po}} \alpha' \longleftrightarrow \alpha \leq^E_{\text{eo}} \alpha' \wedge fst\ E_{[\alpha]} = fst\ E_{[\alpha']}$
synchronisation order:
$\quad \alpha \leq^{P,E}_{\text{so}} \alpha' \longleftrightarrow \alpha \leq^E_{\text{eo}} \alpha' \wedge \alpha \in sync\text{-}events\ P\ E \wedge \alpha' \in sync\text{-}events\ P\ E$
synchronises-with order: $\quad \alpha \leq^{P,E}_{\text{sw}} \alpha' \longleftrightarrow \alpha \leq^{P,E}_{\text{so}} \alpha' \wedge E_{[\alpha]} \rightsquigarrow_{\text{sw}} E_{[\alpha']}$
happens-before order: $\qquad \leq^{P,E}_{\text{hb}} = (\lambda \alpha\ \alpha'.\ \alpha \leq^E_{\text{po}} \alpha' \vee \alpha \leq^{P,E}_{\text{sw}} \alpha')^{**}$

Well-formed and legal executions

$ok\text{-}init\ E \longleftrightarrow (\forall \alpha \in \mathcal{A}_E.\ \neg init_E\ \alpha \longrightarrow (\exists \beta.\ \beta < \alpha \wedge E_{[\beta]} = (fst\ E_{[\alpha]}, TInit)))$

$$P \vdash (E, ws) \checkmark \longleftrightarrow \textit{ok-init } E \wedge$$
$$(\forall \alpha \in \mathcal{R}_E.\ \forall a\ al\ v.\ \textit{snd } E_{[\alpha]} = \textit{Read } a\ al\ v \longrightarrow$$
$$\quad ws\ \alpha \in \mathcal{W}_E \wedge (a, al) \in \textit{locs } P\ E\ (ws\ \alpha) \wedge$$
$$\quad \textit{value-written } P\ E\ (ws\ \alpha)\ (a, al) = v \wedge$$
$$\quad \alpha \not\leq_{\text{hb}}^{P,E} ws\ \alpha \wedge (\textit{is-volatile } P\ al \longrightarrow \alpha \not\leq_{\text{so}}^{P,E} ws\ \alpha) \wedge$$
$$\quad (\forall \beta \in \mathcal{W}_E.\ (a, al) \in \textit{locs } P\ E\ \beta \longrightarrow$$
$$\quad\quad (ws\ \alpha \leq_{\text{hb}}^{P,E} \beta \wedge \beta \leq_{\text{hb}}^{P,E} \alpha \vee \textit{is-volatile } P\ al \wedge ws\ \alpha \leq_{\text{so}}^{P,E} \beta \wedge \beta \leq_{\text{so}}^{P,E} \alpha \longrightarrow$$
$$\quad\quad \beta = ws\ \alpha)))$$

most recent write:

$$\frac{\alpha \in \mathcal{R}_E \quad \beta \in \mathcal{W}_E \quad (a, al) \in \textit{locs } P\ E\ \alpha \quad (a, al) \in \textit{locs } P\ E\ \beta}{\beta \leq_{\text{eo}}^{E} \alpha \quad \forall \beta' \in \mathcal{W}_E.\ (a, al) \in \textit{locs } P\ E\ \beta' \longrightarrow \beta' \leq_{\text{eo}}^{E} \beta \vee \alpha \leq_{\text{eo}}^{E} \beta'}{P, E \vdash \alpha \rightsquigarrow_{\text{mrw}} \beta}$$

$$\textit{sequentially-consistent } P\ (E, ws) \longleftrightarrow (\forall r \in \mathcal{R}_E.\ P, E \vdash r \rightsquigarrow_{\text{mrw}} ws\ r)$$

$$\textit{Allocate } a\ hT \simeq \textit{Allocate } a\ hT \qquad \textit{Read } a\ al\ v \simeq \textit{Read } a\ al\ v'$$

$$\textit{Write } a\ al\ v \simeq \textit{Write } a\ al\ v' \qquad \textit{TStart } t \simeq \textit{TStart } t \qquad \textit{TJoin } t \simeq \textit{TJoin } t$$

$$\textit{SLock } a \simeq \textit{SLock } a \qquad \textit{SUnlock } a \simeq \textit{SUnlock } a$$

$$\textit{Extern } a\ M\ vs\ v \simeq \textit{Extern } a\ M\ vs\ v \qquad \textit{TIntr } t \simeq \textit{TIntr } t \qquad \textit{TIntrd } t \simeq \textit{TIntrd } t$$

$$\textit{TInit} \simeq \textit{TInit} \qquad \textit{TFinish} \simeq \textit{TFinish}$$

$$P \vdash (E, ws)\ \textit{justified-by } (E_i, ws_i, C_i, \varphi_i)_i \longleftrightarrow$$
$$(\forall i.\ P \vdash (E_i, ws_i) \checkmark) \wedge$$
$$(\forall i.\ \textit{inj-on } \varphi_i\ \mathcal{A}_{E_i} \wedge (\forall \alpha \in C_i.\ E_{i[\alpha]} \simeq E_{[\varphi_i\ \alpha]})) \wedge (\forall i.\ C_i \subseteq \mathcal{A}_{E_i}) \wedge$$
$$C_0 = \emptyset \wedge (\forall i.\ \varphi_i\ {}^{\prime}C_i \subseteq \varphi_{i+1}\ {}^{\prime}C_{i+1}) \wedge \mathcal{A}_E = \bigcup_i \varphi_i\ {}^{\prime}C_i \wedge$$
$$(\forall i.\ \leq_{\text{hb}}^{P,E_i}\Big|_{C_i} = \varphi_i^{-1}(\leq_{\text{hb}}^{P,E})\big|_{C_i}) \wedge (\forall i.\ \leq_{\text{so}}^{P,E_i}\Big|_{C_i} = \varphi_i^{-1}(\leq_{\text{so}}^{P,E})\big|_{C_i}) \wedge$$
$$(\forall i.\ \forall \alpha \in \mathcal{W}_{E_i} \cap C_i.\ \forall (a, al) \in \textit{locs } P\ E\ (\varphi_i\ \alpha).$$
$$\quad \textit{value-written } P\ E_i\ \alpha\ (a, al) = \textit{value-written } P\ E\ (\varphi_i\ \alpha)\ (a, al)) \wedge$$
$$(\forall i.\ \forall \alpha \in \mathcal{R}_{E_i} \cap C_i.\ \varphi_{i+1}\ (ws_{i+1}\ (\varphi_{i+1}^{-1}\ (\varphi_i\ \alpha))) = ws\ (\varphi_i\ \alpha)) \wedge$$
$$(\forall i.\ \forall \alpha \in \mathcal{R}_{E_{i+1}}.\ \varphi_{i+1}\ \alpha \in \varphi_i\ {}^{\prime}C_i \vee ws_{i+1}\ \alpha \leq_{\text{hb}}^{P,E_{i+1}} \alpha) \wedge$$
$$(\forall i.\ \forall \alpha \in \mathcal{R}_{E_{i+1}} \cap C_{i+1}.$$
$$\quad \varphi_{i+1}\ \alpha \in \varphi_i\ {}^{\prime}C_i \vee \{\varphi_{i+1}\ (ws_{i+1}\ \alpha), ws\ (\varphi_{i+1}\ \alpha)\} \subseteq \varphi_i\ {}^{\prime}C_i) \wedge$$
$$(\forall i.\ \forall \alpha \in \mathcal{A}_{E_i}.\ \forall \alpha' \in C_i.\ \forall a\ M\ vs\ v.$$
$$\quad E_{i[\alpha]} = \textit{Extern } a\ M\ vs\ v \longrightarrow \alpha \leq_{\text{hb}}^{P,E_i} \alpha' \longrightarrow \alpha \in C_i)$$

$P, \mathcal{E} \vdash (E, ws)$ legal $\longleftrightarrow E \in \mathcal{E} \wedge P \vdash (E, ws) \surd \wedge$
$\quad (\exists (E_i, ws_i, C_i, \varphi_i)_i. \ P \vdash (E, ws) \ \textit{justified-by} \ (E_i, ws_i, C_i, \varphi_i)_i \wedge (\forall i. \ E_i \in \mathcal{E}))$

B.9 The compiler

complete compiler
$J2JVM = compP_2 \circ compP_1$

auxiliary functions
$index \ [] \ y \qquad = 0$
$index \ (x \cdot xs) \ y =$
$\quad (if \ x = y \ then \ if \ y \in set \ xs \ then \ index \ xs \ y + 1 \ else \ 0 \ else \ index \ xs \ y + 1)$

$fresh\text{-}vname \ Vs = concat \ (''V'' \cdot Vs)$

$max \ x \ y = (if \ x \le y \ then \ y \ else \ x)$

B.9.1 Program compilation

compilation of method declarations
$compM :: (mname \Rightarrow ty \ list \Rightarrow ty \Rightarrow 'm_1 \Rightarrow 'm_2)$
$\qquad \Rightarrow 'm_1 \ option \ mdecl \Rightarrow 'm_2 \ option \ mdecl$
$compM \ f \ (M, Ts, T, meth) = (M, Ts, T, Option.map \ (f \ M \ Ts \ T) \ meth)$

compilation of class declarations
$compC :: (cname \Rightarrow mname \Rightarrow ty \ list \Rightarrow ty \Rightarrow 'm_1 \Rightarrow 'm_2)$
$\qquad \Rightarrow 'm_1 \ cdecl \Rightarrow 'm_2 \ cdecl$
$compC \ f \ (C, D, fs, ms) = (C, D, fs, map \ (compM \ (f \ C)) \ ms)$

compilation of program declarations
$compP :: (cname \Rightarrow mname \Rightarrow ty \ list \Rightarrow ty \Rightarrow 'm_1 \Rightarrow 'm_2)$
$\qquad \Rightarrow 'm_1 \ prog \Rightarrow 'm_2 \ prog$
$compP \ f \ (Program \ P) = Program \ (map \ (compC \ f) \ P)$

B.9.2 Compilation stage 1

compilation of expressions
$compE_1 :: vname \ list \Rightarrow 'addr \ expr \Rightarrow 'addr \ expr_1$
$compE_1 \ Vs \ (new \ C) \qquad\qquad = new \ C$
$compE_1 \ Vs \ (new \ T[e]) \qquad\quad = new \ T[compE_1 \ Vs \ e]$
$compE_1 \ Vs \ (Cast \ T \ e) \qquad\quad = Cast \ T \ (compE_1 \ Vs \ e)$

$compE_1\ Vs\ (e\ instanceof\ T) \qquad = (compE_1\ Vs\ e)\ instanceof\,T$

$compE_1\ Vs\ (Val\ v) \qquad\qquad = Val\ v$

$compE_1\ Vs\ (e_1\ «bop»\ e_2) \qquad = (compE_1\ Vs\ e_1)\ «bop»\ (compE_1\ Vs\ e_2)$

$compE_1\ Vs\ (Var\ V) \qquad\qquad = Var\ (index\ Vs\ V)$

$compE_1\ Vs\ (V := e) \qquad\qquad = (index\ Vs\ V) := (compE_1\ Vs\ e)$

$compE_1\ Vs\ (e_1[e_2]) \qquad\qquad = (compE_1\ Vs\ e_1)[compE_1\ Vs\ e_2]$

$compE_1\ Vs\ (e_1[e_2] := e_3) \qquad =$
$\qquad (compE_1\ Vs\ e_1)[compE_1\ Vs\ e_2] := compE_1\ Vs\ e_3$

$compE_1\ Vs\ (e.length) \qquad\quad = (compE_1\ Vs\ e).length$

$compE_1\ Vs\ (e.F\{D\}) \qquad\qquad = (compE_1\ Vs\ e).F\{D\}$

$compE_1\ Vs\ (e_1.F\{D\} := e_2) \qquad = (compE_1\ Vs\ e_1).F\{D\} := compE_1\ Vs\ e_2$

$compE_1\ Vs\ (e.M(es)) \qquad\qquad = (compE_1\ Vs\ e).M(map\ (compE_1\ Vs)\ es)$

$compE_1\ Vs\ \{V: T = vo;\ e\} \qquad = \{|Vs|: T = vo;\ compE_1\ (Vs @ [V])\ e\}$

$compE_1\ Vs\ (e_1;;\ e_2) \qquad\qquad = compE_1\ Vs\ e_1;;\ compE_1\ Vs\ e_2$

$compE_1\ Vs\ (if\ (e_1)\ e_2\ else\ e_3) \qquad =$
$\qquad if\ (compE_1\ Vs\ e_1)\ compE_1\ Vs\ e_2\ else\ compE_1\ Vs\ e_3$

$compE_1\ Vs\ (while\ (e_1)\ e_2) \qquad = while\ (compE_1\ Vs\ e_1)\ (compE_1\ Vs\ e_2)$

$compE_1\ Vs\ (throw\ e) \qquad\qquad = throw\ (compE_1\ Vs\ e)$

$compE_1\ Vs\ (try\ e_1\ catch(C\ V)\ e_2) =$
$\qquad try\ compE_1\ Vs\ e_1\ catch(C\ |Vs|)\ (compE_1\ (Vs @ [V])\ e_2)$

$compE_1\ Vs\ (sync\ (e_1)\ e_2) \qquad =$
$\qquad sync_{|Vs|}\ (compE_1\ Vs\ e_1)\ (compE_1\ (Vs @ [fresh\text{-}vname\ Vs])\ e_2)$

$compE_1\ Vs\ (insync\ (a)\ e) \qquad =$
$\qquad insync_{|Vs|}\ (a)\ (compE_1\ (Vs @ [fresh\text{-}vname\ Vs])\ e)$

compilation of programs

$compP_1 = compP\ (\lambda C\ M\ Ts\ T\ (pns, body).\ compE_1\ (this \cdot pns)\ body)$

B.9.3 Compilation stage 2

compilation of expressions

$compE_2 :: 'addr\ expr_1 \Rightarrow 'addr\ instr\ list$

$compE_2\ (new\ C) \qquad\qquad\quad = [New\ C]$

$compE_2\ (new\ T[e]) \qquad\qquad = compE_2\ e @ [NewArray\ T]$

$compE_2\ (Cast\ T\ e) \qquad\qquad = compE_2\ e @ [Checkcast\ T]$

$compE_2\ (e\ instanceof\ T) \qquad = compE_2\ e @ [Instanceof\ T]$

$compE_2\ (Val\ v) \qquad\qquad\quad = [Push\ v]$

$compE_2\ (e_1\ «bop»\ e_2) \qquad\quad = compE_2\ e_1 @ compE_2\ e_2 @ [BinOp\ bop]$

$compE_2\ (Var\ i) \qquad\qquad\quad = [Load\ i]$

$compE_2\ (i := e) \qquad\qquad\quad = compE_2\ e @ [Store\ i, Push\ Unit]$

$compE_2\ (e_1[e_2]) \qquad\qquad\quad = compE_2\ e_1 @ compE_2\ e_2 @ [ALoad]$

353

$$compE_2\ (e_1[e_2] := e_3) \qquad =$$
$$\qquad compE_2\ e_1\ @\ compE_2\ e_2\ @\ compE_2\ e_3\ @\ [AStore, Push\ Unit]$$
$$compE_2\ (e.length) \qquad = compE_2\ e\ @\ [ALength]$$
$$compE_2\ (e.F\{D\}) \qquad = compE_2\ e\ @\ [Getfield\ F\ D]$$
$$compE_2\ (e_1.F\{D\} := e_2) \qquad =$$
$$\qquad compE_2\ e_1\ @\ compE_2\ e_2\ @\ [Putfield\ F\ D, Push\ Unit]$$
$$compE_2\ (e.M(es)) \qquad = compE_2\ e\ @\ compEs_2\ es\ @\ [Invoke\ M\ |es|]$$
$$compE_2\ \{i : T = vo; e\} \qquad =$$
$$\qquad (case\ vo\ of\ None \Rightarrow [\ ]\ |\ \lfloor v \rfloor \Rightarrow [Push\ v, Store\ i])\ @\ compE_2\ e$$
$$compE_2\ (e_1;; e_2) \qquad = compE_2\ e_1\ @\ [Pop]\ @\ compE_2\ e_2$$
$$compE_2\ (if\ (e_1)\ e_2\ else\ e_3) \qquad =$$
$$\qquad (let\ cnd = compE_2\ e_1;\ thn = compE_2\ e_2;\ els = compE_2\ e_3$$
$$\qquad in\ cnd\ @\ [IfFalse\ (int\ (|thn| + 2))]\ @\ thn\ @\ [Goto\ (int\ (|els| + 1))]\ @\ els)$$
$$compE_2\ (while\ (e_1)\ e_2) \qquad =$$
$$\qquad (let\ cnd = compE_2\ e_1;\ bdy = compE_2\ e_2;$$
$$\qquad\quad loop = [Goto\ (-(int\ (|bdy| + |cnd| + 2)))]$$
$$\qquad in\ cnd\ @\ [IfFalse\ (int\ (|bdy| + 3))]\ @\ bdy\ @\ [Pop]\ @\ loop\ @\ [Push\ Unit])$$
$$compE_2\ (throw\ e) \qquad = compE_2\ e\ @\ [ThrowExc]$$
$$compE_2\ (try\ e_1\ catch(C\ i)\ e_2) =$$
$$\qquad (let\ catch = compE_2\ e_2$$
$$\qquad in\ compE_2\ e_1\ @\ [Goto\ (int\ |catch| + 2), Store\ i]\ @\ catch)$$
$$compE_2\ (sync_i\ (e_1)\ e_2) \qquad =$$
$$\qquad compE_2\ e_1\ @\ [Dup, Store\ i, MEnter]\ @$$
$$\qquad compE_2\ e_2\ @\ [Load\ i, MExit, Goto\ 4]\ @\ [Load\ i, MExit, ThrowExc]$$
$$compE_2\ (insync_i\ (a)\ e) \qquad = [Goto\ 1]^{64}$$

$$compEs_2 :: 'addr\ expr_1\ list \Rightarrow 'addr\ instr\ list$$
$$compEs_2\ [\ ] \qquad = [\ ]$$
$$compEs_2\ (e \cdot es) \qquad = compE_2\ e\ @\ compEs_2\ es$$

exception tables

$$compxE_2 :: 'addr\ expr_1 \Rightarrow pc \Rightarrow nat \Rightarrow ex\text{-}table$$
$$compxE_2\ (new\ C) \qquad pc\ d = [\ ]$$
$$compxE_2\ (new\ T[e]) \qquad pc\ d = compxE_2\ e\ pc\ d$$
$$compxE_2\ (Cast\ T\ e) \qquad pc\ d = compxE_2\ e\ pc\ d$$
$$compxE_2\ (e\ instanceof\ T) \qquad pc\ d = compxE_2\ e\ pc\ d$$
$$compxE_2\ (Val\ v) \qquad pc\ d = [\ ]$$
$$compxE_2\ (e_1\ «bop»\ e_2) \qquad pc\ d =$$
$$\qquad compxE_2\ e_1\ pc\ d\ @\ compxE_2\ e_2\ (pc + |compE_2\ e_1|)\ (d + 1)$$
$$compxE_2\ (Var\ i) \qquad pc\ d = [\ ]$$
$$compxE_2\ (i := e) \qquad pc\ d = compxE_2\ e\ pc\ d$$

---

[64]Since *insync* (_) _ is not part of the input syntax, $compE_2$ outputs a no-op.

$compxE_2\ (e_1[e_2])$ $pc\ d =$
$\quad compxE_2\ e_1\ pc\ d\ @\ compxE_2\ e_2\ (pc + |compE_2\ e_1|)\ (d + 1)$
$compxE_2\ (e_1[e_2] := e_3)$ $pc\ d =$
$\quad (let\ pc_1 = pc + |compE_2\ e_1|;\ pc_2 = pc_1 + |compE_2\ e_2|$
$\quad\ in\ compxE_2\ e_1\ pc\ d\ @\ compxE_2\ e_2\ pc_1\ (d + 1)\ @\ compxE_2\ e_3\ pc_2\ (d + 2))$
$compxE_2\ (e.length)$ $pc\ d = compxE_2\ e\ pc\ d$
$compxE_2\ (e.F\{D\})$ $pc\ d = compxE_2\ e\ pc\ d$
$compxE_2\ (e_1.F\{D\} := e_2)$ $pc\ d =$
$\quad compxE_2\ e_1\ pc\ d\ @\ compxE_2\ e_2\ (pc + |compE_2\ e_1|)\ (d + 1)$
$compxE_2\ (e.M(es))$ $pc\ d =$
$\quad compxE_2\ e\ pc\ d\ @\ compxEs_2\ es\ (pc + |compE_2\ e|)\ (d + 1)$
$compxE_2\ (\{i: T = vo;\ e\})$ $pc\ d =$
$\quad compxE_2\ e\ (case\ vo\ of\ None \Rightarrow pc\ |\ \lfloor v \rfloor \Rightarrow pc + 2)\ d$
$compxE_2\ (e_1;;\ e_2)$ $pc\ d =$
$\quad compxE_2\ e_1\ pc\ d\ @\ compxE_2\ e_2\ (pc + |compE_2\ e_1| + 1)\ d$
$compxE_2\ (if\ (e_1)\ e_2\ else\ e_3)$ $pc\ d =$
$\quad (let\ pc_1 = pc + |compE_2\ e_1| + 1;\ pc_2 = pc_1 + |compE_2\ e_2| + 1$
$\quad\ in\ compxE_2\ e_1\ pc\ d\ @\ compxE_2\ e_2\ pc_1\ d\ @\ compxE_2\ e_3\ pc_2\ d)$
$compxE_2\ (while\ (e_1)\ e_2)$ $pc\ d =$
$\quad compxE_2\ e_1\ pc\ d\ @\ compxE_2\ e_2\ (pc + |compE_2\ e_1| + 1)\ d$
$compxE_2\ (throw\ e)$ $pc\ d = compxE_2\ e\ pc\ d$
$compxE_2\ (try\ e_1\ catch(C\ i)\ e_2)\ pc\ d =$
$\quad (let\ pc_1 = pc + |compE_2\ e_1|$
$\quad\ in\ compxE_2\ e_1\ pc\ d\ @\ compxE_2\ e_2\ (pc_1 + 2)\ d\ @\ [(pc, pc_1, \lfloor C \rfloor, pc_1 + 1, d)])$
$compxE_2\ (sync_i\ (e_1)\ e_2)$ $pc\ d =$
$\quad (let\ pc_1 = pc + |compE_2\ e_1| + 3;\ pc_2 = pc_1 + |compE_2\ e_2|$
$\quad\ in\ compxE_2\ e_1\ pc\ d\ @\ compxE_2\ e_2\ pc_1\ d\ @\ [(pc_1, pc_2, Any, pc_2 + 3, d)])$
$compxE_2\ (insync_i\ (a)\ e)$ $pc\ d = []$

$compxEs_2 :: {}'addr\ expr_1\ list \Rightarrow {}'addr\ instr\ list$
$compxEs_2\ []$ $pc\ d = []$
$compxEs_2\ (e \cdot es)$ $pc\ d =$
$\quad compxE_2\ e\ pc\ d\ @\ compxEs_2\ es\ (pc + |compE_2\ e|)\ (d + 1)$

register size

$max\text{-}vars :: {}'addr\ expr_1 \Rightarrow nat$
$max\text{-}vars\ (new\ C)$ $= 0$
$max\text{-}vars\ (new\ T[e])$ $= max\text{-}vars\ e$
$max\text{-}vars\ (Cast\ T\ e)$ $= max\text{-}vars\ e$
$max\text{-}vars\ (e\ instanceof\ T)$ $= max\text{-}vars\ e$
$max\text{-}vars\ (Val\ v)$ $= 0$
$max\text{-}vars\ (e_1\ «bop»\ e_2)$ $= max\ (max\text{-}vars\ e_1)\ (max\text{-}vars\ e_2)$

$$
\begin{aligned}
&\textit{max-vars} \ (\textit{Var} \ i) &&= 0 \\
&\textit{max-vars} \ (i := e) &&= \textit{max-vars} \ e \\
&\textit{max-vars} \ (e_1[e_2]) &&= \textit{max} \ (\textit{max-vars} \ e_1) \ (\textit{max-vars} \ e_2) \\
&\textit{max-vars} \ (e_1[e_2] := e_3) &&= \\
&\qquad \textit{max} \ (\textit{max} \ (\textit{max-vars} \ e_1) \ (\textit{max-vars} \ e_2)) \ (\textit{max-vars} \ e_3) \\
&\textit{max-vars} \ (e.\textit{length}) &&= \textit{max-vars} \ e \\
&\textit{max-vars} \ (e.F\{D\}) &&= \textit{max-vars} \ e \\
&\textit{max-vars} \ (e_1.F\{D\} := e_2) &&= \textit{max} \ (\textit{max-vars} \ e_1) \ (\textit{max-vars} \ e_2) \\
&\textit{max-vars} \ (e.M(es)) &&= \textit{max} \ (\textit{max-vars} \ e) \ (\textit{max-varss} \ es) \\
&\textit{max-vars} \ (\{i: T = vo; e\}) &&= \textit{max-vars} \ e + 1 \\
&\textit{max-vars} \ (e_1;; \ e_2) &&= \textit{max} \ (\textit{max-vars} \ e_1) \ (\textit{max-vars} \ e_2) \\
&\textit{max-vars} \ (\textit{if} \ (e_1) \ e_2 \ \textit{else} \ e_3) &&= \\
&\qquad \textit{max} \ (\textit{max-vars} \ e_1) \ (\textit{max} \ (\textit{max-vars} \ e_2) \ (\textit{max-vars} \ e_3)) \\
&\textit{max-vars} \ (\textit{while} \ (e_1) \ e_2) &&= \textit{max} \ (\textit{max-vars} \ e_1) \ (\textit{max-vars} \ e_2) \\
&\textit{max-vars} \ (\textit{throw} \ e) &&= \textit{max-vars} \ e \\
&\textit{max-vars} \ (\textit{try} \ e_1 \ \textit{catch}(C \ i) \ e_2) &&= \textit{max} \ (\textit{max-vars} \ e_1) \ (\textit{max-vars} \ e_2 + 1) \\
&\textit{max-vars} \ (\textit{sync}_i \ (e_1) \ e_2) &&= \textit{max} \ (\textit{max-vars} \ e_1) \ (\textit{max-vars} \ e_2 + 1) \\
&\textit{max-vars} \ (\textit{insync}_i \ (a) \ e) &&= \textit{max-vars} \ e + 1
\end{aligned}
$$

$$
\begin{aligned}
&\textit{max-varss} :: \textit{'addr expr}_1 \ \textit{list} \Rightarrow \textit{nat} \\
&\textit{max-varss} \ [] &&= 0 \\
&\textit{max-varss} \ (e \cdot es) &&= \textit{max} \ (\textit{max-vars} \ e) \ (\textit{max-varss} \ es)
\end{aligned}
$$

maximum stack size

$$
\begin{aligned}
&\textit{max-stack} \ :: \textit{'addr expr}_1 \Rightarrow \textit{nat} \\
&\textit{max-stack} \ (\textit{new} \ C) &&= 1 \\
&\textit{max-stack} \ (\textit{new} \ T[e]) &&= \textit{max-stack} \ e \\
&\textit{max-stack} \ (\textit{Cast} \ T \ e) &&= \textit{max-stack} \ e \\
&\textit{max-stack} \ (e \ \textit{instanceof} \ T) &&= \textit{max-stack} \ e \\
&\textit{max-stack} \ (\textit{Val} \ v) &&= 1 \\
&\textit{max-stack} \ (e_1 \ \ll bop\gg \ e_2) &&= \textit{max} \ (\textit{max-stack} \ e_1) \ (\textit{max-stack} \ e_2) + 1 \\
&\textit{max-stack} \ (\textit{Var} \ i) &&= 1 \\
&\textit{max-stack} \ (i := e) &&= \textit{max-stack} \ e \\
&\textit{max-stack} \ (e_1[e_2]) &&= \textit{max} \ (\textit{max-stack} \ e_1) \ (\textit{max-stack} \ e_2 + 1) \\
&\textit{max-stack} \ (e_1[e_2] := e_3) &&= \\
&\qquad \textit{max} \ (\textit{max} \ (\textit{max-stack} \ e_1) \ (\textit{max-stack} \ e_2 + 1)) \ (\textit{max-stack} \ e_3 + 2) \\
&\textit{max-stack} \ (e.\textit{length}) &&= \textit{max-stack} \ e \\
&\textit{max-stack} \ (e.F\{D\}) &&= \textit{max-stack} \ e \\
&\textit{max-stack} \ (e_1.F\{D\} := e_2) &&= \textit{max} \ (\textit{max-stack} \ e_1) \ (\textit{max-stack} \ e_2) + 1 \\
&\textit{max-stack} \ (e.M(es)) &&= \textit{max} \ (\textit{max-stack} \ e) \ (\textit{max-stacks} \ es) + 1 \\
&\textit{max-stack} \ (\{i: T = vo; e\}) &&= \textit{max-stack} \ e \\
&\textit{max-stack} \ (e_1;; \ e_2) &&= \textit{max} \ (\textit{max-stack} \ e_1) \ (\textit{max-stack} \ e_2)
\end{aligned}
$$

$max\text{-}stack\ (if\ (e_1)\ e_2\ else\ e_3)\quad =$
$\quad max\ (max\text{-}stack\ e_1)\ (max\ (max\text{-}stack\ e_2)\ (max\text{-}stack\ e_3))$
$max\text{-}stack\ (while\ (e_1)\ e_2)\qquad = max\ (max\text{-}stack\ e_1)\ (max\text{-}stack\ e_2)$
$max\text{-}stack\ (throw\ e)\qquad\qquad = max\text{-}stack\ e$
$max\text{-}stack\ (try\ e_1\ catch(C\ i)\ e_2) = max\ (max\text{-}stack\ e_1)\ (max\text{-}stack\ e_2)$
$max\text{-}stack\ (sync_i\ (e_1)\ e_2)\qquad = max\ (max\text{-}stack\ e_1)\ (max\ (max\text{-}stack\ e_2)\ 2)$
$max\text{-}stack\ (insync_i\ (a)\ e_2)\qquad = 1$

$max\text{-}stacks\ ::\ 'addr\ expr_1\ list \Rightarrow nat$
$max\text{-}stacks\ []\qquad\qquad\qquad = 0$
$max\text{-}stacks\ (e \cdot es)\qquad\qquad = max\ (max\text{-}stack\ e)\ (max\text{-}stacks\ es)$

program compilation

$compMb_2\ C\ M\ Ts\ T\ body =$
$\quad (let\ ins = compE_2\ body\ @\ [Return];\ xt = compxE_2\ body\ 0\ 0$
$\quad in\ (max\text{-}stack\ body, max\text{-}vars\ body, ins, xt))$

$compP_2 = compP\ compMb_2$

B.9.4 Preprocessor

Annotation rules

$$\frac{V \neq super \qquad E\ this = \lfloor Class\ C \rfloor \qquad P \vdash C\ sees\ V{:}T\ (fm)\ in\ D}{P,E \vdash Var\ V \rightsquigarrow Var\ this.V\{D\}}$$

(with $E\ V = None$ above)

$$\frac{E\ V = \lfloor T \rfloor \qquad V \neq super}{P,E \vdash Var\ V \rightsquigarrow Var\ V}$$

$$\frac{E\ V = None \qquad V \neq super}{E\ this = \lfloor Class\ C \rfloor \qquad P \vdash C\ sees\ V{:}T\ (fm)\ in\ D \qquad P,E \vdash e \rightsquigarrow e'}{P,E \vdash V := e \rightsquigarrow Var\ this.V\{D\} := e'}$$

$$\frac{E\ V = \lfloor T \rfloor \qquad V \neq super \qquad P,E \vdash e \rightsquigarrow e'}{P,E \vdash V := e \rightsquigarrow V := e'}$$

$$\frac{P,E \vdash e \rightsquigarrow e' \qquad P,E \vdash e' :: T}{class\text{-}of\ T = \lfloor C \rfloor \qquad P \vdash C\ sees\ F{:}T_f\ (fm)\ in\ D \qquad is\text{-}Array\ T \longrightarrow F \neq length}{P,E \vdash e.F\{\} \rightsquigarrow e'.F\{D\}}$$

357

$$\frac{P,E \vdash e \rightsquigarrow e' \qquad P,E \vdash e' :: T[]}{P,E \vdash e.length\{\} \rightsquigarrow e'.length}$$

$$\frac{E\ this = \lfloor Class\ C \rfloor}{C \neq Object \qquad class\ P\ C = \lfloor (D, fs, ms) \rfloor \qquad P \vdash D\ sees\ F{:}T\ (fm)\ in\ D'}{P,E \vdash Var\ super.F\{\} \rightsquigarrow (Cast\ (Class\ D)\ (Var\ this)).F\{D'\}}$$

$$\frac{P,E \vdash e_1 \rightsquigarrow e_1' \qquad P,E \vdash e_2 \rightsquigarrow e_2' \qquad P,E \vdash e_1' :: T}{class\text{-}of\ T = \lfloor C \rfloor \qquad P \vdash C\ sees\ F{:}T_f\ (fm)\ in\ D \qquad is\text{-}Array\ T \longrightarrow F \neq length}{P,E \vdash e_1.F\{\} := e_2 \rightsquigarrow e_1'.F\{D\} := e_2'}$$

$$\frac{E\ this = \lfloor Class\ C \rfloor \qquad C \neq Object}{class\ C = \lfloor (D, fs, ms) \rfloor \qquad P \vdash D\ sees\ F{:}T\ (fm)\ in\ D' \qquad P,E \vdash e \rightsquigarrow e'}{P,E \vdash Var\ super.F\{\} := e \rightsquigarrow (Cast\ (Class\ D)\ (Var\ this)).F\{D'\} := e'}$$

auxiliary function: $is\text{-}Array\ T \longleftrightarrow (\exists T'.\ T = T'[])$

Copying rules

$$P,E \vdash new\ C \rightsquigarrow new\ C \qquad\qquad \frac{P,E \vdash e \rightsquigarrow e'}{P,E \vdash new\ T[e] \rightsquigarrow new\ T[e']}$$

$$\frac{P,E \vdash e \rightsquigarrow e'}{P,E \vdash Cast\ T\ e \rightsquigarrow Cast\ T\ e'} \qquad\qquad \frac{P,E \vdash e \rightsquigarrow e'}{P,E \vdash e\ instanceof\ T \rightsquigarrow e'\ instanceof\ T}$$

$$P,E \vdash Val\ v \rightsquigarrow Val\ v \qquad\qquad \frac{P,E \vdash e_1 \rightsquigarrow e_1' \qquad P,E \vdash e_2 \rightsquigarrow e_2'}{P,E \vdash e_1\ \ll bop \gg e_2 \rightsquigarrow e_1'\ \ll bop \gg e_2'}$$

$$\frac{P,E \vdash e_1 \rightsquigarrow e_1' \qquad P,E \vdash e_2 \rightsquigarrow e_2'}{P,E \vdash e_1[e_2] \rightsquigarrow e_1'[e_2']}$$

$$\frac{P,E \vdash e_1 \rightsquigarrow e_1' \qquad P,E \vdash e_2 \rightsquigarrow e_2' \qquad P,E \vdash e_3 \rightsquigarrow e_3'}{P,E \vdash e_1[e_2] := e_3 \rightsquigarrow e_1'[e_2'] := e_3'}$$

$$\frac{P,E \vdash e \rightsquigarrow e'}{P,E \vdash e.length \rightsquigarrow e'.length} \qquad\qquad \frac{P,E \vdash e \rightsquigarrow e' \qquad P,E \vdash es\ [\rightsquigarrow]\ es'}{P,E \vdash e.M(es) \rightsquigarrow e'.M(es')}$$

$$\frac{P,E(V \mapsto T) \vdash e \rightsquigarrow e'}{P,E \vdash \{V : T = vo; e\} \rightsquigarrow \{V : T = vo; e'\}} \qquad\qquad \frac{P,E \vdash e_1 \rightsquigarrow e_1' \qquad P,E \vdash e_2 \rightsquigarrow e_2'}{P,E \vdash sync\ (e_1)\ e_2 \rightsquigarrow sync\ (e_1')\ e_2'}$$

$$\frac{P,E \vdash e_1 \rightsquigarrow e_1' \quad P,E \vdash e_2 \rightsquigarrow e_2'}{P,E \vdash e_1;; e_2 \rightsquigarrow e_1';; e_2'}$$

$$\frac{P,E \vdash e_1 \rightsquigarrow e_1' \quad P,E \vdash e_2 \rightsquigarrow e_2' \quad P,E \vdash e_3 \rightsquigarrow e_3'}{P,E \vdash \text{if } (e_1) \ e_2 \ \text{else } e_3 \rightsquigarrow \text{if } (e_1') \ e_2' \ \text{else } e_3'}$$

$$\frac{P,E \vdash e_1 \rightsquigarrow e_1' \quad P,E \vdash e_2 \rightsquigarrow e_2'}{P,E \vdash \text{while } (e_1) \ e_2 \rightsquigarrow \text{while } (e_1') \ e_2'} \qquad \frac{P,E \vdash e \rightsquigarrow e'}{P,E \vdash \text{throw } e \rightsquigarrow \text{throw } e'}$$

$$\frac{P,E \vdash e_1 \rightsquigarrow e_1' \quad P,E(V \mapsto \text{Class } C) \vdash e_2 \rightsquigarrow e_2'}{P,E \vdash \text{try } e_1 \ \text{catch}(C \ V) \ e_2 \rightsquigarrow \text{try } e_1' \ \text{catch}(C \ V) \ e_2'} \qquad P,E \vdash [] \ [\rightsquigarrow] \ []$$

$$\frac{P,E \vdash e \rightsquigarrow e' \quad P,E \vdash es \ [\rightsquigarrow] \ es'}{P,E \vdash e \cdot es \ [\rightsquigarrow] \ e' \cdot es'}$$

Lifting to programs

$annotate \ P \ E \ e = (if \ \exists! e'. \ P,E \vdash e \rightsquigarrow e' \ then \ \iota e'. \ P,E \vdash e \rightsquigarrow e' \ else \ e)$

$annotate\text{-}Mb \ P \ C \ M \ Ts \ T \ (pns, e) = (pns, annotate \ P \ [this \mapsto Class \ C, pns \ [\mapsto] \ Ts] \ e)$

$annotate\text{-}Prog \ P = compP \ (annotate\text{-}Mb \ P) \ P$

List of Figures

List of Tables

Bibliography

[1] Luca Aceto, Rob J. van Glabbeek, Wan Fokkink, and Anna Ingólfsdóttir. Axiomatizing prefix iteration with silent steps. *Information and Computation*, 127(1):26–40, 1996.

[2] Sarita V. Adve and Hans-J. Boehm. Memory models: A case for rethinking parallel languages and hardware. *Communications of the ACM*, 53:90–101, 2010.

[3] Sarita V. Adve and Kourosh Gharachorloo. Shared memory consistency models: A tutorial. *Computer*, 29(12):66–76, 1996.

[4] Sarita V. Adve and Mark D. Hill. Weak ordering — a new definition. In *Proceedings of the 17th Annual International Symposium on Computer Architecture (ISCA 1990)*, pages 2–14. ACM, 1990.

[5] Klaus Aehlig, Florian Haftmann, and Tobias Nipkow. A compiled implementation of normalization by evaluation. In Otmane Mohamed, César Muñoz, and Sofiène Tahar, editors, *Theorem Proving in Higher Order Logics (TPHOLs 2008)*, volume 5170 of *Lecture Notes in Computer Science*, pages 39–54. Springer, 2008.

[6] Klaus Aehlig, Florian Haftmann, and Tobias Nipkow. A compiled implementation of normalization by evaluation. *Journal of Functional Programming*, 2012. To appear.

[7] Jim Alves-Foss, editor. *Formal Syntax and Semantics of Java*, volume 1523 of *Lecture Notes in Computer Science*. Springer, 1999.

[8] David Aspinall and Jaroslav Ševčík. Formalising Java's data-race-free guarantee. In Klaus Schneider and Jens Brandt, editors, *Theorem Proving in Higher Order Logics (TPHOLs 2007)*, volume 4732 of *Lecture Notes in Computer Science*, pages 22–37. Springer, 2007.

[9] Robert Atkey. CoqJVM: An executable specification of the Java virtual machine using dependent types. In Marino Miculan, Ivan

Scagnetto, and Furio Honsell, editors, *Types for Proofs and Programs (TYPES 2008)*, volume 4941 of *Lecture Notes in Computer Science*, pages 18–32. Springer, 2008.

[10] Michael Backes, Alex Busenius, and Cătălin Hrițcu. On the development and formalization of an extensible code generator for real life security protocols. In *NASA Formal Methods (NFM 2012)*, Lecture Notes in Computer Science. Springer, 2012. To appear.

[11] Project Bali. http://isabelle.in.tum.de/bali/.

[12] Clemens Ballarin. Interpretation of locales in Isabelle: Theories and proof contexts. In Jonathan M. Borwein and William M. Farmer, editors, *Mathematical Knowledge Management (MKM 2006)*, volume 4108 of *Lecture Notes in Artificial Intelligence*, pages 31–43. Springer, 2006.

[13] Gilles Barthe, Pierre Crégut, Benjamin Grégoire, Thomas Jensen, and David Pichardie. The MOBIUS proof carrying code infrastructure. In Frank de Boer, Marcello Bonsangue, Susanne Graf, and Willem-Paul de Roever, editors, *Formal Methods for Components and Objects*, volume 5382 of *Lecture Notes in Computer Science*, pages 1–24. Springer, 2008.

[14] Gilles Barthe, Guillaume Dufay, Line Jakubiec, and Simão de Sousa. A formal correspondence between offensive and defensive JavaCard virtual machines. In Agostino Cortesi, editor, *Verification, Model Checking, and Abstract Interpretation (VMCAI 2002)*, volume 2294 of *Lecture Notes in Computer Science*, pages 325–328. Springer, 2002.

[15] Gilles Barthe, Guillaume Dufay, Line Jakubiec, Bernard Serpette, and Simão de Sousa. A formal executable semantics of the JavaCard platform. In David Sands, editor, *Programming Languages and Systems (ESOP 2001)*, volume 2028 of *Lecture Notes in Computer Science*, pages 302–319. Springer, 2001.

[16] Mark Batty, Kayvan Memarian, Scott Owens, Susmit Sarkar, and Peter Sewell. Clarifying and compiling C/C++ concurrency: From C++11 to POWER. In *Proceedings of the 39th Annual ACM*

SIGPLAN-SIGACT Symposium on Principles of Programming Languages (POPL 2012), pages 509–520. ACM, 2012.

[17] Mark Batty, Scott Owens, Susmit Sarkar, Peter Sewell, and Tjark Weber. Mathematizing C++ concurrency. In *Proceedings of the 38th annual ACM SIGPLAN-SIGACT symposium on Principles of programming languages (POPL 2011)*, pages 55–66. ACM, 2011.

[18] Gertrud Bauer and Tobias Nipkow. Flyspeck I: Tame graphs. In Gerwin Klein, Tobias Nipkow, and Lawrence C. Paulson, editors, *The Archive of Formal Proofs.* http://afp.sourceforge.net/entries/Flyspeck-Tame.shtml, 2006. Formal proof development.

[19] Bernhard Beckert, Reiner Hähnle, and Peter H. Schmitt, editors. *Verification of Object-Oriented Software: The KeY Approach*, volume 4334 of *Lecture Notes in Computer Science*. Springer, 2007.

[20] Nadja Belblidia and Mourad Debbabi. A dynamic operational semantics for JVML. *Journal of Object Technology*, 6(3):71–100, 2007.

[21] Stefan Berghofer, Lukas Bulwahn, and Florian Haftmann. Turning inductive into equational specifications. In Stefan Berghofer, Tobias Nipkow, Christian Urban, and Makarius Wenzel, editors, *Theorem Proving in Higher Order Logics (TPHOLs 2009)*, volume 5674 of *Lecture Notes in Computer Science*, pages 131–146. Springer, 2009.

[22] Stefan Berghofer and Tobias Nipkow. Executing higher order logic. In Paul Callaghan, Zhaohui Luo, James McKinna, Robert Pollack, and Robert Pollack, editors, *Types for Proofs and Programs (TYPES 2000)*, volume 2277 of *Lecture Notes in Computer Science*, pages 24–40. Springer, 2002.

[23] Stefan Berghofer and Tobias Nipkow. Random testing in Isabelle/HOL. In *Proceedings of the Second International Conference on Software Engineering and Formal Methods (SEFM 2004)*, pages 230–239. IEEE Computer Society, 2004.

[24] Stefan Berghofer and Martin Strecker. Extracting a formally verified, fully executable compiler from a proof assistant.

Electronic Notes in Theoretical Computer Science, 82(2):377–394, 2003. Compiler Optimization Meets Compiler Verification (COCV 2003).

[25] Stefan Berghofer and Makarius Wenzel. Logic-free reasoning in Isabelle/Isar. In Serge Autexier, John Campbell, Julio Rubio, Volker Sorge, Masakazu Suzuki, and Freek Wiedijk, editors, *Intelligent Computer Mathematics (AISC/MKM/Calculemus 2008)*, volume 5144 of *Lecture Notes in Computer Science*, pages 355–369. Springer, 2008.

[26] Stefan Berghofer and Markus Wenzel. Inductive datatypes in HOL – lessons learned in formal-logic engineering. In Yves Bertot, Gilles Dowek, Laurent Théry, André Hirschowitz, and Christine Paulin, editors, *Theorem Proving in Higher Order Logics (TPHOLs 1999)*, volume 1690 of *Lecture Notes in Computer Science*, pages 19–36. Springer, 1999.

[27] Jan A. Bergstra, Jan Willem Klop, and Ernst-Rüdiger Olderog. Failures without chaos: A new process semantics for fair abstraction. In *Formal Description of Programming Concepts III (IFIP 1987)*, pages 77–103. Elsevier Science Publishing, 1987.

[28] Jasmin Christian Blanchette. Relational analysis of (co)inductive predicates, (co)algebraic datatypes, and (co)recursive functions. *Software Quality Journal*, 2011.

[29] Jasmin Christian Blanchette, Lukas Bulwahn, and Tobias Nipkow. Automatic proof and disproof in Isabelle/HOL. In Cesare Tinelli and Viorica Sofronie-Stokkermans, editors, *Frontiers of Combining Systems (FroCoS 2011)*, volume 6989 of *Lecture Notes in Computer Science*, pages 12–27. Springer, 2011.

[30] Jasmin Christian Blanchette and Tobias Nipkow. Nitpick: A counterexample generator for higher-order logic based on a relational model finder. In Matt Kaufmann and Lawrence C. Paulson, editors, *Interactive Theorem Proving (ITP 2010)*, volume 6172 of *Lecture Notes in Computer Science*, pages 131–146. Springer, 2010.

[31] Jasmin Christian Blanchette, Tjark Weber, Mark Batty, Scott Owens, and Susmit Sarkar. Nitpicking C++ concurrency. In *Proceedings of the 13th international ACM SIGPLAN symposium on*

Principles and practices of declarative programming (PPDP 2011), pages 113–124. ACM, 2011.

[32] Hans-J. Boehm and Sarita V. Adve. Foundations of the C++ concurrency memory model. In *Proceedings of the 2008 ACM SIGPLAN conference on Programming language design and implementation (PLDI 2008)*, pages 68–78. ACM, 2008.

[33] Sascha Böhme and Tobias Nipkow. Sledgehammer: Judgement Day. In Jürgen Giesl and Reiner Hähnle, editors, *Automated Reasoning (IJCAR 2010)*, volume 6173 of *Lecture Notes in Computer Science*, pages 107–121. Springer, 2010.

[34] John Boyland. An operational semantics including "volatile" for safe concurrency. *Journal of Object Technology*, 8(4):33–53, 2009. Formal Techniques for Java Programs 2008.

[35] Deadlock in class initialization specification, JLS 2nd ed. 12.4.2. Java bug database, ID 4891511 http: //bugs.sun.com/bugdatabase/view_bug.do?bug_id=4891511, 2008.

[36] Lukas Bulwahn. Smart test data generators via logic programming. In John Gallagher and Michael Gelfond, editors, *Technical Communications of the 27th International Conference on Logic Programming (ICLP 2011)*, volume 11 of *Leibniz International Proceedings in Informatics (LIPIcs)*, pages 139–150. Schloss Dagstuhl – Leibniz-Zentrum für Informatik, 2011.

[37] Alex Busenius. Mechanized formalization of a transformation from an extensible Spi calculus to Java. Master's thesis, Information Security and Cryptography Group, Department of Computer Science, Saarland University, 2011.

[38] Pietro Cenciarelli, Alexander Knapp, and Eleonora Sibilio. The Java memory model: Operationally, denotationally, axiomatically. In Rocco De Nicola, editor, *Programming Languages and Systems (ESOP 2007)*, volume 4421 of *Lecture Notes in Computer Science*, pages 331–346. Springer, 2007.

[39] Adam Chlipala. A verified compiler for an impure functional language. In *Proceedings of the 37th annual ACM*

SIGPLAN-SIGACT symposium on Principles of programming languages (POPL 2010), pages 93–106. ACM, 2010.

[40] Jacek Chrząszcz. Implementing modules in the Coq system. In David Basin and Burkhart Wolff, editors, *Theorem Proving in Higher Order Logics (TPHOLs 2003)*, volume 2758 of *Lecture Notes in Computer Science*, pages 270–286. Springer, 2003.

[41] Connected limited device configuration (CLDC) specification 1.1. http://jcp.org/aboutJava/communityprocess/final/jsr139/index.html.

[42] Patryk Czarnik and Aleksy Schubert. Extending operational semantics of the Java bytecode. In Gilles Barthe and Cédric Fournet, editors, *Trustworthy Global Computing (TGC)*, volume 4912 of *Lecture Notes in Computer Science*, pages 57–72. Springer, 2008.

[43] Marc Daumas, Laurence Rideau, and Laurent Théry. A generic library for floating-point numbers and its application to exact computing. In Richard Boulton and Paul Jackson, editors, *Theorem Proving in Higher Order Logics (TPHOLs 2001)*, volume 2152 of *Lecture Notes in Computer Science*, pages 169–184. Springer, 2001.

[44] Maulik A. Dave. Compiler verification: a bibliography. *SIGSOFT Software Engineering Notes*, 28(6):2–2, 2003.

[45] Benjamin Delaware, William R. Cook, and Don Batory. Product lines of theorems. In *Proceedings of the 2011 ACM international conference on Object oriented programming systems languages and applications (OOPSLA 2011)*, pages 595–608. ACM, 2011.

[46] Sophia Drossopoulou and Susan Eisenbach. Describing the semantics of Java and proving type soundness. In Alves-Foss [7], pages 542–542.

[47] Azadeh Farzan, Feng Chen, José Meseguer, and Grigore Roşu. Formal analysis of Java programs in JavaFAN. In Rajeev Alur and Doron Peled, editors, *Computer Aided Verification (CAV 2004)*, volume 3114 of *Lecture Notes in Computer Science*, pages 501–505. Springer, 2004.

[48] Azadeh Farzan, José Meseguer, and Grigore Roşu. Formal JVM code analysis in JavaFAN. In Charles Rattray, Savitri Maharaj, and Carron Shankland, editors, *Algebraic Methodology and Software Technology (AMAST 2004)*, volume 3116 of *Lecture Notes in Computer Science*, pages 132–147. Springer, 2004.

[49] Cormac Flanagan and Martín Abadi. Object types against races. In Jos C. M. Baeten and Sjouke Mauw, editors, *Proceedings of the 10th International Conference on Concurrency Theory (CONCUR 1999)*, volume 1664 of *Lecture Notes in Computer Science*, pages 288–303. Springer, 1999.

[50] Cormac Flanagan and Stephen N. Freund. Type-based race detection for Java. In *Proceedings of the ACM SIGPLAN 2000 conference on Programming language design and implementation (PLDI 2000)*, pages 219–232. ACM, 2000.

[51] Cormac Flanagan, Stephen N. Freund, Marina Lifshin, and Shaz Qadeer. Types for atomicity: Static checking and inference for Java. *ACM Transactions on Programming Languages and Systems*, 30(4):1–53, 2008.

[52] Nate Foster and Dimitrios Vytiniotis. A theory of Featherweight Java in Isabelle/HOL. In *The Archive of Formal Proofs*. http://afp.sourceforge.net/entries/FeatherweightJava.shtml, 2006. Formal proof development.

[53] Dennis Giffhorn. *Slicing of Concurrent Programs and its Application to Information Flow Control*. PhD thesis, Fakultät für Informatik, Karlsruher Institut für Technologie, 2012. To appear.

[54] Li Gong. *Inside Java 2 Platform Security: Architecture, API Design, and Implementation*. The Java Series. Addison-Wesley, 2nd edition, 2003.

[55] James Gosling, Bill Joy, Guy Steele, and Gilad Bracha. *The Java Language Specification, Second Edition*. Addison-Wesley, 2000.

[56] James Gosling, Bill Joy, Guy Steele, and Gilad Bracha. *The Java Language Specification, Third Edition*. Addison-Wesley, 2005.

[57] Matthew Goto, Radha Jagadeesan, Corin Pitcher, and James Riely. Types for relaxed memory models using correspondence assertions. Submitted for publication.

[58] Dan Grossman. Type-safe multithreading in Cyclone. In *Proceedings of the 2003 ACM SIGPLAN international workshop on Types in languages design and implementation (TLDI 2003)*, pages 13–25. ACM, 2003.

[59] Daniel Grunwald, Malte Lochau, Egon Börger, and Ursula Goltz. An abstract state machine model for the generic Java type system. Technical Report 2010-02, TU Braunschweig, 2010.

[60] Florian Haftmann. Data refinement (raffinement) in Isabelle/HOL. This is a draft of an envisaged publication still to be elaborated which, applying the usual rules of academic confidentiality, can be inspected at http://www4.in.tum.de/~haftmann/pdf/data_refinement_haftmann.pdf.

[61] Florian Haftmann and Lukas Bulwahn. *Code generation from Isabelle/HOL theories*, 2011. Availabe at http://isabelle.in.tum.de/dist/Isabelle2011-1/doc/codegen.pdf.

[62] Florian Haftmann and Tobias Nipkow. Code generation via higher-order rewrite systems. In Matthias Blume, Naoki Kobayashi, and Germán Vidal, editors, *Functional and Logic Programming (FLOPS 2010)*, volume 6009 of *Lecture Notes in Computer Science*, pages 103–117. Springer, 2010.

[63] Florian Haftmann and Makarius Wenzel. Constructive type classes in Isabelle. In Thorsten Altenkirch and Conor McBride, editors, *Types for Proofs and Programs (TYPES 2006)*, volume 4502 of *Lecture Notes in Computer Science*, pages 160–174. Springer, 2007.

[64] Christian Hammer. *Information Flow Control for Java - A Comprehensive Approach based on Path Conditions in Dependence Graphs*. PhD thesis, Universität Karlsruhe (TH), Fakultät für Informatik, 2009.

[65] Christian Hammer and Gregor Snelting. Flow-sensitive, context-sensitive, and object-sensitive information flow control

based on program dependence graphs. *International Journal of Information Security*, 8(6):399–422, 2009.

[66] John Harrison. A machine-checked theory of floating point arithmetic. In Yves Bertot, Gilles Dowek, André Hirschowitz, Christine Paulin, and Laurent Théry, editors, *Theorem Proving in Higher Order Logics (TPHOLs 1999)*, volume 1690 of *Lecture Notes in Computer Science*, pages 113–130. Springer, 1999.

[67] Pieter H. Hartel and Luc Moreau. Formalizing the safety of Java, the Java virtual machine, and Java Card. *ACM Computing Surveys*, 33:517–558, 2001.

[68] Martin Hecker. Towards justification of program transformations with regard to the Java memory model. Master's thesis, Westfälische Wilhelms-Universität Münster, Fachbereich Mathematik und Informatik, Institut für Informatik, 2009.

[69] Marieke Huisman and Gustavo Petri. The Java Memory Model: a formal explanation. In *Verification and Analysis of Multi-threaded Java-like Programs (VAMP 2007)*, technical report ICIS-R07021, pages 81–96. University of Nijmegen, 2007.

[70] Marieke Huisman and Gustavo Petri. BicolanoMT: a formalization of multi-threaded Java at bytecode level. In *Bytecode semantics, Verification, Analysis and Transformation (BYTECODE 2008)*, Electronic Notes in Theoretical Computer Science, 2008.

[71] Atsushi Igarashi, Benjamin C. Pierce, and Philip Wadler. Featherweight Java: a minimal core calculus for Java and GJ. *ACM Transactions on Programming Languages and Systems*, 23:396–450, 2001.

[72] International standard ISO/IEC 14882:2011. programming languages – C++. International Organization for Standardization, 2011.

[73] Futoshi Iwama and Naoki Kobayashi. A new type system for JVM lock primitives. In *Proceedings of the ASIAN symposium on Partial evaluation and semantics-based program manipulation (ASIA-PEPM 2002)*, pages 71–82. ACM, 2002.

[74] Jacks is an automated compiler killing suite, 2005.
http://sourceware.org/cgi-bin/cvsweb.cgi/~checkout~/
jacks/jacks.html?cvsroot=mauve.

[75] Radha Jagadeesan, Corin Pitcher, and James Riely. Generative operational semantics for relaxed memory models. In Andrew D. Gordon, editor, *Programming Languages and Systems (ESOP 2010)*, volume 6012 of *Lecture Notes in Computer Science*, pages 307–326. Springer, 2010.

[76] Java platform, standard edition 6 API specification, 2011.
http://download.oracle.com/javase/6/docs/api/.

[77] Cezary Kaliszyk and Christian Urban. Quotients revisited for Isabelle/HOL. In *Proceedings of the 2011 ACM Symposium on Applied Computing (SAC 2011)*, pages 1639–1644. ACM, 2011.

[78] Gary A. Kildall. A unified approach to global program optimization. In *Proceedings of the 1st annual ACM SIGACT-SIGPLAN symposium on Principles of programming languages (POPL 1973)*, pages 194–206. ACM, 1973.

[79] Gerwin Klein. *Verified Java Bytecode Verification*. PhD thesis, Institut für Informatik, Technische Universität München, 2003.

[80] Gerwin Klein and Tobias Nipkow. Verified lightweight bytecode verification. *Concurrency and Computation: Practice and Experience*, 13(13):1133–1151, 2001.

[81] Gerwin Klein and Tobias Nipkow. Verified bytecode verifiers. *Theoretical Computer Science*, 298(3):583–626, 2002.

[82] Gerwin Klein and Tobias Nipkow. Jinja is not Java. In Gerwin Klein, Tobias Nipkow, and Lawrence C. Paulson, editors, *The Archive of Formal Proofs*.
http://afp.sf.net/entries/Jinja.shtml, 2005. Formal proof development.

[83] Gerwin Klein and Tobias Nipkow. A machine-checked model for a Java-like language, virtual machine and compiler. *ACM Transactions on Programming Languages and Systems*, 28(4):619–695, 2006.

[84] Gerwin Klein, Tobias Nipkow, David von Oheimb, Leonor Prensa Nieto, Norbert Schirmer, and Martin Strecker. Java source and bytecode formalizations in Isabelle: Bali. Isabelle sources in Isabelle/HOL/Bali, 2002.

[85] Gerwin Klein, Tobias Nipkow, David von Oheimb, Cornelia Pusch, and Martin Strecker. Java source and bytecode formalizations in Isabelle: μJava. Isabelle sources in Isabelle/HOL/MicroJava, 2002.

[86] Gerwin Klein and Martin Strecker. Verified bytecode verification and type-certifying compilation. *Journal of Logic and Algebraic Programming*, 58(1–2):27–60, 2004.

[87] Gerwin Klein and Martin Wildmoser. Verified bytecode subroutines. *Journal of Automated Reasoning*, 30(3–4):363–398, 2003.

[88] Alexander Krauss. Partial and nested recursive function definitions in higher-order logic. *Journal of Automated Reasoning*, 44:303–336, 2010.

[89] Alexander Krauss. Recursive definitions of monadic functions. In Ana Bove, Ekaterina Komendantskaya, and Milad Niqui, editors, *Workshop on Partiality and Recursion in Interactive Theorem Proving (PAR 2010)*, volume 43 of *Electronic Proceedings in Theoretical Computer Science*, pages 1–13, 2010.

[90] Robbert Krebbers and Freek Wiedijk. A formalization of the C99 standard in HOL, Isabelle and Coq. In *Intelligent Computer Mathematics*, volume 6824 of *Lecture Notes in Computer Science*, pages 301–303. Springer, 2011.

[91] Peter Lammich. Collections framework. In Gerwin Klein, Tobias Nipkow, and Lawrence C. Paulson, editors, *The Archive of Formal Proofs*. http://afp.sf.net/entries/Collections.shtml, 2009. Formal proof development.

[92] Peter Lammich and Andreas Lochbihler. The Isabelle collections framework. In Matt Kaufmann and Lawrence C. Paulson, editors, *Interactive Theorem Proving (ITP 2010)*, volume 6172 of *Lecture Notes in Computer Science*, pages 339–354. Springer, 2010.

[93] Leslie Lamport. How to make a multiprocessor computer that correctly executes multiprocess programs. *IEEE Transactions on Computers*, 28(9):690–691, 1979.

[94] Cosimo Laneve. A type system for JVM threads. *Theoretical Computer Science*, 290(1):741–778, 2003.

[95] Doug Lea. The JSR-133 cookbook for compiler writers. http://gee.cs.oswego.edu/dl/jmm/cookbook.html.

[96] Dirk Carsten Leinenbach. *Compiler Verification in the Context of Pervasive System Verification*. PhD thesis, Universität des Saarlandes, 2008.

[97] Xavier Leroy. Formal certification of a compiler backend or: Programming a compiler with a proof assistant. In *Conference record of the 33rd ACM SIGPLAN-SIGACT symposium on Principles of programming languages (POPL 2006)*, pages 42–54. ACM, 2006.

[98] Xavier Leroy. Formal verification of a realistic compiler. *Communications of the ACM*, 52(7):107–115, 2009.

[99] Xavier Leroy. A formally verified compiler back-end. *Journal of Automated Reasoning*, 43(4):363–446, 2009.

[100] Xavier Leroy and Sandrine Blazy. Formal verification of a C-like memory model and its uses for verifying program transformations. *Journal of Automated Reasoning*, 41(1):1–31, 2008.

[101] Xavier Leroy and Hervé Grall. Coinductive big-step operational semantics. *Information and Computation*, 207(2):284–304, 2009.

[102] Pierre Letouzey. Extraction in Coq: An overview. In Arnold Beckmann, Costas Dimitracopoulos, and Benedikt Löwe, editors, *Logic and Theory of Algorithms (CiE 2008)*, volume 5028 of *Lecture Notes in Computer Science*, pages 359–369. Springer, 2008.

[103] Tim Lindholm and Frank Yellin. *The Java Virtual Machine Specification, Second Edition*. Addison-Wesley, 1999.

[104] Hanbing Liu and J Strother Moore. Executable JVM model for analytical reasoning: A study. In *Proceedings of the 2003 workshop on Interpreters, Virtual Machines and Emulators (IVME 2003)*, pages 15–23. ACM, 2003.

[105] Hanbing Liu and J Strother Moore. Java program verification via a JVM deep embedding in ACL2. In Konrad Slind, Annette Bunker, and Ganesh Gopalakrishnan, editors, *Theorem Proving in Higher Order Logics (TPHOLs 2004)*, volume 3223 of *Lecture Notes in Computer Science*, pages 117–125. Springer, 2004.

[106] Andreas Lochbihler. Jinja with threads. In Gerwin Klein, Tobias Nipkow, and Lawrence C. Paulson, editors, *The Archive of Formal Proofs*. http://afp.sf.net/entries/JinjaThreads.shtml, 2007. Formal proof development.

[107] Andreas Lochbihler. Type safe nondeterminism - a formal semantics of Java threads. In *Proceedings of the 2008 International Workshop on Foundations of Object-Oriented Languages (FOOL 2008)*, 2008.

[108] Andreas Lochbihler. Code generation for functions as data. In Gerwin Klein, Tobias Nipkow, and Lawrence C. Paulson, editors, *The Archive of Formal Proofs*. http://afp.sf.net/entries/FinFun.shtml, 2009. Formal proof development.

[109] Andreas Lochbihler. Formalising FinFuns - generating code for functions as data from Isabelle/HOL. In Stefan Berghofer, Tobias Nipkow, Christian Urban, and Makarius Wenzel, editors, *Theorem Proving in Higher Order Logics (TPHOLs 2009)*, volume 5674 of *Lecture Notes in Computer Science*, pages 310–326. Springer, 2009.

[110] Andreas Lochbihler. Coinductive. In Gerwin Klein, Tobias Nipkow, and Lawrence C. Paulson, editors, *The Archive of Formal Proofs*. http://afp.sf.net/entries/Coinductive.shtml, 2010. Formal proof development.

[111] Andreas Lochbihler. Verifying a compiler for Java threads. In Andrew D. Gordon, editor, *Programming Languages and Systems (ESOP 2010)*, volume 6012 of *Lecture Notes in Computer Science*, pages 427–447. Springer, 2010.

[112] Andreas Lochbihler. Java and the Java memory model – a unified, machine-checked formalisation. In Helmut Seidl, editor, *Programming Languages and Systems (ESOP 2012)*, volume 7211 of *Lecture Notes in Computer Science*, pages 497–517. Springer, 2012.

[113] Andreas Lochbihler and Lukas Bulwahn. Animating the formalised semantics of a Java-like language. In Marko van Eekelen, Herman Geuvers, Julien Schmalz, and Freek Wiedijk, editors, *Interactive Theorem Proving (ITP 2011)*, volume 6898 of *Lecture Notes in Computer Science*, pages 216–232. Springer, 2011.

[114] Jeremy Manson. The proof of DRF guarantee and initialization. Java memory model mailing list, post 62, 2007.

[115] Jeremy Manson, William Pugh, and Sarita V. Adve. The Java memory model. In *Proceedings of the 32nd ACM SIGPLAN-SIGACT symposium on Principles of programming languages (POPL 2005)*, pages 378–391. ACM, 2005.

[116] Filip Marić. Formal verification of a modern SAT solver by shallow embedding into Isabelle/HOL. *Theoretical Computer Science*, 411(50):4333–4356, 2010.

[117] Paul E. McKenney and Raul Silvera. Example POWER implementation for C/C++ memory model. http://www.rdrop.com/users/paulmck/scalability/paper/ N2745r.2011.03.04a.html.

[118] John McLean. A general theory of composition for a class of "possibilistic" properties. *IEEE Transactions on Software Engineering*, 22(1):53–67, 1996.

[119] Robin Milner. A modal characterisation of observable machine-behaviour. In Egidio Astesiano and Corrado Böhm, editors, *CAAP'81*, volume 112 of *Lecture Notes in Computer Science*, pages 25–34. Springer, 1981.

[120] Robin Milner. *Communication and Concurrency*. Prentice Hall, 1989.

[121] Mobius consortium. Deliverable D3.1. Byte code level specification language and program logic, 2006.

[122] J Strother Moore and George Porter. The apprentice challenge. *ACM Transactions on Programming Languages and Systems*, 24(3):193–216, 2002.

[123] Andrew C. Myers. JFlow: practical mostly-static information flow control. In *Proceedings of the 26th ACM SIGPLAN-SIGACT symposium on Principles of programming languages (POPL 1999)*, pages 228–241. ACM, 1999.

[124] Keiko Nakata and Tarmo Uustalu. Trace-based coinductive operational semantics for While. In Stefan Berghofer, Tobias Nipkow, Christian Urban, and Makarius Wenzel, editors, *Theorem Proving in Higher Order Logics (TPHOLs 2009)*, volume 5674 of *Lecture Notes in Computer Science*, pages 375–390. Springer, 2009.

[125] Keiko Nakata and Tarmo Uustalu. Resumptions, weak bisimilarity and big-step semantics for While with interactive I/O: An exercise in mixed induction-coinduction. In Luca Aceto and Pawel Sobocinski, editors, *Proceedings Seventh Workshop on Structural Operational Semantics (SOS 2010)*, volume 32 of *Electronic Proceedings in Theoretical Computer Science*, pages 57–75, 2010.

[126] Tobias Nipkow. Verified bytecode verifiers. In Furio Honsell and Marino Miculan, editors, *Foundations of Software Science and Computation Structures (FOSSACS 2001)*, volume 2030 of *Lecture Notes in Computer Science*, pages 347–363. Springer, 2001.

[127] Tobias Nipkow. Verified efficient enumeration of plane graphs modulo isomorphism. In Marko van Eekelen, Herman Geuvers, Julien Schmaltz, and Freek Wiedijk, editors, *Interactive Theorem Proving (ITP 2011)*, volume 6898 of *Lecture Notes in Computer Science*, pages 281–296. Springer, 2011.

[128] Tobias Nipkow, Lawrence C. Paulson, and Markus Wenzel. *Isabelle/HOL — A Proof Assistant for Higher-Order Logic*, volume 2283 of *Lecture Notes in Computer Science*. Springer, 2002.

[129] Tobias Nipkow and David von Oheimb. Java$_{\ell ight}$ is type-safe — definitely. In *Proceedings of the 25th ACM SIGPLAN-SIGACT symposium on Principles of programming languages (POPL 1998)*, pages 161–170. ACM, 1998.

[130] Tobias Nipkow, David von Oheimb, and Cornelia Pusch. μJava: Embedding a programming language in a theorem prover. In Friedrich L. Bauer and Ralf Steinbrüggen, editors, *Foundations of*

Secure Computation, volume 175 of *NATO Science Series F: Computer and Systems Sciences*, pages 117–144. IOS Press, 2000.

[131] Michael Norrish. *C formalised in HOL*. PhD thesis, University of Cambridge, 1998.

[132] Michael Norrish. Deterministic expressions in C. In S. Swierstra, editor, *Programming Languages and Systems (ESOP 1999)*, volume 1576 of *Lecture Notes in Computer Science*, pages 147–161. Springer, 1999.

[133] Michael Norrish. A formal semantics for C++. Technical report, NICTA, 2008. Available from `http://nicta.com.au/people/norrishm/attachments/bibliographies_and_papers/C-TR.pdf`.

[134] Gary Nutt. *Operating Systems*. Addison-Wesley, 3rd edition, 2003.

[135] David von Oheimb. *Analyzing Java in Isabelle/HOL. Formalization, Type Safety and Hoare Logic*. PhD thesis, Fakultät für Informatik, Technische Universität München, 2000.

[136] David von Oheimb. Hoare logic for Java in Isabelle/HOL. *Concurrency and Computation: Practice and Experience*, 13(13):1173–1214, 2001.

[137] David von Oheimb and Tobias Nipkow. Machine-checking the Java specification: Proving type-safety. In Alves-Foss [7], pages 119–156.

[138] David von Oheimb and Tobias Nipkow. Hoare logic for NanoJava: Auxiliary variables, side effects and virtual methods revisited. In Lars-Henrik Eriksson and Peter Lindsay, editors, *Formal Methods – Getting IT Right (FME 2002)*, volume 2391 of *Lecture Notes in Computer Science*, pages 89–105. Springer, 2002.

[139] OpenJDK 6. `http://openjdk.java.net/`.

[140] Scott Owens. Reasoning about the implementation of concurrency abstractions on x86-TSO. In Theo D'Hondt, editor, *Proceedings of the 24th European conference on Object-oriented programming (ECOOP 2010)*, volume 6183 of *Lecture Notes in Computer Science*, pages 478–503. Springer, 2010.

[141] Sam Owre and Natarajan Shankar. Theory interpretation in PVS. Technical Report SRI-CSL-01-01, Computer Science Laboratory, SRI International, 2001.

[142] Lawrence C. Paulson. Mechanizing coinduction and corecursion in higher-order logic. *Journal of Logic and Computation,* 7(2):175–204, 1997.

[143] Benjamin C. Pierce. *Types and Programming Languages.* The MIT Press, 2002.

[144] Causality test cases for the Java memory model. http://www.cs.umd.edu/~pugh/java/memoryModel/CausalityTestCases.html.

[145] William Pugh. The Java memory model is fatally flawed. *Concurrency: Practice and Experience,* 12:445–455, 2000.

[146] Cornelia Pusch. Proving the soundness of a Java bytecode verifier specification in Isabelle/HOL. In Rance Cleaveland, editor, *Tools and Algorithms for Construction and Analysis of Systems (TACAS 1999),* volume 1579 of *Lecture Notes in Computer Science,* pages 89–103. Springer, 1999.

[147] Quis custodiet – machine-checked software security analyses. http://pp.info.uni-karlsruhe.de/project.php?id=31.

[148] Tahina Ramananandro, Gabriel Dos Reis, and Xavier Leroy. Formal verification of object layout for C++ multiple inheritance. In *Proceedings of the 38th annual ACM SIGPLAN-SIGACT symposium on Principles of programming languages (POPL 2011),* pages 67–80. ACM, 2011.

[149] Tahina Ramananandro, Gabriel Dos Reis, and Xavier Leroy. A mechanized semantics for C++ object construction and destruction, with applications to resource management. In *Proceedings of the 39th annual ACM SIGPLAN-SIGACT symposium on Principles of programming languages (POPL 2012),* pages 521–532. ACM, 2012.

[150] Mikael Rittri. Proving the correctness of a virtual machine by a bisimulation. Licentiate thesis, Göteborg University, 1988.

[151] Marcel Ruegenberg. Semi-automatic proof refactoring for Isabelle. Bachelor's thesis, Technische Universität München, Fakultät für Informatik, 2011.

[152] John Rushby. Formal methods and the certification of critical systems. Technical Report SRI-CSL-93-7, Computer Science Laboratory, SRI International, 1993.

[153] David M. Russinoff. A mechanically checked proof of correctness of the AMD K5 floating point square root microcode. *Formal Methods in System Design*, 14:75–125, 1999.

[154] Susmit Sarkar, Mark Batty, Scott Owens, Kayvan Memarian, Peter Sewell, Luc Maranget, Jade Alglave, and Derek Williams. Synchronising C/C++ and POWER. In *Proceedings of the 33rd ACM SIGPLAN Conference on Programming Language Design and Implementation (PLDI 2012)*. ACM, 2012. To appear.

[155] Ralf Sasse. Taclets vs. rewriting logic - relating semantics of Java. Technical Report 2005-16, Fakultät für Informatik, Universität Karlsruhe, 2005.

[156] Norbert Schirmer. Java definite assignment in Isabelle/HOL. In *Proceedings of ECOOP Workshop on Formal Techniques for Java-like Programs*. Technical Report 408, ETH Zurich, 2003.

[157] Norbert Schirmer. Analysing the Java package/access concepts in Isabelle/HOL. *Concurrency and Computation: Practice & Experience - Formal Techniques for Java-like Programs*, 16:689–706, 2004.

[158] Norbert Schirmer. A verification environment for sequential imperative programs in Isabelle/HOL. In Franz Baader and Andrej Voronkov, editors, *Logic for Programming, Artificial Intelligence, and Reasoning (LPAR 2004)*, volume 3452 of *Lecture Notes in Artificial Intelligence*, pages 398–414. Springer, 2005.

[159] Norbert Schirmer. *Verification of Sequential Imperative Programs in Isabelle/HOL*. PhD thesis, Technische Universität München, 2006.

[160] Jaroslav Ševčík. *Program Transformations in Weak Memory Models*. PhD thesis, Laboratory for Foundations of Computer Science, School of Informatics, University of Edinburgh, 2008.

[161] Jaroslav Ševčík. Safe optimisations for shared-memory concurrent programs. In *Proceedings of the 32nd ACM SIGPLAN conference on Programming language design and implementation (PLDI 2011)*, pages 306–316. ACM, 2011.

[162] Jaroslav Ševčík and David Aspinall. On validity of program transformations in the Java memory model. In Jan Vitek, editor, *Proceedings of the 22nd European Conference on Object-Oriented Programming (ECOOP 2008)*, volume 5142 of *Lecture Notes in Computer Science*, pages 27–51. Springer, 2008.

[163] Jaroslav Ševčík, Viktor Vafeiadis, Francesco Nardelli, Suresh Jagannathan, and Peter Sewell. Relaxed-memory concurrency and verified compilation. In *Proceedings of the 38th annual ACM SIGPLAN-SIGACT symposium on Principles of programming languages (POPL 2011)*, pages 43–54. ACM, 2011.

[164] Peter Sewell, Susmit Sarkar, Scott Owens, Francesco Zappa Nardelli, and Magnus O. Myreen. x86-TSO: a rigorous and usable programmer's model for x86 multiprocessors. *Communications of the ACM*, 53:89–97, 2010.

[165] Daniel J. Sorin, Mark D. Hill, and David A. Wood. *A Primer on Memory Consistency and Cache Coherence*. Morgan & Claypool, 2011.

[166] Robert Stärk, Joachim Schmid, and Egon Börger. *Java and the Java Virtual Machine*. Springer, 2001.

[167] Martin Strecker. Formal verification of a Java compiler in Isabelle. In *Proceedings of the 18th International Conference on Automated Deduction (CADE 2002)*, volume 2392 of *Lecture Notes in Computer Science*, pages 63–77. Springer, 2002.

[168] Martin Strecker. Investigating type-certifying compilation with Isabelle. In Matthias Baaz and Andrei Voronkov, editors, *Logic for Programming, Artificial Intelligence, and Reasoning (LPAR 2002)*, volume 2514 of *Lecture Notes in Computer Science*, pages 403–417. Springer, 2002.

[169] Kohei Suenaga and Naoki Kobayashi. Type-based analysis of deadlock for a concurrent calculus with interrupts. In Rocco

De Nicola, editor, *Programming Languages and Systems (ESOP 2007)*, volume 4421 of *Lecture Notes in Computer Science*, pages 490–504. Springer, 2007.

[170] René Thiemann and Christian Sternagel. Certification of termination proofs using CeTA. In Stefan Berghofer, Tobias Nipkow, Christian Urban, and Makarius Wenzel, editors, *Theorem Proving in Higher Order Logics (TPHOLs 2009)*, volume 5674 of *Lecture Notes in Computer Science*, pages 452–468. Springer, 2009.

[171] Emina Torlak, Mandana Vaziri, and Julian Dolby. MemSAT: checking axiomatic specifications of memory models. In *Proceedings of the 2010 ACM SIGPLAN conference on Programming language design and implementation (PLDI 2010)*, pages 341–350. ACM, 2010.

[172] Kerry Trentelman. Proving correctness of JavaCard DL taclets using Bali. In Bernhard K. Aichernig and Bernhard Beckert, editors, *Proceedings of the Third IEEE International Conference on Software Engineering and Formal Methods (SEFM 2005)*, pages 160–169. IEEE Computer Society, 2005.

[173] VALSOFT/Joana – information flow control in program dependence graphs. `http://pp.info.uni-karlsruhe.de/project.php?id=30`.

[174] Mitchell Wand. Compiler correctness for parallel languages. In *Proceedings of the seventh international conference on Functional Programming Languages and Computer Architecture (FPCA 1995)*, pages 120–134. ACM, 1995.

[175] Daniel Wasserrab. *From Formal Semantics to Verified Slicing – A Modular Framework with Applications in Language Based Security*. PhD thesis, Karlsruher Institut für Technologie, Fakultät für Informatik, 2010.

[176] Daniel Wasserrab and Denis Lohner. Proving information flow noninterference by reusing a machine-checked correctness proof for slicing. In *6th International Verification Workshop (VERIFY 2010)*, 2010.

[177] Daniel Wasserrab, Denis Lohner, and Gregor Snelting. On PDG-based noninterference and its modular proof. In Stephen Chong and David A. Naumann, editors, *Proceedings of the 4th Workshop on Programming Languages and Analysis for Security (PLAS 2009)*, pages 31–44. ACM, 2009.

[178] Daniel Wasserrab, Tobias Nipkow, Gregor Snelting, and Frank Tip. An operational semantics and type safety proof for multiple inheritance in C++. In *21th Annual ACM Conference on Object-Oriented Programming, Systems, Languages, and Applications (OOPSLA 2006)*, pages 345–362. ACM, 2006.

[179] Markus Wenzel. Isar – a generic interpretative approach to readable formal proof documents. In Yves Bertot, Gilles Dowek, Laurent Théry, André Hirschowitz, and Christine Paulin, editors, *Theorem Proving in Higher Order Logics (TPHOLs 1999)*, volume 1690 of *Lecture Notes in Computer Science*, pages 167–183. Springer, 1999.

[180] Andrew K. Wright and Matthias Felleisen. A Syntactic Approach to Type Soundness. *Information and Computation*, 115(1):38–94, 1994.

[181] Francesco Zappa Nardelli, Peter Sewell, Jaroslav Ševčík, Susmit Sarkar, Scott Owens, Luc Maranget, Mark Batty, and Jade Alglave. Relaxed memory models must be rigorous. In *Exploiting Concurrency Efficiently and Correctly $((EC)^2 2009)$*, 2009.

Index